EXPLORER'S GUIDE

NORTH CAROLINA'S OUTER BANKS

EXPLORER'S GUIDE

NORTH CAROLINA'S OUTER BANKS

THIRD EDITION

RENEE WRIGHT

THE COUNTRYMAN PRESS
A division of W. W. Norton & Company
Independent Publishers Since 1923

Copyright © 2018, 2013 by The Countryman Press
Copyright © 2008 by Renee Wright

For information about permission to reproduce selections from this book, write to
Permissions, The Countryman Press, 500 Fifth Avenue, New York, NY 10110

For information about special discounts for bulk purchases, please contact
W. W. Norton Special Sales at specialsales@wwnorton.com or 800-233-4830

Manufacturing by Versa Press
Book design by Chris Welch
Production manager: Lauren Abbate

The Countryman Press
www.countrymanpress.com

A division of W. W. Norton & Company, Inc.
500 Fifth Avenue, New York, NY 10110
www.wwnorton.com

978-1-68268-128-2 (pbk.)

10 9 8 7 6 5 4 3 2 1

DEDICATION

For my Mom, Betty Lou—better known to her many "kids" across the country as RV Momma—who gave me the great gift of travel. Without her, this book could never have been written.

And for Allan Maurer, the editor who helped me find my voice.

And for my sister, Karen, intrepid companion on many shores.

EXPLORE WITH US!

Our guide covers an area stretching from the Virginia border south to the great Marine base of Camp Lejeune, outside Jacksonville, North Carolina. Between the two, you'll find as much water as land, and often a ferry offers a more direct route than a road. We'll island hop from north to south, with a chapter for each of the main destinations on the North Carolina Banks. Scattered throughout, we'll take closer looks at some common denominators, such as Banker horses, lighthouses, and lifesaving stations that stretch all along the coast. Special chapters on the history of the region, suggested itineraries, and a "What's Where on the Outer Banks" section help you design your perfect vacation.

All cities and towns mentioned in this guide are in North Carolina unless otherwise noted. Wherever possible, we've included a website address for more information. We've also included places you can get connected with free Wi-Fi access. We provide lots of specific information for most of the attractions on the Outer Banks, and the information was checked as close to publication as possible. However, the Banks change from month to month and season to season. Please use the phone numbers provided to check for current information before you set out on a long trip to a particular place.

The Outer Banks no longer close down in the winter, as was once the norm. Seasonal closures now are quite random. Most everyone takes a month or two off during the winter; they just don't take the same month off. Even locals sometimes find themselves sitting in front of a favorite restaurant looking at a **CLOSED** sign. Telephone first to avoid disappointment.

LODGING While summer accommodation rates still are the highest of the year, various special events or holiday weeks can bump up prices when you might not expect it. Most places go full tilt from Memorial Day to Labor Day, but we'll steer you to places where you won't notice the crowds.

These rate categories are per room, per night, based on double occupancy, or per unit for cottages or other rentals. They do not include room taxes or any special service fees that may apply. In Dare County, taxes add an additional 5 percent; in Currituck County, 6 percent; in Hyde County (Ocracoke), 3 percent; in Carteret County, 5 percent; and in Onslow County (Swansboro), 3 percent.

$	up to $80
$$	$80 to $150
$$$	$150 to $200
$$$$	$200 and up

RESTAURANTS These categories represent the average cost of an entrée, not including higher-priced specials, that supersize steak or rack of lamb. They also do not include appetizers, desserts, beverages, taxes, or gratuities. Most restaurants on the Outer Banks will add a gratuity to bills for large groups. Be sure to check.

$	under $10
$$	$10 to $20
$$$	$20 to $25
$$$$	$25 and up

GREEN SPACE This special section in each chapter covers the beaches that make the Banks so special and other natural attractions, such as trails.

KEY TO SYMBOLS

❄ Open during off-season

☙ Special-value spots that give you more than you expect

✎ Child-friendly spots that have special children's menus or activities that appeal to families

🐾 Pet-friendly lodgings, restaurants, and shops

♿ Wheelchair-accessible establishments or attractions

☂ Rainy-day activity

⚤ Venue that hosts weddings and civil unions

🍸 Bar or nightspot

▼ LGBT friendly

((ɯ)) Wi-Fi access available

↬ Ecofriendly establishments with green policies, or those that feature local seafood and produce

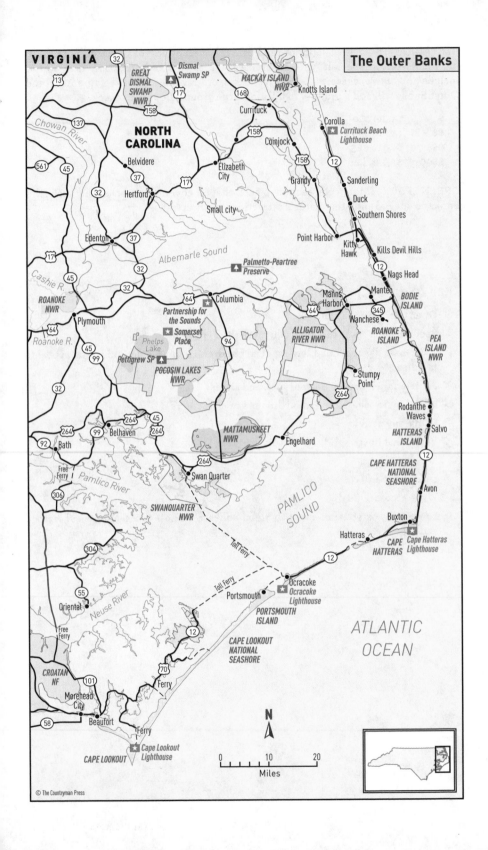

CONTENTS

THE CRYSTAL COAST AND SOUTH BANKS | 319

MAPS

INTRODUCTION

Poised between sky and water, North Carolina's Outer Banks stand as a thin bulwark protecting the rest of the continent behind. A spearhead facing into the wind, a narrow wall marking the separation of land and sea, the Banks exist as they have for centuries, yet are never the same, season to season. Hurricanes and storms created the Outer Banks, mounding up sand scraped from the ocean floor. But Mother Nature is never satisfied. The face of the Banks changes constantly as nature resculpts this work of art. Behind the dunes shelter the rich brackish waters of the Sounds, where North Carolina's great rivers mingle their fresh waters with the incoming tides. The Sounds—Pamlico, Roanoke, and Bogue—are home to a teeming richness of sea life, including many varieties of shellfish and some of the best sportfishing to be found on the globe.

In this land of sky, sand, and water, it takes a special kind of people to thrive. Despite the flood of visitors that now visits the Banks, the families who have lived here for generations remain, practicing their traditions, preserving their heritage. They welcome, as they always have, the castaways who wash up on their shores, fall in love with the place, and stay. In this book, we introduce you to some of these people and help you seek out the authentic experiences the Outer Banks have to offer. Whether you're looking for a classic beach vacation, the thrill of extreme sports, immersion in a unique ecosystem, or a walk through history, the coast of North Carolina can be the destination of your dreams.

SUGGESTED ITINERARIES

Outer Banks Highlights Tour

This trip goes down the Outer Banks then over the ferries to Ocracoke and the South Banks.

Day 1: Start with a day in Corolla on the northern end of the Outer Banks. Visit its elegant **Whalehead Club**, climb the **Currituck Beach Lighthouse**, and take an off-road adventure to see the wild horses of Carova.

Day 2: Travel south on US 158 to visit the **Wright Brothers National Memorial** in Kill Devil Hills, and climb the dunes at **Jockey's Ridge State Park** in Nags Head to see the sunset.

Day 3: Cross the causeway to Manteo, where the **Roanoke Island Festival Park** brings you up to speed on the region's early history. On the way back across the causeway, stop for some fresh local seafood at the **Lone Cedar Restaurant**, owned by Marc Basnight, longtime president pro tempore of the North Carolina Senate. Crossing to Hatteras Island, seek out the **Chicamacomico Life-Saving Station** in Rodanthe for a look into the area's maritime history.

Day 4: Climb the famous **Cape Hatteras Light** for a bird's-eye view of Diamond Shoals, then head for Hatteras Village to tour the **Graveyard of the Atlantic Museum**. Take the free ferry to Ocracoke Island for a swim at one of the country's best beaches. Stop for a meal or beverage at famous **Howard's Pub**, visit the **Village Craftsmen** to meet the local Ocracokers, and watch the sun set over Silver Lake.

Day 5: Take the ferry to Cedar Island and head for **Cape Lookout National Seashore,** where you can climb the diamond-patterned lighthouse and visit the Shackleford horses. Visit the historic town of Beaufort, where you'll find the main campus of the **North Carolina Maritime Museum,** then explore this foodie-friendly town on foot.

OBX for Kids Tour

Thanks to their summer beach patrols, the **best beaches for families** with young children are the Central Beaches of Kitty Hawk, Kill Devil Hills, and Nags Head, and on the Crystal Coast, Emerald Isle. Both areas also have many kid-friendly activities, such as **mini-golf, bumper boats,** and **go-karts**. **Skate parks** can be found in Kitty Hawk, Kill Devil Hills, Nags Head, Buxton, and Manteo, and on the South Banks in Atlantic Beach. The Beach Road running along the Central Beaches still has several old-fashioned ice cream and burger hangouts, such as the **Snowbird** and **Dune Burger**. The **state aquariums** in Manteo and Pine Knoll Shores offer great rainy-day options, and the **Roanoke Island Festival Park** is fun rain or shine. The region's many headboats provide an easy and inexpensive introduction to **fishing** for all ages, as well as an exciting day on the water.

BEST ON THE BANKS

Here are a few suggestions for the best places to satisfy special interests on the Outer Banks.

BEST BIKING Roanoke Island.

BEST KITEBOARDING AND WINDSURFING Hatteras Island—the East Coast hot spot for wind sports.

BEST FISHING Avon Pier on Hatteras Island is the place to hook a giant red drum.

BEST FISHING CHARTERS Oregon Inlet, Wanchese, and Hatteras Village are home to legendary charter fishing fleets—and *Wicked Tuna: Outer Banks*.

BEST SURF FISHING The uninhabited Core Banks in the Cape Lookout National Seashore offer a uniquely untamed opportunity to fish the break.

BEST BEACH Ocracoke! Dr. Beach gave the big nod to the lifeguarded beach here, but we love the miles of undisturbed sand with not a man-made structure in sight just as well.

BEST FAMILY BEACH Emerald Isle on Bogue Banks goes the extra mile with lifeguards, children's entertainment, tons of off-road bike paths, and plenty of family activities.

BEST BOAT TRIP The free North Carolina State Ferry between Hatteras Village and Ocracoke.

BEST EXCURSION Small ferries will take you to the attractions of the often-overlooked Cape Lookout National Seashore, including its diamond-patterned lighthouse, wild horses, and ghost village of Portsmouth.

BEST FOODIE DESTINATION Beaufort, on the Crystal Coast, has the highest concentration of interesting restaurants, all within walking distance of the waterfront. On the upper banks, head for Duck, with many nationally recognized eateries.

BEST PLACE FOR HISTORY AND ART BUFFS Manteo, site of the Lost Colony, has the best history chops on the coast, plus an artist colony inspired by its fishing village charm. On the Crystal Coast, Beaufort is a close runner-up in both categories.

BEST SHOPPING Duck Village connects its many shopping complexes, full of mostly locally owned shops, with boardwalks and paved paths.

BEST BIRDING The Pea Island National Wildlife Refuge has 365 birds on its list, with some species in residence all year.

BEST SURFING Hatteras Island near the Cape Hatteras Lighthouse is the traditional spot for surfers who love both solitude and a challenge. If you're looking for a crowd to applaud your hotdogging, head for Jennette's Pier in Nags Head, home to most of the region's surfing competitions.

BEST PLACE TO LEARN TO SURF The surf in Corolla, with shallow entry and a sand-bar just off shore, is considered a great spot for beginners to catch a wave.

BEST KAYAKING Swansboro on the Crystal Coast, with both saltwater and black-water paddle trails.

BEST OCEANFRONT RV CAMPING The Tri-Villages on Hatteras Island are the last great stronghold of oceanfront RV camping, once so common on the Banks. If you don't mind roughing it (no hookups), plan a vacation moving from one Cape Hatteras National Seashore campground to the next on Ocracoke and Hatteras islands.

WHAT'S WHERE ON THE OUTER BANKS

AREA INFORMATION The destinations discussed in this book stretch across five North Carolina counties. Corolla is part of **Currituck County**, which is located mostly on the mainland. The **Currituck Outer Banks Visitor Center** (www .visitcurrituck.com) offers advice. Kitty Hawk, Kill Devil Hills, Nags Head, Manteo, Roanoke Island, and Bodie and Hatteras Islands make up **Dare County**. For information on Dare destinations, contact the **Outer Banks Visitors Bureau** (www.outerbanks.org). Ocracoke Island is part of **Hyde County** (www.hydecounty .org). Beaufort, Morehead City, and the towns along Bogue Banks are part of **Carteret County** (www.carteretcountync .gov). For visitor information, contact the **Crystal Coast Tourism Authority** (www .crystalcoastnc.org). Swansboro, Camp Lejeune, and Jacksonville are part of **Onslow County** (910-347-4717; www .onslowcountync.gov). For visitor assistance, contact the **Swansboro Area Chamber of Commerce** (910-326-1174; www.swansborochamber.org) or **Onslow County Tourism** (1-800-932-2144; www .onlyinonslow.com).

You'll find information on all these destinations on the main tourism site for the state of North Carolina: **Visit NC** (919-733-8372 or 1-800-VISIT NC; www.visitnc.com); in the **British Isles**: uk.visitnc.com; in **Germany**: de.visitnc .com.

AIRPORTS AND AIRLINES Although no scheduled commercial flights touch down at the small airports that dot the Outer Banks, the heritage of flight is strong here. Kill Devil Hill, where the Wright Brothers National Memorial now stands, is a place of pilgrimage for many pilots. They come to fly over the memorial, and to land and take off at the **First Flight Airport** (252-441-7430 or 252-473-2111; www.nps.gov/wrbr) next to the national monument, flying in the contrail of the Wright brothers themselves.

Most visitors arriving by air land at one of the large commercial airports located near the Banks, where numerous rental cars are available. The major airports located closest to the Outer Banks include: **Newport News/Williamsburg International Airport/PHF** (757-877-0221; www.flyphf.com) and **Norfolk International Airport/ORF** (757-857-3351; www.norfolkairport.com), both about 90 miles from Kitty Hawk; and **Raleigh-Durham International Airport/ RDU** (919-840-2123; www.rdu.com), about 200 miles from Nags Head. **Wilmington International Airport/ILM** (910-341-4125; www.flyilm.com) is the closest major airport to Beaufort and the Crystal Coast. **The Albert J. Ellis Airport/OAJ** (910-324-1100; www.onslowcountync .gov) in Onslow County and **Craven Regional Airport/EWN** (252-638-8591; www.newbernairport.com) in New Bern offer service by smaller regional carriers.

Pilots can request free copies of the current *North Carolina Aeronautical Chart* or *North Carolina Airport Guide* from the **North Carolina Department of Transportation's Aviation Division** website (www.ncdot.org), or by calling 919-840-0112.

AIR CHARTERS **Barrier Island Aviation** (252-473-4247; www.barrierisland aviation.com) and **Outer Banks Air Charters** (252-256-2322; www.outer banksaircharters.com) offer air tours and charters from Dare County Airport in Manteo. **FlightGest** (919-840-4443;

www.flightgest.com) offers charter service from several airports in the Mid-Atlantic region.

AQUARIUMS North Carolina state aquariums (www.ncaquariums.com) can be found in Manteo on Roanoke Island and Pine Knoll Shores on the Crystal Coast.

AREA CODES Area code 252 is used from the Virginia border south to Swansboro, at the southern end of the Crystal Coast, where the area code changes to 910.

ART GALLERIES Manteo, Nags Head, Hatteras Island, Ocracoke, and Beaufort all have active colonies of artists and many galleries.

ATTIRE Whatever the season, dress is relentlessly casual on the coast, and the need for a suit jacket is very rare. Most people get comfortable in shorts and sandals in summer and bundle up when winter comes. A windbreaker is a must all year, and rain gear can come in handy. Closed-toed, rubber-soled shoes are safest on boats. Hats, sunglasses, and plenty of sunscreen and bug repellent make vacations trouble-free, but they can be bought at numerous spots if you forget them.

BARBECUE In North Carolina, barbecue is a noun, and no vacation would be complete without a big order of take-out from one of the local joints. Be sure to order plenty, since ribs and chopped pork are favorite leftovers for many families. North Carolina barbecue is traditionally pork, hickory smoked, and served chopped with bits of fat moistening the mix. In eastern North Carolina, the sauce, served on the side, consists of vinegar with various additions, usually including flecks of red pepper. Farther west, the barbecue parlors in Lexington, North Carolina, the self-proclaimed Barbecue Capital, use a sauce with both vinegar and tomato flavors. Western Carolina barbecue sauce is thicker and tomato based, with a ketchup consistency. South Carolina–style barbecue sauce is based on mustard. Most barbecue restaurants offer versions of all these, so try them all to find your favorite. Another Carolina tradition is putting coleslaw, either traditional or red "barbecue" slaw, on the bun with the chopped (or pulled) pork.

BEACH REGULATIONS North Carolina law says that all the sand below the high-tide line is public property. However, you must enter the beach from a public access, not across private property. Driving on the beach is a treasured local tradition, and one that has come under increasing pressure due to concern for beach-nesting birds and sea turtles. When driving on beaches, especially in the national seashores, it is vital to observe closings established to protect certain areas. Driving on the beaches of the national seashores is especially changeable, with many environmental groups seeking to ban driving completely and locals fighting to maintain their traditional rights. Check with the local park visitor centers to find out which areas are currently available for vehicle and pedestrian access. Currently, the NPS requires those who want to drive on the Cape Hatteras beaches to purchase permits after watching a training video. No permits are currently required to drive on the Core Banks in Cape Lookout National Seashore, but you must ferry your vehicle to the island. Many, although not all, of the communities along the North Carolina coast allow driving on the beach within their townships at certain times of the year, usually October to March. Many towns now ask drivers to buy a permit to drive on the beach. Check the town websites to find out the local laws. When driving on the beach, proceed with extreme caution and follow regular road rules: passing on the left, keeping to the right, wearing seat belts, etc. Speed limits are usually 15 miles per hour.

To avoid getting stuck in the sand, lower the air pressure in your tires to about 20 pounds and stick to the hard-packed sand below the high-tide line. Enter only at beach access ramps, and stay off the dunes if you want to stay out of trouble.

BEACH EQUIPMENT AND LINEN RENTALS You can rent just about anything from the companies that serve the area, and most deliver and pick up for free with a minimum order. Linens and towels, beach chairs and umbrellas, baby equipment, bikes, kayaks, boogie boards, and surfboards are standard items, but you can also rent sports equipment, metal detectors, binoculars, volleyball and horseshoe sets, beach wheelchairs, coolers, charcoal grills, and roll-away beds. Businesses to try include **Just for the Beach Rentals** (www.justforthebeach.com); **Ocean Atlantic Rentals** (www.oceanatlanticrentals.com); **Moneysworth Beach Home Equipment Rentals** (www.mworth.com); on Ocracoke, **Beach Outfitters** (www.ocracokeislandrealty.com); and on the Crystal Coast, **Beach Butler Rentals** (www.beachbutlerrentals.com) and **Island Essentials** (www.islandessentials.com). It's a good idea to make arrangements in advance, especially during the summer season.

BEACHES Dozens of public access points can be found in Corolla, along NC 12 (the Beach Road) and Old Oregon Inlet Road along the Central Beaches, in both the villages and national seashore on Hatteras Island, and along NC 58 on Bogue Banks on the Crystal Coast. Look for signs that identify public access. Regional beach accesses have bathhouses with restrooms where you can shower and change.

BEACH MUSIC AND THE SHAG Shag is the state social dance of North Carolina, and shaggers crowd the dance floors

DRIVING ON SAND REQUIRES SPECIAL PRECAUTIONS

in many beach communities. The R&B tunes that inspire the sweet moves of the shag are heard everywhere on the coast.

BEER Microbrewing is just getting started on the Banks, although with interest in drinking beer on the increase, more breweries are being built all the time. In fact, North Carolina's craft brewing movement began in Manteo back in 1986, when the Weeping Radish began producing fresh beer brewed in accordance with the strict Bavarian purity laws. The **Weeping Radish Farm Brewery** (252-491-5205; www.weepingradish.com) is still making beer, now at a much larger facility on the Currituck mainland. **Outer Banks Brewing Station** (252-449-2739; www.obbrewing.com) produces popular drafts at its windmill-powered brewery in Kill Devil Hills. The **Lost Colony Brewery & Café** (252-473-6666; www.lostcolonybrewery.com) in Manteo crafts British- and Irish-style beers. On the South Banks, **Tight Lines Pub & Brewing Co.** (252-773-0641; www.tightlinesbrewing.com) in Morehead City and the tiny, one-barrel **Mill Whistle**

TOP 10 LIST OF BEACH MUSIC CLASSICS

"Sixty Minute Man," Billy Ward and His Dominoes
"Carolina Girls," General Johnson and the Chairmen of the Board
"Be Young, Be Foolish, Be Happy," The Tams
"Ms. Grace," The Tymes
"I Love Beach Music," The Embers
"Stay," Maurice Williams & the Zodiacs
"My Girl," The Temptations
"Under the Boardwalk," The Drifters
"One Mint Julep," The Clovers
"With This Ring," The Platters

Brewing (252-342-6929; www.facebook.com/MillWhistleBrewing) in Beaufort are gaining fans. The region also has its first small batch kombucha brewery, **Ramblin' Root Kombucha**, produced in Stumpy Point and available at retail outlets and on draft.

BICYCLING Eastern North Carolina is one of the most popular bicycling destinations in the country. In addition to many local bike paths, the area is included in several longer North Carolina Department of Transportation bike trails that lead across the state. **Bike Route 2, Mountains to Sea**, leads from

A BEER SAMPLER AT WEEPING RADISH, NORTH CAROLINA'S FIRST MICROBREWERY

the Great Smoky Mountains to Manteo. **Bike Route 7** runs from Wilson to Cedar Island and the Ocracoke Ferry. The **Wright Brothers Bike Route** runs the length of the Outer Banks, 45 miles from Corolla to Hatteras Village, then over the ferry to Ocracoke. Most of the distance requires on-road riding. **A popular 100-mile round-trip** can be made by traveling from Manteo, down Hatteras Island, over the ferry to Ocracoke, then taking the ferry to Swan Quarter, connecting with US 264, and returning to Manteo. It can be done in one day if you start early in the morning. You can order free maps of statewide and regional bicycling routes from the **North Carolina Department of Transportation website**, www.ncdot.org. North Carolina law requires that all bike riders and passengers 16 and under wear helmets.

BOATING Although most visitors arrive by car, an increasing number of travelers tour North Carolina's shores by boat. A steady stream of power yachts and sailing vessels makes its way along the **Atlantic Intracoastal Waterway** (ICW), the great, 3,000-mile-long water highway that stretches from Boston, Massachusetts, to Key West, Florida. The ICW has one of its longest stretches in North Carolina, making its way down blackwater rivers and salt estuaries. The towns of Elizabeth City, Belhaven, Oriental, Beaufort, Morehead City, and Swansboro are

EXCURSIONS

BIRDING THE BANKS

With over 400 species documented on the Outer Banks, the area is one of the prime destinations for bird-watching on the East Coast. The annual **Wings Over Water festival** (www.wingsoverwater.org) in November introduces many birding hot spots to newcomers through guided expeditions. Among the many exceptional birding locations on the Banks are the **Pea Island National Wildlife Refuge** and the **Pine Island Audubon Sanctuary**, just north of Duck. Stop by the **Sanderling Resort** to see its outstanding collection of bird art. If you are visiting in summer, check out the huge flock of purple martins returning to roost at the **Umstead Memorial Bridge** in Manteo at sunset. In the winter, plan a visit to **Lake Mattamuskeet** to be amazed by the flocks of swans and other waterfowl that visit there. One of the largest colonies of the endangered red-cockaded woodpeckers can be seen at **Palmetto-Peartree Preserve** on the mainland.

The maritime thickets of **Jockey's Ridge State Park** are visited by large numbers of migrating songbirds in late summer and fall, and migrating raptors can be seen along the Soundside Nature Trail. The nature trails around **Bodie Island Lighthouse** yield views of wading birds and wintering waterfowl, while **Coquina Beach** across the road is visited by loons in winter and other shorebirds during the spring and fall migrations. **Nags Head Woods** is the nesting spot of over 50 bird species. **Kitty Hawk Woods** is equally well populated. The Banks are noted for pelagic bird-watching as well, with the world's largest population of black-capped petrels summering just off this coast.

FLOCKS OF SWANS AND OTHER WATERFOWL WINTER AT LAKE MATTAMUSKEET ON THE ALBEMARIE PENINSULA

BOATS ON THE DISMAL SWAMP CANAL, PART OF THE INTRACOASTAL WATERWAY

major stops for mariners passing through, as well as for in-state boaters. An alternate route runs down the back side of the Banks, with stops at Manteo harbor, Hatteras Village, and Ocracoke. Visit the website of the **Atlantic Intra-coastal Waterway Association** (www .atlanticintracoastal.org) for information and updates. You can request a free copy of the official *North Carolina Coastal Boating Guide* by calling 1-877-368-4968 or by visiting www.ncwaterways.com.

BUS SERVICE **Greyhound** (214-849-8100 or 1-800-231-2222; www.greyhound .com) offers scheduled bus service along US 17. Jacksonville (910-346-9832), New Bern (252-633-3100), Washington (252-946-3021), and Elizabeth City (252-335-5183) are the closest terminals to the Outer Banks and Crystal Coast.

CAMPING RV campgrounds are now few and far between on the Outer Banks, except for the **National Park Service campgrounds in Cape Hatteras National**

Seashore, which have very basic amenities. The exception is the **Tri-Villages on Hatteras Island**, where many RV campgrounds, both on the oceanfront and on the sound, welcome campers. Bogue Banks, especially the communities of Emerald Isle and Salter Path, used to have a number of campgrounds. Today, most have disappeared under the wave of development washing across the island. However, a number of RV resorts on the mainland front on Bogue Sound. The Down East region also has several smaller campgrounds, most with boat ramps.

CANOEING AND KAYAKING The coastal region of North Carolina offers a wealth of paddling opportunities for canoes and kayaks. The website of the **OBX Paddlers Club** (www.obxpaddlers .org) lists suggested launch sites from Corolla to Ocracoke, including many spots on the mainland. One of the state's longest paddle trails, the 128-mile **Roanoke River Trail**, is also one of the best developed. It begins near Roanoke Rapids and follows the river to its mouth in Albemarle Sound, near Plymouth. Along the way, it passes through the Roanoke River National Wildlife Refuge, home of black bears, river otters, bobcats, and bald eagles. Camping platforms and boat ramps have been built the length of the river, allowing trips of several days' duration. You can find more information, including links to outfitters offering rentals and guided tours, on the website of the **Roanoke River Partners** (www .roanokeriverpartners.org). On the Crystal Coast, kayaking opportunities are especially rich around Swansboro, with blackwater and saltwater routes available.

CAROLINA FISHING BOATS The unique Carolina-style fishing boats developed from necessity, as the boatbuilders, most of them fishing captains during the summer, adapted the boats they built during the winter months to cope with the unique conditions they faced in Oregon Inlet, bucking the choppy surf at the mouth of the inlet, then venturing far out to sea to fish the Gulf Stream. The most distinctive feature of a Carolina-style fishing boat is the so-called Carolina flare—an exaggerated upward and outward curvature of

A CAROLINA FISHING BOAT WITH THE DISTINCTIVE FLARE HEADS FOR THE WATER

the hull that pushes waves away. Another practical feature is the sharply pointed bow, designed to help the boat cut through the waves and chop. Other features, such as the broken sheerline and extra-wide spray rails, are designed to deflect the spray thrown up during a high-speed trip to the Gulf Stream—and keep the paying customers dry. To find out more about Carolina-style boats and their builders, pick up a copy of *Carolina Flare: Outer Banks Boatbuilding and Sportfishing Heritage*, by John Neal and Jim Conoley.

CHARLES KURALT TRAIL Television journalist Charles Kuralt's love of America, and especially his native state of North Carolina, is well documented in his books *Charles Kuralt's America* and *North Carolina Is My Home*. One of the memorials to him that he might have liked best is the **Charles Kuralt Trail**, linking 11 national wildlife refuges and a national fish hatchery. Located on barrier islands, blackwater swamps, and inland waterways in eastern North Carolina and along the Virginia border, these refuges provide homes for a host of species, many endangered by habitat loss. Each also offers special opportunities for nature lovers to enjoy the splendor and solitude that left Kuralt, in his own words, "a dazzled Odysseus, dizzy with the wonders of the world." For information on the Charles Kuralt Trail, look for red-roofed signboards detailing hiking and paddling routes, boardwalks, observation towers, and scenic drives. You can download a map from the **U.S. Fish & Wildlife website** (www.fws.gov). An audio tour of the refuges, narrated by Kuralt's brother, Wallace, is available and highly recommended.

CHOWDER One local specialty, which you'll find under varying names up and down this coast, is Hatteras clam chowder. It's a whole different take on the genre, having a clear broth with neither cream nor tomatoes. The clam's own

RED-ROOFED SIGNBOARDS AT 12 DIFFERENT WILDLIFE SITES MARK THE CHARLES KURALT TRAIL

juices are used, along with potatoes and onions sautéed in bacon drippings, then seasoned with cracked pepper and salted to taste. Locals often add a splash of Texas Pete, a hot sauce that—despite its name—is made in North Carolina.

CLIMATE The coast of North Carolina generally enjoys a temperate climate, with very few days on which the temperature goes below freezing. In the Nags Head area, January is the coldest

HATTERAS-STYLE CHOWDER GOES BEST WITH A SIDE OF HUSH PUPPIES

month, with average temperatures ranging from 36 to 51 degrees F. July is the hottest month, with lows averaging 72 degrees and highs 86 degrees. The water is warmest in August, when it reaches 80 degrees. However, a steady wind averaging over 10 mph blows all year, cooling even the warmest days and making cold weather very raw. August is generally the wettest month, when thunderstorms frequently develop in the afternoon. The Crystal Coast faces south and is generally a little warmer in the summer, when average July temperatures reach 89 degrees. Some of the best—and worst— weather is experienced in the spring and fall. Hurricane season begins before summer, on June 1. Late summer and fall are prime hurricane season, and storms can approach very quickly. Even outside of the official hurricane season, nor'easters and other big storms can have devastating effects on the coast. The Ash Wednesday Storm of 1962 and the Thanksgiving Storm of 2006 live on in local lore.

DECOYS Decoy carving is a well-established tradition on the Outer Banks, a cottage industry closely associated with waterfowl hunting. The region has several museums exhibiting antique decoys, as well as waterfowl creations by contemporary carvers. The **Outer Banks Center for Wildlife Education** in Corolla contains the important Neil Conoley collection, with examples from all the most famed Currituck Sound school of carvers, and offers classes in carving. Watch for decoys created by the famous carvers of the past, including Ned Burgess of Currituck Sound, Lee Dudley of Knotts Island, and Mitchell Fulcher from Down East. Keep an eye out for hollow canvas-covered decoys, a local style carried on today by Wanchese carver Nick Sapone. Other decoy collections are housed at the **North Carolina Maritime Center** in Beaufort and the **History Museum of Carteret County** in Morehead City. Down east, on Harkers Island, the **Core Sound**

CANVAS-COVERED SWAN DECOYS ARE AN OUTER BANKS TRADITION—AND FOLK ART TREASURES

Waterfowl Museum contains numerous examples of decoys donated by local families who have carved waterfowl for generations. Many of today's carvers gather at the **H. Curt Salter Building**, headquarters of the Core Sound Decoy Carvers Guild, just down the road from the museum. You'll often find carvers at work at these two locations, and auctions are held several times a year.

DRIVING TOURS Several special-interest tours will guide you through the Outer Banks and beyond. Select the itinerary that best suits your interests.

Historic Albemarle Tour (www .historicalbemarletour.org). Founded in 1975, this rambling journey follows brown signs to over 25 sites, most of historical significance, along with natural history and ecotourism highlights. The entire guide can be printed from the website for easy reference.

North Carolina Civil War Trails (www .civilwartraveler.com). Markers tell of little-known battles fought on Roanoke, Ocracoke, and Hatteras islands.

EMERGENCIES Dial 911 for any emergency situation on land or sea anywhere on the Outer Banks. Major hospitals with emergency rooms are the **Outer Banks Hospital** (1-877-359-9179; www.theouter bankshospital.com) in Nags Head and **Carteret General Hospital** (252-808-6000; www.carterethealth.org) in

Morehead City. For boating and water emergencies, contact the **U.S. Coast Guard 24-Hour Search and Rescue** at 252-247-4570.

EVENTS Many events are listed in the individual chapters in this book; however, some events involve the entire region and are a great time to visit the Banks. Check the **Outer Banks visitors website** (www.outerbanks.org), the **Crystal Coast visitors website** (www.crystal coastnc.org), and the **Currituck Visitor website** (www.visitcurrituck.com) for the latest updates.

January: **Outer Banks Wedding Weekend and Expo** (www.obxwa.com). Tour area event venues and score plenty of free swag at the expo.

March: **Taste of the Beach** (www .obxtasteofthebeach.com), a four-day festival for foodies with dozens of events.

April: **Outer Banks Bike Week** (www .outerbanksbikeweek.com).

May: **Spring OBX Restaurant Week** (www.outerbanksrestaurantweek.com).

September: **Bike Fest** (www.outer bankshd.com).

Outer Bank Triathlon (www.outer bankstriathlon.com).

Dare County Beach Sweep (outer banks.surfrider.org). The Outer Banks Brewing Station hosts an after-event, TrashFest, for participants.

October: **Outer Banks Home Builders Parade of Homes** (www.obhomebuilders .org). Tour dozens of homes situated from Corolla to Hatteras.

Fall OBX Restaurant Week (www .outerbanksrestaurantweek.com).

November: **Outer Banks Marathon** (www.obxmarathon.org), Kitty Hawk to Manteo. An expo, art show, and social events are included in this Veterans Day weekend of races. This marathon is a Boston Marathon qualifier.

Wings Over Water (www.wingsover water.org). Weeklong birding festival includes over 100 birding tours, plus special photography workshops, an art show, and social events.

November–December: **Outer Banks Christmas Weekends** (www .obxmasweekends.com). Special events and deals throughout the holiday season.

December: **Festival of Trees** (www .obhotline.org).

Crystal Coast Countdown (www .crystalcoastcountdown.com). A multi-day event with bonfires, live music, tours, hikes, a sand sculpture contest, and more from Beaufort to Emerald Isle leads up to the Pirate Plunge and Crab-pot Drop with fireworks on New Year's Eve.

FERRIES Although most of North Carolina's outer islands are now linked by bridge and causeway to the mainland,

THE NORTH CAROLINA STATE FERRY SYSTEM LINKS MANY OF THE COMMUNITIES ON THE COAST

quite a few still require a journey by boat. Call 1-800-BY-FERRY or visit www .ncferry.org for current schedules and routes. No reservations are taken for free ferries.

The North Carolina ferries run year-round on routes linking Ocracoke Island with Hatteras Island to the north, Cedar Island to the south, and Swan Quarter on the Hyde County mainland to the west. They also cross rivers and sounds, linking the sometimes-isolated communities of the Inner Banks, in addition to creating interesting route options. Any size vehicle can be accommodated on the ferries, and pedestrians and bikers are welcome. Pets must be on a leash or remain in the vehicle. The ferries have restrooms, but no food service beyond vending machines, so a box lunch is recommended for longer voyages. The state ferries run on regular schedules all year and in most weather, although they may be canceled because of high seas or strong winds. Call the terminal in advance to check on current conditions. Current ferry routes in the Outer Banks region include:

Bayview–Aurora across the Pamlico River near Bath. Crossing time: 30 minutes. Fare: Free.

Cherry Branch–Minnesott Beach across the Neuse River below New Bern. Crossing time: 20 minutes. Fare: Free.

Currituck–Knotts Island across Currituck Sound. Crossing time: 45 minutes. Fare: Free.

Hatteras–Ocracoke. Crossing time: 60 minutes. Fare: Free.

Ocracoke Express Passenger Ferry. Direct service from Hatteras Village to Ocracoke Village, May to September. Fare: $15 round-trip.

Ocracoke–Cedar Island. Crossing time: 2.25 hours. Fare: $15 for vehicles less than 20 feet; $1 for pedestrians; $3 for bicycle and rider; $10 for motorcycles; $15–45 for motor homes, with the price increasing with the length of the vehicle. Reservations recommended, especially during the summer season.

Ocracoke–Swan Quarter. Crossing time: 2.5 hours. Fare: Same as Cedar Island Ferry. Reservations recommended.

FIRES While the idea of a campfire on the beach during the evening is an appealing one, many communities along the coast do not permit them or require that you apply in advance for a permit, usually at the local fire station. Check individual town websites, listed in the appropriate chapters, for current information and requirements.

Bonfires are generally permitted in the national seashores if built below the high-tide line. You need a free permit, downloadable from the NPS website, for fires in Cape Hatteras National Seashore. Plan to bring your own wood for your fire, as it is illegal to cut any dead trees or use ship timbers that may have washed up on the shore. A fire should be extinguished with water, not sand, so it will not continue to smolder.

FIREWORKS For many years, Fourth of July fireworks from ocean piers were a treasured and spectacular Banks tradition, with fireworks displays off Nags Head Pier, Avalon Pier in Kill Devil Hills, Avon Pier, and on the Crystal Coast, off Oceana and Bogue Inlet piers. The Independence Day fireworks displays, visible for miles up and down the coast, have returned since a major overhaul of safety regulations prompted by a deadly accident on Ocracoke Island before the 2009 Independence Day festivities.

After a series of near catastrophic brush fires, all private use of fireworks, including firecrackers, torpedoes, skyrockets, and sparklers, has been banned in Dare County, which includes the area from Duck to Hatteras Inlet. Ocracoke and Corolla also ban the private use of fireworks. Fines can range as high as $1,000 and are strictly enforced. Fireworks are prohibited in all national parks and seashores. Regulations for fireworks on the Crystal Coast vary. Check with each township to discover current laws.

In general, the state of North Carolina prohibits the possession of any pyrotechnics that launch or propel into the air, or that explode, making a sound, or "report."

FISHING Fishing is the heart and soul of the North Carolina coast, with generations of watermen heading out to the ocean to make their livings. Some of the largest commercial fishing wholesalers in the country were founded here, including the **Wanchese Fish Company** (www .wanchese.com), established in 1936. Other fishing industries, such as the menhaden fishing fleet once based in Beaufort, have seen their business disappear. In the 1930s, fishing captains, looking for an alternate source of income, began taking amateur fishermen out, first after the big drum in the inlet, then out to the nearby Gulf Stream for blue marlin and other game fish. This was the beginning of the huge and lucrative charter fishing industry, now a year-round activity, on the North Carolina coast. Other fishing enthusiasts prefer to remain on shore, fishing from piers or casting from the beach.

FISHING LICENSES A **North Carolina Coastal Recreational Fishing License** (www.ncwildlife.org) will cover any fishing you might do from the beach, public piers, or private boats in the region. Licenses are required for all individuals 16 years and older. A short-term license good for 10 days costs $5 for North Carolina residents and $10 for those from out of state. Annual licenses are $15 and $30, respectively. Residents age 65 and over can get a lifetime license for $15. Special $10 lifetime licenses are available for the handicapped and disabled veterans. Check the North Carolina Wildlife website for legal sizes, seasons, and bag limits. No license is required in North Carolina for the harvesting of shellfish, including oysters, clams, shrimp, mussels, blue crabs, conchs, and whelks, for personal consumption. However, size limits and bag limits may apply.

WHAT'S BITING WHEN

The location of the Outer Banks at the junction of two huge ocean currents creates an unequaled range of different fish species in these waters.

Winter (November–March): Rockfish (striped bass, called stripers locally), a good eating fish, inshore; giant blue tuna, 100–500 pounds, offshore.

April–May: The hard-fighting bluefish.

June–October: Spanish mackerel, a great eating fish, inshore.

Summer: Cobia, nearshore; the bright and beautiful dolphin (mahi-mahi), possibly the best tasting fish ever, offshore. The fighting game fish arrive in the summer as well: blue marlin, sailfish, wahoo.

July: White marlin, the acrobats of the billfish world and a favorite for light-tackle fishing.

Late summer: Pompano and tarpon in the sounds.

September–October: Runs of spots, a favorite meat fish, rock the piers. A classic Carolina fishing experience, a spot run can hook you on fishing for life.

Fall: King mackerel are hooked all year, but fall brings the big "smoker kings," perfect for the smoker. Fall is also the best time for old drum (channel bass), the inshore fish most prized for eating by locals.

October: Specks (speckled trout), one of the best-tasting fish, inshore; king mackerel, offshore.

All year: Flounder, most often gigged at night; hard-fighting false albacore (fat Alberts), a favorite fly-fishing target.

GETTING THERE The scarcity of causeways and bridges limits automobile access to the Banks to just a few routes. Despite their popularity, the Banks are a bit off the beaten track, far from the major interstates, so allow extra time to reach them, especially if you have an appointment to make.

From the North: There are two main routes from Virginia and points north, and one delightful "back way." Approaching from the Norfolk airport or I-64E, the fastest route to the Outer Banks is VA/NC 168, a toll road. It joins US 158 in Barco, North Carolina, running down to the Wright Memorial Bridge and Kitty Hawk. This route is about 90 miles from airport to bridge, but it may be slow in summer, especially on weekends when people are coming in for their weekly rentals. A new toll causeway across Currituck Sound in the Jarvisburg/Grandy vicinity, intended to cut down on the congestion, is scheduled to open in 2018.

A second route from Virginia follows US 17, which has four lanes from the North Carolina border running parallel with the historic Dismal Swamp Canal. At Elizabeth City, a charming harbor town, you pick up US 158 out to Barco and beyond.

To sneak into the region via the scenic "back way," take VA/NC 618 from Virginia Beach through the Mackay Island National Wildlife Refuge and Knotts Island, noted for its vineyards, then cross via a free ferry to join NC 168. Call ahead (252-232-2683) to make sure the ferry is running, as low water sometimes keeps it at the dock.

GOING FISHING: OBX STYLE

A wide range of fishing experiences are offered on the Banks:

Charter fishing: Charter boats typically accommodate groups of up to six. Prices range well over $1,000 for a full day of offshore action, half that for a nearshore or inshore half-day excursion. All charters include fishing gear, tackle, and bait, plus any license you might need, and—sometimes—ice and fish cleaning.

THE *MISS OREGON INLET* IS ONE OF THE MOST POPULAR AND MOST SUCCESSFUL HEADBOATS ON THE BANKS

- **Makeup charters:** If your group is smaller than six people, ask about a makeup charter to keep down the cost of your day of fishing. The captain matches interests to fill his boat, with the price split among all participants.

- **Offshore charters:** The offshore fleet goes out to the Gulf Stream after the big game fish: sailfish, white and blue marlin; as well as other pelagic fish, such as wahoo and mahi-mahi; plus giant bluefin tuna in the winter months. These are larger boats, especially designed for safety and comfort on offshore trips. It takes about an hour and a half for most boats to reach the Gulf Stream.

- **Nearshore charters:** Nearshore captains fish the inlets or along the edge of the Continental Shelf, or go after bottom fish at one of the many wrecks in the area, home to snapper, grouper, pompano, drum, cobia, sea bass, tile fish, trigger fish, and more.

- **Inshore charters:** The inshore fleet typically is made up of smaller boats that fish within sight of shore, either in the inlets, on Diamond Shoals, or in the sound, for bluefish, king and Spanish mackerel, cobia, flounder, false albacore ("fat Alberts"), striped bass (rockfish), gray and speckled trout, and red drum. Trips on the calm waters of Pamlico Sound are usually the favorite for family fishing trips, offered by many inshore captains.

- **Headboats:** On headboats, or party boats, rates are charged per person (per "head") and are reasonable, usually $30–40 for adults, less for children under 10. Bathrooms and refreshments are available onboard, and gear, bait, and licenses are provided. It's a great introduction to fishing for all ages. Some headboats also schedule 24- or 48-hour marathon trips to the Gulf Stream, or night shark hunts for avid anglers.

- **Pier fishing:** Fishing from piers is a great Carolina tradition—one under attack in recent years due to high values on oceanfront property and a series of savage storms that have knocked down piers year after year. Today, many piers along the coast hang tough, preserving this family activity for future generations. The state of North Carolina has gotten into the mix as well, building concrete, hurricane-proof piers as part of the North Carolina aquarium system. Jennette's Pier in Nags Head has proved a tremendous success, and a similar state pier is in the design stages on Bogue Banks at Emerald Isle. A new pier is also in the planning stages for Hatteras Village. At these commercial piers, you pay a set fee to fish, usually in the $10–15 range, with licenses provided. Fishing tackle and bait, plus refreshments, are generally available at the pier store. Many fishing piers are also located on the sounds. These are often free piers, but you must have a North Carolina fishing license. Pier fishing reaches its peak in the spring and fall.

- **Surf fishing:** Another treasured tradition, fishing from the beach is hugely popular within the Cape Hatteras and Cape Lookout national seashores. As practiced on the Outer Banks, this activity requires a four-wheel-drive vehicle to drive to the surf line, loaded with gear, beach furniture, refreshments, and other necessities. Due to concern for the survival of nesting shorebirds and sea turtles, and an increasing number of accidents on the beach, the National Park Service has enacted a number of often controversial regulations for driving off-road at the Cape Hatteras National Seashore, including ORV permits and closed areas to protect nesting sites. Those who want to experience "old-style" surf fishing, without permit fees, can ferry their vehicles over to the Core Banks at Cape Lookout for up to 14 days of fishing and camping on the beach. A North Carolina Coastal Recreational Fishing License is required for all fishing from the beach or at public piers.

- **Fly and light-tackle charters:** An increasing number of anglers choose to fish with light tackle or with fly-fishing rods for a greater challenge. This is a popular method inshore, especially for sight fishing of red drum and angling for fat Alberts and the tarpon that come into the sounds in the late fall. Some captains also offer light-tackle trips after big game fish on the open ocean.

- **Kayak or SUP fishing:** In this environmentally conscious form of fishing, you paddle out in a specially equipped kayak or stand-up paddleboard (SUP) to fly-fish and enjoy the serenity of nature.

SURF FISHING, A FAVORITE ON THE OUTER BANKS

From the West: To reach Roanoke Island and the Central Banks from the west, you have your choice of two major roads, US 64 and US 264, both of them now four-lane, limited-access highways for most of the distance. The roads start out together from Raleigh, then separate to sweep along either shore of the great Albemarle Peninsula, joining again in Manns Harbor on the mainland opposite Roanoke Island. US 64 is the most direct and fastest route, being four-lane as far as Columbia. The trip from Raleigh to Roanoke Island takes about four hours via this route, with a rest stop in Columbia, or about three hours from I-95. US 70E, a good four-lane, is the most direct route from Raleigh to the Crystal Coast, crossing both I-40 and I-95 along the way. Drive time to Beaufort is about three hours.

From the South: US 17 runs from Wilmington north to the Virginia border, passing through many old Inner Banks towns. To reach the Crystal Coast and Beaufort, turn east on NC 24 in Jacksonville.

GOLF Limited space and high land values make golf courses rare on the Outer Banks. The ones that do exist are wildly busy during the summer season, with tee times scheduled up to a year in advance. The demand has fueled an explosion of golf courses on the mainland just over the Wright Memorial Bridge in Currituck County, North Carolina's newest golf hot spot.

GUIDED TOURS **Hatteras Tours** (252-4754477; www.hatterastours.com). Native historian Danny Couch conducts tours of Hatteras Island and other destinations.

HAPPY HOURS Many North Carolina restaurants and clubs offer happy hours, but these are always specials on food. State law requires drink specials to be offered all day, from open to close. On the Outer Banks, happy hours are often

scheduled earlier than in other areas, usually 3–5 PM, to avoid conflict with the big dinner rush.

HISTORIC DISTRICTS Despite the destruction of storms, the Outer Banks retain several historic districts, including **Old Corolla Village**, the **Nags Head Historic Cottage District**, downtown **Manteo**, and **Ocracoke Village**. Farther south, several recognized historic districts are located along the Crystal Coast, including **Cape Lookout Village** and **Portsmouth Village**, both on Core Banks and today deserted. Other historic districts still occupied are the **Beaufort**, **Morehead City**, and **Swansboro downtowns**, all on the National Register of Historic Places.

HUNTING AND SHOOTING Waterfowl hunting has been a tradition on the North Carolina coast for generations, dating back to Native American days. In the years following the Civil War, many Northern industrialists bought large tracks of marshland, converting them to hunt clubs where they would spend weeks every winter, hunting the numerous ducks, geese, and swans that winter on the Banks. Commercial hunters came as well, shooting huge numbers of waterfowl, until the institution of seasons, bag limits, and other controls as the result of the Migratory Bird Treaty Act of 1918 between the United States and Canada. Currituck County makes a limited number of blinds available to hunters with waterfowl hunting permits from the state. Contact the **Currituck County Game Commission** (252-4293472; www.currituckgamecommission.org) and the **North Carolina Wildlife Resources Commission** (1-888-248-6834; www.ncwildlife.org) to start the process. The National Park Service allows waterfowl hunting at 20 permanent blinds on Bodie Island through a lottery. Visit the **NPS website** (www.nps.gov/caha) to find out how to apply. Ocracoke Island and the Down East region of the South Banks have strong, family-based hunting traditions. One unique style of hunting available only in the area is waterfowl shooting using a curtain box, a similar setup to the now illegal sink box blinds, which allow hunters to hide below the surface of the water. To hunt waterfowl legally, you must have on your person a valid **North Carolina hunting license with North Carolina waterfowl privilege** (1-888-248-6834; www.ncwildlife.org) and a **Federal Duck Stamp** (www.fws .gov/duckstamps). Deer, bear, turkey, and other game are hunted in many national forests and wildlife refuges near the Outer Banks and Crystal Coast, mostly on the mainland. Check the **North Carolina Wildlife Resources website** (www .ncwildlife.org) for opportunities and regulations.

HURRICANES Hurricane season stretches from June 1 to November 30 each year, with the most active period from late August through September. The various islands of the Outer Banks often take the brunt of storms in the Atlantic, with extensive flooding, including overwash, pounding surf, and devastating winds. In recent years, hurricanes have cut new inlets through the Banks, washing out roads and stranding residents. The National Weather Service may issue a mandatory evacuation when a hurricane approaches, and all visitors must leave the area. There are no emergency shelters in Dare, Currituck, or Hyde counties. Evacuation routes are marked with blue signs. If damage is significant, you may not be able to return to the Banks for an extended period of time. Most vacation rental agencies and hotels do not offer refunds if you have to leave during a storm. Some will refund or credit your money if a mandatory evacuation is ordered; however, most do not offer any reimbursement. If you leave before a mandatory evacuation is ordered, you will definitely not receive a refund. This policy makes it a very good idea to have trip cancellation and

interruption insurance in the event of hurricanes or other storms. Most rental agencies now offer this option with your rental agreement. For more information on hurricane preparedness, contact the county emergency management services: **Carteret County Emergency Management** (252-728-8470), **Currituck County Emergency Management** (252-232-2115), **Dare County Emergency Management** (252-4755655), or **Hyde County Emergency Management** (252-926-4372).

KITEBOARDING AND WINDSURFING Steady winds and shallow, protected water stretching for miles create what many boarders consider a paradise for wind-and-water sports. Wind gypsies make their way to the shallow waters of Roanoke and Pamlico sounds to experience the finest conditions on the East Coast. For the more adventurous, the ocean waves are just a few steps away. Hatteras Island is a world-recognized destination for both sports. The Tri-Villages have several top kiteboarding resorts, while Avon is the East Coast center of windsurfing, also sometimes called sailboarding. Equipment for this sport is available for rent from a number of different services on the Outer Banks. Canadian Hole, renowned among windsurfers, is located on the sound side of Hatteras Island. Kiteboarding, sometimes called kitesurfing, has a steep learning curve and requires a great deal of upper-body strength. Equipment for kiteboarding is generally not available for rent, but those interested can take a lesson that includes equipment. Those who complete Professional Air Sports Association–certified training courses may qualify to rent equipment.

LIQUOR Bottles of liquor are only available in North Carolina at state ABC stores. The **ABC website** (www.ncabc .com) has a complete listing of stores and their hours of operation. Generally, the ABC stores are open Monday through Saturday 10–9 and are closed on Sunday.

While a few towns in mostly unincorporated areas along the coast still don't allow liquor by the drink, beer and wine are universally available at restaurants, groceries, and convenience stores until 2 AM. A new law allows restaurants serving brunch to offer cocktails before noon on Sunday and distilleries, such as **Kill Devil Rum** (www.outerbanksdistilling .com) in Manteo, to sell up to five bottles on-site. For a safe, chauffeured night on the town, contact **OBX Pub Crawl** (www .obxpubcrawl.com).

LODGING Weekly cottage and house rentals are still the norm during the summer season; however, overnight and weekend accommodations are now available year-round, although two- and three-night minimums are still the rule on holiday weekends at all but the most expensive hotels. During the off-season, many shorter rentals are available, and most prices drop dramatically. Pay close attention to cancellation policies wherever you rent, including hotels. Many require early notice of cancellations to refund deposits. Trip insurance is a good idea, especially if you are making a considerable outlay in advance. Another thing to take note of is the hurricane or storm policy followed by your accommodation. These vary widely, but very few offer refunds, even for mandatory evacuations. You may receive a rain check or other compensation, or nothing at all. What you see out of your window may affect the price of your room. Ocean-view and oceanfront rooms will cost more than pool-view or so-called dune-view rooms that may look out on the parking lot. Prices are also often higher on the upper floors of hotels for rooms with ocean views, even though you may have to walk up several flights of stairs to get there. If stairs are a problem, it's a good idea to ask specifically whether a property has an elevator.

MAPS Download current maps of North Carolina from the state **Department of Transportation website** (www.ncdot .org), or you can order a free state transportation map to be sent by mail, either from the website or by calling 1-877-DOT-4YOU or 1-800-VISIT NC.

MARINE MAMMALS AND SEA TURTLES Report dead or stranded whales, dolphins, porpoises, or seals as soon as possible to the **North Carolina Marine Mammal Stranding Network** (www .marinemammalsnccnc.com) on its 24-hour hotline at 252-241-5119. Endangered sea turtles also come to the Banks to nest from May to August. The **Network for Endangered Sea Turtles** (www .nestonline.org) maintains a 24-hour hotline at 252-441-8622 for turtle sightings.

MILEPOSTS Along NC 12 from Corolla to Hatteras Inlet, and along the US 158 Bypass from the Wright Memorial Bridge to the Nags Head–Manteo Causeway, milepost markers (marked MP) help visitors find shops, restaurants, hotels, and other destinations. Farther south, Bogue Banks uses a similar MM system along NC 58, although the practice is not as widespread.

NEWSPAPERS AND PERIODICALS *Carolina Coast Online* (252-726-7081; www.carolinacoastonline.com), 4206 Bridges Street, Morehead City.

The Gam (252-728-2435; www.thegam .com), Beaufort. Weekly publication distributed on Thursday in Carteret County and Swansboro.

Island Free Press (www.islandfree press.org), Buxton. Extensive online coverage of Hatteras and Ocracoke islands.

North Beach Sun (252-449-4444; www .northbeachsun.com), Kitty Hawk. Print and online editions cover news, arts, and real estate on the Outer Banks.

Outer Banks Sentinel (252-480-2234; www.obsentinel.com), Nags Head. Local newspaper publishes on Sunday and Wednesday. Online and mail subscriptions available. A blog, **Outer Banks**

PIRATES

Ocracoke, Beaufort, and the Inner Banks village of Bath are the towns most associated with Blackbeard and his fellow pirates. On Ocracoke, visit the Teach's Hole Blackbeard Exhibit, then take a sail on the schooner *Windfall II*, where Captain Temple will entertain you with tales of pirate lore and point out the spot where Blackbeard met his end. In Beaufort, you can see artifacts recovered from the presumed wreck of Blackbeard's ship, *Queen Anne's Revenge*, in the North Carolina Maritime Museum, and take a ghost tour to the pirate's former home, said to be haunted by one of his unfortunate "wives." Websites where you can find out more about Blackbeard's activities in North Carolina are www.blackbeardthepirate.com and www.qaronline.org.

THE OUTER BANKS WERE A POPULAR DESTINATION FOR PIRATES, INCLUDING BLACKBEARD

Entertainment (www.obxentertainment.com), covers local events.

The Virginian-Pilot (252-441-1620; www.pilotonline.com), 2224 Bypass, Nags Head. Daily paper from Hampton Roads, Virginia, has a section of news from the North Carolina coast. A free section called "The Coast," with Outer Banks entertainment listings and news, is published weekly March–December, monthly January–February.

EACH BEACH HAS ITS OWN SET OF PET REGULATIONS

PETS Rules governing pets on the beach vary widely and by season. In general, pets must be leashed. Several communities don't allow pets on the beach at all during the summer season. Again, check each town's website for its current rules. Pets on 6-foot leashes or in crates are permitted within the national seashores, except at designated swimming beaches. Guide dogs may remain with their owners at all times.

RADIO For a local take on the news, community events, and a mix of alternative music, check out **WVOD The Sound 99.1 FM** (www.991thesound.com), broadcasting from Wanchese, and **WOVV FM 90.1, Ocracoke Community Radio** (www.wovv.org), the voice of Ocracoke Village.

RECOMMENDED READING The **Eastern North Carolina Digital Library** (digital.lib.ecu.edu) contains hundreds of works of fiction and nonfiction, much of it from the 1800s and early 1900s, as well as museum artifacts, maps, and other educational material available free online.

SUGGESTED READING Cleary, William J., and Tara P. Marden. *Shifting Shorelines: A Pictorial Atlas of North Carolina Inlets.* Raleigh, NC: NC Sea Grant, 1999.

DeBlieu, Jan. *Hatteras Journal.* Winston-Salem, NC: John F. Blair, 1998. A naturalist writes evocatively about the barrier island ecology.

Fletcher, Inglis. *Men of Albemarle.* New York: Bantam Books, 1970. Prolific author Inglis Fletcher wrote a dozen meticulously researched historical novels covering 200 years of North Carolina history (1585–1789). Hard to find, but worth the hunt.

Fussell, John O. *A Birder's Guide to Coastal North Carolina.* Chapel Hill: University of North Carolina Press, 1994.

Houser, Lynn. Edited by Jeannie Norris. *Seashells of North Carolina.* Raleigh, NC: NC Sea Grant, 2000.

Kaufman, Wallace. *The Beaches Are Moving: The Drowning of America's Shoreline.* Durham, NC: Duke University Press, 1983. Prophetic.

Kraus, E., Jean Wilson, and Sarah Friday, eds. *Guide to Ocean Dune Plants Common to North Carolina.* Chapel Hill: University of North Carolina Press, 1988.

McNaughton, Marimar. *Outer Banks Architecture: An Anthology of Outposts, Lodges & Cottages.* Winston-Salem, NC: John F. Blair, 2000.

Meyer, Peter K. *Nature Guide to the Carolina Coast: Common Birds, Crabs, Shells, Fish, and Other Entities of the Coastal Environment.* Wilmington, NC: Avian-Cetacean Press, 1991.

Pilkey, Orrin H. *How to Read a North Carolina Beach: Bubble Holes, Barking Sands, and Rippled Runnels.* Chapel Hill: University of North Carolina Press, 2004.

Simpson, Bland. *The Inner Islands: A Carolinian's Sound Country Chronicle.* Chapel Hill: University of North Carolina Press, 2006. A guide to the often-forgotten islands of the North Carolina sounds, written by one of the state's top naturalists, a professor at UNC–Chapel Hill and a member of the Tony award–winning string band the Red Clay Ramblers.

Stick, David, ed. *An Outer Banks Reader.* Chapel Hill: University of North Carolina Press, 1998. Excerpts from nearly five centuries of writings about the region, selected by the Banks' top scholar.

RETIRING TO THE OUTER BANKS Thinking of retiring to the Outer Banks? Take a few minutes to stop by the **Thomas A. Baum Senior Center** (252-475-5635; www.facebook.com/BaumCenter), at 300 Mustian Street in Kill Devil Hills, to see all the activities and support services Dare County has to offer seniors. Visitors 55 and over are welcome to attend the center's many exercise classes.

SCENIC BYWAYS The **Outer Banks National Scenic Byway** (www.outerbanksbyway.com) runs 111 miles from Whalebone Junction in Nags Head to Beaufort, crossing two inlets by ferry. Other North Carolina scenic byways cross Roanoke Island, circle the Albemarle Peninsula, and loop through many towns on the Inner Banks. Maps and descriptions of the various routes can be downloaded from the **North Carolina**

Department of Transportation website (www.ncdot.org).

SCUBA DIVING AND SNORKEL-ING The Graveyard of the Atlantic brings divers from around the world to see German U-boats, 18th-century pirate ships, and everything in between on the bottom of the ocean. The hundreds of wrecks just offshore make the North Carolina coast the world's top destination for wreck diving. Warm Gulf Stream waters make diving possible year-round. Water temperatures in the area reach the low 80s, with visibility to 100 feet during the prime season, May to October. Temperatures, however, plummet at deeper depths. In addition to accidental wrecks, numerous ships, fishing boats, World War II Liberty ships, airplanes, landing craft, and even railroad boxcars have been purposely sunk off the Outer Banks. Two Falcon fixed-wing jet aircraft lie on the bottom approximately 8 nautical miles off Oregon Inlet. The original purpose of this program was to improve bottom fishing, but the artificial reefs also make excellent dive sites, harboring a wide variety of sea life, including the sand tiger sharks for which the area is known. A complete list of artificial reefs can be found on the website of the **North Carolina Department of Environmental Quality** (deq.nc.gov). The website of the **Association of Underwater Explorers** (www.uwex.us) has an extensive listing of wrecks in these waters. BFDC, a club that organizes dive trips, lists over 50 frequently visited wrecks off the North Carolina coast on its **North Carolina Wreck Diving website** (www.nc-wreck diving.com).

The Outer Banks is the only place on the East Coast where historic wrecks can be reached from the beach. Because they require you to swim on the surface through the surf, beach dives, while shallower than boat dives, are more physically demanding. You need to be in good physical shape and a strong swimmer. **Snorkeling in Pamlico Sound** is far safer, and it's an interesting experience, with small fish, shrimp, and crabs to be seen. The waters around **Pea Island National Wildlife Refuge** on Hatteras are usually some of the clearest in the area. The **Cape Hatteras National Seashore** (252-995-4474; www.nps.gov/caha) offers sound snorkeling adventures during the summer months.

SEAFOOD The North Carolina commercial fishing fleet brings home a wide variety of seafood, including shrimp, oysters, clams, and blue crab, plus stripers, tuna, mahi-mahi, mackerel, and much more from the rich ocean waters. The **NC Seafood website** (www.nc-seafood.org) has information on the species found in the state, along with local seafood recipes. Two organizations help you find fresh local catch at fish markets, roadside stands, and restaurants. On the Outer Banks, check the website of **Outer Banks Catch** (www.outerbankscatch.com). On the Crystal Coast, consult **Carteret Catch** (www.carteretcatch.org). Look for the logos of these organizations when you shop or eat out, and always ask: "Is it local?"

SEASONS High season on the Outer Banks has traditionally been Memorial Day to Labor Day. However, shoulder seasons are sometimes carved out of this period, and real estate agents seem to have their own formula to determine the price of rental properties. While the Banks continue to host mostly family groups during the summer, other seasons are becoming more popular, and businesses are increasingly open all year.

SHELLING Beachcombers will find plenty to spark their interest on these shores. Although the heavy surf pounds many shells to fragments, a stroll along the beach, especially in early spring at low tide, may yield a trove of shells,

THE SCOTCH BONNET, STATE SHELL OF NORTH CAROLINA AND A RARE FIND

including quahog clams, scallops, pen shells, olives, moon snails, Atlantic giant cockles, and Scotch bonnets, the state shell of North Carolina. Shelling is generally best at the ends of the islands, along the inlet shores. Excellent collections of shells are on permanent display at the **North Carolina Maritime Museum** in Beaufort and the **North Carolina Coastal Federation** in Newport, both on the Crystal Coast. On the North Banks, the **Hampton Inn and Suites Corolla** displays a fine private collection in its lobby.

SMOKING Since 2010, smoking has been banned inside all restaurants and bars, as well as lodging establishments that offer food and drink, in the state of North Carolina. Many restaurants and bars have added smoking patios and decks since then. Lodging establishments must offer nonsmoking rooms, with no more than 20 percent of rooms designated for smoking. Cigar bars and private clubs are exempt from the smoking ban.

SURFING AND SHAPERS The Outer Banks have some of the best breaks on the East Coast, and reports of a storm in the Atlantic set hordes of surfers in motion as they race to catch the big waves. On Hatteras Island, the **Cape** Point area around the lighthouse is considered the Eastern Seaboard's greatest "wave magnet," creating the best surfing available on the Right Coast. Corolla is the North Banks' surfing hot spot, with easy entry and a reliable sandbar, ideal for beginners. Stop by the **Corolla Surf Shop** to find out where the waves are breaking. On the Central Beaches, you'll find surfers catching waves at **Jennette's Pier**. On Ocracoke, surfers meet up at **Howard's**, where they can watch the waves from the rooftop deck.

The great surfing has attracted many professional surfboard makers as permanent residents. Called "shapers" in surf lingo, some of these board artists own local surf shops; others work freelance. Their designs push the boundaries of boarding ever outward. Many shapers

A VINTAGE BOARD ON DISPLAY AT THE COROLLA SURF SHOP

are now branching out into stand-up paddleboards (SUPs). **Wave Riding Vehicles** (www.waveridingvehicles.com), the largest surfboard company on the Eastern Seaboard, makes boards in its Currituck County factory just across the Wright Memorial Bridge and sells its designs in its Kitty Hawk store. **Tim Nolte's shop** (www.timnoltesurfboards .com) is also on the Currituck mainland. Other well-known local shapers include Murray Ross; Mike Rowe, shaper of **Hooked Surfboards** (www .hookedsurfboards.com); Pat McManus; Lynn Shell at the **Outer Banks Boarding Company** (www.obbconline.com); Ted Kearns, creator of **TK Shapes** (www .tkshapes.com), now based in Hawaii; Mike Beveridge; Scott Busbey, creator of **In the Eye** (www.surfintheeye.com); Mike Clark of **Clark Shapes** (www.facebook .com/clarkshapes252); Rascoe Hunt of **Gale Force Glassing**; the late Robert "Redman" Manville, master of the big gun boards; Eric Holmes of **Formula Surfboards**; and Mickey McCarthy of **New Sun**. Other locally made boards to look for include **Ability**, **Avalon**, **Broken Barriers**, **Cherry**, **Future Foils**, **Hot and Nasty**, **Tropix**, and **Secret Spot**. Surf shops in the area typically carry a selection of new and used boards, many by local shapers. Serious surfers can order a board custom crafted by a master just for them. You can catch a surf report on the local radio stations or call any of the local surf shops for expert advice. Online, you can see reports direct from the beach twice a day at www .obxsurfinfo.com.

TRAILS Part of the 900-mile **North Carolina Mountains-to-Sea Hiking Trail** (www.ncmst.org) traverses the length of the Crystal Coast and Outer Banks, crossing the Croatan National Forest via the Neusiok Trail in Carteret County, then leaping to Ocracoke and Hatteras islands on the state ferries before ending at Jockey's Ridge State Park in Nags Head. The sections of trail on Ocracoke, Hatteras, and Bodie islands run along the beach. Camping is available at established campgrounds within the Croatan National Forest and Cape Hatteras National Seashore. Shorter hiking trails can be found at nature preserves all along the Banks.

TRAINS **Amtrak** (1-800-872-7245; www .amtrak.com) offers daily rail service from Boston, New York, and Washington, DC, to Newport News, Virginia, with bus connections to Norfolk and Virginia Beach. The Palmetto, Silver Meteor, and Silver Star trains offer service from New York City; Washington, DC; Charleston, South Carolina; and Florida, with stops in Richmond, Virginia, where you can connect with the train to Newport News. The Carolinian, running daily between New York City and Charlotte, North Carolina, also stops at Richmond, Virginia, as well as Wilson, North Carolina. Amtrak's Thruway bus service connects with the Palmetto in Wilson, bringing travelers to downtown Morehead City daily, with stops in Havelock, New Bern, and Greenville, North Carolina.

VACATION RENTALS Real estate companies offer a wide variety of different properties for weekly rental. Shorter stays are sometimes available, especially off-season. Cottages generally have two to eight bedrooms; some have as many as 18, making them suitable for large family reunions. Most real estate companies rent only to families. With so many properties now available for rental in this area, many management companies are increasing their efforts to make renting from them hassle-free. Linens and towels, formerly a separate charge, are now included with many rentals, and some companies even make up the beds for you in advance. Companies are also dropping some of the many fees that traditionally have been added on, so that the price you see in brochures or online is actually what you pay, without the hundreds of extra dollars in administrative fees, damage waivers, and fees to use a credit card. Increasingly, you can browse available properties online and make your reservations there as well. We make specific suggestions for rental companies in individual chapters. Here are some companies that represent a wide range of properties all along the coast. Some also offer longer, off-season rentals.

Atlantic Realty (1-877-858-4795; www.atlanticrealty-nc.com). Over 200 properties from Corolla to South Nags Head. All renters enjoy the company's Family Fun amenities package.

🐾 **Brindley Beach Vacations** (1-877-642-3224; www.brindleybeach.com), 1215 NC 12. Family-owned realty company represents over 600 rental properties, including many with pools, elevators, and hot tubs.

🐾 **Cola Vaughan Realty** (252-449-2652; www.obxcola.com), 324 W. Soundside, Nags Head. Pet-friendly cottages from Southern Shores to South Nags Head.

Elan Vacations (1-866-760-3526; www.elanvacations.com), 8624 US 158, Powells Point. Early-arrival policy lets you pick up your keys at the check-in office on the mainland. Three-day off-season getaways can be booked in advance.

Joe Lamb Jr. & Associates (1-800-552-6257; www.joelambjr.com), 5101 Bypass, MP 2, Kitty Hawk. Over 500 properties available, most in the Central Beaches.

Kitty Hawk Rentals (252-441-7166 or 1-800-635-1559; www.beachrealtync.com). Amenity package with some rentals. Partial weeks and long-term rentals available.

Outer Banks Blue Realty (1-888-623-2583; www.outerbanksblue.com). Unique "check-in by mail" program eliminates that time-consuming

visit to the real estate office to pick up keys.

Seaside Vacations (1-888-884-0267; www.outerbanksvacations.com). Full-service management company with offices in Kitty Hawk and Corolla handles rentals at over 300 properties from the off-road area in Carova to Nags Head. Last-minute specials and dedicated event properties available.

Sun Realty (252-453-8822 or 1-888-853-7770; www.sunrealtync.com). One of the largest rental companies on the Outer Banks.

🐾 ♿ (((•))) **Twiddy & Company Realtors** (252-457-1110; www.twiddy.com). Twiddy specializes in the North Beaches and off-road area, listing over 700 properties, including more than 100 beyond the end of the road, some truly immense, with 16 to 18 bedrooms sleeping up to three dozen people. Offices in Duck and Corolla.

VEHICLE RENTALS

B&R Car Rentals (252-473-2141; www.facebook.com/BandRRentACar), 404 US 64, Manteo. Owners of the local Ford dealership have been renting cars at the Manteo airport for more than 50 years.

Island Cruisers (252-987-2097; www.islandcruisersinc.com), 26248 NC 12, Rodanthe. Rents fun, street-legal VW buggies, four-wheel drives for heading out to the beach for surf fishing, vintage classics, and golf carts.

Outer Banks Beach Buggies (252-715-1295; www.obxbeachbuggies.com). Rents street-legal golf carts. Free delivery.

Outer Banks Chrysler Dodge Jeep (252-441-1146 or 1-855-459-6555; www.outerbanksjeep.com), 3000 Bypass, MP 5.5, Kill Devil Hills. Rents four-wheel-drive vehicles for beach driving.

WINGED HORSES OF THE OUTER BANKS

During the Centennial of Flight in 2003, 99 life-size fiberglass winged horses and foals, decorated by local artists, lined the streets of the Outer Banks. The sponsor of the project, the Outer Banks Press, selected the horses to represent both the iconic herds of wild mustangs that still roam the Banks and the development of flight. The resulting works of art, each unique, were tremendously popular with residents and visitors alike. Seventy of the winged horses, some a bit battered by wind and rain, can still be seen at locations around the region, from Corolla to Ocracoke. A full listing of the current locations of the winged horses can be found on the Outer Banks Press website, www.outerbankspress.com.

LOOK FOR THIS WINGED HORSE NEAR THE OUTER BANKS CHAMBER OF COMMERCE IN KILL DEVIL HILLS

Outer Banks Harley-Davidson (252-338-8866; www.outerbankshd.com), 8739 US 158, Harbinger. Rents Harleys to tour the Banks.

WINERIES Roanoke Island is the home of the Mother Vine, the oldest scuppernong vine in existence at 400 years and counting. **Sanctuary Vineyards** (www .sanctuaryvineyards.com), with vines growing on the Currituck mainland, produces award-winning wines ranging from French varietal to a popular ice wine, plus The Plank, hearty red muscadine in a pirate-worthy bottle. Several regional vineyards make muscadine wines, including **Martin Vineyards** (www .martinfarmandwinery.com), on Knotts Island; the **Vineyard on the Scuppernong** (www.vineyardsonthescuppernong.com)

in Columbia; and **Bennett Vineyards** (www.bennettvineyard.com) near Aurora, all within an easy drive of the Outer Banks. On the Crystal Coast, **Somerset Cellars Winery** (www .somersetcellars.com) crafts wines from imported grapes while **Lake Road Winery** (www.lakeroadwinery.com) in Newport creates wines from native grapes and berries.

YOUTH HOSTELS **The Adventure Bound Hostel** (252-255-1130; www .adventureboundnc.com) in Kitty Hawk offers dorm and private rooms, plus a tent campground. Closed during the winter months.

THE PLANK, A PIRATE THEMED RED WINE FROM SANCTUARY VINEYARDS

HISTORY AND NATURE

The Outer Banks, an isolated string of islands thrust into the Atlantic Ocean, stretch for about 175 miles from the Virginia border to Beaufort Inlet. These fragile bits of land are made entirely of shifting sand, exposed to extremes of wind and water. To keep a foothold on this uncertain terrain takes a special breed of people. And though they've seen their homesteads washed over with sand, water, and most recently by developers, the Bankers remain—independent, full of stories, and just a bit salty.

✳ The Barrier Islands: A Fragile Ribbon Made of Sand

The island chain now called the Outer Banks juts into the ocean like the bow of a great ship. Here the two great currents of the western Atlantic—the warm, cobalt-blue waters of the Gulf Stream flowing north, and the cold, murky green Labrador Current traveling south—meet and mingle. It is not a peaceful encounter. The maelstrom where the currents meet extends some 8 miles off the tip of Cape Hatteras. The dreaded Diamond Shoals are a place of fog, shifting sandbars, and sudden surf that have led many ships to their ruin and earned the area the name Graveyard of the Atlantic.

The Banks are in constant motion, changed by every storm. Made almost entirely of sand, the land here is forever rolling westward, driven by waves, wind, and rising sea level. During storms, waves wash across the barrier islands, carrying sand from the ocean beach into the sound waters, moving the islands a little westward, and creating new salt marsh. The process, called "overwash," is now considered a necessary part of the health of the island ecology. It is also the reason most cottages stand on tall legs above the sand. This process has been going on for thousands of years and repeats as sea levels rise and fall. Other bands of barrier islands in the past have formed and moved west until they collided with the mainland. Roanoke Island, now situated between the outer islands and the mainland, is one example.

Viewed from above, the temporary nature of the Outer Banks is revealed. The pounding ocean surf is just yards away from the quiet sound waters at some points. Often these are sites where old inlets have closed—or where new ones are in the process of opening.

THE WASH WOODS ON THE BEACH AT CAROVA ARE REMNANTS OF AN ANCIENT FOREST

✳ The Windswept Dunes

Although it is the ocean that provides the material, it is the wind that gives shape to the great dunes of sand that are the most notable feature of Outer Banks geography. **Jockey's Ridge**, at nearly 100 feet, is the largest dune on the East Coast and the most southern in a line of dunes that once stretched north over the Virginia border. Like all dunes, Jockey's Ridge began life with a wind shadow—a tree usually, or even a building—that blocked the wind. Sand behind the obstruction does not blow away, and a dune begins to form.

The prevailing winds of the area come from opposite directions. From March through August, roughly, the winds come from the southwest, off the mainland. The rest of the year, September to February, the winds whistle in off the open ocean, across the cold Atlantic. These opposite winds are ideal for the formation of dunes. The winter winds are stronger, causing the dunes to move slowly to the southwest, usually just inches a year.

Jockey's Ridge has slowly swallowed a hamburger stand and a miniature golf course since it became a state park in 1975. You can sometimes see the final turrets of a castle on the mini-golf course poking above the sand just across the street from Kitty Hawk Kites. Jockey's Ridge State Park presents good exhibits on the processes that form the dunes, as well as a spectacular view from the top of the ridge.

North of Jockey's Ridge stands **Run Hill**, the next in the line of dunes; it can be accessed from West Airfield Road off US 158. From the top of Run Hill, you can see the sand slowly swallowing the forest on the sound side of the dune, while to the north the next dune in line can be seen. This is **Kill Devil Hill**, the dune used by the Wright brothers for their experiments in flight. No longer technically a dune, since it has been planted entirely

DUNES CHANGE WITH EVERY STORM

A CASTLE FROM A BURIED MINI-GOLF COURSE POKES OUT ABOVE THE SAND AT JOCKEY'S RIDGE

with grass to stabilize it for the monument on top, in the Wright brothers' day it was as nude as Jockey's Ridge. The line of dunes continues on toward Virginia, looming to the west as you drive along NC 12 through Duck and beyond. Past the end of the road in Corolla stands the second largest of the untamed dunes, variously called **Penny's or Lewark's Hill**. The old settlement of Seagull, long buried, is slowly emerging from beneath the ever-traveling sand.

Another undisturbed dune system can be found on Bear Island, part of **Hammocks Beach State Park** near Swansboro. On Hatteras Island, **Buxton Woods** is the final remaining remnant of the great forest of cedar and live oaks laced with grape vines that once covered this island. The trees were timbered off for use in shipbuilding by the mid-1800s, and grazing livestock kept vegetation from regrowing.

Huge dunes, called "whaleheads" by locals, developed on Hatteras during this time and swept across the island. Today they are gone, dissipated into the sound, leaving a relatively flat landscape behind. The low dunes along the oceanfront today are the work of a Civilian Conservation Corps project, which constructed sand fences and planted sea grass to rebuild the dune line in the 1930s.

✳ Inlets and Sounds

While the great dunes are the most obvious work of wind and water, inlets that break up the island chain are the most troubling. A single storm can change the face of the Outer Banks, destroying roads and stranding residents. In fact, **Ocracoke Inlet** and

THE BONNER BRIDGE, CONNECTING BODIE AND HATTERAS ISLANDS SINCE THE 1960S, IS BEING REPLACED BY A NEW BRIDGE ACROSS OREGON INLET

Beaufort Inlet are the only breaks in the barrier island chain that remain the same from the time the earliest explorers drew maps of the region in the 1500s. A great hurricane in September 1846 opened the **Hatteras and Oregon inlets** we know today.

The process that gives birth to new inlets originates not from the action of the ocean but from the combination of wind and the fresh water flowing into the sounds from the rivers of the region. **Pamlico Sound**, the largest lagoon-style body of water on the East Coast, receives vast amounts of water from the Roanoke/Chowan river systems via **Albemarle Sound** in the north, as well as the Tar/Pamlico and Neuse rivers farther south. All of this water reaches the ocean through the inlets that pierce the barrier islands. During a hurricane, the water in Pamlico Sound is often driven far northwest during the early hours of the storm, then returns with devastating force as the winds shift to the southeast during the later stages of the hurricane. It is this huge storm surge coming from the landside that opens new inlets in the Outer Banks.

Inlets may close naturally, or they may get some help. In September 2003, with the Centennial of Flight celebration fast approaching, Hurricane Isabel opened a new inlet just east of Hatteras Village, isolating the community and its ferry dock. The U.S. Army Corps of Engineers moved swiftly to pump sand into the breach, closing it within a month, and rebuilding NC 12. By contrast, inlets are generally allowed to open and close as nature dictates on uninhabited Core Banks within the Cape Lookout National Seashore.

Because of the prevailing winds, inlets tend to migrate southwest along with the rest of the barrier island chain. This process can be seen at work at Oregon Inlet. Since the 2.5-mile-long Herbert C. Bonner Bridge opened over Oregon Inlet in 1965, Bodie Island, on the north side of the bridge, has extended nearly a mile south, while, on the opposite shore, Pea Island retreated until the southern end of the bridge was threatened and the Army Corps of Engineers was forced to build a rock seawall to protect the underpinnings of the bridge. This is seen as a temporary measure, however, and a new bridge has been built, despite many construction delays and setbacks, including the Great Blackout of Summer 2017. Meanwhile, dredging continues year-round to keep

Oregon Inlet open for the sport and commercial fishing fleets that depend on this route to reach the open ocean.

✳ The Inner Banks

The sounds to the west of the Outer Banks vary in width from just a few hundred yards to more than 50 miles. Beyond lie the shores, if you can call them that, of the Inner Banks. Here brackish and fresh waters mix together in broad tidal estuaries, marshes, and wetlands, creating one of the richest breeding grounds for sea life on the planet. These swamps provide some of the last refuges for endangered species, such as the red wolf and red-cockaded woodpecker, and are at the northern limit of the American alligator's range. Black bear, deer, raccoon, turkey, squirrel, rabbit, quail, mink, and otter make these wetlands their home, as do a large variety of poisonous snakes and biting insects. Winter is considered the best time to visit. That's when the region's most beautiful visitors arrive for their winter vacations. Some 100,000 tundra swans—plus many more geese, ducks, coots, and other migrating waterfowl—make the lakes of this region their cold-weather home.

The Carolina bays are unusual features found within this wilderness. These round or oval depressions have been variously attributed to giant prehistoric beavers, an ancient asteroid shower, or—most likely—a remnant of falling sea level at the height of the last ice age. Found scattered all along the southern Atlantic seaboard, these bays, also called pocosins, are most numerous in eastern North Carolina, where thousands have been identified. Rimmed with sand, pocosins often contain acidic lakes surrounded by thick layers of peat. Bay trees, vines, and briars survive best in this nutrient-poor soil, and cypress trees grow along the water's edge.

Some pocosin plants have developed unusual behaviors to supplement their diets. This ecosystem is the evolutionary cradle of carnivorous plants, including the Venus flytrap and the less well-known pitcher plant and sundew. The Croatan National Forest in the Southern Outer Banks is home to the nation's largest collection of carnivorous plants.

✳ "A Land of Plentie"

Sir Walter Raleigh's captains sailed into the waters of the Outer Banks in the late 1500s and brought back stories of great abundance to entice settlers to make the voyage into the unknown. They described a land "so full of grapes as the very beating and surge of the Sea overflowed them." These grapes were the native scuppernongs, of which the 400-year-old Mother Vine on Roanoke Island is the oldest surviving example. Scientists speculate that the native tribes in the area began the cultivation of grapes even before the arrival of the English settlers.

The Banks, then and now, are home to white-tailed deer and the occasional

HUGE FLOCKS OF TUNDRA SWANS WINTER ON LAKE MATTAMUSKEET

black bear that makes the swim from the mainland. Today's bears have been known to make use of the causeways to reach the Banks.

Several beach areas provide important nesting grounds for the endangered piping plover. Endangered sea turtles also come to the Banks to nest from May to August. Loggerhead and green are the species most commonly found, with Kemp's ridley, hawksbill, and leatherback turtles making occasional appearances. The **Network for Endangered Sea Turtles** (252-441-8622; www.nestonline.org) maintains a 24-hour hotline for turtle sightings.

✳ Native Tribes

By the time the English first arrived off the Outer Banks, the area had been occupied for thousands of years by tribes of Native Americans. The coast of North Carolina had villages belonging to all three major linguistic groups then inhabiting eastern North America. The most numerous were the Algonquian-speaking tribes occupying the northern Banks and the shores of Albemarle Sound. Although often warring among themselves, the Roanoke, Croatan, and other tribes of the Chowan River valley spoke languages related to those of the tribes of Virginia and the Chesapeake Bay. To the west, the Tuscarora tribes spoke an Iroquoian language, indicating their origin in the eastern Great Lakes region. The southern Banks and the area around today's New Bern were home to tribes speaking Siouan dialects. The Woccon, occupying Ocracoke, and the Coree who gave their name to the Core Banks, belonged to this group. Early maps created by English explorers show dozens of native villages occupying the Banks and the shores of adjacent sounds and rivers. Population at the time of first contact is estimated to have been in the neighborhood of 10,000 souls.

The coastal regions occupied by the native tribes offered a rich selection of foods. In addition to deer, waterfowl, and much other game, the Indians depended on the ample fish and shellfish, including crabs, oysters, clams, scallops, and mussels, found in the waters of the sounds.

Many of the tribes apparently occupied their coastal encampments for just part of the year, retiring periodically to mainland villages to grow crops of various tubers and root vegetables, as well as corn, squash, pumpkins, gourds, beans, and sunflowers. They also gathered wild walnuts, hickory nuts, and chinquapins, wild grains, and fruits. Early explorers reported that the local tribes drank wine made from local grapes, as well as a tea made from the leaves of the yaupon tree, still found abundantly in the maritime forests. Tobacco was grown as a sacred herb.

Roanoke Island was a center of Native American activity in pre-colonial times. Its name indicates it was a manufacturing center for making the shell money used by the native tribes in trade. Roanoke was a type of wampum that consisted of round disks of shell cut from whelk and clamshells. White was the most common color, but black or purple beads were worth more. The name seems to come from the Algonquian word that means to rub, smooth, or polish—a reference to how the beads were made.

The Croatan Indians had their main village, called Croatoan, on what is now the island of Hatteras, near the village of Buxton. Recently, archaeologists conducted excavations, discovering many pottery shards and a few English artifacts amid enormous numbers of discarded oyster shells. Like most tribes, the Croatans also held land on the mainland more suitable for agriculture. Growing crops on the Banks themselves was difficult because of the high salt content of the soil. Hatteras is derived from an Algonquian word, *hatorask*, which has been translated as "place where nothing will grow."

European diseases decimated the tribes, a process completed by the Tuscarora War. This uprising began in 1711 as the tribes protested the taking of their lands and the capture and enslavement of their people. Most tribes in the area joined the rebellion in a last-ditch effort to expel the English and preserve their traditional ways of life. The natives were utterly defeated in 1715, and the survivors were enslaved or driven inland. Most of the Tuscarora migrated north to join with their cousins in the Iroquois Confederacy. The surviving Coree settled near Lake Mattamuskeet, while many of the Croatan people disappeared into the deep swamps surrounding Alligator River. Other Croatans migrated to the shores of the Lumbee River close to the South Carolina border and joined with the remnants of other tribes to become the forefathers of today's Lumbee Indians.

✳ First Contact and the Lost Colony

Spanish explorers visited coastal Carolina as early as 1520, and in 1524 Giovanni da Verrazano, a Florentine captain sailing under the French flag in search of the Northwest Passage, landed on the Bogue Banks in Pine Knoll Shores, and again near today's Kitty Hawk. He was the first to comment on the vast quantities of grapes growing along the shore, but he mistook Pamlico Sound for the Pacific Ocean.

In 1584, Sir Walter Raleigh received a patent from his queen "for the discovering and planting of new lands not possessed by any Christian Prince nor inhabited by Christian People." Raleigh sent a reconnaissance voyage out that very summer. His captains brought back two young Indians, a Croatan named Manteo and a Roanoke brave named Wanchese, and gave such a glowing report about the new land that Queen Elizabeth, the so-called "Virgin Queen," allowed Raleigh to name his colony Virginia in her honor. Subsequent voyages in 1585 and 1586 didn't go as smoothly. Sir Richard Grenville grounded his ship in Ocracoke Inlet, the sailors spread smallpox through the native villages, and the men left on Roanoke Island were soon in conflict with the local tribe.

QUEEN ELIZABETH I AND HER CAPTAIN SIR WALTER RALEIGH BEGAN ENGLISH COLONIZATION IN THE NEW WORLD

RALEIGH'S LOST COLONY

THE SASSAFRAS THEORY AND MORE CLUES TO ITS FATE

Despite the 400 years since the colonists of the short-lived "Citie of Ralegh" disappeared, the mystery continues to attract public interest as well as scientific research and speculation.

Certainly the colonists died, but when, where, and by what means remain matters of debate. Perhaps they perished through starvation, disease, or massacre at the hands of either the Spanish or the native tribes. Perhaps some trusted the sea and tried to sail home on their small pinnace. Perhaps some joined the Croatan tribe, the friendliest of the natives, thanks to the continuing goodwill of Manteo. Most likely several of these theories are correct and the colonists' fates took them down different roads.

In the 1930s, a series of stones emerged that seemed to be engraved with messages from Eleanor Dare to her father, John White, as she moved southwest with Indian friends. They passed several scientific tests in the beginning but today are generally considered bogus.

The Jamestown colonists made several efforts to find traces of the Roanoke Island group less than 30 years after their disappearance. They discovered nothing conclusive, but there was an abundance of rumors about men who dressed in European clothes and lived in two-story houses or who could "talk in a book." One chief claimed to have sent several youths and a "younge maide" to beat copper at his mine up the Roanoke River, but they were never found. Powhatan, the father of Pocahontas, when consulted on the missing colonists' fate, claimed they had been massacred after taking refuge with a Chesapeake tribe. In 1701, the Indians then inhabiting Hatteras Island told naturalist John Lawson that they were descended from English ancestors, and Lawson noted that many of the group had light hair and gray eyes.

John White, who had perhaps the most reason to seek his daughter and granddaughter, initially felt minimal concern for their fate. The carved letters he found at the abandoned stockade indicated clearly to him that the colonists had taken refuge with the friendly Croatan tribe and were not in immediate danger, since he found no carved cross—the agreed-upon sign of distress.

Research into the fate of the colony picked up speed around the 400th anniversary of its disappearance. In the early 1990s, an archaeological dig at the Fort Raleigh site found a metallurgical workshop used by the 1585 expedition, but no trace of the living area of the colonists. Researchers speculate that the site may have washed away and is now underwater. In

In 1587, John White, an artist who had accompanied one of the earlier voyages, arrived with a party of colonists at Roanoke Island. Among the colonists were the first English women to cross the ocean, including White's pregnant daughter, Eleanor. Abandoned on Roanoke Island by the captain of their transport vessel, White's group soon found themselves reliant on the goodwill of Manteo and his mother, head of the Croatan people. Using the superiority of British arms, White drove off the local Roanoke tribe and installed Manteo as duke of much of the Albemarle Peninsula, including the Alligator River region.

After the birth and christening of his granddaughter, Virginia Dare, White was persuaded to return to London for additional supplies, but he was unable to return to "Virginia" until 1590 because of the attack of the Spanish Armada on England. When he finally set foot once again on Roanoke Island, he found only the letters CRO and CROTOAN carved in the logs of the colonists' palisade. A hurricane drove his ship back across the Atlantic before he could visit Manteo's people.

Despite extensive investigations, nothing certain about the fate of the 117 colonists was ever heard, and the enduring mystery of the Lost Colony was born.

1998, excavations conducted on Hatteras Island at the site of a large Indian village, believed to be the Croatan capital, turned up an English signet ring with ties to the English colonists.

Two separate research organizations continue to investigate the mystery. The **First Colony Foundation** (www.firstcolonyfoundation.org), a group of historians, archaeologists, and concerned citizens, is concentrating its efforts on finding the area occupied by the 1587 colonists at the north end of Roanoke Island. They have conducted underwater surveys in the nearby sound, as well as archaeological digs within the national historic park. The **Lost Colony Center for Science and Research** (www.lost-colony.com), a group of interested scientists and historians, is looking further afield for evidence of the Lost Colony. Using satellite technology, remote sensing, oral histories, and primary sources, they are exploring the fate of the lost colonists on several fronts, including DNA studies in America and Britain.

One of the center's most intriguing theories is based on John White's statement that the colonists planned to move 50 miles into the mainland after his departure. Using old maps and other records, Philip McMullan speculates that the colonists relocated to a Croatan village about 50 miles away on the Alligator River, where abundant stands of sassafras trees were located. Sassafras was the main cash crop in the early years of American colonization, before tobacco came to the fore. The roots of the sassafras were at the time believed to cure syphilis, a newly introduced disease then running rampant through Europe. While Raleigh's early voyages are well known, few are aware of the later voyages he sponsored to bring home cargos of sassafras. In 1602, sassafras was selling for up to 2,000 British pounds per ton, and the profits from one voyage in that year permitted Raleigh to fit out two more ships in 1603. The location where Raleigh's captains found these cargos, ready for shipment, was a closely guarded secret and may well have been the Alligator River region.

Recently, an early map drawn by John White himself was discovered in the British Museum. Examination revealed that it has a patch placed over the symbol of a fort at the junction where the Chowan and Roanoke Rivers join to form Albemarle Sound, about 50 miles from the original settlement on Roanoke Island. Researchers speculate that settlers from Roanoke Island established a settlement there so ships from England could easily load sassafras for the voyage home. The patch seems to be in keeping with the remarkable secrecy that surrounded Raleigh's sassafras trade.

The site marked by the patch is opposite Edenton, one of North Carolina's oldest towns, and lies within the exclusive golf community of Scotch Hall. Excavations are ongoing.

✳ Lords Proprietor and the Iron Men of Albemarle

By the 1650s, planters from Jamestown began to move down the Chowan River and into the Albemarle area, spreading gradually south. In 1662, King Charles II granted the lands south of Virginia to eight of his cronies, called the Lords Proprietor, who named the region Carolina in his honor.

Over the next several decades, the new owners of Carolina took measures to tighten their control over the Albemarle colonists, decreasing the power of elected officials. A series of clashes between the Proprietory and anti-Proprietory parties culminated in **Culpeper's Rebellion** in 1677, the first uprising against British tyranny in the colonies. The planters who inhabited the banks of Albemarle Sound earned the name of "Iron Men," thanks to their stiff determination on self-rule.

Beaufort, named for Henry Somerset, Duke of Beaufort, one of the Lords Proprietor, was established in 1713 next to the deepwater inlet then called Topsail, making it the third-oldest town in the colony, following Bath and Edenton farther north.

BLACKBEARD AND THE AGE OF PIRATES

A lthough the name of Blackbeard looms large in North Carolina history, his actual career of piracy was relatively short. Like many eventual pirates, Edward Teach, aka Blackbeard, originally served aboard a privateer with letters of marque from Queen Anne of Britain. These permitted him to capture French and Spanish ships during the War of Spanish Succession, called Queen Anne's War in North America.

After the war ended in 1714, many of the privateers continued to attack foreign ships, but their actions were now considered piracy. In 1717, the royal government offered a one-time pardon to English privateers turned pirates, and most of the active pirates accepted.

Teach (that may or may not have been Blackbeard's true name) first rose to prominence as the magistrate of the short-lived Pirate's Republic on the island of Nassau. In 1717, he and his associate, Captain Benjamin Hornigold, captured the French slave ship *Le Concorde*. Teach equipped the ship with 20 guns and made it his flagship, renaming it the *Queen Anne's Revenge (QAR)*. In May 1718, he committed his most daring feat—a blockade of Charleston harbor. Blackbeard's demand was unusual: he would release his hostages and leave the harbor in return for a box of medicine. Shortly after Charleston met his demands, Blackbeard sailed his fleet of four vessels north, loaded with treasure taken from Spanish ships of the line. The *QAR* ran aground in Beaufort Inlet. Historians speculate that Teach purposely beached the vessel to rid himself of most of his crew. Certainly the flagship could never navigate the shallow inshore waters of the Outer Banks. Divers found what is believed to be the wreck of the *QAR* in 1996 in waters off Fort Macon.

Teach off-loaded most of his treasure onto the *Adventure*, a smaller vessel, left the majority of the crew on a convenient sandbar, and sailed up Pamlico Sound to Bath, where he finally accepted a royal pardon from Governor Charles Eden and reportedly married a local girl. The area was a familiar one for Teach. Legend says he had houses in both Beaufort and Bath at various times. His domestic bliss

THE SHORES OF NORTH CAROLINA WERE POPULAR GATHERING SPOTS FOR PIRATES DURING THE AGE OF SAIL, AND REMAIN SO TODAY, WITH SEVERAL ANNUAL FESTIVALS HOSTING PIRATE INVASIONS

was short-lived, however, and by the fall of 1718 he was once again under sail. By November, reports located him at Ocracoke Inlet, roasting pigs; drinking meal wine, the local liquor; and partying with other pirates. Here Lt. Robert Maynard of the Royal Navy caught up with Blackbeard and, in a pitched battle at a spot called Teach's Hole, cut off the pirate's head, ending the career—but not the fame—of North Carolina's most notorious pirate.

✳ The Civil War on the Banks

The Confederates built numerous fortifications along the Banks in the early days of the Civil War. Gun batteries were built on Huggin's Island (now part of Hammocks Beach State Park), on Beacon Island in Ocracoke Inlet, at the southern end of Hatteras Island, and on Roanoke Island. In April 1861, the Confederates occupied Fort Macon, built in 1826 to defend the port of Beaufort. Union general Ben Butler attacked the forts on Hatteras Island at the end of August 1861, the first amphibious attack of the war. Confederate troops based on Roanoke Island attempted to retake Hatteras in September. The armies chased each other up and down the island for several days, causing the locals to dub the battle the **"Chicamacomico Races."**

Union forces took Roanoke Island on February 7, 1862, and that spring New Bern and Fort Macon fell. The Confederate "mosquito fleet" was defeated off Elizabeth City, and Plymouth and other towns in North Carolina's northeast soon were under Union control. The Confederates managed to defend the Dismal Swamp Canal and the Wilmington & Weldon Railroad, keeping the supply lines to Richmond open. The port of Wilmington, defended by Fort Fisher at the mouth of the Cape Fear River, remained open until the final months of the war.

During the war, the Confederates built many ironclads in the rivers of North Carolina and sent them downstream to do battle with Union gunboats. In April 1864, the Confederates successfully recaptured the port of Plymouth with the support of the ironclad CSS *Albemarle*. This was the last major Confederate victory of the Civil War.

During the war, Roanoke Island hosted a unique social experiment, the **Freedmen's Colony** (www.roanokefreedmenscolony.com). Many enslaved people from nearby

A REPLICA OF THE CONFEDERATE IRONCLAD *ALBEMARIE* FLOATS IN THE RIVER OFF PLYMOUTH

regions escaped and made their way behind Union lines. Declared "contraband" by the U.S. military, these men, women, and children settled in a New England–style village, which included a sawmill, church, and school. By war's end, the population reached an estimated 3,500. The village was dismantled after the war, but many inhabitants of Roanoke Island today trace their family history back to the Freedmen's Colony.

✳ Great Storms, Lost Ships, and Heroic Rescues

No one knows how many ships have been lost off the North Carolina Banks. Estimates range from the hundreds to many thousands. All agree, however, that this shore richly deserves its reputation as the Graveyard of the Atlantic. From the famous ironclad, USS *Monitor*, lost off Cape Hatteras in 1862, to the latest fishing trawler that fails to return to port, the ocean continues to exact its toll.

Storms are the greatest danger, and hurricanes arriving from the tropics June through November cause widespread devastation. But residents of the Banks fear the nor'easters that blow in just as much. Storms such as the Ash Wednesday storm of 1962, the Halloween storm of 1991, and the Thanksgiving storm of 2006 live on in local lore.

As early as 1792, the U.S. Congress authorized the building of lighthouses along this coast to aid navigation. Wooden light towers were constructed at **Bald Head Island on the Cape Fear River** in 1795 and on **Shell Castle Island in Ocracoke Inlet** in 1798. The **first Cape Hatteras Lighthouse** was completed in 1803, and a light tower began operation at **Cape Lookout** three years later. The lighthouses were upgraded over the years, but ships continued to run ashore, with crew and passengers perishing, often just yards from safety. The local fishermen and farmers along the Banks frequently came to the aide of shipwreck victims.

In 1874, the **U.S. Life-Saving Service** (www.uslife-savingservice.org), a division of the U.S. Department of the Treasury, established seven stations along the Outer Banks. One of the earliest was the **Chicamacomico Station** (www.chicamacomico.org) in Rodanthe, where the original buildings have been beautifully restored. In addition to Chicamacomico, several other early lifesaving stations survive, although not in their original forms. The **Kitty Hawk** station today houses the Black Pelican Restaurant, the **Caffey's Inlet** station serves as a restaurant at the Sanderling Resort, and the **Kill Devil Hills** station was moved to Corolla to become a real estate office. The **Little Kinnakeet** station near Avon is being restored by the National Park Service.

Most of the surfmen manning these stations were locals, often descendants of shipwreck victims themselves, seeking to supplement their incomes and carrying on a tradition of service to those in peril at sea. A series of devastating wrecks during 1877 and 1878 caused Congress to authorize an additional 11 stations along the North Carolina coast. Lifesaving stations were eventually located about 4 miles apart along the entire Outer Banks. The surfmen patrolled every mile of beach on foot or horseback 24

THE ORIGINAL 1874 LIFE-SAVING STATION AT CHICAMACOMICO ON HATTERAS ISLAND DISPLAYS THE UNIQUE CARPENTER GOTHIC ARCHITECTURAL STYLE

hours a day. When a ship in distress was sighted, they launched lifeboats through the surf or used a small cannon to send a line from the beach to the wreck, allowing them to bring survivors to safety using the breeches buoy apparatus or a metal life car.

Many of the Life-Saving Service's most daring rescues took place on the Outer Banks. Some of the most notable include the rescue of the crew of the schooner *E. S. Newman* in 1896 by the men of the Pea Island Life-Saving Station, the only station staffed by African Americans, and the rescue by the Chicamacomico station of the crew of the British tanker *Mirlo* after it was torpedoed by a German U-boat in 1918. In 1899, Rasmus Midgett of the Gull Shoal Station single-handedly rescued the 10-man crew of the barkentine *Priscilla*.

The men of the Life-Saving Service had a motto: "You have to go out, but nothing says you have to come back." This same brave spirit and commitment continue today in the U.S. Coast Guard, a service established in 1915 by the merger of the Life-Saving Service and the Revenue Cutter Service. One of the Coast Guard's largest bases is located at Elizabeth City.

✳ Taking to the Air

The first years of the 20th century were important ones on the Outer Banks. The work of the Wright brothers that led to the first airplane flight at Kill Devil Hills in 1903 is well known and the subject of the **Wright Brothers National Memorial** (www.nps.gov/wrbr). Wilbur and Orville Wright began coming to Kitty Hawk in 1900 to conduct glider experiments. They returned to test improved gliders the next two years, and in the fall of 1903 arrived with a powered flyer equipped with a wooden propeller and an aluminum engine created in their bicycle shop. On December 17, they successfully left the ground, and the Age of Flight began.

About the same time and not far away, inventor Reginald Fessenden was

THE WRIGHT BROTHERS MEMORIAL IN KILL DEVIL HILLS COMMEMORATES THE FIRST SUCCESSFUL POWERED AIR FLIGHT

RECOMMENDED READING

Mobley, Joe A. *Ship Ashore! The U.S. Lifesavers of Coastal North Carolina*. Raleigh, NC: Division of Archives and History, North Carolina Department of Cultural Resources, 1994.

Noble, Dennis L. *That Others Might Live: The U.S. Life-Saving Service, 1878–1915*. Annapolis, MD: Naval Institute Press, 1994.

developing another important invention—the wireless telegraph, which led directly to radio and today's wireless technology. Working for the U.S. Weather Bureau, Fessenden successfully sent a message from Hatteras Island to Weirs Point on Roanoke Island on April 26, 1902, a demonstration witnessed by several Navy officers. The development of wireless technology proved a great advance in weather forecasting and an important new aid to keep ships safe at sea.

✳ The German U-Boat Invasion

During World War II, a major battle raged off the Outer Banks, even today largely unknown to the American people. From the time of Pearl Harbor and the American declaration of war, dozens of German U-boats were active along the Atlantic Coast.

FOUR GERMAN U-BOATS ON THE SEA FLOOR NEAR THE OUTER BANKS ARE POPULAR DESTINATIONS FOR DIVERS

RECOMMENDED READING

Hickam, Homer. *Torpedo Junction: U-Boat War Off America's East Coast, 1942.* Annapolis, MD: Naval Institute Press, 1996.

Some came so close they reported seeing the lights from U.S. cities. Afraid of causing panic, the U.S. government did not call for a blackout until August 1942. Sinking tankers and cargo boats along the coast was so easy that German commanders referred to it as "the great American turkey shoot." The U-boats sank nearly 400 Allied ships off the North Carolina coast during this period, with over 5,000 lives lost. The seas off Diamond Shoals earned yet another ominous name: **Torpedo Junction**.

The war in the shipping lanes was no secret to the residents of the Outer Banks, who witnessed great explosions and fires off the coast and found the bodies of burned and drowned seamen washed up on their beaches. The people of Ocracoke buried several British sailors when a submarine sank the HMS *Bedfordshire*. The British Cemetery there is the only official bit of British soil in the United States, outside of the embassy in Washington, DC. By mid-1942, the U.S. military began to counterattack against the German subs. Air submarine patrols took off from the Manteo airport, and naval stations were established on Ocracoke and at Morehead City. The top-secret **Loop Control Station** on Ocracoke intercepted transmissions from German U-boats that helped locate them.

The U.S. Coast Guard and U.S. Navy finally got the better of the German fleet. Four U-boats are known to rest on the ocean bottom off the Banks and are now favorite destinations for divers.

✳ Tourism—Past, Present, Future

The first seasonal visitors to the Outer Banks arrived in the early 1800s as planters in the Albemarle region looked for a healthier place for their families to spend the summer. Francis Nixon, a Perquimans County planter, is the first summer visitor on record. He brought his family to the Banks village at the base of Jockey's Ridge in 1830 to escape an outbreak of malaria. Soon after, Nixon bought 200 acres stretching across the Banks from the sound to the ocean, and Nags Head, the first resort destination on the Outer Banks, was born.

In 1838, the 200-room **Nags Head Hotel**, located on the shore of the sound, opened. Visitors arriving at its dock could look forward to a season of balls and formal dinners, as well as bowling, card games, and ocean bathing. A boardwalk connected the hotel to the beach, and local Bankers made good incomes transporting visitors to the shore in their pony carts. Today that hotel lies buried beneath the dunes of Jockey's Ridge, which slowly swallowed the property in the 1870s. By then, the vacation village had shifted its focus to the ocean beach.

Around 1855, Elizabeth City physician Dr. W. G. Pool bought 50 acres of oceanfront property from the Midgetts, who were then, as they are now, a prominent Banker family. Pool paid a reported $30 and sold lots to his neighbors in Elizabeth City for $1 each. By 1885 there were 13 cottages lining the shore, the first of the "Unpainted Aristocracy" of Nags Head. Several of these historic cottages still survive, although most have been moved back from the ocean several times, as storms washed away the sand

HISTORIC LIGHTHOUSES OF NORTH CAROLINA

Beginning in Corolla and stretching nearly to the South Carolina border, the North Carolina coast has seven historic lighthouses. Built between 1818 and 1958, the lighthouses each sported a distinctive color pattern to help ships distinguish between them during the day; at night each flashed an individual light signature. Most of the North Carolina beacons are still in operation. This list travels north to south.

Farthest north, the **Currituck Beach Light** (www .currituckbeachlight.com), a 162-foot redbrick tower completed in 1875, operates under the stewardship of the Outer Banks Preservationists. Climbing is permitted seasonally.

Bodie Island Light (www.nps.gov/caha), 156 feet tall, is painted in horizontal black and white stripes. Completed in 1872, it is still in operation under the care of the National Park Service (NPS) and retains its first-order Fresnel lens. The lighthouse reopened for climbing in 2013 after an extensive renovation.

Cape Hatteras Light (www.nps.gov/caha), at 198 feet, is the tallest and most famous lighthouse in

THE 162-FOOT CURRITUCK BEACH LIGHT, LOCATED NEAR THE VIRGINIA BORDER

America. Painted in a black and white spiral pattern, it was moved to a new location in 1999 and continues to flash its signal out to sea. The NPS opens the lighthouse to climbers during the summer season.

Ocracoke Light (www.nps.gov/caha), a 65-foot white tower built in 1823, is the oldest continuously operating lighthouse in North Carolina and the second oldest in the United States. Still owned by the U.S. Coast Guard, the lighthouse is maintained by the NPS. Climbing is not permitted; however, the base is open for limited hours during the summer months.

Cape Lookout Light (www.nps .gov/calo), completed in 1859, is painted in a pattern of black and white diamonds. At 163 feet, it was the first tall lighthouse to be built and served as a model for later construction. The lighthouse can be reached by boat from Beaufort and Harkers Island, where Cape Lookout

THE 1872 BODIE ISLAND LIGHT

THE CAPE HATTERAS LIGHT   THE OCRACOKE LIGHT   THE CAPE LOOKOUT LIGHT

National Seashore visitor centers are located. The lighthouse is still operational and open for climbing May to September.

The remaining two lighthouses marked the treacherous entrance to the Cape Fear River in southern North Carolina: Bald Head Island Light (www.oldbaldy.org), no longer in service, was built in 1818, making it the oldest lighthouse still standing in the state. The 109-foot octagonal structure is built of brick covered with concrete. Open for climbing during the summer months, Old Baldy, as it's called by its fans, can be reached by ferry from Southport. Oak Island Lighthouse (www.oakislandlighthouse.org), a poured concrete 158-foot structure striped gray, white, and black, was built in 1958 to replace several earlier beacons and was one of the last manually operated lighthouses in the world. Tours of the first and second levels are conducted by the Friends of Oak Island Lighthouse.

Several other aids to navigation were used in North Carolina waters. Lightships, the most famous of which was anchored off Cape Hatteras on the Diamond Shoals until torpedoed by German submarines, helped mark extremely shallow waters. In the sounds, screw-pile lighthouses helped guide ships. Replicas of the screw-pile cottage-style lights can be found in Manteo on Roanoke Island and in Plymouth on Albemarle Sound.

For more information, visit the website of the Outer Banks Lighthouse Society (www.outerbankslighthousesociety.org).

SCREW-PILE LIGHTHOUSE ON THE MANTEO WATERFRONT

EARLY BEACH COTTAGES IN NAGS HEAD, MEMBERS OF THE UNPAINTED ARISTOCRACY

in front of them. Early cottages were often constructed on sled runners to make this easier.

In the years following the Civil War, Northern businessmen discovered the superb waterfowl hunting available in the region. Much of the land around the sounds was bought by hunt clubs, where sportsmen were accommodated in varying degrees of luxury during their annual winter visits.

The 1920s brought a new group of tourists to the Outer Banks as the first waves of motorists arrived in their Model Ts, crossing the sounds on ferries or taking an adventurous route along the tide line from Virginia Beach.

The year 1928 saw two causeways built to make access to the Banks easier. In Morehead City, a toll bridge linked the end of the rail line to an ocean bathing pavilion on Bogue Banks in today's Atlantic Beach. And in the same year, the **Washington Baum Bridge** linked Roanoke Island with Nags Head. The Baum project was a true leap of faith. At the time, the only way to reach Roanoke Island was by a lengthy journey on rough roads followed by a ferry ride from the mainland. On the Nags Head end, the bridge ended in sandy ruts leading north and south; no roads had yet been paved on the Banks. However, Baum, then chairman of the Dare County Board of Commissioners, was a big believer in the philosophy "if you build it, they will come."

National attention was focused on the Outer Banks in 1928. It was the 25th anniversary of the Wright brothers' first flight, and the National Aeronautic Association commemorated the event by placing a 10-ton boulder at the point of takeoff. The next year, work began on the 60-foot-tall Wright Memorial pylon, which was dedicated in 1932, the beginning of the **Wright Brothers National Memorial**.

W. O. Saunders, founder and editor of the *Elizabeth City Independent* newspaper, was another of the area's notable boosters. He advocated the development of the Wright Memorial and helped organize the group of Elizabeth City businessmen who built the **Wright Memorial Bridge** from the Currituck mainland to Kitty Hawk. The 3-mile bridge was completed in 1930, and in 1931 the state paved the Beach Road, now NC 12, between the Nags Head and Kitty Hawk bridges. Dubbed the **Virginia Dare Trail**, the new road made it possible for motorists to drive on pavement from the mainland all the way to the gates of the "Citie of Ralegh" on Roanoke Island. This re-creation of Raleigh's colony, originally built by local history buffs, became part of the national park system in 1941.

The Lost Colony **outdoor drama**, another Saunders idea, was first performed in 1937. Franklin D. Roosevelt attended a performance, and the drama, originally intended to be a one-season affair to celebrate the 250th anniversary of Virginia Dare's birth, continues to be produced today, more than 80 years later.

In 1933, Saunders and one of his columnists, Frank Stick, began promoting another project in the *Independent*, this one for a coastal park that would restore and protect the rapidly eroding beaches of the Outer Banks. The idea caught on, and funds for the restoration of the dunes along the bald beaches were allocated at the federal level.

The **Civil Works Administration** and its successor, the **Civilian Conservation Corps**, began work constructing sand fences and planting sea grasses to rebuild the dunes in late 1933. The project was a success, and by 1940 a barrier dune as much as 25 feet high ran down Hatteras Island and along about half of the Ocracoke Island

THE 1932 WRIGHT MEMORIAL PYLON, AN EARLY TOURIST DESTINATION

beachfront. It proved impossible to build dunes as far as Cape Lookout because the Core Banks were still being used as pasturage for free-roaming horses and cattle.

Meanwhile, the **Cape Hatteras Seashore Commission** sought donations of land for the proposed seashore park. In 1935, the owners of a hunt club on Hatteras donated 999 acres surrounding the Cape Hatteras Lighthouse to the project. Other donations followed until the beginning of World War II put seashore protection on the back burner.

The postwar years brought a boom in tourism and a rise in property values that almost put an end to the project, but in 1952 an anonymous donation for the purchase of park lands made the **Cape Hatteras National Seashore** (www.nps.gov/caha) a reality nearly 20 years after it was first approved by the U.S. Congress.

The **Cape Lookout National Seashore** (www.nps.gov/calo) followed in 1966. Together, these national parks preserve a unique and ever-changing ecosystem that continues to attract visitors from around the world.

THE NORTH BEACHES

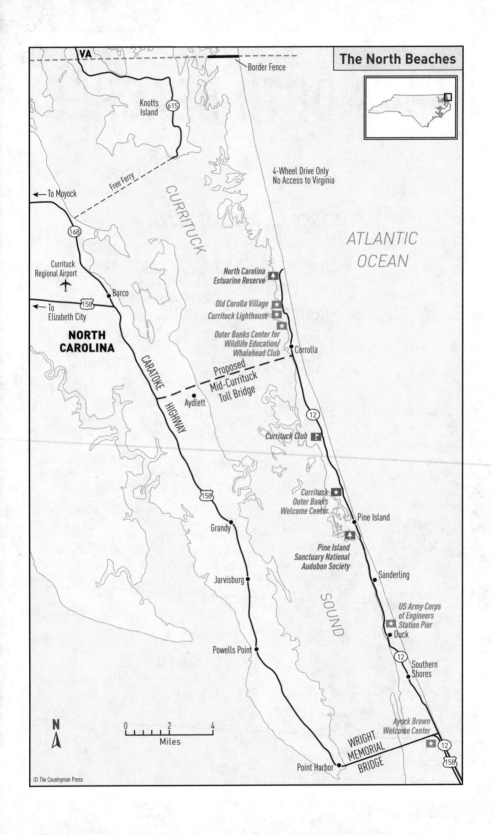

INTRODUCTION
The North Beaches: Where the Road Ends

The North Beaches of the Outer Banks are not islands, but they have been. The original northern boundary of North Carolina was set at Currituck Inlet back in 1663. When the inlet closed in 1828, the island became a peninsula, connected to the Virginia mainland.

In the mid-1900s, many inhabitants of the North Beaches commuted up the beach to jobs in Virginia. But in 1974, a fence at the border blocked the route. On the Virginia side, protected by the fence, lie pristine **False Cape State Park** and the **Back Bay National Wildlife Refuge**, neither of which allows any vehicular access. The border fence has become a tourist attraction in its own right for visitors on the North Carolina side. Numerous proposals were made over the years to build a paved road connecting the Virginia and North Carolina coastlines. But these all came to nothing, and NC 12 today ends at a beach access ramp about 12 miles south of the Virginia line.

The human history of the North Beaches is largely the story of NC 12, originally just a sandy track behind the dunes. Most locals drove on the beach. But when the **Wright Memorial Bridge** joined the mainland with the Banks in 1930, attention inevitably turned to the stretch of Banks to the north, more than 30 miles of dunes and marshes dotted here and there with fishing villages and lifesaving stations. As NC 12 was paved farther north over the following four decades, tourism moved with it up the Banks.

✻ Bridge to the Future

As the summer population in Corolla multiplied, so did the traffic trying to reach the area up narrow, two-lane NC 12. Calls came to expand the road to four lanes, a move much opposed in Duck, where it would mean the sacrifice of a considerable portion of the trees that line the road through town. An alternative solution to the problem was found: a new toll bridge and causeway across Currituck Sound. Stretching from US 158 to NC 12 in Corolla north of TimBuck II, the 7-mile-long Mid-Currituck Bridge will join mainland Currituck County with its beachfront area, diminish drive-through traffic farther south, and cut the drive time to Corolla. The bridge, placed on hold in 2013, has been approved by the North Carolina legislature, but awaits updated environmental impact statements before construction begins.

GETTING AROUND *By bicycle:* The North Beaches are great for biking, with dedicated multiuse paths stretching along NC 12 from Corolla all the way to the junction with US 158 in Southern Shores. Bike paths wind through Historic Corolla Village and Historic Corolla Park, then paved paths parallel both sides of NC 12 as it heads south, reverting occasionally to a wide shoulder. A paved path runs along the road from the Dare County line through Duck and Southern Shores to the US 158 intersection, then turns west along 158 to Kitty Hawk Elementary School. From there you can cross 158 to the Woods Road multipurpose path through Kitty Hawk Woods. Other paved and unpaved paths lace the neighborhoods in Southern Shores, Duck, Sanderling, and Corolla.

TOP ACTIVITIES ON THE NORTH BEACHES

1. Go off-road to see the **Banker horses**.
2. Climb the **Currituck Lighthouse**.
3. Have a picnic at scenic **Historic Corolla Park** after visiting the **Whalehead Club**.
4. Discover the history of waterfowl hunting at the **Outer Banks Center for Wildlife Education**.
5. Have sunset cocktails on a west-facing deck along the **shores of Currituck Sound**.
6. See the bird art at the **Sanderling**.
7. Stroll the **waterfront boardwalk in Duck**, checking out the shops along the way.
8. Plan a **foodie tour of Duck**, with a course at each of its famous restaurants.

By car: Only one road threads north–south along this narrow strip of land, NC 12, named Ocean Boulevard in Southern Shores, Duck Road in Duck, and Ocean Trail in Corolla. Cross streets are short and generally dead-end at the water on both the east and west.

COROLLA AND CAROVA

NC 12 ends in Corolla, pronounced *cuh-RAH-la* by locals. Originally it was a small fishing village and home of the **Currituck Beach Lighthouse**, built in 1875.

Today, the lighthouse is part of a complex of attractions that makes a popular day-trip destination for visitors staying farther south on the Banks. Located on the sound side of NC 12, **Historic Corolla Park** includes the lighthouse, the **Whalehead Club**, and the **Outer Banks Center for Wildlife Education**, all surrounding a boating lagoon and picnic area. On the north side of the lighthouse, the old village of Corolla houses a shopping district of charming shops with an off-the-beaten track appeal.

The Outer Banks Conservationists led the drive to preserve the area's history. Starting in the late 1970s, the group raised more than $1.5 million in private dollars to restore the Currituck Beach Lighthouse and its keepers' quarters. The buildings had been standing open to the elements for over 40 years, and several had been hauled away by local residents, a time-honored Outer Banks tradition.

The restoration of these buildings dating to the late 1800s gives the area a unique group of what is today called "stick style" Queen Anne. Architectural features are notable in the keepers' house, now used as a museum store, and a storage building topped with sharp finials, now used for offices, as well as the **1878 Life-Saving Station** on NC 12, today the office of Twiddy Realty. The design elements found in these buildings have provided inspiration for more recent architects and can be seen reflected in many new buildings in the area.

A mile past the lighthouse, NC 12 comes to its end at a beach access ramp. Beyond a fence and livestock grate lie 12 miles of unpaved North Carolina, variously called the outback, the off-road or 4x4 area, and, most commonly, Carova, thanks to its position between the states of North Carolina and Virginia.

The land is a patchwork of public and private wildlife refuges, traveling sand dunes, and communities where owners and renters travel by four-wheel drive along sandy tracks or on the beach. Wild horses and 12-bedroom vacation cottages exist here side by side, along with a sprinkling of beachcomber shacks and year-round homes.

The best way to explore this area is with one of the local outfitters who know how to get around, where to find the horses, and how to avoid getting stuck in the sand. ATVs are not permitted. Commercial businesses are also not allowed in the area north of the fence. All groceries and other supplies must be brought in by four-wheel-drive vehicle from Corolla.

GUIDANCE The **Currituck County Visitor Center** (252-453-9612 or 1-877-287-7488; www.visitcurrituck.com), at 500

A WILD HORSE EYES ITS NEW NEIGHBOR

Hunt Club Drive, just off NC 12 in the Ocean Club Centre, provides a wealth of information on the area. Ocean Club Centre is the first shopping center you'll pass as you approach Corolla from the south.

Additional information on beach regulations and local attractions is offered by the **Currituck Outer Banks Welcome Center** (252-435-2938; 106 Caratoke Highway, Moyock, NC 27958) and the **Currituck Chamber of Commerce** (252-453-9497; www.currituckchamber.org), both located on the mainland.

POST OFFICE The **Corolla U.S. Post Office** (252-453-2552) is at 1150 Ocean Trail/NC 12. The zip code throughout Corolla is 27927.

PUBLIC RESTROOMS Restrooms open to the public are located at the **Currituck County Visitor Center**, the **Currituck County Southern Beach Access**, the **Light House Ramp Beach Access**, and **Historic Corolla Park**.

PUBLIC LIBRARY **Corolla Public Library** (252-453-0496; www.earlibrary.org/corolla), 1123 NC 12. Closed weekends. Public-use computers, Wi-Fi, and children's area available for visitors.

GETTING THERE *By boat*: A few boaters come to Corolla by water from Back Bay in Virginia Beach or across Currituck Sound from Knotts Island or the Currituck mainland. However, the water here is very shallow, suitable only for flat-bottomed boats. There are no harbors or piers on the oceanfront.

By car: The only road into Corolla is NC 12 coming from the south. There is no approach from the north. You cannot drive down the beach from Virginia. NC 12 is called Ocean Trail in Corolla.

GETTING AROUND If you plan to head north of the paved road into the off-road area, you'll need a four-wheel-drive vehicle. You can use your own vehicle or rent one from several companies located in the area. However, if you plan on venturing off the beach into the interior to look for horses, your best bet is to join a guided tour. Getting stuck in the sand is a very real possibility on the sandy tracks that crisscross the area, and it can throw a serious wrench into your vacation schedule. Tour companies offer trips in both closed and open vehicles to suit weather conditions. You can drive yourself or leave the driving to an experienced guide. Most companies operate year-round.

✳ To See

THIS SANDY LANE IS ONE OF THE MAIN STREETS IN CAROVA

Historic Corolla Park (252-453-9040; www.whaleheadclub.org), MP 11, NC 12.

MUST SEE

Currituck Beach Lighthouse and Keepers' Houses (252-453-4939; www.currituckbeachlight.com), 1101 Corolla Village Road. The 162-foot lighthouse was the last one built along this coast, illuminating the final "dark spot" starting in 1875, and retains its original first-order Fresnel lens. Climb the 214 steps to the top to enjoy an unsurpassed view of the Corolla area from early spring to Thanksgiving weekend (closed Thanksgiving Day) for a fee of $10 a person. Children under eight years old climb for free. The complex of buildings surrounding the lighthouse is remarkably complete, with several restored residences, storage buildings, cisterns, even a privy. The Keepers Quarters and other buildings on the grounds are examples of the Victorian "stick style" architecture, circa 1876, several topped with sharply pointed finials. The restoration of the lighthouse and its sur-

rounding buildings, begun in the late 1970s by the Outer Banks Conservationists, cost more than $1.5 million, and continues with the interior of the main Keepers Quarters still in progress. The smaller keepers' cottage is now a museum gift shop, selling lighthouse replicas and other memorabilia that support the ongoing restoration. The buildings are arranged around a shady green lawn frequented by artists and photographers.

The 39-acre park is a small fraction of the original grounds of the Whalehead Club, but it seems pretty spacious amid today's development. A self-guided interpretive trail tells the history of the area. Launch your boat, kayak, or personal watercraft at the free boat ramp to access the sound. Or just admire the sunset from the arching bridge and gazebo. Many special events, from concerts and wine tastings to Halloween hayrides, are held here annually. Plenty of free parking.

Historic Corolla Village (252-457-1190; www.twiddy.com/history). Old Corolla, once a fishing village that was the largest town between the Virginia border and Kitty Hawk, has been renovated into a district of charming shops, largely through the efforts of the Twiddy family. Highlights include the **1900 Corolla School House** (1126 Schoolhouse Road); the pre-1920 **Parker House** (1129 Corolla Village Road), now housing the museum of the Wild Horse Fund; the **1895 Lewark-Gray House** (1130 Corolla Village Road), now home to Lovie's Wellness; and the **1884 Corolla Post Office**, in the Austin Building on NC 12. The **Village Garden**, located behind the Parker House, offers a delightful retreat featuring native and heirloom species, with herb, vegetable, and butterfly gardens. Services are still conducted in the ♂ **1885 Corolla Chapel** (252-453-4224; www.corollachapel.com) at 1136 Corolla Village Road. Refreshments are available at **Corolla Village BBQ** next to the Parker House.

U.S. Life-Saving Station/Twiddy & Company Realtors (252-457-1190; www.twiddy.com/history), 1142 NC 12. The 1878 Kill Devil Hills Life-Saving Station played an important part in the history of the Banks when surfmen from this station helped the Wright brothers complete their early flights. Preservationist Doug Twiddy moved the

GORGEOUS SUNSETS ARE A REGULAR FEATURE OF HISTORIC COROLLA PARK, ONE OF THE MOST SCENIC SPOTS ON THE OUTER BANKS

derelict building to Corolla and restored it. Visitors are welcome to view the Wright brothers and lifesaving station memorabilia on display and pick up information on Corolla's historic district.

THE 1900 COROLLA SCHOOLHOUSE, A LANDMARK IN OLD COROLLA VILLAGE

Wash Woods Coast Guard Station (252-457-1190; www.twiddy.com/history), North Swan Beach. This landmark in the off-road area served as a lifesaving and Coast Guard Station from 1917 and was restored by Twiddy & Company for use as a real estate office. Visitors are welcome to stop by to view the memorabilia and historic photos on display.

✐ ♂ **The Whalehead Club** (252-453-9040; www.whaleheadclub.org), 1100 Corolla Village Road, Historic Corolla Park. With copper roof shingles, cork floors, Tiffany light fixtures, duck-head doorknobs, and many art nouveau details, the Whalehead Club stands as a monument to a former age. This imposing 21,000-square-foot edifice began life in 1922 as the winter cottage of Northern industrialist Edward Knight and his bride, before becoming the most elegant hunt club on the southeast coast. After decades of other uses ranging from a boys' school to a rocket-testing facility, the sumptuous structure has been restored to pristine condition. Ghost,

THE WHALEHEAD CLUB, AN ART NOUVEAU GEM POISED ON THE SHORE OF CURRITUCK SOUND

children's, and other guided tours are available, as well as a self-guided audio tour. All tours except the audio tour require reservations.

🖉 **Outer Banks Center for Wildlife Education** (252-453-0221; www.ncwildlife .org). Spacious museum in Historic Corolla Park explores the region's rich heritage of waterfowl hunting and fishing with exhibits that include a life-size duck blind, an 8,000-gallon aquarium stocked with native fish, and the 250-piece Neal Conoley collection of antique decoys, one of the finest in the country. A short film discusses Currituck Sound's role in the ecology of the region. The center provides a year-round schedule of classes suitable for ages two through adult, including decoy carving, crabbing, kayaking, fly tying, and nature photography. The classes are mostly free, but registration in advance is highly recommended. The center is open daily all year, including many holidays. Admission is free.

🖉 **Wild Horse Museum** (252-453-8002; www.corollawildhorses.com), 1129 Corolla Village Road. The museum and headquarters of the Corolla Wild Horse Fund, dedicated to preserving and protecting the wild herd of some 100 horses, houses exhibits telling the history of the horses and the challenges they face. Some days, a "gentled" mustang is on hand to greet visitors and offer rides. Children's

AN EXHIBIT AT THE CENTER FOR WILDLIFE EDUCATION DEMONSTRATES WATERFOWL HUNTING FROM A NOW-OUTLAWED SINK BOX

activities are offered in summer for a small fee. Admission to the museum is free. Proceeds from the gift shop help keep the horses wild and free.

✳ To Do

BANKER HORSE TOURS No trip to the Outer Banks can be complete without a journey off-road to see the wild horses coexisting with villagers north of the fence in Corolla. To do this, you'll need a four-wheel-drive vehicle.

Numerous companies offer tours, but your best bet, and a must for horse lovers, is a trip with the Corolla Wild Horse Fund (252-453-8002; www.corollawildhorses .com). These tours, conducted by naturalists who oversee the welfare of the herds, often cost less than similar commercial

DESCENDANTS OF SPANISH HORSES ROAM FREE IN THE OFF-ROAD AREA AT THE NORTH END OF THE OUTER BANKS

tours, and they come with a year-long membership in the fund. Bonus: 100 percent of the tour price goes to help preserve the wild horses.

These companies also offer tours dedicated to wild horse preservation in the off-road area:

Bob's Wild Horse Tours (252-453-8602; www.corollawildhorsetours.com), 817 B Ocean Trail (NC 12). Operating horse tours since 1996, Bob White Jr. is one of the originals. Family-oriented tours go out in open-air, safari-style trucks morning, afternoon, and evening, and guarantee that you'll see wild horses or you get a refund. **The Bier Box** (www.obxcraftbeer.com), featuring craft beers from the Carolinas, is located at the company's base in the Food Lion Shopping Center.

Corolla Outback Adventures (252-453-4484; www.corollaoutback.com), 1150 NC

HORSES HAVE THE RIGHT-OF-WAY IN CAROVA

12. Enjoy a "ride-along" tour that visits several exclusive areas of the wild horse sanctuary donated by tour guide Jay Bender's family, which has been leading off-road adventures since 1962, when the road ended south of Duck.

Wild Horse Adventure Tours (252-489-2020; www.wildhorsetour.com), 610 Currituck Clubhouse Drive. Tours aboard specially equipped Hummers (www .hummeradventuretours.com) take visitors through high sand dune trails and through maritime forest inaccessible to most 4x4 vehicles.

BICYCLING The North Beaches are great for biking, with dedicated multiuse paths stretching along both sides of NC 12, plus paved and unpaved paths lacing

QUICK TIP

Stay 50 feet away from any wild horse you encounter or risk a ticket from local law enforcers. Never feed the horses anything. They have adapted to their sandy, salty environment, and any unfamiliar food, even things domestic horses love, such as carrots or corn, may kill them.

many Corolla neighborhoods. Paved paths and sandy lanes wind through Historic Corolla Village and Historic Corolla Park.

Several companies will deliver a wide-tired beach cruiser to your door. Tandem bikes, tricycles, child seats, and tagalongs are also available from most outfitters. Some also offer bikes with gears. Contact **Just for the Beach Rentals** (1-866-629-7368; www .justforthebeach.com) at the Ocean Club Centre or **Ocean Atlantic Rentals** (252-453-2440; www.oceanatlanticrentals.com) in Corolla Light Town Center. These companies also rent kayaks, surfboards, stand-up paddleboards, tennis rackets, and a variety of other things you might need for your vacation, from high chairs to outdoor grills. They'll even set up your beach chairs and umbrella every day of your vacation so you don't have to bother toting them. Both offer free delivery for orders over $95. Ocean Atlantic delivers to the off-road area.

FISHING Most of Currituck Sound is too shallow for oceangoing charter boats. However, fishing in the sound with light tackle is very good. This was once the sea bass capital of the world. On the beaches, surf fishing reigns, with a world-class red drum run in late fall. No public ocean piers are available along the north coast, but you can fish or crab in the sound from the pier and gazebo at **Historic Corolla Park**. There is no fee, but you'll need a North Carolina Recreational Fishing License.

Corolla Bait and Tackle (252-453-9500; www.corollabaitandtackle.com), with two locations in Corolla (1070 Ocean Trail, next to the Inn at Corolla Light, and the Shoppes at Currituck Club), can set you up for offshore, inshore, backcountry, wreck, or big

WILD HORSES: FREE SPIRITS OF THE BANKS

Manes flying in the wind, hooves leaving their imprint in sand, the herds of wild horses that make their home among the dunes are some of the most popular—and most endangered—tourist attractions of the Outer Banks. Once the herds roamed at will from Virginia to Shackleford Banks. Today they are confined to narrow stretches of land and a few islands, their numbers controlled by park rangers often more concerned with the survival of native grasses than that of the horses, which they consider an "exotic species."

These attitudes are at odds with the beliefs and wishes of most of the local inhabitants. Early settlers reported that the horses were there before them, and the old families of the Banks tell tales of taming the local horses. They pulled pony carts and plows, helped the surfmen of the Life-Saving Service rescue shipwrecked sailors, and raced around Jockey's Ridge.

On Ocracoke, locals held a pony penning on July Fourth every year, rounding up the native ponies and selecting some to be sold off-island, thus stabilizing the size of the herd. The island's Boy Scout troop, established in 1956, was the first mounted troop in the country. Each boy caught, tamed, and trained his own horse.

When most of Ocracoke, including the area where the herds roamed free,

game safari fishing aboard their air-conditioned headboat, the *Jill Louise*. They also offer surf fishing classes, rod/reel and crab pot rentals, plus a huge selection of tackle and bait. Drop by either store for free local fishing advice. Introductory crabbing and fishing trips aboard their pontoon boat are family favorites.

FOR FAMILIES Biking, beachcombing, flying kites, and building sand castles are some of the most popular family activities on the North Beaches. Kids can learn crabbing or fishing at Historic Corolla Park and paint a horse (or ride one) at the ✐ **Corolla Wild Horse Museum** (252-453-8002).

The ✐ **Outer Banks Center for Wildlife Education** (252-453-0221; www.ncwildlife .org) in Historic Corolla Park offers free classes geared to children as young as three throughout the year. Registration is required.

✐ **TimBuck II** (www.timbuckii.com), known for its numerous shopping and dining options, is also a great destination for family activities.

✐ **Corolla Water Sports** (252-453-6900; www.corollawatersports.com), located at the docks along the sound behind TimBuck II, rents kayaks, pontoon boats, and WaveRunners, and offers kayak ecotours that paddle through the protected marsh

became part of the Cape Hatteras National Seashore, the park rangers wanted to remove all the ponies to prevent overgrazing and to protect the ponies themselves from the traffic on NC 12. Local Ocracokers organized a protest and managed to keep some of the ponies on the island. About 25 to 30 ponies remain on Ocracoke, now confined to a 180-acre "pony pen."

Wild or feral horses are still found at several other locations on North Carolina's Banks. About 100 individuals live north of Corolla in the off-road area next to the Virginia state line. Once free-roaming, the Corolla herd is now confined to about 12,000 acres north of a fence and cattle guard near the end of NC 12. The horses were moved behind the fence after collisions with automobiles led to numerous fatalities. In one accident alone, six horses were killed. The Corolla Wild Horse Fund (www.corollawildhorses.com) operates an educational museum and store to support the herd.

Farther south, the horses of Shackleford Banks live much as their ancestors did, running free on a barrier island off Beaufort, with no road or other traffic to threaten them. Nearby, an unrelated herd of feral horses, descended from a herd released here by a local farmer in the 1940s, occupies Carrot Island.

The origin of the Banker ponies and horses has been much debated, but scientific evidence is mounting to support the theory that they are descended from Spanish horses brought to these shores in great numbers by early explorers, as well as from ships wrecked along the coast. Horses are great swimmers and, according to records, were often driven overboard to lighten a ship stuck on a sandbar.

The Corolla, Ocracoke, and Shackleford horses all exhibit typical Spanish traits, including five rather than six lumbar vertebrae. In addition, a unique and rare blood variant found only in horses of Spanish descent is carried by the Shackleford herd. DNA tests are ongoing, and the Horse of the Americas organization recently officially recognized the Corolla and Shackleford herds as Heritage Herds of Colonial Spanish Horses. On a less positive note, the American Livestock Breed Conservancy in 2008 moved both herds from the threatened to the critical category, on the verge of extinction. The U.S. Congress recently passed legislation that will let the Corolla and Shackleford herds expand and interbreed to increase genetic diversity and hopefully assure the survival of these horses—descendants of the first Europeans to reach the Outer Banks.

waterway owned by the Currituck Hunt Club, one of the best paddling routes on the Banks. Parasailing is available for those looking for a thrill, and there's plenty of shady seating if you just want to watch. The complex also includes the Golf Links mini-golf course, with several holes set on an island. Younger kids will enjoy a paddleboat cruise on the canals and a pond full of turtles, fish, and waterfowl.

More fun at TimBuck II? ☄ **Corolla Raceway** (252-453-9100; www.corollaraceway .com) has a go-kart track, bumper cars, and video arcade. ☄ **Kitty Hawk Kites** (252-453-8845; www.kittyhawk.com) offers free kite-flying lessons.

Another mini-golf opportunity, the ☄ **Grass Course**, is located at the **Corolla Light Resort** (252-453-4198).

Public playgrounds in Corolla are located at **TimBuck II Shopping Village** and **Corolla Light Town Center.**

GOLF ☄ **The Currituck Club** (252-453-9518; www.thecurrituckgolfclub.com), 620 Currituck Club Drive. Set amid dunes and marsh, this award-winning Rees Jones course is a links-style par 72, considered one of the top golf experiences in the state. Jones's design makes superb use of the land, formerly part of the legendary Currituck

SUNSET IS A SPECIAL TIME ON THE NORTHERN BANKS, WHERE SOUND-SIDE GAZEBOS OFFER VIEWS TO THE WEST OVER THE MARSHES

Hunt Club, yielding awesome views of the ocean, sound, and nearby lighthouse. 🏌 **The Hunt Club Tavern** serves lunch, dinner, and after-golf libations. Call well in advance for tee times.

HUNTING The 35-mile-long **Currituck Sound** is shallow and grassy, ideal habitat for the migrating ducks, geese, and swans that visit in great numbers every winter. Currituck County makes a limited number of blinds available to hunters with waterfowl hunting permits from the state. Contact the **Currituck County Game Commission** (252-429-3472; www.currituckgamecommission.org) and the **North Carolina Wildlife Resources Commission** (1-888-248-6834; www.ncwildlife.org) to start the process.

You can also arrange a hunt with a local guide service. One of the best known in the region is **Stuart's Hunting Lodge** (252-232-2309), run by the family of Watson Stuart, world swan-calling champion.

SPAS **Eden Day Spa and Salon** (252-453-0712; www.edendayspasalon.com), Monteray Plaza. Get wrapped in rosemary mint or Caribbean seaweed at this spa that specializes in Aveda products.

Lovie's Wellness (252-453-0912; www.loviescorollavillage.com), 1130 Corolla Village Road. Enjoy a facial or massage in a 100-year-old cottage in the heart of the Corolla Village historic district. Salon services, yoga and art classes, energy healing, and more available.

Corolla Yoga (717-503-5716; www.corollancyoga.com). Chelsea Miller offers Vinyasa yoga sessions on the beach and at area resorts.

TENNIS **Pine Island Racquet and Fitness Center** (252-453-8525; www.pineislandrc .com), 290 Audubon Drive off NC 12, Pine Island. This full-service fitness and racket sport center is open to the public, offering day and weekly memberships and tennis lessons. Facilities include two outdoor clay courts and three indoor cushioned courts for tennis, a fully equipped fitness center, and a pro shop.

RECOMMENDED READING

Find out more about the region's hunting traditions in books written by Travis Morris, including *Duck Hunting on Currituck Sound: Tales from a Native Gunner* (2006); *Currituck Memories and Adventures* (2007); *Ducks, Politics and Outlaw Gunners* (2008); and *Untold Stories of Old Currituck Duck Clubs* (2010). All are published by **History Press** (www.arcadiapublishing.com) in Charleston, South Carolina, and are available at area bookstores.

TOURS 🖉 **Back Country Safari Tours** (252-453-0877; www.outerbankstours.com), 1159 Austin Street. In addition to 4x4 tours into a private Spanish Mustang preserve, this outfit offers novice kayak tours that let you see the horses from the water, as well as fat-tire Segway safaris on off-road trails. You can also sign up for a tamer, but still interesting, Segway tour around Historic Corolla.

Corolla Jeep Adventures (252-453-6899; www.corollajeepadventures.com), 1070 Ocean Trail. The Meredith family has purchased a wide swath of land in the off-road area, including Penny's Hill, the second-largest sand dune on the Banks. They offer a variety of tour options, including a self-drive jeep safari and ATV tours to the top of Penny's Hill, as well as kayak tours in the sound. The Mothership boat cruise visits Monkey Island to see the ruins of a historic hunt club and one of the area's largest bird rookeries, before dropping off kayakers to paddle back to the dock. GPS-equipped jeeps are also available for rental.

A SEGWAY TOUR IS A FUN WAY TO SEE THE HISTORIC SITES OF COROLLA

WATER SPORTS 🖉 **Coastal Explorations** (252-453-9872; www.coastalexplorations .com), 1118 Corolla Village Road. This outdoor adventure company has a shop and boardwalk leading to the sound in Historic Corolla Village. Rent a kayak or stand-up paddleboard and launch from their dock to explore Currituck Sound on your own or with a guided tour, or sign up for crabbing or a sunset cruise aboard their boat.

Corolla Kiteboarding (252-202-1227; www.corollakiteboarding.com). Corolla's shallow waters make it a great spot to explore the booming sport of kiteboarding. Equipment rentals available for experienced kiteboarders.

Corolla Surf Shop (252-453-9283; www .corollasurfshop.com), 807 Ocean Trail, Monteray Plaza. With over two decades of experience, this outfit is the most knowledgeable on local surf conditions, with instructors who are experienced in offering lessons for all abilities in surfing, SUP, and kiteboarding. Or go on a surfing safari with shop owner, Gary Smith, a winning pro on the East Coast circuit.

SURFIN' USA: OBX STYLE

The beach at Corolla forms many long, flat sandbars close to shore, making it an easy and safe place to enter the water with your board. *Outside* magazine rated Corolla one of the six best places in the United States to learn how to surf. The off-road beaches north of town are favorites with the surf crowd. Another popular break is found at the end of the Lighthouse Ramp Road, across NC 12 from the lighthouse.

New and used boards are for sale. Rentals include surf, SUP, body and skim boards, kayaks, wetsuits, and bikes. While you're there, check out the classic surfboards on display, including a 1930s hollow-wood board and experimental designs from the 1960s.

Corolla Water Sports (252-453-6900; www.corollawatersports.com), Kitty Hawk Water Sports, TimBuck II. Truly a one-stop shop for fun, this complex behind TimBuck II rents WaveRunners, kayaks, paddleboats, and a flat-bottom party boat, or will take you parasailing. Guided kayak ecotours paddle north to the Whalehead Club or south through the protected marsh waterway owned by the Currituck Hunt Club, one of the best paddling routes on the Banks.

The Island Revolution Surf Company (252-453-9484; www.islandrevolution.com), 1159 Austin Street. Cool shop in Corolla Light Town Center schedules surfing and SUP lessons and rents surfboards, SUPs, surf fishing gear, bikes and beach chairs.

Outer Banks Charter Fishing Adventures/Corolla Bait and Tackle (252-453-9500; www.corollabaitandtackle.com). Relaxing tours aboard the pontoon boat *Currituck Queen* include a sunset cruise and a trip around Monkey Island, once a famous hunt club.

✳ Green Space

With extensive marshes on Currituck Sound and unspoiled beaches on the Atlantic, plus the off-road playground beyond the end of the road, the North Beaches have some of the best ecotourism opportunities on the Banks.

Note that no ATVs are allowed in the off-road area, and four-wheel-drive vehicles are requested to stay on the established sand roads through the communities. No access is available to the Virginia side of the state line through the locked gates.

You must keep 50 feet away from any wild ponies you come upon. Do not feed them any kind of food, even hay or apples. Ponies have died in recent years from well-meaning visitors feeding them food that their digestive systems are not adapted to handle.

BEACHES The beaches at the northern end of the Banks are wide, inviting, clean, and generally not crowded. An excursion onto **Carova Beach** (www.carovabeach.info) north of Corolla at the end of NC 12 is a fascinating journey, best taken with a local who knows how to navigate the maze of largely unmarked sand tracks. If you venture in with your own four-wheel-drive vehicle, stick to the beach, and you can't get lost—but keep an eye on the tides. Public facilities, including restrooms, a picnic area, and a boat launch, can be found at **Carova Beach Park** at Milepost 21, 2100 Ocean Pearl Road. Commercial development is forbidden, but you can buy T-shirts, and perhaps get directions, at the **Carova Beach Volunteer Fire and Rescue Station** (252-453-8690; www.cbvfandr.com) at 2169 Ocean Pearl Road.

Here are some hints for driving on the beach that may keep you from getting stuck. Lower the pressure in your tires to 20 PSI. Be sure you know the weather forecast and the tide tables. High surf can cut you off. Avoid getting too close to the water. If your tires do begin to spin, back up in your tracks for several car lengths, then move forward slowly. You may need to let out more air. Locals usually take along a shovel, wooden planks, and a towrope. Don't forget the sunscreen, hat, cell phone, and extra water.

If you do get stuck, don't call 911. This is not considered an emergency. Instead, use your cell phone to call the local tow service, **A-1 Towing and Recovery** (252-453-4002; www.a1towingcorolla.com). When you come off the beach, re-up your tires with air, and your cooler with beverages, at Winks grocery.

You can drive, walk, or bike onto the beach from Corolla's North Beach Access ramp where NC 12 ends, 24 hours a day, 365 days a year, and drive north on the beach all the way to the Virginia line. Beware of Wash Woods Beach, where many stumps protrude from the sand, remnants of an ancient forest, as well as other hazards, especially the wild horses that frequent the beach during hot weather. Many have been killed or maimed by speeding drivers.

Elsewhere in Corolla, you can access the beach via East Corolla Village Road, the sand road across NC 12 from the lighthouse, also called Lighthouse Ramp Road. Public restrooms are located here.

The Currituck County Southern Beach Access at 471 Ocean Trail (NC 12) has bathrooms, showers, and parking. There is a lengthy walk to the ocean.

Free public parking lots about a block from public beach walkways are available on Whalehead Drive at Sailfish, Bonito, Perch, Sturgeon, and Shad streets. The ban on parking on the shoulders of streets is vigorously enforced.

Another public beach access is located at the Pine Island Audubon Sanctuary, next to the Hampton Inn.

Bonfires, glass, personal watercraft, camping, and ATVs are all prohibited on Currituck County beaches. Pets must be on a leash.

TRAILS **CAMA Sound Boardwalk**, Historic Corolla Park. A short boardwalk just west of the lighthouse leads through an abundance of native plants to a deck with great sunset views over the marsh.

& **Currituck Banks National Estuarine Preserve** (252-261-8891; www.nccoastal reserve.net). Just before the end of NC 12, a boardwalk and hiking trail lead from a parking lot through several barrier island habitats, including mature maritime forest and marsh, to decks overlooking the sound. Interpretive signs explain the ecology of the area.

Currituck National Wildlife Refuge (252-429-3100; www.fws.gov/currituck). Several tracts in the off-road area are included in this national refuge, established to protect the fragile dune ecosystem and endangered species, including piping plover, loggerhead sea turtle, and seabeach amaranth. Visitors must park on the beach and walk in to explore interior areas. No public facilities.

Audubon Center at Pine Island (252-453-0603; www.ncaudubon.org). Occupying one of the last undeveloped parcels

MARSHES AT CURRITUCK WILDLIFE REFUGES HARBOR NUMEROUS WATERFOWL

ANOTHER DAY COMES TO A CLOSE WITH A MAGNIFICENT SUNSET OVER CURRITUCK SOUND

of land between Kitty Hawk and Corolla, this 6,000-acre sanctuary stretches from the ocean dunes to the marshes of the sound. A 2.5-mile, self-guided nature trail runs along the sound side of the sanctuary, beginning behind the Pine Island Racquet & Fitness Center. Two decks on the sound make great spots for birding. The old Pine Island Hunt Club is being renovated as an environmental education center.

✳ Lodging

Corolla has very few hotels and inns, but it boasts some of the most luxurious rental homes on the Banks. During the last few decades, the entire ocean side of NC 12 became lined with tall beach houses, many with private pools, hot tubs, and elevators, well suited to large family get-togethers.

INNS ✳ ♿ ((ᵞ)) **Hampton Inn and Suites Outer Banks Corolla** (252-453-6565; www.obxbeachhotel.com), 333 Audubon Drive, Pine Island. Located north of the Sanderling, this low-rise hotel sits just behind the dune line, halfway between Corolla and Duck. The spacious 123 guest rooms and studio suites all have balconies or patios, and most have a

sleeper sofa. Complimentary breakfast is served daily in the lobby, where you can browse an extensive seashell collection. An indoor pool and hot tub are open all year, while outdoors a pool, kiddie pool, and one of the few lazy rivers on the

AN ARTISTIC COLLECTION OF SHELLS ON DISPLAY IN THE LOBBY OF THE HAMPTON INN ON PINE ISLAND

EXCURSIONS

KNOTTS ISLAND: BETWEEN TWO STATES

Across the sound from Corolla lies a community isolated on an island caught between North Carolina and Virginia. Connected by a causeway to Virginia, Knotts Island is actually a part of North Carolina's Currituck County, although the only connection is by boat. Several boat tours visit the island from the Corolla area of the Outer Banks, just a few miles across the sound, and it's a popular destination for kayakers as well. Once known as the home of duck-hunting preserves, Knotts Island today is a quiet, friendly community. Peaches are the biggest crop here, and the community hosts an annual peach festival in July. The actual name of the town on Knotts Island is Fruitville. The **Martin Farm and Winery** (www.martinfarmandwinery.com) offers wine tastings and pick-your-own apples, peaches, scuppernong grapes, and pumpkins in-season.

The ducks and snow geese still come by the thousands, finding a winter home in **Mackay Island National Wildlife Refuge** (www.fws.gov/mackayisland) along the Virginia border. This land was once the estate of publishing magnate and philanthropist Joseph P. Knapp, founder of Ducks Unlimited, the organization that has done more than any other to preserve the great migrating flocks for future generations. Throughout the refuge, hiking trails and observation decks invite visitors to see the rich wildlife that made this part of the world famous. A free state-run ferry off NC 168 on the Currituck mainland takes 45 minutes to reach this island, surrounded by marsh in Currituck Sound. From the ferry dock, NC 615 travels a dozen miles north to the Virginia border and then on to Pungo, Virginia, just south of Virginia Beach. You can find out more about this unique community at its website, www.knottsislandonline.com.

THE BAY-VILLA MARINA ON KNOTTS ISLAND OFFERS FACILITIES FOR BOATS, AS WELL AS PEARL'S, THE ISLAND'S ONLY RESTAURANT AND BAR

Banks are open seasonally. The hotel has its own game room, coin laundry, and fitness center, and guests also have access to the facilities at the Pine Island Racquet & Fitness Center. Summer $$$; off-season $$.

❄ ♂ ♿ (((•))) **The Inn at Corolla Light** (252-453-3340 or 1-800-215-0772; www .innatcorolla.com), 1066 Ocean Trail/ NC 12. The farthest north of all Outer Banks hotels, this inn sits within the Corolla Light community and shares its extensive amenities, including ocean-front and soundfront activity centers and an indoor sports center with pool, hot tub, and racquetball and tennis courts. The inn itself is charming, with friendly staff and a complimentary continental breakfast buffet served daily in the sunny dining room. Each of the 43 rooms and suites is unique, many with views of Currituck Sound, all with pillowtop beds, refrigerator, TV, and coffeemaker. Guests can enjoy the intimate hot tub and pool with views of the sound, or watch spec-tacular sunsets from the inn's gazebo, which sits at the end of a 400-foot pier. In the summer, kayaks, personal watercraft, sailboats, and other craft are available for rent. Bicycles are free for guests. Summer $$$$; off-season $.

RESORT ♂ **Corolla Light Resort** (252-453-2455; www.corollalightresort.com), 1197B Franklin Street. The largest and most amenity-laden community on the North Beaches, this resort includes 400 homes on 250 acres that stretch from the ocean to the sound. Renters enjoy, among other amenities, an oceanfront recre-ation center with two pools; a soundside swimming pool, pier, and gazebo; kayak rentals; mini-golf; an ecology trail; a fish-ing pond; an indoor sports center; a free summer trolley service; and weekly planned activities during the summer season. $$–$$$$.

VACATION COTTAGE RENTALS 🐾 ♿ ♂ **Corolla Classic Vacations** (252-453-9660 or 1-866-453-9660; www .corollaclassicvacations.com), 1196 NC 12. This property management company represents more than 200 properties in

THE GAZEBO AT THE INN AT COROLLA LIGHT, A FAVORITE SPOT FOR SUNSET COCKTAILS

THE VIEW FROM YOUR COTTAGE IN THE OFF-ROAD AREA MAY INCLUDE A WILD HORSE

the Corolla area, many equipped with elevators, private pools, and hot tubs. Holiday rentals and partial week rentals available.

Karichele Realty (252-453-2377 or 1-800-4532377; www.karichele.com), TimBuck II. Lists many properties, some pet friendly, in Swan Beach and Carova, where you may see wild ponies in your yard.

🐾 ♿ (((•))) ⌁ **Twiddy & Company Realtors** (252-457-1190; www.twiddy.com), 1127A Schoolhouse Lane. Twiddy specializes in the North Beaches and off-road area, listing over 700 properties, including more than 100 beyond the end of the road, some truly immense, with 16 to 18 bedrooms sleeping up to three dozen people.

🐾 ♿ **Village Realty** (252-453-9650 or 1-877546-5362; www.villagerealtyobx .com), 501 Hunt Club Drive, Ocean Club Centre. Represents properties at Corolla Light and the exclusive Currituck Club. Last-minute specials available.

✳ Where to Eat

With the majority of lodgings in Corolla rental houses and cottages, take-out and gourmet markets play a huge role in the local dining scene, so you'll find lots of seafood, barbecue, and pizza take-out

places here. Restaurants typically are accustomed to the large parties that stay at these beach castles, but it's always a good idea to call ahead for reservations.

DINING OUT 🌿 **Agave Roja** (252-453-0446; www.agaveroja.com), 807B Ocean Trail, Monteray Plaza. This upscale Mexican spot is wowing customers with authentic regional cuisine and a big selection of premium tequilas. Try a tequila tasting flight, a mojito, or sangria by the glass or pitcher. Seafood enchiladas, vegetarian entrées, gluten-free items, and lots of Mexican sweets highlight the interesting menu. $$.

🐾 ✳ **Metropolis** (252-453-6167; www .metropolisobx.com), 520K Old Stoney Road, Ocean Club Centre. This intimate spot, serving dinner only, is everything other dining destinations in Corolla are not: no big servings, no children's menu, no split checks for big groups. At this destination of choice for foodies, plates are small, tapas-style. Menus change with the season, featuring truffles, foie gras, and exotic mushrooms. Stop by for a late-night cocktail and a nibble of something interesting at the bar to have a look at the art on walls and plates. $$$$.

🌀 🗲 ♿ 🍸 **Mike Dianna's Grill Room** (252-4534336; www.grillroomobx.com), 777 Sunset Boulevard, TimBuck II. Mesquite-grilled meats and seafood, plus some pasta entrées, are the specialties at

THE BAR AT METROPOLIS MAKES A GREAT DESTINATION FOR COCKTAILS AND TAPAS

IT'S NOT ALL PIZZA AND BARBECUE: DINING IN COROLLA OFFERS LOTS OF INTERESTING OPTIONS

this popular spot in TimBuck II that can accommodate large groups. Steaks and chops are hand-cut and aged in-house before being marinated and seared on the hardwood grill, and come with your choice of house-made sauces and butters. A big wine list recognized by *Wine Spectator* complements the menu with vintages in every price range, including many bottles under $40. Try the mesquite-grilled banana split for dessert. You can eat inside in the white-tablecloth dining room or outside on the casual deck, where you'll enjoy live music in-season. Reservations recommended, especially for large groups. Dinner $$$.

✐ ♿ ♟ ✈ **North Banks Restaurant & Raw Bar** (252-453-3344; www.northbanks .com), 794G Sunset Boulevard, TimBuck II. Popular spot on the upper deck of TimBuck II's west building offers drink specials, a big bar menu, and a wide variety of raw and steamed seafood. The small dining room does not accept reservations, so you may have to wait. Lunch $; dinner $$$$.

✐ ♟ **Oceanfront Grille** (252-453-4748; www.oceanfrontgrille.com), 1197 Franklyn Street. The former private beach club at Corolla Light Resort is now open to the public, serving dinner along with magnificent ocean views from the second floor bar and deck. Seafood, steaks, and lamb chops dominate the menu, with a much-praised giant crab-cake taking center stage. Located in the resort's pool complex, the grille serves lunch for resort guests only. Most seating is open-air at Corolla's only oceanfront restaurant. $$–$$$$.

✐ ♿ **Route 12 Steak & Seafood Co.** (252-453-4644; www.route12obx.com), 786C Ocean Trail, TimBuck II. Menus range from sandwiches at lunch to steak and lobster at dinner, with raw bar selections available all day at this casual spot next to the Brew Thru. The pork ribs are locally famous. Reservations recommended. Lunch $$; dinner $$$.

BARBECUE **Corolla Village Barbecue Shack** (252-457-0076; www.corollabbq .com), 1129 Corolla Village Road. Serving Eastern Carolina–style pork barbecue, hickory-smoked chicken and ribs, soft-serve, and homemade sides in the heart of Old Corolla Village, this local favorite offers take-out only, but you can eat at the picnic tables out front. $.

✐ **Sooey's BBQ and Rib Shack** (252-453-4423; www.sooeysbbq.com), 807 Ocean Trail, Monteray Plaza. Local chain is known for its fried chicken and great dessert menu. Family packs make it easy for your crowd to pig out on Carolina-style barbecue. Additional locations in Duck and Nags Head. $–$$.

BREAKFAST ✐ **First Light Breakfast & Burger** (252-453-4664; www.firstlight corolla.com), 790 Ocean Trail, TimBuck II. Full breakfast menu served until 2 PM in-season, plus lunch, dinner, and a full bar. Specialties include hand-patted burgers, homemade biscuits, and a make-it-yourself Bloody Mary bar. $.

✐ **Lighthouse Bagels & Deli** (252-453-9998; www.lighthousebagels.com), Monteray Plaza. New Jersey natives bring authentic made-from-scratch bagels and old-fashioned doughnuts to the beach. For lunch, build your own sandwich or try a daily special. $.

COFFEE AND SWEETS ⌀ **Big Bucks Homemade Ice Cream & Coffee Bar** (252-4533188; www.bigbucksicecream.com), TimBuck II. More than 50 flavors of homemade ice cream, a dozen flavors of soft-serve, sorbets, sherbets, fruit smoothies, and a full-service espresso bar, plus handmade chocolates and ice cream cakes to die for, earn this local spot Best of the Beach awards. Also in Kitty Hawk and Manteo.

Corolla Scoops & Sweets (252-453-2580; www.corollaicecream.com), 1152 Ocean Trail/Austin Complex. Hand-scooped Hershey's ice cream, milkshakes, sundaes, root beer floats, and a wide variety of candies make this a favorite stop for kids of all ages.

Northern Lights Bakery (252-453-0201; www.facebook.com/northernlightsbakerycorolla), 1159 Austin Street, Corolla Light Town Center. Doughnuts, cinnamon rolls, and other pastries baked fresh daily make a good breakfast with fresh roasted coffee drinks. Small but interesting lunch menu features salads and sandwiches. Special order cakes in advance.

((ᵔ)) **Outer Banks Coffee Company** (252-453-0200; www.obxcoffee.com), 807L Ocean Trail, Monteray Plaza. Beans are fresh roasted on-site, adding to the wake-up aroma as you walk through the door of this full-service coffee shop offering wraps for breakfast and lunch. Try a scoop of Edy's Ice Cream in your coffee for a mean espresso float.

NATURAL FOODS **The Juice Bar** (252-453-0728; www.thejuicejarcorolla.com), 1130 F Corolla Village Road. Fresh spot in Historic Corolla Village serves organic juices, smoothies, acai bowls, and wraps made with natural ingredients, many grown in the garden out back. $.

PIZZA **Pasquale Pizza & Pub** (252-453-0273 or 252-453-6111; www.pasqualepizza.com), 1210 Ocean Trail/NC 12. Located a half mile north of the lighthouse, this spot serves pizzas, calzone, salads, burgers, and subs, plus some sizzling Buffalo wings. Pasquale's real claim to fame, however, is that it delivers to the off-road beaches beyond the end of the paved road, although it will cost you extra. $–$$.

Corolla Pizza and Deli (252-453-8592; www.corollapizza.com), 1152 Ocean Trail/NC 12, Austin Complex. Serving hand-tossed stone-oven pizza, including gluten-free options, plus a variety of hot and cold subs, this longtime local favorite is right next to Winks grocery and Corolla Scoops and Sweets ice cream shop. Free delivery in-season. $–$$.

Cosmo's Pizzeria (252-453-4666; www.cosmospizzeria.com), 1159 Austin Street, Corolla Light Town Center. This popular spot with a great location serves award-winning New York–style pizzas, whole or by the slice, salads, and subs, plus cold beer on tap and a full-service bar. Don't miss the white crab pizza made in a wood-fired oven. Big deck out back offers lighthouse views and frequent live entertainment. New second location at the Ocean Club Centre next to Metropolis. $–$$.

❄ ⌀ ☖ **Tomato Patch Pizzeria** (252-453-4500; www.obxpizza.com), 803 Albacore Street, Monteray Plaza. Family-run spot has a menu that goes way beyond your typical pizza place, offering Italian and Greek classics, seafood, hot subs, gyros, po'boys, and gluten-free and vegetarian specials. Next door the full-service bar hosts tap takeovers and family dance nights. $–$$.

TAKEOUT **Brew Thru Beverage Store** (252-453-2878; www.brewthru.com), 790 NC 12, TimBuck II. The ultimate in convenience: You don't even have to get out of your car to score a six-pack.

Dockside North Seafood Market (252-453-8112; www.docksidenorth.com), 819

NC 12, Monteray Plaza. Full-service market will steam lobster, shrimp, and king and snow crab to order, or you can get a Down East clambake, ready to go. Great for a crowd. $$$.

⌁ **Fat Crabs Rib Company** (252-453-9931; www.fatcrabsobx.com), 1159 Austin Street, Corolla Light Town Center. A large selection of steamed seafood, including Maine lobster, is available à la carte or in steamer pot combos for dine-in or take-out. St. Louis–style ribs and North Carolina pork barbecue make up the flip side of the menu. Seafood and barbecue sandwiches $; platters and steamer pots $$–$$$.

WINE, BEER, AND GROCERIES ⌁ **Bacchus Wine & Cheese** (252-453-4333; www.bacchuswineandcheese.com), 891 Albacore Street, Monteray Plaza. This entertaining place stocks over 750 vintages from around the world plus a big selection of craft beers and all the extras to go with them, from imported cheeses and cured meats to luscious desserts. The wine bar offers daily wine tastings in-season, along with cheese plates, fat sandwiches, and subs stuffed with Boar's Head deli meats. $–$$.

The Bier Box (252-453-2240; www.obxcraftbeer.com), 817B Ocean Trail. Sharing space with Bob's Wild Horse Tours, this beer-only spot specializes in beers from the Carolinas not carried by wholesalers. More than a dozen crafts are on tap, with many more small-batch beers and ciders available in bottles. Samplers and growlers available. Local Bertie County peanuts provide the perfect bar snack . . . try the blister-fried.

Butcher Block (252-453-3663; www.obxbutcherblock.com), 807-E Ocean Trail, Monterey Plaza. Specialties here are Grade A Angus beef cut to order and fresh local seafood, certified by **Outer Banks Catch** (www.outerbankscatch.com), plus house-made sausage, steamed shrimp, Boar's Head deli, fresh produce, wines, and more. A variety of deli sandwiches are available to go.

Corolla Wine, Cigar & Gourmet (252-453-6048; www.corollawinecigar.com), 794M Sunset Boulevard, TimBuck II. Shop with a view specializes in North Carolina wines and beers, champagnes and vintages from around the world, premium cigars and pipe accessories, gourmet food items, and wine-related gifts. Free wine tastings.

Seaside Farm Market (252-453-8285; www.seasidefarmmarket.com), 787 Sunset Boulevard, TimBuck II. Family-run open-air market at the entrance to Tim-Buck II offers locally grown produce fresh from the Grandy family farm, local jams, sauces and cheese, baked pies and breads, and OBX-sourced seafood, plus beer and wine. They stock milk, eggs, and other groceries, too, so stop here before you hit the big chain store.

Winks of Corolla (252-453-8166), 1150 NC12. Once the only spot in Corolla to get groceries, beer, wine, gas, and just about everything else, Winks anchors the shops in the historic Austin building, all local favorites. Lots of beach supplies in stock, plus local T-shirts and crafts.

✳ Entertainment

NIGHTCLUBS ⌁ ⅄ **Sundogs Raw Bar and Grill** (252-453-4263; www.sundogsrawbargrill.com), 807 Ocean Trail/NC 12, Monteray Plaza. Full-service bar serving raw and steamed seafood, burgers, mac-n-cheese, shrimp and wing happy hour, and a late-night bar food menu. Plenty of big screens make this a favorite spot to catch the big game. Bands, DJs, trivia nights, and karaoke keep the joint jumping during the summer season. No cover. $–$$$.

⌁ ⅄ **Uncle Ike's Sandbar & Grill** (252-597-1606; www.uncleikesobx.com), 1159 Austin Street, Corolla Light Town Center. Fun spot serves breakfast, lunch, dinner, and late-night, but is best known for its nightly karaoke, live entertainment, and dance scene. Outside covered deck is a great place for a fish taco. $–$$.

More live music in Corolla can be found at **Mike Dianna's Grill Room**, **Tomato Patch Pizzeria**, **Oceanfront Grille**, and **North Banks Restaurant**.

✲ Selective Shopping

In Corolla, dining, shopping, and entertainment venues are all concentrated in the shopping centers that sit along NC 12, often at the entrance of gated communities. The first, and still the most extensive, shopping destination is **TimBuck II Shopping Village** (www.timbuckii.com), a complex including over 60 shops and restaurants spread through several buildings, with ample parking. The complex backs up to Currituck Sound with a water-sports complex, go-kart track, paddleboat pond, and mini-golf course along the waterfront.

Situated directly across the street from Historic Corolla Park, and within walking distance of the Corolla Light Resort, the **Corolla Light Town Center** houses pizza shops, bakeries, ice cream parlors, and surf shops.

For a very special shopping experience, walk along the sandy streets of **Old Corolla Village**, poking your head into the various shops. Most of them are run by locals, born and bred, and they all have stories to tell.

ART GALLERIES **Dolphin Watch Gallery** (252-453-2592; www.dolphinwatchgallery.com), TimBuck II. Features a wide variety of arts and fine crafts, including gallery owner Mary Kaye Umberger's original works depicting wild horses and local landmarks.

Eclectic Treasures (252-453-0008; www.eclecticgallery.net), TimBuck II. Unique selection of fine art and crafts runs the gamut from blessing bowls to hand-painted glassware to DIY kaleidoscope kits.

Tarheel Trading Company (252-441-3132; www.tarheeltrading.com), TimBuck II. Handcrafted jewelry, gifts, and decorative art from over 200 American artists, including many from North Carolina. Second location in Duck.

BOOKS **The Island Bookstore** (252-453-2292; www.islandbooksobx.com), 1130 Corolla Village Road, Historic Corolla Village. The Corolla location of this independent bookstore occupies a reproduction of the village's original general store. Signings and readings are frequent in-season.

SPECIAL SHOPS ✐ **Corolla Wild Horse Mustang Store** (252-453-8002; www.corollawildhorses.com), 1129 Corolla Village Road. The Wild Horse Fund store carries all sorts of horse merchandise, from books about horses to wild horse clothing, jewelry, and toys. Visitors to the store have an opportunity to meet and even ride a mustang (schedule varies). All proceeds go toward preserving and protecting the wild herds.

Currituck Beach Lighthouse Museum Shop (252-453-6778; www.currituckbeachlight.com), Little Lightkeeper's House, Currituck Beach Lighthouse. Sales of lighthouse and wild horse souvenirs benefit their respective charitable foundations. Look beyond the gifts to see the amazing architecture of this beautifully restored building.

✐ **Flying Smiles Kites** (252-453-8442; www.flyingsmileskites.com), Corolla Light Town Center. Store operated by competitive kite flyers stocks every kind of kite, from snowflakes to four-line stunt models. The experts here will patch up your kite if you crash.

✐ **Outer Banks Popcorn Shoppe** (252-453-4000; www.outerbankspopcornshoppe.com), TimBuck II. Family-owned shop creates popcorn in 20 flavors. Stop by for a free sample of Corolla Crunch.

Spry Creek Dry Goods (252-453-0199; www.sprycreek.com), 1122 Corolla Village Road, Historic Corolla Village. From the outside, the unpresuming building may look like the auto repair shop it once was, but inside, Corolla native Karen Whitfield has gathered a colorful collection of local art, jewelry, and home accents, combining it with handmade crafts from around the world.

Whalehead Club Museum Shop (252-453-9040; www.whaleheadclub.org), Historic Corolla Park. Unique jewelry, ornaments, birdhouses, and other art objects created from the house's original copper shingles join a nice collection of books, posters, and other gifts. Proceeds benefit historic preservation.

✳ Special Events

Check the **website of Currituck County** (www.visitcurrituck.com) for an updated list of events during your stay.

April: **Easter Egg-Stravaganza** (252-453-9040; www.whaleheadclub.org), Historic Corolla Park.

May: **Mustang Spring Jam** (www.mustangmusicfestival.com).

June: **"Under the Oaks" Arts Festival** (252-453-9040; www.whaleheadclub.org), Historic Corolla Park.

July Fourth: **Independence Day Festival of Fireworks**, Historic Corolla Park.

October: **Haunted Corolla Village** (252-453-9040; www.whaleheadclub.org). Evening hayrides and treasure hunts at Historic Corolla Park and Old Corolla Village.

December: **Historic Corolla Park Tree Lighting Celebration** (252-453-9040; www.whaleheadclub.org), Historic Corolla Park, with caroling and carriage rides.

DUCK AND SANDERLING

Today a scenic destination noted for exceptional shopping and gourmet dining, the small fishing village of **Duck** first appears on maps dating to the 1790s. The local folks, who traveled mostly by boat, developed the first crab-shedding business in the area, founding the commercial softshell crab industry. In the 1940s, local residents and crabs alike were subjected to the sound of bombing practice on military land just north of the village. The bombing range is long gone. Its sole remnant is an impressive pier built by the U.S. Army Corps of Engineers, now used to conduct scientific studies of waves and currents.

Duck is Dare County's newest town, having incorporated in 2001. The impressive **Town Park and Boardwalk** lies in the center of town along NC 12 on Currituck Sound. Public parking is available here, as well as at the numerous shopping villages that stretch along the road all the way through town. This stretch of coast is renowned for its sunsets, and many establishments look west over Currituck Sound. Most of the town's many rental condominiums and houses are tucked out of sight amid the maritime forest that makes Duck such a shady, pleasant place in the summer. The town has no public beach access but is still extremely popular as a destination for day trips, a must for dedicated shoppers.

Just north of Duck is one of the narrowest parts of the Banks, once the site of Caffey's Inlet. Today the **Sanderling Resort** occupies this prime property. The old lifesaving station has been restored as a restaurant.

The hotel's builder, Earl Slick, was the first to push the paved road north of Duck, and he put a gate across the road, protecting the exclusive neighborhoods he developed beyond it. The gate remained from 1975 until 1984, when the road became part of NC 12 and the state bulldozed the barrier. NC 12 is called Duck Road in Duck.

GUIDANCE Information on Duck can be found at the Dare County welcome centers. The closest is the **Aycock Brown Welcome Center** (1-877-629-4386; www.outerbanks.org), located at MP 1 in Kitty Hawk on US 158. Contact the **Town of Duck** (252-255-1234; www.townofduck.com), 1240 Duck Road, for information on town events and regulations.

POST OFFICE The U.S. Post Office in Duck is located at 1245 NC 12, inside the

THE SANDERLING RESORT PRESERVES THE CAFFEY'S INLET LIFE-SAVING STATION AS A RESTAURANT

Olde Duck Village Shoppe (252-261-8555; www.oldeduckvillage.com). The zip code for Duck and Sanderling is 27949.

PUBLIC RESTROOMS The town maintains public restrooms in the **Duck Town Park**.

GETTING THERE Until the new toll bridge is completed across Currituck Sound, the only way to reach Duck is from the south along NC 12. It is just two lanes from the junction with US 158 in Kitty Hawk, and traffic frequently backs up, especially on summer weekends as guests check into and out of vacation cottages. Allow plenty of time to reach your destination, relax, and obey all traffic regulations. The slow speed zone through the Sanderling property often catches drivers by surprise.

GETTING AROUND *By bicycle:* Duck is a small village, and many residents and visitors get around by bike. A shady paved bike path, the Duck Trail, runs under the trees through the heart of town. Several local restaurants cater to the two-wheel crowd with to-go windows and outdoor picnic tables.

On foot: Many people who rent vacation cottages in Duck opt to walk to dining and shopping destinations, since most are localized in Duck Village. This can be a big time saver, especially when the traffic gets bad. The paved Duck Trail makes it easy and safe for bikes and pedestrians to navigate the village.

✸ To See

Duck Research Pier/Field Research Facility (252-261-3511; www.frf.usace.army.mil), 1261 NC 12. The equipment on this pier does important research into waves, currents, and other processes that create the Outer Banks. Tours of the pier are no longer offered, but you can get a look from the beach.

Duck Town Hall Art Shows (252-255-1234; www.townofduck.com), 1240 Duck Road. Rotating displays of art by local artists and organizations occupy the town hall's first-floor conference room. The art is free to view and open weekdays, 9 AM to 4 PM. Watch for free opening receptions about every three months.

✸ To Do

BICYCLING A multiuse paved path, the **Duck Trail**, runs parallel with NC 12 from the Currituck/Dare County line through Duck to Southern Shores.

Duck Cycle (252-261-0356; www.duckcycle.com), 1211 NC 12. Shop in Duck Commons rents cruisers for adults and kids, plus jogging strollers, kayaks, SUPs, and other beach gear, by the day or week.

Duck Village Outfitters (252-261-7222; www.duckvillageoutfitters.net), 1207 NC 12. Adult and children's beach cruisers, with or without gear, rent by the week. Training wheels available.

Ocean Atlantic Rentals (252-261-4346; www.oceanatlanticrentals.com), 1194 NC 12. Rents bikes and trikes, plus accessories such as bike lights.

FISHING **Bob's Bait and Tackle** (252-261-8589; www.bobsbaitandtackle.com), 1180 NC 12. A presence in the heart of Duck Village since 1982, Bob's has a big selection

MUST SEE

The Sanderling Resort (252-261-4111 or 1-800-701-4111; www.thesanderling.com), 1461 NC 12. The public rooms of this landmark resort display an outstanding collection of wildfowl art, including porcelain birds by Gunter Granget, the Boehm Studio, and Dorothy Doughty's Birds of North America Royal Worcester collection, as well as many impressive wood and metal bird sculptures by South Carolina artist Grainger McKoy. The lobbies of the main inn display 18 original Audubon prints in addition to a complete copy of Audubon's Baby Elephant Folio.

of equipment and bait, including live minnows, and will teach you how to catch crabs. Bob's also books inshore, offshore, and light-tackle charters, specializing in makeup trips, with boats going out daily.

Sharky's Bait, Tackle and Charters (252-255-2248; www.sharkyscharters.com), 1245 Duck Road/NC 12, Barrier Island Station. Full-service bait and tackle shop across from the Sunset Grille offers rod and reel rentals, surf fishing clinics, and fishing licenses, and arranges charter-fishing trips, including full-day, deep-sea offshore trolling adventures and back country trips, perfect for when the sea is too rough to go offshore. If you aren't part of a group, ask about joining a makeup charter.

FOR FAMILIES ✐ **Duck Town Park** (252-255-1286; www.townofduck.com) has a public playground and hosts numerous family activities during the summer months.

KAYAK TOURS The soundside waterfront, lined with boardwalks, restaurants, and shopping complexes, makes a popular and interesting paddle, especially as the sun sets into Currituck Sound. A public kayak/canoe launch on the Duck Boardwalk is free to use and will put you in the heart of the action.

Coastal Kayak (252-261-6262; www.outerbankskayaktours.com). Guided kayak and stand-up paddleboard trips explore the intricate marsh maze of the Pine Island Audubon Sanctuary.

Duck Village Outfitters (252-261-7222; www.duckvillageoutfitters.net), 1207 NC 12. Sign up here for kayak tours through Kitty Hawk Woods. The store rents single or double, surf or touring kayaks and canoes by the day or week. Delivery available. Or rent by the hour and take your craft directly across the street from the shop and put in at the Duck Town Park public launch.

Ocean Atlantic Rentals (252-261-4346; www.oceanatlanticrentals.com), 1194 NC 12. Rent a surf or touring kayak or stand-up paddleboard. Free delivery on weekly orders over $95. Or rent by the day at the shop along the sound and launch nearby for a peaceful paddle.

SPAS AND FITNESS **Aqua Essence Day Spa** (252-261-9709; www.spasouterbanks .com), 1174 NC 12. Waterfront spa upstairs from the Aqua Restaurant offers Ayurveda treatments, organic facials, spa cuisine, and summertime yoga on the lawn.

The Sanderling Spa (252-261-7744; www.thesanderling.com), Sanderling Resort. This elegant spa overlooking the tranquil waters of Currituck Sound is the perfect setting for the signature Serenity Ritual, in which two therapists work in tandem to give clients a hydro massage, facial, scalp treatment, sea salt glow, and sea mud wrap, then finish up with a Scotch hose massage and Vichy rain shower. The spa also offers yoga classes and salon services. Couple's suite available.

Village Yoga (252-202-4582; www.duckvillageyoga.com), 1240 Duck Road/NC 12, Waterfront Shops. Basic, Flow, Yin, Nidra, Vinyasa, and Kunga classes offered for all abilities. Drop-ins welcome. Private yoga on the beach available.

SURFING **Duck Village Outfitters** (252-261-7222; www.duckvillageoutfitters.net), 1207 NC 12. Centrally located shop rents surfboards, stand-up paddleboards, body boards, skim boards, fins, and wet suits, and will deliver to your rental property. Two-hour surf or SUP lessons include 24-hour board rental.

Kitty Hawk Surf Company (252-261-8787; www.khsurf.com), 1214 NC 12, Wee Winks Square. Rent surfboards, body boards, stand-up paddleboards, and kayaks from this location in the heart of Duck. Surfing and SUP lessons and tours, as well as parasailing and Jet Ski tours, are available.

Outer Banks Surf Shop (252-261-2907; www.obssurf.com), 1176 NC 12. Independent shop run by surfers offers equipment for surfers or skateboarders, as well as surfboard and SUP rentals and lessons for ages six and up.

WATER SPORTS CENTERS From Duck Village to the Sanderling, the shore of Currituck Sound is lined with water-sports emporiums offering a wide variety of water-based fun. Sailing and kayaking are huge here, and parasailing is literally taking off. Kayaks, paddleboards, and personal watercraft, such as Jet Skis and WaveRunners, are widely available. On the other hand, the area is just beginning to explore the sports of windsurfing and kiteboarding. These centers are open seasonally, May to October, or as weather permits. Most have lawns where you can picnic. Bonus: all these docks

CONDITIONS ON CURRITUCK SOUND ARE PERFECT FOR STAND-UP PADDLEBOARD (SUP) EXCURSIONS

THE SUNSET GRILLE'S GAZEBO IS A LANDMARK ALONG THIS PART OF THE BANKS, BOTH DAY AND NIGHT

and marinas face west, so you can expect some awesome sunsets as the day draws to a close.

Kitty Hawk Kites Watersports Center (252-261-4450; www.kittyhawk.com), 1214 NC 12. Wee Winks Square location offers on-site Jet Ski, kayak, bicycle, and surfboard rentals, stand-up paddleboard rentals and lessons, parasailing, waterskiing, and wakeboarding. The less athletic will enjoy a pontoon boat eco-cruise, a voyage across the sound to Sanctuary Vineyards, or an unforgettable sunset experience.

Nor'Banks Sailing & Watersports (252-261-2900; www.norbanks.com), 1314 NC 12. Full-service sailing center offers rentals and instruction, plus parasailing and WaveRunner tours. Weekly racing series are open to visitors. Nor'Banks rents a wide variety of catamarans and sailboats, as well as pontoon boats, kayaks, stand-up paddleboards, WaveRunners, and the new Hobie Eclipse waterbike. The calm waters of the sound are the perfect spot for tubing, waterskiing, wakeboarding, and kneeboarding, and you can try them all in a single afternoon here.

North Duck Water Sports (252-261-4200; www.duckjetskirentals.com), 1446 NC 12, 2.5 miles north of Duck Village. Rent a pontoon boat or Jet Ski for a trip on the sound, or go parasailing to see it all from above.

Soundside Watersports (252-261-0855; www.soundsidewatersports.com), 1566 NC 12, Station Bay Marina. Rent WaveRunners at this casual spot across from the Sanderling, then stop out front at **Station Bay Seafood** (252-261-3267) for some fresh catch for dinner. Boat tours and sunset cruises available, or you can launch your own craft at the boat ramp here for a small fee.

Sunset Watersports (252-261-6866; www.sunsetgrillewatersports.com), 1264 NC 12. Rent kayaks, SUPs, WaveRunners, skiffs, and pontoon boats to explore Currituck

Sound, or sign up for a sunset cruise at the dock behind the Sunset Grille, party place of the North Banks. Follow up with a tropical cocktail at the tiki bar.

✲ Green Space

BEACHES Duck has an excellent 7-mile-long beach, uncrowded and watched over by lifeguards from May 1 to October 31, making it one of the most family-friendly beaches on the Atlantic Coast. However, the town has no beach access open to the public. Only residents, renters, and their guests may use the beach in Duck. Residents may drive on the beach between October 1 and April 30. Pets are allowed to run unleashed on the beach as long as they are with their owner. Fires are not allowed on the beach.

WALKS 🖉 🐾 ♿ **Duck Town Park and Soundside Boardwalk** (252-255-1286; www.townofduck.com), 1200 NC 12. Trails lead through a coastal willow swamp and maritime forest, and a boardwalk edges the Currituck Sound waterfront in downtown Duck. The Duck Boardwalk, famous for its sunsets, begins at Christopher Drive at the south end of Duck Village and ends at the Waterfront Shops north of the water tower, connecting several retail areas in between. A free launch ramp for kayaks and canoes, a fishing and crabbing platform, gazebo, picnic area, public restrooms, and playground, plus an amphitheater used for music, magic, and other programs, cluster in the Duck Town Park behind Duck Town Hall. Four slips for transient boaters can be found at the northern end of the boardwalk. Drinking fountains, including a special one for dogs, are scattered throughout the park. A useful map with parking options can be found on the Town of Duck website. The park is open dawn to dusk. The boardwalk is open dawn–1 AM.

🐾 ♿ **Duck Trail.** This paved multiuse path connects many of the businesses along NC 12/Duck Road. For most of its 7-mile length it runs along the east side of the road as a separate trail. However, through the village's commercial district, the trail runs along both sides of NC 12 and is not separated from traffic. Pedestrians, bicycles, and in-line skaters may use the trail; mopeds, other motorized vehicles, and Segways may not. Pets must be on a leash.

Pine Island Audubon Sanctuary Trail (252-489-5303; www.ncaudubon.org). A 2.5-mile, self-guided nature trail running along the sound begins near the Sanderling and ends behind the Pine Island Racquet & Fitness Center. Two decks on the sound make great spots for birding.

THE DUCK BOARDWALK EDGES THE SHORE OF CURRITUCK SOUND

✳ Lodging

RESORT ☀ ♿ ☄ (ဖ) **The Sanderling Resort & Spa** (252-261-4111 or 1-800-701-4111; www.thesanderling.com), 1461 NC 12. The Sanderling serves up luxurious resort amenities with laid-back Outer Banks style 5 miles north of Duck Village. Two-story, cedar-shingled buildings keep a low profile on this stretch of land between sound and sea. The public rooms of the inn are virtual galleries of art featuring birds and wildfowl. The property recently enjoyed a $4 million refit that equipped guest rooms with king-size beds, 32-inch TVs, wireless Internet, and walk-in showers. Many rooms have private porches where guests can enjoy water views. The 88 guest rooms and suites, plus a conference center, The Lifesaving Station restaurant, and several Jacuzzis, are located along the oceanfront, where a big deck and boardwalk provide access to the beach. Cocktails and sandwiches ($$) are available at the Sand Bar on the deck. Across the road, a full-service spa, indoor pool, and the elegant Kimball's Kitchen restaurant overlook Currituck Sound.

Guests also have access to the championship golf course at the Currituck Club and the indoor courts at the Pine Island Racquet & Fitness Center. The resort offers many activities in-season, including guided kayak trips and live music. The Sanderling also rents five oceanfront villas. A suite atop the conference center with balconies that face both the sunrise and sunset is a favorite with honeymooners. $$–$$$$.

VACATION COTTAGE AND CONDO RENTALS ✳ ☀ **Brindley Beach Vacations** (1-877-642-3224; www.brindleybeach.com), 1215 NC 12. Family-owned realty company represents rental properties in more than two dozen communities in Duck and the surrounding area, including many with pools, elevators, and hot tubs. All homes come with daily newspaper service, beach access, and limited early access beginning at noon. Some communities have indoor pools and tennis courts.

☀ ♿ (ဖ) **Carolina Designs Realty** (252-261-3934 or 1-800-368-3825; www.carolinadesigns.com), 1197 NC 12. Specializes in some of the finest houses in the area.

(ဖ) **Ships Watch** (252-261-2231; www.shipswatch.com), 1251 NC 12. Rental homes in this centrally located community range from three to five bedrooms. Renters have access to a private beach, soundside pier, swimming pool and hot tub, tennis courts, and playground, plus numerous discounts at local establishments. Linens and Wi-Fi included.

✳ Where to Eat

Duck is the foodie capital of the Outer Banks, with numerous spots boasting *Wine Spectator* Awards of Excellence, restaurants practicing farm-to-fork creativity, and the AAA four-diamond Kimball's all within the town limits. There are plenty of spots to grab a casual meal as well, plus soundside decks where you

THE SANDERLING RESORT KEEPS A LOW PROFILE, BUT IS FILLED WITH LUXURIOUS FEATURES

WHAT'S IN A NAME?

Many of the restaurants in Duck feature duck on their menus.

can kick back with a cocktail and watch the legendary sunsets.

Take note that the kitchen and wait-staff at even the best restaurants can get overwhelmed during the busy summer season. Make reservations if possible, or go to eat early. Prices and crowds are both generally smaller at lunchtime.

DINING OUT

IN DUCK VILLAGE

🍴 ♿ 🐾 🍸 🛜 **Aqua Restaurant** (252-261-9700; www.restaurantsouterbanks.com), 1174 NC 12. Big, beautiful house fronting on the sound serves food worthy of its setting: organic, local, and sustainable, although, with a spa upstairs, serving sizes are what you'd expect from "spa cuisine." Fish tacos and crab and corn chowder drizzled with truffle oil are local favorites. The best times here take place on the decks that surround the building, where a bar menu with happy hour prices from 3–6 PM complements the amazing sunset over the water. On summer evenings, live music enhances the deck vibe most nights. Online reservations available. Lunch $$; bar menu $; dinner $$$$.

❄ 🍴 ♿ 🍸 🛜 **The Blue Point Bar & Grill** (252-261-8090; www.thebluepoint.com), 1240 NC 12, Waterfront Shops. Nationally recognized for its innovative cuisine, the Blue Point recently expanded to accommodate more of its avid fans but retains its diner charm, complete with checkerboard floors, red leather stools and booths, and the atmospheric screen porch overlooking Currituck Sound. While there are seasonal changes in the lineup, you'll want to try the much-praised Carolina She-Crab Soup laced with sherry. The crowds—and prices—max out at dinner, but you can eat lunch

here for a much more moderate check. Locals are crazy about the meat loaf, a lunch entrée. Reservations are accepted only for dinner and are very much recommended. You can make them up to a month in advance and online. The open-air Soundside Bar hosts live music (in-season) as the sun sinks into the water. Lunch $$; dinner $$$$.

Eastside (252-715-5033; www.eastsideducknc.com), 1177 NC 12, 11 Scarborough Faire. Something a bit different, and certainly fresh, on the Duck dining scene, this contemporary spot mixes it up with sweet potato nachos, ramen bowls, poke, and Oriental-inspired small plates featuring local, organic, and seasonal ingredients. Dinner only, $$.

🍴 🍸 **Red Sky Cafe** (252-261-8646; www.redskycafe.com), 1197 NC 12, Duck Landing. Located across NC 12 from the Duck Town Park, the Red Sky has many fans despite its small size and sometimes lengthy waits. Chef Wes Stepp puts his wood-burning oven to good use, creating a wood-fired OBX Trio each evening of fresh fish, shrimp, and crabcake. Wood-fired steaks, shrimp and grits, baby back ribs, and seared fish tacos are popular favorites. The Chefs on Call service will

THE BLUE POINT RETAINS ITS DINER CHARM, DESPITE BEING ONE OF THE MOST FAMOUS RESTAURANTS IN DUCK

bring your selected meal to you; no waiting for a table. Lunch $; dinner $$$$.

❋ ▽ **Roadside Raw Bar & Grill** (252-261-5729; www.obxroadside.com), 1193 NC 12. Occupying the oldest house in Duck, this tiny eatery earns raves for its seasonal menu featuring local fish and shellfish. Stained-glass-style windows made of recycled glass brighten the cottage's interior. Visit the upstairs bar for a bowl of the famous clam chowder and a tomato pie. Or have a seat on the pleasant patio, where you'll occasionally encounter live music. If you visit Duck in the off-season, check the schedule for Roadside's oyster roasts. Lunch $; dinner $$$$.

IN SANDERLING

♿ ▽ ↝ **Kimball's Kitchen** (252-261-8419; www.thesanderling.com), 1461 NC 12, Sanderling Resort. Modern, elegant decor highlighted by a bank of windows overlooking Currituck Sound sets off sophisticated menus emphasizing sustainable, organic, artisanal, and local ingredients. Black Angus beef, lamb, bison, and locally sourced seafood team with foie gras, wild mushrooms, and truffles with spectacular results. The restaurant's wine list won approval from *Wine Spectator*. Local oyster specials and cocktails are offered nightly except Monday during the season. The most magical time here occurs at sunset, when the blond onyx bar reflects the sun's glow. Dress code is resort chic: men are asked to wear shirts with collars and "dress shorts" or slacks. Reservations are requested. Children can order half portions. Sunday brunch $$–$$$; dinner $$$$.

❋ ✐ ♿ ↝ **The Lifesaving Station** (252-449-6654; www.thesanderling.com), 1471 NC 12, Sanderling Resort. The Sanderling's casual restaurant, the Lifesaving Station, occupies the renovated 1899 Caffey's Inlet Life-Saving Station boathouse. The paneled interior, beautifully restored, is studded with maritime memorabilia, historical objects, bird decoys, and culinary awards. Menus vary with

THE ONYX BAR AT THE SANDERLING'S KIMBALL'S KITCHEN MAKES A REMARKABLE VENUE FOR COCKTAILS

the season but always feature local fish and shellfish. At breakfast, the Eggs Sanderling atop crabcakes is a standout. Stop by the bar for a bowl of the Sanderling's signature chowder, a creamy blend of blue crab, smoked bacon, and corn. Open all year. Breakfast and lunch $$; dinner $$$$.

The Paper Canoe (252-715-2220; www.papercanoeobx.com), 1564 NC 12. Renovated cottage on the shores of the sound just south of the Sanderling is the latest venture of longtime OBX restaurateur Tom Karole. Locally sourced fish and seafood, handmade ravioli, and house-smoked chicken and duck top the menu. During busy hours, grab a seat in the bar, with windows overlooking the sound, and enjoy a gourmet pizza cooked in the wood oven, accompanied by one of 10 craft beers on draft. Dinner only, $$–$$$$.

EATING OUT

IN DUCK VILLAGE

✐ ▽ **Coastal Cantina** (252-480-0024; www.coastalcantina.com), 1236 Duck

Road/NC 12, Waterfront Shops. Tex-Mex on the boardwalk with great views of the sunset, perfect for kicking back with a margarita. Try a duck confit taco for some local flavor. Live music in-season. $.

❋ ￦ **Coastal Cravings** (252-480-0032; www.cravingsobx.com), 1209 NC 12. One of several restaurants operated by Coastal Provisions, the area's top gourmet grocery, Cravings occupies a former Burger King, complete with drive-through window, the only one in Duck. The restaurant serves breakfast, lunch, and dinner, including Coastal Provisions award-winning crabcakes, complemented by a nice by-the-glass wine list and local microbrews on draft. The take-out window, especially popular for a quick breakfast (truffle oil laced grits or Brie BLT, anyone?), opens at 7 AM. Coastal's Seafood Pots to Go ($$$) have been featured on the Food Network's "Diners, Drive-Ins and Dives" show. Call ahead for the Outer Banks Pot or the Yankee Pot to satisfy your seafood cravings. Free live music nightly on the Tap Shack stage out back. Breakfast $; lunch $$; dinner $$$$.

✎ ☀ ￦ **Duck Deli** (252-261-3354; www .duckdeli.com), 1223 NC 12. A landmark on the Duck Road for over 20 years, this casual spot serves breakfast and hickory-smoked barbecue pork, chicken, fish, and ribs to eat in or take out. The unique T-shirts are popular souvenirs. Beer and wine available. Live jazz in the Picnic Garden during the summer. $–$$.

❋ ✎ **Fishbones Raw Bar & Restaurant** (252-261-6991; www.fishbonesrawbar .com), 1171 NC 12, Scarborough Lane Shoppes. Newly renovated spot matches its fresh sophisticated interior with full-service raw bar plus a big menu of appetizers, burgers, and seafood entrées, served all day and night. For Caribbean flair try the sweet potato coconut curry soup. The chowders here (clam and conch) are award winning. Lunch $$; dinner $$–$$$.

✎ **Sooey's BBQ and Rib Shack** (252-449-2271; www.sooeysbbq.com), 1177

NC 12, Scarborough Faire. Family packs make it easy for your crowd to pig out. Fried chicken is a local favorite. $–$$.

♂ ✎ ￦ **Sunset Grille & Raw Bar** (252-261-3901; www.fishbonessunsetgrille .com), 1270 NC 12. It's hard to miss this edifice along the sound side of NC 12 north of Duck, and usually one look at the tiki bars and long dock stretching out to a gazebo is enough to make travelers hit the brakes. If you like a partying good time and spectacular sunsets, you'll come away singing this spot's praises. White tablecloth dining it's not, but take a seat at one of the outdoor tiki bars, order up an exotic cocktail in a neon glass, hum along to a Jimmy Buffett tune, and you'll soon catch the Key West vibe. Seafood, raw, steamed, and fried, is available all day, and sushi is served nightly on the upper level. The restaurant also offers an interesting breakfast menu. Come early and plan to spend the

THE KEY WEST VIBE IS STRONG AT THE SUNSET GRILLE

DUCK DONUTS

This ever-so-popular shop introduced the design-your-own-doughnuts craze. Fresh, warm doughnuts are dipped in your choice of frosting and sprinkled with your favorite topping. Breakfast sandwiches and ice cream sundaes based on doughnuts expand the menu. Additional locations are found in Corolla, Kitty Hawk, and Kill Devil Hills on the Outer Banks, and much farther afield. Duck Donuts are so good, the franchise is one of the fastest growing in the country, but this shop is the original. Duck Donuts (252-480-3304; www.duckdonuts.com), 1190 NC 12, Osprey Landing.

day. You can rent Jet Skis and kayaks out back. Breakfast and lunch $–$$; dinner $$–$$$$.

IN SANDERLING

♿ (((•))) Y **Sanderling Beach House Bar** (252-261-4111; www.thesanderling.com), 1461 NC 12. Enjoy morning coffee and pastries, and later small plates and cocktails in this comfortable setting. The Firepit outside hosts live music in-season. $–$$.

♿ (((•))) **Sanderling Sandbar** (252-261-4111; www.thesanderling.com), 1461 NC 12. If the weather is good, grab a cocktail and sandwich with a view at the Sandbar on the Sanderling's oceanfront deck. $$.

BREAKFAST Treehouse Coffee and Rope Ladder Kitchen (252-722-3606; www.facebook.com/treehousecoffees), 1177 NC 12. Serene spot in Scarborough Faire serves North Carolina Counter Culture Coffee, cold brews, pour overs, and other gourmet beverages. Breakfasts feature scratch-made biscuits.

COFFEE AND SWEETS ☯ **Donutz On A Stick** (252-261-0484; www.DonutzOna Stick.com), 1216 Duck Road/NC 12, Wee Winks Square. Family-friendly spot on the Duck Boardwalk offers hot doughnuts on a stick with 35 different toppings to choose from, plus coffee drinks, nine flavors of soft serve, frozen yogurt, and more, hosted by a 7-foot-tall rubber duckie.

Duck's Cottage Coffee and Books (252-261-5510; www.duckscottage.com), 1240 NC 12, Waterfront Shops. Run by java junkies, the historic, cedar-shingled cottage that once housed the Powder Ridge Gun Club now provides an early-morning stop for residents and visitors who come to browse the book selection, enjoy an espresso or herbal tea, or hang out on the porch with a cup of joe. $.

Nags Head Shop (252-261-7262; www.nagsheadshop.com), 1171 NC 12, C-6 Scarborough Lane. The oldest espresso bar on the beach also sells a fun selection of hats and beach accessories.

🍦 **Sunset Ice Cream** (252-261-3553; www.facebook.com/SunsetIceCream DuckNC), 1240 NC 12, Waterfront Shops. Take-out window on the boardwalk is a family favorite offering fruit smoothies, M&M cones, espresso shakes, and more, plus a great location for feeding the ducks. Cash only. $.

The Sweet Duck (252-715-1878; www.thesweetduck.com), 1171 NC 12, C-4 Scarborough Lane. Homemade gelato, freshly baked pastries, espresso, and hand-dipped Belgian chocolates from the food artists at Argyles Sea Salt Grille, (www.seasaltgrille.com), considered one of the top catering outfits on the Banks. Gluten-free items, crepes, wines, and craft beers available.

Tullio's Pastry Shop (252-261-7112; www.tulliospastry.com), 1187 NC 12, Loblolly Pines. Top Italian-style bakery offers award-winning cakes, pies, doughnuts, fudge, cupcakes, pastas, breads, and rolls featured at the area's top restaurants at this retail outlet. Come early for breakfast or order a special cake in advance.

WINE AND BEER 🍺 **Growlers To Go** (252-715-1946; www.beerforthebeach.com), 1187 Duck Road/NC 12, Loblolly Pines. Big selection of local and craft brews and ciders (42 on tap) to fill your growlers to take back to the cottage, plus wine, bottled beer, and root beer on tap. Or rent a kegerator for your stay.

((•)) 🍷 **Sweet T's Coffee, Beer & Wine** (252-4802326; www.sweet-ts-duck.com), 1211 NC 12. Go the coffee and pastry route, or relax with a glass of wine or craft draft on the shady deck of this sweet cottage on Duck Road. Wine and beer tastings happen weekly, along with live music in-season.

PIZZA **Duck Pizza Company** (252-255-0099; www.duckpizza.com), 1171 NC 12, Scarborough Lane. Gourmet pizzas in three sizes head a menu of wings, salads, calzone, and stromboli. Free lunchtime delivery in Duck.

Pizzazz Pizza Company (252-261-8822; www.pizzazzpizza.net), 1187 Duck Road, Loblolly Pines. The original location of this local chain offers a lunch buffet. Eat inside, outside, or have your pizza or hot sub delivered (252-261-1111). Online ordering and free delivery from Corolla to Nags Head make this a local favorite.

((•)) 🍷 **The Wave Pizza Café** (252-255-0375; www.thewavepizza.com), 1190 NC 12, Osprey Landing. Take advantage of the free delivery, or enjoy your hand-tossed pie on the waterfront deck with a cold craft beer. Live sunset music on the deck in-season.

TAKEOUT AND GROCERIES ❄ **ABC Store** (252-261-6981; www.ncabc.com), 1216 NC 12. Duck's only outlet for bottles of hard liquor can be found in Wee Winks Square.

🐟 **Dockside N Duck Seafood Market** (252-261-8687; www.docksiden duckseafood.com), 1216 NC 12, Wee Winks Square. Family-owned spot, established in 1987 by local fishermen and farmers, makes a quick stop for Down East clambakes to steam on your stovetop, crabcakes, award-winning she-crab soup, live Maine lobsters, and blue crabs, raw or steamed, along with seafood dips, homemade tomato pies, and desserts. Out front, the Green Acres Farm Market sells sweet corn, vine-ripened tomatoes, watermelons, hot peppers, berries, and more, direct from the family farm in Currituck County.

The Spice & Tea Exchange (252-715-4500; www.spiceandtea.com), 1171 Duck

Road, D-4 Scarborough Lane. Owners Terry Bell and Megan Scott stock a huge selection of spice blends, salts, and sugars sure to spark your culinary creativity, as well as unique gifts and more than 40 different teas.

❧ **Tommy's Natural Foods Market and Wine Shop** (252-261-8990; www .tommysmarketobx.com), 1242 NC 12. Personal service and convenience are the hallmarks of this longtime Duck store that lets you order your groceries, or entire prepared meals, online or by phone. Drop by on Taste It Tuesdays for samples of Outer Banks products or on Wednesday for tastings of wine, cheese, and chocolate.

❈ **Wee Winks Market** (252-261-2937; www.weewinksmarket.com), 1213 NC 12. The first store ever in Duck, still much beloved for its convenience and wide variety of necessities, has a new building and now offers breakfast, salads, subs, hot dogs, burgers, and fries to go, plus a huge selection of craft beer and wine.

EXPAND YOUR TEA VOCABULARY AT THE SPICE & TEA EXCHANGE

✳ Entertainment

The Duck Town Park hosts many special events in its new amphitheater, including concerts several times a week, magic shows, story time, and more. Most events are free. For a schedule and ticket details, visit www.townofduck .com or call the town's event hotline: 252-255-1286

🐾 ▽ **Tap Shack** (252-480-0032; www .facebook.com/cravingsinduck), 1209 NC 12. Open-air stage behind Coastal Cravings books free concerts every night of the summer. Try the local crafts on tap or wine or soda at the outdoor bar, and get in the flow with ping-pong, cornhole, or an open-air game of pool.

Several local spots from our *Dining* section offer entertainment, including **Aqua**, **Blue Point**, **Red Sky**, **Roadside**, **Coastal Cantina**, **Duck Deli**, **Sunset Grille**, the **Sanderling**, **Sweet T's**, and **The Wave Pizza**.

✳ Selective Shopping

Duck's main claim to fame has always been its compact collection of unique and eclectic shops, making it the prime shopping destination (some say the Rodeo Drive) of the Outer Banks. Within a half mile or so along either side of NC 12, you'll find most of the shopping and dining options in Duck. The stores here are linked by paved walkways and boardwalks, making for excellent daylong browsing. Most of the boutiques, shops, and galleries are locally owned and operated, with a smattering of regional chains and high-end nationals.

Scarborough Faire Shopping Center (www.scarboroughfaireinducknc.com), at 1177 Duck Road on the east side of NC 12, was one of the first shopping destinations in the village. Begun in 1983, it set the standard with sprawling live oaks, wooden walkways and porches, and plenty of spots to sit and relax. Next door at 1171 Duck Road is **Scarborough Lane Shoppes** (www .scarboroughlaneshoppesducknc.com), with ample parking beneath the building and even more eclectic shops. **Loblolly Pines**, a bit farther north at 1187 Duck Road, is also on the east or ocean side of NC 12.

On the west or sound side of NC 12, several shopping destinations line the shores of Currituck Sound, offering pleasant decks and great views of the sunset. From south to north, they are **Duck Soundside Shops**, 1180 Duck Road; **Osprey Landing** (www .ospreylandingshops.com), 1194 Duck Road; **Wee Winks Square**, 1216 Duck Road; and **The Waterfront Shops** (www .waterfrontshopsduck.com), just north of the water tower at 1240 Duck Road.

The Waterfront Shops occupy atmospheric buildings, some of them rescued from old hunt clubs, all joined by an expansive deck. This is a great place for lunch, and an even better one at sunset when nature puts on a show. A boardwalk connects the shops with Wee Winks and the Duck Town Park.

THE PORCHES OF SCARBOROUGH LANE ARE LINED WITH FUN SHOPS

ART AND CRAFT GALLERIES **Ocean Treasures Art Gallery** (252-453-2383; www.oceantreasures.net), 1171 NC 12, Scarborough Lane. A 6-foot bronze dolphin welcomes you to the only gallery in the world representing both Wyland, painter of whales, and Thomas Kinkade, Painter of Light. Both are represented by new releases and some sold-out items, as well as licensed gifts and collectibles. The **Ocean Treasures Gift Shop** (1187 Duck Road) in Loblolly Pines features Disney collectibles, Laurel Burch bags, and other artistic gifts.

SeaDragon Gallery (252-261-4224; www.seadragongallery.com), Waterfront Shops. Arts and crafts selected by shop owner Eve Turek are handcrafted by artisans from across the United States, including many based on the Outer Banks. Eve's award-winning photography is featured in the gallery.

Simply Scarborough (252-715-5020; www.facebook.com/simply scarboroughllp), 1-15 Scarborough Faire. One of Duck's original families follows their great-grandfather's tradition, selling hand-carved birds and ducks, as well as sea glass and other unique gifts.

❋ **Solitary Swan** (252-261-7676; www .facebook.com/thesolitaryswan), Scarborough Lane. Longtime Duck favorite stocks folk art, tin signs, decoys, samplers, and OBX photographs.

Tarheel Trading Company (252-441-6235; www.tarheeltrading.com), Scarborough Lane. Handcrafted jewelry, gifts, and decorative art from over 300 American artists, including many from North Carolina.

BOOKS AND MUSIC **Duck's Cottage Coffee and Books** (252-261-5510; www .duckscottage.com), Waterfront Shops. Hand-picked selection of fiction and nonfiction fills this historic, cedar-shingled cottage. Summer signing series and monthly reading group, plus newspapers from up and down the East Coast and great coffee, make this a special spot.

The Island Bookstore (252-261-8981; www.islandbooksobx.com), Scarborough Faire. The original location of this local chain of independent bookstores features carefully selected books for every interest.

JEWELRY **Carolina Moon** (252-619-4298; www.facebook.com/carolinamoon gallery), 6-61 Scarborough Faire. Set in its own pavilion, this New Age shop established in 1982 features vintage clothing and jewelry, including the largest selection of earrings on the East Coast.

The Mystic Jewel (252-255-5515; www .themysticjewel.com), A-4 Scarborough Lane. Handcrafted sterling silver jewelry set with semiprecious stones, designed by sisters Courtney and Christine Davidson, comes with information on the mystical powers of the gems. Second location (252-453-3797) in Corolla's Tim-Buck II.

RECOMMENDED READING

Mercier, Judith D. *Duck: An Outer Banks Village*. Winston-Salem, NC: John F. Blair, 2001.

Tate, Susan. *Bring Me Duck: Folktales and Anecdotes from Duck, N.C. (as told by Ruth Tate)*. Nags Head, NC: Nags Head Art, 1986. Includes many photos and a glossary of local terms.

Sara DeSpain Goldsmith (252-255-0633; www.saradespain.com), Osprey Landing. Seashell charms and OBX and duck beads are among the original designs created by this master jeweler.

SPECIAL SHOPS **Christmas Mouse** (252-261-5404; www.christmasmouse .com), C-1 Scarborough Lane. Specializes in nautical and beach-themed

THE DUCKS OF DUCK ALSO ENJOY THE SUNSETS

SHOPPING LOCAL ON THE OUTER BANKS

As tourism surged, the Banks became an increasingly tempting market for national brands. That's why we send a shout-out to these local chains that have stood the test of time:

Birthday Suits/The OBX Store (www.birthday-suits.com). Frequent winner of the "Best of the Beach" award, this store has been selling swimwear for over half a century. Its sister, the OBX Store, sells some of the most sought-after souvenirs on the Banks. Currently there are three locations: in Duck (252-261-7297) at Scarborough Lane Shoppes; in Corolla (252-453-4862) at Monteray Plaza; and in Kill Devil Hills (252-441-5338) at 2000 Bypass, MP 10.

The Cottage Shop (www.cottageshop.com). Stores feature the latest in OBX-style seaside decor for your vacation cottage or home, plus holiday decorations and gifts. A division of Kellogg Building Supply (www.kelloggsupplyco.com), founded on the Banks in 1946, Cottage Shops are located at the Kellogg store in Duck (252-261-8121), in Corolla's TimBuck II (252-453-3525), and in Nags Head (252-441-2522) at the Outer Banks Mall.

Gray's Department Store (www.grays-sportswear.com). Founded in 1948, the Outer Banks' homegrown department store chain carries the largest selection of Tommy Bahama and Fresh Produce on the Banks, and stocks a huge Vera Bradley collection, said to be the largest in the Mid-Atlantic region. There are locations in Corolla at TimBuck II; in Duck at the Waterfront Shops and Scarborough Faire; and in Kitty Hawk at 3860 Bypass, MP 4.

Nags Head Hammocks (www.nagsheadhammocks.com). Selling relaxation since 1974, the nation's largest retailer of hammocks still handcrafts all its products in North Carolina—a real "Made in America" story. Its stores are very welcoming, inviting you to relax on the many hammocks, swings, and rope chairs spread across the decks, lawns, and porches at each location, and to stay as long you like. Stores are located in Duck (252-261-1062) at 1212 NC 12, with a great deck on the sound; in Corolla (252-453-4611) at TimBuck II; and in Kill Devil Hills (252-441-6115) at MP 9.5 Bypass. At the Kill Devil Hills and Duck locations, you can watch hammocks being made and try your hand at it yourself.

Sound Feet Shoes (www.soundfeet.com). The only full-service shoe stores on the Banks, Sound Feet carries all the top brands and styles, from sheepskin boots to sandals. Find stores in Duck (252-261-0490) at 1194 NC 12; in Corolla (252-453-9787) in TimBuck II; and in Nags Head (252-441-8954) at the Croatan Center, MP 14. A Soundfeet outlet store with great deals can be found in Kitty Hawk (252-441-0715) at 3840 Bypass.

Try My Nuts (www.trymynuts.com). Local company, home of "the world's hottest nuts," hovers on the edge of fame for its Dirty White Trash snack mix. Three locations on the Banks, in Corolla at TimBuck II (252-453-4955); in Duck at Scarborough Lane Shoppes (252-261-0900); and in Kill Devil Hills (252-449-9022) at MP 8.5.

ornaments. Second location in Nags Head on the Bypass (MP 10.5).

Donna Designs Wearable Art (252-261-6868; www.donnadesignsobx.com), Waterfront Shops. Hand-painted clothing and jewelry are created by a local artist inspired by the beach.

Island Attic (252-261-0422; www.theislandattic.com), 16 Scarborough Faire. Eco-friendly tropical décor made from recycled teak fishing boats, Bali imports, ducks crafted from roots, and in the back the Tiki Room with everything to set up your own tropical bar.

✍ **Olde Duck Village Shoppe and Duck Post Office** (252-261-8555; www.oldeduckvillage.com), 1245 NC 12, Barrier Island Station. The tiny Duck post office, founded in 1909, is inside this shop, which features locally crafted jewelry, children's books by local authors, and Duck souvenirs, including rubber duckies for every occasion.

Made in the OBX (252-489-9626; www.madeintheobx.com), 1187 NC 12, Loblolly Pines. Locally made food, crafts, and art by more than 100 artisans on the Outer Banks.

🐾 **Outer Barks** (252-715-4981; www.outerbarks.com), Scarborough Lane. Huge selection of gifts for dogs and dog lovers. Bring your pampered pooch to the Outer Barks Yappy Hour. Second location in the Waterfront Shops.

Plum Crazy (252-261-1125; www.ruplumcrazy.com), Duck Soundside Shops. Step through the looking glass at this local favorite, stocking one-of-a-kind

jewelry, accessories, and functional art furniture, much of it by local artists, plus the hippest national brands.

✳ Special Events

Check the **Outer Banks visitor website** (www.outerbanks.org) for an updated list of events during your stay.

April: **Outer Banks Wedding Show** (www.thesanderling.com), Sanderling Inn.

Coastival Duck & Wine Festival (www.duckandwine.com), Waterfront Shops. Food competition of dishes featuring duck and a wine-tasting festival benefit local children's charities.

July: **Fourth of July Parade and Community Social** (www.townofduck.com), Duck Town Park. The 1-mile annual parade does not travel down NC 12, instead winding its way along side streets.

October: **Duck Jazz Festival** (www.duckjazz.com), Duck Town Park. Columbus Day weekend features great music with free admission topping a week of jazz-themed events all over the village.

December: **Duck Yuletide Celebration** (www.townofduck.com), Duck Town Park. Seasonal caroling, Santa's arrival on the Duck fire truck, the grand finale of the Great Yuletide Elf Hunt sponsored by the **Duck Merchants Association** (www.doducknc.com), and the lighting of the town's Crab Pot Tree highlight this festival in early December.

SOUTHERN SHORES

In 1947, naturalist Frank Stick established the Kitty Hawk Land Company and began the first planned community on the Outer Banks, **Southern Shores**. Interested buyers were advised to cross the **Wright Memorial Bridge** and turn left at the ocean, directions that still hold true today. This left turn onto NC 12 leads through the heart of the original development, today an incorporated town in Dare County. The 4-square-mile community stretches from the oceanfront to the sound. Many of the largest homes are built along the sound side, and many year-round residents live here. Most vacation rentals are located closer to the ocean, along NC 12.

Scattered among the newer cottages are about 30 survivors of the original homes built by Stick and his son David, who took over the company in 1955. Designed to withstand the local weather, these are generally flat-topped houses built of concrete made with local sand. Inside, they are paneled in native juniper (white cedar). The house at **23 Porpoise Lane** is one of the best preserved of the early houses and has been nominated for Historic Landmark status. David Stick took a great interest in Southern Shores, laying out many of the roads himself to take full advantage of the contour of the land.

Today, the community is known for its natural beauty, with roads winding between tall pines, dogwoods, and live oaks draped with Spanish moss. Beautiful lagoons and canals intertwine along the sound.

The local civic association owns and maintains the town's beach accesses and other community resources. No one can park a car inside the town limits except residents, property holders, and those renting cottages here, keeping the beaches free of crowds.

GUIDANCE Information on Southern Shores and Duck can be found at the Dare County welcome centers. The closest is the **Aycock Brown Welcome Center** (1-877-629-4386; www.outerbanks.org), located at MP 1 in Kitty Hawk on US 158.

For more on local ordinances, check in with the **Town of Southern Shores** (252-261-2394; www.southernshores-nc.gov), 5375 N. Virginia Dare Trail, Southern Shores.

POST OFFICE The nearest post offices are in Duck and Kitty Hawk. The zip code for all of Southern Shores is 27949.

GETTING THERE Southern Shores actually begins at the foot of the US 158 bridge from the mainland and runs down the north side of US 158 to its intersection with NC 12. All of the businesses in Southern Shores are located along this stretch of highway and at the junction of the two highways.

NC 12, called Ocean Boulevard at the south end of Southern Shores, then changing to Duck Road at the northern end, runs the entire length of the town from Kitty Hawk to Duck.

GETTING AROUND *By bicycle:* While Southern Shores is a planned community, most of it is not gated. A system of bike trails, both paved and unpaved, runs throughout

Southern Shores, connecting on the north with the Duck Path and to the south with US 158. These provide the best way to explore this unique beach community.

A map of multiuse bike paths can be found on the **Southern Shores town website** (www.southernshores-nc.gov) on the town parking areas map. A paved bike path runs along the northern side of US 158 from the Wright Memorial Bridge all the way to the junction with NC 12, then along NC 12 all the way to the Duck town border.

Parking is available in the **Marketplace Shopping Center** on the north side of US 158 and at **Southern Shores Crossing Shopping Center** at the corner where NC 12 turns off to the north.

MEDICAL EMERGENCY You can reach **Surf Rescue** directly at 252-599-2922.

✳ To Do

BOATING A boat launching area for Southern Shore residents and guests is located off Dogwood Trail on Currituck Sound.

FOR FAMILIES The privacy, low-traffic neighborhoods, uncrowded beaches, and residential quality of Southern Shores make it a favorite with families, especially those with young children. A community playground, basketball court, and soccer field can be found at ✤ **Sea Oats Park**. The ✤ **Soundside Wading Beach** off N. Dogwood Trail has a playground and picnic area. The water here is shallow and suitable for young children. Both facilities are under the management of the Southern Shores Civic Association.

GOLF **Duck Woods Country Club** (252-261-2609; www.duckwoodscc.com), 50 S. Dogwood Trail. Semiprivate course designed by Ellis Maples accepts public play on a limited basis. Duck Woods is most easily accessed from US 158.

✳ Green Space

BEACHES You must have a town parking tag to park in any of the parking lots at beach accesses in Southern Shores. No parking is permitted on the streets. You cannot drive on the beach here. Fires and fireworks are also prohibited. Dogs can go on the beach between 6 PM and 9 AM from May 15 to September 15, anytime the rest of the year. Pets must be leashed at all times. Lifeguards are stationed at the Hillcrest Drive, East Dogwood, and Chicahauk Trail beach accesses from May 1 to October 15.

SOUTHERN SHORES BEACHES ARE RARELY CROWDED

While many realty companies represent one or two properties in town, the original Southern Shores Realty company founded in 1947 offers the greatest selection, including some of the original "flat-tops."

🐾 ♿ (((•))) **Southern Shores Realty** (252-2612000 or 1-800-334-1000; www .southernshores.com), 5 Ocean Boulevard. This real estate company handles 400 rentals in Southern Shores, including some long-term rentals and partial-week stays.

✳ Where to Eat and Selective Shopping

All of the restaurants and retail in Southern Shores are concentrated along its southern edge. No freestanding retail exists in this community once you start up NC 12. Look for Southern Shores listings in our "Central Beaches" section.

Southern Shores Crossing (www .facebook.com/southernshorescrossing), where NC 12 splits with US 158, is the town's premiere shopping destination, with high-end restaurants, shops, and services. Most notable is Coastal Provisions, a foodie destination on this end of the Banks.

✳ Lodging

Available vacation lodging in Southern Shores is composed entirely of cottages, most close to the ocean along NC 12.

THE CENTRAL BEACHES

KITTY HAWK, KILL DEVIL HILLS, NAGS HEAD, SOUTH BODIE ISLAND

THE CENTRAL BEACHES

Kitty Hawk to Oregon Inlet

One hundred years ago, tall sand dunes, migrating with the wind, dominated the landscape of the Central Beaches. Today, this is the most accessible—and the most visited—region of North Carolina's Outer Banks. On this part of the coast, you will find the greatest variety of accommodations, the most restaurants, and the most active nightlife. These beaches have an intimate connection with the history of flight. **Orville and Wilbur Wright** first took to the air from a tall dune in Kill Devil Hills, a flight that changed the world. The persistent breezes that helped lift the Wright brothers into the air today make this one of the premiere destinations for air sports on the East Coast.

The Central Beaches present two faces to the world. The most public face is the well-known beachfront, mile after mile of some of the finest sand and waves in the world. Here you'll find surfers, boogie boarders, sandcastle artists, beachcombers, and surf anglers having the time of their lives. The other, more hidden face of the Central Beaches overlooks Roanoke Sound. The marshes are full of wildlife, attracting both hunters and birdwatchers. The shallow water is perfect for Jet Skis, SUPs, and kayaks, while the steady winds make this an ideal location to learn to windsurf or kiteboard.

In between these two coasts, the Central Beaches hold a wealth of both history and natural wonders. The great dunes that brought the Wright brothers to this neighborhood now lift hang gliders on their own first flights. The deep maritime forests give nature lovers and birdwatchers many pleasant options.

As one of the East Coast's earliest summer getaways, the Outer Banks helped define the beach vacation. The traditions of the Central Beaches are ones of laid-back summers spent in hammocks on the cottage porch, beachcombing, and dancing in the sand on warm summer nights. With the burgeoning of the tourism industry, large hotels and condominiums have made inroads along the beachfront, but the coast here is far from being lined with high-rises, and steps have been taken to preserve reminders of the early days on the Banks. Dare County imposes a 35-foot maximum height on most new development. Numerous public beach accesses make it easy to find a quiet stretch of beach, and small family-run cottage courts preserve the beach vacation of an earlier day.

GUIDANCE Two causeways, the only land accesses from the mainland to the Outer Banks, join the Central Beaches with the rest of the world. In the north, the Wright Memorial Bridge leaps Albemarle Sound, connecting Kitty Hawk and Southern Shores with mainland Currituck County. About 20 miles south, the Nags Head–Manteo Causeway leads to Roanoke Island and the Albemarle Peninsula beyond. Each approach has an Outer Banks welcome center to greet visitors.

The **Aycock Brown Welcome Center** (1-877-629-4386; www.outerbanks.org), located at MP 1 in Kitty Hawk, provides information for vacationers arriving on the Outer Banks from the north via the Wright Memorial Bridge (US 158).

The **Sarah Owens Outer Banks Welcome Center** (252-473-2138 or 1-877-629-4386; www.outerbanks.org) is located on Roanoke Island along the US 64/264 Bypass between the Virginia Dare Memorial Bridge and the Nags Head–Manteo Causeway, providing information for visitors arriving from the west.

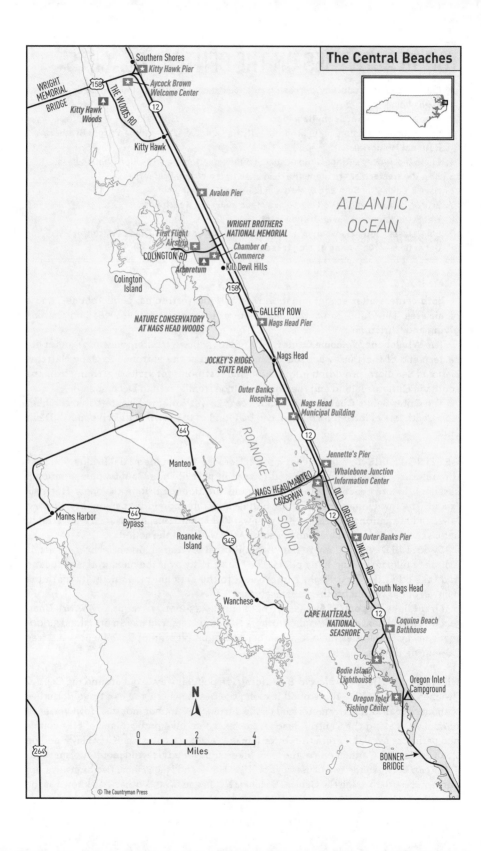

The Central Beaches

Both centers offer accommodation reservations, restrooms, public phones, and a picnic area. The Outer Banks welcome centers close only two days a year, on Thanksgiving and Christmas.

The **Whalebone Welcome Center** (1-877-629-4386; www.outerbanks.org), sits at the eastern end of the causeway from Roanoke Island at the entrance to Cape Hatteras National Seashore, providing information and restrooms for visitors arriving from the south via Hatteras Island and the Bonner Bridge from March to December.

The **Outer Banks Chamber of Commerce** (252-441-8144; www.outerbankschamber .com), with lots of local information, can be found at 101 Town Hall Drive in Kill Devil Hills.

GETTING THERE *By car:* Traveling south from the Wright Memorial Bridge, you pass through three separate incorporated towns, all part of Dare County, plus a national seashore, before reaching Oregon Inlet and the Bonner Bridge to lonely Hatteras Island. The towns may appear alike, but each has its individual personality, history, laws, and attractions. All three, Kitty Hawk, Kill Devil Hills, and Nags Head, stretch across the Banks from the ocean beaches to the waters of the sound.

By air: Kill Devil Hill, where the Wright Brothers National Memorial now stands, is a place of pilgrimage for many pilots. They come to fly over the memorial, and to land and take off at the First Flight Airport next to the national monument, flying in the contrail of the Wright brothers themselves.

First Flight Airport/FFA (252-441-7430 or 252-473-2111; www.nps.gov/wrbr). Unattended airfield next to the Wright Brothers National Memorial has an unlighted 3,000-foot runway. Amenities include a weather and flight planning pilot's facility and free 24-hour tie-downs.

GETTING AROUND *By bicycle:* Bike riding is a popular way to get around the Central Beaches. The best bike route of all is along the beach, where you can travel for miles without encountering any motorized traffic during the summer months. However, each of the towns along the Central Beaches has excellent bike paths. Maps of bike routes and paths are available from the **Outer Banks Welcome Centers** in Kitty Hawk and on Roanoke Island. Contact one of the local bike shops for advice and more information.

By car: Between the two causeways at Kitty Hawk and Nags Head, two highways run north and south through the Central Beaches: NC 12 and US 158, otherwise known as the

Beach Road and the Bypass. The Beach Road (NC 12, also known as the Virginia Dare Trail), is the older and narrower of the two and the most scenic. Sand frequently blows in little drifts across the two lanes, there are few traffic lights, and bicycles are as popular as cars for getting around. Take your time as you drive, and you'll spot raw bars and taverns lining the west side of the road, and beach cottages about to wash into the sea on the east.

The Bypass, just a block or two west, is quite the opposite: a large, fast-moving highway with two lanes in each direction. Although not many hotels are located here, the majority of the newer retail stores and restaurants line both sides in a sometimes bewildering procession of shopping centers and strip malls. The Bypass is officially US 158 and also the Croatan Highway.

Fortunately for visitors, the milepost system is well established along both these roads, and looking for the MP signs will facilitate locating your destination. MP 0 is at the foot of the Wright Memorial Bridge. The milepost distances are not quite the same on the Beach Road and Bypass, but they are helpful anyway. Street addresses can also help with locations, so we include them here. Even-numbered establishments are on the west side of the highways; odd numbers are on the east or ocean side.

Outer Banks Chrysler Dodge Jeep (252-441-1146 or 1-855-459-6555; www .outerbanksjeep.com), on the Bypass MP 5.5 in Kill Devil Hills, rents four-wheel-drive jeeps if you want to drive on the beach. You must also obtain a permit from the National Park Service.

KITTY HAWK

Originally a quiet fishing village and port for arriving visitors, among them the Wright brothers, **Kitty Hawk** became the gateway to the Outer Banks with the completion of the **Wright Memorial Bridge**. The old village lies west of the Bypass, hidden in a deep maritime forest and marsh, with many year-round residences set back in the trees. The Beach Road lies very close to the ocean here, and many seaside cottages have been lost to storms.

The area appears on the earliest maps as *Chickahauk*, a native Algonquin name meaning "goose hunting grounds," which may have evolved into both Kitty Hawk and Currituck, the county across the bridge on the mainland. Certainly, the Native Americans considered the area essential to their welfare and once complained to the colonial government when incoming settlers kept them from hunting here.

Other historians speculate that the name Kitty Hawk came from the skeeter hawk, a local name for the dragonflies that gathered to feast on the mosquitoes so plentiful in earlier days. The name Kitty Hawk was well established by the 1790s.

At the base of the Wright Memorial Bridge, MP 0, Kitty Hawk is on the south side of the highway, and Southern Shores is on the north for about 2 miles to the junction with NC 12. One of the oldest developed parts of the coast lies around Winks Store at MP 2 on the Beach Road.

GUIDANCE For information on beach rules and other local regulations, check with the **Town of Kitty Hawk** (252-261-3552; www.kittyhawknc.gov) or the Kitty Hawk town hall at 101 Veterans Memorial Drive.

POST OFFICE The **Kitty Hawk Post Office** (252-261-2211) is located at 3841 Bypass on the east side at Kitty Hawk Road. The zip code for Kitty Hawk is 27949.

PUBLIC RESTROOMS Public facilities are found at the Aycock Brown Welcome Center at MP 1 on US 158; at Kitty Hawk Park on West Kitty Hawk Road; at Sandy Run Park, on the Woods Road; at Pruitt Park near the junction of US 158 and the Woods Road; and at the public boat ramp on Bob Perry Road. On the Beach Road (NC 12), public facilities are located at the Kitty Hawk Bathhouse at the junction of Kitty Hawk Road next to the Black Pelican restaurant, and at the Byrd Street beach access.

MEDICAL EMERGENCY **Sentara Regional Medical Center** (252-255-6000; www .albemarlehealth.org), 5200 Bypass, MP 1.5, a facility associated with Sentara Albe-marle Hospital in Elizabeth City, offers outpatient surgery, diagnostic imaging and testing, and the services of doctors representing some 20 specialties, as well as urgent care.

KILL DEVIL HILLS AND COLINGTON ISLAND

Referred to by locals as KDH, **Kill Devil Hills** occupies the middle portion of the Central Beaches and was the first town in Dare County to incorporate, taking that step in 1953. The **Wright Brothers National Memorial** was the area's first nonbeach attraction, and many hotels located close to it. More chain hotels and condominiums are found in this part of the beach than any other. The Wrights took flight from a dune called Kill Devil Hill by locals, some say because it was used as a hiding place for scavenged rum that would "kill the devil."

Avalon, centered on the Avalon fishing pier in KDH, was one of the first beachfront neighborhoods on the coast. Today, KDH is Dare County's largest municipality, with over 7,000 year-round residents and a distinctly family focus.

Located west of the Wright Brothers Memorial, **Colington Island**—about 2 miles long by 2 miles wide—is connected by bridges and a single road to Kill Devil Hills. Named for Sir John Colleton, one of Carolina's Lords Proprietor, Colington was the location of one of the earliest plantations on the Banks and eventually became the home of a thriving fishing village where crab-shedding (the process that creates soft-shell crabs) was—and remains—a major industry. Development was slow to come to Colington, but recently upscale subdivisions have appeared among the more modest homes of families who have lived here for generations. The few restaurants and inns set among the old live oaks are worth seeking out for an Outer Banks experience different from both the beach and the Bypass.

KDH runs roughly from MP 5 to MP 10 on both the US 158 Bypass and the Beach Road (NC 12), between the towns of Kitty Hawk and Nags Head.

GUIDANCE **Kill Devil Hills Town Hall** (252-480-4000; www.kdhnc.com), 102 Town Hall Drive, Kill Devil Hills.

POST OFFICE **The Kill Devil Hills U.S. Post Office** (252-441-5666) is at 302 Bypass, MP 8. The zip code in Kill Devil Hills is 27948.

PUBLIC RESTROOMS **Ocean Bay Boulevard Bathhouse**, at MP 8.5 on the Beach Road, along with several public parks off Colington Road, as well as Kill Devil Hills Field on the Bypass, MP 6, behind the KDH fire department, offer public facilities.

PUBLIC LIBRARY (ᵂⁱ-ᶠⁱ) **Dare County Library at Kill Devil Hills** (252-441-4331; www .youseemore.com/EARL), 400 Mustian Street. This library, with a Wi-Fi hotspot and eight computers available for public use, houses a local history collection. Closed on Saturdays in summer and on Sunday year-round.

GETTING AROUND *By car:* KDH runs roughly from MP 5 to MP 10 on both the US 158 Bypass and the Beach Road (NC 12), between the towns of Kitty Hawk and Nags Head.

The KDH town offices, as well as the Outer Banks Chamber of Commerce, a library, recreation facilities, the senior center, the Veterans Memorial, and an arboretum are located west of the Bypass off Colington Road, the first street south of the Wright Brothers Memorial. Turn east on this road instead, and you'll be on Ocean Bay Boulevard, headed for one of the largest ocean bathhouses in KDH.

NAGS HEAD AND WHALEBONE JUNCTION

The unusual name of **Nags Head** appears on maps as early as 1738. Some say it was named for the wild horses that roamed the area, others that it reminded an early settler of a place on the coast of England that bears the same name. The most colorful tale attributes the name to the practice of placing a lantern around a horse's head and leading it along the shore to lure ships to their destruction. In those early days, much of the wood for building homes, as well as other supplies, came ashore from shipwrecks. The practice of luring ships, called "wrecking," has not actually been documented along this coast.

The region became the earliest summer resort on the Outer Banks in the 1830s, when a planter from nearby Perquimans County brought his family to Nags Head to avoid the fevers and insects of the interior. The area along the sound soon housed hotels and cottages, with docks extending far out to accommodate the steamers that put in with vacationing families. By the 1860s, families began to build cottages along the oceanfront, some of which still survive in the historic **Nags Head Beach Cottage Row**, otherwise known as the Unpainted Aristocracy.

The largest surviving dune along the Banks is located in Nags Head. Named **Jockey's Ridge**, possibly for the horse races once held there, the dune is moving slowly southwest with the prevailing wind. The sand has buried many things over the years, including a church and a hotel. Along the Bypass opposite Jockey's Crossing shopping center, the top turrets of a castle, all that remains of a mini-golf course, can sometimes be seen peeking above the sands.

The origin of the name **Whalebone Junction** is another mystery, but the area where the Beach Road joins the Bypass, as well as the causeway coming from Manteo, does provide the backbone and nerve center of the area. Whalebone Junction is the oldest developed part of Nags Head, where you'll find long-lived establishments such as **Sam and Omie's** and **Owens' Restaurant**.

Nags Head stretches from Eighth Street, about MP 10, south to MP 21 on Old Nags Head Road. The Nags Head–Manteo Causeway (US 64) comes from Roanoke Island and the mainland at Whalebone Junction.

GUIDANCE **Nags Head Town Hall** (252-441-5508; www.nagsheadnc.gov), 5401 S. Croatan Highway, on the Bypass, MP 15, Nags Head.

The Whalebone Welcome Center (1-877-629-4386; www.outerbanks.org), at the entrance to Cape Hatteras National Seashore, provides information and restrooms from March to December.

POST OFFICE **The Nags Head Post Office** (252-441-0526) is located at 100 W. Deering Street. The zip code for Nags Head is 27959.

PUBLIC RESTROOMS Bathhouses with restrooms are located on the Beach Road at Bonnet Street, Hargrove Street, Epstein Street, and Jennette's Pier. On the Bypass, the Harvey Sound Access at MP 16 also has public facilities.

GETTING AROUND The Beach Road (NC 12), the Bypass (US 158), and the Nags Head–Manteo Causeway (US 64) all join together in Whalehead Junction. From this junction, NC 12 continues south through the national park along an inland route, while the Beach Road, now named Old Oregon Inlet Road, continues south along the coast for a few miles before rejoining NC 12. This area, almost completely composed of residential and rental properties, is called South Nags Head.

MEDICAL EMERGENCY **Outer Banks Hospital** (1-877-359-9179; www.theouter bankshospital.com), 4800 S. Croatan Highway/US 158, MP 14 on the Bypass. A full-service hospital offering inpatient, outpatient, and emergency services 24 hours a day all year.

Outer Banks Hospital Urgent Care Center (252-261-8040), 4923 Bypass, MP 14.5. Extended hours are available for walk-ins.

✷ To See

IN KITTY HAWK

HISTORIC SITES ら **Monument to a Century of Flight** (1-877-629-4386; www .monumenttoacenturyofflight.org). Adjacent to the Aycock Brown Welcome Center at MP 1 in Kitty Hawk, this memorial commemorates the accomplishments that led from Kitty Hawk to outer space. Stainless-steel pylons and black granite panels chronicle the 100 most significant events of the first 100 years of flight. The poem "High Flight" is engraved on a marker at the entrance. Free.

ら **Old Kitty Hawk Village**. Off Kitty Hawk Road on the west side of the Bypass, turn south onto Moore Shore Drive to drive through Old Kitty Hawk, where the Wright brothers stayed when they came to the Outer Banks. A memorial marks the spot where their boardinghouse stood. Another site associated with the Wright brothers is the old Kitty Hawk Life-Saving Station, now the Black Pelican Restaurant.

ら ⚐ **USS *Kitty Hawk* Exhibit** (252-261-3552; www.kittyhawknc.gov), 101 Veterans Memorial Park Drive. Kitty Hawk's town hall displays artifacts from the supercarrier USS *Kitty Hawk* CV-63, decommissioned in 2009. The Veterans Memorial and Memorial Park are adjacent to the town hall.

IN KILL DEVIL HILLS

GARDEN ら **Outer Banks Arboretum and Teaching Garden** (252-473-4290; dare.ces.ncsu.edu), 300 Mustian Street. Located next to the Thomas A. Baum Senior Center, this pleasant spot has gardens of dune, aquatic, butterfly, and native plants, including many pest- and salt-resistant species, labeled for identification. Free.

MUST SEE

🤿 ♿ ✈ **Wright Brothers National Memorial** (252-473-2111; www.nps.gov/wrbr), MP 7.5, Bypass. Open daily. In late 2018, a renovated and expanded visitor center will open incorporating many features of the former Cen-

tennial Pavilion, including exhibits on the history of aviation, NASA space exhibits, and an interactive area showing what the Outer Banks were like when Wilbur and Orville arrived, as well as a replica of the 1903 flyer, a bookstore, restrooms, and an aviation hall of fame. Close by, the park service has reconstructed the Wrights' living quarters and primitive hangar. The flight line of the first four successful powered flights is marked by a series of granite boulders. A 60-foot granite pylon, the memorial's most noticeable feature, stands atop Kill Devil Hill. On its far side, a life-size group of bronze statues, accurate down to the barefoot photographer snapping the most famous picture in history, captures the moment of the first flight. During the summer months, park rangers give tours and talks throughout the park. Admission $7, good for seven consecutive days; ages 15 and under free.

HISTORIC SITES ♿ ✈ **Paul E. Garber First Flight Society Shrine** (252-441-1903; www.firstflight.org), MP 7.5, Bypass. Over 50 portraits of outstanding figures in the history of aviation hang in the Wright Brothers National Memorial Visitor Center. Reading their biographies is an education in itself. Free with admission to the national memorial.

IN NAGS HEAD AND SOUTH NAGS HEAD

MATTIE MIDGETTE'S STORE SITS AMID THE UNPAINTED ARISTOCRACY

HISTORIC SITES Outer Banks Beachcomber Museum in Mattie Midgette's Store (252-564-5317; www.osob.net), 4008 Beach Road, MP 13. Housed in a 1914 grocery store listed on the National Register of Historic Places, this museum exhibits treasures gathered by Nellie Myrtle Midgette Pridgen during a lifetime of beachcombing, including rare shells, sea glass, whalebone, messages in bottles, driftwood, and all sorts of curious artifacts. Check website for upcoming open house hours.

USS *Huron* Historic Shipwreck Preserve (910-458-9042; www.archaeology.ncdcr.gov), Bladen Street Beach Access, Beach Road, MP 11.5. North Carolina's first shipwreck preserve is the site of the wreck of the *Huron* just north of Nags Head Pier, about 250 yards off the beach. The *Huron*, one of the last iron steamships in the U.S. Navy, sank in heavy seas on November 27, 1877, with many lives lost. In summer, buoys mark the stern and bow of the wreck, now home to a great variety of sea life and a popular destination for divers and snorkelers. A second wreck, a tugboat that went down in 1919, is located halfway between the *Huron* and the pier. Collecting artifacts from the wrecks is prohibited. Look for an information kiosk at the Bladen Street Beach Access.

Shipwrecks (www.nps.gov/caha), Hatteras National Seashore beaches. Several victims of the Graveyard of the Atlantic can sometimes be seen along the South Bodie Island beaches. The remains of the *Laura Barnes*, a four-masted wooden schooner that came ashore in 1921, can be seen at Coquina Beach. Farther south, the wreck of the *Lois Joyce*, a fishing trawler lost in 1981, can be seen on the ocean side of the hook on the north side of Oregon Inlet at low tide.

NATURE MUSEUMS ❄ 🐚 ♿ 🐬 ⌁ **Jennette's Pier** (252-255-1501; www.jennettespier .net), 7223 Beach Road, MP 16.5. Originally erected in 1939, the pier is now part of the North Carolina Aquarium system and has been rebuilt with concrete pilings that, hopefully, will withstand hurricanes. The state facility's goal is to preserve the tradition of family pier fishing for future generations. Nature exhibits in the pier house include a 3,000-gallon aquarium re-creating a coquina rock ledge, the Pier Piling Aquarium that lets visitors see what's under the pier, renewable energy exhibits, and a large collection of mounted trophy fish. Adult and children's fishing passes are available by the day,

JENNETTE'S PIER, PART OF THE NORTH CAROLINA AQUARIUM SYSTEM, ENCOURAGES FAMILIES TO TRY PIER FISHING

MUST SEE

Bodie Island Lighthouse, a 156-foot, black-and-white-striped tower, has been renovated and is open for climbing from mid-April to Columbus Day. Built in 1872, it contains its original first order Fresnel lens. The **Double Keepers' Quarters** building at its base contains exhibits on the history of the lighthouse, a National Park Service visitor center, and a bookstore. Several other historic buildings—the 1878 **Bodie Island Lifesaving Station**, its boathouse, and the 1925 **Bodie Island Coast Guard Station**—have been moved from the oceanfront and are now located along the lighthouse entrance road. Follow the path behind the quarters to a ♿ **boardwalk** where you can spot wading birds and waterfowl in a freshwater pond. Daily ranger programs, including bird walks, turtle talks, soundside seining, and evening campfires, are offered June through Labor Day. Admission to the park is free, but tickets to climb the lighthouse's 200 steps are $8 for adults, $4 for seniors, children 11 and under, and the disabled. **Bodie Island Lighthouse and Keepers' Quarters** (252-473-2111; www.nps.gov/caha), NC 12, South Nags Head.

weekend, or week. Pier fishing classes are offered for all ages. Open all year and until midnight during the summer season. Walking passes are $2 for adults; $1 for children.

♿ **Jockey's Ridge State Park** (252-441-7132; www.nc.parks.gov/jockeys-ridge-state-park), Carolista Drive, MP 12, Bypass. Sunset is the most popular time to visit Jockey's Ridge, when many make the pilgrimage up the 100-foot dune to enjoy a spectacular 360-degree view of the Outer Banks. The visitor center museum provides exhibits and films explaining the unique ecosystems, and two nature trails explore the maritime thickets of stunted live oak slowly being buried by the sand. A handicapped-accessible boardwalk leads out to the dune. Activities available include hang gliding and kite flying, as well as kayaking, windsurfing, and swimming at the Soundside Road access. Sandboarding is allowed with a permit. Activity programs, including birding walks and kayak tours, are offered at the park all year. Admission and all programs are free.

✳ To Do

BICYCLING

IN KITTY HAWK

In Kitty Hawk, the ♿ **Pruitt Multiuse Trail**, a separate paved path, runs along Woods Road through the maritime forest. It connects at its northern end with the Southern

ARCHITECTURE: THE UNPAINTED ARISTOCRACY

Nags Head Cottage Row Historic District. About 40 structures along a 1.5-mile stretch of the Beach Road make up the Nags Head Beach Cottage Row Historic District. Many of them are listed on the National Register of Historic Places. Nine cottages built before 1885 survive today. Most of the others date from 1900 to 1940.

The cottages share design elements that have come to define the Nags Head style: unpainted cedar-shake siding, wide hip-roofed porches with built-in benches, and windows covered by propped shutters.

Cottage Row runs between MP 12 and MP 13.5 on the Beach Road, from the C. H. White Cottage at 3905 S. Virginia Dare Trail on the north end to the Outlaw Cottage at 4327 S. Virginia Dare Trail in the south. Besides the private cottages, historic buildings include St. Andrew's By-the-Sea Episcopal Church (1915), the First Colony Inn (1932), and Mattie Midgette's Store (1914), now a museum. The oldest surviving cottage is the 1859 Spider Villa at 4049 Virginia Dare Trail.

A paved multiuse path runs along the Beach Road past the historic cottages. To see the cottages from the beach side is more difficult, as there are no public beach accesses in the historic district. The closest are at Conch Street (3600 block, Beach Road) at the north end and Small Street (4500 block, Beach Road) at the south end.

This first cottage community was built close to the eastern flank of the Jockey's Ridge dune, and a fine overall view of the historic district can be gained from the observation tower at Jockey's Crossing Shopping Center, built on the site of the old dance pavilion.

In recent years, the Town of Nags Head has encouraged the use of local design elements, including cedar-shake siding, wraparound porches, wooden shutters, gable and hip roofs, cupolas, and lifesaving station watchtowers. These can now be seen in numerous new commercial and residential units along the Banks.

ONE OF THE EARLIEST COTTAGES DISPLAYS THE CLASSIC NAGS HEAD FEATURES

RECOMMENDED READING

Bishir, Catherine. *Unpainted Aristocracy: The Beach Cottages of Old Nags Head*. Raleigh, NC: Division of Archives and History, North Carolina Department of Cultural Resources, 1978.

Roundtree, Susan Byrum. *Nags Headers*. Winston-Salem, NC: John F. Blair, 2001. Oral histories from Nags Head's oldest families.

Roundtree, Susan Byrum, and Meredith Vaccaro. *Nags Head: Then and Now*. Manteo, NC: One Boat Guides, 2004. Walking tour of the Unpainted Aristocracy district.

Siddons, Anne Rivers. *Outer Banks*. New York: Harper Collins Publishers, 1992. This best-selling fiction novel introduced the Unpainted Aristocracy to the world.

Shores bike path along US 158, and at its southern end with a bikeway along the wide, paved shoulders of Kitty Hawk Road. Parking is available at Pruitt Park, near the junction of US 158 and the Woods Road, and at Kitty Hawk Park on W. Kitty Hawk Road.

From Kitty Hawk Road, head south on Moore Shore Road to find the historic village of Kitty Hawk, where the Wright brothers first stayed when they came to the Banks. Moore Shore Road leads down to the & **Wright Brothers Multiuse Path,** which follows a historic roadbed along the sound. This bikeway, a paved road not accessible to motorized traffic, leads to Windgrass Circle and Bay Drive in Kill Devil Hills with a beautiful ride along the sound for several miles.

Another bike route through Kitty Hawk is along a multiuse path running beside Twiford and W. Kitty Hawk roads to Kitty Hawk Landing.

Farther east, Lindberg Avenue, between the highways in east Kitty Hawk, is a popular north–south biking route paralleling NC 12. The Beach Road is narrow here and not recommended for children on bikes.

Kitty Hawk Cycle Company (252-261-2060; www.kittyhawkcyclecompany.com), MP 2.5, Beach Road at Eckner Street. Repairs, rentals, and sales of beach cruisers, road and mountain bikes. Group rides for road bikers offered most days.

Moneysworth Beach Home Equipment Rentals (252-261-6999 or 1-800-833-5233; www.mworth.com), 947 W. Kitty Hawk Road. Bike rentals conveniently located near the Kitty Hawk Woods bike paths.

IN KILL DEVIL HILLS

A paved multiuse path begins at the East Ocean Bay Boulevard beach access on the Beach Road and runs west, crossing the Bypass and following Colington Road along the south side of the Wright Brothers Memorial, then cuts through the woods to connect with First Street, Canal Road, and Bay Drive along the sound. Many paved paths cut off from Colington Road, including paths along Bermuda Bay Boulevard, Veterans Drive, and Mustian Street, connecting the facilities of the Dare County Family Recreation Park and the public schools in the area. The Beach Road has widened paved shoulders for the use of bikes and pedestrians on its stretch through Kill Devil Hills.

The Bike Barn (252-441-3786; www.bikebarnobx.com), 1312 Wrightsville Boulevard. Rents hybrids and road bikes, and also offers repair services and sales.

Just for the Beach Rentals (252-441-6048; www.justforthebeach.com), 1006 Beach Road, MP 9, and **Ocean Atlantic Rentals** (252-441-7823; www.oceanatlanticrentals .com), MP 10, Beach Road. Both these companies rent bikes, kayaks, surfboards, paddleboards, coolers, baby equipment, beach chairs, grills, linens, and every sort of equipment you need at the beach.

Outer Banks Bicycle (252-480-3399), 203 Beach Road, MP 8.5. Dedicated bike store offers rentals of beach cruisers, road bikes, hybrids, and tandem bikes built for two, as well as sales and repairs. Water sports equipment, including kayaks, SUPs, and surfboards also for rent. Delivery available.

IN NAGS HEAD

In Nags Head, a multiuse path runs parallel to the Beach Road from MP 21 on Old Oregon Inlet Road north through Whalebone Junction to Eighth Street (MP 11.5), where it continues as a widened shoulder through Kill Devil Hills.

BOATING

IN KITTY HAWK

A Dare County public boat ramp is located on Bob Perry Road in Kitty Hawk Woods, with a picnic area, public toilets, and parking available for about 30 vehicles. The 200-foot canal leading to Kitty Hawk Bay is approximately 5 feet deep. A floating dock is provided for launching kayaks and canoes.

Dock of the Bay Marina (252-255-5578; www.dockofthebayobx.com). Located just beyond the public boat launch on Bob Perry Road, this marina, with easy access to Albemarle Sound, has a fuel dock, plus a convenience store with all the essentials (beer, wine, ice, snacks) as well as fishing tackle and bait. You can fish or crab for free from the dock, or use the picnic tables.

OBX Sail (1-877-FLY-THIS; www.obxsail.com). Enjoy a daytime or sunset sail of Albemarle Sound aboard the ketch *Movin' On* from the marina on Bob Perry Road.

IN KILL DEVIL HILLS

Kitty Hawk Bay and the canals and streams that surround Colington Island provide peaceful places to paddle or fish. On Colington Island, put your kayak in at the foot of the second bridge, where you'll find a parking area on the western side.

  ♿ **North Carolina Wildlife Boat Ramp and Access** (www.ncwildlife.org), Dock Street at Bay Drive. Open 24 hours. Two paved boat ramps and 12 parking spaces, plus a canoe launch area, give access to Kitty Hawk Bay. Free.

IN NAGS HEAD

Outer Banks Boating Center & Fishing Unlimited Tackle (252-441-5028; www .fishingunlimited.net), 7665 Nags Head–Manteo Causeway. Rent an outboard skiff or pontoon boat for fishing, crabbing, or sight-seeing on Roanoke Sound by the full or half day.

Kitty Hawk Watersports (252-441-2756; www.kittyhawkwatersports.com), 6920 Bypass, MP 16. Rent a Hobie catamaran for a sail on the sound. Beginner sailing lessons are offered here. Jet Skis, paddleboards, kayaks, and surfboards are also for rent. Go tame with a bumper boat, perfect for the youngest kid, or opt for a more thrilling banana tubing or parasail ride.

IN SOUTH NAGS HEAD

The National Park Service operates a free boat ramp at Oregon Inlet behind the fishing center. About 75 vehicles and trailers can park here. You cannot launch personal watercraft (Jet Skis) at this facility.

RECOMMENDED READING

Joe Malat (www.joeknowsfishing.com) wrote the books, literally, on pier fishing, surf fishing, and crabbing.

CRAFTS ✂ ⊤ **Beach Memories** (252-441-7277; www.obxscrapbookersparadise .com), 2236 Bypass, Plaza Del Sol, MP 10, Nags Head. Scrapbook supplies to preserve your vacation memories.

✂ ⊤ **Cloud Nine** (252-441-2992; www.obeadx.com), 3022 Bypass, MP 11, Pirate's Quay Shopping Center, Nags Head. Long-established beading store offers classes for adults and children, with a huge selection of beads, beach glass, and jewelry-making supplies, plus gold and silver jewelry created by local artists.

✂ ⊤ (ᵂ) **OBX Art Studio** (252-449-5055; www.obxbeads.com), 2200 Bypass, Milepost 6 Plaza, Kill Devil Hills. Do-it-yourself studio will help you create a unique souvenir of your vacation. Originally Glazin' Go Nuts, this spot next to the Front Porch Cafe offers paint your own pottery, beading, fused glass art, and canvas painting with two dozen different beach scenes available. A great spot for a rainy day.

DOLPHIN TOURS ♿ **Nags Head Dolphin Watch** (252-449-8999; www.dolphinwatch .com), 7517 Causeway, Whalebone Water Sports. This group of independent researchers studies the Atlantic bottlenose dolphins that make their home in Roanoke Sound. Two-hour journeys aboard a canopied pontoon boat, offered May through September, are guided by naturalists with a wealth of information about the dolphins, many of whom have individual names. Drinks, snacks, and restroom on board.

Kitty Hawk Watersports (252-441-2756; www.kittyhawkwatersports.com), 6920 Bypass, MP 16. Pontoon boat tours to see the local dolphins depart from Wanchese.

FISHING AND CRABBING

IN KITTY HAWK

Havin' Fun Soundside Charters (252-475-0090; www.soundsidecharters.com), Dock of the Bay Marina, 4200 Bob Perry Road. Go fishing or crabbing or take a sunset cruise with Captain Chad on the lovely waters of the sound, and keep what you catch for tonight's dinner.

TW's Bait and Tackle (252-261-7848; www.twstackle.com), MP 4, 3864 Bypass, Kitty Hawk; second location (252-441-4807) at MP 10.5, 2230 Bypass, Nags Head. Custom rods are a specialty at these full-service shops, which also carry hunting accessories, fish decor, and camouflage outfits for all ages.

IN KILL DEVIL HILLS

Colington Road Bridge. The second bridge on Colington Road is noted for its fine crabbing. A paved parking lot is just past the bridge, with a path leading down to the water.

Stop N Shop Gourmet Deli & Beach Shop (252-441-6105; www.stopnshopobx.com), MP 8.5, 100 South Beach Road. Longtime local convenience store is a surf-fishing hot spot offering advice and all the equipment you'll need to bring a string of speckled trout to shore. Deli sandwiches are some of the best on the beach and include vegetarian items.

THE FAMOUS OREGON INLET FISHING CENTER IS HOME TO A LARGE FLEET OF CHARTER FISHING BOATS

IN NAGS HEAD

The so-called little bridge on the eastern end of the Nags Head–Manteo Causeway is a noted spot for fishing. Crabbing is good at the nearby Nags Head Causeway Estuarine Access at the eastern end of the causeway.

Rangers at **Jockey's Ridge State Park** (252-441-2588; www.jockeysridgestatepark .com) offer a free Crabby Clinic during the summer months.

Whalebone Tackle (252-441-7413; www.whalebonetackle.com), 7667 Causeway. Convenient shop in business since 1977 sells tackle, crabbing equipment, ice, and bait, as well as some of the finest custom rods on the Banks.

IN SOUTH NAGS HEAD

Miss Oregon Inlet (252-441-6301 or 1-800-272-5199; www.missoregoninlet.com), Oregon Inlet Fishing Center. Spend a morning or afternoon on the water, fishing with an experienced crew aboard this 65-foot headboat. Family-friendly rates include all the equipment and licenses needed to fish. In summer, a twilight sight-seeing cruise is offered. Does not sail on Sunday.

Oregon Inlet Fishing Center & Marina (252-441-6301 or 1-800-272-5199; www .oregon-inlet.com), 98 NC 12. Nearly 50 charter fishing boats dock at Oregon Inlet Fishing Center, one of the most famous fishing destinations in the world, thanks to the many big fish brought to its docks. On the fishing center's website, you can browse pictures and specs for each boat and visit their individual websites, check availability, book online, or sign up for a makeup charter that will match you with other anglers with similar interests. Prices are standardized and run about $1,500 a day for offshore charters, $900 for nearshore, $600 for inshore and sound fishing in an open boat. Half-day morning or afternoon trips and shorter evening trips also available. The ship's store carries groceries, tackle, sandwiches, and Oregon Inlet souvenirs.

Outer Banks Fly Fishing and Light Tackle Charters (252-449-0562; www.outer banksflyfishing.com). If you prefer fly- and light-tackle fishing, captains Brian Horsley and Sarah Gardner will take you out after bluefish, speckled trout, redfish, little tunny, stripers, and just about anything else that will hit a fly.

FISHING PIERS

IN KITTY HAWK

✐ ♂ **Kitty Hawk Fishing Pier** (252-261-1290; www.hiltongardeninnouterbanks.com), MP 1, 5353 Beach Road. Restored and operated by the Hilton Garden Inn, the pier house is a popular spot for events. The pier is usually open for public fishing for a modest fee. Rental rods and reels available. Contact the inn for access information.

IN KILL DEVIL HILLS

Avalon Pier (252-441-7494; www.avalonpier.com), 2111 Beach Road, MP 6.5. This 696-foot pier, built in 1958, is open 5 AM–2 AM during the summer, shorter hours in spring and fall. No shark fishing. Live pier cam on the website.

IN NAGS HEAD

❋ ✐ ♿ ♂ ↬ **Jennette's Pier** (252-255-1501; www.jennettespier.net), 7223 Beach Road, MP 16.5. A two-story pier house holds a tackle shop, gift shop, and exhibits. Adult and children's fishing passes are available by the day, weekend, or week. Pier and surf fishing classes are offered for all ages. Open all year and 24/7 during the summer season.

Nags Head Pier (252-441-5141; www.nagsheadpier.com), 3335 Beach Road, MP 11.5. The 750-foot Nags Head Pier has a full-featured tackle shop that rents rods and reels, rental cottages, a tiki bar, and a restaurant serving breakfast, lunch, and dinner, where the motto is "You hook 'em, we cook 'em." Open 24 hours a day in-season, with lights for night fishing.

IN SOUTH NAGS HEAD

Outer Banks Pier (252-441-5740; www.fishingunlimited.net), 8901 Old Oregon Inlet Road, MP 18.5. This 600-foot pier operated by Fishing Unlimited is open 24 hours a day and is lit for night fishing. Senior discount passes and rental rods and reels available. ♈ **Fish Heads Bar & Grill** on the pier serves inexpensive sandwiches, appetizers, and drinks, and hosts live music and dancing on the deck. $.

FOR FAMILIES

IN KITTY HAWK

✐ ♈ **Children @ Play Museum** (252-261-0290; www.childrenatplayobx.com), 3809 Bypass, MP 4.5. Play areas include a lighthouse, a fishing vessel, the Teddy Bear Hospital, a grocery store, tree fort, and more. Kids can develop their motor skills on the Living Swell surf activity, or brush

THE KITTY HAWK FISHING PIER IS OPERATED BY THE HILTON GARDEN INN

EXCURSIONS

H2OBX (www.h2obxwaterpark.com), a new $46 million waterpark that opened for the 2017 season, takes family fun to a new level. More than 30 themed rides, slides and swim zones bring the pirates, dunes, storms, surf and wild horses of Outer Banks into the water, with experiences suitable for every thrill level on the 20-acre site just across the Wright Memorial Bridge. You can walk the plank, sail aboard the *Queen Anne's Revenge*, face a rogue wave, slide down a giant watery dune, or catch an endless wave. ✍ **H2OBX** (252-491-3000; www.h2obxwaterpark.com), 8526 Caratoke Highway/US 158, Powells Point, NC 27966.

H2OBX, JUST ACROSS THE WRIGHT MEMORIAL BRIDGE, OFFERS A FULL DAY OF WATER FUN FOR ALL AGES

up on science and math with special interactive exhibits. A new adventure lets kids sift through sand to find shells, gems, and fossils. Birthday party packages available. Closed Sunday. Admission $5, adults; $7 kids; infants 12 months and under free.

✍ **Kitty Hawk Park** (252-475-5920; www.darenc.com/parksrec), 900 W. Kitty Hawk Road. Dare County park has a 5,000-square-foot skate park and a dog park (registration required). There's also a playground, picnic area with grills, restrooms, and a half-mile walking trail.

✍ **Pruitt Park**, 5160 Woods Road at US 158. Small town park surrounded by a fence has play equipment for young children, a picnic area, walking path, restroom, and parking.

IN KILL DEVIL HILLS AND COLINGTON

✍ **Aviation Park**, Veterans Drive off Colington Road. Town park has a fitness trail, skate park, lighted roller-hockey rink, playground, and restrooms. The Kill Devil Derby Brigade (www.thekilldevilderbybrigade.com), the local rollergirl team, practices here.

♂ **Colington Speedway** (252-480-9144), 1064 Colington Road. Find these $5 go-karts off the beaten track on Colington Island.

♂ ☂ **Dare County Youth Center and Recreation Park** (252-475-5920; www.darenc .com/parksrec), 602 Mustian Street. Many activities are offered in this compact area just west of the Bypass, MP 6, off Colington Road. Inside are two full-court gyms for open play of basketball or volleyball, a TV room, foosball, ping-pong, pool table, and computer room. Visitors can use the facilities for a small daily or weekly fee. Outside, lighted tennis courts, volleyball and basketball courts, game fields, horseshoe pits, a picnic pavilion with grills, playground, Alpine Tower, and climbing wall offer more activity options. Public restrooms available.

♂ ❀ **Hayman Boulevard Park** (www.kdhnc.com), W. Hayman Boulevard. Circular town park in a soundside neighborhood offers shady live oaks to climb, a kids' playground, picnic area, restrooms, and parking.

♂ **Lost Treasure Golf** (252-480-0142; www.losttreasuregolf.com), 1600 Bypass, MP 7. Wild West mining theme features a free train ride to the first hole.

♂ **Meekins Field** (252-475-5920; www.darenc.com/parksrec), 1634 Bypass, MP 6. Lighted tennis courts, athletic field, playground, picnic area, and restrooms, behind the KDH fire department.

♂ **Paradise Fun Park** (252-441-7626; www.facebook.com/OBXParadiseFunPark), 3300 Bypass, MP 5.5. Two 18-hole, natural grass courses, go-karts, an arcade, bungee trampoline bounce, and Spin Zone bumper cars appeal to both kids and adults. Kids three and under play free.

IN NAGS HEAD

♿ ♂ **Dowdy Park** (www.nagsheadnc.gov), Bypass and Bonnett Street, has an inclusive playground as well as a nature trail, community garden, bocce ball, and all-purpose court.

♂ **First Flight Adventure Park** (252-715-3622; www.firstflightadventurepark.com), 6714 Bypass, MP 16. New aerial adventure park offers 42 different obstacles and six ziplines arranged in categories of difficulty, from easy to advanced, that challenge strength, skill, and balance. The structure, set along the sound, has a maritime theme and was designed to resemble a hurricane.

♂ **Kitty Hawk Kites** (252-449-2210; www.kittyhawk.com), 3933 Bypass, MP 13, Jockey's Ridge Crossing. Indoor 22-foot rock-climbing wall, lessons in kite flying, and kite-making workshops, plus a shop full of sportswear, colorful kites, and great gifts on-site. Climb the tower for a view of Jockey's Ridge.

♂ **Kitty Hawk Watersports** (252-441-2756; www.kittyhawkwatersports.com), 6920 Bypass, MP 16. Bumper boats, a 26-foot-tall climbing wall, plus Jet Ski rentals, parasailing, banana boat rides, and more are offered at this soundside mecca. This stretch of the Bypass around MP 16 has a wealth of entertainment options, including several go-kart tracks and mini-golf courses.

♂ **Jurassic Putt mini-golf** (252-441-6841) on the Bypass at MP 16 and sister course **Galaxy Golf** (252-441-5875) at 2914 Beach Road both offer all-day play for a single price.

♂ ♿ **Mutiny Bay Adventure Golf** (252-480-6606; www.obxfamilyfun.com), 6606 Bypass, MP 16. This 18-hole pirate-themed course has an arcade and snack bar, plus a pirate ship and a store with pirate souvenirs. **Full Throttle Speedway** (252-441-4499; www.obxfamilyfun.com), 6504 Bypass, close by, offering gas-powered Indy style racing, is operated by the same family.

♂ **Nags Head Raceway** (252-480-4639; www.obxfamilyfun.com), 7000 Bypass, MP 16. Indy-style track also has bumper cars, an arcade, and ice cream.

⚓ **Outer Banks Family YMCA Water Park** (252-449-8897; www.ymcashr.org), 3000 Bypass, MP 11. Water park with two pools and a waterslide is open during the summer.

⚓ ⌁ (((•))) **Outer Banks Gearworks Laser Tag & Video Arcade** (252-480-8512; www.outerbankslasertag.com), 2420 Bypass, MP 10.5, South Beach Plaza. Family amusement center with a wide variety of video games, as well as air hockey, laser tag, and a bounce house for the younger set, is a great place for a birthday party or rainy-day fun.

⚓ ⌁ **Pirates and Pixies Toystore** (252-441-8697; www.toysobx.com), 7332 Beach Road, MP 17. Cool toy store has a playroom with a dollhouse, train set, and plenty of games.

⚓ **Whalebone Park** (www.nagsheadnc.gov) across from Jennette's Pier, Beach Road MP 16.5. Nautically themed playground has shaded picnic tables and bocce and volleyball courts.

GOLF

IN SOUTHERN SHORES

Duck Woods Country Club (252-261-2609; www.duckwoodscc.com), 50 S. Dogwood Trail. Semiprivate course designed by Ellis Maples accepts public play on a limited basis. The course's traditional layout is sheltered by trees along the fairways, making this a good choice for windy days. Duck Woods is most easily accessed from US 158.

IN KITTY HAWK

🍸 **Sea Scape Golf Links** (252-261-2158; www.seascapegolf.com), 300 Eckner Street, MP 2.5, Bypass. The windswept dunes and ocean views at this links-style, par 70 public course just a block from the ocean remind many golfers of Scotland. Pro shop on-site rents clubs. The new public 🍸 **Sandtrap Tavern** (252-261-2243; www.sandtraptavern.com) serves locally sourced, scratch-made dishes for breakfast, lunch, and dinner, plus a nightly happy hour and live music some nights.

IN NAGS HEAD

⛳ **Nags Head Golf Links** (252-441-8073; www.nagsheadgolflinks.com), 5615 S. Seachase Drive. Beautiful Scottish links–style course located in the Village of Nags Head development overlooks Roanoke Sound. The 🍸 **Players Grille** serves lunch and after-golf libations, hosts Friday evening happy hour, and is open to the public.

NORTH OF THE WRIGHT MEMORIAL BRIDGE

Many of the region's best golf courses are located on the mainland north of the Wright Memorial Bridge in Currituck County.

Carolina Club (252-453-3588; www.thecarolinaclub.com), 127 Carolina Club Drive, Grandy. This local favorite, just 15 minutes north of the bridge, is noted for its fine putting surfaces. The on-site **Tucker's Sports Bar & Grille** serves breakfast, lunch, dinner, and drinks.

⚓ **Holly Ridge Golf Course** (252-491-2893; www.hollyridgeobx.com), 8818 US 158, Harbinger. A laid-back, family-friendly 18-hole course with driving range, putting green, a full pro shop, and club rentals. Special rates for junior golfers. LPGA Tour professional Cathy Johnston-Forbes offers instruction. This is the closest mainland course to Kitty Hawk, just 1.5 miles north of the bridge.

⛳ **Kilmarlic Golf Club** (252-491-4220; www.kilmarlicgolfclub.com), 215 West Side Lane, Powells Point. Three miles north of the bridge, this is the newest course in the

HANG GLIDING ON JOCKEY'S RIDGE REMAINS ONE OF THE MUST-DO ACTIVITIES ON THE OUTER BANKS

area and a beauty. The terraced clubhouse houses the ✍ **Black Tartan Taproom** (252-491-8329) offering half-pound hand-patted burgers and Boar's Head deli sandwiches, as well as a full bar.

⛳ **The Pointe Golf Club** (252-491-8388; www.thepointegolfclub.com), 308 Pointe Golf Club Drive, Powells Point. Located 3.5 miles north of the bridge. Designed by Russell Breeden, this was the first course in the country to use A1 bent grass greens. The ⛋ **Greenside Bar & Grille** (252-491-2595; www.greensideobx.com) serves breakfast and lunch, with occasional live music in the evenings.

HANG GLIDING **Jockey's Ridge State Park** (252-441-7132; www.jockeysridgestatepark .com), Carolista Drive, MP 12, Bypass, Nags Head. People with USHGA Hang 1 or other agency-approved certification may hang glide free of charge on the dunes at Jockey's Ridge. Register with the park office.

✍ **Kitty Hawk Kites Hang Gliding Training Center** (252-441-2426; www.kittyhawk .com), MP 12, Bypass, Nags Head. The world's largest hang-gliding school has been teaching students from ages 4 to 84 how to catch the wind since 1974. Lessons are held on the soft sand dunes of Jockey's Ridge State Park. Other ways to get airborne include paragliding under a lightweight glider wing. Or—the ultimate thrill for early airplane buffs—fly a museum-quality replica of the 1902 Wright glider that paved the way for the first powered flight.

HEALTH AND FITNESS

IN KITTY HAWK

❋ **The Gym** (252-255-0609; www.theobxgym.com), 3712 Bypass, MP 4.5. Work out with kickboxing, or jiujitsu or join a beach boot camp.

❋ **Outer Banks Yoga** (757-630-8677; www.outerbanksyoga.com), 5230 Beach Road, MP 1.5, Ocean Centre Shops. Classes in a variety of yoga disciplines as well as Pilates and tai chi are offered in the Kitty Hawk studio, and in summer at Lovie's in Corolla. Beach yoga classes meet at the Kitty Hawk Hilton on weekday mornings. Drop-ins welcome.

TAKING FLIGHT WITH KITTY HAWK KITES FOUNDER
JOHN HARRIS

John Harris, founder of the **Kitty Hawk Kites** empire, arrived on the Outer Banks in 1970 and soon discovered a love of hang gliding, then a sport in its infancy. With a business partner, he established Kitty Hawk Kites in 1974 in an old dance pavilion across from Jockey's Ridge, highest dune and best hang gliding spot on the Banks. Today Harris heads the largest hang gliding school in the world and is one of the guiding forces on the Outer Banks, a major player in establishing it as a destination for outdoor sports. The original location has grown into Jockey's Ridge Crossing and is joined by more than a dozen other locations, now as far afield as Florida and Virginia, as well as other beach destinations along the North Carolina coast.

Over the years, Harris has branched out into many other sports that combine the area's unique blend of wind and water, helping to popularize surf kayaking, parasailing, and the latest extreme sport, kiteboarding. In 2010, he cut the ribbon on Waves Village, a new resort dedicated to the rising sport of kiteboarding, soon to enter the Olympic competitions.

The **KittyHawk.com** website serves as a clearinghouse for a huge number of outdoor activities from horseback riding to parasailing, Segway tours to wine-tasting cruises. Kayak and SUP tours, rentals, and lessons, as well as the new flyboards and jetpacks, expand the Kitty Hawk experience into water sports. You can take flight aboard a replica of the 1902 Wright glider, learn to fly a drone, or go to Mermaid School.

Kitty Hawk Kites sponsors numerous festivals, competitions, and workshops throughout the year. Its retail outlets sell aviation and outdoor clothing, as well as kites and toys, at numerous locations. Adventure towers invite kids of all ages to test their skills. But the heart of Kitty Hawk Kites remains its hang gliding school. Instructors introduce 10,000 visitors annually to the thrill of taking flight. After a lesson, you can spread your nylon wings to the breeze and, like Wilbur and Orville and a million birds before you, take to the sky.

Visit www.kittyhawk.com for a full list of adventure options and upcoming events.

JOCKEY'S RIDGE CROSSING IS LOCATED ACROSS THE BYPASS FROM THE DUNES OF JOCKEY'S RIDGE STATE PARK

IN KILL DEVIL HILLS

Ashtanga Yoga Center (252-202-0345; www.ashtangayogaobx.com), Central Square Shopping Center, 2910 Bypass, MP 11. Introductory to advanced classes, special events, and retreats are offered in several disciplines of yoga.

Outer Banks Family YMCA (252-449-8897; www.ymcashr.org), 3000 Bypass, MP 11. Open daily, this 28,000-square-foot center offers a wide range of equipment, facilities, and classes. Indoor facilities include a lap pool, hot tub, sauna, racquetball courts, cycling studio, and fitness center with FitLinxx strength training. Outdoors, the Y has a water park with waterslides, plus a skatepark. Massage therapy and free child care are available. Nonmembers can purchase day, week, or monthly passes for individuals or families. Many hotels and vacation cottages also offer free passes to the Y.

Outer Banks Sports Club (252-441-8361; www.obxsportsclub.com), 2423 Bypass, MP 10. Fully equipped sports club has the latest in equipment, plus an elevated running track, a variety of classes, and a smoothie bar. Daily and weekly passes available.

> # DID YOU KNOW?
>
> SUP is the abbreviation for stand-up paddleboarding, one of the fastest-growing sports in the country. SUPs can be used on either ocean surf or flat water, and they make excellent substitutes for either a kayak or a surfboard. Plus they give paddlers a great core workout.

HUNTING **Outer Banks Waterfowl and Fishing Guide Service** (252-261-7842; www.outerbankswaterfowl.com). Kitty Hawk resident and decoy carver Captain Vic Berg leads fishing trips in the sound and bird-watching excursions in his flat-bottom skiff, able to navigate in the shallowest water. During the hunting seasons (usually scattered from October to January), he and his experienced guides lead dog hunts after as many as 27 different species of wildfowl.

The National Park Service allows waterfowl hunting on **Bodie Island** by registration request only and limits hunting through a lottery to 20 requests a day. Lottery winners must be present at the Whalebone Junction Information Station for the hunting blind drawing at 4:30 AM on the day of the reservation. Any blinds remaining after the day's drawing are assigned on a first-come, first-served basis to walk-in hunters. The **NPS website** (www.nps.gov/caha) has details.

KAYAKING, CANOEING, AND SUP

IN KITTY HAWK AND KILL DEVIL HILLS

The **floating dock launch facility on Bob Perry Road** gives access both to Kitty Hawk Bay and a paddle trail that runs through the Kitty Hawk Woods nature preserve. The trail follows a canal, variously called High Bridge Creek, Jean Guite Creek, or Ginguite Creek, once used by loggers, and opens into the sound at both ends. Narrow and lined by tall trees on either side, it is protected from the often strong winds that sweep the Banks, besides being a haven for wading birds, turtles, and other wildlife. A covered bridge, the only one in eastern North Carolina, is one of the creek's highlights. This trip is highly recommended and perfect for children and novice paddlers.

After launching at the Bob Perry boat ramp, paddlers have the choice of heading north, deeper into the maritime forest, or south toward the marshy islands lining Kitty Hawk Bay. Experienced paddlers can cross the sometimes choppy open waters of the bay to Colington Island (about 7 miles one-way), or follow High Bridge Creek all the way north to Currituck Sound, then around Martin's Point and back along the shore (about 18 miles round-trip).

A second put-in is located at the point where High Bridge Creek crosses under US 158, near the Wright Memorial Bridge, at the **Kitty Hawk Kayaks Paddling Center** (252-261-0145; www.khkss.com), where you can rent kayaks to explore on your own or sign up for a tour. The covered bridge is located less than a mile south of the paddling center; the public boat ramp is 2 miles south.

Several outfitting companies offer tours along High Bridge Creek, considered the finest paddle on the Banks. Most launch at the Bob Perry boat ramp. The exception is the 🌿 **Kitty Hawk Kayak and Surf School** (252-261-0145; www.khkss.com), at 6150 N. Croatan Highway, MP 1, which specializes in tours of the northern end of High Bridge Creek, including the covered bridge. A portion of proceeds benefits the **1% for the Planet organization** (www.onepercentfortheplanet.org). Sunrise and sunset ocean kayaking tours, full-moon paddles, and overnight kayak trips to platforms around Albemarle Sound, including some key birding areas, are also available.

Outfitters offering tours from the southern end of High Bridge Creek include: **Coastal Kayak** (252-261-6262; www.outerbankskayaktours.com) and **Duck Village Outfitters** (252-261-7222; www.duckvillageoutfitters.net).

The kayak and canoe launch in **Sandy Run Park**, 4351 Woods Road, leads to quiet paddle trails along ponds and canals in the maritime forest. A raised boardwalk makes a fine spot for bird-watching.

♿ **Windgrass Circle Sound Access**, W. Tateway Road at Bay Drive, is a good spot to launch directly into Kitty Hawk Bay.

IN NAGS HEAD

The marshes that stretch between Nags Head and Roanoke Island, both north and south of the causeway, although very shallow, are full of waterfowl and wading birds.

Kayaks and canoes can launch at the **Nags Head Causeway Estuarine Access** on the south side of the causeway near its east end, where you'll also find a parking area, public dock, and fishing gazebo.

KAYAKING SOUTH OF THE CAUSEWAY

EXCURSIONS

Elizabeth City (www.discoverelizabethcity.com), located at the junction of US 17 and US 158, is known as the Harbor of Hospitality, a favorite destination for boaters traveling the ICW and a popular stop when traveling to or from the Outer Banks from the north. The quiet streets of the town, perfect for a walking tour, are lined with historic houses and inns, revitalized shops, even a restored movie palace. On the waterfront, exhibits at the free **Museum of the Albemarle** (www.museumofthealbemarle.com), one of the state museums of history, explore 10,000 years of ecology and culture in the region. An early shad boat, the official state boat of North Carolina, hangs in the museum lobby. Art lovers enjoy the **Arts of the Albemarle Center** (www.artsaoa .com) housed in a historic department store downtown, while kids keep busy at **Port Discover** (www.portdiscover.org), a hands-on science museum. Elizabeth City is also the home of one of the country's largest U.S. Coast Guard bases and TCOM, a company that builds lighter-than-air craft, otherwise known as blimps. Tours of both are available on a limited basis. The **Downtown Waterfront Market** (www.downtownwaterfrontmarket.com), featuring local foods, cooking and craft demonstrations, plus live music, takes place on summer Saturday morning at Mariners Wharf. The rich fields of this region offer an abundance of fresh fruits and vegetables. Elizabeth City is the center of North Carolina's potato farming and hosts the **NC Potato Festival** (www .ncpotatofestival.com) and Miss Tater Tot competition every May.

The four-lane US 17 runs north to Norfolk, Virginia, bordering the historic **Dismal Swamp Canal** along most of its length. About 15 miles north of Elizabeth City, the **Dismal Swamp Canal Welcome Center** (www .dismalswampwelcomecenter.com) offers an orientation to the unique ecology and history of the area. Built by a company headed by George Washington, the canal changed the face of the young nation, providing a safe inland water route for commerce. Today it is a popular alternate route for small boats traveling the Atlantic Intracoastal Waterway and an excellent paddle for kayaks or SUPs. From the welcome center's parking lot, a pedestrian bridge crosses the canal to North Carolina's ♿ **Dismal Swamp State Park** (www.ncparks.gov) with numerous hiking and biking options, as well as exhibits on regional history, including the remains of old stills hidden in the woods. You can rent a kayak or canoe here ($5 per hour) for a paddle on the canal's tea-colored waters.

SHAD BOAT HANGS IN THE LOBBY OF THE MUSEUM OF THE ALBEMARLE

Another good place to put your kayak in is behind Jockey's Ridge State Park at the **Soundside Access** area, found by following the road that runs along the southern boundary of the park to its end. This is also a popular swimming beach for families. See Water Sports Centers for kayak rentals and tours.

KITEBOARDING AND WINDSURFING **Windmill Point and the Nags Head Sound Access** at MP 16 are considered excellent spots for beginners learning both kiteboarding and windsurfing. More advanced boarders can launch from the **sound access at Jockey's Ridge**, considered a prime "bump-and-jump" spot. On the ocean side, the **Jennette's Pier access** is a popular spot to launch.

RUNNING **OBX Running Company** (252-489-8239; www.outerbanksrunningcompany .com), 3712 Bypass, Kitty Hawk. Business owned by a veteran is a great source on upcoming running events on the Banks.

SPAS **Lotus Day Spa & Boutique** (252-261-0800; www.lotusdayspaobx.com), 3810 Bypass, MP 4.5, Buccaneer's Walk, Kitty Hawk. Intimate day spa specializes in Dermalogica skin care products, therapeutic massage, microdermabrasion, reflexology, and mani/pedis.

Windswept Wellness (252-564-8731; www.obxwindsweptwellness.com), 2603 Bypass, Kill Devil Hills. Licensed therapists offer massage, facials, body wraps, and more in the KDH studio, or will come to your vacation cottage for groups.

SHORE SNORKELING AND DIVING **The Triangle Wrecks** (two ships, a freighter and a tanker, now in three pieces) lie about 150 yards offshore in 20 feet of water near Second Street beach access, MP 7.

The **wrecks of the USS *Huron* and the tugboat *Explorer***, both located just north of the Nags Head Pier, are two of the most popular shore diving sites on the Banks. See our description in the *To See* section.

SKATEPARK ✍ **Aviation Park** (www.kdhnc.com), Veterans Drive off Colington Road, Kill Devil Hills. Town of KDH operates a free skatepark with ramps and bowls. Helmets and pads not required, but suggested. Shady picnic area, nature trail, and restrooms available. **The Kill Devil Derby Brigade** (www.thekilldevilderbybrigade.com) practices at the outdoor rink nearby.

Outer Banks Family YMCA Skatepark (252-449-8897; www.ymcashr.org), 3000 Bypass, MP 11. Open to in-line skaters, bikers, and scooters, as well as skateboarders, the YMCA's skatepark, operated by the **Town of Nags Head** (www.nagsheadnc.gov), offers daily and weekly passes. Built by Grindline, the 15,000-square-foot park features a concrete bowl and large street course. Open all year. Helmets required, and pads for those under 18.

SPECTATOR SPORTS Many tournaments featuring some the top names in surfing, surf kayaking, and kiteboarding are held annually on the Banks. The sound behind **Pamlico Jack's** is a good place to check out the kiteboarding action.

Kill Devil Derby Brigade (252-207-6504; www.thekilldevilderbybrigade.com), OBX's resident rollergirl team, competes against teams from other cities in the region. Bouts and practice take place at the rink in Aviation Park, 100 Veterans Drive, Kill Devil Hills.

Outer Banks Daredevils (www.outerbanksdaredevils.com), made up of top-notch college athletes, play ball during the summer against rivals in the **Tidewater Summer**

League (www.tidewatersummerleague.com), one of the oldest and largest collegiate wood-bat summer baseball leagues in the nation. Daredevil logo merchandise is a favorite souvenir. Games are played in June and July at TowneBank OBX Park located in the First Flight Athletic Complex, 109 Veterans Drive in Kill Devil Hills.

SURFING

IN KITTY HAWK

Wave Riding Vehicles (252-261-7952; www.waveridingvehicles.com), 4812 Bypass, MP 2.5. WRV, the largest surfboard manufacturer on the East Coast, is located across the bridge in Currituck County and employs many top shapers. Its retail shop in Kitty Hawk carries the full line of WRV surf-, body-, skim-, snow-, and skateboards, many hard-to-find brands, and cool swim and surf wear with the popular "wave of porpoises" logo, besides offering rentals and repairs.

IN KILL DEVIL HILLS

In KDH, the area around Avalon Pier has some of most rideable waves. Surfing is not allowed within 75 feet of the pier.

The Pit Surf Shop (252-480-3128; www.pitsurf.com), 1209 Bypass, MP 9. A great hangout for surfers of all ages, this shop carries its own line of boards made by expert local shapers and is especially friendly to beginning surfers. Skim boards and accessories are a specialty. Surf, paddle, and skate boards are available for sale or rent, and lessons and surf camps are offered for beginning and intermediate riders.

IN NAGS HEAD

Cavalier Surf Shop (252-441-7349; www.cavaliersurfshop.com), 4324 Beach Road, MP 13.5. Family-run shop, in operation since 1960, offers sales and rentals, as well as private and group surfing lessons.

Farmdog Surf School (252-255-2233; www.farmdogsurfschool.com), 2500 Beach Road, MP 10.5. Located directly across from the beach, this surf shop doubles as an espresso and juice bar, with organic smoothies and other treats. Surfboard and wetsuits come in a wide variety of sizes for an individual fit. Surf and SUP classes and rentals, SUP ecotours, Elite sessions with pro surfer Noah Snyder, three-day adventure camps for kids and teens, and rental wetsuits, boards, and bikes are a few of their services. The staff will even set up your umbrella and chair on the beach.

🦞 ✍ **Hukilau Surf Camp** (252-441-1696; www.surfcampobx.com). Aimed at middle and high school students, these one-day introductions to surfing sponsored by the Nags Head Church are a real bargain, offering one-on-one instruction by experienced surfers, all equipment, and a safe environment.

THE HUKILAU SURF CAMP GETS KIDS RIDING THE WAVES IN A SINGLE DAY

Outer Banks Boarding Company (252-441-1939; www.obbconline.com), 103 E. Morning View Place, MP 10.5, Bypass. The shop of board-shaping legend Lynn Shell carries his signature Shell Shapes, plus high-tech boards from other top designers, and rents surfboards and wet suits.

☙ **Scammell's Corner Surf Shop & Ice Cream Parlor** (252-715-1727), 6406 Beach Road, MP 15.5. Tom Neilson custom-shaped boards are for sale, plus lots of surfer gear, from swimsuits to tie-dye, as well as Hawaiian tikis and artwork. Rental boards and surf lessons available, along with a full menu of ice cream treats.

Secret Spot Surf Shop (252-441-4030; www.secretspotsurfshop.com), 2815 Bypass, MP 11. One of the first surf shops on the Banks, this colorful spot showcases the shapes of founder Steve Hess and other custom and classic boards, plus an eclectic selection of surfer stuff, from beater boards to tiki statues. New and used boards and SUPs are for sale or rent, and lessons are available.

Whalebone Surf Shop (252-441-6747; www.whalebonesurfshop.com), 2214 Bypass, MP 10. Open for more than 40 years, Whalebone stocks boards by top shapers for sale and soft tops for rent. Lessons for beginners never have more than three students per instructor. T-shirts with the shop's skull and crossed surfboards logo are popular even with nonsurfers.

TENNIS Lighted courts for public play are located in KDH at MP 6 on the Bypass next to the Kill Devil Hills Fire Department, and at MP 8.5 on Mustian Street next to the Kill Devil Hills library and water plant. Additional public courts are located at MP 10.

WATER SPORTS

IN KITTY HAWK

☙ **Kitty Hawk Kayak and Surf School** (252-261-0145 or 1-866-702-5061; www.khkss.com), 6150 US 158, MP 1. Experienced instructors conduct surf, kayak, and SUP (stand-up paddleboarding) clinics, private lessons, and three-day camps. Tours via kayaks or SUPs explore many of the waterways on the Banks, and even take you into the Alligator River Wildlife Refuge in search of black bears and into the sound at night. Rentals are available, and used equipment is for sale at the shop. Several packages combine surfing, kayaking, and even yoga, including a "Shredder" package that combines catching waves on boards, SUPs, and surf kayaks. Kids' Coastal Explorer camps are a great value.

☙ **OBX Wakeboard and Waterski** (252-256-2018; www.obxwakeboardwaterski.com), 251 N. Dogwood Trail. Wakeboarding, waterskiing, tubing, wakesurfing, kneeboarding, and sunset cocktail cruises make full use of powerful MasterCraft boats, as seen in the X Games.

IN NAGS HEAD

Causeway Water Sports (252-441-8875; causewaywatersportsobx.com), 7649 Causeway. Sweet spot on the causeway is easy to find thanks to a 30-foot observation tower. Rent a WaveRunner, or sign up for parasailing or an ecotour aboard a Jet Ski.

Kitty Hawk Kites–Whalebone Watersports (252-441-4112; www.kittyhawk.com), 7517 Causeway. Rent single or double kayaks, stand-up paddleboards, or Jet Skis to explore Roanoke Sound. Sign up for kayak ecotours of the Bodie Island marshes or a night bioluminescence tour, or take a Jet Ski tour down to the Bodie Island Lighthouse or north to Roanoke Island. Kiteboarding lessons are also available at this location.

Kitty Hawk Watersports (252-441-2756; www.kittyhawkwatersports.com), 6920 Bypass, MP 16. Windsurfing and kiteboarding lessons are a specialty thanks to the location's shallow waters that are perfect for beginners. Soundside spot also rents kayaks, windsurfers, sailboats, surfboards, SUPs, and Jet Skis; offers Jet Ski and kayak tours; and books parasailing and dolphin tours.

✳ Green Space

BEACHES

IN KITTY HAWK

Many public beach access points line NC 12 (the Beach Road) in Kitty Hawk. Bathhouses with parking and restrooms where you can shower and change are located at **Byrd Street** and at the large **Kitty Hawk Bathhouse**, also known as the Old Station Bathhouse, just south of Kitty Hawk Road. Eight other access points on the Beach Road have parking.

Handicapped access is available at several beach accesses. Beach wheelchairs are available from the **Kitty Hawk Fire Department** (252-261-2666; www.kittyhawkfd .com). Lifeguards are on duty at the **Byrd Street**, **Eckner Street**, and **Kitty Hawk Bathhouse** accesses from Memorial Day to September 30. Roving beach patrols also keep watch. Driving, glass, fires, and fireworks are all prohibited.

Dogs are permitted on Kitty Hawk beaches while under the control of their owners. From Memorial Day weekend to Labor Day weekend, dogs must be on a leash. Check the **town website** (www .kittyhawknc.gov) for current regulations.

& **Kitty Hawk Bathhouse**, Kitty Hawk Road at the Beach Road. Public showers, restrooms, and parking. Free.

IN KILL DEVIL HILLS

Kill Devil Hills (www.kdhnc.com) is particularly rich in beach access points, with nearly two dozen along NC 12 (the Beach Road). Seventeen of them have paved parking, and most of these are handicapped accessible and have open-air showers. The & **Ocean Bay Boulevard Bathhouse** (MP 8.5) has parking, restrooms, and inside showers. Beach wheelchairs are available from the **Kill Devil Hills Fire Department** (252-480-4060). Fires, fireworks, motor vehicles, and glass are not permitted on the beach in Kill Devil Hills. Dogs are not allowed on the beach from 9 AM to 6 PM between May 15 and September 15. They must be leashed at all other times. Lifeguards are

BEACH PATROLS AND LIFEGUARDS MAKE THE CENTRAL BEACHES A TOP CHOICE FOR FAMILIES on duty at many beach access points along this stretch of coast from Memorial Day to Labor Day.

IN NAGS HEAD

More than three dozen public beach access points line NC 12 (the Beach Road) and Old Oregon Inlet Road in Nags Head, between the Eighth Street access on the border with KDH in the north, south to the national seashore.

Bathhouses with restrooms where you can shower and change are located at **Bonnet Street**, **Hargrove Street**, **Epstein Street**, and **Jennette's Pier**. Bathhouse locations have lifeguards during the summer months. ♿ Handicapped access is available at many of the beach accesses. The **Eighth Street** access has a stability mat for easier access. Beach wheelchairs are available from the **Nags Head Fire Department** (252-441-5909), **Jockey's Ridge State Park** (252-441-7132), and the **Bodie Island Lighthouse Visitor Center** (252-441-5711). From Memorial Day to Labor Day, they are also available on a first-come, first-served basis at the **Bonnet Street** (MP 11) and **Hargrove Street** (MP 17) beach access areas. For assistance accessing the beach, call **Nags Head Ocean Rescue** at 252-305-6068. Permits to operate an ATV on the beach are also available for those with disabilities.

Fires on the Nags Head beaches are allowed with a **pit fire permit** from the town's Fire and Rescue Department. Since permits are issued based on current wind and weather conditions, you must obtain the permit between 5 and 9 PM on the day you plan to use it at **Station 16** (252-441-5909), MP 14.5 on the Bypass, or at the **South Nags Head Station 21** (252-441-2910), 8806 S. Old Oregon Inlet Road. Permits are $10.

BUILDING SANDCASTLES IS A FAVORITE FAMILY ACTIVITY ON COQUINA BEACH IN THE NATIONAL SEASHORE

From October 1 through April 30 each year, you can drive on the Nags Head beach with a town permit, available at the Town Hall, Jennette's Pier, and local tackle shops for $25.

Pets are allowed on Nags Head beaches at all times, as long as they are leashed and their owners clean up after them. For current updates on regulations, visit the **Town of Nags Head website** (www.nagsheadnc.gov) or call 252-441-5508.

IN SOUTH NAGS HEAD

The Cape Hatteras National Seashore maintains a large beach facility at the &. **Coquina Beach Bathhouse**, opposite the Bodie Island Lighthouse. Amenities include changing rooms, showers, walkway to the beach, large paved parking lot, and lifeguards (in-season). Beach wheelchairs are available at the **Bodie Island Lighthouse Visitor Center** (252-441-5711).

Street-legal four-wheel-drive vehicles can be driven on the beach with an ORV permit, available from the NPS office at the **north end of the Coquina Beach parking lot** or at **other Cape Hatteras welcome centers**. Permits are currently available for 10 days ($50) or one year ($120). You must show your driver's license and car insurance, and watch a seven-minute informational video to get a permit. Be sure to pick up a map that shows where you may drive. ATVs and motorcycles are not allowed on the beach.

Fires are allowed on the beaches of the national seashore with a free permit, available online. Fireworks, metal detectors, and personal watercraft are forbidden. Pets must be crated or on a 6-foot leash and cannot go on designated swimming beaches.

SOUND ACCESS

IN KITTY HAWK

&. **Windgrass Circle Sound Access**, W. Tateway Road at Bay Drive, Kitty Hawk. This fully accessible town access to the quiet waters of Kitty Hawk Bay is located at the southern end of the &. **Wright Brothers Multi-Use Path** (Moore Shore Road).

IN KILL DEVIL HILLS

Several public access areas are located along **Bay Drive** on the sound side of Kill Devil Hills. **The Hayman Boulevard Estuarine Access**, Bay Drive at W. Hayman Boulevard, has a crabbing pier, gazebo, picnic area, and parking.

N.C. Wildlife Boating Access (www.ncwildlife.org), Dock Street and Bay Drive. Boat-launching area, with picnic tables and free parking, is a popular spot to jump in the water.

Third Street Estuarine Access, Bay Drive at W. Third Street. Gazebo with a pleasant view of the sound. No parking.

IN NAGS HEAD

&. ⚓ **Harvey Sound Access** (252-441-5508; www.nagsheadnc.gov), at MP 16 on the Bypass, is a favorite with windsurfers and kiteboarders. A picnic area, grill, and restrooms are available. This is also a demonstration site for sustainable coastal development, with cisterns, two rain gardens, and educational exhibits.

Jockey's Ridge Sound Access, located at the end of Soundside Road, which runs along the state park's southern boundary, is a popular place for families to swim.

&. **Little Bridge**, on the causeway, is a popular spot for fishing.

♿ **Nags Head Causeway Estuarine Access**, on the south side of the Nags Head–Manteo Causeway near its east end, has a public dock, fishing gazebo, and kayak launch. Bring the chicken necks and string, because the crabbing is great here.

TRAILS

IN KITTY HAWK

🐦 **Kitty Hawk Woods Coastal Reserve** (252-261-8891; www.nccoastalreserve.net), 983 W. Kitty Hawk Road. Nearly 2,000 acres of unspoiled maritime deciduous swamp, forest, and marsh occupy the center of the town of Kitty Hawk. The area contains ancient dunes and bald cypress swamp, and is home to a variety of wildlife and plants, including several rare and endangered species. Birds are numerous, especially wading birds, and bald eagles and ospreys nest here. The Woods Road (NC 1206) runs through the heart of the preserve and is paralleled by a paved multiuse path. Unpaved trails lace the park and can be accessed at the end of Eckner Street, Barlow and Amadas roads, Birch Lane, and Ridge Road, and at Pruitt Park on the Woods Road. Horseback riding and biking are allowed on designated trails. Hunting is permitted in-season with the proper licenses.

✎ ♿ **Sandy Run Park**, 4000 block, Woods Road. A pleasant nature trail with interpretive signs circles a pond, home to wading birds, many turtles, and an osprey nest. A picnic pavilion, crabbing dock, restrooms, and canoe/kayak launch, plus horseshoe pits, shuffleboard court, and basketball half court make this a good destination for a family outing.

IN KILL DEVIL HILLS

✎ 🐦 ♿ **Nags Head Woods Ecological Preserve** (252-441-2525; www.nature.org), 701 W. Ocean Acres Drive, at MP 9.5, Bypass. Located mostly in Kill Devil Hills, this 1,000 acres of maritime forest, protected by the Nature Conservancy, includes pine and hardwoods, with some trees over 500 years old, and provides a nesting area for over 50 species of birds. The property features several ponds full of frogs and other amphibians, plus historical remains of farmsteads and cemeteries. Trails and dirt roads crisscross the preserve, passing through the forest and down to the shore of the sound. The boardwalk trail is fully ADA accessible.

Bikes, horses, and dogs on leashes are allowed on the gravel roads through the preserve, but not on the trails. However, you can take your dog down the Roanoke Trail to the beach on Roanoke Sound. Maps are available at the visitor center.

MILES OF TRAILS CROSS THE NAGS HEAD WOODS PRESERVE

IN NAGS HEAD

⚓ ♿ **Jockey's Ridge State Park** (252-441-7132; www.jockeysridgestatepark.com), Carolista Drive, MP 12, Bypass. Two nature trails explore the maritime thickets of stunted live oak slowly being buried by the sand. One begins at the visitor center, the other at the soundside access. A handicapped-accessible boardwalk leads out to the dune.

⚓ ♿ **Nags Head Town Park and Town Trail** (252-441-5508; www.nagsheadnc.gov), 415 Health Center Drive, off MP 11 on the Bypass at Barnes Road. This shady park has a picnic shelter, grill, playground, and restrooms. The Town Trail, a 1.6-mile round-trip that runs over several forested dune ridges down to the shore of Roanoke Sound, begins at the end of the parking lot. A map of the trail is available on the **Nags Head Woods website** (www.nature.org).

IN SOUTH NAGS HEAD

♿ **Bodie Island Dike Trail** (252-473-2111; www.nps.gov/caha), a short signed nature trail, leads through the marsh to a freshwater pond near the Bodie Island Lighthouse. A longer (and unsigned) trail off the entrance road leads down to the sound, with views of ramshackle fish camps across the water.

✳ Lodging

BED & BREAKFASTS

IN KITTY HAWK

✳ (ᵞ) **Cypress Moon Bed and Breakfast** (252-202-2731; www.cypressmooninn .com), 1206 Harbor Court, at MP 2 Bypass. Innkeepers Greg and Linda Hamby rent three guest rooms that open directly onto the sound. The elegantly appointed inn, furnished with antiques and Greg's professional photography, sits tucked into the maritime forest in Kitty Hawk Village. Rooms each have private bath, private dining area, and semiprivate porch looking out on the water, as well as satellite TV, stereo, and refrigerator. Continental breakfast is served daily. Take one of the inn's complimentary kayaks for a tour of the shoreline, or use one of the inn's bicycles to explore Kitty Hawk's shady bike paths. The inn is nonsmoking and does not accept guests under 18 or pets. You must climb stairs to reach the rooms. The Hambys also rent a fully equipped, self-catering cottage nearby at the same nightly rate. $$–$$$.

ON COLINGTON ISLAND

♿ (ᵞ) **Colington Creek Inn** (252-449-4124; www.colingtoncreekinn.com), 1293 Colington Road. Enjoy waterfront views from the two-story screened porch at this cedar-shingled bed & breakfast on Colington Island, or take a dip in the private pool. The inn's four bedrooms, plus a two-room Luxury Suite, all have private baths, spacious beds, and private sunporches with excellent water views. Boat dockage is available along Colington Creek if you arrive by water. Innkeepers Bob and Mae Lunden sometimes take guests on an evening cruise aboard their private boat to enjoy the sunset. A full breakfast and evening hors d'oeuvres are served daily. The inn has an elevator for handicapped access; children and pets cannot be accommodated. Although the inn enjoys a secluded location off the main highway, public beach access is an easy drive away, without getting into traffic. $$$$.

IN KILL DEVIL HILLS

✳ ♂ (ᵞ) **Cypress House Inn** (252-441-6127; www.cypresshouseinn.com), 500

Beach Road, MP 8. Known to locals as the Cherokee Inn, this 1940s hunting lodge has been designated a local historic landmark. The six guest rooms feature original cypress tongue-and-groove paneled ceilings and walls, with modern amenities, including private baths, small refrigerators, ceiling fans, air-conditioning, and cable TV. Bicycles, beach chairs, and beach towels are complimentary. A public beach access is located directly across the street. Innkeepers Bill and Veda Peters place coffee, tea, and fresh-baked muffins outside each door in the morning for guests to enjoy on the inn's wraparound porch or in front of the fireplace in nippy weather. Room rates include a full breakfast served in the dining room and afternoon tea and cookies. $$.

IN NAGS HEAD

❄ ✧ ♂ (((•))) **First Colony Inn** (252-441-2343 or 1-800-368-9390; www.firstcolonyinn .com), 6720 Beach Road, MP 16. A "grand old lady" of the Outer Banks, this inn first welcomed guests in 1932 and is the sole survivor of the era of shingle-style beach hotels. In 1988, the revered inn was rescued from the ocean by moving it to the other side of the Beach Road, and an extensive renovation began. Placed on the National Register of Historic Places, the inn received an award from the Historic Preservation Society of North Carolina. Charmingly decorated throughout, the inn is a great favorite for wedding parties and other romantic occasions. Two stories of rocking-chair-lined verandas circle the building. Outside, a large swimming pool and hot tub sit amid award-winning landscaping next to a croquet court, with a private beach access just across the street. A hot breakfast buffet and afternoon wine social are included in the daily rate. The property is nonsmoking and kid friendly. Babysitting service and cribs are available. AAA, AARP, and military discounts offered. Open all year. $$$–$$$$.

CAMPGROUNDS AND HOSTEL

IN KITTY HAWK

🐾 ♿ **Adventure Bound Campground and Hostel** (252-255-1130; www .adventureboundnc.com), 1004 W. Kitty Hawk Road, at MP 4.5, Bypass. Tent-only campground in Kitty Hawk Woods has 20 sites, hot-water showers, laundry, a large lawn for games, and a campfire area. The hostel next door offers dorm and private rooms, with shared kitchen and bath. Pets are allowed at the campground, but not at the hostel. Reservations suggested. Closed in winter. $.

❄ 🐾 (((•))) **Kitty Hawk RV Park** (252-261-2636; www.kittyhawkrv.com), MP 4, 3945 Bypass. The last survivor of the oceanside campgrounds on this stretch of beach rents RV sites with full hookups, cable, and Wi-Fi available. Sites stretch from the Beach Road to the Bypass, with a private beach access. The park has no bathhouse or restrooms. No tents or pop-ups. Longer leases available. $.

IN KILL DEVIL HILLS

❄ **Joe & Kay's Campground** (252-441-5468; www.facebook.com/joekay campground), 1193 Colington Road, west of the Bypass at MP 8.5. Dump station, restrooms with warm water, boat ramp. Full-hookup sites are rented by the year. Several grassy tent sites along a canal are available for overnight camping. Tents, $25.

IN SOUTH NAGS HEAD

Oregon Inlet Campground (1-877-444-6777; www.nps.gov/caha), NC 12. The 120 sites at the NPS campground opposite the Oregon Inlet Marina have no utility hookups but are located on level ground. Campground amenities include modern restrooms, potable water, unheated showers, grills, and tables. The ocean is just across the dune line. Open from April to October; 14-day maximum. Reservations recommended at least three days in advance. Tent, trailers, and motor homes $28.

CONDO RENTALS

IN KILL DEVIL HILLS

❄ ((ᵧ)) **Outer Banks Beach Club** (252-441-6321; www.outerbanksbeachclubresort .com), 1110 Beach Road, MP 9. One of the largest condominium groups directly on the ocean rents completely equipped one-, two-, and three-bedroom units by the week year-round. Amenities include indoor and outdoor pools and hot tubs, tennis and shuffleboard, barbecue grills, and a large clubhouse with planned activities all year.

IN NAGS HEAD

♂ ⅙ ((ᵧ)) **Oasis Suites Hotel** (252-441-5211; www.oasissuites.com), 7721 Nags Head–Manteo Causeway. This boutique hotel offers luxurious suites on the north side of the causeway. Leather furniture and Oriental rugs, beds topped with poofs,

flat-screen plasma TVs, full kitchens with stainless-steel appliances, balconies, and Jacuzzi tubs are standard in the family and executive suites, most of which sleep six. Pool and outdoor hot tub are fenced for privacy. Guests can dock their boats behind the hotel or fish from the dock. $$$–$$$$.

HOTELS

IN KITTY HAWK

❄ 🦪 ⅙ ♂ ((ᵧ)) **Hilton Garden Inn Outer Banks** (252-261-1290; www.hiltongarden innouterbanks.com), 5353 Beach Road, MP 1. Conveniently located at the northern end of Kitty Hawk where the Beach Road and the Bypass meet, this Hilton has an added amenity unique on this stretch of beach—its own private fishing pier. You can fish 24 hours a day on the former Kitty Hawk Pier as a hotel guest. This hotel, which opened in 2006, offers every amenity, with the Hilton emphasis on quality, including an indoor pool and whirlpool, fitness center, outdoor

PIER FISHING REMAINS A POPULAR ACTIVITY FOR ALL AGES

seasonal pool, 24-hour convenience shop, and a lobby restaurant serving breakfast, lunch, and dinner. Room service is available in the evenings. The 180 rooms and suites all have private balconies with views of the ocean, and the beach is right out the back door. Standard equipment in each room includes a hospitality center with refrigerator, microwave, and coffeemaker; large-screen cable TV; a large desk with ergonomic chair; and both wired and wireless Internet access. A free business center, open around the clock with remote printing and complimentary fax, makes this a good place to stay when traveling on business. Guest laundry is available. Children under 18 stay free with parents. $$–$$$$.

IN KILL DEVIL HILLS

❄ (ᵖ) **Atlantic Street Inn** (252-305-0246; www.atlanticstreetinn.com), 205 E. Atlantic Street, MP 9.5. Six comfortable suites, all with refrigerator, microwave, cable TV, phone, coffeemaker, and personally controlled heat and air, are available in this recently renovated beach house. Located close to all the action in KDH, the inn is also just down the street from the Atlantic Street Beach Access. Bright colors and local art decorate the suites, which are available by the day or week. Backyard grill, full kitchen, enclosed outdoor showers, and bikes, as well as a full kitchen with ice maker, are available for guest use. Two-night minimum stay required. $$–$$$.

✎ ♿ (ᵖ) **Best Western Ocean Reef Suites** (252-441-1611; www.bestwestern northcarolina.com), 107 Beach Road, MP 8.5. The only all-suite hotel directly on the beach in the Outer Banks, this five-story Best Western received a three-diamond rating from AAA. Each suite accommodates up to six people and has a completely equipped kitchen. Room rates include a full continental breakfast daily, free local calls, cable TV, and access to the hotel's hot tub, sauna, steam room, fitness center, and outdoor heated pool

(open seasonally). The hotel also has a guest laundry room open 24 hours. All rooms are nonsmoking. Children under 13 stay free with paying adult. $–$$$$.

❄ ✎ ♿ (ᵖ) **Days Inn Oceanfront Wright Brothers** (252-441-7211 or 1-800-325-2525; www.obxlodging.com), 201 N. Virginia Dare Trail. The longest continuously operating hotel on the beach, this 52-room property opened in 1948 and has a nostalgic "Old Nags Head" appeal. Built in the style of a mountain lodge, the hotel's inviting lobby features a big fireplace where guests gather for hot cider and popcorn in the cooler months. In summer, lemonade and cookies are the afternoon refreshments. Expanded continental breakfast is included in the room rate. Double, queen, and king rooms, plus efficiencies with a full kitchen, as well as nonsmoking and handicapped-accessible rooms, are available. Children under 13 stay free. The property has a large outdoor pool, open seasonally, and a boardwalk to the beach. Guests also can take advantage of free passes to the local YMCA. Oregon Inlet Fishing Center parties qualify for special discounted rates. $–$$$. The same company operates a number of other properties nearby, including the **Days Inn Mariner** (252-441-2021), located on the oceanfront at MP 7.

(ᵖ) **Outer Banks Inn** (252-715-3507 or 1-888-322-9702; www.theouterbanksinn .com), 1003 Bypass, MP 9. Small hotel two blocks from the beach offers a free beach shuttle, free Wi-Fi and YMCA passes, an outdoor saltwater pool, and complimentary continental breakfast. $$.

❄ ✈ 🐾 (ᵖ) ♿ **Ramada Plaza Resort and Conference Center** (252-441-2151 or 1-800-635-1824; www.ramada plazanagshead.com), 1701 Beach Road, MP 9.5. This five-story hotel offers a host of amenities in a convenient, oceanfront location. Rooms have a king or two queen beds, private balconies, cable TV, Wi-Fi access, microwaves, refrigerators, coffeemakers, hair dryers, and irons. A free guest laundry, fitness center, and business center are located off the spacious lobby, where complimentary coffee and newspapers are available each morning. The large indoor pool and Jacuzzi are open all year. Outdoors, guests enjoy lots of deck space, a seasonal gazebo bar, and a boardwalk to the beach. Free passes to the nearby YMCA and the Kitty Hawk Pier are available by request. Most rooms are nonsmoking. The Ramada's restaurant and bar, ⍦ **Peppercorns**, offers nightly specials, frequent entertainment, and full cocktail service with an ocean view. The breakfast served here is a real bargain. Room service available. The outdoor Dragonfly Deck Bar serves lunch during the summer months. The resort is also home to the OBX Comedy Club (252-207-9950; www.comedyclubobx .com). $$–$$$$.

⚢ ⟨⟨ᵞ⟩⟩ **Sea Ranch Resort** (252-441-7126 or 1-800-334-4737; www.searanchresort .com), 1731 Beach Road, MP 7. Completely renovated in 2004, the Sea Ranch is located on the oceanfront. Amenities include a glass-enclosed pool fronting on an oceanfront deck and a new fitness center. The on-site restaurant, the ⍥ ⍦ ⍤ **Beachside Bistro** (www .obxbeachsidebistro.com), offers room service as well as oceanfront dining all day, with happy hour specials and a walk-up window off the Third Street public beach access. The outdoor deck hosts deck parties with live music. Fishing, golf, and hunting packages are available. $$–$$$$.

❄ ♿ ⟨⟨ᵞ⟩⟩ **Shutters on the Banks** (252-441-5581 or 1-800-848-3728; www .shuttersonthebanks.com), 405 Beach Road, MP 8.5. Recently refurbished with new bedding, furniture, and carpet, the family-owned and family-operated Shutters offers four floors of rooms with two double beds and efficiencies with full kitchens on the oceanfront. Amenities include a new indoor heated pool, whirlpool, family game room, and exercise room, in addition to an outdoor heated pool, gazebo, and walkway to the beach. Rooms on the second through fourth

floors have private balconies. Rates include a deluxe continental breakfast. $–$$$$.

IN NAGS HEAD

☀ ⟨⟨ᵞ⟩⟩ **Nags Head Beach Inn** (1-866-316-1843; www.nagsheadbeachinn.com), 303 E. Admiral Street, off the Beach Road, MP 10.5. Eight guest rooms are available in this historic cottage, once used as a dance pavilion. The Admiral Street beach access is a short walk away, and beach chairs and umbrellas are provided. Closed in winter. $$–$$$.

MOTELS AND COTTAGE COURTS To experience an "Old Nags Head" vacation, make reservations for a week at one of the cottage courts that date from the 1950s to 1970s. A few still survive along the Beach Road, where you can enjoy the simple life filled with traditional beach activities. Cottages typically have kitchen facilities, private baths, and porches. Amenities usually begin and end with air-conditioning and a TV hooked to cable. Linens are usually provided; phones and pools are generally not. Fish-cleaning stations and grills are available for cooking up the daily catch. Some so-called cottages may actually be attached units. Cottage and motor courts usually close during the off-season.

IN KITTY HAWK

❄ ⟨⟨ᵞ⟩⟩ **Saltaire Cottage Court** (252-261-3286; www.saltairecottages.com), MP 2.5, Beach Road. Recently renovated two-bedroom apartments and three-bedroom cottages are across the street from the ocean. All have screened porches. Nightly rentals available off-season. Linens and cable TV included, plus pool, beach access, deck, barbecue pit, and free laundry. No smoking or pets in units. $$–$$$.

♿ **Sea Kove Motel** (252-261-4722; www .seakove.com), MP 3, Beach Road. Efficiencies and cottages on both sides of the Beach Road operated by an old beach family rent by the week in-season, by the night the rest of the year. Outdoor pool and playground. No pets. Off-season $; high season $$.

IN KILL DEVIL HILLS

(⊚) **Driftin' Sands Motor Court** (1-866-316-1843; www.keeshotels.com), 1906 Beach Road, MP 6.5. Small, budget-friendly motel across the street from the beach that offers free Wi-Fi. $–$$.

✿ ☗ **Outer Banks Motor Lodge** (252-4417404 or 1-877-625-6343; www.obxmotorlodge.com), 1509 Beach Road, MP 9.5. Located directly on the ocean, this is one of the Banks' original motels, established in 1961, and is owned by members of the Miller family, which operates several restaurants in the area. Now completely refurbished, the two-story lodge offers both oceanfront and poolside double rooms and efficiencies. A seasonal outdoor pool, plus picnic area and playground, fish-cleaning station, and coin-operated laundry, are on the grounds. Free Wi-Fi in the Coffee Corner. Children under 13 stay free. Open seasonally, April to November. $–$$.

✿ (⊚) **Wright Cottage Court** (252-441-7331; www.obxlodging.com), 301 Beach Road, MP 8. Next door to the Days Inn Oceanfront and enjoying pool privileges there, these two- to six-bedroom oceanfront cottages rent by the day or week at rates that include free linen setup and cable TV, plus full kitchens and, in some, dishwashers and washer/dryers.

IN NAGS HEAD

✿ (⊚) **Cahoon's Cottages** (252-441-5358; www.cahoonscottages.com), 7213 Beach Road, MP 16.5. Oceanfront cottages located next to the new Jennette's Pier and Cahoon's Variety Store, a longtime landmark on the beach, have between two and four bedrooms. Each comes with a full kitchen, linens, TV, and private porch. Weekly and nightly rates available. $–$$$$.

☗ **Nags Head Fishing Pier Cottages** (252-441-5141; www.nagsheadpier.com), 3335 Beach Road, MP 11.5. The pier rents several cottages of various sizes within walking distance. Docks available for small boats. $$.

☗ (⊚) **Pelican Cottages** (252-441-2489; www.pelicancottages.com), 3513 Beach Road, MP 12. Pet-friendly two- and three-bedroom cottages on the oceanfront date from the 1950s. Outdoor hot showers. Complimentary YMCA passes. Linens are not furnished. $$.

✿ **The Sandspur Motel & Cottage Court** (252-441-6993), 6607 Beach Road, MP 15.5. Two-night cottage rentals available off-season. Linens and towels are not provided. Outdoor pool, hot tub, playground, pay phone, coin laundry. Efficiencies and motel rooms also available. $–$$$.

✿ ☗ (⊚) **Colonial Inn Motel** (252-441-7308; www.colonialinnmotel.com), 3329 Beach Road, MP 11.5. This low-rise classic welcoming guests since 1947 enjoys an excellent location directly on the ocean and next door to the Nags Head Fishing Pier. The motel is now open all year. Thirty-one rooms and efficiencies, plus 12 one- and two-bedroom apartments, many paneled in knotty pine, are all first or second floor, with parking in front. The outdoor pool is open seasonally. Free YMCA passes are available to guests. Fall and winter specials provide real bargains. $–$$.

✿ ☗ (⊚) **Sea Foam Motel** (252-441-7320; www.seafoam.com), 7111 Beach Road, MP 16.5. Now on the National Register of Historic Places, this 1948 landmark is hard to miss—it's painted the color of its name. Noted by the register as "one of the last and best preserved" motor courts of the post–World War II era, it's better noted by guests for its well-kept, clean rooms, friendly service, and oceanfront location. Poolside rooms are available at slightly lower rates. Cottages, one- and two-bedroom apartments, and efficiencies come with fully equipped kitchens. During the summer season, these are only rented by the week and have a loyal repeat clientele. The motel wraps around a heated swimming pool, shuffleboard court, and children's playground. Children under 12 stay free. $–$$.

VACATION RENTALS ❋ **Cove Realty** (252-441-6391 or 1-800-635-7007; www .coverealty.com), 105 E. Dunn Street, MP 13.5. Weekly, yearly, and winter rentals, with many located in Nags Head, including Old Nags Head Cove. Some cottages have negotiable rates.

   ❋ 🐾 **Rentals on the Ocean** (252-441-5005; www.rentalsontheocean.com), 7128 Beach Road, MP 16.5. Group of pet-friendly cottages in South Nags Head are available all year.

❋ Where to Eat

DINING OUT

IN SOUTHERN SHORES

🖋 ⚗ ↷ **Coastal Provisions Oyster Bar & Wine Bar Café** (252-480-0023; www .coastalprovisionsobx.com), 1 Ocean Boulevard, Southern Shores Crossing. During the day, the café serves hot and cold sandwiches, seafood tacos, and seafood, steamed, fried and raw. In the evening, dine on antipasti, small plates, fresh local seafood, prime steaks, and other goodies drawn from the gourmet market. Oyster bars, stocking 10 kinds of regional crustaceans, are located indoors and out. Over 20 wines are available by the glass, or select a bottle from the surrounding shelves and enjoy it at retail prices. Live music some evenings. Reservations suggested. Lunch $–$$; dinner $$$$.

IN KITTY HAWK

♿ 🖋 ⚲ ⚗ **Argyles Sea Salt Grille** (252-261-7325; www.seasaltgrille.com), 4716

KEEP IN TOUCH

A unique company, The Village News (252-441-7748; www.obxnews paperdelivery.com), will deliver your hometown daily paper right to the door of your vacation cottage every morning. Daily, weekly, and summer rates, plus delivery from Corolla to Hatteras Village.

Bypass, MP 2.5. Formerly Argyles, one of Kitty Hawk's most sophisticated restaurants and piano bars, this popular destination has been given second life by the original family with a new casual menu of locally sourced burgers and seafood. Breakfast has been added to the lineup, and a daily happy hour lets you sample some of the creative dishes on the menu at low price. $7 martinis and frequent live music add to the fun. Breakfast $; dinner $$–$$$.

   ❋ 🖋 ⚗ ↷ **Black Pelican Oceanfront Restaurant** (252-261-3171; www .blackpelican.com), 3848 Beach Road, MP 4. Located in the 1874 lifesaving station where the Wright brothers came to telegraph news of their successful flight to the world, the Black Pelican makes a great destination before, during, or after a day at the beach. The public beach access is just across the street, and you can even shower off at the adjacent town-operated bathhouse. The restaurant has three levels and a lofty deck with a bar and a view of the ocean. Late-night menu, daily specials, daily happy hour, and vegetarian dishes ensure something for everyone. Lunch $; dinner $$–$$$.

   ❋ ♿ ⚗ **Ocean Boulevard Bistro & Martini Bar** (252-261-2546; www .obbistro.com), 4700 Beach Road, MP 2. A casual spot just steps from the beach, this bistro serves artfully designed dishes that appeal to the upscale palate. *Southern Living* described it as "beachy and swanky all at once." The menu is divided into "Big Plates," which are

CHEF DONNY KING, OWNER OF OCEAN BOULEVARD BISTRO

in classic preparations. The she-crab bisque and crabcakes are legendary, and the homemade desserts, especially the white chocolate crème brûlée, inspire raves. The atmosphere is romantic, with several small rooms downstairs, while larger family groups can be accommodated in the upstairs room. Reservations are highly recommended, especially during the busy summer season. The Colington closes during the winter but often reopens for holidays. Dinner daily, $$–$$$$.

serious entrées of lamb, fresh fish, duck, or beef, sold at equally serious prices, and a nicely varied tapas selection that may range from gourmet macaroni and cheese to an antipasto plate with goat cheese, olives, and cured duck. Menus designed by owner Donny King change with the season. Martinis are a specialty, and the wine list received the *Wine Spectator* Award of Excellence. Live jazz is featured on the OceanSide Patio in-season, and late night on Friday all year. Reservations recommended. $$–$$$$.

ON COLINGTON ISLAND

✎ ♿ ☞ **Colington Café** (252-480-1123; www.colingtoncafe.com), 1049 Colington Road. Located in a lovely Victorian house well away from the crowds on the Bypass, this local favorite is not such a secret since *Southern Living* named it the "Best Restaurant for the Best Price" on the Outer Banks. Inspired by owner Carlen Pearl's French background, the cuisine here features the freshest seafood and other local ingredients

IN KILL DEVIL HILLS

✎ ♼ ☞ **Bad Bean Baja Grill & Cantina** (252-261-1300; www.badbeanobx.com), 4146 Bypass, MP 3.5. Stop by to see what Tex-Mex can be when designed by a professional chef. Created by owner Rob Robinson, formerly a chef at the Left Bank (a fine dining landmark) and a veteran of the James Beard House, the reasonably priced menu features award-winning treatments of classic dishes, such as giant Cali burritos, shrimp ceviche, and black bean quinoa burgers, as well as many vegetarian items, all prepared from local ingredients. The salsas are legendary. Lunch $; dinner $–$$.

♼ **Grandstaff and Stein** (252-441-6894; www.grandstaffandstein.com), 2003 Bypass, MP 9.5. Speakeasy-themed spot offers a menu of steak and local seafood classics, craft cocktails, beer, and wine. Lots of drink specials, live entertainment, and occasional Bootlegger's Burlesque Sunday brunch at the Juice Joint. $$–$$$.

JK's Restaurant (252-441-9555; www.jksrestaurant.com), 1106 Bypass, MP 9. Established in 1984, this fine-dining spot has stood the test of time. Hand-cut house-aged steaks, rack of lamb, grass-fed veal chops, and local seafood are cooked over mesquite coals on the wood-fired grill. Sides are priced separately. A popular special occasion spot for locals, this is definitely a splurge. If you are

PASSING OF AN ICON

Kelly's Outer Banks Restaurant & Tavern (www.kellysrestaurant.com), an OBX institution at MP 10.5 since 1985, closed in late 2017, to be replaced with new development. Kelly's was the flagship of the family of eateries helmed by restaurateur Mike Kelly, who also operates Mako Mike's and Pamlico Jack's. Kelly, a noted community booster, sponsors the annual St. Patrick's Day celebration and other OBX events, activities which he plans to continue. Kelly's Tavern patrons will miss the largest dance floor on the beach, the frequent live entertainment, and the walls covered with Outer Banks memorabilia. However, the famous sweet potato biscuits will still be available on the menus at Kelly's other eateries, along with other popular dishes, and Kelly's Catering, one of the oldest and best loved on the Banks, will continue on its mission to provide exceptional fare for parties of all sizes.

visiting OBX in the off-season, drop by JK's to sample its daily specials at considerable savings. Dinner only, $$–$$$$.

🏄 🍸 ✎ **Kill Devil Grill** (252-449-8181; www.thekilldevilgrill.com), 2008 Beach Road, MP 9.5. Located in an authentic 1939 railroad dining car listed on the National Register of Historic Places, this Beach Road favorite offers meals that far surpass typical diner fare. Talented chefs create daily seafood and blue plate specials (think meat loaf), great crabcakes, white pizza topped with goat cheese and fresh basil, wood-roasted chicken, steaks, and chops. Everything is prepared from scratch here, so specials often sell out. Popular dishes include the chicken wings, the Kahuna burger, and for dessert, award-winning Key lime pie. Closed Sunday and Monday. Lunch and dinner $–$$$.

IN NAGS HEAD

❄ 🏄 ✎ **Blue Moon Beach Grill** (252-261-BLUE; www.bluemoonbeachgrill.com), 4104 Beach Road, MP 13, Surfside Plaza. Earning raves on the Beach Road, this chef-owned restaurant teams a menu of innovative dishes with a friendly family environment. Vegetarian entrées and daily chef specials available. Lunch and dinner $$–$$$.

🏄 ♿ **Old Nags Head Café** (252-441-1141; www.nagsheadcafe.com), 3948 Beach Road, MP 13. Located in an old grocery across from Jockey's Ridge, this

historic property amid the Unpainted Aristocracy has been reinvented as an upscale dining experience, with a full bar, homemade desserts, and daily chef specials. Southern fried chicken and fried green tomatoes are specialties. Breakfast $; lunch and dinner $$–$$$.

🏄 ♿ 🍸 ✎ **Owens' Restaurant** (252-441-7309; www.owensrestaurant.com), 7114 Beach Road, MP 16.5. Bob and Clara Owens opened a 24-seat café on the beach back in 1946, among the first to gamble on the oceanfront property opened up by the causeways. Today, Owens' is still owned by the founding family and is one of the most storied restaurants on the coast, highly praised for its Southern coastal cuisine, fresh seafood, attentive service, and elegant decor. The entrées are classic preparations of softshell crab, shrimp, crabmeat, lobster, and beef, served with a crock of cheese and crackers as a before-meal treat, an old Southern tradition. Ordering fried seafood here is a waste; there are so many delicious and original dishes to choose from. Built to resemble a lifesaving station, Owens' exhibits a collection of logbooks, photographs, and historic memorabilia. The elegant upstairs lounge is a great place for a before-dinner drink. Dinner only, $$$$.

ON THE CAUSEWAY

🏄 ♿ 🍸 ✎ **Basnight's Lone Cedar Café** (252-441-5405; www.lonecedarcafe.com),

7623 Causeway. The family of longtime president pro tem of the North Carolina Senate Marc Basnight operates this local favorite, located on the causeway. Basnight is a native of Manteo and a strong supporter of the local fishing and farming industries. This is one place where you can be sure the fish is from local waters, the vegetables are locally grown, and the beef, pork, and chicken are all natural. **The Osprey Lounge**, named for the ospreys that nest just outside, is a favorite at sunset and late night, when live music is often on tap. Don't miss the mural depicting the history of the Outer Banks fishing fleet painted by the Tillett sisters. Sunday brunch $–$$; dinner $$–$$$$.

  ✎ ♿ ⚲ **Sugar Creek Soundfront Seafood Restaurant** (252-441-4963; www .sugarcreekseafood.com), Causeway, MP 16.5. Located on the north side of the causeway, this soundfront restaurant is a favorite with families, thanks to all the wildlife visible from the dock and outdoor boardwalks. The menu is noted for its prize-winning shrimp and grits, and daily prime rib. The ❄ **Sugar Shack** (252-441-3888), a seafood market selling sandwiches, seafood baskets, steamer buckets, and seafood by the pound, is next door. Lunch $$; dinner $$–$$$$.

BROILED SEAFOOD IS WIDELY AVAILABLE AT OBX RESTAURANTS

✎ ⚲ ☿ **Tale of the Whale** (252-441-7332; www.taleofthewhalenagshead .com), 7575 Causeway. A great choice for large groups; otherwise ask for a private booth with a water view. Prices are high, but portions are huge and recipes are traditional at this longtime favorite. Many diners take advantage of the early-bird discount; seniors receive a price break all the time. Plan to spend any wait time at the outdoor bar and gazebo, where live music entertains at sunset in the summer months. (Or skip the meal and head straight for the water.) Dinner only, $$–$$$$.

EATING OUT

IN SOUTHERN SHORES

❄ ✎ **Steamers** (252-261-0224; www .steamersobx.com), 1 Ocean Boulevard, Southern Shores Crossing. Take a steamer pot of seafood or rack of ribs back to your cottage, or enjoy a relaxed meal on the oceanview deck. The menu features a wide range of seafood sandwiches and entrées, including whole Maine lobsters, plus several vegetarian options. Lunch $$; dinner $$–$$$.

IN KITTY HAWK

❄ ✎ ☿ **Art's Place** (252-261-3233; www .artsplaceobx.com), 4624 Beach Road, MP 2.5. Tiny spot on the Beach Road (look for the cottage covered in cool aquatic murals) serves breakfast, great burgers, and live music all year to a loyal clientele. Join the locals for happy hour on the upper deck with ocean view. $.

✎ ♿ ☿ (((•))) **Barefoot Bernie's Tropical Grill & Bar** (252-261-1008; www .barefootbernies.com), 3730 Bypass, MP 4.5. The menu at Bernie's features tropical flavors drawn from Caribbean, Hawaiian, Jamaican, and other island cuisines, with a bit of Greek thrown in. Fish tacos, gyros, hot subs, and pizzas are on the menu all day, along with gluten-free and health-conscious dishes. In addition to satisfying meals, this

FOODIES ON THE BEACH

Taste of the Beach (www.obxtasteofthebeach.com), a four-day festival for foodies with dozens of events—including wine-pairing dinners, oyster roasts, chowder and barbecue cook-offs, cooking classes, beer and wine tastings, tapas crawls of Manteo and Duck, late night pub crawls, a tasting expo, and more—is held every March. It's a great way to catch the incredible variety and quality of the OBX food scene. The Outer Banks Restaurant Association also sponsors Outer Banks Restaurant Weeks (www.outerbanksrestaurantweek.com) in May and late October with bargain-priced three-course meals at many local eateries.

JUST ONE OF THE STOPS ON THE TASTE OF THE BEACH TAPAS CRAWL

casual spot books live entertainment and is a gathering place for sports fans. Tabletop Sound Dog wireless receivers let you tune in to the audio, too. Lunch $; dinner $$.

❄ ✎ **Henry's Restaurant** (252-261-2025; www.henrysobx.com), 3396 Bypass, MP 5. Classic American food is served all day in a friendly, no-frills environment. A local favorite for breakfast, served until 1 PM. Breakfast and lunch $; dinner $$–$$$.

♈ **Outer Banks Taco Bar** (252-261-8226; www.obxtacobar.com), 3723 Bypass, MP 4.5, Ocean Plaza. Chef-designed tacos and enchiladas made with house-pressed corn tortillas come with a variety of fillings, including vegetarian options. $.

✎ ♈ ⌖ **Rundown Cafe & Tsunami Bar** (252-255-0026; www.rundowncafe.com), 5218 Beach Road, MP 1. Named for the traditional Jamaican fish-and-coconut soup that tops the menu, this cool location right at the head of the Beach Road provides a gathering spot for locals and a favorite dinner stop for those who discover its laid-back charm and eclectic menu. Known for its huge dinner salads and Oriental sesame noodle bowls, both available with a wide variety of toppings, the Rundown successfully combines the flavors of the Caribbean with Asian influences. Vegetarians will be pleased with the numerous offerings designed for them. The Hula Deck hosts frequent live music. Upstairs, a bar offers ocean views, cold brews, and a surfer vibe. $–$$.

ON COLINGTON ISLAND

❄ ♿ ✎ ♈ **SaltBox Café** (252-255-5494; www.thesaltboxcafe.com), 1469 Colington Road. A creative menu, plus fresh, fresh seafood make this a real find several miles out winding Colington Road, or you can arrive by boat at the dock off Colington Creek. Eat inside or take a table on the screened porch, where you can listen to the cicadas sing or to live music most nights in summer. Sunday brunch and lunch $–$$; dinner $$–$$$$.

IN KILL DEVIL HILLS

❄ ✎ ♈ (((•))) **Awful Arthur's Oyster Bar** (252-441-5955; www.awfularthursobx.com), 2106 Beach Road, MP 6. Serving steamed oysters the authentic North Carolina way for two decades, Arthur's has a casual, kicked-back atmosphere much beloved by locals and the regulars who return here each year. Between peeling the famous spiced shrimp (*Esquire* named them one of "67 Things Worth a Detour" in the United States), slurping oysters, and cracking crab legs, things may get a little messy, but that's part of the fun. During summer, the crowds can get thick as the sun heads west. If you want to sit at a table, you may have a long wait. At this point, adopt the local strategy: Head upstairs to the lounge, order some steamed shrimp and a cold beverage, and enjoy the view of the ocean and Avalon Pier, just across the Beach Road. Or order from the take-out window and stake out a picnic table outside. *Coastal Living* magazine named this one of the top 10 oyster bars in the nation, but the menu also offers fried seafood, burgers, barbecue, and steaks. Open every day of the year (another reason the locals love it) for

AWFUL ARTHUR'S IS STRATEGICALLY PLACED ACROSS FROM THE AVALON FISHING PIER

lunch and dinner. You can pick up logo'd souvenirs and gifts, or maybe a hermit crab, or rent a surfboard at the **Awful Arthur's Beach Shop** (252-449-2220), next door to the restaurant. $–$$$.

✎ **Bob's Grill** (252-441-0707; www .bobsgrillobx.com), 1219 Bypass, MP 9. Breakfast is served all day at this restaurant, where the motto is "Eat and Get the Hell Out!" (a great idea to maximize vacation time). Big servings of homestyle food arrive fast, but the line can be long midmorning. Check out the great deals on lunch specials. Full bar; gift shop with logo'd gear. Breakfast and lunch $; dinner $$.

❄ ♈ **Chilli Peppers Coastal Grill** (252-441-8081; www.chilli-peppers.com), 3001 Bypass, MP 5.5. Live entertainment, along with a late-night menu, steamer bar, daily happy hour and specials, and some of the spiciest food on the beach keep regulars coming back. Something is going on here almost every night, from live music to surfer videos. In the off-season, check out the Thursday international tapas nights. The bar features a big selection of premium tequilas and margaritas. Weekend brunch here was voted "Best of the Beach." Brunch and lunch $; dinner $$.

✎ ✣ **Food Dudes Kitchen** (252-441-7994; www.fooddudeskitchenobx.com), 1216 Beach Road, MP 9, Seashore Shops. Two popular OBX chefs team up to offer gourmet food to take out or to eat in the casual dining room. Organic produce and locally sourced seafood are whipped up into a variety of wraps, sandwiches, and blackboard specials. Thursday is taco night. Beer and wine available, along with great bottled hot sauce. Lunch and dinner $–$$.

❄ ✐ ⅄ ((•)) **Jolly Roger Restaurant & Bar** (252-441-6530; www.jollyrogerobx .com), 1836 Beach Road, MP 6.5. A pirate greets you at the Jolly Roger, offering a huge menu of pastas and Italian specialties served nightly. Locals know this is also a great spot for breakfast, served 6 AM–2 PM. Pier-style eggs and Belgian waffles topped with ice cream are specialties, and, for the true pirate, homemade bread pudding with a hearty bourbon sauce. The decor is pure pirate kitsch, but the service is famous for its warmth. The bar offers karaoke or other entertainment nightly, plus Wii and other video games, poker tournaments, a late-night menu, and frequent live music on the outside deck. A gift shop sells

WINGED HORSE "DOUBLOON" GUARDS THE ENTRANCE OF THE JOLLY ROGER

pirate gear. Breakfast and lunch $; dinner $$–$$$.

❄ ✐ ⅄ ↝ **Mako Mike's Beach Grill & Bar** (252-480-1919; www.makomikes .com), 1630 Bypass, MP 7. Promising "killer food" at reasonable prices, Mako Mike's serves all the family favorites, from pizza cooked in a wood oven and a variety of pasta dishes to standard beef, chicken, and pork entrées. Prime rib is a specialty. The long list of seafood features Outer Banks Catch local seafood. Wildly painted decor and huge sharks hanging from the ceilings create an underwater atmosphere popular with children. Early-bird specials make it a favorite with seniors. Head for the Octopus Bar to escape the crowds. Owned by Mike Kelly, this is the sister restaurant of Pamlico Jack's, farther down the Bypass. Reservations available. Lunch and dinner $$–$$$.

🍴 ✐ ⅄ ((•)) ↝ **Outer Banks Brewing Station** (252-449-2739; www.obbrewing .com), 600 Bypass, MP 8.5. Fresh award-winning beer, frequent specials, and live entertainment keep the crowds coming to one of the Outer Banks' most popular establishments. Much of the food served is locally sourced, and the desserts and breads are baked in-house. Gluten-free and vegetarian menus available. The kids' menu is special, too,

A WINDMILL POWERS THE OUTER BANKS BREWING STATION

featuring steak and homebrewed root beer, and there's a pirate-themed playground with picnic tables out back. Stop by the bar (shaped like an old lifesaving boat) for a sampler of some of the Banks' most creative beers and to check out the week's entertainment lineup. This is a hot spot for live regional and national bands. The building itself is inspired by one of the old lifesaving stations that once dotted the Banks and is powered by a wind turbine, making it the first wind-powered brewpub in the US. Bottles and growlers are available to go. Brewery tours available. Sunday brunch $; lunch $–$$; dinner $$–$$$.

❄ 🖍 🍸 **Rooster's Southern Kitchen** (252-441-4594; www.roosterssouthern kitchen.com), 804 Bypass, MP 8.5. New entry from a Banks family experienced in running eateries is one of the best new restaurants in OBX. Scratch kitchen turns out upscale Southern favorites, from fresh Wanchese seafood and house-smoked barbecue to Southern fried chicken atop sweet potato waffles, for lunch, dinner, and weekend brunch. Take a seat at the 20-tap bar featuring regional crafts and enjoy the nightly music from top local musicians. $–$$.

IN NAGS HEAD

🖍 ⇾ **Cafe Lachine** (252-715-2550; www .cafelachine.com), 5000 Bypass, MP 14, Outer Banks Mall. Operated by a husband-and-wife team, Johanna and Justin Lachine, both chefs, this modest spot in the mall rose rapidly to one of the top-ranked eateries on the Banks. This is a great spot to pick up a fast, inexpensive breakfast or lunch that doesn't scrimp on flavor or healthy ingredients. The freshly baked macaroons, cupcakes, fruit tarts, and gluten-free Ho-Ho cakes are irresistible. Stop by for a box lunch for your day at the beach. Breakfast and lunch $–$$.

🖍 ♿ ⇾ **The Dunes Restaurant and R-Bar** (252-441-1600; www .thedunesrestaurant.com), 7013 Bypass, MP 16. Big breakfast menu is reasonably priced. Dinner menu features local seafood and Southern specialties. The R-Bar serves a full selection of cocktails and several North Carolina beers, plus a bar menu. Breakfast $; dinner $$–$$$$.

❄ **It's All Gravy** (252-473-7326; www .itsallgravyobx.com), 6705 Bypass, MP 15.5. When you've had as much seafood as you can hold, this new spot will change it up with Italian specialties, steak and roast pork sandwiches, salads, and pastas. Beer and wine available, plus take-out. $–$$.

❄ 🍸 **Mulligan's Raw Bar & Grille** (252-480-2000; www.mulligansobx .com), 4005 Bypass, MP 13. Fun spot across from Jockey's Ridge has a great second-floor deck and tiki bar with views of the beach and the historic Nags Head cottage district. An Orange Crush cocktail at sunset is rapidly becoming an OBX tradition. Steamed oysters, Greek salads, and buffalo burgers are specialties. Serving breakfast from 8 AM. Breakfast $; lunch $–$$$; dinner $$–$$$$.

🖍 ♿ ⚥ 🍸 ⇾ **Pamlico Jack's Pirate Hideaway** (252-441-2637; www .pamlicojacks.com), 6708 Bypass, MP 15.5. Enjoy a fabulous sunset view from the dining room, huge lounge, or outdoor deck at this soundside landmark, formerly Penguin Isle. The restaurant's wine cellar, which survives from the previous incarnation, received the *Wine Spectator* Award of Excellence many times. Early-bird specials, daily happy hours, and drink specials help visitors stay within budget. The outdoor Sunset Deck, a bar designed to look like a pirate ship, and live entertainment nightly in-season make this a destination for all ages. Reservations available. Dinner only, $–$$.

🖍 ♿ 🍸 ⇾ **Pier House Restaurant** (252-441-4200; www.nhpierrestaurant.com), Nags Head Pier, 3335 Beach Road, MP 11.5. A survivor from another time, this restaurant sits above the surf on the Nags Head fishing pier. The view can't be beat, even on a stormy day. This is a popular breakfast spot, where you'll find

PAMLICO JACK'S SUNSET DECK MAKES A PERFECT BACKDROP FOR HAPPY HOUR COCKTAILS

some unusual local dishes such as salt herring. You can bring your own catch if you like, and the kitchen will prepare it for you. **Capt. Andy's Oceanfront Tiki Bar** hosts daily happy hour and drink specials with live music on summer nights. Dinner includes a free pass to the pier for an after-dinner stroll. Breakfast $; lunch and dinner $–$$.

↝ **Sam & Omie's** (252-441-7366; www .samandomies.net), 7228 Beach Road, MP 16.5 across from Jennette's Pier. Opened in 1937 by a couple of fishermen as a place to eat breakfast before the Oregon Inlet charter fleet set out for the day, Sam & Omie's is still serving breakfast more than 80 years later. Breakfast features "Omie-lettes" and Bloody Marys. Later in the day attention shifts to steamed seafood and cold ones, as fishermen gather to discuss the day's catch. Breakfast and lunch $; dinner $$.

✐ ☂ **South Beach Grille** (252-449-9313; www.obxsouthbeachgrille.com), 6806 Beach Road, MP 16. Enjoy views of both ocean and sound from the lofty covered deck of this Beach Road landmark. The wide-ranging menu is tinged with

Caribbean flavors, with lots of vegetarian dishes and the best gluten-free menu on the beach. There's a special Doggy Menu as well with salmon sliders, turkey fried rice, and other dishes designed for the discerning canine palate. Come early for happy hour backed by fabulous sunsets. Lunch $–$$; dinner $$–$$$$.

IN SOUTH NAGS HEAD

♈ ⚙ **Fish Heads Bar & Grill** (252-441-5740; www.fishheadsobx.com), on Fishing Unlimited's Outer Banks Pier, 8901 Old Oregon Inlet Road, MP 18.5 The closest spot to the Oregon Inlet Campground to get food and drink, this fun location serves inexpensive sandwiches, appetizers, seafood, and drinks, plus hosts live music, karaoke, and dancing on the oceanfront deck. Stop by for a late breakfast, a fish taco, or the steamed shrimp happy hour. $.

BARBECUE ✐ ☂ **Darrell's 2 BBQ & Seafood** (252-449-5400; www.darrells2obx .com), Outer Banks Mall, 5000 Bypass, MP 14, Nags Head. Family of fisherfolk that has operated Darrell's in Manteo since 1960 proves it can smoke meat as well. Hickory-smoked pork barbecue and ribs join Southern fried chicken and the freshest local seafood on this menu of favorites. Party packs available. Outdoor tables are pet friendly. $–$$.

✐ ♿ **High Cotton Barbeque** (252-255-2275; www.highcottonbbq.com), 5230 Beach Road, MP 2, Kitty Hawk. Authentic North Carolina–style pulled pork flavored with vinegar and hot pepper shares the menu with Texas beef brisket, St. Louis–style ribs, and chicken, smoked or fried. The big family packages are a real bargain. Dine in or take out. $–$$.

✐ **Pigman's Bar-B-Que** (252-441-6803; www.pigman.com), 1606 Bypass, MP 9.5, Kill Devil Hills. Besides the usual pork and beef barbecue, this place offers heart-healthy 'cue made from tuna or turkey, plus country ham rolls, smoked chicken and ribs, homestyle sides, and sweet potato fries, washed down with iced tea or a beer. Eat in or take out. $–$$$.

⚲ **Sooey's BBQ and Rib Shack** (252-449-4227; www.sooeysbbq.com), 3919 Beach Road, MP 12.5, Jockey's Ridge Crossing, Nags Head. Southern fried chicken and barbecued pork, beef brisket, and chicken, plus ribs by the rack and Southern-style sides, available for dine in or take out. Other locations in Corolla and Duck. $–$$$.

BEACH BARS

IN KITTY HAWK

✳ ♿ ⛾ ((•)) **Hurricane Mo's Beachside Bar and Grill** (252-255-0215), 120 E. Kitty Hawk Road, at MP 4, Bypass. Fun tropical bar just steps from the beach has nightly happy hours featuring steamed shrimp, wings, and $1 tacos. Lunch and dinner $$.

IN KILL DEVIL HILLS

⚲ ⛾ **Bonzer Shack** (252-480-1010; www.bonzershack.com), 1200 Beach Road, MP 9, Kill Devil Hills. Surfing-themed sports bar is a fun hangout across from the beach. Menu features fresh takes of Southern favorites and daily fresh fish tacos. Big outdoor patio hosts family-friendly games and live entertainment. Open late. Lunch $–$$; dinner $–$$$.

⚲ ⛾ **Goombay's Grille and Raw Bar** (252-441-6001; www.goombays.com), 1608 Beach Road, MP 7. Cool vibes, Caribbean-inspired food, big beer selection, daily happy hour, and live music some nights make this a favorite hangout. A late-night menu features raw and steamed shellfish until 2 AM. Lunch $; dinner $$.

⚲ ⛾ **Mama Kwan's Tiki Bar & Grill** (252-441-7889; www.mamakwans.com), 1701 Bypass, MP 9.5. A favorite hangout for the late-night crowd, Kwan's serves tasty Asian-inspired food and tropical drinks, with weekly live music amid a laid-back vibe. Lunch $$; dinner $$–$$$.

IN NAGS HEAD

✳ ⚲ ⛾ ⇢ **Lucky 12 Tavern** (252-255-2825; www.lucky12tavern.com), 3308 Beach Road, MP 12. A neighborhood favorite for its reasonably priced food, 20 beers on tap, HDTVs tuned to sports, pool table, laid-back attitude, and pizza served until 2 AM. Lunch and dinner $–$$.

⛾ **Red Drum Grille and Taphouse** (252-480-1095; www.reddrumtaphouse.com), 2412 Beach Road, MP 10.5. Over a dozen beers on tap, foosball and pool, plus live entertainment and steamed seafood served late. The ribs in honey habanero barbecue sauce are legendary. Lunch and dinner $–$$$.

⇢ **Tortuga's Lie Shellfish Bar and Grille** (252-441-RAWW; www.tortugaslie.com), 3014 Beach Road, MP 11. Beachside spot features Caribbean-themed dishes made with local catch, late-night steamed seafood, sushi on Wednesday, beach volleyball, and cool vibes year-round. Lunch $; dinner $$.

BEACH FAST FOOD

IN KITTY HAWK

✳ ⚲ ♿ **Capt'n Frank's** (252-261-9923; www.captnfranks.com), 3800 Bypass, MP 4.5. Don't let the boat out front fool you. Hot dogs, topped with everything imaginable, are the main event here, plus North Carolina barbecue, wings, cheese fries, and steamed shrimp in-season. An OBX favorite since 1975. $.

🍴 **John's Drive In** (252-261-6227; www.johnsdrivein.com), 3716 Beach Road, MP 4.5. A longtime favorite across the street from the beach, John's keeps busy, making its signature milkshakes with added fruit, burgers, and legendary fried dolphin (mahi) sandwiches. Take-out only; for fastest service, call ahead (but not from your cell phone; they don't accept calls from off-beach area codes) and pick up your order at the side service window. Closed Wednesday. $.

⚲ **Spanky's Grille** (252-261-1917; www.spankysnc.com), 4105 Bypass, MP 3.5.

Serving 79-cent hotdogs and $3 cheese-burgers, plus fish sandwiches, barbecue, and home-cooked meat loaf (a dinner special), this spot is one of the top-rated eateries on the Banks. Only the 2-pound Viking Burger tops the $10 mark—finish one and you enter the hall of fame. Sides come separately, however, and can add up quick. $.

Winks Market and Deli (252-441-9465), 4626 Beach Road, MP 2. This family-run grocery across from the ocean has stood the test of time by providing what beachgoers need since 1953. Pick up a deli sandwiches or one of the daily specials, such as steamed shrimp or prime rib, for a quick meal. $.

IN KILL DEVIL HILLS

American Pie Pizza and Home-made Ice Cream (252-441-3332; www.americanpieobx.com), 1600 Beach Road, MP 9.5. Award-winning ice cream and pizza converge at this spot, just across Beach Road from the Ramada. In addition to hand-tossed New York–style pies, the menu includes hot subs, corn dogs, salads, and fresh-fruit smoothies. $–$$.

Kill Devil's Frozen Custard & Beach Fries (252-441-5900; www.killdevilsfrozencustard.com), 1002 Bypass, MP 8.5. Real frozen custard, made fresh hourly and so much better than ordinary soft-serve ice cream, comes in a variety of flavors, such as Key lime, egg nog, and, of course, chocolate. Try the waffle sundae for a satisfying treat. The menu also includes never-frozen, hand-cut fries; Coney Island hot dogs; barbecue; and burgers, both meat and veggie. $.

IN NAGS HEAD

Dune Burger (252-441-2441; www.facebook.com/duneburgerobx), 7304 Beach Road, MP 16.5. Get your burgers, hot dogs, fries, and other fast-food favorites from the window at this throwback to another age, strategically placed in

Whalebone Junction across from Jennette's Pier. Open seasonally. $.

Fat Boyz Ice Cream & Grill (252-441-6514; www.fatboyzobx.com), 7208 Beach Road, MP 16.5. Full line of ice cream delights, hand-patted burgers, veggie burgers, fresh grilled tuna, crabcakes, onion rings, and other take-out favorites are served at this pink landmark on the Beach Road. Shady side deck has tables where you can eat. Homemade ice cream cakes for special occasions are a specialty. $.

🍦 **Snowbird Burgers & Cones** (252-480-6632; www.snowbirdobx.com), 3522 Beach Road, MP 12. Try your choice of soft-serve or hand-scooped ice cream, plus burgers, fish tacos, gyros, and seafood "boats" at this sweet little take-out spot on the Beach Road. Don't miss the cool penguin T-shirts. Stays open late in summer. $.

BREAKFAST ❄ 🍦 **Stack'em High** (252-261-8221; www.stackemhigh.com), 3801 Bypass, MP 4.5, Kitty Hawk. Family-owned and family-operated cafeteria-style breakfast restaurant offers made-to-order French toast, pancakes, omelets, and eggs, plus unusual items such as clam hash and red flannel hash from 7 AM to 2 PM daily. Kids love the specialty pancakes in flavors like banana

PENGUINS—AND TOURISTS—KEEP COOL AT THE SNOWBIRD, A LANDMARK ON THE BEACH ROAD

MUST SEE

❄ ✎ ☂ ((ρ)) **Front Porch Cafe** (www.frontporchcafeonline.com), founded some two decades ago by a young couple seduced by the dream of living on the Outer Banks year-round, has become the Banks' preeminent local purveyor of fine, fresh roasted coffee, voted the best beans on the beach many times, with three locations in Dare County. The Front Porch Cafes all serve their own Kill Devil Coffee, purchased as green beans, sourced from small sustainable farms around the world, and roasted on the Outer Banks in small batches to ensure the freshest taste.

Although each Front Porch Cafe is a bit different, all are open every day all year and provide free Wi-Fi for customers. The **original Front Porch is in Kill Devil Hills** (252-449-6616) in the Milepost 6 Plaza, 2200 Bypass. This location is rather small but offers both sweet and savory baked goods, baked fresh on-site every day, and a special children's menu, as well as full espresso service. A new power strip provides a place to recharge electronics. The OBX Art Studio, with DIY arts and crafts projects, is adjacent, making this a great place to spend a rainy day.

The **Front Porch Cafe in Nags Head** (252-480-6616; MP 10.5, 2515 Bypass), located in the Food Lion plaza, is larger, with a special Wi-Fi bar with comfy couches and plenty of plug-in space. Events of various kinds are scheduled here, from live music performances to kids' story hours. All the coffee roasting is done at this location.

The **third and newest Front Porch Cafe is located in Manteo** (252-473-3160; 300 US 64) on Roanoke Island. The spacious free-standing building offers seating inside and on the porch, with secure Ethernet available in addition to Wi-Fi.

KILL DEVIL COFFEE SELECTION AT THE ORIGINAL FRONT PORCH CAFE LOCATION IN KILL DEVIL HILLS

split. Reasonably priced lunch features sandwiches and Greek specialties. Senior menu. $.

❀ **Grits Grill** (252-449-2888; www.gritsgrill.com), 5000 Bypass, MP 14, Outer Banks Mall, Nags Head. Retro diner serves breakfast and burgers from 6 AM to 2 PM. Huge biscuits, fresh Krispy Kreme doughnuts, and reasonable prices on everything from corned-beef hash to shrimp and grits make it a real find. $.

COFFEE ✍ ☀ ((ɰ)) **Morning View Coffee House** (252-441-4474; www.themorningview.com), 2707 Bypass, MP 11, Forbes Candies Shopping Center, Nags Head. Fair-trade and organic beans from around the world are roasted on-site by Ashley Barnes, owner of this laid-back, dog-friendly café. Organic teas, plus fruit and veggie smoothies round out the menu.

DELI ✍ **Country Deli** (252-441-5684; www.countrydeliobx.com), 1900 Bypass, MP 9.75, Kill Devil Hills. Overstuffed subs, classic deli meats, cheeses and salads, plus a selection of beverages available to take out or delivered free along the Central Beaches. Select one of the deli's designer sandwiches, a classic Reuben, a grilled cheese, or create your own combo from the meats and cheeses in stock. Breakfast bagels served all day. New location has room to dine-in, but this place is famous for delivering right to your beach chair. $–$$.

✍ ((ɰ)) **Good Life Gourmet** (252-480-2855; www.goodlifegourmet.com), 3712 Bypass, MP 4.5, Kitty Hawk. A real find, this place is a bakery and coffee shop in the morning and a deli with a big menu of salads and subs at lunchtime. Breads and sweets are baked on-site, the in-house wine shop carries unusual vintages and beers, the whole place has free Wi-Fi, and prices are some of the most reasonable on the Banks. $–$$.

❀ **N.Y. Bagels** (252-480-0990; www.outerbanksbagels.com), 1708 Bypass, MP 7.5, Dare Center, Kill Devil Hills.

More than a dozen flavors of scratch-made bagels are baked fresh daily. Open all year, serving lunch sandwiches made with Boar's Head deli meats, as well as breakfast sandwiches and treats. Order bagels by the dozen in advance, as they do sell out. $.

✍ ((ɰ)) ➳ **Waveriders Coffee, Deli & Pub** (252-715-1880; www.waveriderscoffeeanddeli.com), 3022 Bypass, MP 11.5, Pirates Quay Shops, Nags Head. Bagel breakfast sandwiches, muffins, smoothies, and Boar's Head panini-style sandwiches, plus a full coffee bar, beer, and wine, served in a friendly family environment. Take a seat at the computer bar if you need to catch up on your email. $.

HEALTHY FOOD **Outer Bean Juice & Java** (252-261-6000; www.outerbean.com), 3701 Bypass, MP 4.5, Kitty Hawk. Healthy spot in the Dunes Shops serves organic fair trade coffee, organic juices, fruit smoothies, and protein shakes. A big menu of salads, panini, sandwiches, and breakfast items features many vegan and vegetarian selections, including a Turkish breakfast plate, tapenade bagels, and kale salad. $.

✍ **Single Fin Bistro Bar & Grille** (252-715-3983; www.singlefinobx.com), 2424 Bypass, MP 10.5, Nags Head. Chef Phongrit "Pok" Choeichom grew up on the Outer Banks working at his family's Thai restaurant. After studying in New York City, he returned to OBX to create some beautiful dishes at his own restaurants. His first venue, **Pok's Art Asian Fusion Kitchen** (252-715-4421; www.obxtogo.com), at 3701 Bypass, in the Dune Shops, Kitty Hawk, offers dishes derived from many Asian cuisines, including vegetarian items, for take-out or delivery. Pok's newest venture, Single Fin, offers a menu that fuses Asian and Western cuisines, as well as an exceptional selection of sushi and sashimi. $–$$$$.

✍ ❀ **Thai Room Restaurant** (252-441-1180; www.thairoomobx.com), 710 Beach

Road, MP 8.5, Oceanside Plaza, Kill Devil Hills. Longtime Asian spot on the Beach Road is a local favorite for its many vegetarian dishes and specials featuring local seafood, as well as its classic Thai and Chinese menu. Take-out and full bar available. Lunch $; dinner $–$$.

Vilai Thai Kitchen (252-441-8424; www.vilaithai.com), 5230 Beach Road, MP 2, Kitty Hawk. Classic Thai dishes, including several vegetarian selections, plus hand-rolled sushi every night all summer. In-home catering available. $–$$.

MARKETS **Cahoon's Market and Deli** (252-441-5358; www.cahoonscottages .com), 7213 Beach Road, MP 16.5, Nags Head. Family owned and operated Cahoon's, since 1962 a one-stop shopping destination along the Beach Road, has gone gourmet, adding cheese, pâté, and locally grown vegetables to its offerings of wine, beer, meats cut in-house, and other groceries, plus beach, fishing, and camping supplies. Salads, sandwiches, and subs, plus a big, inexpensive breakfast menu, are made-to-order and grab-and-go. $.

❋ ✐ ❡ **Coastal Provisions Market and Wine Shop** (252-480-0023; www .coastalprovisionsmarket.com), 1 Ocean Boulevard, Southern Shores Crossing, Southern Shores. The mother ship of the Coastal Provisions food empire, this market stocks prime and natural meats, fresh local seafood, seasonal produce, a wide variety of imported and gourmet groceries, and a huge selection of wines. Chefs on staff create the market's famous crabcakes, gourmet deli sandwiches, and other prepared dishes. Coastal's Seafood Pots to Go (www.cravingsobx.com; $$$) have been featured on the Food Network's "Diners, Drive-Ins and Dives" show. Call ahead for the Outer Banks Pot full of local shrimp and crab or the Yankee Pot with Maine lobster to satisfy your seafood cravings. $–$$.

❋ ✐ **Stop-N-Shop Beach Shop, Deli & Wine Shop** (252-441-6105; www .stopnshopobx.com), 100 Beach Road, MP 8.5, Kill Devil Hills. Everything you'll need for a picnic is available here, including creative deli sandwiches (with cool names) made of Boar's Head cold cuts, along with convenience and gourmet food items, beach supplies, unique souvenirs, and a wide selection of wines and beers, including kegs. $.

PIZZA

IN SOUTHERN SHORES/KITTY HAWK

❋ **Cosmo's Pizzeria** (252-261-8388; www .cosmospizzaobx.com), 5591 N. Croatan Highway, The Marketplace, Southern Shores. Same name as the popular Corolla hangout, but different recipes and vibe. Try the hot tunnel stuffed sandwich or the dinnertime pasta specialties.

((ᵠ)) **Max's Pizza Company** (252-261-3113; www.maxspizzaobx.com), 3733 Bypass, MP 4.5, Ocean Plaza, Kitty Hawk. Family-owned spot serves hand-tossed New York–style pizzas, baked subs, panini, calzone, stromboli, and Italian pasta specialties, all made from scratch and cooked in a stone oven. Free delivery to Southern Shores, Kitty Hawk, and Kill Devil Hills. Or eat in and enjoy beer and wine, local art, surfing videos, and free Wi-Fi. $–$$.

The Pizza Stop (252-261-7867; www .pizzastopobx.com), 5385 N. Virginia Dare Trail, Sandy Ridge Center, Southern Shores. Hand-tossed New York–style thin-crust pizza is baked in a stone oven. Organic toppings are available. Hoagies on Amoroso's rolls, salads, and pasta dishes made with organic marinara fill out the menu. Best of all, this pizzeria delivers for free from Duck to Kill Devil Hills—and will deliver beer with your order.

Southern Shores Pizza (252-715-3940; www.southernshorespizza.com), Southern Shores Crossing. The folks at Corolla Pizza bring their expertise to Southern Shores, offering New York–style pizzas, gigantic stromboli, and super-size

Sicilian thick crust to dine in or take out. Beer, wine, and delivery available.

IN KILL DEVIL HILLS

Y **Dare Devil's Pizzeria** (252-441-6330; www.daredevilspizzeria.com), 1112 Beach Road, MP 9, Kill Devil Hills. A landmark along the Beach Road since 1987, this cool spot shows surf videos while you wait for your pizza or stromboli, created with dough and sauces made in-house. Or chow down on some wings or nachos at the full-service bar. $–$$.

IN NAGS HEAD

Maxximmuss Pizza (252-441-2377; www .facebook.com/maxximmusspizzaobx), 5205 Bypass, MP 14.5, Nags Head. New York–style thin-crust pizza, stromboli, and calzone, plus hot subs, jumbo wings, and salads, mingle with Middle Eastern specialties, including gyros and falafel, available to eat in or take out. Gluten-free pizzas and desserts are a specialty, along with lots of vegetarian items. Beer available. $$.

Pizzazz Pizza Company (252-261-1111; www.pizzazzpizza.net), 2512 Bypass, MP 10.5. Locally owned and operated pizzeria, with other locations in Duck, Corolla, and Grandy on the mainland, has been making pizza lovers happy since 1986, with lunch buffets, hot wings, and oven-baked pies and subs. Dine in or order online and have your pie delivered free. $–$$.

SEAFOOD

IN KITTY HAWK

Carawan Seafood (252-261-2120; www .carawanseafood.com), 5424 Bypass, MP 1. Family-owned market next to the Walmart specializes in fresh local seafood, steamed shrimp, lobster, and crab, plus beer, wine, organic produce, and other groceries.

❄ ✎ ↩ **I Got Your Crabs Shellfish Market & Oyster Bar** (252-449-2483;

www.igotyourcrabs.com), 3809 Bypass, MP 4.5. Local family pulls blue crabs out of Currituck Sound daily and brings them direct to market. Order them live to cook at home or steamed to eat at this casual spot. Hard-shell and softshell available, along with crab dip, seafood platters, sandwiches and pots, local veggies, and fresh oysters (raw, steamed, or fried), served with ice-cold beer and local wines. Call ahead for large take-out orders. $$–$$$.

♫ **Jimmy's Seafood Buffet** (252-261-4973; www.jimmysobxbuffet.com), 4117 Bypass, MP 4. If you decide to forgo the 100-plus-item all-you-can-eat buffet, which includes lobster, Southern specialties, and a wealth of desserts, call ahead for a seafood bucket to steam at home, or have the kitchen do it for you and pick it up curbside. Dinner is also served à la carte. Kids 4–12 pay their age plus $2 for the buffet. Dinner $$; buffet $$$$.

ON COLINGTON ISLAND

↩ **Billy's Seafood** (252-441-5978; www .billysseafoodobx.com), 1341 Colington Road, Colington Island. This little grocery, open since 1971, sits in the heart of the Colington Island crabbing scene, making it a great place to pick up local blue crabs and oysters, "shedders," shrimp, or other seafood, plus groceries, beer, and wine. They'll even steam the crabs for you. A gold member of **Outer Banks Catch** (www.outerbankscatch .com).

IN NAGS HEAD

((ip)) ↩ **Austin Fish Company** (252-441-7412; www.austinfishcompany.com), 3711 Bypass, MP 12.5. Family owned and operated, Austin's has been selling fresh fish and seafood from the same location next to Jockey's Ridge for over 50 years. Freshness is guaranteed, and most of the seafood here is fished sustainably from local waters. Fried seafood dinners and sandwiches, as well as a variety of steamed seafood and locally famous mac and cheese, are available to go or to eat at the picnic tables outside. Lunch $–$$.

⚓ Dirty Dick's Crab House (252-449-2722; www.dirtydickscrabs.com), 2407 Bypass, MP 10.5. Fun place with a menu of all types of seafood that is constantly being updated, this is one of Nags Head's most popular spots. AYCE and a breakfast buffet available. **Second location in Avon** (252-995-3425) on Hatteras Island. Breakfast and lunch $–$$; dinner $$–$$$.

⚓ ❄ The Sugar Shack (252-441-3888; www.sugarcreekseafood.com), 7340 Nags Head–Manteo Causeway, MP 16.5. Get a bucket of seafood to "go-go" or a seafood sandwich or steamed combo from the shack, located at the edge of the sound next to sister restaurant Sugar Creek. Delivery of raw or steamed seafood available. A seating area overlooks the sound where paddleboats, kayaks, and other watercraft are available for rent. $$–$$$$.

SWEETS AND ICE CREAM **Big Buck's Ice Cream** (252-715-0779; www .bigbucksicecream.com). 3810 Bypass, MP 4.5, Buccaneer's Walk, Kitty Hawk. Ice cream made in house, plus sorbet, sherbets, smoothies, and handmade chocolate goodies.

Booty Treats (252-715-3385; www .bootytreats.com), 2600 Beach Road, MP 10.5, Nags Head. Hawaiian-style shaved ice, handmade ice cream cookie sandwiches, old-fashioned malts and sundaes, and the original "booty freeze" are the specialties here. Second location on the Bypass at MP 9.

Distinct Delights (252-715-0779; www .distinctdelights.com), MP 4.5, Bypass, Buccaneer's Walk, Kitty Hawk. Small-batch chocolates and caramels made by hand, plus delicious fudge and ice cream cakes. Additional locations in Manteo and Corolla.

Forbes Candies (252-441-7293; www .forbescandies.com), 6321 Bypass, MP 15.5, Nags Head. Second location (252-441-9411) at 2707 Bypass, MP 9.

Established in Virginia Beach in 1933, this chain of candy stores is known for its salt water taffy and peanut brittle. New additions include sea glass candy; fudge; hand-dipped chocolates, including many sugar-free varieties; and beach-themed silver charms containing a real pearl. For dog-lovers, Forbes now carries the popular all-natural **Salty Paws Dog Biscuits** (www.saltypawsbiscuits.com), handmade on the Outer Banks.

The Fudgery (252-480-0163; www .fudgeryfudge.com), 3933 Bypass, MP 12.5, Jockey's Ridge Crossing, Nags Head. Now found in a dozen states, the very first Fudgery got its start in OBX back in 1980. Handcrafted fudge is cooked in copper kettles the old-fashioned way by a fun singing staff. Additional local locations can be found in Corolla at the Currituck Club Center and TimBuck II, and in Duck at Scarborough Lane.

OBX Frozen Yogurt (252-261-2697; www.obxfroyo.com), Southern Shores Crossing. New expanded location of this family-owned and -operated shop offers candy, craft sodas, Dipping Dots, and ice cream in addition to froyo soft serve with your choice of toppings.

Scoops Ice Cream Parlor (252-441-4485), 3941 Bypass, MP 12.5, Jockey's Ridge Crossing. Old-fashioned ice cream shop conveniently located across from the often burning sands of Jockey's Ridge.

((•)) Surfin' Spoon (252-441-7873; www .surfinspoon.com), 2408 Beach Road, MP 10.5. Frozen yogurt with a difference at this spot, operated by a former professional surfer. There's a game room, walls covered with local surfing and OBX memorabilia, and creative frozen yogurt and sorbet creations by Jesse Hines and his wife, Whitney.

WINE, BEER, AND SPIRITS **ABC Liquor Store** (252-261-2477; www.ncabc .com), MP 1, 5441 Bypass, Kitty Hawk. Additonal location in **Nags Head** (252-411-5121; 2104 Bypass), as well as

Manteo, **Duck**, and **Grandy**. All liquor by the bottle is sold at these state-run stores, which are closed on Sunday.

((•)) **Chip's Wine and Beer Market** (252-449-8229; www.chipswinemarket.com), 2200 Bypass, Milepost 6 Plaza, Kill Devil Hills. Additional location in Moyock (252-435-1629) on the Currituck mainland. With 2,000 different wines and the Great Wall of Beer offering 500 brews, Chip's may well have the largest selection of adult beverages on the Outer Banks. The Tasting Lounge offers your choice of wines dispensed by an automated wine station, or try a flight of draft beers. Chip's also offers fun and informative wine classes conducted by a pro, and free beer and wine tastings each week.

🍴 ❄ ♀ ((•)) **Trio** (252-261-0277; www.obxtrio.com), 3708 Bypass, MP 4.5, Harbor Bay Shops, Kitty Hawk. Unique store stocking a huge selection of wine, beer, cheese, and gourmet food items from around the world lets you taste before you buy. Downstairs, sample 24 different wines by the taste or the glass from automat-style WineStations, or try one of the two dozen draft beers at the copper-top bar in the Tap Room. A menu of cheese and charcuterie plates, panini, and other small dishes makes a great lunch or light supper. Champagne brunch served on weekends. Upstairs, the Carolina Tasting Room offers free samples of North Carolina wines and beers, along with free a pool table and Wi-Fi. Live music plays most nights. $–$$.

❋ Entertainment

LIVE MUSIC Spots in Kitty Hawk offering live entertainment in-season include the **Black Pelican**, **Ocean Boulevard Bistro**, **Art's Place**, **Barefoot Bernie's**, the **Rundown Cafe**, **OBX Taco Bar**, **Trio**, and the **Sandtrap Tavern** at the Sea Scape Golf Course.

Hot spots for nightlife in Kill Devil Hills include the **Outer Banks Brewing Station**, **Roosters**, **SaltBox Cafe**, **Jolly Roger**, **Peppercorns** in the Ramada Plaza, **Beachside Bistro** in the Sea Ranch Resort, **Goombay's Grille and Raw Bar**, **Bonzer Shack**, and **Chilli Peppers Coastal Grill**.

In Nags Head check out the lineup at the **Red Drum**, **Miller's Waterfront**, **Mulligan's**, **Fish Heads** on the Outer Banks Pier, and **Capt. Andy's Oceanfront Tiki Bar** on the Nags Head Pier. All summer, special sunset concerts are hosted at the **Soundside Event Site** at MP 16.

NIGHTCLUBS ♀ **Blue Crab Tavern** (252-441-5919; www.seabbaticals.com), 1180 Colington Road, Kill Devil Hills. Hidden away on Colington Island, this former fish house is a local favorite and worth seeking out. The loyal clientele, many of whom arrive by boat, come for inexpensive beers, 50-cent pool, and a jukebox stocked with decades' worth of hits. Step out the back door, where you'll find a yard with cornhole and horseshoe pits and a new waterfront gazebo, perfect for watching magnificent sunsets and the setting of frequent live music.

♪ ♀ **Longboards Island Grill** (252-261-7377; www.longboardsobx.com), 3833 Bypass, Kitty Hawk. Casual Hawaiian vibe provides a great setting for live music, dancing to DJs, and the best karaoke on the beach. Daily happy hour appetizer deals, drink specials, and a late-night menu of pizza, wings, and apps served until 1 AM. $$.

CONCERT SERIES **Outer Banks Forum for the Lively Arts** (252-202-4289; www.outerbanksforum.org), First Flight High School Auditorium, 100 Veterans Drive, Kill Devil Hills. Nonprofit brings top international classical and popular music groups to town September to May. Tickets $12 (student) to $25.

COMEDY CLUB ♀ **The Comedy Club of Kill Devil Hills** (252-207-9950; www.comedyclubobx.com), Ramada Plaza Resort, 1701 Beach Road, MP 9.5, Kill

EXCURSIONS
CURRITUCK TRADITIONS: WINE, BEER, AND MONSTER TRUCKS

John Wright's family has lived in Currituck County for seven generations, ever since ancestor Jacob Wright was shipwrecked on the shores of Duck. His descendants became farmers, experts at coaxing crops from the sandy soil. The latest generations have taken on the challenge of growing grapes on their seaside farm, and not just the native muscadines that the region is famous for. The Wrights have planted Italian, Spanish, and French hybrid grapes among the native vines, and at Sanctuary Vineyards they demonstrate their expertise in making delicious wines from their crops.

Located in Jarvisburg, at 7005 Caratoke Highway/US 158, **Sanctuary Vineyards** (252-491-2387; www.sanctuaryvineyards.com) is along the route many take to and from the Outer Banks from the north. Free tastings are offered daily at the winery, with tours on Mondays and Wednesdays. Next door, the **Cotton Gin** (252-491-2387; www.cottongin.com) occupies one of the family's original farm buildings, offering a huge selection of home decor, beachwear, gifts, and souvenirs. The shop opened in 1929, and became such a popular stop that branches can now be found in Corolla, Duck, and Nags Head. All offer tastings and sales of Sanctuary wines.

SANCTUARY VINEYARDS' AWARD-WINNING WINES

Devil Hills. Touring comedians keep the laughs coming at the longest-running comedy club on the beach.

DANCE CLUB **Outer Banks Shag Club** (www.obxshagclub.com). Friendly folk promoting beach music and shag dancing on the Banks are currently dancing at the Duck Woods Country Club, 50 S. Dogwood Trail off US 158 in Southern Shores, on Monday nights. Check the website for updates. Visitors are welcome.

DINNER THEATER ✑ **OBX Murder Mystery Dinner Show** (252-305-2976; www

A SAMPLING OF THE WEEPING RADISH SELECTION OF SAUSAGES, INCLUDING THE NOT-TO-BE-MISSED SWEET POTATO LIVERWURST, FEATURED ON *DINERS, DRIVE-INS AND DIVES*

A short distance north on US 158, the **Weeping Radish Farm Brewery & Eco Farm** (252-491-5205; www.weepingradish.com) represents another Outer Banks tradition. Formerly located in Manteo, the Weeping Radish is North Carolina's oldest micro-brewery, founded in 1986. The Butchery sells award-winning homemade sausages and sweet potato liver pâté, a Guy Fieri favorite, plus fresh beer brewed in accordance with strict Bavarian purity laws. Meals featuring these products, including sausage sampler platters and German dinner entrées, are served in the **Weeping Radish Pub**. Sign up for a Brat & Brew tour to see how it all happens. Hint: stop on your way to the beach to pick up sausages for the grill.

Keep heading north on US 158 and the **Grave Digger Dungeon** (252-453-4121; www.gravedigger.com) soon comes into view, unmistakable thanks to the monster truck out front. Fans can have their pictures taken sitting in the Grave Digger, pick up logo merchandise, or get a bite to eat at the shiny diner next door.

.obxmysterydinner.com), Ramada Plaza, 1701 Beach Road, MP 9.5, Kill Devil Hills. Murder mystery with plenty of comedy mixed in is wrapped around a four-course meal. Rated PG, this is a hit with kids.

SPORTS BARS **BK Shuckers** (252-261-7800; www.bkshuckers.com), 4020 Bypass, MP 3.5, Kitty Hawk. Sports and oyster bar carries all DirecTV sports packages, NFL ticket, and pay-per-view events, including UFC fights, plus live music on the patio and hermit crab racing. Menu features wings, steamed seafood, and bar favorites. $–$$.

🦪 ♉ 🐟 **Just George's Sports Bar** (252-4806677; www.captaingeorges.com), 705 Bypass, MP 8.5, Kill Devil Hills. Located next to Captain George's Seafood Buffet, this state-of-the-art sports bar has 28 flat-screen TVs carrying all the major sports packages. An à la carte menu featuring local seafood is served until close, or you can go next door and raid the buffet all through the game. Dishes $–$$$; buffet $$$$.

❄ Selective Shopping

ART GALLERIES **Nags Head Gallery Row** (www.obxgalleryrow.com), located around MP 10 between the Beach Road and the Bypass, has the greatest concentration of galleries on the Banks. This area, encompassing both **Gallery Row Road** and **Driftwood Road**, was set aside by the town especially to encourage local arts and crafts. Most artists here live on the property. While several of the galleries have closed in recent years, you'll still find **Glenn Eure's Ghost Fleet**

Gallery and **Jewelry by Gail** well worth a stop. Galleries and other neighborhood businesses throw open their doors the annual **Roll & Stroll** event in July.

The Bird Store (252-480-2951; www.thebirdstore.biz), 807 Bypass, MP 8.5, Kill Devil Hills. Antique decoys and fishing and hunting equipment on display, plus new carvings, paintings, and prints of wildfowl and other wildlife by local and regional artists.

🐾 **Copper Mermaid Art Gallery & Gifts** (252-715-5330; www.coppermermaid.com), 300 E. Driftwood Street, Gallery Row, Nags Head. Mermaid-themed gallery is the row's newest member, featuring photography by OBX beach bum Roy Edlund, handmade jewelry, glass treasures, and beach art.

Glenn Eure's Ghost Fleet Gallery (252-441-6584; www.glenneureart.com), 210 E. Driftwood Street, Gallery Row, Nags Head. Unique gallery displays the sculptural watercolors and oils, woodcuts, and etchings of the talented Eure, a fixture for over 40 years on the local art scene.

UNIQUE ART AT THE GHOST FLEET GALLERY

WINGED HORSE "STARRY STARRY FLIGHT" GUARDS THE ENTRANCE TO THE KDH COOPERATIVE ART GALLERY

🐾 🕊 **KDH Cooperative Gallery & Studios** (252-441-9888; www.kdhcooperative .com), 502 Bypass, MP 8.5, Kill Devil Hills. Artist-operated gallery exhibits the works of more than 40 local artists in media ranging from sea glass to ironwork. Classes for adults and kids and openings are hosted year-round. Look for the mirrored flying horse out front.

Nags Head Town Hall (252-441-5508; www.nagsheadnc.gov), 5401 Bypass, MP 15. The town's ever-growing collection of local art in all media is on display free, Monday through Friday 8:30–5.

Seagreen Gallery (252-715-2426; www .seagreengallery.com), 2404 Beach Road, MP 10.5, Nags Head. Gallery specializing in art made from found or cast-off items has a huge collection of jewelry made from sea glass and natural seeds, plus gourds, fishing floats, oyster shell flowers, and more. Around back is a garden full of art and a fishpond.

❄ **Seaside Art Gallery** (252-441-5418; www.seasideart.com), 2716 Beach Road, MP 10, Nags Head. Established in 1961, this gallery carries over 2,000 originals by local and contemporary artists, plus a selection of lithographs and woodcuts by past masters. Special collections of original animation art from Disney and Hanna-Barbera, estate jewelry, and more.

Yellowhouse Galleries (252-207-4274; www.yellowhousegallery.com), 4711 Bypass, MP 13.5, Croatan Shopping Centre, Nags Head. Now in a new location, this gallery, owned by award-winning photographer Eve Turek, specializes in contemporary fine art photography and fine American crafts, as well as antique maps, charts, and prints.

BOOKS **The Island Bookstore** (252-255-5590; www.islandbooksobx.com), 3712 Bypass, MP 4.5, Ocean Plaza, Kitty Hawk. With sister stores in Corolla and Duck, the Island Bookstore is a powerhouse on the local literary scene, hosting book signings, author readings, book clubs, and many special events. Local subjects are a specialty, as well as large collections of children's titles, audiobooks, and magazines. *New York Times* best-sellers are discounted.

FASHION Chameleon Clogs (252-202-4047; www.chameleonclogs.com), 115 Hamilton Court, Powells Point. Design your own Swedish-style wooden clog with your choice of leather, velvet animal print, or customized handwoven textile upper. This Amazon and Etsy favorite is operated by a longtime local crafter.

Shore-Fit Sunwear (252-441-4560; www.obxsunwear.com), 100 E. Helga Street, at MP 5.5, Bypass, Kill Devil Hills. Featured on national TV, swimwear boutique operated by a local designer offers fashionable solutions to fit every figure, including many plus-size selections and mix-and-match tops and bottoms, as well as beach cover-ups, bags, and sandals.

JEWELRY Creative Jewelers (252-255-2015; www.obxjeweler.com), 2501 Bypass, MP 5.75, Kill Devil Hills. Custom jewelers let you design you own ring using virtual technology, and sell signature Outer Banks Destination bracelets and unique lighthouse and Outer Banks beads.

Dare Jewelers (252-441-1112), 5000 Bypass, MP 14, Outer Banks Mall. Handcrafted 14-karat gold sea-life jewelry, OBX watches, and locally created stained-glass designs.

Gulf Stream Gifts (252-441-0433; www.gulfstreamgifts.com), 2512 Beach Road, MP 10.5, Nags Head. Specializing in 14K gold and sterling silver jewelry, including the popular Lone Wolf Trading Company line, along with a wealth of nautical and sea-themed decor and souvenirs.

Jewelry by Gail (252-441-5387; www.jewelrybygail.com), 207 E. Driftwood Street, Gallery Row, Nags Head. Award-winning jeweler Gail Kowalski creates original pieces using diamonds, colored pearls, amethysts, and corals. Her designs include a popular line of Outer Banks lighthouse charms. The shop features a magnificent amethyst chandelier.

♪ **Michael's Gems and Glass** (252-441-4449; www.michaelsgems.com), 4711 Bypass, MP 14, Croatan Centre, Nags Head. A big selection of crystals, agate geodes, fossils, and shells is supplemented by sterling silver jewelry set with larimar, amber, and gemstones, plus glass suncatchers, framed insects, and Florida gator heads. Kids are invited to dig through treasure barrels and to make their own pieces of jewelry to take home. Second location in TimBuck II, Corolla.

SHOPPING CENTERS Along US 158, shopping centers pass in sometimes bewildering profusion. Here we list the major shopping destinations and some of their outstanding features, starting at the north end, where Kitty Hawk and Southern Shores face off on either side of the highway. Even-numbered addresses are on the west or soundside of the road. Odd numbers are on the east or ocean side. The street numbers, which don't relate much to the MP address, rise as you drive north or south from the Wright Memorial in Kill Devil Hills. Here are shopping centers to watch for, arranged from north to south:

IN KITTY HAWK/SOUTHERN SHORES (ARRANGED NORTH TO SOUTH)

Shoreside Center, 5400 Bypass, MP 1. National chains including Walmart, Harris Teeter grocery, and Dollar Tree are found at this large complex, as well as several locally owned shops.

The Marketplace, located across from the Walmart, is anchored by a **Food Lion** grocery, plus a **CVS pharmacy** and a **UPS Store**. Here you'll find a **Starbucks** (252-255-0790), **Cosmo's Pizzeria**, and **Shun Xing Chinese** (252-261-0202 or 252-251-5099), serving classic Chinese dishes to eat in or take out for 20 years.

Sandy Ridge Center (5385 N. Virginia Dare Trail/US 158), located across from the Home Depot, is a smaller shopping area, home to a **Tropical Smoothie Cafe** (252-441-9996; www.tropicalsmoothie

MADE ON THE OUTER BANKS

Local entrepreneurs are busy producing a variety of food and gift items that make great souvenirs of your vacation. Here are a few to look for at local produce markets, groceries, restaurants, and stores.

Hatteras Saltworks (www.hatterassaltworks.com). Buxton company uses solar evaporation to extract nutrient-rich salts from ocean water.

Hollow Daze Surf Designs (www.facebook.com/hollowdaze). Natural handmade Castile soap scented with local herbs.

Kill Devil Rum Ball Co. (570-220-6375; www.killdevilrumballs.com).

Made in the OBX (www.facebook.com/MadeintheOBX), with stores in the Dune Shops in Kitty Hawk and Loblolly Pines in Duck, stocks a selection of local food and art items handcrafted by over 100 local artisans.

Outer Banks Bees Honey (252-441-8277). Made from hives in Wanchese.

Outer Banks Kettle Corn (252-202-2469; www.obxkettlecorn.com). Created by two teenage sisters from family recipes, this company's products are widely available at special events and festivals.

Outer Banks Rum Cakes (252-441-9090; www.outerbanksrumcakes.com).

Outer Banks Sea Salt (252-267-7884; www.obxseasalt.com). All-natural salt hand-harvested from Atlantic Ocean water using heritage techniques.

.com), with several healthy menu options, and the **Pizza Stop**.

Ocean Centre, MP 1, 5230 Beach Road. Strip of shops at the northern end of the Beach Road houses barbecue and ice cream shops and the oh-so-tasty **Duck Donuts** (252-261-3312; www.duckdonuts.com), plus an art supply store.

Southern Shores Crossing (www.facebook.com/southernshorescrossing), where NC 12 splits with US 158, is the Southern Shore's premiere shopping destination, with high-end restaurants, shops, and services. Most notable is **Coastal Provisions**, a foodie destination on this end of the Banks.

Kitty Hawk Plaza, MP 4, 3836 Bypass. Specialty stores include a sporting goods store, a party store, a **Sound Feet Shoes outlet** (www.soundfeet.com), and an excellent thrift store with lots of bargains.

Buccaneer's Walk, MP 4.5, 3810 Bypass. Specialty stores crowd this nautically themed center, including two antiques stores and shops specializing in chocolates, wine, homemade ice cream, and peanuts.

Ocean Plaza, MP 4.5, 3723 Bypass. Home of the Island Bookstore, a bakery, and a tobacco and beer store.

Harbor Bay Shops, MP 4.5, 3708 Bypass. Home of gourmet food emporium **Trio**.

Dunes Shops, MP 4.5, 3701 Bypass. **Outer Bean Juice and Java** serves healthy snacks here. Shop for local products at the **Made in the OBX** store.

IN KILL DEVIL HILL (ARRANGED NORTH TO SOUTH)

Seagate North, MP 5.5, 3105 Bypass. Shops include a fun thrift and consignment store, **Cyber Dog**, and a skateboard shop that stocks vintage vinyl records.

Milepost 6 Plaza, MP 6, 2200 Bypass. Anchored by the original location of the **Front Porch Cafe** family, this strip of shops houses a DIY art studio, **Chip's Wine and Beer**, and a salon, as well as the **Beach Music Shop** (252-573-0067; www.facebook.com/beachmusicshop), selling new and used musical instruments, vinyl records, and more.

Dare Center, MP 7.5, 1708 Bypass. Shopping center near the hospital is

JOCKEY'S RIDGE CROSSING OFFERS A FREE SLATE OF FUN ACTIVITIES, AS WELL AS VIEWS OF THE UNPAINTED ARISTOCRACY AND JOCKEY'S RIDGE HANG GLIDING ACTION

home to several national chains as well as **N.Y. Bagels'** flagship location.

IN NAGS HEAD, ARRANGED NORTH TO SOUTH:

Gallery Row, MP 10. Set between the highways, this is the largest concentration of galleries on the beach.

Central Square, MP 11, 2910 Bypass. Noted for its antiques stores.

Pirate's Quay Shoppes, MP 11.5, 3022 Bypass. Sophisticated and fun shops and boutiques next to the YMCA skate park. Look for the huge boat propeller out front.

Jockey's Ridge Crossing (www .jockeysridgecrossing.com), MP 12.5, 3933 Bypass. Located at the site of the original Nags Head Pavilion across from the Jockey's Ridge dunes, this two-story center offers refreshments, shopping, and an indoor climbing wall, plus planned activities and daily sunset celebrations throughout the summer.

Outer Banks Mall (www .nagsheadshopping.com), MP 14, 5000 Bypass. Over two dozen specialty shops, restaurants, department stores (including **Sears**), and a **Food Lion** grocery are located next to the Outer Banks Hospital. Restaurants here include **New China** (252-449-8000), **Taiko Japanese Sushi Bar** (252-449-8095; www.taikosushiobx .com), **Cafe Lachine**, a **N.Y. Bagels, Darrell's BBQ**, and **Grits Grill**. Check website for coupons.

Tanger Outlet Mall (252-441-5634; www.tangeroutlet.com/nagshead), MP 16.5, 7100 Bypass. Discount shopping for name brands. Check for coupons on the website.

SPECIAL SHOPS

IN KITTY HAWK/SOUTHERN SHORES

CHKD Thrift Store (252-255-5437; www.chkd.org), 3838 Bypass, MP 4.5, Kitty Hawk Plaza, Kitty Hawk. Thrift store benefits the Children's Hospital of the King's Daughters.

Goodwill Community Foundation Store (252-255-5111; www.gcfglobal.org), 5381 N. Virginia Dare Trail, Southern Shores. Located next to the Southern Shores Town Hall, this is a great place to pick up some gently used clothes, toys, and books to read on the beach.

Islander Flags (252-261-6266; www.islanderflags.com), 6146 Bypass, MP 0, Kitty Hawk. Blink as you come over the Wright Memorial Bridge and you'll miss this spot, selling flags, banners, and wind socks in colorful profusion.

Made in the OBX (252-581-0001; www.madeintheobx.com), 3701 Bypass, MP 4.5, Dune Shops, Kitty Hawk. Locally made food, crafts, and art by more than 100 artisans on the Outer Banks.

IN KILL DEVIL HILLS

A Penny Saved Thrift & Consignment Shop (252-441-8024), Seagate North, MP 5.5, 3105 Bypass, Kill Devil Hills. Great spot to browse on a rainy day.

BrewThru Outlet (252-453-2878; www.brewthru.com), 3101 Bypass, MP 5.5, Kill Devil Hills. Licensed beer apparel and memorabilia, plus over 50 different Brew Thru T-shirts, including annual designs dating back to 1977.

The Cyber Dog USA Holistic Pet Shop & School for Dogs (252-449-0331; www.outerbanksschoolfordogs.com), 3105 Bypass, Seagate North, MP 5.5, Kill Devil Hills. Healthy pet foods and remedies, plus grooming and training, as well as doggie day care available by the hour.

Mom's Sweet Shop (252-423-1206; www.sweetstuffinside.com), 3105 Bypass, Seagate North, Kill Devil Hills.

Husband-and-wife skateboarders operate this rad shop filled with vintage vinyl records and T-shirts, collectible skateboards, along with Quiet Life, Herschel Supply, and other hot brands of shoes, hats, and clothing. Snacks and sweets are equally hip, with vintage and vegan candies, kombucha, acai bowls, milkshakes, and cold brew.

Parrot Bay (252-480-1774; www.parrotbayobx.com), 808 Bypass, MP 8.5, Kill Devil Hills. Large shop carries name brands, including Simply Southern, Fish Hippie, Southern Fried, and Salt Life, with many exclusive designs with OBX maps and lighthouses. An exclusive line of 50 OBX-themed beads compatible with the Pandora and Chamilia collections includes sterling silver lighthouses and colorful glass beads crafted from Outer Banks beach sand.

IN NAGS HEAD

Absolutely Outer Banks (252-255-1606; www.absolutelyouterbanks.com), Outer Banks Mall, 5000 Bypass, MP 14, Nags Head. Unique items crafted by Outer Banks artists include jewelry and home decor created from shells, beach glass, driftwood, and license tags.

🌲 **Christmas Mouse** (252-441-8111; www.christmasmouse.com), 2401 Bypass, MP 10.5, Nags Head. It's Christmas all year at this huge store, full of holiday cheer and gift ideas. The nautical room stocks hundreds of OBX-themed ornaments. Additional location in Duck.

The Cotton Gin (252-449-2387; www.cottongin.com), 5151 Bypass, MP 14.5, Nags Head. Southern tradition meets coastal charm in room after room of gifts, home and garden decor, decoys, dolls, collectibles, and holiday decorations. Each store offers free tastings of the family's Sanctuary wines. Additional locations in Corolla and Duck. The original store in Jarvisburg (252-491-2387; US 158), open since 1929, has an even bigger selection.

EXCURSIONS

Pronounced *Bah-dee Island* by natives, and named supposedly for the many bodies that washed up here during the worst years of the Graveyard of the Atlantic, this end of the peninsula forms the northernmost segment of **Cape Hatteras National Seashore**. The **Bodie Island Lighthouse, Coquina Beach,** and a campground are maintained by the park rangers.

NC 12 is the only through road on this stretch of the Outer Banks. It runs from Whalebone Junction to the Bonner Bridge and beyond. Old Nags Head Road, a continuation of the Beach Road, runs through South Nags Head before joining NC 12.

Bodie Island comes to an end at Oregon Inlet and the newly rebuilt Bonner Bridge, stretching to Pea Island, Hatteras Island, and beyond. Just before the Bonner Bridge, **Oregon Inlet Fishing Center** (252-441-6301; www.oregoninlet.com) is home to one of the world's most storied fishing fleets.

Take the kids down to the south end of the fishing center in the late afternoon when the charter boats come in to see the different fish that have been caught and watch the crews weigh the really big ones. The store here can provide an impromptu picnic. Check out the world record blue marlin and the 805-pound bluefin tuna mounted in cases outside the store.

The history of the famous **Oregon Inlet Fishing Fleet** began about 1951, when the state paved the sand road from Whalebone Junction to Oregon Inlet. Sambo Tillett, a local fisherman and owner of a little restaurant named Sambo's, decided to dock his boat in a canal at the southern end of the road where he would be closer to the inlet and the open ocean waters beyond. Others followed, and soon a marina was built, the first at Oregon Inlet. Today, the little restaurant in Whalebone Junction, renamed **Sam and Omie's** after Sambo's son Omie joined the business,

THE OREGON INLET CHARTER FISHING FLEET AT THE END OF A BUSY DAY

is still serving breakfast and beer to fishing captains, and the Tillett family remains a force on the Oregon Inlet fishing scene. Omie and his brother Tony went on to become two of the most famous captains the inlet has ever known.

Omie is retired after a lifetime of building and captaining boats, but Tony Tillett is still taking out charters aboard his famous *Carolinian*, built by the legendary Warren O'Neal, the father of Roanoke Island boatbuilding, and considered the epitome of the Carolina-style boat.

KIDS LOVE WATCHING THE FISHING FLEET COME IN AT OREGON INLET AND DISCOVERING WHAT A TUNA LOOKS LIKE WITHOUT A CAN

Carolina boats, constructed by hand in the traditional manner with juniper planks, last just about forever. Many of these boats, built by the big names in Roanoke Island boatbuilding such as O'Neal, Buddy Cannady, Sheldon Midgett, Buddy Davis, Rick Scarborough, and Omie Tillett himself, still dock at Oregon Inlet. Other boats in the Oregon Inlet marina built by O'Neal include the **Sinbad** (252-473-2398; www.sinbadsportfishing .com).

Several boats built by Omie Tillett at his famous Sportsman Boatworks are also still on the water. Look for the *Fight-N-Lady*, *Fintastic*, and *Rigged Up*. Cannady-built boats working out of Oregon Inlet, many with captains bearing famous names in the Outer Banks fishing world, include the *Skirt Chaser*, skippered by Captain Barry Daniels; *High Return*, *Tuna Fever*, and *Trophy Hunter*. Cannady's grandson, Jordan Croswait, captains the sportfisher **Legacy** (252-305-7960; www.legacyfishingobx.com).

All of these boats are available for a day of fishing through the **Oregon Inlet Fishing Center website** (www.oregoninlet.com). Many of the captains also offer sunset cruises, ecotours, bird-watching, and other trips. The headboat *Miss Oregon Inlet* makes reasonably priced half-day trips from May through the end of October, perfect for those learning to fish or who just want to sightsee.

See our "Manteo" section for more information on Warren O'Neal, and the "Wanchese" section for more on Dare County boatbuilders.

RECOMMENDED READING: Brown, William K. *Mullet Roar and Other Stories by an Outerbanker*. Manteo, NC: Maritime Kids' Quest Press, 2007. Written by the founder of the Oregon Inlet Fishing Center and the son of legendary photographer and early PR genius Aycock Brown, these fascinating stories of fishing and hunting in the "old days" are illustrated by the author's original artwork.

WILLIAM BROWN, FOUNDER OF THE OREGON INLET FISHING CENTER

❉ ♂ **Karma Blue and Endless Possibilities** (252-715-3870; www.facebook.com/KarmaBlueOuterBanks), 4711 Bypass, MP 13.5, Nags Head. Thrift shop benefiting the **Outer Banks Crisis Hotline** (www.obhotline.org) shares space with **Endless Possibilities** (www.facebook.com/endlesspossibilities.hotline), a unique program that recycles fabric into woven rugs, bags, and more which are sold to fund the hotline. Come by and try your hand at the loom.

♂ ⇡ **Life on a Sandbar** (252-449-9066; www.lifeonasandbar.com), Jockey's Ridge Crossing, MP 12.5, Bypass, Nags Head. Popular logo'd souvenirs are available all over the Banks, but the shop at Jockey's Ridge offers the full range, plus local art and jewelry, Del Sol products that change color in the sun, make-your-own sand art, and hair wraps and braiding.

Rock-A-Bye Baby (252-480-2297; www.rockabyebabyobx.com), 4711 Bypass, MP 14, Croatan Centre, Nags Head. New and used baby clothes, furniture, toys, and maternity and baby shower supplies, plus info on baby equipment rentals for vacationing families.

Shipwreck (252-441-5739), 7746 Causeway. Stop on the causeway for driftwood and shells, plus local crafts and scenic views.

❉ Special Events

Check the **Outer Banks visitors website** (www.outerbanks.org) for an updated list of events during your stay.

February: The **Elizabethan Rendezvous** (252-473-1061; www.elizabethrandco.org), Pamlico Jack's. Fun-filled gala produced by Elizabeth R and Company benefits Outer Banks Arts and Education.

Annual Chili Cookoff (www.chilli-peppers.com), sponsored by Chilli Peppers Restaurant.

March: **Taste of the Beach** (www.obxtasteofthebeach.com), a four-day festival for foodies with dozens of events.

St. Patrick's Day Parade (252-441-4116; www.kellysrestaurant.com), Beach Road, MP 12–10.5.

Annual George Barnes Oyster Roast (252-441-7132; www.jockeysridgestatepark.com), Jockey's Ridge State Park. Help create new oyster beds, then enjoy the party afterward for free.

Outer Banks Polar Plunge (252-449-8897; polarplungeobx.passioncff.org), Ramada Plaza Resort. Benefits the Cystic Fibrosis Foundation.

First Flight Cruisers Shamrock Car Show and Poker Run (www.firstflightcruisers.com).

April: ♂ **Wilbur Wright's Birthday** (252-441-7430; www.nps.gov/wrbr), Wright Brothers National Memorial.

Kitty Hawk Kites Easter Egg-stravaganza & Fly into Spring (252-449-2210; www.kittyhawk.com), Nags Head. The largest egg hunt on the Outer Banks is held at the Kitty Hawk Kites store while kite flyers from around the country demo stunt kites and teach lessons at Jockey's

MISS BARBARA HIRD IS THE FORCE BEHIND ELIZABETH R AND COMPANY

Ridge State Park in honor of National Kite Month. Free.

Earth Day OBX (252-255-1501; www.jennettespier.net), Jennette's Pier.

Flying Pirate Half-Marathon & Pirate Expo (www.flyingpiratehalfmarathon.com).

May: **Coastal Gardening Festival** (252-473-4290), Outer Banks Arboretum and Teaching Garden. Educational lectures, plus plant sale and vendors. Free.

Nags Head Woods 5K and 1-Mile Fun Run (www.nagsheadwoods5krun.org). A beach party and buffet at the Ramada Plaza Resort follow the races.

⚑ **Artrageous Art Extravaganza Day** (252-473-5558; www.darearts.org), Dowdy Park, Nags Head.

Dare2Care OBX Shred Fest (www.dare2careobx.com), Soundside Event Site. Professional skateboarders, BMX riders, female roller derby competitors, live music, Kidz Zone, and art vendors.

Kitty Hawk Kites Hang Gliding Spectacular and Air Games (252-4412426; www.kittyhawk.com), Jockey's Ridge State Park. The world's longest running hang gliding competition.

June: **Rogallo Kite Festival** (252-449-2210; www.kittyhawk.com), Jockey's Ridge State Park, MP 12.5. Weekend festival honors the inventor of the flexible wing. Night flight on the beach at the Ramada Plaza Resort.

Family Fishing Tournament (252-255-1501; www.jennettespier.net), Jennette's Pier.

Storm The Beach (www.stormthebeach.org). OBX's only obstacle and adventure race.

July: ⚑ **Wright Kite Festival** (252-441-4127; www.kittyhawk.com), Wright Brothers National Memorial, MP 8. Giant animal and stunt kites fly over the national monument, and kids get to build a kite of their own. Free with NPS admission.

Roll and Stroll (www.obxgalleryrow.com), Gallery Row, Nags Head. Free evening open house crawl of local galleries and businesses.

August: **Sandbar 5K** (252-261-2004; www.outerbanksrelieffoundation.com), Beach Access at MP 4.5. Charity run/walk takes place on the sand in front of the historic Old Station public bathhouse in Kitty Hawk.

⚑ **National Aviation Day** (252-441-7430; www.nps.gov/wrbr). Celebrate Orville Wright's birthday at the Wright Brothers National Memorial.

⚑ **Outer Banks Pirate Festival** (252-441-4127; www.outerbankspiratefestival.com). Weekend festival sponsors swashbuckling events at various venues, with a pirate encampment and a Scallywag School for Young Scoundrels at Jockey's Ridge Crossing. Free.

September: **Outer Banks Arts and Crafts Festival** (www.facebook.com/obxartfestival), Hilton Garden Inn.

ESA Eastern Surfing Championships (757-233-1790 or 1-800-937-4733; www.surfesa.org), Jennette's Pier. The grand finale of the amateur surfing competition season on the East Coast.

Outer Banks Stunt Kite Competition (www.kittyhawk.com), Soundside Event Site, Nags Head. Kite competition set to music. Free stunt and power kite lessons.

Kayak Fishing Tournament (www.khsurf.com), Kitty Hawk Surf Co., Nags Head.

Nags Head Surf Fishing Club Invitational Tournament (www.nagsheadsurffishingclub.org).

SAGA Outer Banks Triathlon (www.outerbankstriathlon.com).

October: **Outer Banks Seafood Festival** (www.outerbanksseafoodfestival.org), Soundside Event Site, MP 16, Bypass. Free festival with live music, cooking demonstrations, and kids' activities showcases Outer Banks seafood.

OBX Brewtag (252-441-4127; www.obxbrewtag.com), Soundside Event Site, MP 16, Nags Head. Local brews meet flying beer kegs. Free.

Halloween International Film Festival and Parade of Costumes (www.obxhalloween.com), Kill Devil Hills. Part of the annual HalloWeek festivities.

November: **Kites with Lights & Hanging with Santa** (252-441-4127; www.kittyhawk.com). Giant illuminated kites fly over Jockey's Ridge State Park beginning at sunset. The Kitty Hawk Kite store in Jockey's Ridge Crossing serves refreshments and offers free Hanging with Santa pictures in a demo hang glider. Free.

Outer Banks Gobbler 5K and Little Giblet Fun Run (www.outerbanksrunningclub.org). Course follows Roanoke Sound.

December: **OBX Festival of Trees** (252-473-5121; www.obhotline.org), Ramada Plaza. Annual event benefits the crisis hotline serving victims of sexual and domestic abuse. Holiday bazaar features items from Hotline Thrift Shops and original weavings.

First Flight Anniversary (252-473-2111; www.nps.gov/wrbr), Wright Brothers National Memorial. Free December 17 celebration includes flybys and guest speakers.

Man Will Never Fly Memorial Society Annual Banquet (www.manwillneverfly.com). Held the night before the First Flight Anniversary, this evening event centers around disputing the "myth" of manned flight and traditionally lasts all night. The society's motto: "Birds fly, men drink." Open to the public.

Poulos Christmas Lights, 622 W. Ocean Acres Drive, Kill Devil Hills. The Poulos family was the 2005 national winner of NBC's *The Today Show* lights contest, thanks to their unique, extensive, and ever-growing holiday lights display. Their house, decorated during the month of December, has become an annual beach tradition.

New Year's Eve 5K (252-441-7299; www.tortugaslie.com), Tortuga's Lie Restaurant, Beach Road, MP 11.5. Go for a run, then head back to the restaurant for a champagne toast.

ROANOKE ISLAND AND THE ALBEMARLE PENINSULA

■

MANTEO AND PIRATE'S COVE

WANCHESE

INTRODUCTION

Roanoke Island and the Albemarle Peninsula:
Mystery and the Mother Vine

Only 12 miles long and about 3 miles wide, **Roanoke Island** packs a lot of history into a small, conveniently toured area. Visitors staying elsewhere on the Outer Banks often make a day trip to Roanoke. However, if you are especially interested in history, you'll find a stay on the island rewarding. This is the location of the famous **Lost Colony**, the earliest attempt by England to settle families in the New World. No one is sure what became of the colony, although speculation and archaeological investigations continue. Visitors have plenty of opportunity to form their own opinions. *The Lost Colony* outdoor drama, **Fort Raleigh National Historical Park**, and the state-run **Roanoke Island Festival Park** all present pieces of the puzzle.

The island of Roanoke rose to importance even before Sir Walter Raleigh attempted to place his ill-fated colony there. Its Native American name, unchanged from then until now, indicates that it was a major manufacturing point for roanoke, elsewhere called wampum, the shell beads used as currency by the natives. The word *roanoke* most literally meant "money."

Early settlers thought they were coming to a paradise. Besides the ample fish and shellfish in the surrounding waters, the area was renowned for its grapevines. The colonists all disappeared, but one of the grapevines growing then lives on. The so-called **Mother Vine**, estimated to be more than 400 years old, continues to thrive in Manteo.

Many landmarks refer to the island's history. The two major towns, **Manteo** and **Wanchese**, are named for two Native American chiefs, who as youths were taken to England by an early voyage of exploration and returned with Raleigh's expeditions. Their roles in the history of the settlement are part of the mystery, but Manteo is generally believed to have been friendly with the newcomers, while Wanchese proved to be hostile. The story is told in fictionalized form in a film shown daily at Roanoke Island Festival Park. Oddly, the feelings of the two chiefs are reflected today in the attitudes of the two villages on the island. Manteo, at the northern end of Roanoke, welcomes guests with a wide variety of attractions and accommodations. Wanchese, on the island's southern tip, works hard to maintain its traditions as a fishing village. You'll find few restaurants here and fewer hotels. But the natives these days are friendly.

GUIDANCE **The Sarah Owens Welcome Center** (252-473-2138 or 1-877-629-4386; www.outerbanks.org), located on the US 64/264 Bypass just over the Virginia Dare Memorial Bridge, is the logical first stop as you reach the Banks. Besides an abundance of information on Outer Banks attractions in Dare County, the expansive complex also offers an accommodation reservation service, a picnic area, and restrooms that are open 24/7. Staffed by friendly natives, the center is open 9–5 every day except Thanksgiving and Christmas. RVers will appreciate the free dump station, available 24/7.

Dare County (252-475-5000; www.darenc.com), 962 Marshall C. Collins Drive, Manteo.

GETTING THERE *By air:* **Dare County Regional Airport/MQI** (252-475-5570; www.darenc.com/airport), Manteo. General aviation airport offers car rentals, air tours, an

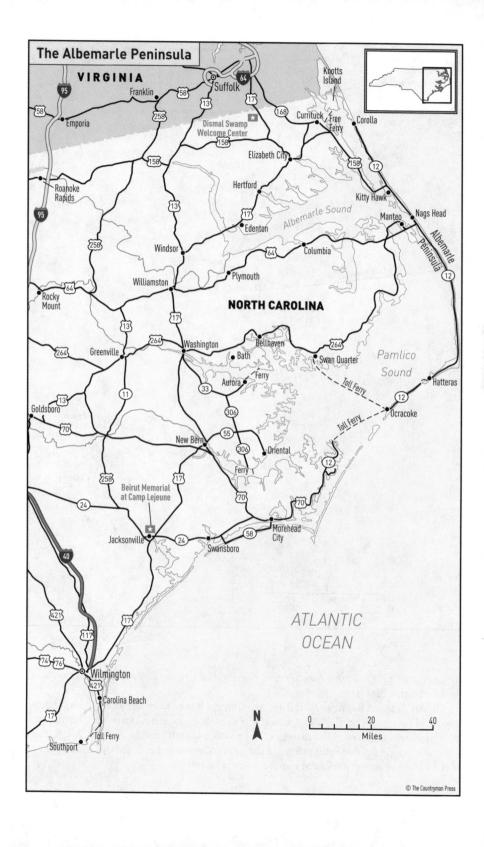

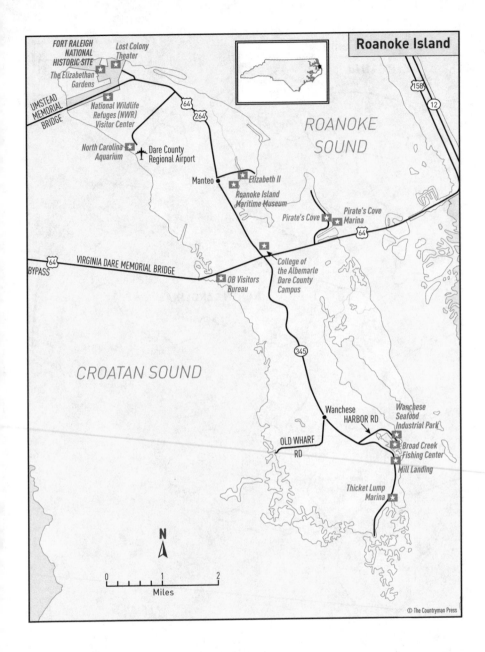

aviation museum, 24-hour fuel service, two lighted runways of 3,300 and 4,300 feet, and amenities for visiting pilots.

By car: To reach Roanoke Island and the Central Banks from the west, you have your choice of two major roads, US 64 and US 264, both of them now four-lane, limited-access highways for most of the distance. The roads start out together from Raleigh, then separate to sweep along either shore of the great Albemarle Peninsula, joining again in Manns Harbor on the mainland opposite Roanoke Island.

TOP 10 ACTIVITIES ON ROANOKE ISLAND

1. Walk the **Manteo boardwalk** and circle **Roanoke Island Festival Park's** island.
2. Bike to the **Umstead Memorial Bridge** and learn the history of the **Freedmen's Colony**.
3. Discover the history of flight in Manteo at the **Dare County Regional Airport Museum**, then take a **flight-seeing tour** to see the Banks from above.
4. Go backstage at *The Lost Colony*.
5. See a film at the **Pioneer Theatre**.
6. Enjoy a glass of wine at the copper bar in the **Tranquil House's 1587 Restaurant**.
7. See the purple martins fly in to roost under the **Umstead Memorial Bridge**.
8. Hear the red wolves howl and see the black bears stroll at **Alligator River Wildlife Refuge**.
9. Visit **Roanoke Island Festival Park** to learn the story of chiefs Manteo and Wanchese.
10. Get lost in the **maze at the Elizabethan Gardens**.

US 64 is the most direct and fastest route, being four lanes as far as Columbia. The trip from Raleigh to Roanoke Island takes about four hours via this route, with a rest stop in Columbia, or about three hours from I-95.

US 264 is currently four-lane as far as Washington, NC. Beyond, it makes its winding way past Lake Mattamuskeet and tiny fishing villages on the peninsula's southern and eastern shores. You can turn off US 264 at Swan Quarter to catch a toll ferry to Ocracoke.

Once they join, the highways split again in Manns Harbor, this time into the older US 64 and the newer US 64/264 Bypass. Each route has its own causeway bridge to Roanoke Island: the older William B. Umstead Memorial Bridge at the northern tip of the island, and the newer Bypass bridge, dubbed the Virginia Dare Memorial, the longest bridge in the state at 5.25 miles.

The Nags Head–Manteo Causeway (US 64/264), an extension of the Bypass, crosses marshy Roanoke Sound, connecting Manteo and Wanchese with NC 12 on the Central Beaches.

GETTING AROUND The island is easy to navigate. The Bypass bisects the island east-west and continues on to Nags Head and the main beaches of the Outer Banks via the Nags Head–Manteo Causeway. A second road runs north/south down the length of the island from the Umstead Memorial Bridge to the docks in Wanchese. The two roads meet at a traffic light.

B&R Car Rentals (252-473-2141; www.facebook.com/BandRRentACar), 404 US 64, Manteo. Owners of the local Ford dealership have been renting cars at the Manteo airport for more than 50 years.

MEDICAL EMERGENCY **Sentara Family Medicine** (252-473-2500; www.sentara.com), 715 N. US 64, Manteo. A family practice associated with Sentara Albemarle Hospital in Elizabeth City.

MANTEO AND PIRATE'S COVE

To outward appearances, Manteo might be any other small fishing village turned to tourism. Narrow streets lead down to the bay. Waterside shops offer practical goods and souvenirs. Boats from far and wide line the docks. But in most fishing villages, you won't find ladies and gents dressed in the finery of 400 years ago strolling the streets and gardens. In Manteo it's not unusual to encounter Queen Elizabeth I, dressed in her brocades, lace ruffs, and strings of pearls, several times a day.

The northern end of Roanoke Island is virtually a historical park, where the year 1587, when Raleigh's colony is believed to have occupied the site, is celebrated. Here, under live oak trees hundreds of years old, the outdoor drama *The Lost Colony* has been presented nightly every summer for over 75 years. Its **Waterside Theatre** sits adjacent to **Fort Raleigh National Historic Site**, where a visitor center displays the latest archaeological findings, and the **Elizabethan Gardens**, a living tribute to the 16th century.

The main town of Manteo lies a few miles south down a broad avenue. Many of the town's restaurants, motels, and a new complex of government buildings lie along this road, US 64, which runs along the back of the town's historic downtown. Stretching from the highway to the waterfront, this historic district, about 10 blocks square, is small, charming, and easily walked. A boardwalk rims the water's edge, with great views any time of day that turn superb at dawn and dusk. Locally owned shops and bed & breakfast inns have colonized the historic homes and renovated storefronts.

An ambitious 20-year plan revitalized the historic waterfront of Manteo. Adopted to prepare the town for the 400th anniversary of Raleigh's original colony, the plan resulted in the building of the *Elizabeth II* replica ship, christened at a ceremony attended by Princess Anne of Britain in 1984. In the years since, many other elements of the plan have come to fulfillment, including a boardwalk and public marina, as well as shops and condominiums along the waterfront. **The Tranquil House Inn**, built to resemble a hotel that welcomed guests in the early 1900s, opened its doors in 1988.

The state of North Carolina has taken an active interest in Manteo and its history, resulting in a cluster of government-subsidized attractions. **Roanoke Island Festival Park**, which completely transformed the environmentally challenged Ice Island, is located directly across Dough Creek from the historic waterfront.

ELIZABETHAN LADIES OFFER REFRESHMENTS UNDER THE ANCIENT LIVE OAKS

THE ELIZABETH II, A RECREATION OF THE SHIPS THAT BROUGHT THE LOST COLONISTS TO THE NEW WORLD, MAKES A COLORFUL BACKDROP FOR THE MANTEO WATERFRONT

It provides the community with a history museum, indoor and outdoor performance venues, plus much more, including a large, free parking lot close to downtown. Other state-funded attractions in Manteo include branches of the **North Carolina Aquarium** and the **Roanoke Island Maritime Museum**.

Manteo's most precious resource, however, is the people who make this their home. A mix of old boat-building families and newer residents who fell in love with the small town's story, the citizens of Manteo extend a warm welcome to visitors from near and far.

PIRATE'S COVE

Located between Roanoke Island and the main beaches to the east, Pirate's Cove is clearly visible—some would say all too visible—from the Manteo waterfront.

Today the site of a gated community, a resort, and a marina boasting a large and successful charter fishing fleet, Pirate's Cove was once called Midgett's Hammock, and before that, Ballast Point. Various bars and restaurants were established on the Hammock, and in the late 1980s development began on one of the region's first gated communities. Developer Glenn Futrell remains committed to keeping Pirate's Cove compatible with its unique location in the midst of a salt marsh. Nearly 500 acres here are protected as a bird sanctuary and wildlife preserve. Pirate's Cove, officially part of the town of Manteo (and sharing its zip code, 27954), is located at the western end of the Washington Baum Bridge on the Nags Head–Manteo Causeway (US 64/264). Many visitors arrive by boat and either stay onboard at the marina or rent a vacation home with its own dock.

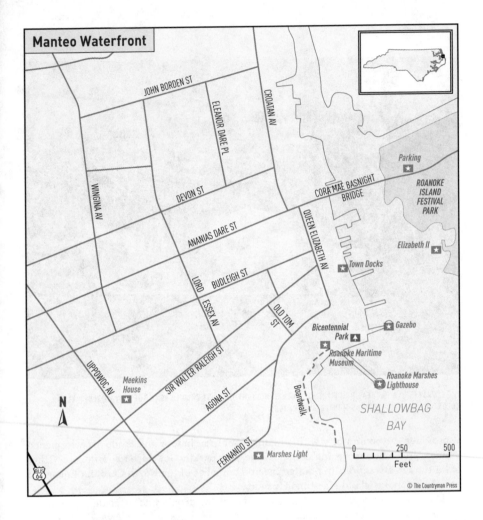

GUIDANCE **Manteo Town Hall** (252-473-2133; www.townofmanteo.com), 407 Budleigh Street.

POST OFFICE The **Manteo Post Office** (252-473-2534) is located at 212 US 64. The zip code for Manteo is 27954.

PUBLIC LIBRARY 🖉 (ᵖ) **Dare County Library** in Manteo (252-473-2372; www.youseemore.com/EARL), 700 US 64.

GETTING AROUND *By bicycle:* Bicycling is an excellent option for getting around the island, thanks to the paved multiuse path that runs from the Business/Bypass junction all the way to the Umstead Memorial Bridge. Several bike rental companies are located along US 64 and down by the boardwalk.

By car: US 64 is the main drag through Manteo, running from the William B. Umstead Memorial Bridge in the north to the traffic light where it meets Bypass US 64/264. Locals usually just refer to it as US 64 or "the highway." Although many businesses are found along this stretch of road, the main business district lies just off it, a compact and walkable 10 square blocks along the waterfront of Shallowbag Bay.

✳ To See

ARCHITECTURE Residents of Manteo have taken a remarkable interest in the community's architectural character through the years, and the town enacted measures to preserve the village's traditional character.

Much of the downtown waterfront was destroyed by a catastrophic fire in 1939. Local historians used the rebuilding process as an opportunity to rename the streets with more evocative titles. Water Street became Queen Elizabeth Avenue, with other streets named for Sir Walter Raleigh, Ananias Dare, and other characters from *The Lost Colony*. Tudor-style architectural details became popular in the 1940s and can still be found in some commercial structures, such as the **Pioneer Theatre**.

Several buildings escaped both fire and development. Today, Manteo's historic downtown is a mix of architectural styles ranging from late Victorian to the Western Plains style popularized by Frank Lloyd Wright. There's even a Sears mail-order arts-and-crafts cottage at 505 Croatan Street.

Two properties are on the National Register of Historic Places: the Queen Anne–style **Meekins House** at 319 Sir Walter Raleigh Street, today the **White Doe Inn**; and the **George W. Creef Jr. House**, at 308 Budleigh Street. The **Manteo Preservation Trust** (www.manteopreservationtrust.com) places bronze MPT plaques on buildings that predate the 1939 fire.

To protect its historic look and small-town atmosphere, Manteo adopted guidelines that all new construction and renovations must follow. At **the Manteo Town website**, www.townofmanteo.com, you can download both a sketchbook of historic properties and a manual of the *Manteo Way of Building*, illustrated with numerous photos. Picket fences are encouraged. Cul-de-sacs are not.

You can see the Manteo Way in action at the new **Marshes Light development** (www.marsheslight.com) at the southern end of the Manteo waterfront, designed to blend seamlessly with the historic village.

ART EXHIBITS Manteo's historic waterfront district makes an attractive location for a variety of art studios and galleries. Most are located within a few blocks of each other. The town's monthly First Friday celebrations include a gallery crawl. See the *Selective Shopping* section for a listing of commercial galleries.

College of the Albemarle Professional Arts Gallery (252-475-9248; www.albemarle.edu), 205 S. US 64. The new Professional Arts Building overlooking Roanoke Sound on the COA Roanoke Island campus houses a gallery that presents changing shows, many associated with the Professional Crafts programs in jewelry and pottery offered at the college.

Dare County Arts Council Gallery (252-473-5558; www.darearts.org), 300

THE HISTORIC COUNTY COURTHOUSE NOW SERVES AS A GALLERY FOR THE ARTS COUNCIL

The story of the Pea Island Life-Saving Station and Richard Etheridge's struggle for civil rights in the 1880s is told in the book *Fire on the Beach*, written by David Wright and David Zoby and recently made into the documentary film *Rescue Men*. For younger readers, Carole Weatherford's *Sink or Swim: African-American Lifesavers of the Outer Banks* tells the story of the heroes of the Pea Island Life-Saving Station.

Queen Elizabeth Avenue. The arts council sponsors several competitions every year, as well as art classes and changing exhibitions at its gallery on the first floor of the historic 1904 Dare County Courthouse in the heart of historic Manteo. Highlights on the gallery calendar include monthly First Friday exhibit openings.

Tuesday Craft Fairs at Magnolia Market Place (252-473-6010; www.townof manteo.com), Magnolia Market Place, corner of Ananias Dare and Queen Elizabeth Streets. Open-air pavilion hosts a Tuesday series of art shows, craft demonstrations, and more May through September.

Roanoke Island Festival Park Art Gallery (252-475-1500; www.roanokeisland.com), 1 Festival Park Boulevard. Part of the state-operated Festival Park complex, this gallery presents important shows of local and regional art in many media.

ATTRACTIONS IN DOWNTOWN MANTEO ♪ **Manteo Weather Tower** (www .townofmanteo.com), Manteo waterfront. One of the few remaining Coastal Warning Display towers left in the country, and possibly the only one with all its original signal lights intact, this tower was restored and moved back to the Manteo waterfront. An information board at the base of the tower explains the meaning of the various flag combinations.

❄ ♿ **Outer Banks History Center** (252-473-2655; www.ncdcr.gov), 1 Festival Park Boulevard, Roanoke Island Festival Park. Open weekdays. This branch of the North

RICHARD ETHERIDGE STILL STANDS GUARD NEAR THE PEA ISLAND LIFE-SAVING STATION MUSEUM

MUST SEE

Roanoke Island Festival Park, located across from the Manteo docks, offers a full roster of activities and amenities to visitors and the Manteo community. Its most visible attraction, the **Elizabeth II**, a replica of a 16th-century sailing vessel like the ones that carried Sir Walter Raleigh's colonists, is docked opposite the Manteo waterfront. Her bright colors advertise the fact that the history interpreted here, the Elizabethan Age, has little in common with the grim groups of Puritans who later settled farther north. The ship is staffed by costumed characters speaking Elizabethan dialect. The **Settlement Site** explores the daily life of the settlers both at work and play. Nearby at the newly updated **American Indian Town**, visitors experience a different way of life, building a log canoe, working a fish trap, harvesting crops, and participating in tribal dances.

There's plenty of inside fun at the Festival Park as well, making it a popular rainy-day destination. In the **Roanoke Adventure Museum**, kids can dress in Elizabethan ruffs and bum rolls or American Indian skin tunics, become sailors, pirates, lifesavers, and duck hunters. The excellent docudrama **The Legend of Two-Path**, exploring Native American attitudes toward the settlers in their midst, screens several times a day in the film theater.

Admission is charged to visit the interpretive areas, the film, and the museum, but other areas of the park, which covers a small island, are free to the public. These include an excellent museum store with many pirate-, Elizabethan-, and American Indian–themed gift items; an art gallery with changing exhibits; the **Outer Banks History Center**; an interpretive boardwalk; picnic tables; and a fossil pit. Not least of the free attractions is the spacious parking lot, located across a short bridge from the busy Manteo waterfront, where parking is often hard to find during the summer season. Art gallery and grounds are free; admission to the **Elizabeth II**, the museum, film, and historical interpretation areas: adults $10, students (6–17) $7, children 5 and under free; tickets are good for two consecutive days. 🐚 ✎ ⚷ ⚙ 🏛 **Roanoke Island Festival Park** and **Elizabeth II** (252-475-1500; www.roanokeisland.com) are open March through December, daily 9–5.

REENACTORS AT ROANOKE ISLAND FESTIVAL PARK SPEAK IN ELIZABETHAN DIALECT

DRESSING UP IN ELIZABETHAN GARB IS ONE OF THE FUN INTERACTIVE ACTIVITIES IN THE ROANOKE ADVENTURE MUSEUM

Carolina State Archives collects and preserves documentary evidence relevant to Outer Banks history, including books, magazines, newspapers, photographs, maps, and a collection of oral histories. The center is open to all, and most services are free. Permanent and temporary exhibits are on display in the History Center Gallery.

⚲ **Pea Island Cookhouse Museum and Herbert M. Collins Boathouse at Collins Park** (252-474-1964; www.townofmanteo.com), 622 Sir Walter Raleigh Street at Bideford Street. Free tours are available; check the town website for hours. This new museum preserves the history of the Pea Island Life-Saving Station, the only one to have an all African American crew. Exhibits detail the many daring rescues performed by these brave men, awarded the Gold Lifesaving Medal in 1996, 100 years after they rescued the crew of the *E. S. Newman* in hurricane-force seas. The museum is housed in the station's original cookhouse, moved to this site and restored by descendants of the lifesavers. Next door, a replica boathouse displays a historic surf boat like those used in sea rescues. Across the street, a bronze statue honors Richard Etheridge, the first African American United States Life-Saving Service keeper at Pea Island Station. Free.

Roanoke Heritage Art Gallery and Military Museum (252-473-2632), 543 Ananias Dare Street. Artist and collector Herbert Bliven displays his original photographs and artwork of local wildlife, lighthouses, and other local scenes, plus driftwood carvings and handcrafted wooden frames at a rustic shop behind his home. The outside is surrounded by buoys, driftwood, and fig trees, all for sale. Inside, glass cases display finds Bliven has made in a lifetime of relic hunting on the Outer Banks, including artifacts from the Civil War, antique hunting decoys, old bottles, and Native American artifacts, plus his collection of uniforms and equipment from World War I through the Korean War. Call for hours. More of Bliven's work can be seen at his son's Roanoke Heritage Extended gallery downtown (see *Selected Shopping*).

⚲ ⚙ ⚳ **Roanoke Island Maritime Museum** (252-475-1750; www.townofmanteo.com or www.roanokeisland.com), 104 Fernando Street. The historic **Creef Boathouse** on the

Manteo waterfront is named for George Washington Creef, creator of the shad boat, the official state boat of North Carolina. On exhibit are several traditional small watercraft, including an 1883 Creef shad boat, dubbed the "pickup truck of the Banks"; spritsail skiffs; and a 1948 Buddy Davis runabout. The *Elizabeth II* replica at Roanoke Island Festival Park was built on-site. Volunteers and staff repair historic boats and build new ones, take visitors on sailing excursions in a shad boat, give classes in boatbuilding and maritime skills, and every summer teach hundreds of children how to sail in the **Outer Banks Sailing Program** (www .townofmanteo.com).

⚙ *⚲* **Roanoke Marshes Lighthouse** (252-475-1750; www.townofmanteo.com), end of the pier on the Manteo waterfront. A reproduction of the cottage-style screw-pile lighthouses that once aided navigation in nearby sounds now helps

SAIL AROUND SHALLOWBAG BAY ON AN AUTHENTIC SHAD BOAT WITH THE ROANOKE ISLAND MARITIME MUSEUM

THE ROANOKE MARSHES LIGHTHOUSE ON THE MANTEO WATERFRONT AND O'NEAL'S CLASSIC CAROLINA BOAT, *ISLAND TIME*

mariners enter Shallowbag Bay. Inside are exhibits on the history of the lighthouse, a wooden hydroplane used in local speedboat races in the 1960s, and an exhibit on local pioneering boatbuilder Warren O'Neal. Outside, you may find *Island Time*, considered one of O'Neal's masterpieces, berthed at the dock. Visiting boaters can tie up to this pier for complimentary overnight mooring. Free.

A STATUE IN THE ELIZABETHAN GARDENS CELEBRATES THE QUEEN ELIZABETH ROSE

ATTRACTIONS AT THE NORTH END OF ROANOKE ISLAND ❋ ♿ **Dare County Regional Airport Museum** (252-475-5575; www.darenc.com/departments /airport/museum), 410 Airport Road. Open daily 8–7. The aviation history of Dare County may have begun with the Wright brothers, but it didn't end there. Find out the rest of the story at these exhibits, housed in the regional airport at the north end of Roanoke Island. The airport, commissioned as a Naval Auxiliary Air Station during World War II, served as a base for Civil Air Patrol antisubmarine searches and as a training facility for many famous Navy air squadrons, including the VF-17 "Jolly Rogers." The Ready Room of aviator Dave Driscoll details the history of aviation in the region, from the barnstorming days of the 1920s to the dawn of the jet era. Free.

WARREN O'NEAL AND ROANOKE ISLAND BOATBUILDING

Credited as the father of boatbuilding on Roanoke Island and the originator of the Carolina style of sportfishing boat, Warren O'Neal was born in Manteo in 1910 and worked as a commercial fisherman and charter boat captain. In 1959, he designed and built a boat with a deep V-shaped hull to help him cut through the chop in Oregon Inlet and the rough seas beyond. Up until then, most boats on the Banks had flatter bottoms to help them keep afloat in the shallow inshore waters, but blue marlin had recently been striking in the Gulf Stream, and charter captains and their customers were eager to go out after this legendary game fish. Many of the boatbuilders who would become famous for their Carolina-style sportsfishing boats worked with O'Neal in the early years, including Omie Tillett, Sheldon Midgett, and Buddy Davis. To delve deeper into the O'Neal legacy, visit the Outer Banks History Center at Roanoke Island Festival Park, where the papers from his boatworks are archived. (See the "South Bodie Island and Oregon Inlet" chapter for more on the Carolina-style boat, and the "Wanchese" chapter for boats being built on Roanoke Island today.)

✳ 🐾 ♿ ✒ ⚥ **The Elizabethan Gardens** (252-473-3234; www.elizabethangardens.org), 1411 National Park Drive. Open daily; hours vary seasonally. Begun as a project of the Garden Club of North Carolina during the 1950s, the site, on the shores of Roanoke Sound, has developed into a rich complex of gardens that delights history lovers, art lovers, and nature lovers alike. The gardens are embellished with many works of sculpture and include a Shakespearean herb garden, a sunken garden, a maze, and superb collections of camellias and rhododendrons, with something in bloom year-round. The Queen's Rose Garden features the Queen Elizabeth rose, a gift from Queen Elizabeth II. Many special programs are included with admission, including weekday programs for children during the summer season. Adults $9; youths $6; children 5 and under $2; dogs $3; reduced admission on Virginia Dare's birthday, August 18.

✳ ✒ ♿ **Fort Raleigh National Historic Site** (252-473-5772; www.nps.gov/fora), 1401 National Park Drive. The NPS visitor center is open 9–5 daily year-round (except Christmas Day), and grounds are open dawn to dusk. June–Labor Day, the visitor center stays open until 6 PM, and the grounds remain open until the completion of *The Lost Colony* outdoor drama. Located between the Elizabethan Gardens and *The Lost Colony*'s Waterside Theatre, the Lindsay Warren Visitor Center exhibits artifacts found on Roanoke Island and tells the story of early explorations and the first English attempts at colonization in the New World. A documentary, *Roanoke: The Lost Colony*, is shown daily. The site contains an earthen fort built in the style used by the adventurers and a nature trail with signs that identify the native plants found in the area in 1585 by naturalist Thomas Harriot. A longer trail leads to an interpretive display on the Freedmen's Colony on the shores of Roanoke Sound. Archaeological investigations are ongoing. In summer a range of free activities is

WINDMILLS WERE A FREQUENT SIGHT ON THE OUTER BANKS IN THE EARLY DAYS

offered, including nature hikes and visits to the park's museum collection building, as well as special programs on the Freedmen's Colony. Free.

The Freedmen's Colony of Roanoke Island (www.roanokefreedmenscolony .com) existed from 1862 to 1867 and was home to an estimated 3,500 people, nearly all of them enslaved people who had fled Confederate-controlled areas and sought protection from the Union army. The actual site of the timber town remains lost. It's yet another of Roanoke Island's archaeological mysteries. An interpretive display is located at the northern end of the Manteo Bike Path at the foot of the Umstead Memorial Bridge in a small park, which also has a sandy beach and parking lot on the sound. Another site connected with the Freedmen's Colony is **Cartwright Park** at 303 Bideford Street. The park sits on the grounds of the first church, dated to 1865, of Andrew Cartwright, founder of AME Zion churches in the Albemarle area. Cartwright Park has a picnic shelter, restrooms, grills, and a playground. Free.

THE NATIONAL WILDLIFE REFUGES GATEWAY CENTER INCLUDES EXHIBITS ON 11 DIFFERENT REFUGES

✿ **Island Farm** (252-473-5440; www .theislandfarm.com), 1140 US 64 at Buzzy Lane. Open April–November. The last remaining pre–Civil War farmhouse on Roanoke Island is now a living history museum. A dozen farm buildings have been restored, including a windmill relocated from Nags Head. Farm animals of the types raised in the 1850s, including sheep, oxen, chickens, and Banker horses, now live in the barns and pastures. A new welcome center houses exhibits on island culture, boatbuilding, windmills, and the Freedmen's Colony. Admission $8; children 5 and under free.

✿ ⛏ **National Wildlife Refuges Gateway Visitor Center** (252-473-113; www.fws.gov/ ncgatewayvc), 100 Conservation Way. Open daily except Thanksgiving and Christmas. Manteo's newest attraction, located across US 64 from Fort Raleigh, offers exhibits and information on 11 different wildlife refuges along the Carolina and Virginia coasts. Interactive exhibits include a Cessna "fly-over" of the refuges; dioramas of many indigenous species, including red wolves, black bears, and eagles; exhibits of wildlife art; and a theater showing three different productions, including the story of Buffalo City, a moonshining town once hidden in the depths of the Alligator River swamp. Four nature trails cross the center's 35 acres if you want to stretch your legs. Free.

✳ ✿ ⚬ ⛏ ✿ **North Carolina Aquarium at Roanoke Island** (252-473-3494 or 1-800-832-3474; www.ncaquariums.com), 374 Airport Road. Open daily 9–5 year-round. Closed Thanksgiving Day, Christmas Day, and New Year's Day. One of three state aquariums located along the North Carolina coast, this one presents exhibits exploring the waters of the Outer Banks, from the rivers pouring into the sounds to the marine communities offshore in the deep ocean. Highlights include a one-third scale model of the USS

THE RED WOLVES OF NORTH CAROLINA

Alligator River and a few other refuges in eastern North Carolina are home to over 100 free roaming wild red wolves. The species was declared officially extinct in the wild in 1980. The wolves in eastern North Carolina are descended from a captive breeding program using 14 wolves from southern Louisiana. In 1987, some of these wolves were released at the Alligator River refuge, where they continue to multiply and expand their territory. For more about the Red Wolf Recovery Program, visit the Fish and Wildlife Service website (www.fws.gov/redwolf) or contact the Red Wolf Coalition (252-796-5600; www.redwolves.com).

EXHIBIT ON RED WOLVES AT THE NATIONAL WILDLIFE REFUGES GATEWAY CENTER

Monitor in the Graveyard of the Atlantic gallery and the *Operation: Sea Turtle Rescue* exhibit. A nature trail leads to exhibits along the sound. A changing menu of activities is offered daily, including films, feedings, and dive shows. Adults $8; seniors (62+) $7; children (3–17) $6; 2 and under free.

✳ To Do

AIR TOURS Aviation companies based at the **Dare County Airport** (252-475-5570; www.darenc.com/Airport), located at the northern end of Roanoke Island, take you high above dunes and surf, providing a unique view of the fragile environment we call the Outer Banks. Lighthouses, marine wildlife, shipwrecks on the bottom of the ocean—all can be seen best from above.

Barrier Island Aviation (252-473-4247; www.barrierislandaviation.com), 407 Airport Road. Air tours in a vintage Waco biplane or a high-winged Cessna. Sunrise and sunset flights available.

Coastal Helicopters (252-475-4354; www.obxhelicopters.com), 410 Airport Road. Get pictures from high above the Banks in a three-seat, air-conditioned 'copter.

OBX Biplanes (252-216-7777; www.obx biplanes.com), 407 Airport Road. Tour the Banks in an open-cockpit 1990 reproduction Waco biplane.

Outer Banks Air Charters and Tours (252-256-2322; www.outerbanks aircharters.com), 410 Airport Road. Five people can tour aboard this Piper craft. Charter flights are available to any OBX airport from your home airport as well.

MUSCADINE GRAPE VINES CONTINUE TO FLOURISH ON ROANOKE ISLAND

BICYCLING **Roanoke Voyages Corridor Bike Path** (252-475-1500; www.roanoke voyagescorridor.com). Manteo is blessed with this wide, paved multiuse path, suitable for walking, jogging, cycling, and roller-blading, that runs along US 64 from the Umstead Memorial Bridge to the junction with

KITTY HAWK KITES CREATE A COLORFUL DISPLAY IN MANTEO'S DOWNTOWN

THE MOTHER VINE

Now located on private property along Mother Vineyard Road in Manteo, this scuppernong vine still produces fat, white grapes. Experts estimate its age to be at least 400 years old and speculate that it may have been first cultivated by the American Indians in the area before Raleigh's English colonists arrived. The Mother Vine has a central trunk about 2 feet around, and its vines cover about half an acre.

In 2010, the ancient vine had a brush with destruction when a contractor killing weeds under power lines inadvertently sprayed an outlying runner with a powerful herbicide that follows vines to their roots. The Mother Vine began to wither and die. Agriculture specialists rushed to Manteo to treat the injured plant, and the vine seems to have survived the attack.

Early explorers reported that the shores of North Carolina, when first discovered, were thick with grape vines. These grapes, native to the Southeast, were muscadines, a particularly hearty species with an extra chromosome that defends them from the diseases and insects that plague European varietals planted here. Scuppernongs are one of the 250 varieties of muscadine.

The discovery of the many health benefits of the muscadine grape has sparked increased interest in both the grape and the wine made from it. Two extremely powerful antioxidants—resveratrol and quercetin—are found in concentrated form in muscadine juice. The Mothervine Nutraceutical Company (www.themothervine.com) uses grapes grown from Mother Vine cuttings to create supplements, juices, and other healthful products. You can even order your own Mother Vine cutting, ready for planting. Part of the company's proceeds go to support the nonprofit Outer Banks Conservationists, who preserve the Currituck Lighthouse and Manteo's Island Farm, and one day will have the care of the Mother Vine itself.

Other companies have used cuttings from the Mother Vine to create new vineyards. Duplin Winery (www.duplinwinery.com), in Rose Hill, North Carolina, just off I-40, is the world's largest muscadine wine producer and has mature vines grown from Mother Vine cuttings. Its Mother Vine Scuppernong Wine, first released in 2008, was the first wine made from Mother Vine grapes in 100 years.

NC 345 and the US 64/264 Bypass. From the light at that intersection, it continues as a wide paved shoulder over the Washington Baum Causeway Bridge to Whalebone Junction in Nags Head. More than 8 miles long, the multiuse path joins downtown Manteo with the Lost Colony district at the north end of the island, ending at the Freedmen's Colony Memorial. The ride is both cool and colorful, running beneath live oak trees and crape myrtles that bloom all summer. A nice side trip takes bikers around a loop composed of Scuppernong and Mother Vineyard roads. Along the way you'll pass the oldest-known grapevine in the country, the so-called Mother Vine, estimated to be more than 400 years old. The vine is now on private property, so take a look from the road.

If you are coming to Manteo to ride the bike path, good paved parking areas are located at **Roanoke Island Festival Park**, the **Fort Raleigh National Historic Site**, and the end of the path at the **Umstead Memorial Bridge**. The paved paths within the national park are also open for biking.

Manteo Cyclery (252-305-0306; www.manteocyclery.com), 312 US 64. Road and fat-tire bikes available to rent. Repairs available.

Manteo Kitty Hawk Kites (252-473-2357; www.kittyhawk.com), 307 Queen Elizabeth Street. Single, tandem, and children's bikes, plus infant seats and trailers, are available by the hour, day, or week at this shop on the Manteo waterfront.

BIRD-WATCHING Roanoke Island and the adjacent Albemarle Peninsula contain exceptional opportunities for birding year-round. **The North Carolina Birding Trail** (919-604-5183; www.ncbirdingtrail.org) identifies 11 places to look for birds in the area. Popular spots for birding on Roanoke Island include the area around Dare County Airport (swallows, martins, upland sandpipers); the freshwater pond at the foot of Umstead Memorial Bridge (warblers); Sunnyside Lane (hummingbirds); and the Roanoke Island Marsh Game Land (wading and shore birds).

Country Girl (252-473-5881; www.countrygirlcharters.com), Pirate's Cove Marina. Charter this boat that can carry up to 27 people for pelagic birding expeditions on the Gulf Stream led by experts.

Manns Harbor Purple Martin Roost (252-305-5753; www.purplemartinroost.com). The Umstead Memorial Bridge at the north end of Roanoke Island has gained fame as a roosting location for huge flocks of purple martins every summer. Over 100,000 birds can be observed returning to roost under the bridge at dusk. The **Coastal Carolina Purple Martin Society** coordinates educational programs at the Betty Dean "BeBop" Fearing fishing pier and observation platform on the Manns Harbor side of the bridge on selected evenings from July 15 to August 25, when the martins reach their greatest numbers. The *Crystal Dawn* **headboat** (www.crystaldawnheadboat.com) out of Pirate's Cove offers guided sunset ecocruises during the last two weeks of July and the first

THE *DOWNEAST ROVER* SETS OUT ON A WEDDING SAIL

two weeks of August to watch the martins come in to roost. Funds raised benefit the Coastal Carolina Purple Martin Society. Call 252-473-5577 for reservations.

BOATING AND BOAT CRUISES ♿ **North Carolina Fish and Wildlife** (www.ncwildlife .org) maintains free public boat ramps into Croatan Sound at the west end of Bowsertown Road in Manteo and in Manns Harbor on US 64.

Manteo has a public boat ramp downtown at Edward's Landing, on Queen Elizabeth Avenue at the foot of the Basnight Bridge.

Public docks are available for daytime use on the Manteo waterfront along the boardwalks leading to the Roanoke Marshes Lighthouse and the town gazebo.

Charter Private Sailing (252-473-2719; www.sailouterbanks.com), Manteo waterfront. Charter the *Sea'Scape*, a 41-foot Gulfstar ketch, for a private sight-seeing or sunset sail with up to six people.

⚜ *Downeast Rover* **Sailing Cruises** (252-473-4866; www.downeastrover.com), Manteo waterfront. If you are visiting Manteo late spring through early fall, you're sure to notice the lovely ship with red sails entering Shallowbag Bay. This is the *Downeast Rover*, a 55-foot topsail schooner, offering three cruises a day, including one at sunset, from the Manteo boardwalk.

⚓ **Shallowbag Bay Sail About** (252-475-1750; www.townofmanteo.com), Roanoke Island Maritime Museum, 104 Fernando Street. Every Tuesday during the summer months, volunteers from the maritime museum take visitors out for a free sunset sail on an authentic shad boat, the official state boat of North Carolina. Suggested donation $5.

CANOEING AND KAYAKING **Kitty Hawk Kayak and Surf School** (252-261-0145 or 1-866-702-5061; www.khkss.com). Experienced guides offer paddling tours of the Alligator River National Wildlife Refuge, as well as Roanoke Island ecotours and full-moon paddles.

Manteo Kitty Hawk Kites (252-473-2357; www.kittyhawk.com), 307 Queen Elizabeth Street. Rent single or tandem kayaks or stand-up paddleboards right on the waterfront to explore Shallowbag Bay and surrounding waters. You can launch from a floating dock behind the shop. This location also offers guided kayak trips along the Manteo waterfront as well as paddles into the Alligator River National Wildlife Refuge to explore the cypress swamp that concealed one of Prohibition's most famous moonshine capitals. For reservations, call 1-877-359-8447.

🛶 **Roanoke Island Outfitters** (252-473-1356; www.roanokeislandoutfittersanddivec enter.com). Pam Malec Landrum, the author of *Guide to Sea Kayaking in North Carolina*, leads kayak ecotours and special children's activity tours. Her company also offers kayaking lessons and rents kayaks, including fishing kayaks, with free delivery to put-ins on Roanoke Island and Nags Head.

DOLPHIN WATCH *Capt. Johnny's* **Outer Banks Dolphin Cruises** (252-473-1475; www.outerbankscruises.com). Dolphin watches (sightings guaranteed) on the *Capt. Johnny*, a covered, pontoon-style boat (complete with restroom), depart from the Manteo waterfront June to October. Dolphin mating and births are often observed. Private charters and shrimping/crabbing cruises also available.

Miss Bodie Island **Dolphin Watch Cruises** (252-449-8999; www.nagsheaddolphin watch.com), Shallowbag Bay Marina, 1100-B S. Bay Club Drive. Naturalists from the **Outer Banks Center for Dolphin Research** (www.obxdolphins.org) conduct tours, explaining the dolphin life cycle and identifying individual dolphins aboard a 35-foot pontoon boat with padded seats, a top for shade, and a restroom.

DRIVING TOUR **Civil War Trail Sites** (www.civilwartraveler.com). Although fortified by Confederate troops, Roanoke Island fell to the Union army in February 1862. Former slaves came to the island to be under the protection of the federal authorities and built the Freedmen's Colony on a site now lost. Several brown markers recounting Civil War events are scattered around the island. A sign about the **Battle of Roanoke Island** is located on the east side of NC 345 just south of the US 64/264 traffic light. One on the **Burnside Expedition of 1862**, describing the Union capture of the island, is at the Manteo Outer Banks Welcome Center on US 64/264 Bypass. The **Gateway to the Albemarle** marker, explaining the strategic importance of Roanoke Island, is located on the mainland side of the Umstead Memorial Bridge on US 64.

FISHING A North Carolina Coastal Recreational Fishing License is required at these free public piers.

♿ **BeBop's Multi Purpose Pier** (www.darenc.com), west end of the Umstead Memorial Bridge in Manns Harbor. Noted for purple martin viewing (see *Bird-Watching*), crabbing, fishing, and photography.

♿ **Roanoke Sound Boat Access and Fishing Pier** (www.ncwildlife.org), western end of the Nags Head–Manteo Causeway.

♿ **Washington Baum Bridge Roanoke Sound Boating Access Area** (www.ncwildlife.org). The public dock and pier under the Washington Baum Bridge on the south side of the Nags Head–Manteo Causeway, just opposite Pirate's Cove, is a popular spot for crabbing and fishing. Large parking lot, restrooms, and public boat ramp available.

FISHING TOURNAMENTS **Pirate's Cove Big Game Tournaments** (252-305-3610; www.pcbgt.com). The Tournament Pavilion at Pirate's Cove serves as the headquarters of many fishing tournaments each year. Most include a variety of events, including meals, open to the public for a fee. Highlights include the family-friendly **Small Fry Tournament** in June; the **Carolina Boat Builders Challenge** (www.dcbbf.org), open only to those with custom boats built in North or South Carolina; and in August a double bill of billfish, with the **Alice Kelly Memorial Ladies Only Billfish Tournament** followed by the **Pirate's Cove Billfish Tournament**. November brings the **Inshore Slam** (www.rockfishrodeo.org), formerly the Rockfish Rodeo, benefiting the scholarship fund of the Manteo Rotary Club.

FOR FAMILIES Public playgrounds are located in Manteo next to the Old Fishing Hole on Airport Road; at Manteo Elementary School, 701 N. US 64; at Cartwright Park, Sir Walter Raleigh Street; and on the Manteo waterfront.

♪ **Ghost Tours of the Outer Banks** (252-573-1450; www.ghosttoursoftheobx.com). Walking tours begin at the Manteo Town Center Kiosk. Reservations required.

♪ ☗ **Lost Colony Children's Show** (252-473-2127; www.thelostcolony.org), Waterside Theatre. Selected weekday afternoons, June–August. Every year, the cast of *The Lost Colony* presents a special play just for kids. Performances are held in the air-conditioned Gazebo Theatre. Tickets $10. The company also offers five-day Theatre Arts Camps with sessions for kids from rising first-graders to age 12.

♪ **Pirate Adventures of the Outer Banks** (252-473-2007; www.pirateadventuresobx.com), 408 Queen Elizabeth Avenue, Manteo waterfront. The pirate ship *Sea Gypsy* sets sail from the Manteo docks several times a day during the summer for a pirate adventure complete with messages in a bottle, sunken treasure, and battles with water cannon. Arrive early for dress-up and face painting to transform the young ones into pirates or mermaids.

♪ ☗ **Roanoke Island Festival Park Children's Shows** (252-475-1500; www.roanokeisland.com). University theater departments and touring companies from around the state offer special plays for children, often with audience participation, on selected mornings. Tickets $5 for six and up; five and under free. The park also sponsors one-day summer activities for kids ranging from crabbing to watercolor painting. Fees vary.

HEALTH AND FITNESS ☞ **Dare County Center** (252-475-9270; www.darenc.com/DCCenter), Dare County Government Complex, 950 Marshall C. Collins Drive off US 64. This facility for all ages has a state-of-the-art fitness room, a variety of exercise classes offered at low rates, health and wellness programs, plus arts and crafts classes, trips, and a media room with free computers to use as well as free Wi-Fi. Most programs are free for seniors. Stop by for an orientation tour.

Nautics Hall Health & Fitness Complex (252-473-2101; www.elizabethaninn.com), 814 US 64. The Elizabethan Inn's fitness center offers exercise equipment, a free-weight room, and the largest heated indoor pool on the Outer Banks, plus a whirlpool and sauna. Passes available for those not staying at the inn.

HEADBOATS *Country Girl* (252-473-5881; www.countrygirlcharters.com), Pirate's Cove Marina. The 57-foot *Country Girl*, owned by the family who runs Big Al's Grill, takes larger groups out for private Gulf Stream charters and winter rockfish trips, plus headboat-style bottom fishing, Ashes at Sea memorial services, and pelagic birding expeditions.

Crystal Dawn (252-473-5577; www.crystaldawnheadboat.com), Pirate's Cove Marina, 2000 Sailfish Point. A 65-foot party boat, sister to the *Country Girl*, takes up to 150 anglers out for half-day fishing trips in inlet and sound. All bait, tackle, and licenses furnished. Families with children welcome. Sunset sight-seeing cruises are also available at very reasonable rates.

SAILING LESSONS The ⚓ **Outer Banks Sailing Program at the Roanoke Island Maritime Museum** (252-475-1750; www.townofmanteo.com) gives school-age sailors five days of sailing experience, with special classes in racing. Applications can be submitted as early as January 1 and can be found online.

SKATEPARK ⚓ **Manteo Skateboard Park** (252-473-2133; www.townofmanteo.com), Uppowac Street, between Marshes Light and College of the Albemarle's Roanoke Island campus. Free and open to the public.

SKYDIVING **Skydive OBX** (252-678-5867; www.skydiveobx.com), Dare County Regional Airport, 410 Airport Road. Discounts available for students and military.

TENNIS Tennis courts at **Manteo Middle School** (252-473-5549; mms.daretolearn .org), 1000 US 64, and at **Manteo High School** (252-473-5841; mhs.daretolearn.org), 829 Wingina Avenue, are open for public use after school hours.

WATER SPORTS **Manteo Kitty Hawk Kites** (252-473-2357 or 1-877-359-8447; www .kittyhawk.com), 307 Queen Elizabeth Street, Manteo waterfront. In addition to kayak and bike rentals, this location offers SUP rentals and lessons, and parasailing for singles, doubles, or triples over Shallowbag Bay. Prices rise with the altitude, up to 1,200 feet. This is also the place to try some of the newest water sports thrills: Jetpaks or Flyboards.

Roanoke Island Outfitters and Dive Center (252-473-1356; www.roanokeisland outfittersanddivecenter.com), 627 US Hwy 64/264. Formerly Nags Head Diving, this outfitter, operated by Matt and Pam Landrum, has expanded to offer even more outdoor adventures. On the diving side, a wide variety of scuba courses are available, plus boat or shore dives and night dives to historic wrecks, are available, along with rental scuba and snorkel gear, spearfishing charters, and inshore fishing charters.

✳ Green Space

SWIMMING HOLES While you won't find much surf on the shores of Roanoke Island, you can join the locals at their favorite swimming holes. It's a long-standing community tradition to

THE BASNIGHT BRIDGE IN DOWNTOWN MANTEO LEADS TO FESTIVAL PARK

THE JOCKEY'S RIDGE DUNE CAN BE SEEN ACROSS THE SOUND FROM ROANOKE ISLAND FESTIVAL PARK

swim just off the Manteo waterfront, and you'll often see local kids keeping cool next to the Basnight Bridge, which arches over Dough Creek to Festival Park. Look for the swim platform on the south side of the bridge.

For a more structured experience, take a dip at the **Old Swimming Hole** (252-475-5910; www.darenc.com/ParksRec), on Croatan Sound at 410 Airport Road next to the North Carolina Aquarium. Maintained by Dare County, the park has a sandy beach, playground, volleyball court, picnic tables, grills, and restrooms. A lifeguard is on duty daily 10–6 from Memorial Day to Labor Day.

WALKS **Manteo High School Wetland Boardwalk** (252-473-5841), Manteo High School, 829 Wingina Avenue. Students worked with the UNC Coastal Studies Institute to build a cistern, rain garden, and public education boardwalk, located behind the high school.

(((•))) ⟿ **Manteo Waterfront Boardwalk and Roanoke Island Festival Park** (www.town ofmanteo.com or www.roanokeisland.com). Take a stroll along the Manteo water-front for relaxing views of marsh and sound. The boardwalk stretches all the way to the Marshes Light Marina, curving around a bit of marsh, and passes in front of the maritime museum. Continuing along the town docks, you pass a pirate-themed playground, the Roanoke Marshes Light, and the town gazebo. Next walk over the Cora Mae Daniels Basnight Bridge. The sidewalk will take you to another boardwalk, this one along the shores of the island that houses Festival Park, with a view of the high, white dunes of Jockey's Ridge across the sound. Interpretive signs tell of the environmental restoration of this once badly damaged shoreline. Public restrooms and parking are located at Roanoke Island Festival Park and next to the maritime museum on Fernando Street.

Roanoke Island Marsh Game Land (252-482-7701; www.ncwildlife.org), NC 345, south of Manteo. Short walking trail leads to views of a 40-acre waterfowl impoundment and a black needlerush marsh.

  Trails at Fort Raleigh National Historic Site (252-473-5772; www.nps.gov/fora), 1401 National Park Drive. The 1.25-mile **Freedom Trail** leads from the parking lot in front of the Elizabethan Gardens to the Freedmen's Colony exhibit at the foot of the Umstead Memorial Bridge. Along the way, signs identify plants used in the native Algonquian culture. The shorter **Thomas Harriot Nature Trail** winds on sandy paths under old live oaks down to the shore. Signs here hold quotes from Harriot's journals on the local flora he found in the New World and the ways colonists used them. Both trails are paved and open to both pedestrians and bicycles.

❋ Lodging

Roanoke Island is a rarity among major vacation destinations. Not even one chain hotel or motel has taken root here. Nearly all accommodations are locally owned and operated, often by families who have lived on the Outer Banks for generations.

Seasonal demand can drive up prices to extravagant heights. A room that rents for $59 a night in January may go for $199 in July. Valentine's Day weekend is also a time of high tariffs in Manteo, with its many romantic bed & breakfasts, as are May and June, when wedding parties come to town.

Many accommodations require two-night minimum stays on the weekends and three-night minimums on holiday weekends. Some also require notice of cancellations many days in advance in order to retrieve your deposit, up 50 percent of the total price. Many accommodations on Roanoke Island are now pet friendly, often with an additional pet fee required.

BED & BREAKFASTS (ᐧᐧ) **Burrus House Inn Waterfront Suites** (252-475-1636; www.burrushouse.com), 509 S. US 64. Away from the bustle but within walking distance of the Manteo waterfront, this classic Carolina beach house offers views of Shallowbag Bay from all eight elegantly appointed guest suites, all with both bedrooms and sitting rooms, fireplaces, ceiling fans, refrigerators,

microwaves, and coffeemakers. Baths feature Jacuzzi tubs and showers big enough for two. Kitchens are stocked with continental breakfast items, coffee, tea, wine, cheese, and crackers. The tower suites with cathedral ceilings are popular with honeymooners. Private and quiet with few distractions, the Burrus is best suited to couples seeking a romantic getaway. $$$$.

🐾 🐶 ♂ (ᐧᐧ) **Cameron House Inn** (252-473-6596 or 1-800-279-8178; www.cameronhouseinn.com), 300 Budleigh Street. Just a block from the Manteo waterfront, this restored 1919 Arts and Crafts bungalow features comfortable rooms with period decorations, plus lots of common areas where you can relax and mix with other guests. Favorite gathering places are the front porch, furnished with wicker furniture and an antique swing, and a large jasmine vine-covered back porch, where rocking chairs surround a fireplace. Breakfasts of muffins, juice, coffee, or tea are served in the dining room, and fresh-baked cookies and other goodies are available around the clock. The innkeepers are guidebook writers and very helpful in suggesting local activities. The inn is home to several cats. Children are welcome. Bicycles are included in the room rate. No smoking is allowed inside. $$–$$$.

🐾 ♂ (ᐧᐧ) **Roanoke Island Inn** (252-473-5511 or 1-877-473-5511; www.roanokeislandinn.com), 305 Fernando Street. With an unsurpassed Manteo location and a long tradition of

EXCURSIONS

WALK ON THE WILDSIDE: ALLIGATOR RIVER AND THE ALBEMARLE PENINSULA

Just over the bridges from Roanoke Island lies the Dare County mainland, a network of wildlife refuges, state parks, conservation and game lands, preserves, a wilderness of brackish marsh, freshwater lakes, and wooded wetlands. US 64 and US 264, which run together through Roanoke Island, divide as they reach the mainland and sweep out north and south to embrace this immense area of undeveloped land called the Albemarle Peninsula. Man has made few inroads into this wilderness, although not for lack of trying. Numerous land development companies over the years have sought to drain Lake Mattamuskeet and convert the rich bottomland into farms, and a great pumping station still stands as a monument to the endeavor. But the water always comes creeping back. Today, a few farms grow cotton, sweet potatoes, and onions as sweet as Vidalias. Along the marshy coast, US 264 passes the little fishing villages of Stumpy Point, Engelhard, and Swan Quarter, largely untouched by tourism. The towns along US 64, Columbia and Plymouth, once important seaports along Albemarle Sound, quietly dream of their historic pasts. Most of the vast interior is managed by a patchwork of federal and state agencies.

THE MATTAMUSKEET LODGE, A FORMER PUMPING STATION INTENDED TO DRAIN THE LAKE, IS BEING RESTORED

Wildlife, including black bear, deer, and American alligator, is found here in abundance. The U.S. Fish and Wildlife Service is reintroducing the endangered red wolf into the area. Every winter, the lakes in the region host huge flocks of migrating tundra swans, ducks, and snow geese, making this one of the best bird-watching areas on the East Coast. Bald eagles, ospreys, and wading birds live here all year. Spring and fall, migrating songbirds stop here on their journeys, filling the forests and swamps with their music.

🖉 🌲 The **National Wildlife Refuges Visitor Center** (252-473-1131; www.fws.gov/ncgatewayvc), on the Manteo side of the Umstead Memorial Bridge, provides an overview of the natural preserves on the Albemarle Peninsula and beyond, and takes reservations for programs. Open 9–4 daily, except Thanksgiving and Christmas. Free.

🖉 ♿ **Alligator River National Wildlife Refuge** (www.fws.gov/alligatorriver) is one of the most accessible of the area's refuges, thanks to its location just west of Roanoke Island and the Outer Banks. ♿ The **Creef Cut Wildlife Trail**, on US 64, a paved, half-mile interpreted trail, leads to an accessible fishing platform. Several ranger programs begin here, including 🖉 **Red Wolf Howlings**, bear interpretive talks, and

GREAT BLUE HERONS ARE AMONG THE WADING BIRDS THAT FREQUENT THE LAKES AND MARSHES OF THE ALBEMARLE PENINSULA

tram and van tours. **Peterson Wildlife Drive**, a 5-mile unpaved road for cars or mountain bikes, where sightings of black bears are very frequent, also begins here. Other public-use areas are located at the end of unpaved Buffalo City Road, including & **Sandy Ridge Wildlife Trail**, a half-mile earth path and boardwalk through a cypress swamp, and a boat ramp for the refuge's 15 miles of paddling trails on Milltail Creek.

Mattamuskeet Lodge (www.mattamuskeet lodge.com), the grand pumping station on the shores of Lake Mattamuskeet, presides over one of the country's largest gatherings of swans and other waterfowl every winter.

Palmetto-Peartree Preserve (www.palmetto peartree.org), northeast of Columbia, is about 38 miles from Manteo. Known locally as P3, the preserve is home to one of the last large populations of the endangered red-cockaded woodpecker. Several trails and boardwalks lead through the preserve, as does a paddling trail with a camping platform on Hidden Lake for overnight stays. Free.

Pettigrew State Park (www.ncparks.gov), centered on Lake Phelps, one of the cleanest lakes in North Carolina, is a paradise for paddling, bass fishing, and hiking through sweet gum and cypress forests. **Somerset Place State Historic Site** (www.nchistoricsites.org), also on the shores of Lake Phelps, was one of the largest plantations in the upper South before the Civil War. Its reconstructed buildings offer a realistic view of the life of all its inhabitants, from the plantation owners to the workers of African descent, both enslaved and free. Located south of US 64, about an hour's drive west of Manteo, both the state park and historic site are free to visit.

In Columbia, the **Tyrrell County Visitor Center** (www.visittyrrellcounty.com) provides a welcome stop at the foot of the bridge on US 64, offering restrooms and travel information. The **Scuppernong River Interpretive Boardwalk**, along the waterfront, introduces the river ecosystem.

Farther east on US 64, **Plymouth** (www.visitplymouthnc.com) is home to the **Port O' Plymouth Museum** (www.livinghistoryweekend.com) with a working 63-foot replica of

WATERFOWL ARE SOME OF THE MOST NUMEROUS RESIDENTS OF THE WILDLIFE REFUGES LOCATED ON THE ALBEMARIE PENINSULA

a Confederate ironclad tied to the dock outside. In-season it cruises the river, firing its guns. Stroll down Water Street to discover the **Roanoke River Lighthouse and Maritime Center** (www.roanokeriverlighthouse.org) and the **Rail Switch Nature Trail**, plus unique eateries and shops.

THE ROANOKE ISLAND INN OFFERS UNIQUE LODGING OPTIONS ON THE MANTEO WATERFRONT

hospitality, the Roanoke Island Inn garners rave reviews from guests. Built in the 1860s for the current innkeeper's great-great-grandmother, the white building is surrounded by distinctive gardens and has grown into a sprawling hostelry looking out over the marsh at Shallowbag Bay. The inn's eight guest rooms each have a private entrance and access to a big porch overlooking the water. Two of the rooms are family suites that have small adjoining rooms with twin beds for children. Through the arched carriageway, you'll find a lush garden and koi pond, as well as a two-bedroom bungalow. Bicycles, crab dip nets, and continental breakfast are included, and the innkeeper's pantry offers refreshments 24 hours a day. The Roanoke also has a private boat dock and a wedding chapel on the grounds. Open seasonally. $$–$$$$.

The same innkeeper rents other unique properties in the area. The **Island Camp** is on a private island accessible only by boat and comes complete with crab traps. You must have your own boat and cell phone. The **Croatan Cottage** is a restored Sears kit home with three bedrooms and three baths. The backyard faces the water.

(((•))) **Scarborough House Bed & Breakfast** (252-473-3849; www .scarboroughhouseinn.com), 323 Fernando Street. Innkeepers Sally and Phil Scarborough, both natives of the Outer Banks, frequently chat with guests in their comfortable living room or while rocking on their porch overlooking the garden. All the guest rooms are furnished with genuine antiques and mementos of Roanoke Island history. The house enjoys a terrific location facing the harbor, just a block from the activity on Queen Elizabeth Avenue. The Scarborough rents five rooms in the main house, plus two suites in a separate guest house and a cottage loft on the grounds. A light continental breakfast is offered in your room. The guest house suites have Jacuzzi tubs for two and complete kitchens. $–$$.

&. (((•))) **Scarborough Inn** (252-473-3979; www.scarboroughinnmanteo.com), 524 US 64. The younger generation of the Scarborough family operates this inn on the main highway with the same island hospitality, outstanding cleanliness, and reasonable rates found at the Scarborough homestead not far away. The cedar-shake main inn has two-story covered porches to catch the island breezes. Fourteen rooms, each with private bath, cable TV, refrigerator, microwave, and coffeemaker, are distributed among three buildings. A light continental breakfast is served. $–$$.

🐾 ✈ &. (((•))) **Tranquil House Inn** (252-473-1404 or 1-800-458-7069; www .tranquilhouseinn.com), 405 Queen Elizabeth Avenue. Located directly on the Manteo boardwalk across from the *Elizabeth II*, this elegant inn is top-of-the-line among local hostelries. Richard Gere and Diane Lane stayed here while filming *Nights in Rodanthe*, and other notables seem to find their way here as well. Maybe it's the room service. The hotel's restaurant, **1587**, is one of the finest in the area. Built of cypress, cedar, and stained glass to resemble historic inns of the past, the Tranquil House is in the heart of downtown Manteo, but its focus is outward toward Shallowbag Bay. The spacious second-floor patio overlooking the harbor is a favorite gathering spot at sunset. Each of the inn's 25 rooms is unique. The three-story hotel does not have an elevator, but a ramp makes the first floor accessible to wheelchairs, with one guest room equipped for the handicapped. Up to two children under 18 may stay free with their parents. Continental breakfast, daily newspaper, bicycle rental, and an afternoon wine and cheese reception are included in the room rate. $$–$$$$.

♂ ▼ (((•))) **The White Doe Inn** (252-473-9851 or 1-800-473-6091; www .whitedoeinn.com), 319 Sir Walter Raleigh Street. Its turret, wraparound porches, elaborate woodwork, balconies, and extensive gardens make the Queen Anne–style Theodore Meekins house, built in 1910 and on the National Register of Historic Places, stand out. Today it is the White Doe Inn, Manteo's most romantic bed & breakfast. Decorated in the Victorian style, its eight uniquely designed bedrooms offer a range of amenities, including private gardens, balconies, canopied beds, stained-glass windows, soaking tubs, and Jacuzzis for two. Both masculine and feminine color schemes are available. All rooms have guest bathrobes and a fireplace. Room rates include a four-course seated breakfast served in the dining room or on the veranda, as well as coffee, dessert, and sherry every evening. In-room spa services are available, as are special picnic, wedding, honeymoon, champagne, and chocolate packages; a 24-hour butler's wine pantry; and cappuccino and espresso service. $$$–$$$$.

CONDO RENTALS **Shallowbag Bay Club** (252-475-1617; www.shallowbag baymarina.com), 90 N. Bay Club Drive. Several of the fully equipped, luxury one- to four-bedroom condos in this soundfront community are available as rentals. Community amenities include a swimming pool and hot tub, fitness center, and game room, as well as the popular **Stripers Bar & Grille**. Slips at the marina are available for transient boaters.

THE TRANQUIL HOUSE INN, BUILT TO RESEMBLE HOSTELRIES OF THE PAST, IS A FAVORITE WITH VISITING CELEBRITIES

⚲ 🏠 ♿ **Pirate's Cove Realty** (1-800-537-7245; www.pirates-cove.com), 1 Sailfish Drive. A wide variety of vacation rentals are available in the gated Pirate's Cove community, from seven-bedroom homes to smaller villas and condominiums, including some with private boat slips. Many rental units come complete with bicycles and beach and fishing equipment, and some are equipped for infants. Rentals include linen service and housekeeping. Guests can use the community amenities, including a clubhouse, game room, pool and hot tub, fitness center, playground, volleyball courts, fossil search area, horseshoe pits, putting green, and lighted tennis courts, and receive reduced greens fees at the nearby **Nags Head Golf Links**.

GUEST HOUSES AND COTTAGES

♂ **Booth Guest House** (252-305-1205 or 252-473-3515; www.theboothhouse.com), 135 Morrison Grove Road. Located on the sound at the north end of Roanoke Island, this home, filled with family antiques, is within walking distance of *The Lost Colony* theater. The soundfront gazebo is a popular spot for weddings. $–$$.

🏠 **Cottages on Roanoke Island** (804-640-4440; www.cottagesonroanoke island.com). Collection of rental cottages scattered around the Manteo historic district range from the cozy two-bedroom Clemons Cottage to the historic Magnolia Cottage and Neva Midgett House, among the town's most distinguished residences. You can even book a stay aboard a luxury yacht docked at on the Manteo waterfront. Weekly rates are available. $$–$$$$.

🏠 ♂ 📶 **Island Guesthouse and Cottages** (252-473-2434; www.theislandmotel.com), 706 US 64. This guest house, a cottage located on the main highway through town, offers friendly service and bright, clean accommodations at surprisingly reasonable rates both on- and off-season. The 14 rooms each have two double beds with foldout cots available, plus cable TV and air-conditioning. The property is popular with wedding parties, and an on-site wedding planner is available. A block away, at 708 Wingina Avenue, three themed cottages that offer more privacy as well as more upscale amenities are operated by the same proprietors. Each cottage has a full kitchen, Dolby surround sound home theater with a flat-screen TV, bath with two-person whirlpool tub, fireplace, and Wi-Fi. $–$$$$.

MARINAS Several marinas on Roanoke Island welcome transients who want to cruise in and stay aboard their boats or just stop by for dinner on the docks. Most host excursion boats or charter fishing vessels, so a marina can be an exciting place to hang out, even if you don't have a boat.

📶 **Manteo Waterfront Marina** (252-473-3320; www.townofmanteo.com), 207 Queen Elizabeth Avenue. Numerous transient berths with full hookups are available on the waterfront in downtown Manteo. Showers, a laundromat, ship's store, and many onshore amenities are nearby. The town hosts free Wi-Fi along the entire waterfront.

Marshes Light Marina (252-475-9863; www.marsheslight.com/marina), 201 Fernando Street. New marina with full-service transient slips is connected to downtown Manteo by a boardwalk. Shower and laundry available, plus a ship's store.

Pirate's Cove Yacht Club (252-473-3906 or 1-800-367-4728; www.fishpiratescove.com), 2000 Sailfish Drive. The 20 or so charter fishing boats based here head out to the Gulf Stream for tuna, dolphin, wahoo, and marlin; stay nearshore for cobia or Spanish mackerel; or fish the inlet for trout, flounder, bluefish, and striped bass. Makeup charters available. Transient slips include electric, water, and cable TV in the dockage rate, with access to the gated community's pool and hot tub, fitness center, sauna, and tennis courts,

SLIPS AT MANTEO'S TOWN MARINA ARE A FAVORITE WITH VISITING BOATERS THANKS TO THEIR CENTRAL LOCATION AND FREE WI-FI

plus laundry facilities, showers, private fish-cleaning house, and a courtesy van. Internet access is available in the ship's store.

Shallowbag Bay Marina (252-305-8726; www.shallowbagbaymarina.com), 100 Bay Club Drive. Boat slips come with all club amenities, including a pool and hot tub, fitness center, bicycles, cable and phone hookups, laundry and shower facilities, and a courtesy car. A ship's store and restaurant are located on-site, with slip space available for customers.

MOTOR LODGES 🐾 (ᵖ) **Dare Haven Motel** (252-473-2322; www.darehaven .com), US 64. The 26 courtyard units in this family-run motel have been recently renovated. Each has a color TV, phone, and mini-fridge. Pleasant porches have swings and rockers. Room service and boat trailer parking available. $–$$.

🐾 ♿ (ᵖ) **The Elizabethan Inn** (252-473-2101 or 1-800-346-2466; www .elizabethaninn.com), 814 US 64. Roanoke Island's largest accommodation, with 78 units, has an attractive,

Tudor-style, timbered exterior that fits in well with the island's historic theme. Opened in 1954 and renovated in 2003, the motor lodge now has a professionally staffed spa with heated indoor pool, whirlpool, sauna, aerobic and yoga classes, and the latest fitness equipment, as well as a seasonal outdoor pool. A variety of room types are available, including deluxe rooms with whirlpool bath and king bed, handicapped-accessible rooms, smoking and nonsmoking rooms, pet-friendly rooms, and efficiencies. All rooms have cable TV, and most have refrigerators. 🍴 **La Dolce Vita Italian Cuisine & Pizzeria** (252-473-9919; www.ladolcevitamanteo.com) is on-site. $–$$$.

✳ Where to Eat

With the exceptions of McDonald's, Subway, and Pizza Hut, Roanoke Island remains free of chain restaurants. Most eateries are family owned and operated. Often the fresh seafood on the menu

A SPECIALITY PIZZA AT AVENUE WATERFRONT GRILLE MAKES A PERFECT LIGHT LUNCH

comes directly from the family's fishing boat to the table. Keep an eye out for blackboard specials. These change frequently and usually represent what is literally "the catch of the day."

DINING OUT ♂ ♈ ⊕ **Avenue Waterfront Grille** (252-473-4800; www.avenuegrilleobx.com), 207 Queen Elizabeth Street, Waterfront Shops. Closed Sunday and Monday. This chef-owned spot is a favorite location for weddings and other events, thanks to its lofty views over Shallowbag Bay and clean contemporary decor, but it is also a favorite with diners looking for something a little upscale. Chef Thomas Williamson creates a seasonally changing menu, with plenty of vegan, vegetarian and gluten-free options. There's a nice lounge area as well, with seasonal live entertainment. For something light, try a specialty burger or pizza. Lunch $$; dinner $$$–$$$$.

♂ ♂ ♈ **Blue Water Grill & Raw Bar and Mimi's Tiki Hut** (252-473-1955; www.bluewatergrillobx.com), Pirate's Cove Marina, 2000 Sailfish Drive. Big windows and a porch offer great views of the Pirate's Cove Marina, accompanied by impressive presentations of freshly caught fish and locally sourced vegetables. Seafood dominates, but the menu offers vegan and vegetarian dishes as well. If your charter brought in a catch, the kitchen here will cook it for you to order. A big selection of oysters, mostly locally sourced, come, raw or steamed with several unusual sauces. Out on the dock, Mimi's Tiki Bar brightens up the night with a fun menu of appetizers and live music in-season. Lunch $$; dinner $$–$$$$.

♂ ♿ ⊕ **1587 Restaurant** (252-473-1587; www.1587.com), Tranquil House Inn, 405 Queen Elizabeth Avenue. Relax over a glass of wine and watch the moon rise over Shallowbag Bay, then order up a selection of the creative cuisine from the Tranquil House Inn's signature restaurant. The chefs here exhibit a fine touch with the fresh local ingredients at hand and are constantly designing new, but always delicious, combinations. The menu changes seasonally and features fresh local seafood, chargrilled chops, and, often, local game. A full vegetarian menu is available upon request. If you're just in the mood for something light, stop by the restaurant's copper-top bar, a work of art in itself, for an appetizer or a glass of wine. The cellar selection at 1587 received favorable mention in *Wine Spectator*. You'll be favorably surprised by the prices, both for bottles and wines

TUNA SASHIMI GETS AN ARTFUL PRESENTATION AT THE BLUE WATER GRILLE IN PIRATE'S COVE

SAMPLER OF BRITISH AND IRISH STYLE BEERS AT THE LOST COLONY BREWERY

by the glass. One of the Outer Banks' unique fine-dining experiences, this is a don't-miss. Reservations recommended. Dinner only, $$$.

🦐 🐾 ♿ ➷ **Lost Colony Brewery & Café** (252-473-6666; www.lostcolony brewery.com), 208 Queen Elizabeth Avenue, Creef's Corner. Catch the laid-back pulse of Manteo at this restaurant, formerly the Full Moon Café, located in the heart of it all, under the town clock. The eclectic menu brings together cuisines from several continents, ranging from hummus to shrimp-and-crab enchiladas, and includes many creative vegetarian suggestions. Owner Paul Charron's microbrewery creates unique small-batch British and Irish-style beers. You can sample them all, as well as a selection of outstanding North Carolina drafts, at the beer pub on-site. Pets are welcome on the patio. Lunch $–$$; dinner $$–$$$.

➷ **Ortega'z Southwestern Grill & Wine Bar** (252-473-5911; www.ortegaz .com), 201 Sir Walter Raleigh Street. Closed Sundays. Occupying a location with a history of fun—former site of the Green Dolphin Pub and before that Fernando's Ale House—in downtown Manteo, this classy spot offers indoor and outdoor dining and fresh takes on Southwestern cuisine, featuring slow-cooked

beef and pork, gluten-free dishes, house-made desserts, and fish tacos featured on the Food Network's *Diners, Drive-ins and Dives*. The convivial bar in the center of the restaurant is a favorite gathering spot for locals. Check out the restored mural of the Albatross Fleet on the back wall. Lunch $–$$; dinner $–$$$.

➷ ♿ 🍸 **Stripers Bar & Grille** (252-473-3222; www.stripersbarandgrille.com), 1100 S. Bay Club Drive, Shallowbag Bay Club. This restaurant is a little hard to find, tucked away from the road inside the Shallowbag Bay Club. The secret to finding it: Turn east between McDonald's and Darrell's on US 64. Or come by boat. You can tie up at the dock outside. The three-story building sits right on the waterfront, guaranteeing great views from every seat. Downstairs, the steamed and raw bar is a fun-loving hangout where locals gather for happy hour, with an outdoor patio and screened porch overlooking the docks. Upstairs, you'll find sophisticated dining with quiet background jazz, a lounge, and roof-top deck. Signature dishes include the Rockfish Reuben, a tasty take on the classic featuring the restaurant's namesake fish, the rockfish or striped bass, known locally as a striper. The Sunday brunch, voted a favorite by locals, features a variety of eggs Benedict creations. Live music some evenings. Sunday brunch $; lunch and dinner $–$$$.

EATING OUT 🦐 ➷ ♿ **Big Al's Soda Fountain & Grill** (252-473-5570; www .bigalsobx.com), 716 S. US 64. Local fishing boat captain Al Foreman, known as Big Al to his friends, grew up around ice cream and always wanted his own old-fashioned soda fountain. Big Al's ended up as a complete 1950s-themed restaurant with multiple dining rooms, a big dance floor next to a jukebox full of rock 'n' roll classics, and a soda fountain counter long enough for a dozen people to spin around on those shiny red stools. Kids can get all their favorites here for about what you'd pay for a Happy Meal.

LOADS OF MEMORABILIA ON DISPLAY AT THE '50S-THEMED BIG AL'S SODA FOUNTAIN & GRILL

Meanwhile, adults and teens enjoy a wide selection of burgers, melts, finger food, blue-plate specials, and fresh local seafood, straight off Big Al's *Country Girl* and other local fishing boats. The dessert menu features all the classics, from a banana split to peanut butter pie. You'll have fun here just reading the menu, but there's plenty more to do: play the jukebox, admire the incredible collection of Coke memorabilia, visit the game arcade, or browse the gift shop full of 1950s-themed souvenirs. Lunch and dinner $–$$.

🖋 ♿ ✈ **Darrell's Seafood Restaurant** (252473-5366; www.darrellsseafood .com), 523 S. US 64. Closed Sunday. The motto on the menu says it all: "Eat More Fish." This family-owned favorite, operated by the Daniels family, has been serving local fish and other seafood straight from the boat for over 50 years. The fried oysters are what people rave about, but Darrell's does things like marinated grilled tuna well, too. The surf and turf is a local favorite, as is the super-budget take-out lunch. Dessert features a legendary hot fudge ice cream cake. If you'd rather eat at home, Darrell's has a great family-style take-out menu featuring hickory-smoked barbecue and Southern fried chicken. Breakfast and lunch $; dinner $$.

Garden Deli & Pizzeria (252-473-6888; www.gardendelipizza.com), 512 S. US 64. Known for its New York–style thin-crust pizzas, including a delicious white Greek

pie, this spot has chefs who like to press the envelope. The menu also has vegan pizzas and salads. Free delivery in Manteo, or eat on the shady deck. $–$$.

🖋 **Hungry Pelican Deli and Ice Cream** (252-473-9303; www .thehungrypelican.com), 205 Budleigh Street, Waterfront Shops. Sandwiches at this shop next to the Pioneer Theatre are made with Dietz & Watson "Healthier Lifestyle" deli meats on breads baked on-site. Salads, dressings, soups, and sides are all made in-house, as are the desserts. $.

🍸 (ᵞ) **Poor Richard's Sandwich Shop** (252-473-3333; www .poorrichardsmanteo.com), 303 Queen Elizabeth Avenue. A presence on the Manteo waterfront since 1984, Poor Richard's is easy to find, with a door opening onto Queen Elizabeth Avenue and another leading directly onto the docks. A full breakfast menu is served until 10:30 AM. Hot and cold sandwiches are made with Boar's Head meats and cheeses or house-made deli salads. You can check your email, thanks to the complimentary Wi-Fi access along the waterfront. Live entertainment most nights, and the newly enlarged pub opens at noon on Sunday. $.

T. L.'s Country Kitchen (252-473-3489), 812 S. US 64. Breakfast is served anytime at this family-owned local favorite where Southern home cooking is the specialty. Lunch and dinner feature homestyle dishes, sandwiches, and a salad bar. Don't miss the homemade pies. $.

COFFEE SHOPS ❄ (ᵞ) **Front Porch Cafe** (252-473-3160; www.frontporchcafe online.com), 300 US 64. Front Porch's newest location, on the road into town, has both Wi-Fi and secure Ethernet options at its "wireless bar," plus a wine bar with a selection of vintages available by the glass or to-go in bottles. They host wine tastings on First Fridays.

KILL DEVIL RUM

Outer Banks Distilling (252-423-3011; www.outerbanksdistilling.com) at 510 Budleigh Street in the heart of Manteo's historic downtown is the first (legal) distillery on the Banks. Two brewers from the Outer Banks Brewing Company joined forces with two bartenders to revive the tradition of rum that runs strong through the region. Kill Devil Hills itself is named for the Caribbean spirit once called kill-devil, after barrels washed up on its shores from shipwrecks. The four entrepreneurs restored a wonderful old building and set up their stills. The result: a world-class, fine drinking rum that's found favor with bartenders up and down the Banks and beyond. Kill Devil Rum is available in several varieties, including an award-winning pecan flavor, classic Silver and Gold, a spiced Winter Solspice rum, and limited edition small batches, named for shipwrecks. Make a reservation for a tasting and tour, or stop by the distillery shop for up to five bottles of rum or a bag of rum-flavored pecans.

(((ρ))) 🐾 **Island Perk** (252-423-3565; www.islandperkobx.com), 101-A Budleigh Street. Full espresso bar in the heart of downtown serves hot and cold beverages, including single-origin pour-overs and fruit smoothies, plus a nice selection of pastries and muffins.

FARMERS' MARKET **Manteo Farmers' Market** (252-473-2133; www.townofmanteo.com), George Washington Creef Park. Held in the park next to the maritime museum on the Manteo waterfront every Saturday morning from mid-May to early September, this market, sponsored by the Town of Manteo, features local produce, jellies and pickles, home-baked goodies, and crafts.

ICE CREAM AND SWEETS **Big Buck's Ice Cream and Distinct Delights Chocolates** (www.bigbucksicecream.com). Two

Manteo locations: 106-A Sir Walter Raleigh Street (252-423-3400), and 207 Queen Elizabeth Avenue in the **Waterfront Shops** (252-423-3118). Ice cream made in-house, plus sorbets, sherbets, smoothies, and handmade chocolate goodies are Outer Banks favorites.

❄ 🐾 🎵 **Olde Towne Creamery** (252-305-8060; www.oldetownecreamery.com), 500 US 64. Located on the main road into town, this full-service ice cream shop stocks a wide range of both ice cream and frozen yogurt flavors, plus Italian ice, fudge, gourmet chocolates, an espresso bar, and a huge menu of desserts. The creamery serves "real food" as well; choose between North Carolina barbecue, beef franks, grilled chicken sandwiches, or an authentic Italian meatball sub.

WINE AND SPIRITS **Dare County ABC Store** (252-473-3557; www.ncabc.com), US 64. Most state ABC stores are open Monday to Saturday 10–9 and are closed Sunday.

❄ Entertainment

CINEMA 🐾 🎵 **Pioneer Theatre** (252-473-2216), 113 Budleigh Street. The first, and still the only, movie theater in Manteo, Pioneer opened in 1918 and is the oldest cinema still run by the original family in the country. Today, the Creef family continues to operate the local landmark and keeps prices low to make it affordable for families. One first-run movie plays each week (Friday to Thursday) at 8 PM nightly. The theater, the largest in both seating and screen size in the county, recently was updated with an extra-powerful digital projector and new surround-sound speakers. Tickets are $7; add freshly made popcorn and a drink, and you'll still be spending under $10 for the evening.

LIVE MUSIC You'll usually find a crowd of locals lifting a glass at **Poor Richard's**

After Hours (252-473-3333), 303 Queen Elizabeth Avenue, the pub located adjacent to Poor Richard's Sandwich Shop on the Manteo waterfront. Live music is offered nearly every night of the week.

Other spots with live entertainment include **Ortega'z**, **Striper's Bar & Grille**, **Avenue Grille**, and the **Lost Colony Brewery & Café**. Concerts are hosted at the **Old Dare County Courthouse**, now home to the Dare County Arts Council, and **Roanoke Island Festival Park**.

First Friday on Roanoke Island (252-473-5558; www.darearts.org/firstfriday), downtown Manteo waterfront. Organized by the Dare Arts Council, Manteo's galleries, boutiques, and restaurants host open house First Friday events from April to December. Look for live music, family activities, historical interpreters in period costumes, a rock-climbing wall, and more, 6–8 PM.

🐾 🍸 **Mimi's Tiki Hut** (252-473-1955; www.bluewatergrillobx.com), Pirate's Cove Marina, 2000 Sailfish Drive. Live music on the dock at Pirate's Cove as you watch the charter fishing fleet unload its catch.

Pickin' On The Porch (252-423-3039; www.bluegrassisland.com), 107 Budleigh Street. Free bluegrass music concerts at the Phoenix Shops on Fridays all summer.

Roanoke Island Festival Park Concert Series (252-475-1500; www.roanokeisland.com). Outdoor Festival Stage hosts bands and music festivals throughout the year.

THEATER 🎵 *The Lost Colony* **Outdoor Drama** (252-473-2127; www.thelostcolony.org), Waterside Theatre, 1409 National Park Drive. Nightly except Sunday, June–August. Over 4 million visitors have seen the outdoor drama *The Lost Colony* since it debuted in 1937. Commissioned by the residents of Manteo, the symphonic drama, scripted by Pulitzer Prize winner Paul Green, was the first of its kind, telling the story of the original English colony and of Virginia Dare, the

PIRATE'S COVE MARVEL

Don't miss the huge blue marlin displayed outside near Mimi's Tiki Hut. It's the North Carolina state record holder, a giant weighing in at 1,228.5 pounds, caught in the 25th Annual Pirate's Cove Billfish Tournament in 2008.

first English child born in the New World, through song, dance, and dramatic narrative. The show has always been lucky in its talent. **Andy Griffith** started his career playing Sir Walter Raleigh here. The magnificent costumes are created by **William Ivey Long**, winner of multiple Tony awards for production design and himself a local boy who began his theatrical career at the Waterside Theatre. In the event of rain, tickets are honored at a future performance.

Theatre of Dare (252-462-1776; www.theatreofdareobx.com). An all-volunteer cast and crew present several musicals and comedies every fall and spring in the company's new home, the auditorium of the College of the Albemarle Roanoke Island campus in Manteo.

Waterside Theatre Backstage Tours (252-473-2127; www.thelostcolony.org). Evening tours conducted before each show give a behind-the-scenes look

at *The Lost Colony* theater, prop rooms, and costume shop as the actors warm up to go onstage. Summer only. $10. VIP tickets include the backstage tour, *The Lost Colony* performance, souvenirs, and more. You can also enjoy a pre-show buffet dinner with the queen and other costumed characters or take a ghost tour of the grounds with an astral plane investigator.

✱ Selective Shopping

Manteo has no malls and only one strip shopping center. Most of the shopping options are located in downtown Manteo close to the historic waterfront. There you'll find numerous shops offering a variety of practical and gift items.

GALLERIES Manteo's historic waterfront district makes an attractive location for a variety of art studios and galleries. Most are located within a few blocks of each other. The town's monthly First Friday celebrations include a gallery crawl.

Andrus Gallery & Studio (252-305-5411; www.andrusgallery.com), Waterfront Shops, Queen Elizabeth Street. Longtime Banks resident and founder of the local high school arts program, Steve Andrus, displays his light-drenched watercolors of boats, harbors, and other marine subjects.

Inspired by the Sea (252-473-9955; www.furnitureinspiredbythesea.com), 107 Budleigh Street, Phoenix Shops. Hand-painted scenes of lighthouses, shells, and seascapes grace functional furniture items.

John Silver Studio (252-473-8245; www.johnsilverpaintings.com), 103 Sir Walter Raleigh Street. Oils by John Silver, including many of local scenes, as well as artwork by other professional artists. Silver also conducts plein air painting workshops.

Nancyware Pottery (252-473-9400; www.nancywareobx.com), 402 Queen Elizabeth Avenue, Magnolia Market. Nancy Huse creates high-fired functional pottery in her studio. In the gallery next door, her collectible ornaments and God jars are customer favorites.

Red Drum Pottery II (252-473-4747; www.reddrumpottery.com), 207 Queen Elizabeth Avenue. Second gallery of Hatteras-based artists and musicians Rhonda Bates and Wes Lassiter displays their original artwork and pottery, including a collection of hand-painted beach and nautical-themed Christmas ornaments. Rhonda can often be found working on-site.

✿ ⚓ **Roanoke Heritage Extended** (252-475-1442), 100 Sir Walter Raleigh Street, Suite 109. The home of Stumpy the Pirate Cat, hero of several popular children's books written by Jeremy Bliven, exhibits artwork by its illustrator Herbert Bliven, Jeremy's father. The building is full of fascinating treasures, including seashells, driftwood, duck decoys, handcrafted ceramic jewelry, and nautically themed gifts for children and adults. You can even create your own driftwood sculpture.

Silver Bonsai Jewelry & Art Gallery (252-475-1413; www.silverbonsai.com), 905 S. US 64. The home gallery of jewelry artists Ben and Kathryn Stewart also exhibits the fine arts and crafts of other select artists, as well as a large collection of bonsai. Among the art and miniature trees, you'll find Ben Stewart's secret passion: Etch A Sketch art.

Wanchese Pottery (252-473-2099), 107 Fernando Street. Potters Bonnie and Bob Morrill create handcrafted pottery in this attractive building, facing George Washington Creef Park on the Manteo waterfront.

BOOKS ✿ ⚓ **Duck's Cottage Downtown Books** (252-473-1056; www.duckscottage.com), 101 Sir Walter Raleigh Street. The much-loved Manteo Booksellers closed after suffering extensive flood damage in Hurricane Irene, but Duck's Cottage, a stalwart on the North Banks scene, stepped in to continue the location's reputation as a refuge for book lovers. The hand-picked selection includes regional titles and local authors, cookbooks, graphic novels, best-sellers, and more, with a special area devoted to young readers. The shop also carries a large selection of toys and games that encourage creativity, including the popular Melissa & Doug series, and has a comfy refreshment corner offering fresh brewed coffee, tea, and treats.

SHOPPING CENTERS **Chesley Mall**, 210 S. US 64. All the stores you simply have to find—grocery, post office, drugstore—are conveniently centralized in this strip mall, anchored by a Food-A-Rama IGA grocery, on the main highway.

SPECIAL SHOPS **Bluegrass Island Trading Co.** (252-423-3039; www .BluegrassIslandTradingCo.com), 107

Budleigh Street, Phoenix Shops. Lots of bluegrass music–themed items and thousands of CDs share space with a collection of original props from *The Andy Griffith Show* and an exhibit on the bootlegging ghost town of Buffalo City. Tickets to local music events are sold here.

♂ ♈ **The Christmas Shop and General Store** (252-473-2838; www .outerbankschristmas.com), 621 S. US 64. Originally established in 1967, one of Manteo's most popular shops, famous for its Christmas displays, has reopened. It now includes a Halloween room, plus fudge, candy, antiques, jewelry, craft, and book shops. Wander around the grounds for a great shopping experience.

Mackey's Ferry Peanuts (252-423-3015; www.mfpnuts.com), 107 C Budleigh Steet, Phoenix Shops. Try the famous French-fried peanuts, or the blister-fried, flame-thrower, Cajun-roasted, or sugarcoated varieties. Plenty of nonpeanut goodness in this shop as well, including fudge and chocolates, molasses cookies, preserves, and more. Stop by for a free sample of fudge and a refreshing muscadine cider slushy.

Mike Keller Ltd. (252-473-5007 or 1-800-683-8464; www.mikekellerltd.com), 416 Russell Twiford Road. Sports outfitter carries foul-weather gear, crabbing supplies, cast nets, fishing accessories, and Grundens' "Eat Fish" line of clothing.

Modern Heirloom (252-475-1413; www .modernheirloom.com), 905 US 64. Husband-and-wife team Ben and Kathryn Stewart create timeless masterpieces from precious metals and gemstones.

Muzzie's Antiques (252-473-4505; www.muzziesantiquesobx.com), 107-A Budleigh Street. Vintage, estate, and antique jewelry is Muzzie's specialty, along with vintage clothing, garden statuary, and unique engagement rings.

My Secret Garden (252-473-6880; www.facebook.com/ MySecretGardenOBX), 101 Sir Walter Raleigh Street. Manteo's oldest gift shop is a favorite stop for residents and visitors alike, with a wealth of ornaments for your garden, plus gift items, jewelry, stuffed animals, mermaids, and fairies.

Outer Banks Quilts and Antiques (252-473-4183; www .obxquiltsandantiques.com), 108 Sir Walter Raleigh Street. An antiques mall with more than a dozen different dealers shares space with quilting fabrics and supplies. Antique quilts are on display.

Shoreline Handwerks (252-473-2271; www.shorelinehandwerks.com), 4250 Maritime Woods Drive. Full-service sewing and quilting shop stocks lots of fabric and kits with beach and ocean designs, and offers quilting and sewing classes. Exclusive dealer for the OBX fabric map.

✳ Special Events

Check the **Outer Banks visitors website** (www.outerbanks.org) for an updated list of events during your stay.

January: **Frank Stick Memorial Art Show** (252-473-5558; www.darearts.org), DCAC Historic Courthouse Gallery. Juried show honoring Outer Banks preservationist Frank Stick runs through February.

March: **Outer Banks Community Quilt Show** (252-475-1500; www.roanoke island.com), Roanoke Island Festival Park Gallery. Annual quilt show includes a vendor day. Free.

April: **Easter Eggstravaganza** (252-473-3234; www.elizabethangardens.org), Elizabethan Gardens. Celebrate spring with Easter egg hunts, live bunnies, egg rolls, an Easter bonnet contest, and a day of fun at the gardens.

May: **Mollie Fearing Memorial Art Show** (252-473-5558; www.darearts.org), DCAC Courthouse Gallery. Juried show honors the founder of the Dare County Arts Council.

Kidfest (252-441-0614; www.darekids .org), Roanoke Island Festival Park Outdoor Pavilion. Lots of free activities for kids.

June: **Dare Day** (252-475-5629; www .townofmanteo.com), downtown Manteo. Annual all-day free festival with music,

RECOMMENDED READING

Harrison, Molly, and Meredith Vaccaro. *Roanoke Island: Then and Now*. Manteo, NC: One Boat Guides, 2014. Walking tour with map and many old photos of Manteo.

Hird, Barbara, and lebame houston, eds. *Roanoke Revisited: The Story of the First English Settlements in the New World and the Fabled Lost Colony of Roanoke Island*. Manteo, NC: Penny Books, 1997. Hird and houston, the team behind the successful Elizabeth R theatrical troupe, translate the documents relating to the Lost Colony into modern English.

Hudson, Marjorie. *A Journey into History, Memory, and the Fate of America's First English Child*. www.searchingforvirginiadare.com, 2007.

Tate, Suzanne. *Memories of Manteo and Roanoke Island, N.C. (as told by the late Cora Mae Basnight)*. Nags Head, NC: Nags Head Art, 1988. Oral history recalls details of Basnight's 25 years performing in *The Lost Colony*.

boat race, kids zone, and vendors takes place on the waterfront.

July: **Fourth of July Celebration and Fireworks** (252-475-5629; www.townofmanteo.com), downtown Manteo. Old-fashioned event with apple pie eating contest, bike parade, free band concert in Roanoke Island Festival Park, and fireworks.

August: **New World Festival of the Arts** (252-473-5558; www.darearts.org), Manteo waterfront. Two-day outdoor event features a juried exhibition of works by more than 80 select artists.

OBX Summer Send Off Concert (252-475-1500; www.roanokeisland.com), Roanoke Island Festival Park Outdoor Pavilion. Benefits the Mustang Outreach Program.

Roanoke Island American Indian Cultural Festival & Powwow (757-477-3589; www.ncalgonquians.com), Airport Pavilion Lawn, Airport Road.

Virginia Dare Day (252-473-3234; www.elizabethangardens.org), Elizabethan Gardens. Annual celebration of the birthday of the first English child born in America.

Pirate's Cove Big Game Tournaments (252-305-3610; www.pcbgt.com), Pirate's Cove Marina. The Alice Kelly Memorial Ladies Only Billfish Tournament followed by the Pirate's Cove Billfish Tournament provide a couple weeks of big game fishing action.

September: **The Lost Colony Wine & Culinary Festival** (252-473-2127; www.tlcwinefest.com), Waterside Theatre. Grand Tasting, samples of wines from the New World and Old, and the best dishes from local eateries.

Surfalorus Film Festival (252-473-5558; www.surfalorus.com), sponsored by Dare County Arts and Wilmington, North Carolina's Cucalorus Film Festival. Films highlighting the culture and art of surfing screen at several venues, including the DCAC Courthouse Gallery.

Harvest Hayday (252-473-3234; www.elizabethangardens.org), Elizabethan Gardens. Harvest festival with hayrides, apple rolls, scarecrow stuffing, and other seasonal fun.

October: **Outer Banks Bluegrass Festival** (www.bluegrassisland.com), Roanoke Island Festival Park.

Wooden Boat Show (252-473-2133; www.townofmanteo.com), Creef Boathouse and Park.

Trick or Treat Under the Sea (252-473-3494 or 1-866-332-3475; www.ncaquariums.com), North Carolina Aquarium at Roanoke Island.

Outer Banks History Weekend (www.firstcolonyfoundation.org), U.S. Fish & Wildlife Visitor Center. Weekend of presentations, exhibits, and tours related to the latest research on Raleigh's Lost Colony.

November: **Manteo Rotary Inshore Slam** (252-473-6644; www.rockfishrodeo.com), Roanoke Island Festival Park. Family-oriented tournament features competitions for several inshore species.

OBX Marathon and Southern Fried Half-Marathon (www.obxmarathon.org). Annual road races conclude in downtown Manteo with a block party open to all.

December: **Christmas by the Sea** (252-473-2133; www.townofmanteo.com), downtown Manteo. Friday night lighting of the town tree; Saturday Christmas parade featuring Queen Elizabeth I and Santa.

Holiday Small Works Show (252-473-5558; www.darearts.org), Historic Courthouse Gallery.

WinterLights (252-473-3234; www.elizabethangardens.org), Elizabethan Gardens. The gardens transform into an illuminated winter wonderland full of holiday decor, accompanied by gift shop and plant sales, from late November through early January.

Holiday Tour of Homes (www.manteopreservationtrust.com). Local homes beautifully decorated for the holidays open their doors for this fund-raiser for the Manteo Preservation Trust.

St. Nicholas Arrives at Island Farm (www.theislandfarm.com). Santa arrives via ox-drawn wagon, then visits with kids around the fire.

WANCHESE

No one is sure what the word *wanchese* meant in the native Algonquian language, but there's no doubt what the word stands for today. The village of Wanchese is all about fishing and all about preserving this traditional way of life. A leisurely drive or bicycle ride along the village's winding roads takes you past houses with boats, crab pots, and horses in the backyard. Family homes often have their own docks and piers, with fishing boats tied up alongside. There may be a boat-building shed around back. A recently adopted zoning plan preserves the traditional right of families to both live and work on their land. It also puts some major roadblocks in the way of development, which local residents feared would drive up their property values, a process already witnessed in Manteo.

Many of the roads bear the names of local families, some of whom have been here for centuries, including Etheridge, Daniels, Baum, and Tillett. The Etheridge and Daniels families founded the now international **Wanchese Fish Company** (www.wanchese .com), which remains under family control.

Wanchese has a venerable history as a center of boatbuilding. If you find yourself in a long line of slowly moving traffic, be patient. A new boat is likely making its way from boat shed to water. These frequent events turn into impromptu parades as utility teams take down and replace wires to let the big boats pass.

So Wanchese residents continue, as they have for centuries, to harvest the sea. There are only a few restaurants and a couple of bed & breakfast inns. The tourists who do find their way here come to board a charter fishing boat, to shop for a boat of their own, or to buy seafood snatched fresh from the ocean.

The state has been busy in Wanchese, as in Manteo—but with a different aim. The state-sponsored **Wanchese Seafood Industrial Park**, devoted exclusively to marine-focused industries, opened in 1988. Locals were slow to warm to it, but in recent years the park on Harbor Road has become a beehive of boatbuilding and boat repair, specializing in custom sportfishing boats and commercial trawlers.

GUIDANCE Wanchese is an unincorporated community in Dare County. Information is available at the **Sarah Owens Welcome Center** (252-473-2138 or 1-877-629-4386; www.outerbanks.org), located on the US 64/264 Bypass, and at **the offices of Dare County** (252-475-5000; www.darenc.com), 962 Marshall C. Collins Drive, Manteo.

POST OFFICE The **Wanchese Post Office** (252-473-3551) is at 3525 Mill Landing Road. The zip code for Wanchese is 27981.

PUBLIC RESTROOMS Public facilities are located at **"Pigum" Walker Park** (252-473-6638; www.darenc.com/parksrec) on Pond Road.

GETTING THERE To find Wanchese, head south down the main highway from Manteo to the other end of Roanoke Island. The road, now NC 345/Mill Landing Road, meanders through marsh before reaching the more populated area at the southern tip of the island. You'll look in vain for a downtown commercial district. All the business of Wanchese takes place on the docks.

GETTING AROUND The quiet streets at the southern end of Roanoke Island are excellent for exploring by bicycle. Be prepared to turn around a lot. Most roads end at the water's edge.

✳ To See

↝ **Coastal Studies Institute** (252-475-3663; www.coastalstudiesinstitute.org), 850 NC 345. Located in the Skyco neighborhood, about halfway between Manteo and Wanchese, this institute affiliated with the University of North Carolina is dedicated to the study of estuarine ecology, ocean energy, sustainability, and North Carolina's maritime heritage, and hosts a variety of educational and outreach community programs, as well as summer camps. The LEED-certified campus, located amid marshland, is landscaped with native plants.

Decoys by Nick Sapone (252-473-3136), 292 The Lane. Call ahead to visit the studio of Sapone, a carver of traditional Outer Banks–style canvas-covered hunting decoys.

Wanchese Seafood Industrial Park (252-473-5867; www.nccommerce.com/wanchese), 615 Harbor Road, off NC 345. North Carolina's ocean industries are on display in this bustling compound. Fishing boats dock to unload their catch at seafood processing plants, and shipbuilders create and repair everything from custom yachts to seagoing commercial trawlers. A large charter fishing fleet makes its home here at the **OBX Fishing Center** (formerly Broad Creek). **O'Neal's Sea Harvest** offers fresh seafood at a dockside market.

BOATBUILDERS If you're in the market for a sportsfishing boat or cruising yacht of your own, you've come to the right place. Boats custom built in Carolina are considered the best available by many anglers and mariners around the world. Contact local professional boatbuilders to see their prebuilt models, or design your own customized boat. Many also offer repair and upgrade services, haul-out, and storage.

✳ To Do

BOATING The free **Dare County boat ramp** (www.darenc.com) is on Mill Landing Road between the Fisherman's Wharf Restaurant and Moon Tillett's Fish Company. **Thicket Lump Marina** also offers a public boat ramp.

DOLPHIN WATCHING & **Paradise Dolphin Cruises** (252-573-0547; www.paradise dolphincruises.com), Wanchese Marina, 408 Harbor Road. Dolphin sightings are guaranteed aboard the *Kokomo*, a 40-foot catamaran with restroom, cushioned seats, and sun shade.

FISHING Wanchese is home to a large charter fishing fleet as well as a commercial fishing fleet that ships its catch around the world. Check these marina websites for charter fishing options departing from their docks:

OBX Marina (252-473-9991; www.obxmarina.com), Wanchese Seafood Industrial Park, 708 Harbor Drive. This fully equipped marina offers new floating dock slips for boats from 28 to 70 feet and smaller transient slips with all the amenities, plus an enomous indoor dry stack storage facility. A big charter fishing fleet calls this marina home, offering light-tackle sound fishing, shrimping, and shark trips, as well as inshore, offshore, and deepwater wreck fishing. The marina has a full-service ship's store, engine

BOATWORKS ON ROANOKE ISLAND

Boatbuilders in Wanchese include:

Bayliss Boatworks (252-473-9797; www.baylissboatworks.com), Wanchese Seafood Industrial Park, 600 Harbor Road. Custom boats are built the old-fashioned way here—from the keel up. A marine supply store is located on-site.

Blackwell Boatworks (252-473-1803; www.blackwellboatworks.com), Wanchese Seafood Industrial Park, 932 Harbor Road. In business for over 20 years, Blackwell's owner formerly worked for the famed Buddy Davis.

Bluewater Outer Banks Yacht Service (252-475-1420; www.bluewateryachtsales.com), Wanchese Seafood Industrial Park, 920 Harbor Road.

Briggs Boatworks (252-473-2393; www.briggsboatworks.com), Wanchese Seafood Industrial Park, 370 Harbor Road. Boats from Briggs are noted for speed.

Scarborough Boatworks (252-473-3646; www.scarboroughboatworks.com), 273 Thicket Lump Road. Ricky Scarborough, a major proponent of the Carolina style and 30-year boat-building veteran, hand builds his boats from juniper planks.

Spencer Yachts Inc. (252-473-6567; www.spenceryachtsinc.com), 31 Beverly Drive. Producers of high-performance sportfishing yachts.

A couple of other boatbuilders, both famous for their skill, operate in the Roanoke Island area. In Manns Harbor, Mann Custom Boats Inc. (252-473-1716; www.paulmanncustomboats.com), 6300 US 64, builds boats that are proven winners in fishing tournaments. In Manteo, legendary boatbuilder Buddy Cannady teams up with charter captain Billy Maxwell to create custom Carolina-style boats at BB Boats (252-473-1097; www.bbboatsinc.com), 135 Berry Drive.

BAYLESS BOATWORKS, IN WANCHESE INDUSTRIAL PARK, BUILDS BOATS THE OLD-FASHIONED WAY

and canvas repair, and a professional fish-cleaning station, plus a seasonal tiki bar. This is the southern home base of the National Geographic Channel's hit show *Wicked Tuna: Outer Banks*.

Thicket Lump Marina (252-473-4500), 219 Thicket Lump Road. Located just 5 miles from Oregon Inlet by sea, this full-service marina at the end of Thicket Lump Road offers fuel, a ship's store, and private slips. Dolphin tours, charter fishing, and headboat trips are available from the docks. The shaded patio of the on-site **Great Gut Deli** is a favorite lunch stop.

Wanchese Marina (252-619-2695; www.wanchesemarinaandlandinggrill.com), 4447 Mill Landing Road. The town's original docks, where the Danielses launched their international seafood company, today is a laid-back spot offering a variety of charters, including clamming trips, crabbing and shrimping, dolphin tours, and your choice of fishing styles and destinations. To see the shrimp trawlers unloading their catch, visit around lunchtime from mid-July through September on a Friday or Saturday. **The Landing Grill** (252-473-3247) serves breakfast and lunch. The beloved **Fisherman's Wharf Restaurant** (www.fishermanswharfobx.com), a Wanchese landmark since 1974, is currently closed—at least until another member of the Daniels family decides to try their hand at foodservice.

FOR FAMILIES ✐ **"Pigum" Walker Park** (252-473-6638; www.darenc.com/parksrec) on Pond Road has a playground, picnic shelter, tennis courts, and restrooms.

✐ ♿ **Grandpa Shrimp and Crab Charters** (252-305-8862; www.grandpascharters .com), OBX Marina, 705 Harbor Road. Experience the life of a professional fisherman with Captain Russell Firth as he drags a commercial-style shrimp net behind the boat, then takes you to check a line of crab pots. You sort the catch and keep everything of legal size—a favorite with families. Light tackle, inshore fishing, and half-and-half crabbing/shrimping and fishing also available.

HEADBOAT *Chief Wanchese* (252-423-1422; www.headboatchiefwanchese.com), 4457 Mill Landing Road. Sailing from the Wanchese Marina, this 50-foot catamaran was built in 2016 specifically for fishing the shallow waters of Roanoke Sound. Sunset and sight-seeing cruises also available.

✳ Lodging

BED & BREAKFASTS 🌾 (ᵗᵞ) **Island House of Wanchese Bed & Breakfast** (252-473-5619; www.islandhouse-bb.com), 104 Old Wharf Road. Located in a rambling historic home, this inn serves a full country-style breakfast buffet every morning. Guests are welcome to use the freezer to store their catch, or borrow beach chairs, umbrellas, and towels for trips to the beach. They also have access to a 24-hour pantry with refrigerator, microwave, and ice machine. A screened gazebo is available for smokers or just to relax. $$–$$$.

(ᵗᵞ) **Timothy O Tillett Homeplace Bed & Breakfast** (252-216-7702; www .timothyotillett.com), 188 Old Schoolhouse Road. Lorraine Tillett, a descendant of the couple who built the house in 1891, welcomes couples only to rent a three-room suite with private outdoor porch, all decorated with family heirlooms. Rates include a full (and memorable) breakfast, plus homemade dessert. Stables are available if you want to trailer-in your horses. Two-night minimum. $$$.

✳ (ᵗᵞ) **Wanchese Inn Bed and Breakfast** (252-475-1166 or 252-473-0602; www .wancheseinn.com), 85 Jovers Lane. Especially popular with anglers, this

BODIE ISLAND OYSTERS

Oysters were once a major product of the local fisheries, with some 800,000 bushels of the bivalves pulled from Outer Banks waters in 1902. Numbers steadily declined from there, however, as overfishing and pollution decimated the population of local oysters, known as Crab Sloughs. However, in recent years, oyster farming techniques have taken giant leaps forward, and in 2013 a Wanchese waterman named Joey Daniels took note and decided to get in the game. He pitched his business plan to the board at Wanchese Fish Company, the now worldwide business founded by his great-grandfather 80 years ago. The board, made up of family members, thought it was a great idea. Today, Joey farms oysters seeded in off-bottom trays on his lease situated between Bodie Island and Oregon Inlet, where the mix of fresh and salt water is optimum for oyster growth. Bodie Island Oysters are going strong, appearing at oyster bars across the Banks, and soon, if Joey has his way, around the world.

OYSTER FARMING IS BRINGING BACK THE TASTY BIVALVES TO LOCAL WATERS AND RESTAURANTS

historic house in Wanchese offers four rooms, including a master suite with king bed and Jacuzzi. A full breakfast is served every morning. After that, you can lounge on the porch, take the complimentary beach towels and chairs to the shore, or go fishing. There's a freezer to stash your catch and a 35-foot boat slip where you can dock your boat. Boat and trailer parking is available on-site. Pets are not allowed, but the inn will help you arrange boarding nearby. Smoking is not permitted inside the building. Winter $–$$; otherwise $$.

RV RESORTS While overnight parking or camping is not permitted there, the **Outer Banks Roanoke Island Welcome**

THE WANCHESE INN BED & BREAKFAST IS ONE OF THE FEW ACCOMMODATIONS IN THE VILLAGE

Center (252-473-2138) on the US 64/264 Bypass provides visiting RVers with a free waste dump station.

&. ((ᵱ)) The **Refuge on Roanoke Island** (252-473-1096; www.therefuge-roanokeisland.com), 2881 NC 345. Campground offers full hookups, including some waterfront sites. Amenities include a bathhouse, pavilion with picnic tables and grills, fishing pond, outdoor pool, Wi-Fi, cable TV, and a dock and boardwalk over the marsh.

✳ Where to Eat

✒ **Great Gut Deli** (252-473-2479), 219 Thicket Lump Road, Thicket Lump Marina. Closed Sunday. The deli upstairs in Thicket Lump Marina serves sandwiches made of Boar's Head meats and cheeses, plus delicious house-made shrimp, chicken, and tuna salads and

pizza. Eat indoors or out on the shaded deck. Beer and wine available. $.

🦀 **The Landing Grill** (252-473-3247; www.wanchesemarinaandlandinggrill .com), 4447 Mill Landing Road. Friendly spot in the Wanchese Marina serves breakfast and lunch, including breakfast sandwiches and quesadillas. $.

Mann's Luncheonette (252-473-3787), NC 345. Friendly staff will fill your orders at the counter located next to Mann's Grocery and Hardware. Spencer sausage, a local favorite, is the featured meat in breakfast sandwiches, or you can have eggs with your choice of sausage, bacon, "city ham," or country ham. The luncheonette serves rib eyes, barbecue, daily specials, and buckets of fried chicken (but no seafood) until 5 PM. $.

🍸 **OBX Marina Tiki Bar** (252-473-9991; www.obxmarina.com), Wanchese Seafood Industrial Park, 708 Harbor Drive. Meet the locals, and possibly the cast and crew of *Wicked Tuna*, around this tiki bar with daily drink specials and icy cold beer. There's generally a food truck nearby and live music on Fridays and some Saturday nights during the season.

⌗ ↪ **O'Neal's Sea Harvest Restaurant and Retail Store** (252-473-4535; www .onealsseaharvest.com), Wanchese Seafood Industrial Park, 622 Harbor Road. Closed Sunday. This casual café serves fried fish or shrimp baskets and softshell crabs with your choice of fries or fried okra. Add a crabcake or oysters to your order for a small additional fee. In the retail store, fresh seafood is available according to the season, but most varieties are also available flash frozen year-round. The store will pack your cooler full of seafood to take home or will ship it directly to you. Lunch only, $.

✳ Selective Shopping

Mann's Sentry Hardware and Mann's Red and White (252-473-5664), 2991 NC 345/Mill Landing Road. Owned and operated by the Mann family, Wanchese's version of a shopping center includes a grocery store, an old-fashioned hardware store, and a luncheonette, all connected by interior doors. You can fill up on gas out front.

HATTERAS ISLAND

■

PEA ISLAND

THE TRI-VILLAGES: RODANTHE,
WAVES, AND SALVO

AVON (KINNAKEET)

BUXTON

FRISCO

HATTERAS VILLAGE

HATTERAS ISLAND
One Road On, One Road Off

atteras Island is the most fragile section of the Outer Banks and the heart of the **Cape Hatteras National Seashore**. Here you can see nature at work, as wind and water compete to build land and to wash it away. In the past, one continuous strip of sand stretched from the Virginia border to the tip of Ocracoke. A great unnamed storm opened both the Oregon and Hatteras inlets in 1846, creating the Hatteras Island we know today.

Experts say that within not too many years, Hatteras will break into separate islands as new inlets open across the sandy barrier, which at some points is less than a quarter-mile wide. In fact, this process is already in motion. In 2011, Hurricane Irene moved these speculations out of the realm of possibility into the world of fact. Overwash coming from the sound side created several breaches, both in the **Pea Island Refuge** and in the Mirlo Beach neighborhood of **Rodanthe** near the famous S curves. These breaches have continued to reopen in the years since, and the state is currently building new causeway bridges at both the Pea Island Refuge and Rodanthe that will bypass the new inlets and better preserve the birds and wildlife of the region.

At the same time that tides and storms are washing away parts of the Banks, the ocean is also building new islands. In June 2017, a new island appeared off the tip of Cape Point, just past the **Cape Hatteras Lighthouse**. About a mile long, the sandbar, dubbed **Shelly Island** by a young visitor, was originally separated from Cape Point by a 50-yard-wide channel with strong riptides flowing through. The channel eventually filled in, with the island becoming part of Hatteras Island. The coast in this area changes constantly as storms continue to sculpt Mother Nature.

GUIDANCE The islands south of the Bonner Bridge are long and narrow. For the first 13 miles, the **Pea Island Visitor Center** (252987-2394) is the only place to stop. The villages on the rest of Hatteras are broken into two groups. Rodanthe, Waves, and Salvo, sometimes called the Tri-Villages, and Avon, a few miles farther south, form Kinnakeet Township, still unincorporated but pulling together for mutual benefit. Hatteras Island takes a sharp bend to the west at Cape Point, where the famed Hatteras Lighthouse is located, with Buxton, Frisco, and Hatteras Village, the unincorporated villages that make up Hatteras Township, strung east to west.

A note on addresses: The somewhat charming method of giving addresses on Hatteras Island combines the number address along NC 12 with the name of the (short) cross street.

For information on attractions and traveling conditions on Hatteras Island, consult the **Whalebone Welcome Center** (252-441-6644 or 1-877-629-4386; www.outerbanks .org) on NC 12 in South Nags Head, or the **Outer Banks Visitors Bureau Hatteras Welcome Center in the historic U.S. Weather Station** (252-986-2203; www.outerbanks .org), 57190 Kohler Road in Hatteras Village.

GETTING THERE *By ferry:* At the southern end of Hatteras Island, free ferries run from Hatteras Village to Ocracoke Island, where NC 12 continues south. The ferries run every day on a regular schedule that changes with season and demand. Ferry

TOP 10 ACTIVITIES ON HATTERAS ISLAND

1. Climb the **Cape Hatteras Lighthouse**, at night, by flashlight, if you dare.
2. Enjoy a sunset cocktail on the deck of a **Hatteras Village marina**.
3. Discover the heroic deeds of lifesavers at **Chicamacomico Life-Saving Station**.
4. Explore 400 years of shipwrecks at the **Graveyard of the Atlantic Museum**.
5. Catch the kiteboarding action at **Kite Point** and the windsurfing at **Canadian Hole**.
6. Fish for red drum at **Avon Pier**.
7. Board a **headboat** for a day of fishing the Atlantic or a pirate adventure.
8. Eat with the Hatteras Island locals at a **Saturday-night fish fry** in Avon or Hatteras Village.
9. Photograph birds at **Pea Island National Wildlife Refuge**.
10. Try surf fishing at **Cape Point**.

service will, however, occasionally be canceled in times of storms or high seas. Check the **ferry website** at www.ncferry.org for the schedule. You can call 252-986-2353 or toll-free 1-800-368-8949 for current conditions. The crossing takes about 40 minutes.

By car: Without taking a boat or airplane, there is only one way on and off Hatteras Island: the Herbert C. Bonner Bridge. Built in 1962, it replaced the state ferry service that began in 1935. Now showing its age, the Bonner Bridge is being replaced by a new, four-lane bridge parallel to the current span. If all goes well, it is scheduled to open in 2018. A part of the old bridge will be retained for use as a fishing pier. If storm or other accident should render the Bonner impassable, the state plans to immediately begin ferry service across Oregon Inlet. For updates on Bonner Bridge construction and background information, visit the **North Carolina Department of Transportation website** (www.ncdot.gov/nc12).

NC 12, THE MAIN ROAD ON HATTERAS ISLAND, IS FREQUENTLY OVERWASHED WITH SAND AND WATER

GETTING AROUND NC 12, here part of the Outer Banks National Scenic Byway, is the only through road on Hatteras Island. It is just two lanes wide and subject to frequent traffic backups. Tucked just behind the dunes, the narrow roadway is frequently overwashed by storm waters and covered with sand. However, the state's Department of Transportation remains committed to keeping the road open and invests considerable manpower and equipment in this ongoing project. Currently new causeway bridges are underway in the Pea Island–Rodanthe region, but the state plans to keep traffic flowing throughout the construction process.

Island Cruisers (252-987-2097; www.islandcruisersinc.com), 26248 NC 12, Rodanthe, will rent you a fun, street-legal VW buggy, a four-wheel drive for heading

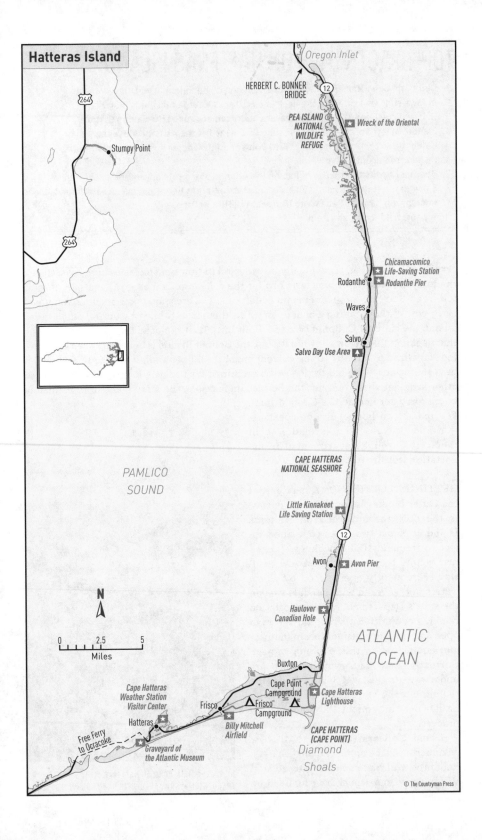

Hatteras Island

264

Stumpy Point

Oregon Inlet

HERBERT C. BONNER
BRIDGE

12

*PEA ISLAND
NATIONAL
WILDLIFE
REFUGE*

⭐ *Wreck of the Oriental*

*Chicamacomico
Life-Saving Station*

Rodanthe ⭐

⭐ *Rodanthe Pier*

Waves

Salvo

Salvo Day Use Area ⛺

264

PAMLICO
SOUND

*CAPE HATTERAS
NATIONAL SEASHORE*

*Little Kinnakeet
Life Saving Station* ⭐

12

Avon ⭐ *Avon Pier*

*Haulover
Canadian Hole* ⭐

N

0   2.5   5
Miles

ATLANTIC
OCEAN

Buxton

*Cape Hatteras
Weather Station
Visitor Center*

Frisco

Cape Point
Campground

⛺ *Frisco
Campground*

⭐ *Cape Hatteras
Lighthouse*

Hatteras ⭐

*Free Ferry
to Ocracoke*

⭐ *Billy Mitchell
Airfield*

*Graveyard of
the Atlantic Museum*

*CAPE HATTERAS
(CAPE POINT)*

Diamond

Shoals

© The Countryman Press

EXCURSIONS

The Outer Banks National Scenic Byway (www.outerbanksbyway.com) begins at Whalebone Junction and follows NC 12 south over the Bonner Bridge and down Hatteras Island, across the ferry to Ocracoke Island, then takes the ferry to Cedar Island to meander through the small Down East communities where decoy carving and boatbuilding still rule. The 138-mile route (plus two ferry rides) passes through 21 maritime villages with strong traditions tied to the sea, as well as some of the most spectacular coastal scenery accessible by automobile. The byway runs past four lighthouses, plus several wildlife refuges and museums, and is a great trip any time of year. The route is also a North Carolina Scenic Byway, and an interactive map can be found on the **North Carolina Department of Transportation website** (www.ncdot.gov/travel/scenic). The *NCDOT: Scenic Byways* book, containing a detailed description of the Outer Banks Scenic Byway as well as other scenic drives in the region, can be downloaded from the same website. A new book from University of North Carolina Press, *Living at the Water's Edge: A Heritage Guide to the Outer Banks Byway*, by Karen Amspacher and Barbara Garrity-Blake, collects stories of people who live along the byway's route.

out to the beach for surf fishing, or a vintage classic for cruising the island roads. Golf carts are also available. A full-service garage, **Hatteras Island Performance** (252-987-1250), is located next door.

Island Hopper Shuttle (252-995-6771) offers taxi and limo service on Hatteras Island and beyond.

MEDICAL EMERGENCY **Outer Banks Family Medicine Avon** (252-995-3073; www.vidanthealth.com), 40894 NC 12, Avon. Center associated with the University Health Systems of Eastern Carolina offers family medicine by appointment, with a doctor on call 24 hours.

PEA ISLAND

As you come across the Bonner Bridge from Bodie Island, the abandoned Oregon Inlet Life-Saving Station sits awash in sand, its tower just peeking above the dunes. Just beyond, sand crowds close to the narrow pavement of NC 12, frequently blowing over the road. Waves often wash across this area during storms. The first 13 miles south of the bridge are part of the 6,000-acre **Pea Island National Wildlife Refuge**, the wintering grounds of more than a dozen waterfowl species. Large fresh and brackish water impoundments and natural ponds take up most of the width of the island. Biologists studying the ecosystem have determined that periodic overwash is a natural process and an essential part of maintaining the habitat. NC 12, running between the ponds and the dunes, is in the way.

GUIDANCE The **Pea Island Visitor Center** (252-987-2394) is the best place to stop. Here you can pick up a map of the very easy walking trails in the refuge and get help identifying the species you will see. If you cross the dunes here to walk along the ocean, you may see the boiler of a steamer that wrecked in 1862, the *Oriental*, above the waves. Public restrooms are available here as well.

✳ To See

& **Pea Island National Wildlife Refuge** (252-987-2394; www.fws.gov/pea island), NC 12. The refuge offers superb bird-watching and handicapped-accessible hiking trails, as well as a pristine stretch of beach where endangered shorebirds and loggerhead sea turtles nest. Paved parking areas are located at the base of the Bonner Bridge next to Oregon Inlet, and at the visitor center, about 4 miles south of the bridge. The & visitor center, with a bookstore and spotting scope trained on the North Pond, is open 9–4 daily; hours are shorter December–March.

✳ To Do

BIRD-WATCHING The **Pea Island National Wildlife Refuge** is considered one of the finest birding destinations in North Carolina, with habitats ranging from salt marsh to freshwater impoundments to beach and dune. The bird list for the refuge includes 365 different species.

During the winter months, large numbers of ducks, geese, and swans are in residence. Several observation decks overlook the refuge, as well as a more remote blind for photography or serious birding. Ask about access.

✳ **Pea Island Bird Walks** (252-473-1131; www.fws.gov/peaisland). Free bird walks are offered year-round from the visitor center. Special ecotours focus on shorebirds and sea turtles during the summer months.

BOATING Kayaks are a very popular way to tour the wildlife refuge, both to spot birds and to see the aquatic life through the usually extremely clear, shallow water. The **New**

THE OLD OREGON INLET LIFE-SAVING STATION IS NEARLY BURIED IN SAND

Inlet Boat Ramp, a free public ramp, accommodates only small boats with very shallow drafts. The parking lot is on the west side of NC 12, about a half-mile south of the bridge over the new Pea Island Inlet caused by Hurricane Irene, and about 6 miles south of Oregon Inlet.

Pea Island Canoe Tours (www.fws.gov/peaisland). Canoe tours in Pamlico Sound led by a naturalist are offered for a fee, with a special tour for families. Call 252-216-9464 to register.

Several commercial outfitters offer kayak and SUP (stand-up paddleboard) tours of the Pea Island Refuge. Among them, **Kitty Hawk Kites Sunset Tour** (252-987-2528; www.kittyhawk.com) and **Coastal Kayak** (252-441-3393; www.outer banskayaktours.com), are recommended for birders.

Pea Island is also extremely popular for kayak fishing. **Kitty Hawk Kites** (252-987-2528; www.kittyhawk.com), **Kitty Hawk Surf Co.** (252-441-4124; www.khsurf.com) and **Ocean Atlantic Rentals** (1-800-635-9559; www .oceanatlanticrentals.com) all rent kayaks equipped for fishing. Rob Alderman of **Outer Banks Kayak Fishing** (252-305-2017; www.outerbankskayakfishing.com) will take you on a guided outing in the sound or the ocean.

FISHING **Bonner Bridge,** NC 12. A catwalk from the southern end of the Bonner lets you fish around the pilings out in

PEA ISLAND'S PONDS ARE A FAVORITE STOP FOR BOTH WATERFOWL AND PHOTOGRAPHERS

MANY SPECIES OF WADING BIRDS INHABIT PEA ISLAND YEAR-ROUND

Oregon Inlet. There's a large paved parking lot at the base of the bridge. When the Bonner is replaced in the next few years, the old bridge will be adapted as a fishing pier. It is free to fish here, but you do need a North Carolina Coastal Recreational Fishing License.

SHORE SNORKELING AND DIVING Strong swimmers can reach a few of the wrecks along the Hatteras Island coast. The *LST 471*, which sank in 1949, is about 100 yards offshore, a mile north of the **Rodanthe Fishing Pier**, in 15 feet of water. The *Oriental*, also called the Boiler Wreck, a federal transport that sank in 1862, lies off the beach opposite the **Pea Island National Wildlife Refuge** visitor center in 20 feet of water. The boiler is usually visible above the waves.

✴ Green Space

& **Pea Island National Wildlife Refuge Trails**. The refuge has two handicapped-accessible trails around North Pond, where bird-watching is good all year, and spectacular in the winter months when the migratory waterfowl are in residence. The **North Pond Trail** leads along the south side of the pond to a dual-level observation tower. The shorter **Salt Flats Wildlife Trail** leads along the north side of the pond to an observation deck. A service road connects these two trails along the west side of the pond, and many people walk the entire loop. The final leg of the loop, however, runs along the shoulder of NC 12, a sometimes dangerous proposition. Instead, cross over the dunes and return along the beach, where you'll see the boiler of the *Oriental* about 100 yards offshore. No vehicles are allowed on the beach in the refuge, and fires and camping are prohibited. The refuge trails and beach are open during daylight hours all year.

✴ Special Events

June: **Pea Island Crabbing and Fishing Rodeo** (www.fws.gov/peaisland), Pea Island National Wildlife Refuge. North Pond is open for fishing and crabbing for three hours, once a year, on the second Saturday in June.

THE TRI-VILLAGES: RODANTHE, WAVES, AND SALVO

Towering above the wild dunes, the tall cottages of Mirlo Beach are the first signs of human habitation on Hatteras. Named for a torpedoed ship that sank close by and a famous rescue, Mirlo is the most quickly eroding stretch of beach on Hatteras.

In the late 1800s, villages formed around lifesaving stations established by the federal government, when numerous shipwrecks gave this coast the well-deserved name, Graveyard of the Atlantic. With no reliable means of summoning help, lifesavers patrolled every foot of coast, 24 hours a day, on the watch for ships in distress. In the shadow of the Mirlo Beach cottages, the **Chicamacomico Life-Saving Station** sits facing the ocean, as it has since 1874. The restored buildings are filled with memories of heroic rescues, violent storms, daily drills, and the harsh life along these shores.

The village of Chicamacomico was renamed **Rodanthe** (*roe-DAN-thee*) when the U.S. Postal Service arrived in 1874. Over time, South Rodanthe and Clark received new postal service names as well, becoming **Waves** and **Salvo**. Today you have to look closely to see boundaries between these villages. In fact, there is a growing trend to refer to this section of Hatteras as the Tri-Villages. It's noted for its many campgrounds and great king mackerel fishing from the pier.

One name you're sure to encounter here is Midgett. Descended from a man who purchased land in this area as early as 1717, members of the family today run stores and restaurants, operate one of the area's largest real estate firms, and continue the family's long tradition of serving in the Coast Guard. At the time of the *Mirlo* rescue, five of the six lifesavers on duty were named Midgett. The sixth was married to a Midgett girl.

Most recently, the Tri-Villages have become a nationally recognized hot spot for the growing sport of kiteboarding, due soon to become an official Olympic sport. Two large resorts dedicated to kiteboarding have opened along the shores of Pamlico Sound, with numerous other water sports venues offering rentals and lessons.

POST OFFICE The **Rodanthe Post Office** (252-987-2273) is located at 25969 NC 12. The zip code for Rodanthe is 27968; for Salvo and Waves, 27982.

PUBLIC RESTROOMS Restrooms are located inside the **Rodanthe-Waves-Salvo (R-W-S) Community Center** (252-987-2575), at 23186 Myrna Peters Road, and at the **Salvo Day Use Area** (see *To See*) south of the villages.

GETTING AROUND As you drive into the Tri-Villages from the north, you will pass first through Rodanthe, then Waves, then Salvo, before reentering the national seashore. Avon is about 10 miles to the south.

Across the street from the lifesaving station, a short road leads down to Rodanthe Harbor, site of a Civil War battle.

For additional information or a visitor guide, visit www.rodanthewavessalvonc.org.

✳ To See

Civil War Trails (www.civilwartraveler .com). A marker across NC 12 from the Chicamacomico Life-Saving Station in Rodanthe tells the tale of the infamous Chicamacomico Races, during which Confederates and Federals chased each other up and down the island in October 1861. A marker in a picnic area on the sound nearby describes the capture of the *Fanny*, a Union supply ship, on October 1, 1861.

   Rodanthe Fishing Pier (252-987-0030; www.rodanthepierllc.com), 24251 Atlantic Avenue, Rodanthe. Repaired after extensive damage in the stormy 2012 season, Rodanthe Pier, one of the island's longest, played a cameo role in the 2008 movie *Nights in Rodanthe*. The large pier house has an air-conditioned game room with pool table, air hockey, arcade games, a snack bar, and a jukebox. The tackle shop sells bait, tackle, gifts, and snacks, and rents rods, reels, and other equipment. Sightseers can walk out on the pier for $2. Call for hours.

   Kiteboarding. One of the most watchable sports around, kiteboarding is booming in the Tri-Villages and could soon be an Olympic sport. To check out the action (without getting wet), visit the **Waves Village Sports Resort** (252-987-2297; www.kittyhawk .com) or **REAL Lesson Center** (252-987-6000 or 1-866-REAL-548; www.realwatersports .com), both located along the west side of NC 12 in Rodanthe. Both have restaurants and decks overlooking Pamlico Sound where you can kick back with a microbrew and enjoy the show.

   Island Art Shows (252-987-2575; www .rwscivic.org), R-W-S Community Center, 23186 Myrna Peters Road. Changing art shows showcase the work of local artists.

   Pea Island Art Gallery (252-987-2879; www.peaislandartgallery.com), 27766 NC 12, Salvo. Housed in a replica of one of the lifesaving stations, a work of art in itself, Kim Robertson's gallery exhibits her own artwork as well as the work of some 100 other talented artists. A portion of sales benefits the Pea Island National Wildlife Refuge and the Chicamacomico Life-Saving Station.

   Salvo Day Use Area (www.nps.gov/ caha), NC 12. As you leave the Tri-Villages and enter the national seashore, this former campground along Pamlico Sound is a great rest stop where you can check out the shallow waters, sunbathe, or windsurf. There's an old cemetery here as well, with many local names on the headstones.

KITEBOARDING IS EXPECTED TO BECOME AN OLYMPIC SPORT SOON, THANKS TO ITS EXCITING ACTION

EARLY LIFESAVING STATION ARCHITECTURE

In 1874 the U.S. Life-Saving Service began building stations along the East Coast. The earliest stations were designed by architect Frances W. Chandler in an eclectic style with medieval and Renaissance influences. The stations' architecture, called Carpenter Gothic, used a board-and-batten style put together with wooden pegs that reminds many people of Scandinavian ski lodges. Most of these stations have been lost to fire or flood, or altered over the years, but Hatteras Island has two of the best preserved of all the 1874 stations, plus one very authentic replica of this unique architectural style.

The best, most completely restored station is the very first one built along this coast, now part of the Chicamacomico Historic Site (252-987-1552; www.chicamacomico.org). The National Park Service is restoring the Little Kinnakeet Station (www.nps.gov/caha), also built in the 1870s, located just north of Avon. The Pea Island Art Gallery (252-987-2879; www.peaislandartgallery.com), the last building on the sound side as you leave Salvo heading south, authentically reproduces much of the intricate woodwork that is the hallmark of Carpenter Gothic style.

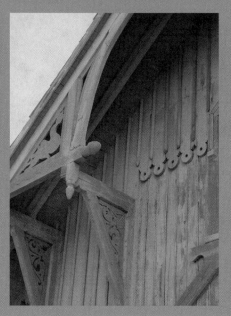 

Salvo Post Office, NC 12, Salvo. Famous as the country's second-smallest post office until it was decommissioned in 1992, the tiny white building with blue and white trim is now listed on the National Register of Historic Places. It sits on private land along the west side of NC 12 just south of the Park Road junction.

The Inn at Rodanthe, 23289 Beacon Road, Rodanthe. Mirlo Beach's most northern oceanside house, then known as Serendipity, served as a major location in the movie *Nights in Rodanthe*, starring Richard Gere and Diane Lane. After filming concluded, waves gradually eroded the beach away and left the towering cottage standing with its pilings in the surf. New owners moved the house about a half-mile south to a new oceanfront location and added the blue shutters and lofty porches seen in the movie.

MUST SEE

The vintage **Chicamacomico Life-Saving Station Historic Site & Museum** is dedicated to the amazing history and valiant heritage of the U.S. Life-Saving Service, which gave birth to the U.S. Coast Guard in 1915. Life-savers, drawn from the local population, achieved many daring rescues along this coast in the days when the area was earning its title as Graveyard of the Atlantic. The complex of buildings in Rodanthe is the most complete lifesaving station complex remaining on the East Coast. It includes the 1874 station, the first to be built on the Outer Banks, and the 1911 Life-Saving Station, now restored as a gift shop and museum. Exhibits detail the daily drills of the lifesavers, as well as the many rescues and wrecks that took place along this coast. Other buildings on the site include the 1907 Midgett House, with original furnishings. Volunteer crews from nearby Coast Guard stations reenact the breeches buoy drill every week during the summer season. ✆ ⚲ ♂ **Chicamacomico Life-Saving Station Historic Site & Museum** (252-987-1552; www.chicamacomico.org), 23645 NC 12, Rodanthe.

RESTORED TO ITS 1874 APPEARANCE, THE CHICAMACOMICO LIFE-SAVING STATION TELLS TALES OF HEROIC RESCUES AND DEDICATION TO DUTY

The interior has been decorated to match the on-screen decor as well. It's not open to the public, but it is available for rental through **Sun Realty** (252-987-2766; www.sunrealtync.com).

Wreck of the G.A. Kohler, NPS Ramp 27, 4 miles south of Salvo. The charred remains of this four-masted schooner that was driven ashore in a hurricane in 1933 are sometimes visible through the shifting sands.

✳ To Do

BIKING A paved off-road multiuse path parallels the west side of NC 12 through the Tri-Villages, from the Rodanthe-Waves-Salvo Community Building, at 23186 Myrna Peters Road, to the Salvo Day Use Area. In addition, a 3- to 6-foot-wide paved shoulder runs along NC 12 all the way to Hatteras Village. In Salvo, the Colony Road loop offers nice ocean views.

Duck Village Outfitters (252-987-1222; www.duckvillageoutfitters.net), 26689 NC 12, Salvo. DVO rents beach cruisers for the whole family, plus geared bikes, surfboards, kayaks, and a variety of other useful beach equipment.

BOATING AND KAYAKING It is easy to launch kayaks and other shallow-bottom craft at any soundside access point. Jet Skis and powerboats are allowed only in the waters off the island's villages, as the National Park Service does not allow you to launch or operate power craft within park boundaries.

The **Dare County boat ramp** (www.darenc.com) in Rodanthe is on Myrna Peters Road. If you are staying at **Camp Hatteras Campground** (252-987-2777; www.camphatteras.com), you can launch your boat there.

The **Salvo Day Use Area** (see *To See*), south of the Tri-Villages, is a great alternative to the crowds at Canadian Hole and an excellent spot to launch a kayak, windsurfer, or kiteboard. A bathhouse provides showers and restrooms.

Charlie's Boat Rentals (757-477-6475; www.charliesboatrentals.com), 25628 NC 12, Waves. Rent flat-bottomed skiffs or pontoon boats that seat 5–16 people, or a three-seater Yamaha WaveRunner, by the hour, day, or week. You can launch at Charlie's soundside location.

Kitty Hawk Kites (252-987-2297; www.kittyhawk.com), 24502 NC 12, Rodanthe. Rental kayaks and other sport equipment available.

CRAFTS ✄ ☂ **Beads & Beans OBX** (252-305-2352; www.facebook.com/beadsandbeans obx), 24267 NC 12, Rodanthe. Create your own jewelry from the thousands of beads in stock while you stoke your creativity with the wide selection of coffees and teas available.

FISHING **Hatteras Jack** (252-987-2428; www.hatterasjack.com), 23902 NC 12, Rodanthe. Master caster Ryan White's shop will build you a custom rod and reel, repair the equipment you've got, or provide guide services for whatever kind of fishing you have in mind. Casting instruction available.

((ᵧ)) **Mac's Tackle & Island Convenience** (252-987-2239), 23532 NC 12, Rodanthe. Mac Midgett's tackle shop also has a wrecker service if you get stuck in the sand, plus gas, beer, and all the usual convenience store items. The popular **Marilyn's Deli** inside serves homemade biscuits for breakfast, fried chicken, sandwiches, and boiled peanuts all day.

Rodanthe Fishing Pier (252-987-0030; www.rodanthepierllc.com), 24251 Atlantic Avenue, Rodanthe.

FOR FAMILIES ✄ **R-W-S Community Center Playground** (252-475-5650; www.darenc.com/parksrec), 23646 NC 12, Rodanthe. Playground and picnic area. Restrooms inside the community center.

SURF SHOPS **Rodanthe Surf Shop** (252-987-2412; www.facebook.com/rodanthe surfshop), 23580 NC 12, Rodanthe. Run by hard-core surfers, this shop sells Hatteras Glass Surfboards, shaped on-site and a longtime local favorite. Call 252-987-2435 for the daily Hatteras surf report.

WATER SPORTS Among the numerous water sports shops on Hatteras Island, several provide good destinations for a daylong excursion, with rentals of watercraft, plus showers, restrooms, and picnic facilities. All are located on the shores of Pamlico Sound.

Hatteras Island Surf & Sail (www
.hatterasislandsurfshop.com). The two
HISS shops offer expert water sports
equipment, lessons, and local knowledge
dating to the 1970s, when the legendary
Barton Decker founded his first shop in
Waves. The **HISS Surf Shop** (252-987-
2296), 25920 NC 12, carries many top-
of-the-line brands of boards. Sister store
HISS Sail Shop (252-987-2292), on Lela
Court behind the Dairy Queen in Waves,
offers kayak, paddleboard, windsurfing,
kiteboarding, and sailboat rentals and
lessons, with an on-site launch.

MANY SPOTS ON HATTERAS RENT JET SKIS FOR
EXCURSIONS ON THE SOUND

Hatteras Watersports (252-987-2306;
www.hatteraswatersports.com), 27130
NC 12, MP 42.5, Salvo. Rent Jet Skis, kayaks, SUPs, and Hobie Cat sailboats at this
friendly, family-operated water sports
mecca located in the former Pea Island Life-Saving Station. A large lawn with picnic
tables, observation deck, and volleyball court; restrooms with hot showers; plus a
beach on the sound make this a great place for all ages to spend a relaxing afternoon.

Rodanthe Watersports and Campground (252-987-1431; www.watersportsand
campground.com), 24170 NC 12, Rodanthe. Rent Jet Skis, kayaks, SUPs, and sailboats
here, and enjoy the soundside beach and hot showers. Wet suits, beach equipment,
and surf, boogie, and skim boards also for
rent.

KITEBOARDING IS THE BIGGEST SPORT ON THE HATTERAS
ISLAND SCENE

WATER SPORTS RESORTS ✍ **REAL
Kiteboarding Center** (252-987-6000 or
1-866-REAL-548; www.realwatersports
.com), 25706 NC 12, Waves. Founded by
Trip Forman and Matt Nuzzo, both leg-
ends in kiteboarding, REAL offers a wide
variety of kiteboarding lessons for all
ability levels, from beginner to advanced,
including the award-winning Zero 2 Hero
course and special lessons for young riders, as well as stand-up paddleboarding
and surfing instruction. The rental shop
offers top kiting, surfing, and stand-up
gear. A huge deck overlooks the action on
"the Slick," and music plays throughout
the property. The launch site is reserved
for customers. **Watermen's Bar & Grill** is
part of the complex, as are as the **Watermen's Retreat condos**. Check the **REAL
website** (www.realwatersports.com) for a
map of the best kiting and surfing "session" spots on Hatteras Island, rated by
ability level.

Waves Village Watersports Resort (252-987-2297; www.wavesvillage.com), 24502 NC 12, MP 40, Rodanthe. Located on the sound side, Kitty Hawk's new kiteboarding resort offers kiteboard, surfing, and SUP rentals and lessons, kayak and bike rentals, plus kiteboarding camps, private lessons, and the popular "Fly & Ride" one-day introductory course. The free launch site here, with restrooms and hot showers, is open to the public. A new Adventure Tower ropes challenge course combines 15 climbing elements. Waves Village also has a coffee shop, the **Good Winds Restaurant**, several retail stores, and on-site accommodations.

✲ Green Space

BEACHES Hatteras Island faces the Atlantic with a long, unspoiled beach for some 50 miles, from the Bonner Bridge to the spit south of Hatteras Village. The island bends to the west after Cape Hatteras, and the water and waves along the southern shore are often warmer and less wild than the eastern-facing Kinnakeet beaches farther north. Most of the beach is under the management of the National Park Service as part of the **Cape Hatteras National Seashore** (www.nps.gov/caha), which maintains several spots along NC 12 where you can park and cross the dunes. It's not advisable to pull off on the shoulders of NC 12, as the sand can be deceptively deep. There are no lifeguards along this stretch of beach. If your car has four-wheel drive, you can drive onto the beach at off-road vehicle ramps located along the island after obtaining a permit from the NPS. The beaches in front of the island's villages are generally closed to vehicle traffic from March 15 to September 15.

THE BEACH IN THE TRI-VILLAGES GETS CROWDED DURING THE SUMMER MONTHS

On the sound side of the park, the **Salvo Day Use Area**, formerly a national park campground, is just south of the village of Salvo and has a nice, shallow beach for children, plus restrooms and a shower. It's a favorite spot to launch kayaks, kiteboards, and windsurfers as well.

Dare County maintains a beach access (252-475-5650; www.darenc.com/parksrec) at 23731 NC 12 in Rodanthe Village.

✳ Lodging

CAMPGROUNDS The Tri-Villages are the last stronghold of oceanfront camping, once prevalent from one end of the Banks to the other. Frequent devastating storms have made this stretch of coast less attractive to developers, keeping oceanfront property prices low and allowing campgrounds to continue this longtime tradition.

✳ 🐾 ♂ ☀ (ဲ) ♂ **Camp Hatteras RV Resort & Campground** (252-987-2777; www.camphatteras.com), 24798 NC 12, Rodanthe. Located on both sides of NC 12, this camping resort stretches from the ocean to the sound. Some 400 full-hookup sites with cable TV enjoy numerous amenities, including three swimming pools (one indoors); a hot tub; clubhouse; lighted tennis courts; miniature golf; a soundside marina and boat ramp; stocked fishing ponds; a dog park; and free Wi-Fi access. Jet Ski, kayak, and bike rentals are located on-site. Off-season $; summer $$.

✳ ♂ ☀ (ဲ) **Cape Hatteras KOA Resort** (252-987-2307 or 1-800-562-5268; www.capehatteraskoa.com), 25099 NC 12, Waves. Large campground on the ocean side of NC 12 has over 300 campsites for RVs and tents, plus upgraded one- and two-bedroom Kamping Kabins. Amenities include a pool, a hot tub, snack bar, game room, playground, and planned activities, including campfires and outdoor movies. Additional fees for rides on the kids' train, jumping pillow, minigolf, bike rentals, Wi-Fi access, cable TV hookups, and pancake breakfasts. Canine campers enjoy a fenced dog

park where they can run free. Off-season $; summer $$.

♿ **Lazy Days Campground** (252-207-2060; www.obxlazydays.com), 26153 NC 12, Salvo. Small campground with 16 full hookup sites was built in 2013. Beach access. $.

☀ (ဲ) **Midgett's Campground** (252-986-2284 or 252-216-7033; www.midgettscampground.com), 23444 NC 12, Rodanthe. Sites available for tents and RVs behind Island Convenience, with full bathhouse, indoor and outdoor hot showers, and playground for the kids; propane, diesel, and gas sales; and an on-site store and deli. The beach is a 5-minute walk. $.

✳ (ဲ) **Ocean Waves Campground** (252-987-2556; www.oceanwavescampground.com), 25313 NC 12, Waves. Quiet oceanfront campground has over 60 sites with full hookups, cable TV, game room, camp store, swimming pool, hot showers, laundry, free Wi-Fi, and direct access to the ocean. Tent sites available. $.

Rodanthe Watersports and Campground (252-987-1431; www.watersportsandcampground.com), 24170 NC 12, Rodanthe. This small campground on Pamlico Sound is a favorite with windsurfers, kiteboarders, and kayakers, who can launch on-site. Water and electric hookups for 15 RVs under 25 feet and 20 tents; full bathhouse. Campers get discounts on water sport rentals on-site. $.

(ဲ) **Saint Clair Landing Campground** (252987-2850; www.stclairlandingcampground.com), 25028 NC 12 at Mac Oca Drive, Rodanthe. Small, quiet campground on the sound for RVs and tents was completely rebuilt after Hurricane Irene. Boat rentals and Wi-Fi on-site. $.

MOTELS ☀ ((ၦ)) **Sea Sound Motel** (252-987-2224; www.seasoundmotelobx.com), 24224 Sea Sound Road, Rodanthe. Just a short walk from the beach, this family favorite is noted for its hospitality and economical rates, with many guests returning every year. Guests can enjoy an outdoor pool, fish-cleaning table, and picnic area with grills. $.

RESORTS ♂ ((ၦ)) **Watermen's Retreat** (252987-6060; www.watermensretreat .com), 25682 NC 12, Waves. Luxuriously appointed two- and three-bedroom condo units next to the REAL flagship store have teak floors, leather furniture, flat-screen TVs with cable, down duvets, granite cocktail bars, and full kitchens. Each unit has a private balcony with water views. The **Watermen's Bar & Grill** on-site serves meals and hosts frequent live music. Off-season $$; high season $$$$.

☀ ♿ ((ၦ)) **Waves Village Water-sports Resort** (1-866-595-1893; www .wavesvillage.com), 24502 NC 12, MP 40, Rodanthe. Part of the Kitty Hawk Kiteboarding Resort, these condominiums each have three bedrooms and three baths, electric fireplace, full kitchen with granite counters, multiple LCD TVs with cable, washer/dryer, plus a private balcony with a hot tub, gas grill, and view of the sound. Each unit sleeps up to eight people. Guests have access to an outdoor pool, an on-site restaurant, and kayak, SUP, surfing, and kiteboarding rentals and lessons just outside the door. Minimum stay may be required. $$$$.

�֎ Where to Eat

DINING OUT ♂ ♿ ↝ **Boardwok South** (252-987-1080; www.boardwoksouth .com), 26006 NC 12, MP 41.5, St. Waves Plaza, Waves. Specialties at the Boardwok are Asian stir-fried dishes made with rice, lo mein, or rice noodles. There

are surf and turf entrées as well, including an excellent crabcake and a tasty crab bisque, plus chocolate egg rolls for dessert. Dinner only, $$–$$$.

♂ ♿ ♈ ↝ **Good Winds Seafood & Wine Bar** (252-987-1100; www .goodwindsrestaurant.com), 24502 NC 12, Rodanthe. This restaurant, above the Kitty Hawk Kites store in Waves Village, has a casual vibe, but the chef-designed cuisine goes beyond the usual beach menu. The views of the sound, the sunset, and the kiteboarders are terrific. Ditto the fresh local catch and other chef creations. Or drop by the bar to try the dozen local crafts on draft. Live music some nights. Lunch $$; dinner $$–$$$.

♂ ♈ ((ၦ)) **Watermen's Bar & Grill** (252-987-1600; www.watermensbarandgrill .com), 25706 NC 12, Waves. Located on the sound behind REAL's flagship store, this new hot spot has it all—awesome sunsets, cold drafts of the local microbrew variety, seafood quesadillas and ribs that have folks raving, plus premieres of surfing movies and live music on the waterfront stage right through the fall. Drop by for a breakfast smoothie starting at 9 AM or come later to explore the Rum Bar. Lunch and dinner $$.

EATING OUT ♂ ((ၦ)) ↝ **Atlantic Coast Café** (252-987-1200; www .atlanticcoastcafe.com), 25150 NC 12, Waves. This Internet hotspot is a favorite with campers from the KOA just across NC 12. A big breakfast menu is served from 7 AM, with breakfast wraps and sandwiches available all day. For lunch or dinner, try a crabcake or shrimp Reuben "Hatteras style" with slaw, a dish of mac and cheese laced with crab, or a platter of local seafood. Beer and wine are served. Take-out and party trays available. $–$$.

((ၦ)) **Marilyn's Deli** (252-987-2239), Island Convenience, 23532 NC 12, Rodanthe. Popular stop with surfers and locals for the home-cooked specials at breakfast and lunch. $.

⚓ **Top Dog Café** (252-987-1272; www.topdogcafeobx.com), 27982 NC 12, Waves. Enjoy huge burgers, fish tacos, seafood, hot dogs, and beer and wine on the deck or screened porch of this casual, family-friendly spot with a pirate theme. Lunch $; dinner $–$$.

BEACH BARS ⚓ ☀ Ⴤ **Sting Wray's Bar & Grill** (252-987-1500; www.facebook.com/stingwrays), 24394 NC 12, MP 40, Rodanthe. Fun spot in the former Uncle Pauly's location has good fish sandwiches, cold beer, and live entertainment during the summer months. The dog-friendly outdoor deck yields great sunset views. $–$$.

COFFEE SHOPS ⚓ ☂ **Beads & Beans OBX** (252-305-2352; www.facebook.com/beadsandbeansobx), 24267 NC 12, Rodanthe. A wide selection of coffees and teas are served at this interesting bead store.

(((ɢ))) **Forbes Candies, Coffee and Tea** (252-987-2320; www.forbescandies.com), Waves Village, 24502 NC 12, Rodanthe. In addition to the candies, taffy, brittles, and fudge this candymaker is known for, this location also has a full-service espresso and coffee bar, teas, smoothies, and a variety of baked goods for a fast breakfast.

ICE CREAM **Village Conery** (www.facebook.com/VillageConery), 26204 Monitor Lane, MP 42, Salvo. Soft-serve and hand-dipped ice cream and frozen yogurt come in your choice of shakes, sundaes, splits, or cones.

PIZZA **Leonardo's Pizza** (252-987-6522; www.facebook.com/leonardospizzaobx), St. Waves Plaza, 26006 NC 12, MP 41.5, Waves. In a new location since Hurricane Irene, this little spot operated by locals is the go-to choice for thin-crust New York–style pizza. Delivery available after 5 PM. $–$$.

⚓ **Lisa's Pizzeria** (252-987-2525; www.lisaspizzeria.net), 24158 NC 12, Rodanthe. A tradition on the beach since 1986,

Lisa's serves hand-tossed pizza along with lasagna, spaghetti, burgers, subs, and more. Eat in, take out, or get free delivery. $–$$.

TAKEOUT ✳ **Waves Market and Deli** (252-987-2352; www.facebook.com/wavesmarket), St. Waves Plaza, 26006 NC 12, Waves. Small grocery has a good selection of craft beer, wine, and seafood, plus barbecue smoked in-house, burritos, Boar's Head sandwiches, thick-cut Belgian-style fries, homemade chicken salad, and lots of vegetarian options. Popular with the kiters and surfers who frequent the area, this store stays open really late all summer. $.

Ocean Gourmet and Sea Treasures (252-987-1166), 24753 NC 12, Rodanthe. Shop offers homemade fudge, ice cream, taffy, and pastries, plus a wealth of souvenirs, all within walking distance of Camp Hatteras.

✳ Entertainment

During the summer season, check the schedules at **Sting Wray's**, **Watermen's Bar & Grill**, and **Good Winds** in Waves Village for live music.

Skye Blue Summer Concert Series (252-987-6000 or 1-866-REAL-548; www.realwatersports.com), REAL, 25706 NC 12, Waves. Live concert series on the waterfront March through November is family friendly and free.

✳ Selective Shopping

Blue Whale (252-987-2335), 27307 NC 12, Salvo. Fun stop sells groceries, including steaks and chops, gas, beer, and wine, plus a popular logo T-shirt and a huge selection of hot sauces.

⚓ ☂ **Pirates of Chicamacomico** (252-489-9022), 23881 NC 12, Rodanthe. Ahoy, mateys: this is the spot to score your pirate garb.

✳ Special Events

Check the **Outer Banks visitors website** (www.outerbanks.org) for an updated list of events during your stay.

January: **Old Christmas** (252-987-2575; www.rwscivic.org), Rodanthe-Waves-Salvo Community Building. Celebrated on the Saturday closest to January 6, this 100-year-old custom includes an appearance by "Old Buck," plus oyster roasts, music, and bonfires.

May: **Hatteras Demo Days** (252-987-2297; www.wavesvillage.com), Waves Village. Kiteboarding demos and clinics, giveaways, and a stand-up paddleboarding race.

Endless Summer Weekend (252-987-6000; www.realwatersports.com), REAL. Surf sessions, live music, screening of original *Endless Summer* movie. Free.

June: **Triple-S Invitational and Annual Sunset Swim Charity Fashion Show** (252-987-6000; www.triplesinvitational.com), REAL. Weeklong Surf, Slick and Slider competition brings top kiteboarding pros and fans together for riding, live music, dancing, and autograph sessions, topped with an awards ceremony by the sound.

July: **Fourth of July Celebration** (252-987-2575; www.rwscivic.org), Rodanthe-Waves-Salvo Community Building. A reading of the Declaration of Independence precedes a patriotic musical performance.

Light Up the Night (252-987-2297; www.wavesvillage.com), Waves Village. Free demos of NOCQUA underwater lighting systems for SUPs, surfboards, and kayaks, plus a movie by the sound.

August: **Anniversary of the *Mirlo* Rescue** (252-987-1552; www.chicamacomico.org), Chicamacomico Life-Saving Station Historic Site, Rodanthe. Descendants the *Mirlo* crew and the lifesavers who rescued them gather to talk story.

October: **Halloween Parade and Party** (252-987-2575; www.rwscivic.org), Rodanthe-Waves-Salvo Community Building. Pumpkin signs indicate homes and businesses welcoming trick-or-treaters after the parade.

December: **Community Holiday Dinner** (252-987-2575; www.rwscivic.org), Rodanthe-Waves-Salvo Community Building.

AVON (KINNAKEET)

Ten miles farther down NC 12, Avon is another village that received a name change from the U.S. Postal Service. Many residents still refer to it by its earlier name, Kinnakeet, a village that grew up between the Little Kinnakeet and Big Kinnakeet lifesaving stations. The main part of the town lies west of NC 12 along the sound. The **Avon Fishing Pier** is the town's most notable landmark, famed as a spot to catch red drum.

Recent years have seen the arrival of the **Koru Village Resort**, which has changed the face of Avon. In addition to high-end accommodations, Koru has added a spa, salon and fitness and yoga center to the local scene, as well as a restaurant, the **Pangea Tavern**, and an open air **Beach Klub**, which hosts frequent live music. The resort has also thrown its support behind the Avon Pier, badly in need of repair after a series of storms.

Just south of Avon, back in the national seashore, you'll pass **Canadian Hole**, famous among windsurfers worldwide. The National Park Service calls it the **Haulover Day Use Area** and provides restrooms and showers here. The name refers to a pre-windsurfing use of the area, when locals would haul their boats across this narrow stretch of island to avoid the long sail around.

Avon remains a worldwide center for windsurfing and wavesailing, and is the only East Coast stop on the international **American Windsurfing Tour** (www.americanwindsurfingtour.com). Many shops specializing in windsurfing rentals and lessons are found near the Avon Pier.

Avon occupies the widest spot on the north–south section of Hatteras. Its soundside harbor was once an important port for boatbuilding, using the stands of live oaks and cedar that grew here. For more information on Avon or a free visitor guide, visit www.hometownavonnc.org.

POST OFFICE The **Avon Post Office** (252-995-5991) is at 41196 NC 12. The zip code in Avon is 27915.

GETTING THERE NC 12 runs through Avon. The Avon Pier is on the east or ocean side of the road. Turn west at the Harbor Road traffic light to find the village of Avon, on the shores of Pamlico Sound.

GETTING AROUND Bikes are a great way to explore old Avon Village, with its many scenic lanes and older cottages. Rent a bicycle at Island Cycles (see *To Do—Bicycling*).

✳ To See

✿ **Avon Fishing Pier** (252-995-5480; www.avonfishingpier.com), 41001 NC 12. This 600-foot pier is a hot spot for red drum and stays open late when the fish are running. The pier house store stocks a full range of fishing gear and tackle for sale or rent; bait, snacks, and beverages; plus some cool souvenirs. You can walk down the pier and have a look without fishing for $1, or fish all day for about $10.

ONE OF THE MOST RECOGNIZED LANDMARKS ON HATTERAS ISLAND: THE AVON PIER

Little Kinnakeet Life-Saving Station (252-995-4474; www.nps.gov/caha), Cape Hatteras National Seashore, NC 12. Located down a short road on the sound side of NC 12, just north of the town of Avon, the Little Kinnakeet station is being restored by the National Park Service. The station complex includes an 1870s building and a 1904 building, both similar to the already restored buildings at **Chicamacomico**, and offers an interesting perspective on the challenges faced by preservationists. The National Park Service is also restoring stations at Bodie Island and Creeds Hill, near Frisco.

✳ To Do

BICYCLING A 4-foot-wide paved shoulder for bikes and pedestrians runs along NC 12 through Avon. Plans will extend this as far as national seashore ramps to the north and south of town. Avon Village west of NC 12 makes a pleasant place to bike, with little traffic and some shade.

Island Cycles (252-995-4336; www.islandcycles.com), 41074 NC 12. Shop across from the Avon Pier rents bikes, including tandems, recumbent, and adult trikes; baby joggers; bikes with training wheels and little red wagons; kayaks, and surf, SUP, body, and skim boards; plus racks to carry it all around. Professional mechanics here also repair bikes. Delivery available.

Ocean Atlantic (252-995-5868 or 1-800-635-9559; www.oceanatlanticrentals.com), 40809 NC 12. Beach cruisers for adults and kids, plus surfboards, kayaks, and a variety of beach equipment for rent. Or rent a street-legal golf cart to haul everything to the beach. Delivery available.

BOATING AND KAYAKING Avon has a boat ramp, but it can be tricky to find. Ask for directions at one of the local bait and tackle stores. Kayaks and other nonpowered craft can be launched at ocean and soundside access points in the national seashore. You can rent kayaks to use in the ocean or sound at the shops listed under *Bicycling*.

Avon Harbor Sailing (252-305-6839; www.avonharborsailing.com), 40073 Harbor Road. Book a sunset cruise, daily charter, or sailing lessons aboard the 19-foot *Flying Scot*.

✐ **The Kinnakeet Experience** (252-475-0151; www.kinnexp.com), 40073 Harbor Road. Hit the water with Captain Buddy O'Neal for a day of swimming, fishing, clamming, or just relaxed cruising on Pamlico Sound.

CRAFTS ⊤ **The Cosmic Octopus** (252-995-0566; www.facebook.com/thecosmic octopuscapehatteras), 40530 NC 12. Gift and tobacco shop offers tie-dye classes.

✐ ⊤ **The Glass Bead** (252-995-7020), 39774 NC 12. Make your own jewelry from this shop's huge selection of beads and jewelry supplies.

✐ ⊤ **Kinnakeet Clay Studio and Showroom** (252-995-0101; www.kinnakeetclay .com), 40462 North End Road. The showroom features handcrafted pottery, much of it with an ocean theme, by local fourth-generation artist Antoinette Gaskins Mattingly and other regional artists. Sign up for a class to learn to hand build your own fish tiles, wall hangings, mugs and bowls, or even a fairy house.

✐ ⊤ **Studio 12** (252-995-7899; www.studio12hatteras.com), 41008 NC 12. Create your own pottery, mosaic, and glass projects or browse local art at this popular spot for rainy days and parties. **Samantha's Coffee & Smoothie** is located inside.

✐ ⊤ **Uglie Mugs** (252-995-5590), 40534 NC 12. Another spot to get your bead on in the Kinnakeet Shoppes.

FISHING **Frank and Fran's Fisherman's Friend** (252-995-4171; www.hatteras-island .com), 40210 NC 12. This friendly, family-run gathering spot for anglers carries everything you'll need for fishing from surf or pier, including North Carolina fishing licenses, the best bait for the season, and cigars for when the fish aren't biting. The 94.2-pound world-record red drum, caught from the beach just south of the Avon Pier in 1984, and

AVON PIER IS ONE OF THE HOTTEST SPOTS ON THE COAST FOR CATCHING RED DRUM

the rod that brought it in, are on display. Fishing advice, weather reports, and coffee are all complimentary.

☙ **Avon Fishing Pier** (252-995-5480; www.avonfishingpier.com), 41001 NC 12. The place for red drum on the Banks. Kid's Fishing Frenzy tournament every summer.

FOR FAMILIES ☙ **Avon "Kinnakeet Village" Playground** (252-475-5650; www .darenc.com/parksrec), 40184 Harbor Road. Fenced-in grassy area has a nice playground and picnic pavilion. Turn off NC 12 at the light toward Avon Village.

☙ **Ketch 55 Seafood Grill** (252-995-5060) has a large game arcade with pool tables and video games.

SPAS AND FITNESS **Spa Koru** (252-995-3125; www.koruvillage.com), 40920 NC 12. Salon and spa offers a full menu of beauty and body treatments, including Serenity exfoliation with local organic sea salt.

MANY VISITORS COME TO AVON FOR THE WINDSURFING ACTION ON THE OCEAN AND SOUND

The Beach Klub at Koru Village (252-995-3125; www.koruvillage.com), 40920 NC 12. A complete fitness center with daily exercise and yoga classes is located on-site, with daily and weekly passes available.

WATER SPORTS The combination of steady winds and shallow water makes Hatteras Island the best destination in the East for windsurfing and kiteboarding. Pamlico Sound, with its 35-mile-wide expanse of waist-deep water, provides some of the best flatwater riding in the world. Avon itself is the region's top hot spot for windsurfing shops, with kiteboarding and surf shops running close behind.

Located just south of Avon, **Canadian Hole**, officially named the **Haulover Day Use Area**, is a favorite with windsurfers (no kiteboarding). Just across NC 12 and over the dunes lies **Ego Beach**, a hot spot for wavesailing.

Kiteboarders congregate just south of Canadian Hole at **Kite Point**. At **Ramp 34**, about a mile north of Avon, kiters frequently launch for oceanside downwinders.

Hatteras Island Boardsports (252-995-6160; www.hiboardsports.com), 41056 NC 12. Surfing specialists offer some of the best intro to surfing lessons around and rent kayaks, surf, SUP, and body boards, wet suits, and fins. A two-bedroom, two-bath apartment over the shop is available for rent by the night or week.

Kite Club Hatteras (202-549-7693; www.kiteclubhatteras.com). Kiteboarding school offers kite camps and lessons for women and beginners, including a three-day course leading to certification by the **International Kiteboarding Organization** (www .ikointl.com), foil board lessons for experienced riders, plus SUP rentals and lessons. Accommodations available.

(ᵍ) **OceanAir Sports** (252-995-5000; www.oceanairsports.com), 39450 NC 12. At this great water sports hangout right on the sound, you can enjoy windsurfing, kiteboarding, kayaking, and stand-up paddleboarding; rent a Hobie Cat or Jet Ski; enjoy a session of waterfront yoga; or just watch all the action from the shore.

Outer Banks Kiting (252-305-6839; www.outerbankskiting.com). Kiteboarding specialists offer private lessons for all abilities using the latest Core Kiteboard gear, plus kite charters, kite camp, SUP lessons and tours, wakeboarding instruction, and sunset cruises.

Ride Hatteras (252-995-6755; www.ridehatteras.com), 40168 NC 12. Shop specializing in windsurfing lessons and rentals also offers personalized kiteboarding and surfing lessons, plus kayak and stand-up paddleboard rentals. New and used gear for sale.

✳ Green Space

There are many places to access the typically quiet waters of Pamlico Sound along the west side of Hatteras Island. Most are reached via sand roads suitable for four-wheel-drive vehicles. The national seashore's **Haulover Day Use Area** (www.nps.gov/caha), just south of Avon on NC 12, has a bathhouse with showers and restrooms, as well as paved parking. The water here is shallow, making this a good spot for youngsters to get into the water if the windsurfers aren't too numerous.

Several public access points to the ocean-side beaches can be found in Avon around the pier. Other ocean beach accesses lie within the national seashore and are subject to closures for nesting birds and turtles. Check with one of the Cape Hatteras National Seashore visitor centers or visit the seashore's Facebook page (www.facebook.com/CapeHatterasNS) for an up-to-the-minute list of ramp and beach closures, as well as rip current and other hazards.

✳ Lodging

Accommodations in Avon are mostly of the weeklong, vacation cottage rental variety.

CAMPGROUND ((ᵧ)) **Sands of Time Campground** (252-995-5596; www.sandsoftimecampground.com), 125 North End Road. Quiet park set in a fishing village has full hookups with free cable TV for 57 RVs, plus a two-bedroom rental cottage and 15 shady tent sites with water and electric, plus Wi-Fi, bathhouse, laundry, lighted fish-cleaning table, and a fish freezer.

MOTEL 🐾 ((ᵧ)) **Avon Motel** (252-995-5774; www.avonmotel.com), 40230 Younce Drive at NC 12. Located on the same block as an ocean beach access, this clean but slightly dated family-owned property at the north end of Avon offers 45 first-floor motel rooms, as well as two- and three-room efficiency apartments, a fish-cleaning station, and coin laundry. The same family operates the Avon Cottages (see *Vacation Rentals*). Off-season $; high season $$.

RESORT ♂ ((ᵧ)) **Koru Village** (252-995-3125; www.koruvillage.com), 40920 NC 12. Six fully equipped two- and three-bedroom villas located in the resort's **Meditation Garden** are themed to nature: Air, Earth, Water, Fire, Sun, and Stars. Guests enjoy free access to the **Koru Fitness Center**, with yoga classes, Zumba, and more; backyard volleyball and horseshoe area; the **Beach Klub**, with ocean access, parking, and pool; and free beach bikes. A boutique offering salon and fitness products, local art, and a gourmet tea bar are located on the property. Minimum stay may be required. Off-season $$; summer season $$–$$$.

VACATION RENTALS 🐾 ((ᵧ)) **Avon Cottages** (252-995-4123; www.avoncottages.com), 40279 Younce Road. Owned and operated by the same family since 1954, these cottages with two to four bedrooms rent mostly by the week, but a few efficiencies are available by the night. $$–$$$.

Colony Realty (252-995-5891 or 1-800-962-5256; www.hatterasvacations .com), 40197 Bonito Road at NC 12. Specializing in smaller, affordable homes suitable for one or two families, Colony also has longer rentals available on Hatteras Island.

🍴 ⚓ **Hatteras Realty** (252-995-5466 or 1-800-HATTERAS; www.hatterasrealty .com), 41156 NC 12. The more than 500 vacation homes of every description represented by Hatteras Realty come with member privileges at **Club Hatteras**, the company's private clubhouse in Avon, with a large heated pool, tennis courts, putting green, playground, snack bar, and changing rooms with showers. Many homes are also part of the **Klub Koru program**, offering access to the Koru Fitness Center and daily schedule of classes. Last-minute three-night stays available.

🐾 ♿ **Outer Beaches Realty** (252-995-4477 or 1-800-627-3150; www .outerbeaches.com), 40227 Tigrone Boulevard. Additional offices in Hatteras Village (252-986-2900) and Waves (252-987-2771). Operating exclusively on Hatteras Island, Outer Beaches lists over 550 properties, including cottages especially suited to windsurfers and handicapped-accessible properties.

✳ Where to Eat

DINING OUT ⚓ ♿ ⇨ **Dolphin Den** (252-995-7717; www.dolphindenrestaurant .com), 40126 NC 12, MP 55. Owned by an island family who took root here in the 1700s, this longtime favorite serves fresh seafood, broiled or fried, including locally sourced softshell crabs; house-smoked pork, ribs, and wings; Italian pasta dishes; and grass-fed, hormone-free steaks cut in-house. Desserts are homemade, and the Key lime pie is award winning. Early-bird specials before 5 PM. Full bar. Take-out available and large groups welcome. Dinner only, $$–$$$.

⚓ ♿ 🍷 **Ketch 55 Seafood Grill** (252-995-5060; www.ketch55.com), 40396 NC 12. Creative seasonal menu is full of seafood options, such as baked fish crusted with pesto, tuna tartar, and Ocracoke oysters, steamed or on the half shell. Full bar plus a large selection of wines by the glass and microbrews on tap, plus daily specials, oyster roasts on the deck, and live music some nights. Dinner only, $$–$$$.

✳ ⚓ ♿ 🍷 **Oceana's Bistro** (252-995-4991; www.oceanasbistro.com), 40774 NC 12. Restaurant across from Outer Beaches Realty is the only eatery in Avon serving breakfast, lunch, and dinner all year. Sit at the bar and enjoy a blackened tuna griller or a rare sesame seared tuna appetizer, both house specialties. Occasional live entertainment, creative cocktails, and a large TV make this a local favorite for hanging out. Breakfast and lunch $–$$; dinner $–$$$.

🍴 ⇨ **Open Water Grill** (252-505-0159; www.openwatergrill.com), 39450 NC 12. Lovely sunsets on the waterfront deck and excellent food are good reasons to visit. Inside, it's a bit elegant, especially for Hatteras Island, with actual tablecloths, or you can sit on the patio overlooking the water. Chocoholic alert: don't miss the World's Ugliest Chocolate Cake. Full bar. Lunch $$; dinner $$–$$$.

⚓ **Pangea Tavern** (252-995-3800; www .pangeatavern.com), 41001 NC 12. Koru Village's pub keeps it light all day, then gets its cuisine on with some serious entrées at dinner. The pub vibe kicks back in with post-dinner darts. Lunch $$; dinner $$–$$$.

EATING OUT ⚓ **Bros Sandwich Shack** (252-995-9595; www.brossandwichshack .com), Hatteras Island Plaza, 41934 NC 12. Local favorite begun by brothers (and culinary school grads) Matt and Josh serves the area's best burgers, along with grilled tuna po'boys, quinoa veggie burgers, and sweet potato waffle fries. House-smoked barbecue and wings are a specialty. $.

✎ ♿ ((•)) **Dirty Dick's Crab House** (252-995-3425; www.dirtydickscrabs.com), Hatteras Island Plaza, 41934 NC 12. In honor of Hatteras Island's new liquor-by-the-drink rules, Dirty Dick's built a large new restaurant in Hatteras Island Plaza. (No more tent!) Crabs every which way, from a crab martini to crab lasagna, are the name of the game at this fun spot, with lots of different kinds of crustaceans on the menu, from local blue crabs and softshells to king, snow, and Dungeness brought in from the Pacific. Barbecue, steaks, and Louisiana specialties, such as crawfish and frog legs, fill out the menu. Stop by the on-site store for the world-famous "I Got My Crabs at Dirty Dick's" logo'd attire. Breakfast is served during the summer season. A second Dirty Dick's (252-449-2722) is in Nags Head at MP 10 on the Bypass. Lunch $$; dinner $$–$$$.

✎ ♿ ♟ **Froggy Dog Restaurant** (252-995-5550; www.froggydog.com), 40050 NC 12. A landmark in Avon, the Froggy Dog provides food early to late, plus entertainment and some great souvenirs. The pub offers happy hour in the afternoon and stays open late with karaoke and sports on the surfboard TV. Kids enjoy the Tadpole Corner play area and the kids meals served on a Frisbee. **Ribbit's Gifts**, upstairs, offers a variety of froggy mementos. Live music and karaoke on the outside deck in-season. Breakfast and lunch $; dinner $$–$$$.

✎ ♿ ♟ **Mad Crabber** (252-995-5959; www.themadcrabber.com), 40369 NC 12. New location of this longtime favorite has a cool log cabin vibe accented with homespun quilts. The food that made it popular remains the same—huge piles of fresh seafood. To get a taste of everything, order the Mad Crabber Platter, a pizza pan heaped high with steamed crab legs, mussels, clams, oysters, crawdads,

shrimp, and scallops. Pool and poker tournaments, plus live music and sushi, make this a nightlife destination. Lunch $–$$; dinner $$–$$$.

BARBECUE **Surf'n Pig BBQ** (252-216-2022; www.surfnpig.com), 40618 NC 12, Kinnakeet Korner. Hickory-smoked brisket, pork, chicken, and ribs available in sandwiches, platters, and party packs, plus an amazing Cuban sandwich and some fine Southern sides. Takeout only. $–$$.

BEACH FAST FOOD Avon is unique among the villages on Hatteras Island for having several chain fast-food restaurants, including **Dairy Queen** (252-995-5624) and **Subway** (252-9957827). For a more local experience, try ✎ **Burger Burger** (252-995-0311; www.facebook .com/obxburgerburger), in Kinnakeet Corner at the corner of NC 12 and Harbor Road. It's a chain, too, but a local one. The original store is in Buxton. Locals are crazy for the Smile Burger, which comes with a crispy layer of cheese bigger than the bun. The burgers here are all hand-patted and cooked to order.

COFFEE AND SWEETS 🐾 ✎ ♿ **Island Time Cups and Cones** (252-995-0202; www.pinkicecreamshop.com), 40146 NC 12. Coffee is just one of the offerings at this bright pink spot along the main highway. Get a Hawaiian shaved ice, smoothie, hand-dipped scoops of Hershey's ice cream, or an Italian ice. There are games and puzzles to play, and on summer evenings Island Time is open late, with family films playing on an outdoor screen.

✎ ☂ **Samantha's Coffee Smoothie** (252-995-7899; www.obxcoffeesmoothie .com), 41008 NC 12. Located adjacent to Studio 12, this sweet spot from the same owners offers smoothies made with 100 percent fruits and veggies, frappes, pour-over coffees, and espresso drinks, hot and cold.

🖊 ☂ ((ᵞ)) **Uglie Mugs Coffee House** (252-995-5590), 40534 NC 12, Kinnakeet Shoppes. Internet hotspot next to the Subway has a computer you can use, plus a creative selection of high-octane espresso and tea drinks, cinnamon buns, and breakfast goodies. You can create your own bead jewelry here as well, or browse works by local artists.

MARKETS **Breeze Thru Avon** (252-995-3347; www.breezethruobx.com), 40374 NC 12, MP 55. No need to get out of your car to score beer (including kegs) at this drive-through convenience store.

Island Spice & Wine (252-995-7750), 40246 NC 12. Fun store stocks hundreds of wines and champagnes, microbrews, and imports, plus locally made jellies and tons of supplies for gourmet cottage meals, including sushi-making sets. Check the schedule for wine tastings.

PIZZA ❋ 🖊 ((ᵞ)) **Gidget's Pizza and Pasta** (252-995-3109; www.pizzagidget.com), 41934 NC 12, Hatteras Island Plaza. Family-run local favorite, formerly Toppers, serves specialty pizzas, pastas, calzone, and oven-baked subs, plus daily specials made from family recipes. Beer and wine available. Delivery in Avon. $–$$.

Nino's Pizza (252-995-5358), 41188 Palazzolo Road. Hand-tossed pizzas by the pie or by the slice, seafood pastas, Italian specialties such as stuffed peppers and baked ziti, plus burgers, subs, and salads. Beer available. Free delivery in Avon. $–$$.

SEAFOOD TO GO **Surf's Up Seafood Market** (252-995-3432; www .surfsupseafood.com), 41838 NC 12, Hatteras Island Plaza. Local and imported seafood includes live lobsters, king and snow crab legs, salmon, and red snapper. Get some shrimp steamed and ready to

eat, or pick up a clambake with all the fixings to cook at home.

❋ Entertainment

Entertainment is sparse in Avon during the winter, when many spots close or cut back their hours. The nightlife scene gathers steam during the summer months, when you'll find live entertainment at the **Froggy Dog**, the **Mad Crabber**, **Oceana's Bistro**, **Ketch 55**, and the **Open Water Grill**.

☖ **Papawack Theater** (252-995-3125; www.koruvillage.com). Located in the **Koru Village Beach Klub** next to the Avon Pier, this 4,000-square-foot theater's large stage brings a major entertainment venue to Avon with plenty of space out front to dance. Live bands every week during the summer season.

☖ **Turner's High Moon Bar** (252-995-6666; www.turnershighmoon.com), 40618 NC 12. Live music venue stays open late, serving up craft beers, wine, and cocktails accompanied by a menu that ranges from crispy crust pizza and Surf'n Pig BBQ to seafood specials. In accordance with North Carolina law, this is a private club, with a membership fee of $1.

✳ Selective Shopping

ART GALLERIES **Kinnakeet Clay Studio and Showroom** (252-995-0101; www
.kinnakeetclay.com), 40462 North End
Road. Stop by the studio of Antoinette
Gaskins Mattingly, the fourth generation
of her family creating art on Hatteras
Island, to see her distinctive tiles, stoneware pottery, and other handmade items,
as well as art by other local artists.

Sandcastles (252-995-0147; www
.sandcastlesavon.com), 39774 NC 12,
Dairy Queen Shops. Eclectic gallery
carries locally produced arts and crafts,
from paintings, handblown glass, and
metal work to mosaics, stained glass, and
jewelry, including a big selection of sea
glass and shells.

SPECIAL SHOPS **Askins Creek Store**
(252-995-6283; www.askinscreek.com),
42676 NC 12. This convenience store at
the far southern end of Avon carries a
wide variety of souvenirs, including
authorized OBX merchandise, beach
stuff, groceries, and grab-and-go meals,
but its real claim to fame is its car wash,
where you can rinse the sand and salt off
your car.

⚓ **Fisherman's Daughter** (252-995-
6148), 39455 NC 12. Two stories of fashion, accessories, home decor, books, and
just cute stuff make for a great day of
browsing.

Mill Creek Gifts (252-995-3188; www
.millcreekgifts.com),41074 NC 12, in the
same building as the Breeze Thru. Nice
selection of beachy gifts and local art.

✳ Special Events

Check the **Outer Banks visitors website**
(www.outerbanks.org) for an updated list
of events during your stay.

March: **St. Baldrick's Day** (www
.stbaldricks.org). The Avon Volunteer
Fire Department sponsors this St. Patrick's Day head-shaving event to raise
money for childhood cancer research.

April: **OBX-Wind.com Windsurfing Festival** (www.obx-wind.com).
The only East Coast stop on the
American Windsurfing Tour (www
.americanwindsurfingtour.com) features
five days of competitions and parties at
local venues.

May: **Shore Break 5K and Tide Pool
Fun Run** (www.hatterasyouth.com), Koru
Village Beach Klub. Benefit held annually on Memorial Day weekend.

June: **Rock the Cape** (www.darearts
.org). A week dedicated to the arts features an art show, a crawl of Hatteras
Island galleries, and concerts at local
venues.

July: **Fourth of July Fireworks** (www
.avonfishingpier.com), Avon Pier.

August: **Junior Fishing Tournament**
(www.avonfishingpier.com), Avon Pier.

October: **Frank and Fran's Red
Drum Tournament** (252-995-4171; www
.hatteras-island.com).

North Carolina Beach Buggy Association Red Drum Tournament (www.ncbba
.org).

**Hatteras Island Cancer Foundation
Positively Pink 5K** (www.hicf.org). Fun
run and festivities in support of Breast
Cancer Awareness begins at Sun Realty
in Avon.

November: **Veterans Day History Potluck Dinner**, Avon Fire Station. Honors
local veterans.

Hatteras Island Oyster Roast (252-
305-1722), Avon Volunteer Fire Department. Buy tickets in advance for this
benefit for wounded warriors. Contact
Kinnakeet Civic Association (P.O. Box
291, Avon, NC 27195) for details.

BUXTON

Traveling south from Avon, you often see kiteboarders' foils above the sound, and up ahead the Banks' most famous landmark, the spiral-striped **Cape Hatteras Light**, comes into view. A climb up the lighthouse offers a staggering panorama of the cape. To the west and south stretches **Buxton Woods**, one of the largest remaining maritime forests on the East Coast. To the east, the treacherous **Diamond Shoals** stretch 8 miles out to sea, a constant menace to navigation.

Before the post office renamed it for a Fayetteville judge, this area was called simply The Cape. Buxton has a reputation as a casual, family-oriented resort, popular for surf fishing, surfing, and—on the sound side—windsurfing and kiteboarding.

GUIDANCE The **Double Keepers' House** at the base of the Cape Hatteras Lighthouse (252-995-4474; www.nps.gov/caha), Lighthouse Road, houses the visitor center for the area. You can also sign up for beach driving permits here. For additional information on Buxton and a free visitor guide, visit www.hometownbuxtonnc.org.

POST OFFICE The **Buxton Post Office** (252-995-5755) is located at 48042 NC 12. The zip code in Buxton is 27920.

PUBLIC RESTROOMS Facilities are located at the **Cape Hatteras Lighthouse Welcome Center** (252-995-4474; www.nps.gov/caha), on Lighthouse Road, and at the **Dare County Fessenden Center** (252-475-5650; www.darenc.com/ParksRec), 46830 NC 12.

GETTING THERE NC12 takes a sharp turn to the west as it reaches Buxton, doglegging past Cape Point.

GETTING AROUND *By bicycle:* Bicycles are a great way to explore the many roads and trails running through Buxton Woods and the small residential roads leading off NC 12. The loop formed by NC 12 and the Buxton Back Road is a popular biking excursion.

By car: Most commercial development in Buxton lies along NC 12 and the Buxton Back Road. Old Lighthouse Road runs along the Atlantic coast, with many motels along its length. The newer Lighthouse Road leads to the Cape Hatteras Light itself, as well as camping and hiking in the Cape Point area.

✳ To See

The Old Gray House (252-995-6098; www.outerbanksshells.com), Light Plant Road. Take a (virtual) step back in time with a visit to this traditional homestead, owned by a family who has been on the island since the 1600s. Built largely from salvaged ship timbers, the house today is filled with local crafts. A path leading through the woods to the **Cape Pines Motel** is posted with signs about island lore. Free.

MUST SEE

Cape Hatteras Lighthouse, the iconic landmark of Hatteras Island, continues to flash its warning out to sea, as it has since 1870. The 210-foot tower, the tallest lighthouse in the nation, is painted with a distinctive black-and-white spiral pattern and flashes every 7.5 seconds. Visitors at least 42 inches tall can climb the 268 steps to the walkway at the top of the light for great views over Hatteras Island and Diamond Shoals. Next to the lighthouse, the two-story **Double Keepers' Quarters** has been restored and houses a visitor center, bookstore, and the **Museum of the Sea,** with exhibits on the history and ecology of the Outer Banks and information on the lighthouse and its dramatic move inland in 1999. A video, *The Move of the Century,* is shown daily at the museum. During the summer months, park rangers offer a variety of free programs on shipwrecks, lifesavers, and pirates. Climbing tour tickets are $8 for adults; $4 for seniors 62 or older and children 11 and under. **Full Moon Climbs** are scheduled June through September (reservations required). Bring a flashlight, as there are no lights inside the tower. Admission to the park and museum is free. ❃ ✐ **Cape Hatteras Lighthouse** (252-995-4474; www.nps.gov/caha), Lighthouse Road.

CLIMBING THE 210-FOOT CAPE HATTERAS LIGHTHOUSE IS A MUST FOR EVERY VISITOR

❃ To Do

BIRD-WATCHING **Buxton Woods** and the **Cape Point area** of the Cape Hatteras National Seashore are noted birding destinations and important stops for birds on the East Coast Flyway. The trails in Buxton Woods are good for sighting songbirds during the spring and fall migrations; ponds within the woods harbor wading birds in summer and diving ducks in winter. **Salt Pond**, near the tip of Cape Point and best reached by four-wheel-drive vehicle, yields views of a variety of fowl, both summer and winter. After severe winter weather, the Point is a refuge for many varieties of gulls, and in late May, pelagic species, such as storm petrels, shearwaters, and jaegers, migrate north along this route.

A **Birds of the Outer Banks** checklist is available on the NPS site and at the visitor center. Maps and site descriptions can be found online at the website of the **North Carolina Birding Trail** (www.ncbirdingtrail.org).

FISHING One of the most storied beaches for surf fishing in the United States is located at **Cape Point** south of the lighthouse, accessed by four-wheel-drive vehicle from Ramps 43 and 44. A beach driving permit from the NPS and a fishing license from

WILDFLOWERS BLOOM ALONG MANY TRAILS IN THE NATIONAL SEASHORE

the state of North Carolina are required. Talk to the folks at local tackle shops about what's biting where and how to catch them.

Dillon's Corner (252-995-5083; www.dillonscorner.com), 47692 NC 12. Downstairs you'll find a complete selection of fishing gear and tackle, upstairs a gallery of gifts, apparel, and art. Fishing cottage rentals available.

The Red Drum (252-995-5414; www.reddrumtackle.com), 46813 NC 12. Serving the fishing public since 1954, the tackle shop anchors a gas station and market complex.

FOR FAMILIES Mini-golf and ice cream just go together in Buxton. See our listings under *Where to Eat* for info on **Uncle Eddy's Frozen Custard and 18-Hole Mini-Golf**, next to the Falcon Hotel in Buxton, and **Cool Wave Ice Cream Shoppe and Mini-Golf**, another spot in Buxton offering the popular ice cream/mini-golf combination.

The game room in the back of ✿ **Angelo's Pizza/Burger Burger Arcade** (252-995-6364), with pool tables, air hockey, and lots of video games, is a hit with kids. Small children have their own section.

The entire lower floor of the **Sandbar and Grille** (252-995-3413; www.sandbarandgrille.com) is given over to a game room equipped with a jukebox, pool table, pinball, and classic video games. It's a popular hangout for teens while the parental units enjoy a sunset cocktail on the deck upstairs.

✿ **Junior Ranger and Seashore Ranger** programs at the Cape Hatteras National Seashore (252-995-4474; www.nps.gov/caha) include a variety of free, family-friendly activities during the summer months at the Cape Hatteras Lighthouse Visitor Center.

HEALTH AND WELLNESS **Hatteras Island Chiropractic** (252-489-1688; www.hatterasislandchiropractic.com), 47761 NC 12. Dr. Howard Ruderfer offers adjustments, therapeutic massage, reflexology, aromatherapy, cranial-sacral work, and chakra balancing. House calls available as far away as Ocracoke.

VIEW FROM THE TOP OF THE CAPE HATTERAS LIGHT REVEALS THE GEOGRAPHY OF CAPE POINT AND THE TREACHEROUS DIAMOND SHOALS

KAYAK TOURS **Fatty's Treats N Tours** (252-995-3288; www.capehatterasmotel.com/fattys-treats-n-tours), 46618 NC 12. Take a guided kayak tour along the soundside waterfront to discover the history of Hatteras, once the home of the Croatan people.

SKATE PARK ✐ **Dare County Fessenden Center** (252-475-5650; www.darenc.com/ParksRec), 46830 NC 12, Buxton, boasts a state-of-the-art skateboard park with street course and a reportedly gnarly bowl. Helmets are required. The Fessenden is a Dare County community activity center with a full roster of classes and activities for all ages.

TENNIS On Hatteras Island, tennis courts are located in Buxton at the **Fessenden Center** (252-475-5650; 46830 NC 12) and at the **Cape Hatteras High School** (252-995-5730; 48576 NC 12). Courts at the school are available for public use after school hours.

WATER SPORTS **Fox Watersports** (252-995-4102; www.foxwatersports.com), 47108 NC 12. Founded by the late surfboard shaper and windsurfing pioneer Ted James, Fox is still run by his family and carries custom boards based on his best designs, as well other top brands, plus quality equipment for windsurfing and SUP. You can rent windsurfers, kayaks, SUPs, and surfboards; get lessons to bump you to the next level; or just stop by and talk surf. Repairs available.

Kite Hatteras (252-305-5290; www.kitehatteras.net). Ty Luckett's custom kite boats and tower apparatus let you develop boarding skills in a controlled environment. Kite camps, charters, and wakeboarding also available.

Natural Art Surf Shop (252-995-5682; www.surfintheeye.com), 47331 NC 12. Owner Scott Busbey shapes his custom In the Eye boards at this shop in Buxton, a haven for surfers since 1977. Board rentals and repairs, plus rad surf gear for sale. Locally made **Shortbus Skimboards** (www.shortbusskims.com) are also sold here.

✳ Green Space

BEACHES ♿ **Cape Hatteras National Seashore** (252-995-4474; www.nps.gov/caha), Lighthouse Road. The beach next to the old lighthouse site is the only one on Hatteras with a lifeguard, on duty Memorial Day to Labor Day. The park service offers a busy schedule of free activities on Hatteras every summer, ranging from bird walks to snorkeling trips on the sound. Beach wheelchairs can be borrowed from the park service by calling 252-995-4474 or 252-473-2111.

Driving on the beaches of the national seashore is a hot topic these days, with bird lovers battling it out with fishermen. The NPS has worked out a court-ordered compromise that puts in place closures of various parts of the beach to protect nesting shorebirds and sea turtles. Those who want to drive their four-wheel-drive vehicles on the sand must now purchase a permit and watch a short film before proceeding. Permits are available at the **Cape Hatteras Lighthouse Visitor Center**, which has expanded hours during the summer season, as well as the **Coquina Beach** and **Ocracoke visitor centers, and online**. Check the **NPS website** (www.nps.gov/ca) for current regulations and requirements, and a map of current ORV routes. Some stretches of beach are also reserved for pedestrians.

TRAILS **Buxton Woods Coastal Reserve** (252-261-8891; www.nccoastalreserve.net), NC 12. Over 1,000 acres of maritime forest, the largest remaining on the Banks,

ONLY THE FOUNDATION REMAINS AT THE ORIGINAL LOCATION OF THE CAPE HATTERAS LIGHT, JUST STEPS FROM THE SURF

occupy the southeast coast of Hatteras Island from Cape Point to Hatteras Village. Rare plants and animals make their homes here, and the woods are noted for their abundance of birds and rare butterflies, including the giant swallowtail and gossamer-winged northern hairstreak. A number of trails and multiuse paths run through this maritime forest.

NPS Buxton Woods Nature Trail (252-261-8891; www.nps.gov/caha) begins at a picnic area just beyond the Cape Hatteras Lighthouse. This shady three-quarter-mile loop runs along pine-needle-covered paths where interpretive signs explain the ecosystem of the area. Many creatures are seen along this trail, including cottonmouth snakes, so be wary. The **Open Ponds Trail** begins farther down the road near the old British cemetery and connects with other trails that enter the woods from roads off NC 12, eventually reaching the NPS campground in Frisco. An information kiosk and parking are found at the end of Old Doctors Road

COLORFUL WILDFLOWERS GROW ALONG MANY TRAILS IN BUXTON WOODS AND THE CAPE HATTERAS NATIONAL SEASHORE

off NC 12. Four-wheel-drive vehicles can drive down this road to another parking area near the **Lookout Loop Trail**. Two-wheel-drive vehicles can follow Water Association Road off NC 12 to a parking area and information kiosk. The reserve is open year-round. ATVs are not allowed on trails, and horses can only use the **Piney Ridge Trail**. Camping and campfires are not permitted. Pets must stay on a leash. Be cautious during hunting season, as some hunting is allowed.

❋ Lodging

BED & BREAKFASTS ✒ ♂ ((ᵖ)) **Cape Hatteras Bed & Breakfast** (252-995-6004; www.capehatterasbandb.com), 46223 Old Lighthouse Road. Enjoy a stay in one of this inn's eight guest rooms, each named for a famous hurricane. Located a short walk from the beach, the inn is smoke-free and received three diamonds from AAA. You can watch the Cape Hatteras Lighthouse from the great room or the large sundeck furnished with comfortable tables and chairs and a gas grill. Guests have the use of bicycles, beach chairs, and coolers, as well as lockable surfboard and sailboard storage. Gourmet breakfasts are a highlight of a stay

here, with menus that change daily. $$–$$$.

🦐 ♿ ♂ ((ᵖ)) **The Inn on Pamlico Sound** (1-866-726-5426; www.innonpamlicosound.com), 49684 NC 12. A favorite for honeymoons and romantic getaways, this quiet inn enjoys a lovely setting along the sound where stunning sunsets are nightly events. Innkeeper Steve Nelson has created a retreat that manages to be both casual and elegant. The inn's 12 rooms range from modest queens to new king rooms with whirlpool tubs and private porches. The rate includes a gourmet three-course breakfast with menus that change daily; afternoon cookie breaks; complimentary beverages and snacks; use of the inn's kayaks, stand-up paddleboards, bicycles, beach chairs, towels, and field glasses; and all the chocolate you can eat. Other amenities include a pool, a 14-seat HD theater with 1,800 DVD titles, computers, and a lending library of books to enjoy on the many porches and decks where hammocks and lounge chairs overlook the sound. The property was ranked as the top hotel on the North Carolina coast in 2012 by TripAdvisor readers. The inn's restaurant, **Cafe Pamlico** (see *Where to Eat*), is locally renowned for its cuisine. Reservations are highly recommended. Chef Forrest Paddock and his staff prepare everything from elegant picnics to breakfast in bed for guests. They'll also cook the fish or ducks you catch. The inn excels at special events, hosting weddings, private film festivals, and corporate retreats with equal ease. $$–$$$$.

CAMPGROUNDS AND CABINS ✖

Cape Woods Campground (252-995-5850; www.capewoods.com), 47649 Buxton Back Road. Occupying a shady pondside location in Buxton Woods, this family-run campground has sites for RVs and tents, plus cabin rentals, pool, heated bathhouse, laundry, playground, and fish-cleaning stations. Fifty-amp service available.

(ᵞ) **Island Hide-A-Way Campground** (252-995-6628; www.alphaadv.net/hideaway), 1254 Buxton Back Road. Small, quiet campground accommodates 30 RVs and 15 tents, with hookups, cable TV, and a bathhouse.

National Park Service Cape Point Campground (252-473-2111; www.nps.gov/caha), 46700 Lighthouse Road. Located within walking distance of the lighthouse and the beach, 202 sites for RVs and tents are paved, with picnic tables and grills but no hookups. Stays limited to 14 days. Restrooms, cold-water showers, drinking water, dump station, and pay phone provided. Open summer only.

COTTAGE COURTS ✖ ✖ (ᵞ) **Dillon's Corner Cottages and Village Homes** at

the **Outer Banks Motel** (252-995-5601 or 1-800-995-1233; www.outerbanksmotel.com), 46577 NC 12. Located in Buxton just north of the lighthouse, this complex offers a wide range of accommodations, from motel rooms and oceanfront cottages to homes in the village, at great prices. All guests can use the pools, hot tub, rowboats with crab nets, and Wi-Fi at the motel. Off-season $; in-season $$.

MOTELS ✖ ♂ (ᵞ) **Cape Hatteras Motel** (252-995-5611 or 1-800-995-0711; www.capehatterasmotel.com), 46556 NC 12, MP 61. With units on both the ocean and the sound, this low-key inn has nonsmoking rooms, efficiencies, and apartments for rent close to the lighthouse. A lighted swimming pool, hot tub, two fish-cleaning stations, and a fish freezer make this a popular spot both for anglers and families. The inn also anchors a complex of retail, restaurants, and recreation at the entrance to Buxton Village. **Fatty's Treats N Tours** (see *Where to Eat*), located next to the motel office, offers light meals, ice cream, and kayak tours on the sound. Off-season $; in-season $$$.

✖ ✦ ✖ (ᵞ) **Cape Pines Motel** (252-995-5666; www.capepinesmotel.com), 47497 NC 12. Located just a half-mile from the Cape Hatteras Lighthouse, the Cape Pines is an older property but is immaculately maintained and professionally run. It offers clean, comfortable, freshly renovated rooms in a two-story main building and cottages set amid lush landscaping. Guests enjoy a large pool, gas and charcoal grills in the picnic area, a fish-cleaning station, and a playground with swings, horseshoe pit, and croquet. The property is very pet friendly. Off-season $; in-season $$.

✖ ✦ (ᵞ) **Lighthouse View Motel** (1-800-225-7651; www.lighthouseview.com), 46677 NC 12. Located directly on the oceanfront, with no road to cross to get to the beach, the Lighthouse View has been operated by the Hooper family since the 1950s. Over the years, the property has grown to include 85 diverse units ranging from standard rooms and efficiencies to one- and two-bedroom villas and cottages. A heated pool and hot tub are located on the oceanfront. Other amenities include a playground, barbecue grills, and lighted fish-cleaning tables. Most units require guests to climb at least one flight of stairs. No pets, although a number of cats make their homes here. Off-season $; in-season $$$.

❋ Where to Eat

DINING OUT ♂ & ♟ ↝ **Cafe Pamlico** (252-995-4500 or 252-995-7030; www .innonpamlicosound.com), 49684 NC 12. Definitely the class act when it comes to dining on Hatteras Island, the restaurant at the elegant Inn on Pamlico Sound accepts a limited number of outside reservations for dinner. Menus change nightly as the talented chefs create gourmet dishes based on the freshest local produce and seafood available, as well as organic grain-fed beef and vegetable-fed chicken. Vegetarian and vegan choices are available. The café is also open to the public for breakfast, named "Best on the Outer Banks" by *National Geographic Traveler*. You can dine on the deck overlooking Pamlico Sound or in the white-tablecloth dining room. Reservations are highly recommended. Extensive wine and cocktail lists and bar menu served on the deck along with live music in season. Breakfast $$; dinner $$$–$$$$.

♂ & ↝ **The Captain's Table** (252-995-3117; www.thecaptainstablenc.com), 47048 NC 12. Locally owned restaurant receives high marks for both its fresh, wild-caught seafood and its friendly service. Donna Scarborough, the owner, is married to a commercial fisherman, so the Captain's Catch of the Day is always a good bet here. Sides and desserts are made in-house. Beer and wine available. Lunch $; dinner $$–$$$; senior menu $.

🍴 ♂ & ♟ ↝ **Diamond Shoals Restaurant, Sushi Bar, and Lounge** (252-995-5217; www.diamondshoals.net), 46843 NC 12. Reliable local spot serves satisfying meals, including an AYCE salad bar, at reasonable prices. The creamy clam chowder, made with local Ocracoke clams, is award winning. Sushi is served nightly in the lounge, one of the first on Hatteras to offer cocktails, where you'll also enjoy live music. Diamond Shoals has numerous aquariums filled with tropical fish—the largest collection on the island—making it a favorite with kids. An on-site seafood market (252-995-5521), is open daily 10–7. Breakfast $; lunch $–$$; dinner $$–$$$.

♂ & ♟ **Rusty's Surf and Turf** (252-995-4184; www.rustyssurfnturf.com), 47355 NC 12, Osprey Shopping Center. This popular seafood restaurant, operated by Rusty Midgett, a local boy who went to the big city to learn to cook and traveled the islands of the world in pursuit of big surf, brings his experience of both back home, preparing local seafood with tropical touches—a nice change from the fried-or-broiled selection at most Hatteras restaurants. The full bar carries several local microbrews and is a popular hangout for locals. Dinner $$–$$$.

EATING OUT ((ᵧ)) ↝ **Buxton Munch Company** (252-995-5502; www .buxtonmunch.com), 47355 NC 12, Osprey Shopping Center. Closed Sunday and Monday. Small sandwich shop serves fish tacos, crabcakes, wraps, quesadillas, fried chicken, and vegetarian dishes, plus beer and wine, all at low prices, amid '70s music and groovy memorabilia. Lunch only, $.

❋ & ♟ **Pop's Raw Bar** (252-995-7734), 48967 NC 12. Closed Sunday. Pop's is open all year, and most evenings it's crowded with locals playing darts, watching sports on TV, and enjoying fresh steamed seafood, bowls of Hatteras chowder, burgers, and barbecue. Locally made crabcakes and fish cakes, spicy steamed shrimp, really cold beer, occasional live music, and lots of local gossip make this place an experience. Not good for large groups, as most seating is at the bar or small tables. $–$$.

❄ ✐ ♿ ♙ ♟ **Sandbar and Grille** (252-995-3413; www.sandbarandgrille.com), 49252 NC 12. Great location on the sound along NC 12 makes a super destination for sunset cocktails with a view and live acoustic music on the back deck. The bar crowd loves the place, too, thanks to a late-night menu, poker tournaments, and schedule of live entertainment and karaoke. Downstairs, the game room is a draw for all ages. Dinner only, $–$$$.

BEACH FAST FOOD ❄ ✐ **Angelo's Pizza** (252-995-6364; www.facebook.com/AngelosPizzaBuxtonNC), 46903 NC 12. Nice eat-in or take-out spot has good deep-dish pizza, plus other Italian favorites, wings, burgers, and a mean Philly cheesesteak sub. Kids like the arcade room and jukebox. $.

✐ **Burger Burger** (252-995-0065), 46903 NC 12. Sharing the same building (and arcade room) as Angelo's, this popular spot has hand-patted burgers cooked to order, sweet potato fries, veggie wraps, wings, and freshly squeezed lemonades. Several specialty burgers are on the menu, but the Smile Burger, surrounded by a crispy ring of cheddar cheese bigger than the bun, is the favorite. $.

Fatty's Treats N Tours (252-995-3288; www.capehatterasmotel.com/fattys-treats-n-tours), 46618 NC 12. Located next to the office at the Cape Hatteras Motel, Fatty's is a good spot for Hershey's ice cream, root beer floats, and fudge, or made-from-scratch beignets, cinnamon rolls, brownies, and other goodies. A brief menu of wings, chicken fingers, and hot dogs fills the bill for a quick lunch. Sign up for a kayak tour of the sound here as well. $.

BREAKFAST **Orange Blossom Bakery & Cafe** (252-995-4109; www.orangeblossombakery.com), 47206 NC 12. Open mornings only, 6:30–11 in-season. Famous for its huge Apple Uglies, this café, located near the entrance to Cape Hatteras Lighthouse, also serves breakfast sandwiches and burritos, fair-trade organic coffees, yummy Meyer's rum raisin cinnamon rolls, hand-glazed doughnuts, and the soon-to-be-famous Chocolate Ugly. The bakery sells freshly baked bread and special-order cakes as well. $.

ICE CREAM AND MINI-GOLF ✐ **Cool Wave Ice Cream Shoppe and Mini-Golf** (252-995-6366), 47237 NC 12. Both soft-serve and hand-scooped ice cream are served in homemade waffle cones at this shop, next to the mini-golf course at the fork where the Back Road cuts off from NC 12. Play cornhole or have a turn on the swings for free.

✐ **Uncle Eddy's Frozen Custard and 18 Hole Mini-Golf** (252-995-4059), 46860 NC 12. Enjoy homemade frozen custard in an ever-expanding list of custom flavors, including fig (a local favorite), sorbet smoothies, or coffee drinks while the kids play unlimited mini-golf for a single fee next door or chat with the resident parrots.

MARKETS **Buxton Seafood** (252-995-5085), 49799 NC 12. Fresh local seafood, plus steaks, wine, produce, and other groceries.

Conner's Supermarket (252-995-5711; www.connerssupermarket.com), 47468 NC 12. Three generations of the Conner family have operated this grocery, serving locals and visitors for half a century.

Diamond Shoals Seafood Market (252-995-5521; www.diamondshoals.net), 46843 NC 12. Stocks a variety of locally caught seafood, crabcakes, soups, seafood salads, pick-your-own herbs, and kids' meals to-go.

❄ Entertainment

Hatteras Island is something of a hot spot for live music, especially of the acoustic variety, perhaps because of its proximity to Ocracoke Island, where many musicians make their homes. During the summer season, look for live music in Buxton at **Cafe Pamlico**, **Diamond Shoals**, the **Sandbar and Grille**, and **Pop's**.

✳ Selective Shopping

BOOKS **Buxton Village Books** (252-995-4240; www.buxtonvillagebooks.com), 47918 NC 12. Located in a Civil War–era cottage, this charming store carries an amazing range of new and used books for all ages. Specialties include sea stories, fishing guidebooks, Southern fiction, and books on Hatteras history. Owner Gee Gee Rosell hosts frequent book signings and stocks note cards by local artists.

SHOPPING CENTER **Osprey Shopping Center**, 47355 NC 12. This strip of shops houses the island's **ABC Liquor Store** (252-995-5532) and **Buxton Munch** (252-995-5502), a retro-themed sandwich shop. Out front there's a picnic area and **Rusty's Surf and Turf** (see *Where to Eat*), a popular seafood restaurant.

✳ Special Events

Check the **Outer Banks visitors website** (www.outerbanks.org) for an updated list of events during your stay.

Early August: **Hatteras Island Arts and Craft Guild Arts and Crafts Show** (252-441-1850), Cape Hatteras Secondary School, 48576 NC 12. Money raised sponsors scholarships for local students. Free.

October: **Capital City Four Wheelers Annual Surf Fishing Tournament** (www.capitalcityfourwheelersva.com).

Early November: **Annual Invitational Surf Fishing Tournament and Bob Bernard Open Individual Tournament** (252-995-4253; www.capehatterasanglersclub.org), 47231 Light Plant Road. Guinness World Record holder as the largest surf fishing tournament in the world. Registration for the individual tournament is free for youth and juniors, $10 for adults.

Late November: **Hatteras Island Arts and Craft Guild Holiday Show** (252-441-1850), Cape Hatteras Secondary School, 48576 NC 12. Local food and artwork, held annually on the Friday and Saturday after Thanksgiving. Free admission.

FRISCO

Formerly the town of Trent, Frisco is a quiet family resort town once famous for its fishing pier on the ocean. Known for the numerous king mackerel caught from its deck, the landmark was destroyed by a series of storms culminating in the 2010 blow from Hurricane Earl, which left the pier in ruins. Attempts to rebuild it have been delayed by the economic downturn, but fishermen who fished here still hope for a reprieve.

Back in the 1920s, locals had front-row seats as **Gen. Billy Mitchell**, a World War I flying ace and early supporter of airpower, struggled to build an airfield in the sand. A squad of airplanes soon arrived, then bombed and sank two former battleships just off-shore. This early demonstration of airpower is credited with sparking the development of the U.S. Air Force as well as naval aviation.

Mitchell was later court-martialed for his outspoken statements, but his views were vindicated by events. Frisco's airport, not far from the fishing pier, is named for Mitchell, as was the famous B-25 Mitchell bomber, a key to victory in World War II.

The area was also the location of an immense Indian town, perhaps **Croatoan**, the home of Manteo, friend of the Lost Colony. The site is being excavated in sections by East Carolina University and other archaeological teams.

For more information on Frisco history and attractions, visit the village website: www.hometownfrisconc.org.

POST OFFICE The **Frisco U.S. Post Office** (252-995-5017) is located at 53590 NC 12. The zip code for Frisco is 27936.

PUBLIC RESTROOMS ♿ **Frisco Beach Bathhouse**, on the south side of NC 12 just beyond the cutoff to the old pier, has public restrooms.

GETTING THERE *By air:* **Billy Mitchell Airfield**/HSE/HNC (252-995-3646; www.nps .gov/caha) in Frisco is an unattended airfield with 3,000 feet of runway but no facilities. Air tours available.

By car: Frisco occupies a narrow section of Hatteras Island, with NC 12 the only through road.

GETTING AROUND Frisco is a good spot for biking, particularly down Billy Mitchell Road to the NPS campground at the end, set on the highest natural point on Hatteras Island. You can pedal out the boardwalk here and along the beach.

❋ To See

Cape Hatteras Fishing Pier, 54221 Cape Hatteras Pier Drive. Better known as Frisco Pier, this was a noted spot for catching king mackerel. The pier was destroyed by Hurricane Earl in 2010 and needed a complete rebuild. The pier became a scenic ruin, with just portions standing in the surf, a popular spot for photographers looking for an atmospheric shot. In 2013, the National Park Service acquired the pier from its final private owner, and in 2016 announced plans to demolish whatever remained. Fishermen would often cast into the surf around the pilings from the beach. At time of press, pier demolition had begun. A NPS bathhouse is located nearby.

✍ **Frisco Native American Museum & Natural History Center** (252-995-4440; www.nativeamericanmuseum.org), 53536 NC 12. Open Tuesday–Sunday 11–5. Built close to the site of an early American Indian village, this museum displays an amazing collection of Native American artifacts from precolonial to modern times. Of special interest are the dugout canoe found on the property and items from the archaeological dig nearby. Several galleries in the 100-year-old building display Native art from across the nation, while a special gallery and natural history room focus on the local tribes and their way of life. A bookstore and a gift shop offering the work of over 30 Native American artists carry many

THE FRISCO NATIVE AMERICAN MUSEUM TELLS THE STORY OF THE NEARBY VILLAGE OF CROATOAN AS WELL AS OTHER NATIVE AMERICAN TRIBES

unique items. The museum is also the repository of a marvelous collection of historic photos of the Chiracahua Apache, the people of Geronimo, available to researchers by prior arrangement. Outside, enjoy the bird garden or follow the nature trail that begins in the back of the parking lot and winds through 3 acres of maritime forest. Special programs, including nature walks, are offered for the visually impaired. $5 per person; $15 per family; $3 seniors.

✳ To Do

FISHING **Frisco Rod and Gun** (252-995-5366; www.friscorodandgun.com), 53610 NC 12. Bryan Perry, chief of the Frisco Volunteer Fire Department, owns and operates this tackle and gun shop, along with the Frisco Market next door, at the junction of NC 12 and Billy Mitchell Road. This is an official weigh station, and it sells North Carolina fishing licenses.

FOR FAMILIES ✍ **Frisco Mini-Golf and Go-Karts** (252-995-6325; www.frisco minigolfandgokarts.vpweb.com), 50212 Trent Lake Lane, MP 65, NC 12. Kids under six play free on the 18-hole mini-golf course. Other fun things to do include a game room with pool table and video games, a snack bar, go-karts, and bumper cars. The nicely landscaped property has a deck and goldfish pond, and stays open until late in the evening.

HORSEBACK RIDING Horses are allowed on the beaches of the national seashore but must follow the same rules and use the same access ramps as off-road vehicles.

HORSEBACK RIDING ON THE BEACHES OF THE NATIONAL SEASHORE IS A SPECIAL EXPERIENCE

Driftwood Ranch (252-489-8488). If you'd like to bring your horses with you on vacation to ride on the beaches or in Buxton Woods, you can board at this Frisco stable with easy access to trails. Dry camping also available.

Equine Adventures (252-995-4897; www.equineadventures.com), Piney Ridge Road. Horseback rides take groups through the maritime forest and onto the beach, where you can trot or canter, depending upon your riding ability. Rides are offered all year.

SPAS AND FITNESS **Hatteras Yoga** (252-996-0713; www.hatterasyoga.com), 53013 NC 12. Full schedule of classes and workshops in a variety of yoga styles. Beach yoga sessions available.

In Touch Massage and Wellness Center (252-995-4067; www.intouchmassage andwellness.com), 50840 NC 12. Spa treatments here use only natural and organic products. Massage, raindrop therapy, Reiki, Thai foot massage, and organic facials are offered, along with a selection of organic and Oriental beauty products.

WATER SPORTS **Cape Hatteras Kiteboarding** (252-216-7228; www.capehatteras kiteboarding.com), Frisco Woods Campground. Learn the basics or improve your skill with a kiting camp or private lesson that launches from Frisco Woods, well away from the busy waters off Avon and Rodanthe. Captain Billy Stark will also take your family out in his Carolina skiff for clamming, a sunset cruise, or a session of wakeboarding.

✳ Green Space

BEACHES The **Cape Hatteras National Seashore** (www.nps.gov/caha) has two facilities close to each other along NC 12 in Frisco. The ♿ **Frisco Beach Bathhouse**, on the south side of NC 12 just beyond the cutoff to the old pier, has restrooms, changing rooms, showers, and a fully wheelchair-accessible beach-access boardwalk. The **Sandy Bay Sound Access** offers a large parking area on the north side of NC 12 with paths over to Pamlico Sound and, across the street, a stairway to the ocean beach. Kiteboarders have recently renamed this soundside beach **Isabelle's Inlet** after the hurricane that opened a new inlet here (now filled in) back in 2003.

BOTH OCEAN AND SOUNDSIDE BEACHES ARE AVAILABLE IN THE CAPE HATTERAS NATIONAL SEASHORE

✳ Lodging

CAMPGROUNDS ♂ ☀ (ᵒᵖ) **Frisco Woods Campground** (252-995-5208; www .thefriscowoodscampground.com), 53124 NC 12. Large, shady campground with 150 RV sites, 100 tent sites, and air-conditioned cabins is popular with windsurfers and kayakers, thanks to its easy launch on Pamlico Sound. Full hookups with cable, pool, laundry, LP gas sales, fish-cleaning station, and a camp store are available, plus kayak, stand-up paddleboard, kiteboard, and windsurfing rentals and lessons. $.

National Park Service Frisco Campground (252-473-2111; www.nps.gov/ caha), 53415 Billy Mitchell Road. Located amid sand dunes on the oceanfront, the 127 sites here have no hookups. Restrooms, cold-water showers, and drinking water are available. Fourteen-day maximum stays. Open April to October. Day-use passes available. $.

MARINA **Scotch Bonnet Marina & Campground** (252-995-4242), 51684 NC 12. Twenty slips with water and electric are available for transients up to 30 feet long, with showers, ice, and marina store, as well as a boat ramp open to the public for a fee. Scotch Bonnet is worth hunting out for the awesome fudge sold in the marina store, even if you never set foot on a boat.

✳ Where to Eat

DINING OUT ♂ ↪ **Quarterdeck Restaurant & Bar** (252-986-2425; www .quarterdeckhi.com), 54214 NC 12. There's a bit of a time warp as you enter this spot that's been serving since 1978. The local seafood is fried or broiled, steaks are hand-cut and chargrilled, and the pies are homemade. Inexpensive sandwiches and a no-frills salad bar round out the menu. The Hatteras chowder and crabmeat in butter are memorable. Full bar. Large groups welcome. Lunch is served some days. $–$$$.

EATING OUT ⓨ **Capt'n Rolo's Raw Bar & Grill** (252-995-3663; www.facebook.com/captnrolo), 53060 NC 12. Fun eatery serves up local seafood, along with live music on weekends and happy hour specials. Best bets are the award-winning Hatteras-style clam chowder, shrimp burger, fish tacos, and steamed oysters. With a full bar and cheap PBR on draft, things can get rowdy at this local hangout as the evening wears on. $–$$.

⌇ **Frisco Sandwich Company** (252-995-3354), 53674 NC 12, Frisco Shopping Center. This cool shop, with a great location across from the Ramp 49 beach access and the NPS campground, serves gourmet-level sandwiches, wraps, panini, and house-smoked barbecue that are very much worth seeking out. The fried pickles are great, when available, or get a jar of house-made pickles or a pickle-themed T-shirt to take home. Ice cream sandwiches are made fresh in-house. Lunch only, $.

⌇ ♿ **Gingerbread House Bakery & Pizza** (252-995-5204; www.gbhbakery.com), 52715 NC 12. Hansel and Gretel–style cottage serves some of the best pizza on Hatteras Island, plus wings and a salad bar. A full espresso bar with hot and cold creations, fresh-squeezed orange juice, plus a variety of fresh baked goodies, from cookies to éclairs, add to the mix. A favorite with kids. Dinner $$.

ICE CREAM AND SWEETS **Hatteras Sno-Balls** (252-995-5331 or 252-562-4488), 53203 Delmar Willis Road off NC 12, MP 67.5. Hatteras-style snowballs, combining ice cream and shaved ice, are a unique treat well worth a try. Mix and match your way through 44 snow cone flavors and 12 ice creams.

Scotch Bonnet Fudge & Gifts (252-995-4242; www.scotchbonnetfudges.com), 51684 NC 12, MP 65.5. Making fudge on Hatteras for over 60 years, this spot in a marina has been featured on the Food Network. Offers more than two dozen flavors of homemade fudge (try the Chocolate Sandbar), plus 21 flavors of saltwater taffy, Jelly Belly jelly beans, seashells, and other beachy gifts. Stop by on Friday afternoons in summer for the hermit crab races.

✳ Selective Shopping

ARTS AND CRAFTS **Blue Lagoon** (252-986-5065; www.facebook.com/bluelagoonobx), 53688 NC 12. New gallery offers art, jewelry, fashion, and home decor by local artists, as well as some fabulous chocolate.

Empty Nest Studio & Gallery (252-995-5605), 52193 Cardinal Street at NC 12. The working studio of artist Crystal Blackmon where she crafts gorgeous sea-inspired jewelry from precious metals, pearls, and gemstones. Her photographs, acrylics, and watercolors are also available.

Indian Town Gallery (252-995-5181; www.indiantowngallery.com), 50840 NC 12. One-of-a-kind artwork by Outer Banks and regional artists are displayed at this gallery, where you may catch Wayne Fulcher, grandson of a Cape Hatteras lightkeeper, or other local artists at work. Locally made jewelry and pottery are specialties, as well as clever pieces made from repurposed objects. Classes are available as well, including photography classes with Pulitzer-nominated photographer Don Bowers. Arts and craft shows are held every Memorial Day and Columbus Day, with music and barbecue dinners.

Lightkeepers Gallery (252-995-3400; www.lightkeepersgallery.com), 53460 NC 12. Locally owned and operated gallery specializes in beach-themed art, jewelry, and home decor.

Red Drum Pottery & Coffee (252-995-3686; www.reddrumpottery.com), 53561 NC 12, across from the Native American Museum. The studio of potters Rhonda

Bates and Wes Lassiter displays their original pieces, including a collection of hand-painted beach and nautical-themed Christmas ornaments. Wes, familiar to Molasses Creek fans as "Banjo Wes," is often at work in the studio or tending the espresso machine. Watch for shows and weekly bluegrass concerts in the **Martin Parker Theater** on the grounds. The pottery has a second location on the Manteo waterfront at 207 Queen Elizabeth Avenue.

Sandy Bay Gallery (252-216-5666; www.facebook.com/sandybaygallery), 53013 NC 12. Art in a variety of media from local and regional artists includes original oils and sculpture, shark tooth jewelry, watches and clocks, tie-dyed silk, and more.

Sunsational Designs Gallery and Beads of Paradise (252-995-5960), 53255 NC 12. Owned by a family of artists native to Hatteras Island, this little gallery carries jewelry and unique island works painted on rocks, shells, and driftwood. They will help you make your own jewelry from the huge selection of beads, charms, and sea glass they have in stock. A great rainy-day stop for kids.

HATTERAS VILLAGE

Soon after **Hatteras Inlet** opened in 1846, watermen began moving to the area to enjoy easy access to the rich fishing grounds offshore. In 1935 the Hatteras Development Co. installed an electric generator and ice plant where Oden's Dock now stands, bringing Hatteras into the modern age. Two years later, Captain Ernal Foster began taking anglers out after blue marlin aboard his boat, the *Albatross*, founding the charter fishing industry in North Carolina. Despite booming tourism and lots of new construction, the village of Hatteras is actively seeking to preserve its traditional commercial and sportfishing culture. Life here still revolves around the town's marinas and docks, and many of the inhabitants are members of old island families. The Hatteras watermen share their heritage every September at the annual **Day at the Docks** and **Blessing of the Fleet.**

In September 2003, Hurricane Isabel cut the village off from the rest of the island, throwing a new inlet across NC 12 north of town and causing widespread devastation. The Army Corps of Engineers filled the new inlet in record time, but this section of the island is still considered unstable.

At the southern end of NC 12 sit the ferry docks where the free state ferry leaves for **Ocracoke Island** every day, year-round. Just beyond the ferry landing, the **Graveyard of the Atlantic Museum** presents the dramatic tales of many ships and sailors brought to grief.

GUIDANCE **Hatteras Welcome Center** (252-986-2203 or 1-877-629-4386; www .outerbanks.org), in the restored 1901 U.S. Weather Bureau Station, is located next to the Burrus Red & White grocery in the heart of Hatteras Village, at 57190 Kohler Road, and is open daily 9–5 all year.

POST OFFICE The **Hatteras U.S. Post Office** (252-986-2318) is at 57689 NC 12. The zip code for the town of Hatteras is 27943.

PUBLIC RESTROOMS Public facilities are found at the **Hatteras Welcome Center** (252-986-2203), 57190 Kohler Road; at Hatteras Landing, 58848 Marina Way; and at the state ferry docks at the end of the road.

PUBLIC LIBRARY (ゆ) **Dare County Library in Hatteras** (252-986-2385; www .youseemore.com/EARL), 56658 NC 12, has a section on local history and exhibits of Croatoan Indian artifacts discovered nearby in digs by the Croatoan Archeological Society (252-216-7118; www .cashatteras.com).

THE 1901 WEATHER BUREAU BUILDING NOW SERVES AS A WELCOME CENTER

Hatteras Village

PAMLICO SOUND

Oden's Dock
Foster's Quay
Village Marina
Hatteras Harbor Marina

Hatteras Welcome Center

KOHLER RD

Hatteras Library

12

FLAMBEAU RD

12

EAGLE PASS RD

Free Ferry to Ocracoke

Teach's Lair

LIGHTHOUSE RD

Hatteras Landing

CAPE HATTERAS NATIONAL SEASHORE

Graveyard of the Atlantic Museum

Beach Access

ATLANTIC OCEAN

0   0.25   0.5
Mile

© The Countryman Press

GETTING THERE *By ferry:* If you are arriving on Hatteras from Ocracoke, the **North Carolina State Ferry** (252-986-2353 or 1-800-368-8949; www.ncferry.org) runs 5 AM– midnight every day, unless conditions are too rough, departing about every half hour from May to October, every hour the rest of the year. Free. In 2018, the state began a new passenger-only ferry service, directly from Ocracoke Village to Hatteras Ferry Landing, May to September. Fare: $15 round-trip.

By car: Hatteras Village is hard to miss as you come down Hatteras Island on NC 12. Just keep going south. NC 12 runs directly to the state ferry docks.

GETTING AROUND *By bicycle:* Hatteras Village has a quiet residential side, with streets lined with historic houses and old family cemeteries—perfect for getting around by bike. Take a right on Kohler Road at the Burrus Red & White, or turn off on Eagle Pass Road, to discover this side of island life.

Waterboy Equipment Rentals (252-986-2222), along NC 12, rents bikes and golf carts to help you get around, as well as rental kayaks and SUPs.

By car: Most of the action—lodging, food, activities—in Hatteras Village centers on the six marinas located here. However, since they are oriented toward the water, these can be a bit hard to find. All are located on the northwest (or sound) side of NC 12. Four are next to each other just past the traffic triangle marked by the Burrus Red & White grocery. North to south, these are: **Oden's Dock, Foster's Quay** (home of the Albatross

FREE FERRIES TO OCRACOKE ISLAND DEPART FROM THE DOCKS IN HATTERAS VILLAGE

Fleet), **Village Marina**, and **Hatteras Harbor Marina. Teach's Lair** is a large marina a bit farther down NC 12, followed closely by **Hatteras Landing**, next to the state ferry docks, where the (paved) road ends.

MEDICAL EMERGENCY **Hatteras Village Medical Center** (252-986-2756; www .hatterasmedicalcenter.org), 57635 NC 12. Community nonprofit rural health center offers care for children and adults.

✳ To See

Albatross Fleet at Foster's Quay (252-986-2515; www.albatrossfleet.com), 57976 NC 12. The Outer Banks' very first charter fishing fleet originated here in 1937 and still takes anglers to the Gulf Stream after the big ones. Stop by to see the unique Hatteras-style boats with sharp, flared prows and rounded sterns, designed to help boats safely run the breaking waves of the inlet. A history of the Albatross Fleet and the early days of sportfishing can be found on its website.

Barnett Graveyard, Hatteras Landing, NC 12. An evocative graveyard dating to 1859 can be reached by a boardwalk over the marsh north of Hatteras Landing. Buried amid the twisted cedars are Stephen and Rebecca Barnett, lost when

THE BARNETT GRAVEYARD PRESERVES THE MEMORY OF A YOUNG COUPLE LOST AT SEA

their schooner broke up on the Ocracoke shoals.

Civil War Trails (www.civilwartraveler .com). Markers in the parking lot of the Graveyard of the Atlantic Museum describe the capture of Fort Hatteras and Fort Clark in 1861, the sinking of the USS *Monitor* in 1862, and other wartime shipwrecks. A marker in the parking lot of the Hatteras Village Civic Center on NC 12 describes the amphibious assault on Forts Hatteras and Clark. Nearby, a marker located at 57197 Kohler Road, a block west of NC 12, describes the Hatteras islanders' attempt to reconstitute a Union-oriented government.

❋ **U.S. Weather Bureau** (252-986-2203 or 1-877-629-4386; www.outerbanks.org), 57190 Kohler Road. Open daily 9–5 all year. Built in 1901, this first U.S. Weather Bureau Station played a key role in the nation's developing meteorological network and in the lives of local residents, giving warning of oncoming storms. The building in Hatteras Village, now on the National Register of Historic Places, has been restored to its original appearance, with a cedar-shingled widow's walk. Today it houses an Outer Banks visitor center as well as history exhibits. Free.

✐ ᕦ ⵝ ⭁ **Hatteras Island Ocean Center Ecology Park** (www.hioceancenter.org), 57204 NC 12, MP 71, Beacon Shops. The first phase of a project that may eventually include a fishing pier, this indoor/outdoor nature center has exhibits on sea turtles, local history, the fishing fleet, and local ecology. An easy launch for paddlesports is located on the grounds with a marsh walk, ecology exhibits, and a crabbing dock. Programs include kayak tours, sea turtle walks, and stargazing campfires. Free admission; program fees vary.

❋ To Do

BICYCLING Hatteras Village is a pleasant spot to bike, with lots of roads besides NC 12 to tour. You can also take your bike on the ferry to Ocracoke to explore there.

Bike rentals are available at **Nedo Shopping Center** (252-986-2545), **Waterboy Rentals** (252-995-2295), and **A. S. Austin Company** (252-986-1500).

BIRD-WATCHING Charter trips out of Hatteras Village offer unique opportunities to see species of sea birds that rarely come to shore but migrate along the Gulf Stream, feeding off schools of fish found in its warm waters. The best times for birding trips at sea are May–September and January–March.

Seabirding Pelagic Trips (252-986-1363; www.seabirding.com), Hatteras Landing Marina. Pelagic trips aboard the *Stormy Petrel II*, operated by Captain Brian Patterson and an experienced band of volunteer bird experts, have made some impressive sightings, including a rare black-browed albatross. Participants may also sight sea turtles, dolphins, and whales. Private trips and makeup charters available.

BOATING In Hatteras Village you can launch your boat at the Dare County boat ramp at **Village Marina** (www.villagemarinahatteras.com), or for a fee at **Teach's Lair Marina** (www.teachslair.com). Rent a Carolina skiff or kayak from **Hatteras Parasail & Kayak** (252-986-2627 or 252-986-2243; www.hatterasparasail.com), at Oden's Dock. See the *Water Sports* section for more options.

MUST SEE

Graveyard of the Atlantic Museum, now a part of the North Carolina state history museum system, is dedicated to conserving the maritime heritage of the area and memories of the hundreds of shipwrecks that line the coast. On display are shipwreck artifacts from the Age of Pirates through World War II, including some recovered from the wreck of the ironclad *Monitor*, an Enigma machine from a German submarine, and relics from the *Titanic*. The star of the collection is the 1854 Fresnel lens from the first Cape Hatteras Lighthouse, which disappeared during the Civil War and was only recently recovered and restored. Maritime movies, history lectures, children's programs, and other special events take place daily. The dramatic building, with a sweeping design resembling the bones of a shipwreck, sits at the end of NC 12, beside the state ferry docks. **Graveyard of the Atlantic Museum** (252-986-2995; www.graveyardoftheatlantic .com), 59200 Museum Drive. Free.

RECOMMENDED READING: For more on the Fresnel lens in the Graveyard of the Atlantic Museum, read *The Lost Light: The Mystery of the Missing Cape Hatteras Fresnel Lens* (Raleigh, NC: Looking Glass Productions, 2003) by Kevin Duffus, a factual and dramatic account of how the author found the lens, missing since the Civil War.

For more on the Graveyard of the Atlantic, read Bland Simpson's *Ghost Ship of Diamond Shoals: The Mystery of the Carroll A. Deering* (Chapel Hill: University of North Carolina Press, 2005).

THE ORIGINAL FRESNEL LENS FROM CAPE HATTERAS LIGHT WENT MISSING DURING THE CIVIL WAR AND REMAINED LOST FOR MORE THAN 100 YEARS

THE DRAMATIC GRAVEYARD OF THE ATLANTIC MUSEUM TELLS THE TALES OF MANY SHIPS COME TO GRIEF IN THE WATERS OFF THE OUTER BANKS

RECOMMENDED READING

Carlson, Tom. *Hatteras Blues: A Story from the Edge of America*. Chapel Hill: University of North Carolina Press, 2005. Memoirs of deepwater fishing and the families of Hatteras.

If you're looking for something a little more laid-back than a charter out to the Gulf Stream, contact Hatteras native Timothy Midgett, captain of the ***Happy Hour*** **catamaran** (252-996-0487; www.hatteraslanding.com), for a trip that can include snorkeling, clamming, fishing and shelling, a sunset booze cruise, or some nighttime gigging.

The free trip aboard the **Hatteras-Ocracoke Ferry** (252-986-2353; www.ncferry.org) is not to be missed. Ferries run 5 AM–midnight every day unless conditions are too rough.

DRIVING TOUR Download a self-guided tour of Historic Hatteras Village from the website of the **Hatteras Village Civic Association** (www.hatterasonmymind.com) to see the local side of life here.

FISHING Just 12 miles from the docks in Hatteras Village is the **Gulf Stream**, the highway used by the big-game fish, here closer to shore than at any point north of Stuart, Florida. Because this is the southernmost range of some species and the northernmost of others, the waters off Cape Hatteras where the cool Labrador Current, headed south, meets the warm Gulf waters flowing north earned the name **Gamefish Junction**, with more types of fish caught here than any other destination on the East Coast. Billfish anglers from around the world come to attempt the rare Grand Slam by catching a blue marlin, a white marlin, and a sailfish. Tarpon and wahoo, renowned for their fighting spirit, swim these waters as well.

The fishing is equally good for "meat fish" in the area, with numerous bass, bluefish, king mackerel, tuna, and dolphin (mahi-mahi) brought to boat. In winter, giant bluefin tuna, often weighing 200 to 500 pounds, are the most sought-after fish, as documented in the National Geographic Channel's reality show, *Wicked Tuna: Outer Banks*.

Follow the links in our listings under *Marinas* to find an offshore or nearshore sportfishing charter.

North Carolina State Sport Fishing School (919-515-2261; go.ncsu.edu/fishing). For more than 60 years, North Carolina State University's Office of Professional Development has sponsored an annual sportfishing school in Hatteras every June, with two days of classroom instruction, two offshore excursions hunting big-game fish, and a half-day of inshore fishing, plus fish fries and social events. Open to the public.

FOR FAMILIES ✐ **Kitty Hawk Kites** (252-986-1446) supervises a 32-foot outdoor climbing wall at Hatteras Landing. There's also a playground at this location.

The evening ✐ **Little Pirate Adventure Cruise aboard the *Cap'n Clam*** (252-986-2365; www.hatterasfishingcaptain.com) out of Oden's Dock is a must for Jack Sparrow fans. The fee includes free swords, eye patches, root beer grog, and plenty of swashbuckling. Birthday parties are a specialty.

✐ **Custom Sound Charters** (252-216-6765; www.customsoundcharters.com), Oden's Dock. Captain Rick Caton offers educational Happy Crabber trips especially suitable for families and children. The trips include pulling blue crab traps and identifying the species caught, followed by rod and reel fishing in the calm back waters of the sounds. Inlet adventures involve several different types of fishing, with anglers trying sight casting, trolling, and light-tackle wreck fishing.

🐾 **Family Water Adventures** (252-216-5683; www.captaintamigray.com), Hatteras Landing Marina. Captain Tami Gray offers family-friendly ecotours on the water that include your choice of shelling, tubing, clamming, snorkeling, fishing, bird-watching, and more. Captain Tami appeared on *Wicked Tuna: Outer Banks* with her boat, *Reel Action.*

HEADBOATS 🎣 *Cap'n Clam* (252-986-2365; www.hatterasfishingcaptain.com), Oden's Dock. The 68-foot *Cap'n Clam* makes daily trips in-season around Hatteras Inlet fishing for flounder, sea bass, trout, and other inshore and sound fish. In the evening the headboat offers the inexpensive **Little Pirate Adventure Cruise**, a great way for kids to go to sea.

🎣 *Miss Hatteras* (252-986-2365; www.hatterasfishingcaptain.com), Oden's Dock. To experience fishing on the Gulf Stream, sign up for this headboat's 10-hour trip and bottom fish for snapper, triggerfish, grouper, and sea bass. A shorter four-hour trip is offered to nearshore waters, or try the **Dolphin and Live Music Sunset Cruise.**

Stormy Petrel II (252-986-1363 or 252-473-9163; www.thestormypetrel.com), Hatteras Landing Marina. This 61-foot boat is able to handle larger groups, up to 15 people, for bottom or inshore fishing or trolling in the Gulf Stream. It also offers party boat cruises for sight-seeing or pelagic bird-watching.

HORSEBACK RIDING 🎣 ♿ **Hatteras Island Horseback Riding** (252-216-9191; www.hatterasislandhorsebackriding.com), Ramp 55, NC 12. Ultra-safe rides on the beach can accommodate any age, kids to seniors, even those in a wheelchair or with other disabilities. The family package is a great bargain, with the whole family riding for a single price. Rides happen on the NPS beach at the end of NC 12.

THE CHARTER FISHING FLEET HEADS HOME TO THE MARINAS OF HATTERAS VILLAGE AFTER A DAY OF TROLLING THE GULF STREAM

HUNTING Ken Dempsey's Guide Service (252-986-2102; www.kendempseyguide
.com), Hatteras Landing Marina. Dempsey takes hunters to blinds located in Pamlico
Sound. Charters include use of Ken's handcrafted decoys. He also offers light-tackle
inshore charters.

MARINAS Each of the marinas in Hatteras Village hosts its own charter fleet, with
each offering something a little different. Check the websites listed for current details.
Charter boats typically accommodate groups of up to six. If your group is smaller, ask
about a makeup charter.

Trips on the calm waters of Pamlico Sound are usually the favorite for family fishing
trips offered by many inshore captains.

Albatross Fleet at Foster's Quay (252-986-2515; www.albatrossfleet.com), 57976
NC 12. The experienced captains of the Outer Banks' very first charter fishing fleet
can take you out to the Gulf Stream after the big game fish or on a hunt for good-eating
Spanish mackerel and other nearshore fish. See the Albatross website for good pictures and descriptions of the fish caught in these waters.

Hatteras Harbor Marina (1-800-676-4939; www.hatterasharbor.com), 58058 NC 12.
Protected, full-service marina is home to the area's largest charter fishing fleet and
offers deepwater slips with water and electric for transients up to 60 feet. Showers and
a coin laundry are available for visiting boaters, or you can rent an efficiency apartment over the marina. Makeup charters available. **The Harbor Deli** (252-986-2500)
specializes in bag lunches for charters.

Hatteras Landing Marina (252-986-2077; www.hatteraslanding.com/marina),
58848 Marina Way. Located in the Hatteras Landing Resort immediately adjacent
to the ferry docks, this marina has a 9-foot-deep basin and more than three dozen
slips that can accommodate boats up to 75 feet. Hookups include cable TV and telephone. Showers, laundry, and a huge ship's store and deli are on-site. Inshore and offshore charters, sight-seeing cruises, clamming, bird-watching, and makeup charters
available.

Oden's Dock (252-986-2555 or 1-888-544-8115; www.odensdock.com), 57878 NC 12.
Oden's is a center of activity in Hatteras Village, the home of charter fishing and duck
hunting outfitters, kayak tours, WaveRunner rentals, and parasailing; the **Breakwater
Inn and Restaurant** and **Risky Business Seafood Market**; and two headboats offering
fishing and sight-seeing cruises. Transient boat slips with utility hookups are available
by the night or month.

Teach's Lair Marina (252-986-2460; www.teachslair.com), 58646 NC 12. Transient
boaters can dock at this 87-slip marina, one of the farthest south in Hatteras Village,
by the day, week, or month. Dry storage, boat ramp, ship's store, bait and tackle shop,
and restaurant are on-site. More than a dozen offshore and inshore charter boats dock
here. Makeup charters available.

 ♿ ((•)) **Village Marina** (252-986-2522; www.villagemarinahatteras.com), 57980 NC
12. This full-service marina caters to anglers bringing their own boats to Hatteras,
offering slip rentals, a boat ramp, dry storage, a ship's store, and a 12-suite motel, plus
Dinky's Waterfront Restaurant.

SCUBA DIVING Some of the following dive outfitters offer trips to the *Monitor
National Marine Sanctuary* (www.monitor.noaa.gov), open only by permit.

 ♿ **Capt. J. T.'s Wreck Diving** (757-537-6524; www.capt-jt.com), Hatteras Landing
Marina. The dive boat *Under Pressure* is available for dive charters or open boat recreational dives. The boat is equipped with a diver lift to make it easier for those with
mobility issues to enter and exit the water.

Dive Hatteras (703-818-1850 or 703-517-3724; www.divehatteras.com), Saxon Cut Drive. Specializing in the shipwrecks of Diamond Shoals, dive masters Ann and Dave Sommers take small groups to some of the deeper, more challenging sites, including German U-boats. They also offer blue-water spearfishing charters for scuba or free divers.

THE CHARTER FISHING FLEET TIED UP AT HATTERAS LANDING MARINA

WATER SPORTS Crisscrossed by creeks, inlets, and canals, and surrounded by salt marsh, Hatteras Village is a super spot to kayak or SUP, and especially good for beginners who want to practice without going out into the open water.

A. S. Austin Company (252-986-1500; www.asaustinhatteras.com), 57698 NC 12. The Austin family store opened in Hatteras Village back in 1915 and is still operated by the latest generation, who help visitors discover the island's secrets by kayak or SUP. They offer guided eco-tours, including highly recommended sunset kayak trips, or will map out a self-guided tour for you. Sit-on-top or fishing kayaks and SUPs rent by the hour, and you can put-in right next to the shop. Surfboard lessons and rentals, bike rentals, and surf-fishing expeditions are other options, or you can rent clamming or flounder gigging equipment or a rod and reel. Austin's rents a large selection of helpful stuff, including beach wheelchairs and carts, golf carts, coolers, and jogging strollers. The shop also sells local artwork, crabbing equipment, beach attire, hats, and more.

Hatteras Parasail (252-986-2627; www.hatterasparasail.com), Oden's Dock. Single, double, and triple parasail rides depart from Oden's Dock. WaveRunner, Carolina skiff, and pontoon boats available for rent.

Kitty Hawk Kites (252-986-1446; www.kittyhawk.com), 5848 Hatteras Landing. Kayaks and stand-up paddleboards available for rent. Launch into the sound from Hatteras Landing.

Sailor Jo's SUP Adventures (252-216-6123; www.sailorjo.com), 57171 Kohler Drive. Jody Stowe offers guided SUP tours and SUP yoga. You can also rent rooms in her historic Hatteras cottage.

Waterboy Equipment Rentals (252-986-2222; www.waterboyessentials.com), NC 12. This stand along the main drag through town rents bikes, kayaks, surfboards, and stand-up paddleboards, along with fun stuff like cornhole games and golf carts to help you get around.

⁂ Green Space

BEACHES In Hatteras Village, the **Ramp 55 Public Beach Access boardwalk** is located across from the Graveyard of the Atlantic Museum parking lot, where there's plenty of free parking. A second beach access is located at the **end of Flambeau Road off Eagle Pass Road**.

Beyond the ferry docks, sand roads run on through the national seashore to the tip of Hatteras Island. A popular surfing break called the **Water Tower** is located along the ocean side. Check with the NPS for current ORV routes.

TRAILS The **Sea Breeze Trail** in Hatteras Village Park on Eagle Pass Road has a boardwalk leading to a scenic overlook of the salt marsh. Other nature trails can be found behind the new **Hatteras Island Ocean Center** on NC 12.

✳ Lodging

BED & BREAKFASTS 🏠 ♿ ⚲ (ɯ) **Seaside Inn** (252-986-2700 or 1-800-635-7007; www.coverealty.com), 57321 NC 12. Originally named the Atlantic View Hotel, this was the first hostelry to receive guests in Hatteras Village. The historic 1928 inn was completely renovated with modern amenities after Hurricane Isabel, but it retains its cedar-shingle charm. Six suites and four standard rooms are furnished in antiques and wicker. Several, including a honeymoon suite, have Jacuzzi tubs. Spacious decks with grills and common rooms with fireplaces make this a popular place for special events, including weddings. Room rate includes a continental breakfast. The inn is a block from the ocean. No smoking permitted. $–$$.

CAMPGROUNDS AND CABINS ⚲ 🏠 (ɯ) **Hatteras Sands RV Resort** (252-986-2422 or 1-888-987-2225; www.hatterassands rvpark.com), 57316 Eagle Pass Road. Highly rated Good Sam campground has over 100 full-hookup and tent sites, as well as six 2-story air-conditioned cabins that look like dollhouses. Resort-style amenities include a large pool area with kids' pool and spa, fitness room, a bathhouse that is both heated and air-conditioned, laundry, adult lounge, free cable TV, and a game room with pool tables and ping-pong. $.

CONDO RENTALS 🏠 (ɯ) **Hatteras Cabanas** (1-800-338-4775; www .hatterascabanas.com), 57980 NC 12. Each efficiency condo in this oceanfront complex has a kitchen, two sundecks, covered parking, and is topped by a "crow's nest." Originally built in 1968, every unit was extensively remodeled (or rebuilt entirely) in 2005. Weekly and shorter stays available. $–$$.

SeaWorthy Condos (252-986-6510; www.seaworthygallery.com), 58401 NC 12. Fully equipped luxury condos above the SeaWorthy Gallery rent by the week. $–$$$.

(ɯ) **The Villas at Hatteras Landing** (252-986-1110; www.villasofhatteras .com), 58822 Marina Way. This complex, next to the Hatteras ferry dock, formerly a Holiday Inn Express, has 53 one-bedroom units available for nightly or weekly rental. Each condominium has a king bed and sleeper sofa, fully equipped kitchen, and a private balcony or patio. Free guest laundry, swimming pool, sundeck, and boardwalk to the beach. Smoke-free. $$–$$$.

MARINA LODGING ✳ 🏠 (ɯ) **Breakwater Inn** (252-986-2565; www.breakwater hatteras.com), 57896 NC 12, Oden's Dock. The former Hatteras Harbor Motel continues its tradition of welcoming anglers and hunters. A newer soundfront building houses 21 nonsmoking rooms, each with two queen beds, a kitchenette, cable TV, and private deck with fabulous sunset views. The older Fisherman's Quarters building offers standard rooms that can accommodate pets, and some are smoker friendly. Guests enjoy a continental breakfast and a pool. The **Breakwater Restaurant** and **Oden's Dock and Marina Store** are next door. Off-season $; in-season $$.

⚲ (ɯ) **Hatteras Harbor Marina Efficiencies** (252-986-2166 or 1-800-676-4939; www.hatterasharbor.com), 58058

NC 12. Five efficiency units on the second floor of the marina building have private balconies overlooking the harbor, full kitchens, cable TV, and sleep six. $$.

❀ ♿ ⟨⟨ᵧ⟩⟩ **Village Marina Motel** (252-986-2522; www.villagemarinahatteras .com), 57980 NC 12. A dozen suites, new in 2004, overlook the sound, each with a living area equipped with a daybed, flat-screen TV, kitchenette, and bedroom that sleeps three. Boat slips, restaurant, marina store, and laundry are on the property. $$.

MOTOR LODGES ❀ 🐾 ⟨⟨ᵧ⟩⟩ **Sea Gull Motel** (1-866-316-1843; www.keeshotels .com), 56883 NC 12. Completely refurbished after Hurricane Isabel in 2003, the Sea Gull sits on the oceanfront with its own beach. Amenities include morning coffee, an oceanfront swimming pool, a picnic area with grills, and a fish-cleaning table. Off-season $; in-season $$$.

VACATION RENTALS **Dolphin Realty** (252-986-2562 or 1-800-338-4775; www .dolphinrealtyhatteras.com), 56821 NC 12. Small realty company handles rentals from Avon to Hatteras Village, ranging in size from efficiencies to four-bedroom cottages.

🐾 **Midgett Realty** (252-986-2841 or 1-866-348-8819; www.midgettrealty .com), 57783 NC 12. Run by an old island family, this realty company established in the 1960s lists more than 500 properties on Hatteras Island ranging in size from condos to multistory vacation homes equipped with pools, docks, hot tubs, elevators, and more.

❀ Where to Eat

DINING OUT 🍴 ⍨ ↬ **Breakwater Restaurant & Bar** (252-986-2733; www .breakwaterhatteras.com), 57878 NC 12, Oden's Dock. Enjoy the fabulous sunset views from this restaurant on the second floor of Oden's Marina. The menu is creative, offering unusual appetizers and specials, including a highly praised Tuna Tort and Sticky Bottom Salad. You can eat in the white-tablecloth dining room, in more casual surroundings at the bar, or on the large covered deck, where you'll often encounter a band playing music to end the day in style. Dinner only, $$–$$$.

❀ 🍴 ♿ **Dinky's Waterfront Restaurant** (252-986-2020; www.dinkysrestaurant .com), 57980 NC 12, Village Marina. Open all year, this is a hot spot for locals who gather around the mahogany bar after the fishing fleet comes in. Fresh fish is served in numerous tasty preparations, and regulars recommend the crabcakes, soups, and Friday night's prime rib. The restaurant is small, with just 48 seats, but offers great sunset views over the water. An elevator is available. If you were lucky on your fishing trip, ask Dinky's to cook up your catch. Full bar. Dinner only, $$–$$$$.

🍴 ⍨ **Hatteras Sol Waterside Grill** (252-986-1414; www.hatterassol.com), 58646 NC 12, Teach's Lair Marina. Awesome views of Pamlico Sound and the docks team with a creative menu based on the freshest fish, with influences that range deliciously from Asian to Cajun, Italian to Southern, reflecting the eclectic background of the chefs. Sunset celebrations on the outdoor deck are a Hatteras tradition. Dinner $$–$$$.

EATING OUT ↬ Hatteras Harbor Deli (252-986-2500; www.hatterasdeli.com), 58058 NC 12, Hatteras Harbor Marina. Enjoy breakfast and lunch sandwiches at dockside tables or on the enclosed, air-conditioned porch. If you like seafood, don't miss the unique grilled shrimp burger or the family-recipe Islander fish-cake sandwich. The deli case has grab-and-go items. Opens at 5 AM most days; closed Sunday. Breakfast and lunch $.

🍴 ❀ **Rocco's Italian Restaurant** (252-986-2150), 57331 NC 12, MP 70. Thin- and thick-crust hand-tossed pizzas are the

HATTERAS VILLAGE FISH FRY

Every Saturday for the past six decades, the fine folk of Hatteras Village (www.facebook.com/HatterasVillage) have fried up a batch of locally caught fish to raise money for the Hatteras Fire Station, the local food pantry, and the Hatteras Village Civic Association. The Ladies Auxiliary whips up great coleslaw, potato salad, desserts, iced tea, and hush puppies to go with. Don't miss this fun family tradition and authentic taste of local cuisine, served every Saturday evening between Memorial Day and Labor Day, from 5 PM to 7 PM or until the fish is gone. Hatteras Fire Station, 57689 Hwy 12. $.

draw, plus subs, calzone, Italian pastas, and burgers. $–$$.

Sonny's Waterfront Restaurant (252-986-2922; www.sonnyshatteras.com), 57947 NC 12. Opens at 6 AM for breakfast. After more than three decades serving Hatteras diners, Sonny's has breakfast figured out: homemade biscuits and homefries, big servings, friendly service. Full bar. Breakfast and lunch $; dinner $$.

The Wreck Tiki Bar (252-996-0162; www.thewreckobx.com), 58848 Marina Way, Hatteras Landing Marina. Rockin' spot right next to the ferry docks, with seating indoors and out, live music at sunset, a menu of panini and Tex-Mex fare, plus beer chilled down in ice. Take-out available. $.

BEACH FAST FOOD **Ferry Bites** (252-986-2191), Hatteras Landing Marina. Quick grab-and-go shack right next to the ferry dock offers burgers, tacos, fish sandwiches, fries, hush puppies, and other finger food to get you through your ocean voyage. $.

The Hatterasman (252-986-1005; www.facebook.com/hatterasmandrivein), 57449 NC 12. Small family spot serves inexpensive breakfast, lunch, and dinner. Better-than-fast-food burgers and fries are joined by pork barbecue, fried veggies, crabcakes, fresh fish sandwiches, and beer. Take a moment to look at the **Veterans Memorial**. Next door, sister spot **Old Hatteras Village Ice Cream Shop** serves ice cream, shakes, cookies, and warm stuffed

pretzels in a laid-back environment. Relax on the porch and enjoy free Wi-Fi. Cash only. $.

COFFEE AND SWEETS **The Dancing Turtle Coffee Shop** (252-986-4004; www.thedancingturtle.com), 58079 NC 12. Dog-friendly Internet hotspot across from the harbor serves a full menu of coffee and tea drinks, plus tasty muffins, cookies, chocolates, breakfast croissants, even cookies for your dog. Open mic nights are a community event.

Scratchmade Snackery (252-986-0048; www.scratchmadesnackery.com), 57544 NC 12. Avid bakers Kitty Kellum and her husband Kyle make traditional French pastries, cinnamon rolls, cheesecakes, cookies, cupcakes, scones, Danish, and dog treats, too, all from scratch.

ICE CREAM **Happy Belly Ice Cream, Smoothies and Candies** (252-986-0018), 56910 NC 12, Stowe on 12 Shops. Score a big waffle cone full of ice cream or sorbet, iced coffee, fruit smoothie, local fudge, or a chocolate treat to enjoy on the screened porch.

MARKET **Burrus Red & White Supermarket** (252-986-2333; www.burrusmarket.com), 57196 Kohler Road. Located in the heart of Hatteras Village, this family-run grocery has been serving locals since 1866. Excellent deli items, ready-to-eat hot dogs, salad bar, plus fresh meat, seafood, produce, and all the necessities brought to you by a friendly staff.

SEAFOOD TO GO ✎ **Harbor House Seafood Market** (252-986-2039; www .harborhouseseafoodmarket.com), 58129 NC 12. Owned by the Harrison family, this market sells raw seafood off the family's own trawler, plus lots of prepared items seasoned with home-grown herbs, including oven-ready sea-food dishes, shrimp and crab enchiladas, chowder, shrimp dip, seafood salads, smoked fish, crabby patties, steamed North Carolina shrimp, and clams.

✎ ✎ **Risky Business Seafood** (252-986-2117; www.riskybseafood.com), 57878 NC 12, Oden's Dock. Run by a former commercial fisherman, this market, where the quality of the sea-food is anything but risky, offers a variety of fresh-caught local seafood, plus spiced steamed blue crabs and shrimp, smoked tuna and tuna spread, famous secret-recipe crabcakes, clam chowder, and cocktail sauce. They will also clean, vacuum pack, and freeze your catch then pack it for travel when you leave, or ship it to you. Kids enjoy watching the fish being cleaned at this spot under the **Breakwater Restaurant**. A member of **Outer Banks Catch** (www .outerbankscatch.com).

❊ Entertainment

Look for live music at the **Wreck Tiki Bar**, **Hatteras Sol**, and **Breakwater**, most often around sunset during the summer. **The Dancing Turtle** sponsors open mic nights.

❊ Selective Shopping

ART GALLERIES The beauties of storm and ocean have attracted a large colony of artists to Hatteras, including many fine photographers specializing in wild-life, sunsets, and surfscapes.

QUICK TIP

A few pounds of steamed shrimp make an inexpensive and delicious meal. Most seafood markets will steam shrimp or crabs for you at no additional charge.

Blue Pelican Gallery Gifts & Yarn (252-986-2244; www.bluepelicangallery .com), 57762 NC 12. Hatteras Island native Jenn Johnson displays her pho-tography and unique jewelry, along with the work of other local artists, and sells a variety of yarn, fibers, notions, and more in this vintage cottage next to the Burrus Red & White. Workshops are offered in both fine and fiber arts.

SeaWorthy Gallery (252-986-6510; www.seaworthygallery.com), 58401 NC 12, MP 72. Stop by to browse the wide selection of art, including a huge col-lection of North Carolina pottery, in the bright blue building. Artist Carole Nun-nally has arranged everything by sub-ject—boats, birds, lighthouses, marine life—for a uniquely compelling display. Classes are offered in jewelry making, painting, and other media.

SHOPPING CENTERS ✎ (ⁱᵖ) **Hatteras Landing** (252-986-2205; www.hatteras landing.com), 58848 Marina Way. Located next to the ferry docks, this large, modern center contains a number of shopping, dining, and activity options. Turnover is rather high, with new shops moving in every year, but there's always something fun to see and tasty to eat while you wait for the ferry. The **Hatteras Landing Marina Ship Store** (252-986-2077) is the one perennial, with snacks, souvenirs, beach necessities, and free Wi-Fi.

Shops at Stowe on Twelve (252-986-2024), 56910 NC 12. Fun shops are run by some of the island's coolest ladies. A gourmet deli and surf shop add to the mix.

SPECIAL SHOPS A. S. Austin Company.
See *To Do—Water Sports.*

Family Jewels (252-782-1115; www
.hatterasjewels.com), 56910 NC 12, Stowe
on Twelve. Wendy Stowe Sisler designs
jewelry from Murano glass beads she
makes herself, freshwater pearls, and
semiprecious stones. See her at work in
her fun shop full of antiques, glass, and
many objects d'art.

Lee Robinson's General Store (252-
986-2381; www.leerobinsongeneralstore
.com), 58372 NC 12. This island classic,
opened in 1948 and the survivor of many
hurricanes, stocks lots of necessary
items, fun souvenirs, local jams and jellies, books, wine, and over 100 different
beers. Don't miss the upstairs gallery of
gifts. In-season, Robinson's operates the
Sticky Bottom produce stand just across
the street.

Nedo Shopping Center (252-986-
2545), 57866 NC 12. They aren't kid-
ding when they say Nedo's has a little
of everything. If you like to browse in
hardware stores, this is your spot. You'll
find shoes, hats, fishing tackle, and toys
among the tools and nails. You can also
rent a bike here.

✳ Special Events

Check the **Outer Banks visitors website**
(www.outerbanks.org) for an updated list
of events during your stay.

April: **Underwater Heritage Symposium** (www.graveyardoftheatlantic.com).

May: **Hatteras Village Offshore
Open** (252-986-2579; www.hatteras
offshoreopen.com), Hatteras Village
Civic Association. Cash and trophies for
largest billfish and blue marlin, followed
by evening events, including a Taste of
the Village.

British War Graves Ceremony (www
.graveyardoftheatlantic.com).

Hatteras Storytelling Festival (www
.hatterasonmymind.com). A weekend of
top storytellers and local music.

June: **Hatteras Marlin Club Invitational Tournament** (252-986-2454; www
.hatterasmarlinclub.com), Hatteras
Marlin Club. The state's oldest billfish
tournament.

July: **Fourth of July Golf Cart Parade**,
Hatteras Village.

September: **Day at the Docks—A Celebration of Hatteras Island Watermen**
(252-986-2515; www.dayatthedocks.org),
Hatteras Village. Chowder cook-off, kids'
fishing contest, crab races, traditional
wooden boat exhibits, Taste of North
Carolina, and a working boat parade followed by the Blessing of the Fleet.

**Hatteras Village Invitational Surf
Fishing Tournament** (252-986-2579;
www.hatterasonmymind.com), Hatteras
Village Civic Association.

November: **United Methodist
Women's Holiday Craft Bazaar** (252-
986-2149), Hatteras Village Civic Association. Community lunch made by the
local ladies is served.

**Thanksgiving Day Surfin' Turkey
5K and Drumstick Dash Fun Run** (www
.hatterasyouth.com), Hatteras Village
Civic Center. Benefits the Hatteras Island
Youth Education Fund and OBX Go Far.

December: **Christmas Parade** (252-
986-2579; www.hatterasonmymind.com),
Hatteras Village. Parade is followed by
open houses at area businesses.

MANY HOUSES AND SHOPS ARE DECORATED WITH FLOATS
AND OTHER ITEMS THROWN UP BY THE SURF

OCRACOKE ISLAND

OCRACOKE ISLAND
Off the Grid

If once you have slept on an island / You'll never be quite the same . . .
—RACHEL FIELD

Ocracoke is a true island. No bridge links it to the mainland, so to get here you must take a boat or plane. The state of North Carolina obligingly provides three different ferries to Ocracoke. The one from Hatteras is free, while the other two charge a fee; but however you arrive, the trip lends a sense of isolation to the island. You cannot easily leave this place. Someone must ferry you away. Although, locals say, once the sand gets between your toes, you may not ever want to leave.

For eons the island belonged to the birds and the waves. Later, the ponies arrived and flourished, survivors perhaps of Spanish attempts to establish colonies along the Carolina coast. The local natives, the Woccon tribe, used to come to the island for oyster roasts. Their name for the island, "Wococon," appears on John White's 1585 map. The island's name had morphed into Occocok by Blackbeard's day. No one is sure how the "r" sneaked into the present-day name of Ocracoke. Locals today will tell you: "Pronounce it like the vegetable and the soft drink."

The island's location, next to an inlet that gives access to the great Pamlico and Albemarle sounds, gave Ocracoke a unique prominence during the age of sail. In colonial days, two-thirds of all North Carolina shipping passed through Ocracoke Inlet, the only gap in the northern Outer Banks that has remained open continuously since the 1500s.

The first to take advantage of this position were the pirates. Blackbeard and his cohorts would lurk here, waiting for rich ships to pass. Between raids they came ashore to drink rum and roast pigs. The island became a known gathering spot for pirates, and it was here that Lieutenant Maynard of the British Navy hunted Blackbeard down. The fateful battle, which ended with the pirate's head hanging from the bowsprit of Maynard's ship, took place just offshore at a place known today as **Teach's Hole**.

The constantly shifting sands of the inlet made passage dangerous for ships, and in 1715 the North Carolina colonial government sought to establish a community of pilots on Ocracoke to guide ships through. By the 1730s, **Pilot Town** was well established at what is today Springer's Point. Many of the families who live on the island are descendants of those early pilots. The names of Howard, Williams, Garrish, Balance, O'Neal, Gaskill, Stryon, and Wahab all appear on census records from the 1700s, and you'll meet people with the same names running the shops, charter boats, and restaurants of Ocracoke today.

Perhaps most notable among these are the Howards, descended from a William Howard, who bought the island in 1759. Legend connects him with Blackbeard's quartermaster, also a William Howard, the only member of the pirate crew to escape hanging. Look for the **Village Craftsmen** shop on Howard Street, established by the eighth generation of the family to live on Ocracoke.

The first lighthouse built in the area, a wooden structure on **Shell Castle Island** constructed in 1798, was replaced in 1823 by the current white tower of the **Ocracoke Light**.

ALL THE ACTION IN OCRACOKE VILLAGE CLUSTERS AROUND SILVER LAKE HARBOR, WITH THE OCRACOKE LIGHT NEARBY

It's the oldest operating lighthouse in North Carolina and the second-oldest continuously operating lighthouse in the United States.

In 1846, a great storm opened Hatteras and Oregon inlets, and from that date the importance of Ocracoke Inlet began to decline. Shipwrecks along this coast did not, however, and many local families joined the Life-Saving Service or turned to commercial fishing and hunting.

During World War II, the U.S. Navy established a base on Ocracoke to chase the German subs that were decimating shipping along the coast. The 500 men stationed there complained it was "the Siberia of the East Coast" due to the lack of amusements navy men typically enjoyed, but more than one ended up marrying a local girl and staying on after the war.

The navy base has disappeared except for a large cistern, but the military left a lasting legacy on the island's footprint. **Cockle Creek**, until then just a swampy inlet in the marsh, was dredged for the navy boats, becoming **Silver Lake Harbor**, today the centerpiece of Ocracoke Village. This, the island's lone town, occupies less than a third of the island on the southwest Pamlico Sound side.

The 16 or so miles of oceanfront beach remain completely undeveloped, part of the **Cape Hatteras National Seashore** established in 1953. This is one of the last places on the East Coast of the United States where you can look both ways, up and down the shore, and not see a single structure built by man.

Until the 1950s, when North Carolina began regular ferry service, Ocracoke remained largely isolated from the rest of the world. Through the centuries, the local residents developed their own unique style of speech, known to linguists as the Ocracoke brogue. Visit the docks around Silver Lake, and you may hear the boat captains and mates still using terms you won't hear elsewhere and commenting on the "hoi toide."

The ferries brought a steadily increasing tide of visitors to Ocracoke, and tourism is now the major industry. The village of 800 year-round residents swells to over

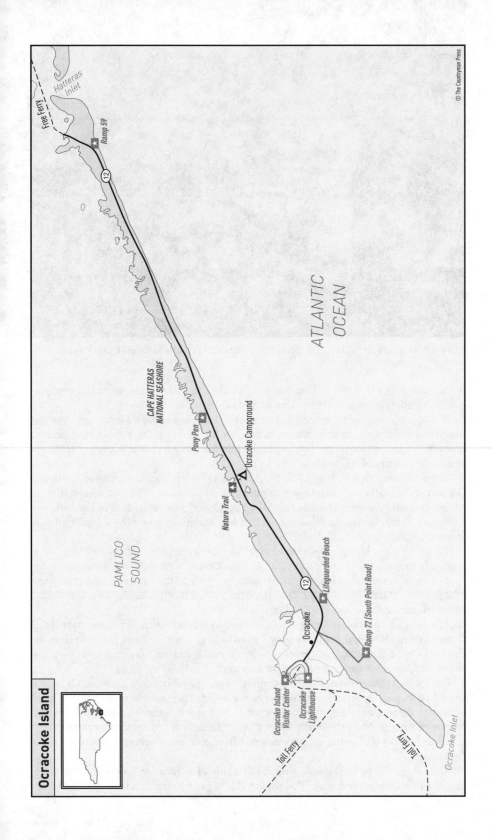

Ocracoke Island

Hatteras Inlet

Free Ferry

★ Ramp 59

12

CAPE HATTERAS
NATIONAL SEASHORE

PAMLICO
SOUND

Pony Pen ★

△ Ocracoke Campground

Nature Trail ★

ATLANTIC
OCEAN

12

★ Lifeguarded Beach

Ocracoke ●

★ Ramp 72 (South Point Road)

Ocracoke Island
Visitor Center ★
★
Ocracoke
Lighthouse

Toll Ferry

Toll Ferry

Ocracoke Inlet

7,000 during the summer season. Tourism reached storm force after Dr. Beach named Ocracoke the best beach in America in 2007. Ferry operators reported an immediate jump in number of visitors to the island.

Locals, feeling the glare of the spotlight, hope that all the publicity doesn't attract a new breed of pirates to their island. It's hard to imagine waterslides or mini-golf courses on Ocracoke. But the year-round residents also welcome the increase in tourism—and the income it brings. Villagers, both the descendants of the old residents, who call themselves the O'Cockers, and newer settlers, are determined to preserve the family traditions, laid-back lifestyle, and close-knit community that make Ocracoke special.

Many visitors catch just the briefest glimpse of Ocracoke and its unique qualities as they drive from one ferry landing to the other. To them, the island is just a traffic jam around the harbor and another two-lane stretch of road through the dunes. However, for those who park their vehicles in the large lot behind the **National Park Service Ocracoke Island Visitor Center** next to the docks and wander out into the village on foot, Ocracoke often becomes a favorite vacation memory.

Visit the dockside watering holes. Wander the old lanes paved with oyster shells. Look for galleries hidden amid the gnarled live oaks. Listen to some local music. Stroll the beach, looking for shells or shipwrecks. Take time to watch the sun set. Relax. You're on island time.

GUIDANCE A good place to begin a tour of the island is the **National Park Service Ocracoke Island Visitor Center** (252-928-4531; www.nps.gov/caha), 38 Irvin Garrish Highway, NC 12. Located next to the ferry docks in Ocracoke Village, the visitor center offers information on both the national seashore and the town, along with a bookshop full of local-interest books. Rangers lead programs during the summer at various locations around the park, including history and ecology talks, bird walks, and excursions that teach crabbing and seining techniques.

The **Village of Ocracoke's official website** (www.visitocracokenc.com) offers guidance on dining, lodging, fishing, places of worship, events, and entertainment. The **Ocracoke Civic & Business Association Information Center** is located in Community Square at 278 Irwin Garrish/NC 12. The **Ocracoke Community Center** (252-928-3162; www.ocracokecommunitycenter.com), at 999 NC 12, is the setting for many local events. Check the billboard there and others at the Variety Store and Community Square for notices of interest.

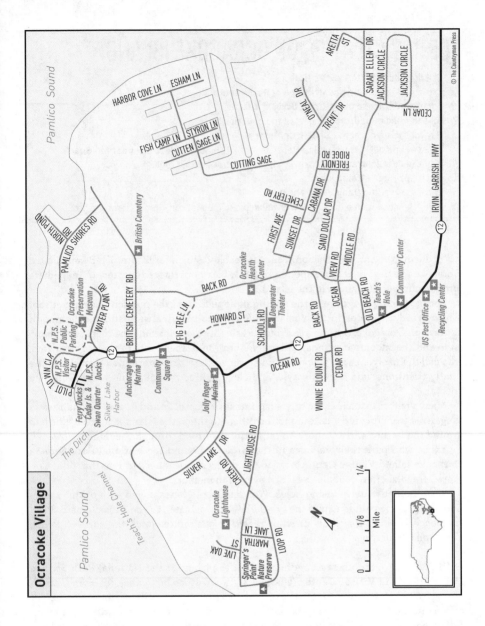

Another resource is the **Ocracoke Navigator** (www.ocracokenavigator.com), available as an app for cell phones as well as online, with interactive maps, historical photos, and audio tours, as well as walking and paddle tours.

Ocracoke is an unincorporated town in Hyde County, which is otherwise located on the mainland Albemarle Peninsula. Additional tourism information is available from:

Hyde County (252-926-4178; www.hydecountync.gov), 30 Oyster Creek Road, Swan Quarter NC, 27885.

Hyde County Chamber of Commerce (252-926-9171 or 1-888-493-3826; www.facebook.com/hydecountychamber), 20191 US 264, Swan Quarter, NC 27885.

LOCAL UPDATES

For more information and news from the island, visit the Ocracoke Current website (www.ocracokecurrent.com) or listen to Ocracoke's excellent community-based radio station, WOVV (www.wovv.org), at 90.1 FM and streaming live online. Broadcasting 24 hours a day, WOVV programming features an eclectic mix of local and regional music, plus interviews with local celebs and coverage of island events.

POST OFFICE The **Ocracoke U.S. Post Office** (252-928-4771) is located at 1122 Irvin Garrish Highway/NC 12. The zip code for the entire island is 27960.

PUBLIC RESTROOMS Public facilities can be found at **both of the ferry docks**; at the **national park visitor center in Ocracoke Village**; at the **Community Square docks**; at the **Lifeguarded Beach**, about 1.5 miles north of the village; and at the NPS campground.

PUBLIC LIBRARY The 🐾 ⛵ 📶 **Ocracoke Community Library** (252-928-4436; www.bhmlib.org) shares its location at 225 Back Road with the Ocracoke School. Hours vary due to school activities but are generally late afternoons and evenings on weekdays, mornings on Saturdays during the school year, with expanded hours in summer. The library's collection includes works on the Civil War, World War II, and pirate and Ocracoke family history. Free Wi-Fi is available at the library, and several computers are available for public use. The Friends of the Library host an annual book sale during the month of July on the library's porch.

GETTING THERE *By air:* You can reach Ocracoke Island by air—if you have a private plane. The ✈ **Ocracoke Island Airport/W95** (919-814-0550; www.airnav.com/airport/w95), a 3,000-foot asphalt strip operated by the National Park Service, is unattended and unlighted. Tiedowns are available but no fuel. The beach is just 100 yards away.

By ferry: A typical Outer Banks island, about 16 miles long and just 5 miles across at its widest point, Ocracoke lies about 20 miles off the mainland. **State-operated ferries** arrive at both the north and south ends. NC 12 runs between the ferry docks.

The **free ferry at the north end of the island** connects with Hatteras Village, a trip that takes about 60 minutes.

In 2018, the Ocracoke Express, a new passenger-only ferry, began runs directly to Silver Lake Harbor in Ocracoke Village from the Hatteras Ferry Landing, allowing visitors to skip the busy summer traffic. Ferries run May to September, $15 round-trip, which includes rides aboard the Ocracoke visitors tram and bike transport to the island.

Two ferries come to the docks in the south at the far side of Ocracoke Village. From here you can go to Cedar Island,

NC STATE FERRIES PROVIDE DAILY CONNECTIONS BETWEEN OCRACOKE AND THREE OTHER HARBORS

THE OCRACOKE LIGHT STANDS OUT AGAINST THE SUNSET

where a short drive brings you to Beaufort and the Crystal Coast; or to Swan Quarter, the Hyde County seat, on the Albemarle Peninsula. Both trips take about an hour and a half. Reservations are recommended for these ferries, especially in the summer, and a fee is charged. Contact the **North Carolina Ferry Division** (1-800-BYFERRY; www .ncferry.org) for prices and schedules. For immediate information on local conditions, contact the Ocracoke ferry docks at 252-928-1665.

A note on hours: As the tourist trade increases into the spring, fall, and winter seasons, hotels, restaurants, and other establishments are expanding their hours to meet demand. Although a listing may say that the place you'd like to go is closed seasonally, a telephone call will often reveal that the welcome mat is out.

Ocracoke Village is the only town on Ocracoke Island, and all establishments listed here, except the National Park Service campground and beach, the pony pens, and the ferry docks to Hatteras Island, are located within its boundaries.

GETTING AROUND *By bicycle or golf cart:* Bikes and golf carts (locally referred to as "Ocracoke turtles") are two of the best ways to get around Ocracoke Village. Numerous bike and cart rental stands are located throughout the village. Golf carts are only permitted on public streets within the limits of the village, and not on NPS land. Children under 18 cannot drive golf carts on public streets.

Beach Ride Rentals (252-916-0133; www.ocracoke4x4rentals.com), 1070 NC 12. Four-wheel-drive vehicles rent by the day or half day and include ORV beach driving permits. Shuttles are also available.

Ocracoke Island Golf Carts (252-928-0090; www.ocracokeislandgolfcarts.com), 216 Irvin Garrish Highway. Carts rent by the hour, day, or week.

Wheelie Fun Golf Cart Rentals (252-921-0216; www.wheeliefunocracoke.com), 990 Irvin Garrish Highway/NC 12. Rents electric or gas carts by the hour, day, or week.

On foot: There's a large parking lot behind the visitor center. Leave your vehicle there and set off on foot to explore the town, or rent a bike or golf cart at one of the nearby stands. Walking tour maps are available at the **visitor center** and at the **Ocracoke Preservation Society Museum** next door, on the other side of the parking lot.

By tram: A new, eco-friendly tram takes to the village streets in 2018 along with the new passenger ferry service. Routes from the Silver Lake ferry dock will run along Irvin Garrish Highway (NC 12) within Ocracoke Village.

A note on addresses: Who was Irvin Garrish anyway? Many of the addresses listed here are officially located on Irvin Garrish Highway, named for the first Hyde County commissioner from Ocracoke and one of the first captains of the Cedar Island Ferry. This road is identical to NC 12, the scenic byway that runs south from the Hatteras ferry dock down the length of the island until it reaches the waterfront. There, it makes a sharp right turn to the west, running along the water to the ferry docks that will take you to Cedar Island or Swan Quarter. At this T intersection (sometimes referred to as Kayak Corner) where NC 12 meets the water, Silver Lake Drive is to your left, running around the eastern edge of the harbor.

MEDICAL CARE **Ocracoke Health Center** (252-928-1511; after hours: 252-928-7425), a certified rural health clinic at 305 Back Road, offers nonemergency health care. Call for an appointment.

✳ To See

Thanks to their centuries of isolation, Ocracoke islanders developed a unique culture, creating their own forms of entertainment and creativity. Sea chanteys blended with folk music around winter fires, decoy carving developed into fine art, and always there was—and is—the inspiration of sea, wind, and sand.

This remarkable commitment to community has helped the islanders retain their unique spirit and, equally remarkable, find ways to share it with visitors without losing their island's identity.

ARCHITECTURE Some 200 acres of the village (about half the total area) is officially identified as the **Ocracoke Historic District**. Concentrated around Silver Lake, the district includes 232 historic buildings, 15 cemeteries, plus the lighthouse, cisterns, picket fences, and docks dating from 1823 to 1959, when Ocracoke is considered to have entered the modern era. Many of the older houses are traditional "story-and-a-jump" cottages with steep gable roofs, front porches, chimneys on the end, tongue-and-groove interior walls, and rooms in the attic. The outside is usually covered with cedar shakes, and there may still be a cistern to catch the rain, the island's only source of

TRADITIONAL STORY-AND-A-JUMP COTTAGE IN PORTSMOUTH VILLAGE, LOCATED ACROSS THE INLET FROM OCRACOKE

fresh water in the early days. Many of the homes in the historic district display wooden plaques giving the construction date and name of the original occupant.

Sam Jones, a native son turned Norfolk industrialist, was another major influence on Ocracoke architecture. During the 1950s Jones engaged local craftsmen in a variety of construction projects, most of his own fanciful design. Two significant examples survive along the waterfront: the many-gabled **Castle** (www.thecastlebb.com), now a bed & breakfast inn, and **Berkley Manor** (www.theberkleymanor.com), recently renovated as an event and adventure destination by **Dare To Hyde** (www.daretohyde.com).

HISTORIC SITES **Beach Jumper Historical Marker on Loop Shack Hill** (www .beachjumpers.com). This granite marker on the west side of NC 12 just before Ocracoke Village commemorates an almost forgotten episode in World War II history. During the war, German submarine activity was monitored from a facility on Loop Shack Hill via a top-secret magnetic cable that ran between Ocracoke and Buxton. In 1943, Loop Shack became a training base for an undercover Navy program, dubbed the Beach Jumpers, amphibious commando units deployed on tactical missions, a precursor of the famed Navy Seals of today. The original idea for the Beach Jumper commando units came from Lt. Douglas Fairbanks Jr., a famous movie star both before and after the war.

British Cemetery (www.nps.gov/ caha), British Cemetery Road. The bodies of four British sailors who lost their lives when a German submarine torpedoed HMS *Bedfordshire* on May 12, 1942, are buried here under a British flag. The U.S. Coast Guard performs an honor guard ceremony every year on the anniversary of the ship's sinking.

Community Square (www.ocracoke foundation.org), NC 12 and Silver Lake. Centered around the beloved **Community Store**, the shops and docks at this location have been the center of Ocracoke life since the days when mailboats, once the island's only contact with the outside world, tied up here. Since 1918, local folks have gathered on the porch, or around the

THE BRITISH CEMETERY, THE FINAL RESTING PLACE OF FOUR BRITISH SAILORS

potbellied stove, of the Community Store to share news and talk story. Today, the complex includes several historic buildings, including those housing the **Working Watermen's Exhibit**. The Community Store itself is being transferred to the ownership of the Ocracoke Preservation Society. The complex provides an Ocracoke Village visitor center, educational exhibits on the Ocracoke Clean Water Initiative, increased shoreline access for pedestrians, and a venue for many special events.

Fort Ocracoke Historical Marker. Located at the back of the parking lot behind the National Park Service visitor center, this marker gives information about Fort Ocracoke, once located just offshore. The site of the Civil War fort is now underwater but has been excavated by divers, and some of the artifacts are on display in the Ocracoke Preservation Museum.

Howard Street (www.visitocracokenc.com). Shaded with live oak, yaupon, and myrtle trees, this lane, paved with oyster shells, was once one of the village's main streets. The houses still belong to the island's oldest families, and the live oaks here are the most ancient on the island.

North Carolina Center for the Advancement of Teaching Campus at Ocracoke Island (www.nccat.org). The historic 1940 U.S. Coast Guard station, located beyond the ferry docks at the mouth of Silver Lake Harbor, has been restored for use as a campus offering enrichment programs for North Carolina teachers. A historic bell, on loan from the Coast Guard, sits on the harbor side of the facility. Around back, a boardwalk leads to a dock on the sound.

Ocracoke Lighthouse (252-928-4531; www.nps.gov/caha), Lighthouse Road. Most visitors to the island make their way to its most prominent landmark, the 70-foot

LIKE ALL NORTH CAROLINA LIGHTHOUSES, OCRACOKE HAS A KEEPER'S QUARTERS, BUT THIS ONE IS NOT OPEN TO THE PUBLIC

lighthouse that continues to help guide ships today as it has since 1823. A short board-walk leads to the base of the lighthouse, past the old keeper's cottage surrounded by twisted trees. The lighthouse is not open for climbing, but during the summer you can have a look inside the base if a docent is on duty. Free.

Ocracoke Pony Pens (252-928-4531; www.nps.gov/caha), NC 12. Ocracoke, like other Banks islands both north and south, has its own herd of wild horses. No one has ever been sure where they came from, but they played an important role in island life for several centuries, serving as mounts for local residents and pulling lifesaving equipment to wreck sites. In the late 1950s, when the road, now NC 12, was paved down the length of the island, collisions between cars and ponies, which then numbered in the hundreds, became a problem. The National Park Service initially wanted to remove all the ponies from Ocracoke, but at the request of island residents agreed to keep a small herd in a 180-acre pasture. A boardwalk leads from a parking area along NC 12 to a viewing deck where the ponies, now numbering under two dozen, can be observed. National Park Service rangers present a program on the ponies during the summer months. Genetic testing reveals that they are likely the descendants of Spanish horses who were stranded or shipwrecked on these shores. The pony pens are located on the sound side of NC 12, about 6 miles south of the Hatteras Ferry docks and 7 miles north of Ocracoke Village. Free.

Ocracoke Preservation Society Museum (252-928-7375; www.ocracokepreservation .org), 49 Water Plant Road. Located in a historic 1900 house next to the National Park Service visitor center, this museum is a community-based effort with strong support from local families. The rooms are furnished with donated antiques, decoys, model boats, and quilts. Special exhibits explore the island's hunting and fishing traditions, Civil War and World War II history, and the distinctive Ocracoke brogue. Outside, the yard, enclosed in a rose-twined picket fence, contains an original cistern, a life car used by the U.S. Life-Saving Service, and a 1934 fishing boat. During the summer, local

THE REMNANT OF THE OCRACOKE WILD HORSE HERD CAN BE SEEN IN THE NPS PONY PENS

residents, many of them cultural treasures themselves, give talks on the porch. The museum's gift shop is an excellent source of books on local history and culture. Free.

Ocracoke Seafood Company Fish House (252-928-5601; www.ocracoke seafood.com), 416 NC 12. The last surviving fish house on Ocracoke remains in its historic spot on the waterfront due to an intense community effort led by the nonprofit **Ocracoke Working Watermen's Association** (www.ocracokewatermen.org). Visitors are welcome. Come by to watch seafood being unloaded on the dock or to pick up some fresh catch for dinner.

Ocracoke Working Watermen's Exhibit (www.ocracokewatermen.org). The historic **Will Willis Store & Fish House** on the Community Square docks houses exhibits explaining the crucial connection between fishing and the local economy, past, present, and future, through historic photos and artifacts, plus video clips on many related topics. It also serves as a clearinghouse for classes, birding tours, and community events. Free.

Ocrafolk Performances. Ocracoke is home to an impressive number of musicians and storytellers who have developed a unique "Ocrafolk" style based on island traditions. Annual festivals and folk schools, plus an island-based recording studio, help spread the sound. During the summer, performances are held several nights a week at the Deepwater Theater, featuring Molasses Creek, the Ocrafolk Opry, and local storytellers. See the *Entertainment* section for more info.

Teach's Hole Blackbeard Exhibit (252-928-1718; www.teachshole.com), 935 NC 12. This pirate store, with over 1,000 pirate-related items, offers educational exhibits, including weapon and pirate flag displays, old bottles, and a film on Ocracoke's most famous resident and his pirate associates.

Village Craftsmen (252-928-5541; www.villagecraftsmen.com), 170 Howard Street. Gallery in an old island cottage stocks a wide variety of crafts by over 300 American crafters, including many from the Outer Banks. Gallery founder Philip Howard, an eighth-generation Ocracoker, is a wealth of information on the island, past, present, and future, and admits he just may be descended from one of Blackbeard's pirate crew. Drop by to chat, or check out his wonderful blog on Ocracoke life at www.villagecraftsmen.blogspot .com. The store also offers history and ghost tours of Ocracoke Village.

✳ To Do

If you want to play golf on vacation or have young ones who need to ride roller coasters, Ocracoke is not the destination for you. The attractions here are walking and swimming at one of the best beaches

OCRACOKE STILL HAS AN ACTIVE FISHING INDUSTRY

MUST SEE

Portsmouth Village (252-728-2250; www.friendsofportsmouth island.org or www.nps.gov/calo). Once larger and more prosperous than Ocracoke on the other side of the inlet, today Portsmouth is a ghost town, maintained in pristine yet lonely splendor by the National Park Service as part of **Cape Lookout National Seashore.** The NPS offers guided tours of the village, or you can take a self-guided tour. Maps, restrooms, and historical exhibits can be found at the visitor center, close to the dock where boat shuttles drop off day-trippers. Several buildings are open to the public and contain exhibits on village history, including the general store and post office, the Methodist church, and the lifesaving station.

THE METHODIST CHURCH IN PORTSMOUTH IS OPEN FOR VISITORS

in the country, exploring the historic village, slowing down, reading a book, or just relaxing. You can find more action out on the water, but even there you'll encounter the island's laid-back vibe, locally referred to as the Ocracoma.

BICYCLING The best way to see Ocracoke Village is by bike. Ride the **Loop Road** to the lighthouse, visit **Springer's Point** and the **British Cemetery**, and gallery-hop along the **Back Road**. Especially seek out the old lanes paved with crushed oyster shell, such as **Howard Street** and **Fig Tree Lane**.

A paved multiuse path connects the village with the **National Park Service campground** and the **Lifeguarded Beach**.

Most hotels and inns rent bicycles if they aren't included for free in the room rate. Shacks and stands along NC 12 also offer convenient daily rentals.

Anchorage Marina Scooter and Bike Rentals (252-928-6661; www.the anchorageinn.com), Anchorage Marina, 180 NC 12. Shop at the marina rents both bikes and scooters by the hour or day. Helmets provided.

Beach Outfitters (252-928-6261; www.ocracokeislandrealty.com), 1053 NC 12. Large bike stand sits outside the Ocracoke Island Realty office at the north end of the village.

The Slushy Stand (252-928-1878; www.theslushystand.com), 473 NC 12. Popular ice cream stand near the Silver Lake T intersection rents adult, kid, and tandem bikes; adult tricycles; and baby seats by the hour, day, or week. Locks are included.

BIRD-WATCHING The sections of the Cape Hatteras National Seashore located on Ocracoke are some of the most isolated and undisturbed on the East Coast and are popular nesting sites for a variety of shorebirds, including the endangered piping plover. Sections of the national seashore are frequently closed during the summer to protect nesting shorebirds and sea turtles. On offshore islands, brown pelicans, black skimmers, and terns can be seen during nesting season.

Wading and marsh birds, as well as migrating songbirds, are often seen along the Hammock Hills Nature Trail, across NC 12 from the National Park Service campground, and at Springer's Point.

BROWN PELICANS NEST ON AN OFFSHORE ISLAND WHILE THE BEACHES ARE HOME TO A WIDE VARIETY OF SHOREBIRDS, MANY ENDANGERED

In spring and fall, **Portsmouth Island ATV Excursions** (252-928-4484; www .portsmouthislandatv.com) offers bird-watching trips from the Jolly Roger Marina over to Portsmouth Island's tidal flats to see shorebirds such as rare curlew sandpipers and bar-tailed godwits.

Captains Rudy and Donald Austin at Austin Boat Tours (252-928-4361 or 252-928-5431; www.portsmouthislandboattours.com) take visitors to Beacon Island to see an amazing brown pelican rookery in-season.

BOATING Most of the recreation on the island, beyond the beach, is found at the docks along **Silver Lake**. Several fun establishments have sprung up on the waterfront, where you can kick back with a cold beverage and watch the nautical action.

Those who arrive by boat will find consistent depths of 8 feet in **Silver Lake Harbor** and in the well-maintained channels leading to it.

Several boat ramps are available in the village. The National Park Service maintains a **free boat ramp** at the back of the large parking lot next to the visitor center, but you cannot launch personal watercraft such as Jet Skis from here—they are not allowed in the waters of the national seashore. Boat ramps charging a fee are located at the **Anchorage Marina** and the **Harborside Motel**.

Anchorage Marina (252-928-6661; www.theanchorageinn.com), 180 NC 12. Full hookups including cable, fuel, and pump-out service are available for transient boaters, with access to showers and a swimming pool. Vessels up to 100 feet can dock. **SMacNally's Raw Bar** serves local seafood and cold ones on the dock in-season. Bikes and scooters are rented by the hour, day, or week. **Restless Native Small Boat Rentals** (252-921-0011; www.ocracokeboatrentals.com) operates out of this marina.

Community Square Docks, 324 NC 12. Sign up here for boat tours and ferry service to historic Portsmouth or sunset sails aboard the *Windfall II* or *Wilma Lee*. Fuel for boats is available, as are occasional slips for transients, a dinghy dock, and kayak launch area.

Gun Barrel Point Marina, located at the T intersection where NC 12 meets the water, sometimes referred to as Kayak Corner.

⛵ **Jolly Roger Pub & Marina** (252-928-3703; www.jollyrogerocracoke.com), 410 NC 12, across the street from the Silver Lake Motel. **Ocracoke Parasail**, **Ocracoke Wave Runners**, **Native Son Boat Tours**, and several charter-fishing boats dock here, convenient to the refreshments and fun served up daily by the pub.

National Park Service Docks (252-473-2111; www.nps.gov/caha). Located next to the ferry docks at the far end of Silver Lake, these government-run docks host boats up to 80 feet at low rates. Dockage is first come, first served, and there is a 14-day limit on stays during the summer. Services include electric hookup, available in summer only; low-pressure water connections; and bathrooms across the street.

BOAT RENTALS AND BOAT TOURS ⚓ **Beach Ride Rentals** (252-928-0007; www .ocracoke4x4rentals.com), 294 NC 12, Community Square Docks. Rent a pedal boat for a family-friendly cruise on Silver Lake.

Portsmouth Island Boat Tours (252-928-4361 or 252-928-5431; www.portsmouth islandboattours.com), Community Square Docks. Captains Rudy and Donald Austin run a shuttle service from the Ocracoke waterfront to the ghost village of Portsmouth. $20 round-trip. The Austins also offer a narrated sight-seeing tour of Pamlico Sound, visiting the sites of **Fort Ocracoke**, **Shell Castle Island**, **Pelican Island**, and other local landmarks. During the tour the Austins tell local tales in the fast-disappearing Ocracoke brogue.

CAPTAIN RUDY AUSTIN AND HIS FAMILY RUN BIRDING AND DOLPHIN TOURS, AS WELL AS THE SHUTTLE TO PORTSMOUTH VILLAGE

Restless Native Small Boat Rentals (252-921-0011 or 252-928-1421; www .ocracokeboatrentals.com), Anchorage Marina, 180 NC 12. Be your own captain in a flat-bottom skiff with outboard motor. After a brief orientation, explore the harbor and sound on your own, go fishing or clamming, or head over to Portsmouth Village for the day. Daily and package rates available.

℘ **Sail Ocracoke** (252-928-7245; www.schoonerwindfall.com), Community Square Docks. Captain Rob Temple takes small groups on sails aboard the *Windfall II* schooner, April through October. Onboard, Temple tells tales about Ocracoke's most infamous resident, Blackbeard, including many little-known facts. Captain Temple also offers sunset sails aboard the *Wilma Lee*, flagship of **Ocracoke Alive** (www.ocracokealive .org). The restored 1940 shipjack, able to carry up to 42 passengers, is a popular venue for weddings conducted by the captain, ordained by the Universal Life Church.

DOLPHIN- AND WHALE-WATCHING

The waters of Pamlico Sound and offshore on the ocean side are rich in sea life year-round. Boats making their way through Ocracoke Inlet often encounter groups of bottlenose dolphins. More rare are whale sightings. Whale hunting was once a lucrative pursuit in these parts. Today, more different species of whales migrate along the coast of North Carolina than any other stretch of the East Coast. While no organized whale-watching tours are taking place at this time, the experienced captains of Ocracoke know where to look, if asked. Sperm whales and the extremely rare northern right whales migrate past the coast in springtime; humpback and fin whales pass in fall. Pilot whales can be seen all year. Some whales, such as the orcas, stay far from shore in deep water, but juvenile humpbacks can sometimes be seen from the Ocracoke beaches, breaching and forming bubble nets in the rich waters. Seals also haul out on the beach occasionally.

CAPTAIN ROB TEMPLE CAPTAINS THE SAILING VESSELS *WILMA LEE* AND *WINDFALL II*, IN ADDITION TO BEING ONE OF THE ISLAND'S TOP STORYTELLERS

Austin Boat Tours (252-928-4361 or 252-928-5431; www.portsmouthislandboat tours.com). Captains Rudy and Donald Austin take visitors out to see the dolphins in Pamlico Sound.

Devereux II (252-921-0120; thedevereux.tripod.com), Anchorage Marina. Locals recommend contacting Captain Reid Robinson, one of the area's top charter fishing captains, about whale-watching trips.

FISHING CHARTERS Docked less than 20 miles from the Gulf Stream, Ocracoke's charter-fishing fleet conducts some of the most successful, and reasonably priced, offshore trips on the coast, and the rich waters of Pamlico Sound are just outside the harbor.

Many of Ocracoke's charter fleet captains are descendants of families who have fished this region for generations, and they will take you to productive spots that the out-of-town fisherman will never find.

Although Ocracoke has no fishing piers, surf fishing is tremendously popular along the unspoiled beaches of the island. A four-wheel-drive vehicle is a must. A permit is required to drive on the beach. Consult the **National Seashore website** (www.nps.gov/caha) for current regulations and closures.

Drum Stick (252-921-0011 or 252-928-1421; www.drumstickocracoke.com), Anchorage Marina. Capt. Farris O'Neal's charter boat has the distinction of catching the state-record king mackerel, an 82-pound, 66-inch monster, and also a world-record snowy grouper. A wide variety of excursions are possible, including makeup trips, night drum fishing, shark fishing, Gulf Stream trolling, and winter fishing for giant bluefin tuna.

Fish Tale (252-921-0224; www.facebook.com/FishTaleCharters), Jolly Roger Marina. Educational family trips using light tackle on Pamlico Sound include lessons in fish identification, perfect for first-time anglers. The Catch Your Dinner special offers a quick two-hour trip after good "eating" fish. Tackle, bait, ice, and fish filleting are included in per-person rates.

Ocracoke Sportfishing (252-928-4841 or 252-928-8064; www.ocracokesportfishing .com), Community Square Docks. The O'Neals, father and son, belong to a native Ocracoker family with a fishing heritage that dates back to the 1600s. Join Captain Ronnie O'Neal (252-928-8064) for a full or half day aboard the *Miss Kathleen.* Or set out with Ronnie's son, Captain Ryan O'Neal (252-928-9966), in the 24-foot *Tarheel* for a day of inshore light-tackle fishing, clamming, or a night trip to gig flounder. Makeup charters available.

FISHING TACKLE SHOPS ✳ **Ocracoke Variety Store** (252-928-4911; www .ocracokevarietystore.com), 950 NC 12. This one-stop shop offers groceries and microbrews, as well as bait and tackle, beach supplies, and much more. Open all year.

Tradewinds Tackle Shop (252-928-5491; www.fishtradewinds.com), 1094 NC 12. The place to find the right gear for surf, inshore, and offshore fishing, plus clam rake rentals, crab nets, and camping and beach supplies. Surf fishing is a passion of the owners, and they have an official weigh station where you can register your citation fish.

FITNESS CLASSES ✳ ((ᵠ)) **Angie's Gym** (252-928-2496; www.angies-gym.com), 141 Sand Dollar Road. Full-service gym offers cardio and strength machines, plus exercise classes, yoga, and a sauna. Daily and weekly passes available.

✳ **Free Fitness Classes at Ocracoke Community Center** (252-928-3162; www .ocracokecommunitycenter.com), 999 NC 12. Free exercise classes for all ages and abilities are offered on weekday mornings.

OCRACATS

Island visitors often comment on the large number of feral cats on Ocracoke. Many locals believe they arrived along with the island ponies, survivors of shipwrecks along this coast, since the cats seem to have been here even before the village. Perhaps some are even descendants of cats that lived aboard Blackbeard's pirate ship, because every captain kept cats aboard to battle rats. Ocracats (252-921-0281; www.ocracats.org) is a nonprofit organization dedicated to caring for these community cats through catch-and-release vaccination and spay-neuter services. Donations to this cause are tax-deductible and greatly appreciated. You can sign up on the Ocracat website to adopt an Ocrakitten.

❊ **Yoga with Amy** (www.yogawithamy.net). Local health professional Amy Hilton teaches Anusara yoga classes at the Angie's Gym. Drop-ins welcome.

FOR FAMILIES If you have a young pirate in the family, Ocracoke is a great place to explore the real episodes of Blackbeard's life, with lots of pirate-themed attractions to visit. You can stay at **Blackbeard's Lodge**, tour a **Blackbeard exhibit**, take a pirate cruise to the site of **Blackbeard's final battle**, eat at the **Jolly Roger Pub**, and stroll through **Springer's Point**, where Blackbeard once made his camp. Check the schedule at the **Deepwater Theater** (www.ocracokealive.org) to see if its hit musical, *A Tale of Black-beard* (www.ataleofblackbeard.com), is playing.

Ocracoke Alive (www.ocracokealive.org) sponsors a full schedule of fun, free events through the summer that includes dockside talks about pirates and sailing next to the **skipjack *Wilma Lee*** docked at **Community Square**, dances at the **Ocracoke Community Center** (www.ocracokecommunitycenter.com), and more.

The village also offers a growing list of water sports that appeals to the younger set, including surf camps, boat cruises, Jet Ski rentals, and parasailing. The **Windfall Sailing School** (252-928-7245) offers basic sailing, cruising, and navigation lessons for the novice sailor.

The **NPS rangers at Cape Hatteras National Seashore** (www.nps.gov/caha) also offer many family-friendly activities and programs on pirates, sea turtles, Banker ponies, Ocracoke history, cast netting, crabbing, and more. Most are free.

Ocracoke Community Park (www.ocracokecommunitypark.com), at 148 Maurice Ballance Road, offers a ballpark with various baseball and softball activities, as well as fitness and walking trails.

HORSEBACK RIDING ✧ ❋ **Morning Star Stables** (252-921-0383; www.facebook.com/ ocracokehorserides), 213 British Cemetery Road. Horseback rides on the beach are available all year.

HUNTING Shooting waterfowl is a treasured winter tradition for many Ocracoke families. Some native Ocracokers now offer guide services, taking visiting hunters after the redheads, bluebills, black ducks, pintails, brants, widgeons, and geese that winter in Pamlico Sound. You'll find a unique kind of blind in use here: the curtain blind, a kind of sink box developed in the area that is legal only in Hyde and Dare counties.

Curtain Box Hunting (252-588-0185). Native guide Russell Williams specializes in curtain blind trips.

Dare To Hyde Outdoor Adventures (252-926-9453; www.daretohyde.com), named for two adjacent counties, seeks to make the outstanding outdoor opportunities of the region more available to visitors. Hunting tours include trophy hunts for 500-pound black bear, turkey and deer hunting, and shooting for duck, tundra swan, and snow and Canada geese. Birding and photography trips are another popular option. All-inclusive packages available.

Ocracoke Sportfishing & Hunting (252-928-4841 or 252-928-8064; www.ocracoke sportfishing.com). Ronald O'Neal Jr., descended from eight generations of Ocracokers, takes hunters out to the family duck blinds in Pamlico Sound during the winter season.

Ocracoke Waterfowl Hunting (252-928-5751). Native Monroe Gaskill provides bush blinds, transport, and a resting area for dogs, and deploys more than 100 decoys at each blind.

Open Water Duck Hunting (252-928-7170). Wade Austin is the fourth generation of his family to guide hunters. Curtain boxes and bush blinds available.

KAYAKING AND STAND-UP PADDLEBOARDING Ocracoke Village is an ideal location for kayaking and stand-up paddleboarding (SUP). The calm waters of Silver Lake, with the lighthouse visible in the background, make a safe and scenic spot for a family paddle. Just stay clear of the ferry docks.

Outside the harbor, the sound side of the island is covered in salt marsh where many wading birds can be seen, especially at dawn and dusk. A favorite paddle is southeast along the coast toward **Springer's Point**. More experienced paddlers may want to cross **Ocracoke Inlet** to **Portsmouth** but should get local advice on winds, tides, and weather before setting out.

Kayak fishing is quite rewarding in the area. Ask the folks at **Tradewinds Tackle** for advice.

Kayaks and other nonmotorized craft can launch at the **Community Square Docks** and at a sandy, soundside launch at the back of the parking lot next to the national seashore visitor center.

Rental kayaks and SUPs are available at **several stands along the harborfront**; at **Kitty Hawk Kites** (252-928-4563; www.kittyhawk.com) in Community Square; and at **Ride the Wind Surf & Kayak** (252-928-6311; www.surfocracoke.com), which also offers a variety of tours, including a paddle out to a secluded beach for a session of tai chi and yoga. See *Water Sports* for more information.

SHELLING Some of the best shelling in the state is found along the Atlantic side of Ocracoke. Lucky beachcombers may collect a variety of different whelks, sand dollars, and possibly a rare Scotch bonnet, the North Carolina state shell. The best time to search for shells is right after high tide or after a storm. The northern end of the island has a gentle slope, good for finding unbroken shells.

SPAS AND WELLNESS **Ann Ehringhaus Massage Therapy** (252-928-1311; www .annehringhaus.com), 660 NC 12. Licensed massage therapist offers treatments and classes in a variety of bodywork techniques, including Reiki, Chinese acupressure, and the Rosen Method of emotional healing. Ann is the innkeeper at **Oscar's House B&B** (see *Lodging*).

Deep Blue Bodywork & Massage Therapy (252-921-0182; www.deepbluebodywork .com), 260 O'Neal Drive. Amy Hilton offers Structural Integration sessions, craniosacral therapy, and a variety of massage and body treatments.

Float with Grace (919-418-5472; www.floatwithgrace.com). Licensed massage therapist offers Watsu treatments, a gentle form of therapeutic massage conducted while the client floats in a warm-water indoor pool, as well as tai chi classes.

Island Path Massage and Retreats (252-475-0859; www.islandpath.com). Ruth Fordon and Ken DeBarth offer therapeutic massage, life coaching, personal path retreats, and creativity camps. Ken trained at the Cayce/Reilly School of Massage.

Stillwater Spa and Wellness (252-588-0267; www.stillwaterspaandwellness.com), 72 Back Road. Licensed therapists offer bodywork and spa treatments. All-natural handcrafted aromatherapy and herbal products are for sale.

WALKING TOURS **Ocracoke Ghost and History Tour** (252-928-6300; www.village craftsmen.com), Village Craftsmen, 170 Howard Street. Eighth-generation Ocracoker Philip Howard and his trained staff lead two different walking tours of Ocracoke Village, and both include plenty of ghost stories. Tours last about 90 minutes and cover 1.5 miles. Adults $12; ages 12 and under $6. Self-guided MP3 tours also available.

WATER SPORTS Although the water-sports industry here is not yet as organized as you'll find farther north on the Banks, the area has plenty of opportunities for extreme water fun.

Surfing experts say Ocracoke has some of the best, and least crowded, waves on the East Coast. Locals here consider surfing an important part of island life. Ocracoke's high school was the first east of the Mississippi to offer a surfing class.

Ocracoke Parasail (252-928-2606; www.ocracokeparasail.com), Jolly Roger Marina, 410 NC 12. Get the big picture as you fly high with this locally owned outfitter. A kiosk outside the Jolly Roger takes reservations.

Ocracoke Wave Runners (252-928-2600; www.ocracokejetski.com), Jolly Roger Marina, 395 NC 12. Half-hour and hour-long rentals let you explore Silver Lake and the waters of Ocracoke Inlet on your own. Tours also available.

Ride the Wind Surf & Kayak (252-928-6311; www.surfocracoke.com), 486 NC 12. Kayak and surf specialists offer kayak tours, including full-moon tours, a history tour to **Teach's Hole**, and a morning yoga/tai chi paddle. Kayaks (including boats equipped for fishing), surfboards, stand-up paddleboards, skimboards, and boogie boards with fins rent by the hour, day, or week. From May to August, students ages 9–17 can attend a three-day Surf Camp to learn both technique and safety procedures. Members of the staff surf every morning of the year and invite island visitors to join them.

✳ Green Space

BEACHES Ocracoke Island's undeveloped beach, more than 16 miles long, is managed by the National Park Service as part of the **Cape Hatteras National Seashore** (www .nps.gov/caha) and is the island's greatest asset. In recent years the beach brought Ocracoke to international prominence. After ranking Ocracoke for four years among his top three, in 2007 Dr. Beach named **Ocracoke's Lifeguarded Beach** the best in the country. The shoreline's wide, uncrowded, and unpolluted sands, plus the warm Gulf Stream waters that allow swimming into the late fall, attracted Dr. Beach's attention. Surfing, shelling, surf fishing, bird-watching, and just plain old loafing are the favorite activities on this beach, where no high-rises block the sun. Parts of the 16.5 miles of beach on Ocracoke Island are open to both off-road vehicles (ORVs in park parlance) and pedestrians. There are six places where you can park and walk over the dunes to the beach, and several beach access ramps for four-wheel-drive vehicles.

Driving on the beach requires an ORV permit from the National Park Service. You can get one at the ORV Permit Office at the Cape Hatteras National Seashore Visitor Center in Ocracoke Village. See the **seashore's website** (www.nps.gov/caha) for current updates on prices, regulations, and maps of ORV routes. The northern end of the island, accessed via Ramp 59, and the southern end, accessed by Ramp 72, also known as **South Point Road**, are popular spots for surf fishing, although they are subject to closures to protect nesting birds and sea turtles.

The boardwalk opposite the pony pens is a popular spot to cross to the beach. Ramp 70, also called the **Airport Road**, is the beach access most used by locals. The parking lot for the award-winning Lifeguarded Beach can be found about a half-mile north of Ramp 70, about 1.5 miles north of the village, on NC 12. This beach also has changing rooms and showers. Look for the brown swimmer sign. Lifeguards are on duty Memorial Day to Labor Day.

Fires are allowed on the beach only with a free permit, available on the park website or at the Ocracoke Visitor Center next to the village ferry dock. From May 1 to November 15, beach fires can only be lit in the Ocracoke Day Use Area. Pets are allowed if kept on a 6-foot leash or in a crate, but they cannot be brought onto the lifeguarded swimming beach.

Current information on beach closures, activities, and regulations can be found on the **Cape Hatteras National Seashore website** (www.nps.gov/caha) or by calling 252-473-2111.

For an even more remote beach adventure, cross the inlet to the unspoiled beaches of **Portsmouth Island, part of the Cape Lookout National Seashore** (www.nps.gov/calo). Primitive beach camping is allowed on the beach just beyond Portsmouth Village for a maximum of 14 days without a permit. Beach fires are allowed on the ocean side of the dunes below the high tide line, but you should plan on bringing your own wood. A compost comfort station is located at the gate into the historic district on the beach side, with flush toilets available at the visitor center near the ferry dock (open April–November). Pets must remain leashed at all times.

Personal watercraft (Jet Skis, etc.) and other boats and kayaks may land at the **Wallace Channel** dock located east of the ferry dock in Portsmouth Village and on the beach to the east of this dock. The water here is very shallow.

MANY OCRACOKE BUILDINGS ARE CONSTRUCTED FROM WOOD AND OTHER ITEMS SALVAGED FROM THE OCEAN

For a do-it-yourself tour to the Portsmouth beaches, **Portsmouth Island Boat Tours** (252-928-4361; www.portsmouthislandboattours.com) runs a shuttle service from the Community Square Docks on the Ocracoke waterfront to the ghost village of Portsmouth. You have time for quick self-guided tour of the town, a swim, and some beachcombing on the unspoiled beach before your pickup four hours later. Bring insect repellent, drinking water, sunscreen, a hat, and good walking shoes. The beach is 1.5 miles from the village. The shuttle may transport pets on request. It can also drop you off and pick you up nearer the beach, depending on current conditions. Be sure to set this up in advance. The shuttle costs $20 round-trip.

✒ **Portsmouth Island ATV Excursions** (252-928-4484; www.portsmouthislandatv .com), Jolly Roger Marina. Wade and Gwen Austin take groups to Portsmouth Island for a four-hour tour of the deserted village and nearby beach April through November. The ATVs can accommodate a family of four.

TRAILS **Hammock Hills Nature Trail** (252-473-2111; www.nps.gov/caha), Cape Hatteras National Seashore, NC 12, 3 miles north of Ocracoke Village, across NC 12 from the National Park Service campground. This 30-minute hike over remnant dunes covered with maritime forest and through salt marsh leads to an overlook on Pamlico Sound. There is ample parking and good birding here.

Springer's Point Nature Preserve (252-449-8289; www.coastallandtrust.org), Loop Road. The North Carolina Coastal Land Trust protects 121 acres of maritime forest overlooking Ocracoke Inlet and Teach's Hole. Once known as **Teach's Plantation**, legend says the infamous Blackbeard, aka Edward Teach, had an island outpost here where he roasted pigs and drank rum with his fellow pirates. The property today is heavily wooded with significant stands of ancient live oaks. A nature trail leads down

EXCURSIONS

Mattamuskeet National Wildlife Refuge, in Swan Quarter, is North Carolina's largest natural lake and the winter home of huge flocks of tundra swans, snow geese, Canada geese, and ducks. A paved road (NC 94) runs on a causeway across the center of the refuge. A 5-mile unpaved wildlife drive leads to park headquarters, next to the historic **Lake Mattamuskeet Pumping Station** (www.mattamuskeet.org). A short nature trail begins in this area. Other refuge amenities include three boat ramps and several observation decks and towers. The lake is very shallow and appropriate only for small boats, including canoes and kayaks. A paddle trail leads along the lake's southern shore. Fishing is permitted March through October. Sign up well in advance for the open-air wildlife tram tours offered during **Swan Days**, the annual open house every December. **Swan Quarter** can be reached via US 264 from Manteo or aboard the Swan Quarter Ferry from Ocracoke Village. **Mattamuskeet National Wildlife Refuge** (252-926-4021; www.fws .gov/mattamuskeet), 38 Mattamuskeet Road off US 264, Swan Quarter. Free.

to the sound where a sand path runs along the beach. Teach's Hole, where Blackbeard met his fate, lies just offshore. Plaques along the trail identify local plants. The preserve is an excellent birding spot, with a rookery containing white ibis, heron, and egret nests. Keep an eye out for ruins from the original pilot's village and the grave of entrepreneur Sam Jones, who is buried next to Ikey D, his favorite horse, marked by a rearing horse statue. Locals claim the grave site, in fact the entire point, is haunted. No parking is available, so walk or bike to the gate off the Loop Road.

Windmill Point (252-928-7375; www.ocracokepreservation.org), 211 Silver Lake Road. A conservation easement protects the area on the far side of Silver Lake from future development. Once the site of a windmill used to grind grain, the area is now heavily wooded. Locals recommend taking Robbie's Way, a sandy path found at the end of Silver Lake Road, out to an uninhabited beach along Pamlico Sound to catch a spectacular sunset. This is also a great spot to dig for clams or to launch a kayak.

✳ Lodging

Like the village itself, Ocracoke inns generally have a little more character than those elsewhere on the Banks. You may find yourself passing a family of cats in the hall or renting a room from a published author. What you won't find is cookie-cutter resorts or chain hostelries.

Lodgings in Ocracoke Village are eclectic, no two the same. Mostly the inns are owned by local families, some of whom have returned to their roots to open hostelries after successful careers off-island.

While more innkeepers are staying open all year, Ocracoke Island is still a very seasonal place, quiet in the winter months but welcoming to visitors. In fact, for many regular guests, this is their favorite time of year, when the traffic dies down and the beach is deserted.

In-season and out, rental fees tend to be a bit less than in other areas of the Banks—another advantage of an island that can't be reached by bridge.

BED & BREAKFASTS (ⁱᵖ) **Cove Bed & Breakfast** (252-928-4192; www .thecovebb.com), 21 Loop Road. Closed January. The Cove's location at the far end of Lighthouse Road guarantees a peaceful experience but is only a short walk from village attractions. Suites designed for romantic getaways, with queen beds, two-person Jacuzzis, and private decks, occupy the top floors of each wing, and a suite with private entrance and screened porch is located on the first floor. Several rooms can accommodate three guests, but all must be at least age 15. Innkeepers John and Kati Wharton serve a full plated breakfast and afternoon wine and "goodie" hours. Bicycles and beach chairs are complimentary. You can launch a kayak from the inn's dock. The inn is smoke-free, but smoking is allowed on balconies. A shuttle will pick guests up from the airport or docks. Off-season $$; in-season $$$.

Crews Inn Bed & Breakfast (252-928-7011; www.ocracokers.com), 503 Back Road. Step into the lives of old-time Ocracokers at this historic 1908 inn, once the home of the O'Neal and Garrish families. It sits in the midst of live oaks at the end of an oyster shell driveway, not far from Silver Lake. Rooms are furnished with iron bedsteads, quilts, and the simple antiques typical of island homes. They do not have TVs or phones, but do have individual air conditioners. Two rooms on the first floor have private baths, while the two on the second share a bath. Up top is the Captain's Quarters, with private deck and claw-foot tub. A continental breakfast is served every morning. The wraparound porch, partially screened and furnished with rockers and swings, is a great place to read *Ocracokers*, a book on local history written by the inn's owner, Alton Ballance. Proceeds from the sale of the book benefit Ocracoke School, where Ballance once taught English and journalism. $–$$.

Oscar's House Bed & Breakfast (252-928-1311; www.oscarsbb.com), 660 NC 12. Closed winters. Built in 1940 by one of the island's last lighthouse keepers, Oscar's has four charming guest rooms with original beadboard walls, private half-baths, and a laid-back, creative vibe nourished by innkeeper Ann Ehringhaus, a photographer, massage therapist, and interfaith minister. Guests share a private outdoor shower under a cedar tree. Ann serves a healthy breakfast daily and can accommodate special diets. A deck with barbecue grill and bicycles are free for guests to use. $$.

☀ (ᵗᵖ) **Pam's Pelican Bed & Breakfast** (252-928-1661; www.pamspelican.com), 1021 NC 12. This inn, located close to the airport, the beach, and Howard's Pub, rents four rooms, each with private bath, mini-fridge, microwave, and cable TV. Rates include a home-cooked breakfast. Guests can relax on the deck on top of the building or in a shady gazebo. Complimentary shuttle to airport or marina. Free bikes, grills, and coolers are available for guest use. $$–$$$.

♿ (ᵗᵖ) **Thurston House Inn** (252-928-6037; www.thurstonhouseinn.com), 685 NC 12. Operated by members of an old island family, this charming historic cottage rents nine rooms, surrounded by several lovely outdoor porches and a courtyard with outdoor shower. The generous Southern-style breakfast, served on the porch when weather allows, features homemade Ocracoke Fig Cake, a local specialty. $$–$$$.

CAMPGROUNDS Because it takes a boat trip to reach the island, it's a good idea to always make advance reservations to camp, especially during the busy summer season.

❄ ♂ ☀ ☂ **Beachcomber Campground** (252-928-4031; www.ocracokecamping.com), 990 NC 12. This big-rig-friendly campground, situated behind Ocracoke Station, a busy gas station and convenience store at the north end of the village, has water and electric sites for 29 RVs, plus a few tent sites, a bathhouse with hot showers, dump station, picnic tables, and grills. Cable TV at some sites. Bike, golf cart, and four-wheel-drive rentals available. Free Sunset Music series during the summer months.

☀ ♿ **Ocracoke NPS Campground** (252-928-5111; reservations: 1-877-444-6777; www.nps.gov/caha), 4352 NC 12. Closed November to April. The National Park Service operates this 136-site campground on the oceanfront about 4 miles from the village ferry docks. Paved sites can be used by either tents or RVs. An unspoiled beach is just over the dunes. Amenities are basic: cold showers, running water, flush toilets, dump station, picnic tables, and grills. Rangers lead evening programs and campfires during the summer months. Maximum stay is 14 days. Reservations and mosquito repellent recommended.

☀ (ᵠ) **Teeter's Campground** (252-588-2030 or 1-800-705-5341; www .teeterscampground.com), 200 British Cemetery Road. Open March through November. Located in the historic district, Teeter's has the island's only full hookups (two sites), plus a dozen more shady sites with water and electric, and 10 for tents. Hot showers, picnic tables, grills, and cable TV are available.

COTTAGE AND CONDO RENTALS

The vast majority of rentals on Ocracoke are cottages handled by local real estate companies. While a few of the newer

ones are large, multiroom constructions, the majority are small, neat houses crouched among gnarled live oaks that protect them from the weather. Some have waterfront locations on canals leading to Pamlico Sound, but none is on the beach. The Atlantic side of the island remains totally undeveloped, under the care of the National Park Service.

☀ ♿ **Blue Heron Vacation Rentals** (252-928-7117 or 1-866-576-7117; www .blueheronvacations.com), 585 NC 12, Spencer's Market. This company, started by an island native, Jennifer Esham, offers friendly, personal service and a variety of houses all over the village, including several historic cottages. You can browse and book online. Bicycle, golf cart, and linen rentals available.

☀ (ᵠ) **Ocracoke Island Realty** (252-928-6261 or 1-877-646-2822; www .ocracokeislandrealty.com), 1075 NC 12. The island's premiere real estate company handles the rental of over 300

A TYPICAL RENTAL COTTAGE IN OCRACOKE VILLAGE SITS AMID TWISTED LIVE OAKS

privately owned properties that run the gamut from small historic cottages to luxurious soundfront properties with private docks and swimming pools. Most rent by the week, but some shorter getaway packages are available, especially off-season. Most properties come without linens, but you can rent them and other vacation essentials from **Beach Outfitters on Ocracoke Island Realty's website**, where you'll also find extensive pictures of all rental properties.

HISTORIC INNS AND RESORTS ❄ ✎ 🐾
♿ (ᵞ) **Blackbeard's Lodge** (252-928-3421 or 1-800-892-5314; www.blackbeards lodge.com), 111 Back Road. The hotel that started Ocracoke's tourism industry in 1936 has been completely refurbished and is now back in the family of the original owner. Stanley "Chip" Stevens, who bought the hotel in 2007, is the great-grandnephew of the man who built the hotel, Robert Stanley Wahab. Today, a statue of Blackbeard the Pirate greets guests as they enter the spacious lobby. Comfortable couches and a wood-burning stove invite both hotel guests and day-trippers to sit and relax awhile. The yellow frame lodge has 38 air-conditioned units with a wide variety of sleeping arrangements, from regular doubles to full-kitchen efficiency apartments that sleep eight, all nonsmoking. The lodge has a heated pool, wide porches furnished with rocking chairs and swings, and a game room with a pool table, foosball, and video and board games. Bicycles and golf carts are available for rent, and a free shuttle takes guests to the harbor or airport. Rates are higher if you stay only one night during the peak season or on weekends. Free Wi-Fi in common areas. Off-season $; in-season $$$.

(ᵞ) **The Castle on Silver Lake and Castle Courtyard Villas** (252-928-3505 or 1-800-471-8848; www.thecastlebb .com), 155 Silver Lake Drive. Once the domain of the legendary Sam Jones, this house, built by local craftsmen in the mid-1900s, soon earned the nickname of "The Castle" thanks to its many-gabled roof and lofty cupola. After many years of neglect, the landmark building has been completely refurbished as a bed & breakfast inn with 11 elegant rooms, all paneled with beautiful wood. Each has a private bath with shower. A hot breakfast buffet is served daily. The common rooms are spectacular, including a den with big-screen TV and custom pool table, a parlor, formal dining room, and a screened porch with swings. High atop the inn, occupying the entire third floor, the Lighthouse Suite is the inn's most requested accommodation. The bed & breakfast does not allow children under eight. Behind the Castle, the ✎ (ᵞ) **Castle Courtyard Villas**, 11 units ranging from studios to three-bedroom suites, are available for larger parties or families with young children. All guests can enjoy the Castle's amenities, which include an outdoor heated pool, pool house with sauna and steam shower, bicycles, and complimentary dockage at the inn's dock. Be sure to climb the outside stairs up to the widow's walk around the inn's cupola for a spectacular view. B&B $$–$$$; villas $$$–$$$$.

Island Inn and Villas at 25 Lighthouse Road, long one of Ocracoke's favorite hostelries, is currently closed and for sale. Built of shipwrecked wood in 1901, the part of the inn fronting on Silver Lake is the island's oldest commercial building, originally built as an Oddfellows Lodge and reputedly haunted.

MOTELS ❄ (ᵞ) **Bluff Shoal Motel** (252-928-4301; www.bluffshoal.com), 306 NC 12. Small, '60s-era motel has seven well-maintained rooms, each with a small refrigerator; a great location in the center of the village action; and a nice waterfront deck out back. Parking is right outside your room. Off-season $; in-season $$.

(ᵞ) **Edwards of Ocracoke** (252-928-4801 or 1-800-254-1359; www .edwardsofocracoke.com), 226 Old Beach Road. Laid-back motel rooms, efficiencies, and private cottages, all with screened porches or covered decks, are located on a quiet street and have plenty of simple island charm. The courtyard is a favorite location for cookouts. The **Duck Cottages**, three larger properties located near the lighthouse, rent by the week. $–$$.

(ᵖ) **Harborside Motel** (252-928-3111; www.ocrakeharborside.com), 244 NC 12. Closes mid-November to Easter. Located just across the street from the waterfront, Harborside has been a popular destination since 1965. Family owned and operated, the motel offers 14 rooms, each with two double beds, refrigerator, television, and private bath, plus four efficiencies. Room rates include continental breakfast, making this a good bargain. A sundeck with seats overlooking the harbor, boat dock, and boat ramp are across the street. Guests share the motel with a colony of cats. AAA and senior discounts are available. Nonsmoking. Off-season (April and November) $; in-season $$.

❄ (ᵖ) **Pony Island Motel & Cottages** (252-928-4411 or 1-866-928-4411; www.ponyislandmotel.com), 785 NC 12. One of the largest inns on the island, Pony Island rents 50 guest rooms and efficiencies, plus four classic island cottages. All rooms are air-conditioned and nonsmoking, and all have TVs and refrigerators. Several suites have Jacuzzi tubs. A swimming pool, picnic area with grills, and a popular family restaurant are on-site. Bike rentals and boat docks available. Off-season $; in-season $$.

❄ (ᵖ) **Sand Dollar Motel** (252-928-5571 or 1-866-928-5571; www.sanddollarmotelofocracoke.com), 70 Sand Dollar Road. Motel built in the 1960s has 11 motel-style rooms paneled in knotty pine renting by the night, plus a suite and several cottages that rent by the week. Guests can enjoy a pool and picnic area with grills. Off-season $; in-season $$.

PET ACCOMMODATIONS 🐾 **Sandy Paws Bed & Biscuit Inn** (252-928-3093),

136 West End Road. Hotels and rental cottages that don't allow pets recommend you board your family friend at Sandy Paws. Doggie day care is also available.

WATERFRONT INNS 🐾 ♿ **Anchorage Inn & Marina** (252-928-1101; www.theanchorageinn.com), 180 NC 12. Located on Ocracoke's harbor, the Anchorage Inn has its own marina, a private pool, a sundeck, a café, plus terrific views of the harbor at sunset. The four-story brick inn contains 35 modern rooms and two suites served by an elevator. Small boats, bikes, golf carts, and scooters are available for rent. Open from March to November, the inn accepts reservations only by phone. $$–$$$$.

♿ (ᵖ) **Captain's Landing** (252-928-1999; www.thecaptainslanding.com), 324 NC 12. Located directly on the Silver Lake waterfront, Captain's Landing lets guests put the traffic literally behind them. Owner Betty Chamberlin, a descendant of some of the island's oldest families, designed this inn on the old Howard property to maximize views of the harbor and the island's renowned sunsets. Eight spacious suites each sleep four and have a full kitchen and one-and-a-half baths, as well as a private deck. A penthouse with all the comforts of home sleeps eight. The **Captain's Cottage**, formerly a 1950s post office building, sits next to the inn, and offers modern amenities, including a big-screen LCD television and gourmet kitchen, in a private setting. All guests enjoy access to a DVD library, bicycles for exploring the island, and complimentary boat dockage with hookups just outside their doors. $$$–$$$$.

♿ (ᵖ) **Ocracoke Harbor Inn and Cottages** (252-928-5731 or 1-888-456-1998; www.ocracokeharborinn.com), 144 Silver Lake Road. Modern lodging on the quiet end of the harborfront offers 16 standard rooms and seven suites on three floors, all with Jacuzzi tubs, plus apartments and cottages for longer stays. Guests can access a picnic area with grills and outdoor showers. Boat docking is complimentary with advance reservation. Bikes and golf carts can be rented. A continental breakfast is included. $$–$$$.

✳ ☀ (())) **Silver Lake Motel & Inn** (252-928-5720; www.theinnonsilverlake.com), 395 NC 12. Located across the street from the Jolly Roger Pub and Marina, this property has two segments: an older two-story motel-style unit and a newer three-story inn with both motel rooms and suites with full kitchens. Many of the inn units have private balconies with hammocks, while the motel units share a balcony furnished with rocking chairs. A continental breakfast is included. Off-season $; in-season $$.

✳ Where to Eat

If you plan on doing a lot of cooking in your vacation rental, consider shopping on your way to the island to pick up your favorite foods and essential items. Groceries are limited on Ocracoke, although improving, and a specialty store now offers many gourmet-cooking items. The one thing you won't need to bring is fish; the **Ocracoke Seafood Company** should be able to meet your needs with its fresh catch.

A major change came to the Ocracoke dining scene in 2007 when liquor by the drink arrived in Hyde County.

DINING OUT & ⊸ **Back Porch Restaurant and Wine Bar** (252-928-6401; www.backporchocracoke.com), 110 Back Road. A favorite with local Ocracokers, the Back Porch has a warm, inviting atmosphere, with low lights and white tablecloths. Twisted trees and a fence of cacti shield the outside of the old building, increasing the intimacy. The menu changes seasonally but always features fresh fish caught locally. Many of the preparations, such as the Vietnamese lime sauce available on the fresh catch,

have an Asian fusion slant. Big appetites will enjoy the seafood platter, a local favorite loaded with broiled fish, sautéed shrimp, scallops, and signature crab beignets. Half portions of some dishes are available for smaller appetites. Cocktails and a casual bar menu are available, along with an extensive wine list. Dinner only, $$–$$$$.

⊘ ☀ & ⊤ **Dajio Restaurant and Patio Bar** (252-928-7119; www.dajiorestaurant.com), 305 NC 12. Located across from the waterfront in the historic house once occupied by the popular Pelican Bar, this new addition to the Ocracoke scene retains the relaxed atmosphere and shady, dog-friendly patio of its predecessor while updating the menu with touches like ceviche, a blue plate special of local fish tempura, and vegan salads, all featuring locally sourced ingredients. The Pelican's "Shrimp Hour," 3–5 PM, and the live music that followed remain in place, making Dajio a favorite party place after a day on the water. This laid-back spot also serves breakfast daily, featuring apple pancakes, shrimp and grits, and crème brûlée French toast. A take-out menu offers flatbread pizzas baked in a wood-fired oven. Breakfast $–$$; lunch and dinner $$–$$$.

⊘ & ⊸ **The Flying Melon** (252-928-2533), 181 Back Road. Calling the menu eclectic doesn't really do it justice, but whatever you order, you will likely come away singing the praises of the Flying Melon. The bright, even funky dining room is the scene of meals that span the globe in culinary influences, from Creole- and Cajun-style dishes to Thai curries to classic French preparations. Ocracoke broth-based chowder and fresh local seafood prepared with creative flair star at dinner, the homemade desserts are to die for, and there are plenty of dishes to keep vegan and vegetarian diners happy. Dinner only, $$–$$$$.

⊘ & ⊤ **Ocracoke Oyster Company** (252-928-0200; www.ocracokeoystercompany.com), 875 NC 12. Like the name says, this new restaurant specializes in oysters, served raw, steamed, fried, or baked, all in an impressive number of creative preparations (oysters sushi, oysters ceviche, barbecue oysters, to name a few). The rest of the menu is equally interesting, with local fish and shrimp, a rib eye seared in a cast-iron skillet, burgers, Mexican dishes, and a selection of sandwiches and po'boys. Don't miss the barbecue smoked over local fig wood. You can watch sports or live music, or enjoy happy hour on the screened porch. $–$$$.

FIG CAKE

If you'd like to re-create some authentic Ocracoke recipes at home, look for *The Island Cookbook*, containing all the favorite recipes of the Methodist Women of Ocracoke Island. Be sure to try Frances O'Neal's Fig Cake, a real island treat. Several local restaurants publish volumes of their best recipes as well, including the Back Porch and the late, lamented Café Atlantic. The Preservation Society museum bookstore is a great place to find local books and music.

EATING OUT ❄ Y (W) **Gaffer's Sport Pub** (252-928-3456; www.gafferssportspubocracoke.com), 1050 NC 12. Enjoy live music and sports on numerous TVs at this fun pub, with a bar-oriented menu featuring a dozen flavors of wings, famous blackened shrimp nachos, wing happy hour, and daily drink specials. And this is the place to go if you want a Bloody Mary with breakfast. Breakfast $; lunch $$; dinner $$–$$$.

✐ ♿ Y **Howard's Pub & Raw Bar** (252-928-4441; www.howardspub.com), 1175 NC 12. Open seasonally. For lots of Outer Banks visitors, a trip to Howard's is an annual pilgrimage. Some of them ride over on the free ferry and never make it any farther than this restaurant and bar, which sits at the northern limit of Ocracoke Village. An on-site store sells the famous Howard's T-shirts, license plates, and other collectibles. Barbecued ribs, chargrilled rib eyes, steamed shrimp, and the Ocracoke oyster shooter (served with hot sauce and a shot of beer or vodka in a souvenir glass) are the specialties, but everyone will find something to like on the extensive menu. After a day of fishing or beachcombing, relax with a cold one from the pub's list of 200 beers on the big screened porch or up on the rooftop deck with a view over the dunes to the ocean. This is entertainment central, with live bands, bar games, and sports on the numerous TVs. Kids' meals come served on a take-home Frisbee. $–$$$.

✐ ♿ ⟴ **Jason's Restaurant** (252-928-3434; www.jasonsocracoke.com), 1110 NC 12. Closed Sunday. Casual low-key spot is a favorite hangout for locals and visitors alike. The big bar here offers several beers on tap, by the glass or pitcher, plus a complete selection of all the most popular bar food, but daily specials reveal gourmet touches. Take a seat on the screened porch and enjoy Ocracoke fish cakes, authentic Mexican tacos, Portuguese seafood stew, and ever-changing specials, along with fresh local vegetables and the regular menu of pastas, vegetarian lasagna, and subs. Tuesday is sushi night. Full bar. $–$$.

✐ ♿ Y **Jolly Roger Pub & Marina** (252-928-3703; www.jollyrogerocracoke.com), 410 NC 12. A casual, open-air spot that sits right on the docks next to the Ocracoke Fish House serves sandwiches and baskets of fried or grilled fish, shrimp, crabcakes, ribs, and wraps, plus burgers and some Mexican offerings. The best bet is the catch of the day. The setting is casual, with outside tables on a deck or under umbrellas and food in plastic baskets with throw-away utensils. The main attraction here is the location, directly on the waterfront. In fair weather, a crowd gathers at cocktail hour to see what the charter fleet brings in. Live music adds to the sunset vibe. A great place to develop that Ocracoma. $$.

⚓ 🍸 **Ocracoke Bar & Grille** (252-928-6227; www.ocracokebarandgrille.com), 621 NC 12. Eat on the screened porch or on the patio at this casual, surf-themed spot featuring fresh local seafood and a Baja Mexican menu. Guacamole is made fresh for every order. Fish and shrimp tacos and enchiladas are favorites, along with seafood specials such as bacon-wrapped scallops. Clams here are local and a specialty. Everything is available to-go, including a menu for your canine friend, with a late-night menu until 1 AM. Live music on the patio in-season. $–$$.

⚓ ♿ 🍸 🐾 **SMacNally's Raw Bar and Grill** (252-928-9999; www.smacnallys.com), 180 NC 12, Anchorage Inn Marina. Located on the docks at the Anchorage Inn Marina, this is a great place to kick back with a cold one while you check out the catch of the charter fishing boats. SMacNally's keeps its beer on ice and claims it's the coldest in town. Local seafood comes grilled or fried, but this place is best known for its juicy half-pound Angus burgers dressed in a variety of toppings. Live music all summer features local songsmiths. $–$$.

BAG LUNCHES AND TAKEOUT Many, if not most, of the restaurants in town offer takeout or have self-serve windows. This reflects the big need for bag lunches and picnics experienced by both locals and visitors. People stock up on provisions before heading to the beach, boarding a charter fishing boat, or taking the shuttle to Portsmouth Island. Getting a bag lunch to take on the state-run ferries is also a good idea, as they offer very limited food options—vending machines and coffee. If you have a ferry to catch or other time constraint, call ahead to order.

⚓ 🐾 **Back Porch Lunch Box** (252-928-3651; www.backporchocracoke.com), 747 NC 12. Pick up a gourmet bag lunch for the ferry at this to-go window, located next to the Pony Island Motel but operated by the Back Porch Restaurant's kitchen. Unique sandwiches, drinks,

ice cream, smoothies, and home-baked cookies are available. $.

⚓ **Graceful Bakery** (www.facebook.com/gracefulbakery), 110 Back Road. Enjoy a morning bite at a café table under the trees at this food stand, set at the corner of the Back Road and Old Beach Road, offering freshly baked artisanal breads, sweet and savory pastries, cookies, breakfast biscuits, fresh squeezed orange juice, and more. $.

❄ **Eduardo's Taco Stand** (252-928-0234; www.facebook.com/amadowoch), 950 NC 12. Eduardo Chavez Perez, a Back Porch chef alumnus, serves authentic gourmet Mexican cuisine, made with love, at this food truck in the Variety Store parking lot. Don't miss the wonderful breakfast menu. $–$$.

⚓ **Fig Tree Bakery and Deli and the Sweet Tooth** (252-928-3481), 1015 NC 12. The Fig Tree/Sweet Tooth combo has what it takes to assemble a great picnic or bag lunch for ferry or beach. Try a deli sub or the pimento cheese sandwich, a Southern favorite. Breakfast sandwiches and sweet potato biscuits are also available, along with delish cinnamon rolls, homemade fudge, and chocolates. Shady outdoor seating. $.

❄ 📶 🍸 **Ocracoke Station Deli** (252-928-4031; www.ocracokecamping.com), 990 NC 12. Locals drop by this gas station and deli in front of the Beachcomber Campground for breakfast biscuits and the latest news. Candyland section features a self-serve ice cream bar and lots of sweets. A popular spot to pick up a box lunch of fried chicken, sub sandwiches named for the fishing fleet, or local fried fish for the ferry, this is also the island's only gas station. There's an evening Beachcomber Cantina as well, serving beer and wine during the nighttime entertainment. Free Wi-Fi and charging station. $.

Thai Moon Carry-Out and Sushi (252-928-5100; www.facebook.com/ThaiMoonOcracoke), Spencer's Market, 589 NC 12. Take-out-only spot that earned a write-up in *Gourmet* magazine

Ocracoke Station, near the north end of Ocracoke Village, is the only spot on the island to fill up with gas.

serves traditional Thai dishes such as tom yum soup, curries, and pad thai, plus Asian takes on local seafood, sushi, and vegetarian choices. Cash only. $–$$.

T J Outfitters (256-541-7891), 285 NC 12. Food truck across from Community Square offers the unique Walkin' Taco, based on a bag of Fritos, plus dogs and sausages with a big selection of toppings. Browse flea market–style for beachwear, pirate gear, and bamboo stuff. You can rent bikes, golf carts, and watercraft here as well.

BREAKFAST ✳ ❧ **Pony Island Restaurant** (252-928-5701; www.ponyisland motel.com), 51 Ocean View Road. Big breakfasts at reasonable prices keep Ocracoke's oldest eatery a favorite with families. Try the famous Pony Potatoes, topped with cheese, sour cream, and salsa, and the awesome biscuits. Open for breakfast every day all year. Breakfast $.

COFFEE ☕ ▼ **Magic Bean Coffee Bazaar** (252-928-0253 or 252-588-2440; www .magicbeanocracoke.com), 35 School Road. Organic fair-trade coffees in eco-friendly cups spark discussions in this laid-back community gathering spot that hosts painting parties, open mics, and reggae vibes.

🦆 ((•)) **Ocracoke Coffee Co. & Island Smoothie** (252-928-7473; www .ocracokecoffee.com), 226 Back Road. With a wide porch, a shady yard, coffee drinks created with specially selected roasted beans, fruit smoothies, fresh baked goods, and free Wi-Fi, this coffee shop is a community gathering spot for island residents as well as visitors. $.

ICE CREAM **Corkey's Store** (252-921-0058; www.facebook.com/corkeysstore

ocracoke), 58 Creek Road. Corkey Mason and her brother Shane reopened their granddad's general store in hopes of helping new generations of kids make memories. They serve old-fashioned treats like cinnamon roll sundaes and hot dogs; homemade pies like chocolate peanut butter, Key lime, and cherry cheesecake; plus an assortment of grab-and-go items. Take them away or enjoy at a picnic table in the yard.

((•)) **The Slushy Stand** (252-928-1878; www.theslushystand.com), 473 NC 12. Located at the three-way junction where NC 12 meets the water, this landmark serves ice cream, sundaes, floats, smoothies, breakfast pastries, coffee, and—of course—slushies. You can read the paper or check your email on the porch. The stand rents bikes as well.

MARKETS **ABC Store** (252-928-3281; www.ncabc.com), 950 NC 12, Variety Store Shops. The state-run liquor store here has some unusual hours, especially off-season. Check for the latest.

Farm 2 Fork Farmers Market (252-207-4027), lot of the Native Seafood Company, 800 NC 12. Weekly produce market featuring fresh veggies from North Carolina farms sponsored by the Coastal Farmers Co-op.

((•)) **Zillie's Island Pantry** (252-928-9036; www.zillies.com), 538 Back Road. A godsend to gourmet cooks on the island, Zillie's stocks items from around the world, including pâtés, smoked salmon, cheeses, and much, much more, as well as lots of local products. The shop also has a huge selection of wine and the island's best stock of imported beers and microbrews. Enjoy a beer or glass of wine on the Wine and Wi-Fi Deck or make reservations for the frequent beer and wine tastings.

SEAFOOD ✳ ♂ ➻ **Ocracoke Seafood Company** (252-928-5601; www.ocracoke seafood.com), 416 NC 12. To see what's biting in local waters, visit this historic fish market on the waterfront where local fishing trawlers land their catch. Some seafood is available for retail sale; some makes its way to local restaurants. The friendly staff here will help you identify what you see. You may want to check out some of the more unusual local fish, such as sheepshead or spadefish, said to taste much like grouper and red snapper, respectively. Shrimp, clams, oysters, and blue crab are plentiful in these waters.

Native Seafood (252-928-2722), 800 NC 12. Fresh seafood right off the family boats. Shrimp is a specialty.

✳ Entertainment

For a small island, Ocracoke makes a lot of music. The island traditions of impromptu back-porch jam sessions, potluck dinners, and community square dances have morphed into something the locals call Ocrafolk, a unique form of American music melded from old and new musical styles.

The original members of **Molasses Creek** (www.molassescreek.com), Gary and Kitty Mitchell and Fiddler Dave, began the movement. The trio played a fusion of folk, bluegrass, and humorous ballads, writing songs inspired by their location on Pamlico Sound. They started out performing weekly at the **Deepwater Theater** and inviting local talents, such as native legend Martin Garrish, leader of the **Ocracoke Rockers**, and Roy Parsons, a local boy who toured with the **Barnum & Bailey Circus band** way back when, to sit in. Band membership has changed and grown in the years since the band formed. Along the way Molasses Creek won an award on Garrison Keillor's *Prairie Home Companion*, and in recent years has toured extensively off-island.

In 1996 Gary Mitchell recorded a compilation album of songs by local musicians, called *Ocrafolk*. Its popularity led to recurring performances by the **Ocrafolk Opry** and to the ever-growing **Ocrafolk Festival of Music and**

Storytelling (www.ocracokealive.org), held every year in June.

During the summer you'll have several choices for live music most nights of the week. In addition to the Deepwater Theater shows, you can regularly find music at **Howard's Pub**, the **Jolly Roger**, **Ocracoke Bar & Grill**, **SMacNally's**, **Ocracoke Oyster Bar**, **Gaffer's**, **Beachcomber Campground**, and **Dajio**.

Coyote Music Den (252-928-6874 or 252-256-2081; www.coyotemusic.net), 288 NC 12, Community Square. Duo Marcy Brenner and Lou Castro, known as Coyote, along with their talented friends such as Martin Garrish, perform several nights a week in this historic spot next to Silver Lake.

Deepwater Theater and Music Hall (252-921-0260; www.ocracokealive.org), 36 School Road. From June to September, you can catch some of the brightest stars of the local music scene at the Deepwater Theater, a venue that has changed considerably (and acquired air-conditioning) since its original incarnation as an overgrown screened porch. While schedules vary every year, performers often include *Prairie Home Companion* award-winners **Molasses Creek** (www.molassescreek.com), **Captain Rob Temple** telling sea tales and singing sailor shanties, and the ever-evolving **Ocrafolk Opry**. The musical *A Tale of Blackbeard* (www.ataleofblackbeard.com) returns to the lineup periodically.

✳ Selective Shopping

Most shops on Ocracoke Island are small and eclectic, mixing practical items with souvenirs for visiting tourists. The "necessities" can be found in general-store-type shops, which carry a large variety of different and useful groceries and goods, but perhaps not the selection of brands that people are used to at home. Locals make regular runs "up the beach" across the Hatteras Ferry to get items unavailable on Ocracoke,

Lots of local music is made—and recorded—on Ocracoke. Here are some CDs to look for. *CoastalFolk* and the *Ocrafolk Sampler* compilations, for great tunes and fascinating stories.

Molasses Creek's *Ocracoke Island*, 2008 (remastered). New version of the original 1993 recording by the group that is the guiding force behind the folk music revival on Ocracoke, with a dozen CDs to date.

Roy Parsons, *Songs and Tales from Ocracoke Island*, 1999. An Ocracoke original, much missed by the community.

Coyote recordings, including their latest release, *My Live Oak*.

Captain Rob Temple's recording, *The Rumgagger*, 2006. Features sea stories, pirate poetry, and nautical tunes from the captain of the schooner *Windfall II*.

returning as quickly as possible with full trunks and sighs of relief.

ANTIQUES **Annabelle's Florist and Antiques** (252-928-4541), 324 Back Road. Local floral designer and folklorist Chester Lynn sells treasures and artifacts related to Ocracoke's past, as well as seedlings of the island's some dozen varieties of figs.

Ocracoke Restoration (252-928-2669 or 252-291-0060; www.ocracokerestoration.com), 341 NC 12. Fascinating shop in an old cottage stocks a huge selection of English antique stained glass, vintage jewelry, wrought-iron yard art, and locally made spa products.

ARTS AND CRAFTS The funky personality, natural beauty, and relative isolation of the island have led many creative folk to settle here. Information on Ocracoke's galleries and artists, plus gallery openings, the annual Art Walk, and other events, can be found at www.ocracokecurrent.com.

Bella Fiore Pottery (252-928-2826), 80 Back Road. The vivid hues of Sarah Fiore's microwave- and oven-safe stoneware pottery reflect the beauty of the island environment. Watercolors, silk mobiles, handblown glass, and other locally created artwork also on display.

Deepwater Pottery (252-928-3936), 34 School Road. Dedicated to artful living, Deepwater is a focus of Ocracoke culture. The pottery shares the historic 1898 **Dezzie Bragg** house with **Books to Be Red**, and the **Deepwater Theater** is next door.

Down Creek Gallery (252-928-4400), 260 NC 12. This waterfront gallery, winner of a 2009 award from *Niche* magazine as one of the "Top 25 Retailers for American Craft in North America," represents over 125 local and regional artists and craftspeople. Art openings during the summer season showcase local artists.

Downpoint Decoys (252-928-3269), 340 NC 12. David O'Neal, a noted carver and collector of decoys, carries on the historic traditions of his forefathers. The shop is full of decoys, old fishing lures, scrimshaw, and other nautical memorabilia.

Island Artworks (252-928-3892; www.islandartworks.com), 89 British Cemetery Road. Artist Kathleen O'Neal's original jewelry, made of precious metals, gemstones, and beachcombed treasures, forms the heart of a collection of works by local and regional artists.

Knife and Pen Shop (252-928-7180; www.knifeandpenshop.com), 290 Sunset Drive. Artist and owner John Moss handcrafts unique wooden pens and duck calls on-site, and carries handcrafted knives and other treasures from around the world at this small shop.

Over the Moon (252-928-3555; www.overthemoongiftshop.com), 64 British

Cemetery Road. Handmade arts and crafts of every kind, selected by Cathy Scarborough, a sixth-generation islander, crowd this old island house.

Secret Garden Gallery (252-928-2598; www.facebook.com/SecretGardenGallery), 72 Back Road. Jewelry designer Barbara Hardy and her husband, Ray, a painter and collage artist, exhibit their own art, plus works by many other artists, including 20 jewelry designers. An upstairs gallery hosts rotating exhibits.

Sunflower Center for the Arts (252-921-0188), 170 Back Road. Carol and Jim O'Brien present their original hand-crafted jewelry as well as a large collection of estate pieces. The upstairs gallery is devoted to art and glass by local artists. Classes in arts and crafts are also offered, and there's an herbal pharmacy on-site.

Tree Top Studio (252-928-9997), 402 Back Road. Featuring paintings and photography by local artists, this little studio also does professional framing.

Village Craftsmen (252-928-5541; www.villagecraftsmen.com), 170 Howard Street. Gallery in an old island cottage stocks a wide variety of crafts by over 300 American crafters, including many from the Outer Banks. The staff here

OCRACOKERS CAN CREATE ART FROM JUST ABOUT ANYTHING

are old-time islanders and can tell great stories.

Woccocon Nursery and Gifts (252-928-3811), 439 Lighthouse Road. Della Williams preserves many old Ocracoke crafts and sells the results at this shop next to the Assembly of God church. Fruit butters, fig jams and preserves, peach rum jam, plus needlepoint, beaded jewelry, and hand-loomed bags, are a few of the treasures found here.

BOOKS AND MUSIC **Books to Be Red** (252-928-3936; www.bookstobered.com), 34 School Road. Sharing a historic building with **Deepwater Pottery**, this small bookstore has an excellent selection of local and regional book titles and music CDs. Redheaded owner Leslie Ann Lanier stocks her shelves with titles ranging from light beach reading to historical research, with a special section of books and puzzles for children. If you prefer to write your own story, you'll find a nice selection of journals here as well.

Ocracoke Preservation Society Museum Gift Shop (252-928-7375; www.ocracokepreservation.org), 49 Water Plant Road. The museum's gift shop stocks a range of books relating to Ocracoke for all ages, plus cookbooks published by local churches and restaurants, DVDs of local storytellers, and music CDs by local musicians. Sales benefit the society.

THE MUSEUM OF THE OCRACOKE PRESERVATION SOCIETY SITS AMID A GARDEN OF ROSES

BOOKS BY (AND ABOUT) OCRACOKERS

The people who live on Ocracoke year-round are a creative bunch and find plenty of time to write during the long off-season. Some books to look for:

Digging Up Uncle Evans: History, Ghost Tales & Stories from Ocracoke Island (www .blacksquall books.com), as told by Philip Howard.

Hoi Toide on the Outer Banks: The Story of the Ocracoke Brogue, by Walt Wolfram and Natalie Schilling-Estes, the definitive 1997 work published by Chapel Hill's University of North Carolina Press.

The Lady and the Moon, a novel written by Mary Chandler Newell, once co-owner of the Island Inn.

Ocracoke Odyssey: A Naturalist's Reflections on Her Home by the Sea, by Pat Garber.

Ocracokers, written by Alton Ballance, historian and owner of the Crews Inn, considered the definitive book about the islanders and their culture.

The Sheltering Cedar, a children's book written by Anne Marshall Runyon, about a Christmas Eve storm that threatens the wildlife on Ocracoke. For ages four to eight.

FASHION **Harborside Gift Shop and Art Gallery** (252-928-3111; www .ocracokeharborside.com), 229 NC 12. Shop at the Harborside Motel carries top-label resort wear, batik dresses, popular Sea Dog T-shirts, and the original island art of Douglas Hoover.

Island Vibe Cafe (252-588-0244; www.islandvibecafe.com), 213 British Cemetery Road. Not so much a café as a cool spot, this cottage carries colorful clothes and accessories made by artisans in Nepal and Thailand, as well as jewelry made on Ocracoke. The homemade Greek yogurt and selection of granolas make this a healthy stop as well.

Mermaid's Folly (252-928-7347; www .mermaidsfolly.com), 259 NC 12. The former owners of the **Island Ragpicker** present a selection of their best-selling "sea-spirited" clothing.

SHOPPING DESTINATIONS **Back Road Loop.** Over a dozen interesting shops and galleries line these shady lanes, and traffic is generally light, making it ideal for a stroll or a bike ride. Here you'll find a gourmet restaurant, a neat coffeehouse and bookstore, and the Ocracoke Library, with Internet access and a porch full of rocking chairs.

Captain's Landing Shops, NC 12 and Silver Lake. Clustered around **Captain's Landing Hotel** are several shops, most in historic buildings that once housed the post office, which has since moved to the north end of town.

Community Square Shops and Dock, NC 12 and Silver Lake. Centered around the beloved **Community Store**, the shops and dock at this location have been the center of Ocracoke life since the days when mail boats, once the island's only contact with the outside world, tied up here. Today, the complex houses the **Working Watermen's Exhibit** and the **Ocracoke Civic and Business Association Visitor Center**, as well as several shops and the **Coyote Den**, a music venue. The *Wilma Lee* docks here, as do several other boat tours.

❋ **Ocracoke Variety Store and True Value Hardware** (252-928-4911; www .ocracokevarietystore.com), 950 NC 12. A one-stop store where you'll find groceries, fresh meats, beer, wine, and ice, plus souvenirs and beach, boating, and camping gear. The **ABC store** is located here, as well as a **gourmet Mexican food truck**. Check the bulletin board for local events.

The Shops at Spencer's Market, NC 12 and School Road. This complex, set a bit back from the harbor, contains an international selection of shops.

SPECIAL SHOPS **Albert Styron Store** (252-921-0100; www.facebook.com/ AlbertStyronsStore), 300 Lighthouse Road. This 1920 landmark on the National Register of Historic Places lives on, thanks to its initials, offering T-shirts with the popular ASS and Fat Boys Fish Company logos, plus a wide variety of wine, gourmet food items, gifts, and ice cream. The leather-bound ledgers dating to 1925, antique cash register, and original adding machine, feed scales, and roll-top desk raise Styron's to near-museum status.

Captain's Cargo (252-928-9991; www.thecaptainslanding.com), 326 NC 12. Former post office on the Captain's Landing property displays an eclectic collection of nautical gifts, shells, bath products, and island arts and crafts tucked into the old postal boxes.

Island Ragpicker (252-928-7571; www.facebook.com/IslandRagpicker), 515 NC 12. Seemingly assembled from driftwood, the 10 rooms of this shop near The Slushy Stand contain original hand-loomed Ragpicker rugs, created here since 1973, plus crafts, apparel, wind chimes, and the Title Wave Room, filled with cards and books of local interest.

Ocracoke Island Woodworks (252-928-7001; www.ocracokeisland woodworks.com), 158 Ocean View Road. Comfortable Adirondack chairs, swings, and other outdoor furniture are hand-crafted by local Ocracokers from white cedar, the same wood used to build boats. It doesn't splinter and looks better the longer is sits out in the weather.

Pirates Chest Gift Shop (252-928-4992), 11 Back Road at NC 12. Fun shop has a huge selection of shells and driftwood, plus an upstairs full of discounted T-shirts.

Teach's Hole Pirate Specialty Shop (252-928-1718; www.teachshole .com), 935 NC 12 at West End Road. All things pirate are on sale at this shop, stocking over 1,000 items of "piratical piratephernalia."

Village Thrift Store (252-928-2855), 271 NC 12, across from Community Square. Proceeds from the sale of used items at this shop benefit the **Ocracoke Youth Center** and its **Ocracoke Community Park** (www.ocracokecommunitypark .org).

✳ Special Events

April: **Portsmouth Village Homecoming** (www.friendsofportsmouthisland .org), Portsmouth Village, Cape Lookout National Seashore. Held on even-numbered years, this old-fashioned homecoming brings together descendants of Portsmouth residents and visitors for music, fellowship, and a picnic dinner. Open to all.

Clam Chowder Cookoff (www .visitocracokenc.com). Local chefs compete to create the best Ocracoke-style chowder to benefit **Ocracoke Child Care** (www.ocracokechildcare.org).

Blackbeard Half-Marathon (www .visitocracokenc.com). A 5K/10K and family fun run, held the day before the half-marathon, award medals to all participants.

May: **Ocracoke Invitational Surf Fishing Tournament** (www.ncbba.org), Ocracoke Community Center. Some 400 anglers hit the beach for this competition, which concludes with a big community dinner open to all.

British Cemetery Military Honors Ceremony (www.ocracokecommunity center.com). Graveside ceremony at the British Cemetery is followed by a reception at the Ocracoke Community Center.

Ocracoke Volunteer Firemen's Ball (www.ocracokevfd.org). A pig pickin' is followed by live and silent auctions and a dance at the Ocracoke Community Center.

June: **Ocrafolk Music and Storytelling Festival** (252-921-0260; www .ocracokealive.org), Deepwater Theater and other venues. A free weekend of acoustic music, storytelling, art exhibits, a live auction, potluck dinner, and community square dance.

Women's Arm Wrestling Tournament (wovv.org). Fundraiser for local radio station features ladies with big biceps and bigger egos in pro-wrestling garb.

July: **Ocracoke Island Independence Day Celebration** (www.visitocracokenc.com). A sand sculpture contest, patriotic parade, classic car contest, community square dance, beach bonfires, and fireworks mark the Fourth of July.

August: **Ocracoke Fig Festival** (www.visitocracokenc.com). Celebrating all things fig with two days of fig tastings, a fig cake bake-off, community square dance, and old-fashioned crafts and games, concluding with a dance party.

October: **Annual Halloween Carnival and Spook Walk,** Ocracoke School.

Blackbeard's Pirate Jamboree (www.visitocracokenc.com). Ocracoke festival features a pirate encampment on the grounds of the **Wahab House** and the reenactment of the **Battle at Ocracoke,** where Blackbeard lost his head, on Silver Lake.

November: **Festival Latino de Ocracoke** (www.ocracokealive.org). Traditional Mexican and Latin American games, folkloric dancing, and foods at the Ocracoke School, followed by Latin dancing at the Community Center.

December: **Island Caroling** (252-928-5541; www.villagecraftsmen.blogspot.com). Meet at the United Methodist Church.

Ocracoke Seafood Company Oyster Roast and Shrimp Steam (252-928-5601; www.ocracokewatermen.org), Ocracoke Fish House.

Wassail and Tree Lighting (252-928-7375; www.ocracokepreservation.org), Ocracoke Preservation Museum.

THE CRYSTAL COAST AND SOUTH BANKS

■

DOWN EAST

CAPE LOOKOUT AND THE
CORE BANKS

BEAUFORT

MOREHEAD CITY AND NEWPORT

THE BOGUE BANKS:
Atlantic Beach, Pine Knoll Shores,
Indian Beach, Salter Path,
and Emerald Isle

SWANSBORO, CEDAR POINT, AND
CAPE CARTERET

INTRODUCTION
The Crystal Coast and South Banks

The Crystal Coast, sometimes known as the **Southern Outer Banks**, is a place of contrasts. Recorded history here stretches back over 300 years and has always had a close relationship with the sea. **Beaufort**, North Carolina's third-oldest town, was an early seaport of vital importance to the state during the **Age of Sail**. Pirates and privateers made cameo appearances throughout the region's history, including the infamous **Blackbeard**, who wrecked his flagship, *Queen Anne's Revenge*, on the shoals off **Bogue Banks**. Commercial fishing and boatbuilding have been the backbone of the economy here for centuries.

In 1858, the railroad arrived when former North Carolina governor John Motley Morehead extended the rails to the deepwater port he built across the inlet from Beaufort. The community that grew up around the port took its name from the visionary governor, becoming **Morehead City**. The area's first beach resort, **Atlantic Beach**, was established on Bogue Banks across from Morehead City to serve travelers arriving by rail.

Atlantic Beach and **Emerald Isle**, communities at either end of Bogue Banks, evolved into popular vacation destinations for families and servicemen from the Marine Corps at nearby Camp Lejeune and Cherry Point air station. Today, Bogue Banks is home to a string of increasingly upscale resort communities catering to vacationers attracted by the area's largely undiscovered white-sand beaches and family-friendly activities.

However, the **South Banks** have another face. The area north of Beaufort, called **Down East** by locals, has been among the last along the coast to be caught up in development. Here families still carve decoys, build boats, and sew quilts as their ancestors have done for generations. Just offshore lie the islands of **Core** and **Shackleford Banks**, areas once home to thriving communities that were swept away by storms in the 1890s. Today, National Park Service caretakers and herds of wild ponies are the only year-round inhabitants of these lonely isles.

GUIDANCE The **Visitor Center for Carteret County and the Crystal Coast** (252-726-8148; www.crystalcoastnc.org), 3409 Arendell Street, Morehead City. The **Emerald Isle branch of the visitor center** (252-393-2008) is located at 8401 Emerald Isle Drive.

GETTING THERE *By air:* The largest commercial airport near the Crystal Coast is **Wilmington International Airport/ILM** (910-341-4125; www.flyilm.com), Wilmington, about 85 miles from Beaufort, with major service from both national and international destinations.

Smaller regional carriers schedule flights to:

Albert J. Ellis Airport/OAJ (910-324-1100; www.flyoaj.com), Richlands. This airport, operated by Onslow County, is about 60 miles from Beaufort.

Craven Regional Airport/EWN (252-638-8591; www.newbernairport.com), New Bern. About 45 miles from Beaufort.

By car: **From the west,** US 70E, a good four-lane road, is the most direct route from Raleigh and points west to the Crystal Coast, crossing both I-40 and I-95 along the way. Drive time from Raleigh to Beaufort is about three hours.

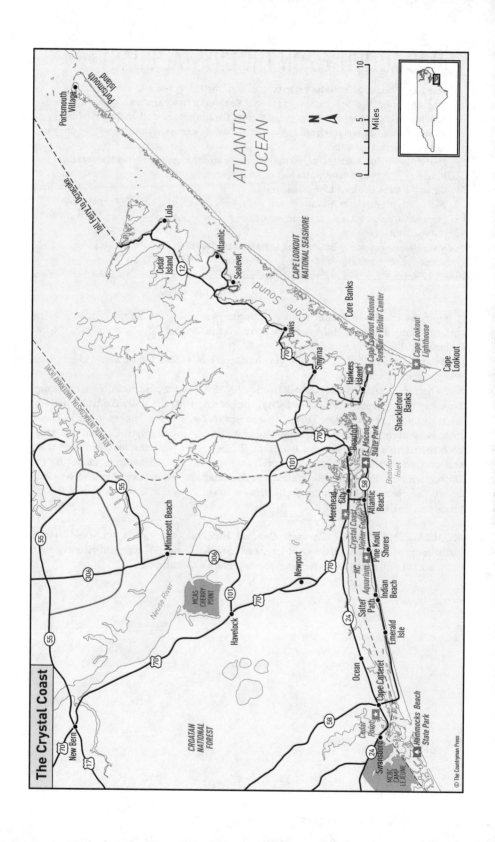

The Crystal Coast

TOP 10 ACTIVITIES ON THE CRYSTAL COAST

1. Take a boat ride to **Shackleford Banks** to pick up shells and see wild horses.
2. Plan a progressive dinner that visits some of **Beaufort's fine eateries**.
3. Paddle—or take a boat taxi—over to the **Rachel Carson nature trail on Carrot Island**.
4. Stroll the **downtown waterfront in Morehead City**, checking out the artwork, the seafood restaurants, and the otters.
5. Take a day trip to Jacksonville, North Carolina, to visit the moving **Beirut Memorial**.
6. Hunt down a **Bogue Sound watermelon**, chill, and enjoy.
7. Climb the **Cape Lookout Lighthouse**.
8. Visit the iconic **Circle at Atlantic Beach** and take in a concert at historic **Fort Macon**.
9. Look for endangered red-cockaded woodpeckers among the longleaf pines at **Patsy Pond Nature Trail**.
10. Make the journey out to **Bear Island in Hammocks Beach State Park** to see a truly unspoiled dune system—and swim on an uninhabited beach.

From the south, US 17 runs from Wilmington north to the Virginia border, passing through many old Inner Banks towns. To reach the Crystal Coast, turn east on NC 24 in Jacksonville.

From the north, NC 12 arrives via the Ocracoke–Cedar Island ferry, then heads south to meet US 70.

By train and bus: In 2012, **Amtrak** (1-800-USA-RAIL; www.amtrak.com) began a new **Thruway bus service to Morehead City**, connecting with the **daily Amtrak Palmetto train** running between New York City and Savannah. The bus makes stops in Havelock, New Bern, and Greenville before arriving in Wilson, North Carolina, to meet both the north and southbound Palmetto. Buses depart from the restored 1905 **train station** (252-808-0440) at 1001 Arendell Street, used as a community center by the **Downtown Morehead City Revitalization Association** (www.downtownmoreheadcity .com). The return of passenger train service to the area is one of the organization's long-term goals.

MEDICAL EMERGENCY **Carteret General Hospital** (252-499-6000; www.carteret health.org), 3500 Arendell Street, Morehead City. A full-service hospital offering inpatient, outpatient, and emergency services 24 hours a day all year.

DOWN EAST

A Downeaster is best defined as one who prefers salt fish (notably spots) for breakfast. But mostly it is a state of mind, where the people like wooden boats and build them in back yards beneath big live oak trees...
—FROM *WHEN THE WATER SMOKES* BY BOB SIMPSON

As you leave the Cedar Island Ferry from Ocracoke, you enter a region of marshes and forests dotted with small communities where generations of Down East families continue their traditions of boatbuilding, decoy carving, hunting, fishing, and farming. The people here retain an exceptional sense of place and are actively involved in preserving their way of life.

The **Down East** region includes more than a dozen small unincorporated towns, spread on the shores and streams that lace this area. Most are dedicated to fishing and during much of their history could be reached only by boat. Some, such as Portsmouth on North Core and Diamond City on Shackleford, no longer exist, swept away by storms or passed over by history.

Harkers Island is the largest community Down East, and there is no better place to discover the region's maritime traditions than the **Core Sound Waterfowl Museum and Heritage Center** located here. Next door, the recently expanded **Cape Lookout National Seashore Visitor Center** offers exhibits on the ecology, history, and culture of the region. **Island Road**, the main drag on Harkers, is lined with marinas offering trips to uninhabited islands that draw tourists, beachcombers, and surf fishers year-round.

GUIDANCE To become acquainted with the history and lore of these fascinating small villages just north of Beaufort, take the **virtual Down East Tour** (www.downeasttour .com), developed by members of the Core Sound Waterfowl and Heritage Museum. Another online tour of the Core Sound region is maintained by the **North Carolina Folklife Institute** at www.ncfolk.org.

POST OFFICES Many of the little towns Down East have a U.S. Post Office and a unique zip code:
  Atlantic (252-225-5081), 755 Seashore Drive. Zip code: 28511.
  Cedar Island (252-225-2131), 3553 Cedar Island Road. Zip code: 28520.
  Harkers Island (252-728-2924), 823 Island Road. Zip code: 28531.
  Sea Level (252-225-4791), 751 US 70. Zip code: 28577.
  Smyrna (252-729-4951), 467 US 70. Zip code: 28579.

PUBLIC RESTROOMS Public facilities are available at the **ferry docks on Cedar Island** and at the **National Seashore Welcome Center on Harkers Island**.

PUBLIC LIBRARY **Down East Public Library** (252-728-1333; carteret.cpclib.org), 702 US 70, Otway. Computers available for public use, plus many classes and a used-book sale on Fridays and Saturdays.

GETTING THERE *By car:* **From the south,** the Down East communities are reached by following US 70 from Beaufort. NC 12, leading out to the ferry docks, branches off from US 70, passing through many miles of marsh and forest before reaching the dock, with no services along the way—not a fun trip in the dark. At the end of the road, on Cedar Island, there's a convenience store, campground, and boat ramp, plus many miles of unspoiled beach. The Driftwood Motel and Restaurant, long a landmark next to the ferry docks, has closed, to be replaced by the new Cedar Island Resort.

By ferry: The **North Carolina State Ferry** (1-800-BYFERRY; www.ncferry.org) makes between three and six trips a day between Ocracoke and Cedar Island, depending on the season. Scenic Byway NC 12 crosses over with the ferry. The trip takes about two and a half hours. One-way fares at the time of publication are $1 for pedestrians; $3 for a bicycle and rider; $10 for motorcycles, scooters, golf carts, and ATVs; and $15 for passenger cars, with higher fees for longer vehicles and trailers. Reservations are strongly recommended but not required. You can reserve online at the state ferry website or by calling 1-800-293-3779.

The ferries are sometimes canceled due to rough weather or other emergencies. If you need to check on whether the ferry is running, call the **Cedar Island terminal** at 252-225-7411 or the Ocracoke terminal at 252-928-1665.

GETTING AROUND US 70, one of the major east–west highways in the nation before the interstate system was built, begins in Arizona and runs 2,385 miles before ending in the little Down East community of Atlantic.

MEDICAL EMERGENCY **Eastern Carteret Medical Center** (252-225-1134), US 70, Sea Level. Down East clinic associated with Carteret General.

✳ To See

Several of the area's top attractions are concentrated along the Island Road, the main drag of Harkers Island.

✳ ⚅ **Cape Lookout National Seashore Harkers Island Visitor Center** (252-728-2250; www.nps.gov/calo), 1800 Island Road, Harkers Island. Open daily 9–5, except Christmas and New Year's days. Located at the very tip of Harkers Island, this visitor center provides an introduction to the Cape Lookout islands. An award-winning documentary, *Ribbon of Sand*, is shown daily. Nearby on the waterfront, ferries, licenced by the NPS, will take you across to South Core Banks, where you can climb the lighthouse from mid-May to late September. Admission to the visitor center is free; the ferry across the inlet costs $16 and up for adults, depending on the season; tickets to climb the lighthouse cost $4–8. For more things to do in the national seashore, see our section on "Cape Lookout and the Core Banks."

✐ **Core Sound Decoy Carvers Guild Hall** (252-838-8818; www.decoyguild.com), 1574 Harkers Island Road, Harkers Island. Local carvers and waterfowling enthusiasts gather at the historic H. Curt Salter Building, located at the foot of the Harkers Island bridge. Classes for adults and children are available, as well as decoy merchandise. Thursday is Guild Carving Day; stop by to meet the carvers and talk decoys. Kids Carving Days are held on the third Saturday of the month; preregistration required. Free.

✳ ⚅ **Core Sound Waterfowl Museum and Heritage Center** (252-728-1500; www.coresound.com), 1785 Island Road, Harkers Island. Near the end of the road on Harkers Island, this important museum is filled with hand-carved decoys, boat models, quilts, and other artifacts donated by local families. Each of the Down East communities has

THE NPS VISITOR CENTER ON HARKERS ISLAND SITS NEXT TO SHELL POINT, A POPULAR PUT-IN FOR KAYAKS AND WINDSURFERS

its own exhibit, and traditional decoy carvers and quilters demonstrate their crafts on-site. Outside, a nature trail leads to a pond frequented by migrating waterfowl. Several full-size boats built locally have been restored, including the *Jean Dale*, a 40-foot Harkers Island sink netter with a classic flared bow, hand-built by the legendary Brady Lewis. The center sponsors a full schedule of activities featuring Down East cooking, music, and crafts, including the **Waterfowl Weekend** every December. Climb the lookout tower for a great view of the lighthouse. $5.

Snug Harbor on Nelson Bay (252-225-4411; www.snugharboronnelsonbay.com), 272 US 70, Sea Level. Now an upscale retirement community, this originally was **Sailor's Snug Harbor**, a home for retired sailors founded on Staten Island in 1833. The sailors were moved to this location in 1976, while the original location in New York became an outstanding cultural center. The Sea Level facility has lovely grounds with several statues.

✳ To Do

BOATING Fishing and hunting from small boats, as well as ecotouring, are hugely popular Down East, with the many boat ramps in the area seeing heavy use. The **North Carolina Wildlife Resources Commission** (www.ncwildlife.org) has boat ramps at ♿ **Straits Landing** (1648 Harkers Island Road), at the northern end of the bridge to Harkers Island; ♿ **Oyster Creek** (1300 US 70, Davis), into Core Sound; **Salters Creek** (200 Wildlife Ramp Road, Sea Level), under the US 70

EXAMPLES OF A MASTER DECOY CARVER'S CRAFT

THE CORE SOUND WATERFOWL MUSEUM & HERITAGE CENTER IS FULL OF DECOYS AND OTHER LOCAL CRAFTS, PLUS EXHIBITS ON BOATBUILDING, HUNTING AND FISHING, ALL IMPORTANT PARTS OF TRADITIONAL LIFE DOWN EAST

high-rise bridge; and **Cedar Island** (115 Driftwood Drive), into Pamlico Sound. No public facilities at any of these ramps.

The Cedar Island National Wildlife Refuge (252-225-2511 or 252-926-4021; www.fws.gov/cedarisland) maintains two free boat ramps. One, at the end of Lola Road past the refuge office at the east end of Cedar Island, gives access to the sounds; the other, at the Thorofare Bridge on NC 12, puts you into the heart of the marsh. These are available for both powerboats and kayaks or other unmotorized craft.

On Harkers Island, you can use boat ramps at several marinas for a fee, including the **Harkers Island Fishing Center** (252-728-3907; www.harkersmarina .com), **Rose's Marina** (252-728-2868; www.rosesvacationrentals.com), and **Cape Pointe Marina** (252-728-6181; www .capepointemarina.com).

A harbor of refuge is located near the mouth of the North River at the southern end of Harkers Island.

DRIVING TOUR Follow the **Outer Banks National Scenic Byway** (www.outerbanks scenicbyway.org) through the small towns and fishing villages of Down East, where you'll see working fish houses, docks full of fishing boats, yards full of crab pots and skiffs, plus many historic structures. The **Down East Green Map** (www.greenmap.org) identifies numerous points of interest and maritime history along the route.

FISHING A public fishing pier is located on the small island that sits in the middle of the bridge to Harkers Island. A North Carolina fishing license is required. The inshore waters near Harkers Island are considered some of the finest on the East Coast for light-tackle and fly-fishing, especially in the late fall when the giant false albacore (little tunny or "fat Alberts") run, and in the late summer when tarpon enter the sounds.

A number of Down East charter captains will take you out for light-tackle or saltwater fly-fishing. False albacore, king and Spanish mackerel, cobia, red drum, trout, lady fish, and shark are the most frequent catches. The shallow waters are also great for flounder gigging. You can even fish for them with bow and arrow.

Noah's Ark Fishing and Tour Charters (252-342-6911 or 252-504-3139; www .noahsarkfishingcharters.com), at Cape Pointe Marina, 1390 Harkers Island Road, Harkers Island. Specializes in light-tackle spinning and fly-fishing.

HORSEBACK RIDING Outer Banks Riding Stables (252-225-1185; www.horseback ridingonthebeach.com), 120 Driftwood Drive, Cedar Island. Rides aboard well-trained horses offer opportunities to trot and canter and ride through the water on the open beach. Located next to the Cedar Island ferry docks.

HUNTING Hunting waterfowl during the winter months is a treasured tradition among Down East families. Loons were a favorite target, both for eating and for their leg bones, used to make fishing lures, until loon shooting was outlawed. Today, huge numbers of ducks, geese, and swans arrive each year to winter in the marshes and protected waters. The **Cedar Island National Wildlife Refuge** (www.fws.gov/cedarisland) has 400 acres open to waterfowl hunters with the proper permits. Hunting is also allowed on the **Core Banks of Cape Lookout National Seashore.**

   Lucky Duck's Guide Service (252-723-8711; www.capelookout.com), 476 US 70, Bettie. Captain Bernie Corwin will accompany you on a hunt for ducks or geese. Dogs are welcome. Corwin also offers light-tackle and saltwater fly-fishing, including fall trips after fat Alberts.

KAYAKING Sea kayaking is a popular activity in the region. You can launch on the sandy beach at the picnic area in front of the NPS visitor center on Harkers Island, or at nearby Shell Point at the end of Island Road, and park your car in the large picnic area lot. It's a 2- to 3-mile paddle over to the Core Banks from this spot, and conditions can sometimes be hazardous. The National Park Service asks that you file a float plan before setting off. Paddle maps are available inside the center.

US 70 RUNS ALL THE WAY ACROSS THE US, ENDING AT THE DOWN EAST FISHING VILLAGE CALLED ATLANTIC

The many streams and canals that lace the Down East region are ideal for kayaking and stand-up paddleboarding. The canals through the black needlerush marsh of the **Cedar Island National Wildlife Refuge** are good spots for birding or fishing from a kayak. Other popular spots to launch kayaks include the beach at Cedar Island and the boat ramp areas in Cedar Island National Wildlife Refuge.

⏎ **Cape Lookout Cabins & Camps Ferry Service** (252-729-9751; www.cape-lookout-cabins-camps-ferry-davis-nc.com), 125 Grady Lane, Davis. You can rent a kayak here, or put your craft aboard the ferry for a day of paddling over on Core Banks.

Down East Kayaks (252-838-1336; www.downeastkayaks.com), 1604 Harkers Island Road, Straits. You can rent kayaks and SUPs at this shop on the north side of the Harkers Island bridge, with an easy launch into the North River, or sign up for a guided ecotour.

Island Express Ferry Service (252-728-7433; www.islandexpressferryservices.com) will ferry your kayak to Cape Lookout.

WATER SPORTS **Shell Point**, at the end of Island Road on Harkers Island, is a popular spot for windsurfers to launch. You can park in the lot at the NPS visitor center. The **beach at Cedar Island** is another option.

❊ Green Space

BEACHES Public beaches are located at the **southeast end of the Harkers Island drawbridge** and **next to the ferry docks on Cedar Island**, but neither offers any facilities besides parking. Most beach fans head to **Core** or **Shackleford Banks** for their day on the sand.

TRAILS **Cedar Island National Wildlife Refuge** (252-225-2511 or 252-926-4021; www.fws.gov/cedarisland), 829 Lola Road, Cedar Island. This refuge, about 40 miles north of Beaufort, contains nearly 15,000 acres, about 10,000 of it brackish marsh, the rest pocosin and woodland, and is part of the largest remaining marsh on the East Coast, rated "world class" by geologists. This refuge is home to more than 270 species of birds, including the reclusive black rail, as well as large numbers of dragonflies. Kayaks or canoes are the best way to explore the black needlerush marshes, and the best time to visit is in winter, when huge numbers of redhead ducks are in residence and the local mosquitoes are least fierce. A number of gated, unimproved roads can be used for hiking, biking, or horseback riding. The refuge is open during daylight hours. No camping or motorized vehicles are allowed.

Harkers Island Trails. Two connecting trails are located in the maritime forest behind the NPS visitor center and the Core Sound Waterfowl Museum. The **Willow Pond Trail**, a short trail with interpretive signs, begins at the Core Sound Waterfowl Museum and circles a freshwater pond where waterbirds can be observed. The longer **Soundside Loop Trail** leads from the Cape Lookout National Seashore Visitor Center out to the marsh.

☀ Lodging

BED & BREAKFASTS **Cape Lookout Bed & Breakfast** (252-728-3662; www
.capelookoutbedandbreakfast.com), 349 Bayview Drive, Harkers Island. Two pleasant rooms offer great views over the marsh and of the wild horses on Browns Island, across Core Sound Straits. A hot breakfast is served on your schedule. $$.

((ᵞ)) **Davis Bed & Breakfast** (252-723-0893; www.davisbandb.com), 811 US 70, Davis. Two suites are available in this B&B near the Core Banks ferries. A full hot breakfast and an afternoon wine reception are included, plus Netflix. Screened porch with swimming pool for summer; fireplace for winter. Duck hunting packages available. $$$.

☀ ᴧ **Otway House Bed & Breakfast** (252-728-5636; www.otwayhouse.com), 68 US 70, Otway. Located on 6 acres in the quiet little town of Otway, this dog-friendly inn rents four elegantly furnished rooms with private baths, ceiling fans, and cable TV. The canine members of the party enjoy quality dog food, indoor and outdoor kennels, and a doggy play area. Human guests can indulge in a full breakfast, often including the inn's signature whole-wheat pancakes with bananas and pecans, before an active morning of rocking on the porch. Several free boat ramps are located close by, and the property has plenty of room for boat trailers. $$.

CAMPGROUNDS **Cape Pointe Marina & Campground** (252-728-6181; www
.capepointemarina.com), 1390 Harkers Island Road, Harkers Island. Boat slip rentals, boat ramp, ship's store, and RV site rentals. $.

((ᵞ)) **Cedar Creek Campground & Marina** (252-225-9571; www
.cedarcreekcampgroundandmarina
.com), 111 Canal Drive, Sea Level. Family-run Good Sam park has swimming pool, boat ramp, saltwater fishing dock, and game room. Tent area available. Cash or checks only. $.

☀ **Cedar Island Campground** (252-515-0201; www.cedarislandresort.com), 3557 Cedar Island Road, Cedar Island. Located next to the Cedar Island Ferry, this campground, now part of the Cedar Island Resort, recently got an upgrade with new full hookup sites and new electric and plumbing throughout the park. Amenities include a beautiful quartz sand beach; private boat ramp; kayak, canoe, and golf cart rentals; pontoon boat ecotours; fishing and duck-hunting guide service; horseback riding; and an on-site bar and grill. The dump station here is available for RVers passing through. The motel next door is being renovated as well. $

Harkers Island RV Resort (252-725-0820; www.harkersislandrvresort.com) 288 Guthrie Drive. New RV campground has its own fishing pier, pool, boat slips, and boat ramp, plus boat storage. $–$$.

MARINAS AND MOTELS ((ᵞ)) **Harkers Island Fishing Center** (252-728-3907; www.harkersmarina.com), 1002 Harkers Island Road, Harkers Island. Basic budget motel rooms and efficiencies, transient boat slips, boat ramp, fly- and light-tackle fishing charters (252-504-3823). Food and supplies available at the marina. $.

((ᵞ)) **Rose's Vacation Rentals** (252-728-2868; www.rosesvacationrentals.com), 287 Bayview Drive, Harkers Island. An old island family rents several well-maintained units next to Rose's Marina. A few RV sites and boat slips are also available. The boatbuilding sheds of the L. R. Rose Boatworks are still intact on the property. $.

☀ Where to Eat

EATING OUT ✿ ⤳ **Captain's Choice Restaurant** (252-728-7122; www
.captainschoicerestaurant.com), 977

Island Road, Harkers Island. Longtime favorite established in 1986 offers authentic Down East–style dining amid boat models, porthole windows, and framed posters from past Decoy Festivals, or on a breezy patio. Specials include certified local seafood prepared many ways, surf and turf platters, secret-recipe prime rib, and all-you-can eat seafood buffets on Friday and Saturday nights, plus a Sunday brunch buffet. Come for a weekday lunch special when a complimentary dessert may include Down East lemon pie. Lunch and dinner $–$$$.

✐ ⟿ **Fish Hook Grill** (252-728-1792; www.fishhookgrillharkersisland.com), 980 Island Road, Harkers Island. Southern-style diner food is served by friendly locals at this unpretentious spot near the Cape Lookout Visitor Center. Order a platter of local seafood, a North Carolina pork barbecue sandwich, or a Southern veggie plate with squash casserole, pickled beets, and fried okra, washed down with fresh brewed tea. Don't miss the local broth-based clam chowder, crabcakes, and delicious pies, all specialties of Ms. Faye, the 80-year-young owner. $–$$.

Morris Marina Grill (252-225-4261; www.portsmouthislandfishing.com), 1000 Morris Marina Road, Atlantic. A favorite stop for breakfast before catching the ferry to North Core Banks for a day of surf fishing. Try the Core Sound shrimp burger or the famous Morris Burger for lunch. $.

Outer Island General Store (252-504-2672; www.facebook.com/OuterIslandGeneral), 499 US 70, Otway. This family-owned convenience store and grill serves home cooking, Down East style. $.

Seaside Harkers Island (252-728-5533; www.facebook.com/hiseaside), 311 Island Road. Little convenience store on Harkers Island's main drag serves breakfast, lunch, and dinner, featuring certified local seafood and the recipes of native Down Easter Mila Guthrie,

famous for her tartar sauce. Try the clam chowder. $.

Sharky's Bar and Grill (252-515-0201; www.cedarislandresort.com), 3557 Cedar Island Road, Cedar Island. New eatery at the Cedar Island Resort next to the ferry dock offers a full bar and daily specials on food and drink, including a Thursday night prime rib and Taco Tuesdays. $–$$.

White Point Take-Out (252-225-1500), 101 Core Sound Loop Road Extension, Atlantic. Those in the know follow US 70 all the way to its end to find this little purple take-out spot run by the Stryon family. The softshell crabs are shed on-site, the shrimp and flounder are caught by the boat out front, and the crabcakes are made from "local swimmers." Sides include fried okra, hush puppies, and clam strips, and prices are so low you won't believe it. $.

✳ Selective Shopping

Captain Henry's Gift Store (252-728-7316), 1341 Island Road, Harkers Island. Browse a wide variety of gifts and collectibles, including locally carved decoys.

Core Sound Waterfowl Museum Store (252-728-1500; www.coresound.com), 1785 Island Road, Harkers Island. Features art and crafts by local people,

Black Head (Lesser Scaup)
Alvin Harris, Atlantic, NC

LOCAL SHOPS PROVIDE OPPORTUNITIES TO PURCHASE HANDCRAFTED DECOYS, AN AUTHENTIC AMERICAN FOLK ART including decoys, locally produced books and music, and **Core Sound crab pot Christmas trees** (www.crabpottrees .com), invented by local Nicky Harvey— the must-have souvenir of a trip to the Crystal Coast.

✳ Special Events

Check the **Crystal Coast visitors website** (www.crystalcoastnc.org) for an updated list of events during your stay.

February: **Taste of Core Sound– Winter Edition** (252-728-1500; www .coresound.com), Core Sound Waterfowl Museum and Heritage Center, Harkers Island. Enjoy a dinner of Down East specialties and lots of local welcome.

May: **Loon Day Carving Competition** (252-838-8818; www.decoyguild.com), Core Sound Decoy Carvers Guild, Harkers Island. Auction and vintage decoy display.

August: **Taste of Core Sound–Summer Edition** (252-728-1500; www.coresound .com), Core Sound Waterfowl Museum and Heritage Center.

North Carolina Wildlife Artists Society Fall Exhibition Opening Reception (252-728-1500; www.ncwas.com), Core Sound Waterfowl Museum and Heritage Center.

December: **Core Sound Decoy Festival** (252-838-8818; www.decoyguild.com), Core Sound Decoy Guild, Harkers Island. Weekend of decoy competition includes a decoy auction, retriever demonstrations, loon calling, and children's decoy painting.

Core Sound Waterfowl Weekend (252-728-1500; www.coresound.com), Core Sound Waterfowl Museum and Heritage Center, Harkers Island. Held the same weekend as the decoy festival, this event celebrates Down East traditions of boatbuilding, fishing, music, arts and crafts, cooking, and fellowship.

CAPE LOOKOUT AND THE CORE BANKS

The five uninhabited islands stretching from Ocracoke Inlet to Beaufort Inlet, making up the Cape Lookout National Seashore, have more than 55 miles of pristine ocean beach wiped nearly clean of all traces of human occupation. Originally used as hunting and fishing grounds by the Coree Indians, from whom they take their name, the Core Banks remain today, as then, a rich ecological treasure, one of the most significant undeveloped barrier island systems in the world.

At the north end of Core Banks, once-prosperous **Portsmouth Village**, now a ghost town administered by the National Park Service, is most easily reached from Ocracoke Island. See our coverage in that chapter. The national seashore is generally divided into the **North Core and South Core Banks islands**, plus **Shackleford Banks** nearer Beaufort, although the park service has decided to let the shape of these islands be determined entirely by natural causes. Inlets open and close, depending on storms and tides.

THE DIAMOND PATTERN SPORTED BY THE CAPE LOOKOUT LIGHT MAKES IT ONE OF THE WORLD'S MOST BEAUTIFUL AND DISTINCTIVE LIGHTHOUSES

Cape Lookout Lighthouse is located near the southern hook of South Core. Nearby lie the remnants of **Cape Lookout Village**, including an old lifesaving station. This area is reached via passenger ferries from **Harkers Island**, where the **Seashore's Visitor Center** is located, and from Beaufort's waterfront. Private watercraft can also land on the Banks at designated spots.

From **Cape Lookout**, the Shackleford Banks stretch west to a point opposite Fort Macon on Bogue Banks. Once the location of the whaling village of **Diamond City**, Shackleford was abandoned by its inhabitants after a hurricane in 1899 sent a storm surge over the island. Today, the island's sole residents are about 150 ponies of Spanish descent who have adapted to the harsh conditions.

GUIDANCE For a complete rundown on things to do on Cape Lookout, how to get there, and reservations at the NPS cabin camps, visit the website of the **Cape Lookout National Seashore** (252-728-2250; www.nps.gov/calo) or go by the **NPS visitor center on Harkers Island**. From March to November, an additional NPS visitor center is located on the first floor of the Beaufort Town Hall (701 Front Street), with information and maps, as well as ecology and history exhibits. Additional information centers are located on the Core Banks at the Light Station Visitor Center and the cabin offices at Great Island and Long Point. Services at the centers include first aid, NPS passport stamps, restrooms, and free beach wheelchair rental. Portsmouth Village, the deserted village at the northern tip of Core Banks, has its own visitor center, best reached via boat shuttle from Ocracoke.

GETTING THERE During the summer months, ferries licensed by the National Park Service make their way to the national seashore's islands from several ports on the mainland and Harkers Island. Ferries from **the village of Atlantic** go to North Core. Ferries from **Davis** go to the middle of South Core. The ferries from these ports carry vehicles, including passenger vehicles, ATVs, golf carts, and utility vehicles, as well as passengers, and dock near cabin camps maintained by the National Park Service. Ferries from **Harkers Island** carry only passengers and go to the Cape Lookout Lighthouse area and Shackleford Banks. Ferries from **Beaufort** also carry passengers to the lighthouse and Shackleford.

Ferry service from Harkers Island and Beaufort changed dramatically during the last few years, as the National Park Service consolidated and standardized services. Where a number of ferry companies once made the run from the Harkers Island and Beaufort docks, now only one concessionaire holds the NPS license. Ferries now depart from NPS terminals on Harkers and the Beaufort waterfront, instead of a host of different marinas and docks.

From Beaufort and Harkers Island: **Island Ferry Adventures** (252-728-7433; www .islandferryadventures.com) holds the license to ferry visitors from both Harkers Island and Beaufort. The Harkers Island Gateway terminal is located at 1800 Island Road; the Beaufort Gateway terminal is located on the waterfront at 600 Front Street. Ferries run all year. Leashed pets are accepted on most ferries. Rates are standardized by NPS. From the Harkers Island Gateway (15-minute ferry ride), expect to pay $16 per person for adults; $9 for children under 12; $7 for pets, round-trip to either Cape Lookout or the east end of Shackleford Banks. From the Beaufort Gateway, rates are $35 for adults, $25 for children under 12 to Cape Lookout (a 45-minute ferry ride); $16 and $9 to the west end of Shackleford (a 15-minute trip). All fares are round-trip. Excursions stopping at both Shackleford and the lighthouse are available for an additional fee. See the website for current fees and hours, and to reserve online.

From Atlantic: **Morris Marina Ferry Service** (252-225-4261; www.portsmouth islandfishing.com), 1000 Morris Marina Road, Atlantic. Ferries carrying pedestrians, vehicles, trailers, and ATVs depart for the Long Point Cabin Area on the North Core Banks daily from March to mid-December.

From Davis: ♿ **Cape Lookout Cabins & Camps Ferry Service** (252-729-9751; www .cape-lookout-cabins-camps-ferry-davis-nc.com), 125 Grady Lane, Davis. Passenger and vehicle ferry departs from Davis to Great Island on South Core. Kubota utility vehicles, four-wheel-drive trucks, and kayaks available for rent. Guided waterfowl hunting and fishing charters to Drum Inlet and other hot spots can be arranged here.

Davis Shore Ferry Service (252-729-3474; www.davisferry.com), 148 Willis Road, Davis. Fourth-generation local family operates vehicle and passenger service to the Great Island Cabins and Camp. Ice, bait, and tackle available, as well as fishing guides.

From Ocracoke: **Rudy Austin's Portsmouth Island Boat Tours** (252-928-4361; www .portsmouthislandboattours.com). The Austin family holds the NPS licence to run passenger ferries to the dock at Portsmouth Village on the northern tip of the Core Banks from Ocracoke's Community Square Docks.

MUST SEE

Cape Lookout Lighthouse & Keepers' Quarters Museum (252-728-2250; www.nps.gov/calo), South Core Banks. The 169-foot-tall Cape Lookout Lighthouse was first lit in 1859 but didn't receive its distinctive black and white diamond paint job until after the Civil War. Its 207 steps are roughly the equivalent of a 12-story building. The adjacent Keepers' Quarters holds a free museum detailing the history of the lighthouse and the Core Banks. Ferries make the run from Harkers Island, the nearest land access, and Beaufort, docking near the Light Station Visitor Center, which houses a ranger station, bookstore, and restrooms, along with an exhibit on local seashells. During the summer months, park rangers conduct free programs on the history of the lighthouse and the surrounding area. A ferry ride is required to reach South Core Banks, and the fare does not include lighthouse-climbing tickets. The lighthouse is open for climbing May–September; the free Keepers' Quarters Museum, at the base of the tower, and the Light Station Visitor Center are open daily, April–November. Buy tickets to climb, currently $4–8, at the Light Station Visitor Center the day of your visit. Check the NPS website to see if advance reservations are available. The view is well worth both the price and the climb.

THE VIEW FROM THE OBSERVATION DECK ATOP THE CAPE LOOKOUT LIGHT

GETTING AROUND *By four-wheel drive:* Much of the ocean beach and the unpaved sand roads on North and South Core Banks within the Cape Lookout National Seashore are open to ORV use. Vehicles can reach the seashore aboard ferries located at Atlantic (for North Core) and Davis (for South Core). No permit is required for driving on the beach; however vehicles must display an ORV Education Certificate decal, available free online and at the park.

Most driving is done on the harder surface along the tide line, although a sandy road, referred to as the Back Road, runs behind the dunes. Vehicles must remain on the beach or the sand roads and are not allowed on dunes or in areas restricted due to bird or sea turtle nesting activities. Four-wheel-drive vehicles are strongly recommended; there are no tow trucks or emergency vehicles on the Core Banks. You are on your own, so come prepared.

By shuttle: **Island Express Ferry Service** (252-728-7433; www.islandexpressferry services.com) offers shuttle service from the light station to the Cape Point beaches. The Beach Shuttle is $10 and includes a narrated tour of Cape Point and its historic ruins, plus on-your-own time to enjoy the beach or explore. Call for hours and information.

On foot: The sand on Core Banks is soft and difficult to walk through. A boardwalk leads across to the beach from the ferry dock near the lighthouse.

RECOMMENDED READING

Prioli, Carmine. *The Wild Horses of Shackleford Banks*. Winston-Salem, NC: John F. Blair, 2007.

✳ To See

Cape Lookout Village (252-728-1500; www.friendsofcapelookout.com), Cape Point, South Core Banks. Located about a mile south of the lighthouse, this cluster of buildings on the National Register of Historic Places is all that remains of the village that once thrived here. There are currently 16 buildings, built from 1887 to 1960, including the 1887 Life-Saving Station and its boathouse, and various private residences and fishing cottages, all unoccupied. The 1915 Coast Guard Station is just across the bight. Interpretive signs are located throughout the village. The village can be reached by foot, by private vehicle or boat, or by shuttle service from the Light Station Visitor Center.

Portsmouth Village (252-728-2250; www.friendsofportsmouthisland.org or www.nps.gov/calo). This eerie ghost village is located at the northern tip of North Core Banks and is most easily reached by ferry from Ocracoke. **Austin Boat Tours** (252-928-4361 or 252-928-5431; www .portsmouthislandboattours.com) holds the NPS license for the service. A **visitor center in the restored Theodore and Annie Salter House**, open seasonally, has restrooms, maps of the village, and exhibits on Portsmouth history. Free tours of the village are offered by rangers during

THE HERD OF WILD HORSES ON SHACKLEFORD BANKS HAVE BEEN CONFIRMED BY DNA TO BE OF SPANISH COLONIAL STOCK

the summer months. You can also reach Portsmouth Village by bringing your vehicle across to North Core on the ferry from Atlantic, then driving about 16 miles up the beach.

Shackleford Banks Horses. A herd of about 100 horses descended from Spanish stock lives the wild life on Shackleford Banks. The island can be reached only by boat. A tour guided by a naturalist is recommended for the best and safest views of the wild horses.

✳ To Do

BOATING You can get to the various deserted islands aboard your private boat, although caution is advised since the average depth in the sound is just 5 feet, and there are numerous shifting sandbars. Docks where you can off-load passengers are located just north of the lighthouse on South Core and at the western end of Shackleford near Beaufort. Two docks are located near Portsmouth Village at the tip of North Core. You cannot tie up at any of these docks, but must anchor offshore. Many shallow draft boats simply pull up on the sandy beach.

Sailboats and deeper draft vessels can best moor in Cape Lookout Bight behind the Cape Point spit, a truly beautiful anchorage with awesome views of both the lighthouse and the Shackleford horses. You can anchor for a maximum of 14 days in national seashore waters.

Personal watercraft (PWC) such as Jet Skis and WaveRunners can currently land on the islands of Cape Lookout National Seashore at 10 designated soundside locations. However, these regulations change frequently, so check with the National Park Service before launching your watercraft.

In addition to shuttles to Cape Lookout, **Island Express Ferry Service** (252-728-7433; www.islandexpressferryservices.com) also offers a heritage tour of the region aboard a catamaran that circles Harkers Island and passes by Shackleford and Cape Point, with great views of the lighthouse, dolphins, and wild horses, plus many stories shared by a local. Tours depart from 1800 Harbor Road, Harkers Island.

FISHING Next to the lighthouse, surf fishing is Cape Lookout's biggest draw, with numerous fishing enthusiasts bringing their four-wheel-drive vehicles over on the ferries from Atlantic and Davis, and spending weeks at a time roaming the tide line, camping out, and fishing the break, then cooking their catch for dinner. Fall and spring are the busiest seasons for fishing, highlighted by the Cape's famous run of red drum during the autumn months.

HUNTING Waterfowl hunting is allowed on the Core Banks islands, with the correct permits, during certain times of the year. Contact the park service for more details.

SHELLING Core and Shackleford Banks and other islands of Cape Lookout National Seashore are great places to find shells, including Scotch bonnets, olives, petrified clams, whelks, conchs, and Queen's helmets. The beach on the west side of Cape Point south of the lighthouse is noted for the large whelk shells, some a foot long, found there.

Sand dollars are also abundant, especially on the small sandbar called **Sand Dollar Island** that lies between Carrot Island and Shackleford Banks. This little sandbar is barely above water and is only accessible at low tide.

A limit of 2 gallons of shells a day may be taken from national seashore beaches. Shelling is best in the early spring, about two hours before or after high tide, and especially after big storms.

SNORKELING AND SCUBA The rock jetty near the west end of the Cape Lookout spit (officially Power Squadron Jetty) is a great spot for seeing the local aquatic life. The area is best reached by boat.

SWIMMING The Cape Lookout National Seashore does not have a lifeguarded beach. All swimming is at your own risk.

WATER SPORTS The uninhabited beaches of Cape Lookout offer surfers, kiteboarders, and windsurfers a unique opportunity to practice their sports in a truly natural environment.

✳ Green Space

🐾 **Core Banks, Cape Lookout National Seashore** (www.nps.gov/calo) has more than 55 miles of pristine, undeveloped beaches stretching from Portsmouth Island in the north to Cape Point, south of the lighthouse. Accessible only by boat, the seashore's beaches have few amenities and can be hard to travel by foot. A boardwalk stretches from the **Light Station Pavilion** near the ferry dock, over to the ocean beach and to the **Keepers' Quarters** museum. Drinkable water, restrooms, and picnic areas are located at **Cape Point**, the **Light Station** area, and **Great Island** on South Core; and at **Long Point** and **Portsmouth Village** on North Core. North Core and South Core are separated by the fairly deep **New Drum Inlet**. Check the park service website for current amenities and recommended supplies. (Such as insect repellent, a must for a trip to Cape Lookout. The insects here have well-deserved reputations for ferocity.) During the summer, rangers and volunteers from the **North Carolina Coastal Federation** (252-808-3301) lead free programs exploring barrier island ecology.

Endangered sea turtles and shorebirds nest along the shore, especially in the Cape Point area. Wading birds frequent the marsh. Visitors can hike along the shores of the ocean or sound to observe birds, or along the sandy roads and trails.

Beach wheelchairs are available on a limited basis at the **Light Station Pavilion** and at the NPS Visitor Center in Beaufort. Fires are permitted only on the beach below the high tide line. Plan to bring your own wood. Pets are allowed within the national seashore but must be leashed at all times.

Shackleford Banks (252-728-2250; www.nps.gov/calo). Home to a herd of wild horses (proved through DNA studies to be descended from colonial-era

THE SHACKLEFORD WILD HORSES LIVE A PROTECTED LIFE ON AN ISLAND THAT CAN ONLY BE REACHED BY BOAT

Spanish stock) and little else, this island is a popular spot for shelling and sunning. Access is by ferry or private boat. Park rangers offer **Horse Sense and Survival Tours** during the summer season. Reservations required. Restrooms are located near the passenger ferry landing at the western tip of the island, and at Wade's Shore, a short distance east. See "Beaufort" section for details on tours and ferries to Shackleford.

✱ Lodging

CAMPING There are no established campgrounds within the national seashore; however, primitive camping with both tents and vehicles is allowed. Tents are permitted anywhere except on dunes or within 100 feet of any structure.

Vehicles, allowed on the Core only, must park on the ocean side of the dune line. Because of the softness of the sand and the likelihood of becoming stuck, large RVs are not recommended. There are no stores on the Banks, and campers should bring along all supplies they'll need, including drinking water, and plan to carry out all trash. Dump stations and restrooms are available at the picnic area near Cape Point and at the two cabin areas. Showers for public use and fuel for vehicles are available at the cabin camps. Camping is limited to 14 consecutive days. Free.

CAPE LOOKOUT CABINS **Two groups of cabins on Core Banks** are available for rent, and they are popular with fishers and kayakers, and for family getaways. Rentals are available from mid-March through the end of November. Rates are higher during the spring and fall fishing seasons, and less during the summer. Renters must provide their own linens, bedding, cookware, food, and other supplies. Gas and ice are sold at the camp offices. Pets are allowed in cabins, but they must be kept in crates or tied up on the cabin porch and not left unattended. Each cabin camp also has a hot shower and restroom facility open to campers. Reservations for these cabins can be made online at the **Recreation.gov website,** or by calling 1-877-444-6777.

Reservations are accepted beginning in early January. Plan ahead, as these cabins book up quickly.

♿ **Great Island Cabin Camp** (1-877-444-6777; www.nps.gov/calo), South Core Banks. The 26 rustic cabins sleep 4–12 people; one is fully accessible. Accommodations are basic, with screened porches, bunk beds, hot water, full baths with showers, and propane stoves, but no electricity. Most are wired for generators, which must be provided by individual renters. Great Island is reached by ferry from Davis or by private boat. $–$$.

♿ **Long Point Cabin Camp** (1-877-444-6777; www.nps.gov/calo). Ten duplex cabins each sleep up to six people on each side. Units 1–8 are in hexagonal buildings; four of these units have air-conditioning. The other units are in rectangular buildings with propane heaters. All cabins have electricity, private baths, ceiling fans, bunk beds, and kitchen stoves. Cabins at Long Point are reached by ferry from Atlantic or by private boat. One cabin is accessible. $$.

For additional camping and lodging options on the mainland and Harkers Island, see our "Down East" listings.

✱ Special Events

April: **Junior Ranger Day** (www.nps.gov/calo).

October: **Davis Island Fishing Foundation Surf Fishing Tournament** (www.diffclub.com), Great Island Camp and South Core Banks.

BEAUFORT

The charming village that is today the seat of Carteret County began life as Beaufort-by-the-Sea back in 1709, making it the state's third-oldest town. Pronounced in the French manner with a long o (*BO-furt*, in contrast with the South Carolina Beaufort, pronounced *BYOO-furt*), the town is a favorite stop for yachts cruising the **Atlantic Intracoastal Waterway** (ICW) as well as visitors seeking history, water-based recreation, and fine cuisine. *Travel & Leisure* magazine named this "America's Favorite Town."

The pedestrian-friendly historic district centers on **Front Street**, facing the town docks. Here you'll find a variety of restaurants, bed & breakfasts, historic houses, and boat tours and water taxis to nearby islands. The **wild ponies on Carrot Island** can often be seen just across the water.

Shops along the waterfront offer an eclectic blend of nautical items, antiques, and local artwork. The **Beaufort Historic Site** and the **North Carolina Maritime Museum** provide context on the area's rich background of pirates, merchants, and commercial fisheries. Beaufort is also the home port of North Carolina's last privateer, Captain Horatio Sinbad. His ship, the brigantine *Meka II*, can often be found at the **Gallants Channel** docks, and the captain himself frequents the establishments along Front Street.

CAPTAIN SINBAD'S *MEKA II* MAKES FREQUENT VISITS TO BEAUFORT DOCKS

GUIDANCE The historical center at the **Beaufort Historic Site** (252-728-5225; www .beauforthistoricsite.org), on the first block of Turner Street, serves as a welcome center for the town of Beaufort. The **Town of Beaufort's visitor website** can be found at www.beinbeaufort.com.

Additional information can be found at:

Beaufort Town Hall (252-728-2141; www.beaufortnc.org), 701 Front Street, Beaufort, and the **NPS Visitor Center for the Cape Lookout National Seashore** (www.nps.gov/ calo), with exhibits and information on the park.

Carteret County Offices (252-728-8450; www.carteretcountygov.org), Courthouse Square at Cedar and Turner streets, Beaufort.

POST OFFICE The **Beaufort U.S. Post Office** (252-728-1812) is at 1903 Live Oak Street. The zip code in Beaufort is 28516.

PUBLIC RESTROOMS Public facilities are found at the **Beaufort Historic Site's historical center**; the **Town Docks** on Front Street; **Perry Park** at the east end of Front Street; and the **W. Beaufort Road Water Access**. On the US 70 causeway to Morehead City, look for restrooms and bathhouses at the **Newport River Park** on the north side of the road, and across the street at the **Radio Island Water Access**.

PUBLIC LIBRARY The main branch of the ((ŋ)) **Carteret County Public Library** (252-728-2050; carteret.cpclib.org) is at 1702 Live Oak Street in Beaufort. Services include children's story time, faxing, public-use computers, and a paperback exchange.

GETTING THERE *By air:* **Michael J. Smith Field Airport/KMRH** (252-728-2323; www .crystalcoastaviation.com), 150 Airport Road, Beaufort. Car rentals, fuel, and tie-downs, as well as air tours and aircraft rentals, are offered at this field, named for the astronaut, a local man who commanded the space shuttle *Challenger* on its final, fatal flight.

By boat: Beaufort is a popular stop for boats traveling the Atlantic Intracoastal Waterway. Boat slips for transients are located at the **Beaufort Town Docks** (252-728-2503), 500 Front Street, in the heart of town.

By car: US 70 comes over the bridge from Morehead City, then runs along the north side of Beaufort's historic district before making a sharp turn to the north and heading toward the Down East communities.

GETTING AROUND *On foot:* Beaufort is a great walking destination. Everything you need for a great vacation is within a block or two of Front Street. Many visitors arrive, park their car at the hotel, and walk to museums, restaurants, and nightlife. Even boat tours are easy to reach, with the docks right on Front Street.

MEDICAL EMERGENCY The nearest emergency room is located at **Carteret General Hospital** (252-499-6000; www.carterethealth.org), 3500 Arendell Street, Morehead City.

✷ To See

ARCHITECTURE The **Beaufort Historic District** contains over 100 buildings bearing plaques listing the original owner and date of construction. Victorian and Queen Anne influences are reflected in the elaborate millwork found on many of the houses.

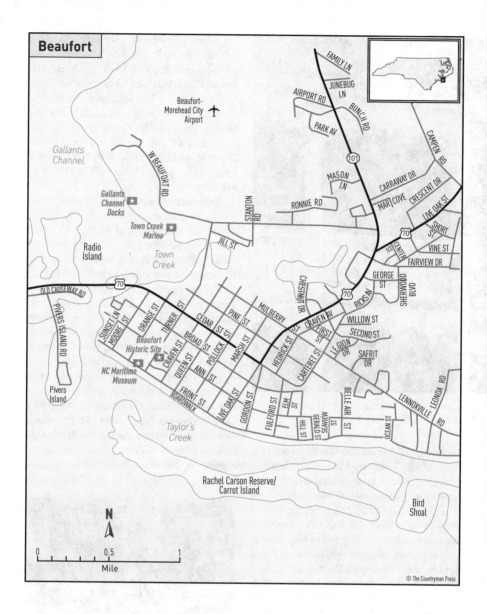

Beaufort also has a distinctive style of picket fence, characterized by an undulating, up-and-down top line and square pickets. The **Beaufort Historical Association** (252-728-5225 or 1-800-575-7483; www.beauforthistoricsite.org) sponsors an Old Homes and Gardens Tour every June.

❄ ♂ **Beaufort Historic Site** (252-728-5225 or 1-800-575-7483; www.beauforthistoric site.org), 100 block, Turner Street. The Beaufort Historical Association, a private, membership-based organization formed in 1960, has gathered, restored, and furnished six historic buildings—including the 1732 **Rustell House**, now an art gallery, and Federal and Victorian residences—in the 100 block of Turner Street. Other buildings around the wide green lawn include the 1786 **Carteret County Courthouse**; the **Old Jail**, reputed to be haunted; and the 1859 **Apothecary and Doctor's Office**, filled with

ELABORATE MILLWORK GRACES MANY OF THE BUILDINGS IN BEAUFORT'S HISTORIC DISTRICT

fascinating medical artifacts. Gardens on the grounds include a colonial-era kitchen garden and herb gardens. The **Safrit Historical Center** houses exhibits, the museum gift shop, and restrooms, in addition to serving as an information center. Free admission to grounds, gardens, and art gallery; guided tours of the historic buildings, **Old Burying Ground**, and double-decker bus tours of the town are available for a fee.

Beaufort Town Hall (252-728-2141; www.beaufortnc.org), 701 Front Street. Step into the lobby of Beaufort's town hall, formerly the post office, to see four large murals depicting scenes related to the town's history and culture, including the 1886 wreck of the schooner *Crissie Wright*, a mailboat, a hunting scene, and the "sand ponies" still found on several islands. The murals are the work of immigrant artist Simka Simkhovitch, who began work soon after the post office opened in 1937, as part of a federally funded project that put artists to work during the Great Depression. The lobby also houses exhibits from the NPS, which operates its ferry concession from this location; the **Rachel Carson Reserve**; and other organizations. Free.

❋ ✐ ♿ ⚓ **North Carolina Maritime Museum in Beaufort** (252-728-7317; www.ncmaritime.org or www.maritimefriends.org), 315 Front Street. Open daily except Thanksgiving, Christmas holidays, and New Year's Day. The state's maritime museum in Beaufort includes three separate facilities: **the main galleries on Front Street**; the **Watercraft Center**, across the street on the waterfront; and the **Gallants Channel Docks**, about 1 mile west of downtown. The main galleries contain an extensive shell collection, examples of traditional boats, an excellent collection of hand-carved decoys, and the skeleton of a 35-foot sperm whale, as well as a new Blackbeard's *Queen Anne's Revenge* exhibit, featuring artifacts from the pirate ship and interactive activities. The Watercraft Center specializes in the building and restoration of wooden boats and houses a ship model-making shop. The maritime museum sponsors a wide

AN 1859 APOTHECARY, PART OF THE BEAUFORT HISTORIC SITE

BEAUFORT'S PRIVATEER

Capt. Horatio Sinbad (www.pirate-privateer.com) and his ship, the brigantine *Meka II*, are familiar sights around the town of Beaufort. Captain Sinbad built the *Meka II*, a 2/3-scale replica of a two-masted pirate brigantine, and for five decades has made Beaufort his home port. Officially commissioned as a privateer (sort of a legalized pirate) by the governor of North Carolina and President Ronald Reagan, Sinbad spends his time sailing the high seas in search of adventure, participating in historical reenactments, tall ship parades, and pirate festivals. The *Meka II*'s eight cannons come into frequent use at the annual Pirate Invasions of Beaufort (August) and Ocracoke (October), both ports with an intimate connection to Blackbeard and the Age of Pirates.

CAPTAIN HORATIO SINBAD, ABOARD THE *MEKA II*

variety of boatbuilding, boating, and environmental education programs, including kayak tours, throughout the year. Free.

Old Burying Ground (252-728-5225; www.beauforthistoricsite.org), bounded by Ann, Craven, and Broad streets. Open dawn to dusk. A leisurely walk beneath the 100-year-old live oaks that shade the Old Burying Ground is a fascinating trip through local history. The nearly 300-year-old cemetery contains some 400 graves dating back to 1731. Two notable occupants are Otway Burns, the famous privateer whose grave is marked with a cannon from his ship, and a young girl buried in a barrel of rum, whose grave is decorated with toys and gifts left by visitors over the years. A self-guided tour booklet is available at the Beaufort Historic Site, and costumed interpreters offer guided tours ($10) with many additional stories several times a week. Free.

SIGN UP TO BUILD YOUR OWN BOAT IN A DAY AT THE WATERCRAFT CENTER ON THE BEAUFORT WATERFRONT

THE TOMB OF PRIVATEER OTWAY BURNS IN THE OLD BURYING GROUND IS TOPPED WITH A CANNON FROM HIS SHIP

Rachel Carson National Estuarine Research Reserve (252-728-2170; www.nccoastalreserve.net), 135 Duke Marine Lab Road. The complex of islands, accessible by ferry, includes Carrot Island, Town Marsh, Bird Shoal, and Horse Island, all less than a mile wide. Feral horses, not related to the Spanish descendants on Shackleford Banks, roam the islands. A local farmer released them here in the 1940s. The horses on Carrot Island, located directly across Taylor's Creek from the Beaufort waterfront, are frequently sighted from dockside restaurants.

✳ To Do

AIR TOURS **Southern Air** (252-728-2323; www.crystalcoastaviation.com), 150 Airport Road. For a unique perspective, see Cape Lookout, the wild ponies, and Fort Macon from the air. You can also take an introductory flight lesson or rent an aircraft.

BICYCLING The **Beaufort Bicycle Route** makes a signposted 6-mile loop around the historic village. The quiet side streets generally make for good riding.

Beaufort Bicycles (252-728-1203), 127 Briar Patch Lane, rents bikes.

THE FERAL HORSES OF CARROT ISLAND CAN BE SEEN FROM MANY RESTAURANTS ALONG THE BEAUFORT WATERFRONT

❋ ♂ **Hungry Town Tours** (252-648-1011; hungrytowntours.com), 400 Front Street. Local tour company rents bikes and offers a range of fun biking and walking tours exploring Beaufort's history, maritime heritage, and cuisine. Special tours highlight local shrimp and oysters, while the "Ride to Remember" visits spots mentioned by author Nicholas Sparks in his books *The Choice* and *A Walk to Remember*.

BOATING The **Friends of the Maritime Museum** (252-728-1638; www.maritimefriends .org) sponsors many different boating programs, including two-week long Junior Sailing Programs, the Beaufort Oars Rowing Club, and family sailing on traditional skiffs or a 30-foot keelboat available by reservation.

Several free boat ramps are available to the public. ♿ **Curtis A. Perry Park**, at the east end of Front Street, has four boat ramps maintained by the **North Carolina Wildlife Service** (www.ncwildlife.org), plus a dock, picnic area with grills, tennis courts, and restrooms. ♿ **Town Creek Water Access** (Turner Street and W. Beaufort Road) has two ramps, easiest to use at high tide, plus a boardwalk, fishing pier, floating docks, and restrooms, with access to Gallants Channel.

Rent a Carolina skiff or pontoon boat from **Ahoy Boat Rentals** (252-726-1900; www .ahoyboatrentals.com), 232 W. Beaufort Road at the Town Creek Marina.

Beaufort is a popular destination for boaters traveling the Intracoastal Waterway. Several marinas cater to live-aboards and transients:

((ɐ)) **Beaufort Town Docks** (252-728-2503), 500 Front Street. Transient slips are located in the heart of historic Beaufort.

Beaufort Yacht Basin (252-504-3625; www.beaufortyachtbasin.com), 103 Cedar Street.

Homer Smith Docks and Marina (252-728-2944; www.homersmithdocksandmarina .com), 101 Cedar Street.

Town Creek Marina (252-728-6111; www.towncreekmarina.com), 232 W. Beaufort Road. Transient slips, restaurant, waterside bar with live entertainment, and terrific sunset views.

BOAT TOURS The Beaufort waterfront is very active, with many tours leaving from docks all along Front Street. The trip over to Shackleford Banks for shelling and viewing the wild horses, offered by several different companies, is not to be missed. Naturalist-led tours are recommended and well worth the small additional cost.

The National Park Service operates a ferry concession out of the Beaufort Town Hall, recently moved to the old post office building at the corner of Front and Pollock streets. The ferries depart for Shackleford Banks and the Cape Lookout Lighthouse from a dock in **Grayden Paul Park** (252-728-2141; www.beaufortnc.org) at 718 Front Street, directly across from the Town Hall. **Island Express Ferry Service** (252-728-7433; www.islandexpressferryservices.com) holds the exclusive NPS concession to operate ferries to the national seashore from Beaufort.

♂ **Carolina Ocean Studies** (910-458-7302; www.carolinaoceanstudies.com). Naturalists offer educational, hands-on programs on Shackleford and Core Banks, featuring dolphins, Banker ponies, tidal flats, fishing, and coastal science for grades K-12 from the Beaufort waterfront.

♂ **Crystal Coast Lady Cruises** (252-728-8687; www.crystalcoastlady.com), 617 Front Street. The largest and newest cruiser on the Beaufort waterfront hosts narrated harbor tours, lunch cruises, sunset dinner cruises, dolphin watches, and family fishing trips.

🐎 **Island Ferry Adventures** (252-728-4129; www.islandferryadventures.com), 610 Front Street. Award-winning boat tours include a horse and waterfront sight-seeing

THE ISLAND ADVENTURES WATER TAXI WILL DROP YOU OFF AT SEVERAL DIFFERENT ISLANDS WHERE YOU CAN ENJOY A DAY AT THE BEACH WITHOUT THE CROWDS

cruise that circles the islands in front of Beaufort. Others take you to Harkers Island for views of the lighthouse, and along the Morehead City waterfront. Water taxi service will drop you off for a day of relaxation on Bird Shoal, Sand Dollar Island, or Carrot Island. Small dogs can ride along.

Lookout Cruises (252-504-7245; www.lookoutcruises.com), 600 Front Street. A 45-foot sailing catamaran offers dolphin-watching day trips to Cape Lookout with lunch and snorkeling, plus sunset and moonlight cruises.

❋ **Shackleford Wild Horse and Shelling Safari** (252-838-1167; www.shackleford wildhorseandshellingsafari.com), 600 Front Street. Naturalists licensed by the NPS to offer tours of Shackleford guide visitors around the island to see herds of wild ponies, then search for shells along the oceanfront, one of the best shelling destinations on the East Coast.

Water Bug Harbor Tours (252-342-3577; www.waterbugtours.com), 610 Front Street. Cruise the historic Beaufort waterfront on a one-hour tour or take in the sunset from the water.

FISHING Public-access fishing piers are located at the ♿ **Town Creek (West Beaufort) Water Access** (298 W. Beaufort Road) and ♿ **Newport River Park**, on the causeway between Beaufort and Morehead City. A North Carolina Coastal Recreational Fishing License is required.

Crystal Coast Lady Cruises (252-728-8687 or 252-728-7827; www.crystalcoastlady .com), 617 Front Street. Headboat operating from the Beaufort waterfront offers reasonably priced half-day bay fishing trips, with lower rates for children, seniors, and spectators. All equipment, bait, and licenses are included.

✽ **Waterdog Guide Service** (252-728-7907 or 919-423-6310; www.waterdogguide service.com). Captain Tom Roller offers light-tackle and fly-fishing charters, operated with the highest ethical standards.

FOR FAMILIES The ⚓ **North Carolina Maritime Museum** (252-728-1638; www .ncmaritime museums.com) offers a weeklong Summer Science School for students entering grades 1–10, introducing the natural environments and maritime history of coastal North Carolina.

Beaufort Escape Room (252-772-9925; www.pctourco.com), 108 Middle Lane. Work as a group to solve the mystery and escape the room.

Beaufort Pirates Revenge (252-728-7827; www.beaufortpiratesrevenge.com), 600 Front Street. The *Revenge,* a 40-foot replica pirate ship, offers treasure cruises with sword fighting and water cannon battles, and a sunset Ghost Float with stories of pirate ghosts.

Legend of Blackbeard (252-772-9925; www.pctourco.com), 108 Middle Lane. Interactive activity for all ages brings the Age of Pirates to life on a tour across Beaufort.

GHOST TOURS **Beaufort Ghost Walk** (252-772-9925; beaufortghostwalk.com), 108 Middle Lane. On Beaufort's most popular tour, a pirate guide leads you to the Hammock House, once the residence of Blackbeard, then on to a 300-year-old cemetery for more tales of horror.

Haunted Webb Memorial (252-772-9925; www.pctourco.com), 168 S. Ninth Street at the Webb Memorial Library. Investigate the Crystal Coast's most haunted building with a paranormal investigator using professional ghost-hunting equipment.

Port City Pirates & Ghosts Tour (252-772-9925; www.pctourco.com). Tour a haunted house, learn to fight with a sword, and fire a cannon on this fun tour.

GOLF **Beaufort Club** (252-728-5525; www.beaufortclub.com), 300 Links Drive. Course designed by award-winning architect Bob Moore offers daily fee play.

KAYAKING Thanks to the many close-by islands, Beaufort is a great kayaking destination. One favorite paddle crosses **Taylor's Creek** from the town waterfront to **Carrot Island**. Several small beaches along Front Street are good for launching a kayak, including **Topsail Marine Park** at the end of Orange Street and **Fisherman's Park** at the end of Gordon Street.

A handicapped-accessible kayak and canoe put-in is located at the ♿ **Town Creek Water Access** (298 W. Beaufort Road).

Kitty Hawk Kites (252-504-2039; www.kittyhawk.com/beaufort), 412 Front Street. Kayak and SUP tours visit Taylor's Creek and the Rachel Carson Reserve. Lessons and rentals available.

PARASAILING **Beaufort Inlet Watersports** (252-728-7607; beaufortwatersports.com), 600 Front Street. Parasailing offers a bird's-eye view of the lighthouse and other area attractions.

SCUBA AND SNORKELING **Sand Dollar Island** in the Rachel Carson Reserve is a popular spot for snorkeling in the tidal pools that stretch between it and Bird Shoal.

Discovery Diving Company (252-728-2265; www.discoverydiving.com), 414 Orange Street. Full-service dive shop offers headboat trips on three dive boats to more than 30 offshore wrecks, plus lobster-hunting and spearfishing trips, classes and equipment sales, repairs, and rentals.

✳ Green Space

BEACHES The uninhabited islands that make up the **Rachel Carson Reserve**, especially **Carrot Island**, are popular beaches and are uncrowded since they are accessible only by boat. **Island Ferry Adventures** (252-728-7555; www.islandferryadventures .com) offers inexpensive ferry service to **Sand Dollar Island**, **Carrot Island**, and **Bird Shoals**. No concessions are available on any of these islands, so take a cooler, sunscreen, hats, and plenty of water along.

On the causeway between Beaufort and Morehead City, ♿ **Newport River Park** has a bathhouse, pier, sandy beach, and shallow-water boat ramp. Across US 70 is the entrance to **Radio Island**, where a popular regional beach access has a picnic area with grills, sandy beach, bathhouse, and a great view of **downtown Beaufort** and **Carrot Island** across the channel.

TRAILS ✳ **Rachel Carson National Estuarine Research Reserve Nature Trails** (252-838-0890; www.nccoastalreserve.net), Carrot Island, across from the Beaufort waterfront. Two nature trail loops introducing this unique island habitat are each about 1 mile long. Access is by boat from the northwest beach on Carrot Island. Low tide is the best time to hike. You can also hike about 1.5 miles down sandy **Bird Shoal**, with perhaps some wading. The **Carrot Island Boardwalk** is located farther east, directly across from the boat ramp at Front Street and Lennoxville Road. It leads across the island to a viewing platform that is a good spot for birding. Carrot Island is home to a small herd of feral horses.

THE WHITE SAND BEACHES OF BEAUFORT'S ISLANDS ARE PERFECT FOR WATERSPORTS OR JUST RELAXING

Sea Gate Woods Preserve (910-790-4524; www.coastallandtrust.org). Located about 8 miles west of Beaufort off NC 101, this unique habitat preserves one of the rarest community types, a nonriverine wet hardwood forest, and provides a critical feeding and nesting area for more than 25 species of migrant songbirds. Contact the Coastal Land Trust to join one of their guided walks.

✳ Lodging

CAMPGROUNDS **Coastal Riverside Campground** (252-723-0505; www.coastalriverside.com), 216 Clark Lane. Shady campground just north of the village has a 320-foot pier and a boat ramp.

HISTORIC BED & BREAKFASTS **Ann Street Inn** (1-877-266-7814; www.annstreetinn.com), 707 Ann Street. Beautifully restored 1832 house has porches lined with wicker and rocking chairs; a full hot breakfast; afternoon cocktails; and an award-winning water garden. $$$.

🍴 (ᯤ) **Cousins Bed & Breakfast** (252-728-3917 or 1-877-464-7487; www.satansbreath.com), 305 Turner Street. Three brightly decorated rooms loaded with amenities are available for guests in this casual, friendly B&B in the 1820s **Jarvis Brown House**. Downstairs, Chef Elmo whips up goodies in the kitchen, making for memorable breakfasts. There's a spice shop on-site. $$.

🍴 (ᯤ) **Pecan Tree Inn** (252-728-6733 or 1-800-728-7871; www.pecantree.com), 116 Queen Street. Relaxation and charm are the norm at the Pecan Tree, housed in a Victorian building that started life as the town's Masonic lodge back in 1866. Rock the morning away on the upstairs balcony, have a cup of tea on the wraparound front porch, or just chill out on the brick patio. The seven guest rooms are elegantly appointed with antiques. One room is pet friendly. An ample breakfast buffet is served in the dining room, with afternoon refreshments in the downstairs parlor, stocked with books of local interest. Conveniently located just a few steps from Front Street. Children under 10 cannot be accommodated. $$–$$$.

HOTELS AND INNS ♂ (ᯤ) **The Cedars Inn and Restaurant** (252-838-1463 or 1-800-548-2961; www.cedarsinn.com), 305 Front Street. Located directly on Front Street facing the water, The Cedars occupies the 1768 William Borden House. Set amid cedars and lush landscaping, the inn rents six guest rooms and suites furnished with clawfoot tubs and antiques. The Cedars is also home to the **much-acclaimed new**

THE PORCH AT THE PECAN TREE INN INVITES GUESTS TO LINGER AWHILE

Cedars Inn Restaurant (www.thecedars
innrestaurant.com), now serving dinner
and Sunday brunch. Reservations recommended. Rooms $$–$$$. Meals
$$–$$$$.

🔍 📶 **Inlet Inn** (252-728-3600 or 1-800-
554-5466; www.inlet-inn.com), 601 Front
Street. Located at the corner of Front
and Queen streets, the 36-room Inlet Inn
enjoys the best location in town. Several
fine restaurants are just across Queen
Street, the boat-tour docks lie directly
across Front Street, and all the town's
dining and shopping action is just steps
away. The three-story building has an
elevator and a top-floor lounge where
a widow's walk balcony overlooks the
waterfront. All rooms are spacious and
have private, but no-frills, baths. All
rooms have refrigerators, cable TV, hair
dryers, telephones, and coffeemakers,
and many of the first-floor rooms have
gas fireplaces. A call in the morning
brings a complimentary tray of freshly
baked muffins, bagels, and juice, plus a
newspaper, to your door. Boat slips are
available. $–$$.

HOUSEBOAT RENTALS 🐾 **Outer Banks
Houseboats** (252-728-4129; www
.outerbankshouseboats.com), 324 Front
Street. Houseboats for weekend, weekday, or full-week rentals come with a Carolina skiff for getting around. An
experienced captain pilots your houseboat to your preferred mooring place.

VACATION RENTALS **Beaufort Realty**
(1-800-548-2961; www.beaufortrlty.com),
325 Front Street. Lists cottages and condos in Beaufort, including many on the
waterfront and in the historic district.

✳ Where to Eat

DINING OUT ♿ ↬ **Aqua** (252-728-7777;
www.aquaexperience.com), 114 Middle
Lane. Seasonal menus at Aqua showcase
fresh local seafood and produce in creative combinations, and fine wines from
around the world. The menu is divided
into tapas, small plates, and large plates.
Small plates may range from a Japanese
bento box with seared yellowfin tuna and
seaweed salad to lamb lollipops. Large
plates are sturdier fare but still creative:
a fillet of choice beef rubbed with coffee,
or fresh triggerfish crusted with wild
mushrooms. The wine menu is extensive,
and a nightly "wine discovery" is available by the glass at a special price. You
can dine in the stylishly decorated contemporary dining room or outside on the
roofed patio. The whole place is quite a
contrast to the company's other restaurant, **Clawson's**, around the corner. Din-
ner only, $$–$$$$.

♿ **Beaufort Grocery Co.** (252-728-
3899; www.beaufortgrocery.com), 117
Queen Street. A casual spot for lunch,
this local favorite becomes a sophis-
ticated fine-dining experience every
evening. Executive chef/owner Charles
Park gives many creative twists to sea-
sonally changing menus. All desserts,
including a variety of cheesecakes and
a great pecan pie, are homemade. The
take-out deli counter is a great spot to
assemble a quick lunch. Lunch and Sun-
day brunch $$; dinner $$$$; extra charge
for sharing.

🎣 🍸 ↬ **Blackbeard's Grill &
Steam Bar** (252-728-3335; www
.blackbeardsgrillandsteambar.com),
1644 Live Oak Street. Diners young and
old will enjoy this pirate themed eatery
specializing in design-it-yourself pots of
steamed seafood, fresh locally sourced
fish, steaks, and burgers. Later, the specialty grogs based on rum infusions and
29 drafts start to flow in the tiki bar and
billiards room, with live music to lubri-
cate the action. Complimentary shuttle

THE *MEKA II* AT THE GALLANTS CHANNEL DOCKS

makes this an easy spot to visit. Free delivery too. Dinner $–$$$.

❄ ↬ **Blue Moon Bistro** (252-728-5800; www.bluemoonbistro.biz), 119 Queen Street. The menu at this restaurant in a historic 1827 house in the heart of downtown epitomizes the local, sustainable farm-to-fork movement. Desserts are made at the in-house bakery. Dinner only, $$–$$$$.

𝖸 ↬ **City Kitchen Restaurant and Tiki Bar at Town Creek Marina** (252-648-8141; www.facebook.com/citykitchenfoods), 232 W. Beaufort Road. This restaurant, located above the Town Creek Marina, is a great place to meet for a cocktail as the sun sets. Local seafood is featured in the daily specials, and the sunset view is great from the veranda. Diners arriving by boat can tie up at the dock. Live entertainment at the tiki bar in summer. Dinner $$–$$$.

❄ ☕ ♪ ♿ ↬ **Clawson's 1905 Restaurant & Pub** (252-728-2133; www.clawsonsrestaurant.com), 425 Front Street. This landmark on the Beaufort waterfront occupies a series of historic buildings over 100 years old. Decorated with memorabilia from the town's history and other period items, the restaurant is often crowded with tourists during the summer months. The menu ranges from seafood burgers to some excellent seafood bisque and chargrilled steak. The mud pie, made with Oreos and rocky road ice cream, is another local favorite and well worth the calories. The cozy bar is a favorite retreat among locals who know they can find the best beer selection in town here, including many North Carolina microbrews. Order a beer sampler and settle in to watch the game on the big-screen TVs. Lunch $–$$; dinner $$–$$$.

𝖸 **Front Street Grill & Rhum Bar at Stillwater** (252-728-4956; www.frontstreetgrillatstillwater.com), 300 Front Street. Casual waterfront setting meets creative cuisine in the best possible combination. The unpretentious street front belies an interior dining room lined with windows. Or have your meal beneath an umbrella on the casual Afterdeck, with unexcelled views of the harbor. Sunsets here are spectacular, and after dark the deck is romantically lit with hurricane lamps. The outdoor Rhum Bar stocks a great selection of imported rums and serves a fun, casual menu. Dock space is available for diners

The annual **Beaufort Wine and Food Festival** (www.beaufortwineandfood .org), a weeklong event held in April, has been a tremendous success in this foodie town, expanding to include a beer festival and a retail store.

arriving by boat. Lunch and Sunday brunch $-$$; dinner $$-$$$.

&c& **Spouter Inn** (252-728-5190; www.the spouterinn.com), 218 Front Street. Superb waterfront views and friendly service make this a winner for lunch or dinner. You can dine inside or out on the partially covered deck, where you may spot porpoises or the Carrot Island horses. On Sunday, a special brunch menu offers Eggs Orleans, sitting atop crabcakes, and seafood crêpes. Desserts prepared in the on-site bakery are fabulous, as is the Banana Crème Crêpe, a house specialty for over 30 years. Freshly baked breads and luscious desserts, including éclairs and napoleons, fill the bakery's display case. Dock available. Full bar. Lunch and Sunday brunch $-$$; dinner $$-$$$.

EATING OUT **No Name Pizza & Subs** (252-728-4978; www.nonamepizzaand subs.com), 408 Live Oak Street. The No Name serves much more than pizza and subs, including pasta and Greek dishes, in its dining room and at the drive-through window. Beer and wine available. Second location (252-773-0654) at 5218 US 70W in Morehead City, with delivery available. $.

Roland's Barbecue (252-728-1953; www.rolandsbarbecue.com), 1507 Live Oak Street. Stop by this top caterer for some eastern North Carolina pulled pork and ribs accompanied by Roland's famous vinegar-based sauce, or "pig out" on classic fried chicken or catfish, pork chops, shrimp, scallop or oyster burgers, and a full list of Southern-style vegetables and desserts. $.

&c& **Royal James Cafe** (252-728-4573), 117 Turner Street. Beaufort's oldest business in continuous operation is this casual spot, named after a pirate ship. Take a seat at the counter for a Southern breakfast or one of the café's signature cheeseburgers, topped with secret chili sauce. The menu features Beaufort's version of fast food: shrimp burgers, local steamed shrimp, and Down East clam chowder, all washed down by your choice from a lengthy list of beers. The bar is a local hangout and a favorite spot to "rack up" on the antique Brunswick pool tables, so expect to meet some characters if you visit late in the evening. $.

&& **The Spot Grill** (252-728-4020; www.spotgrillbeaufort.com), 202 Wellons Drive. This unassuming spot is easy to overlook, but locals have been going here for breakfast and lunch since 1950. Hand-patted burgers, Carolina reds hot dogs, and onion rings share the menu with fresh local seafood, including flounder sandwiches, shrimp burgers, and softshell crabs. The Spot is under the

CHEESEBURGER TOPPED WITH SECRET CHILI SAUCE AT THE ROYAL JAMES CAFÉ

same ownership—and shares the same local seafood, but not the same prices—as the **Southern Salt Seafood Company**, now in the Capt. Bill's location in Morehead City. $.

BEER **Mill Whistle Brewing** (252-342-6929; www.facebook.com/MillWhistle Brewing), 1354 Lennoxville Road. Carteret County's first microbrewery produces just one barrel at a time of small-batch beers in a variety of styles. Located on site of the historic **Safrit Lumber Mill**, the brewery blows the original shift-change whistle every day at 4:45. Call for tap room hours.

CANDY AND ICE CREAM **The Fudge Factory** (252-728-6202; www.thefudge factory.com), 400 Front Street, Somerset Square. Old-fashioned handmade fudge, ice cream, and frozen yogurt available overlooking the docks.

❋ **The General Store** (252-728-7707; www.beaufortgeneralstore.com), 515 Front Street. Carries 32 flavors of ice cream, fudge made in-house, plus souvenirs and gifts. Out back you'll find a coin laundry, great for campers or boaters. Closed Sundays.

COFFEE AND WINE **Beaufort Wine and Food** (252-515-0708; www .beaufortwineandfood.org), 129 Middle Lane. This store features Beaufort Wine and Food private label Bordeaux wines as well as many of the wines poured at the annual Beaufort Wine and Food events.

𝖸 (ᵗᵖ) **Cru Wine Bar and Beaufort Coffee Shop** (252-728-3066; www .beaufortcru.com), 120 Turner Street. Comfortable, sophisticated shop sells wine by the bottle or glass, along with a light menu. Draft beers and cocktails also available at the bar. The coffee shop featuring artisan chocolate made in Beaufort is just through the archway, serving breakfast sandwiches and baked goods. Locals love this place for the live music several nights a week. $.

WINE, CHEESE, AND CHUTNEY AT THE CRU WINE BAR

MARKETS ♂ **Chandlery at Front Street Village** (252-838-1524; www.frontstreet village.com), 2400 Lennoxville Road. This ship's store, located next to the boathouse at Front Street Village, has a huge selection of boutique wines and ice-cold beers, along with gourmet groceries, fishing supplies, outdoor gear, and souvenirs.

⬩ **Coastal Community Market** (252-728-2844; www.coastalcommunity market.com), 606 Broad Street. Earth-friendly store carries locally grown and organic produce; dried fruits, wines, and soy products; locally baked bread; and free-range eggs.

⬩ **Fishtowne Seafood Center** (252-728-6644; www.fishtowneseafood.com), 100 Wellons Drive. Certified Carteret Catch retailer sells locally sourced fish and shellfish, including conch meat, raw oysters, blue crabs, and clams.

Martha's Spices and Gifts (1-877-464-7487; www.satansbreath.com), 305 Turner Street. Stock up on Chef Elmo's award-winning hot sauces, spice blends, and handmade sausages.

✳ Entertainment

LIVE MUSIC CLUBS ✳ 🐾 ♈ **Backstreet Pub** (252-728-7108; www.facebook.com/TheBackstreetPub), 124 Middle Lane. Cool little spot behind Clawson's features a big wine list, cold beer, and live music year-round. No food here—unless it's free. Check out the upstairs lending library.

♈ **Dock House Restaurant & Bar** (252-728-4506), 500 Front Street. This landmark on the docks serves up daily live music on the boardwalk during the summer season. The inside is quite small, but you can get some pub grub or a big mug of coffee and breakfast with a view in the upstairs lounge.

Hannah's Haus (252-728-3757; www.facebook.com/hannahshaus), 900 Live Oak Street. Fun pub inside old Gaskill's Hardware (now part of Lennoxville Commons) has 16 beers on tap, live music, darts, ping-pong, and TVs tuned to sports.

Queen Anne's Revenge (252-504-7272; www.facebook.com/QARBeaufort), 510 Front Street. Choose a beverage from the huge selection of craft beers and wines, then enjoy it on the covered deck along with some sunset music and views of the docks.

Additional spots to hear live music in Beaufort include the **Cru Wine Bar, City Kitchen at Town Creek Marina, Front Street Grill, Royal James Cafe,** and **Blackbeard's Grill.**

✳ Selective Shopping

On Beaufort's historic Front Street, a multitude of nautically themed shops carry everything you might need for a life at sea, from books and charts, to Bloody Mary mix, to shipboard cat and dog accessories.

ANTIQUES **Marketplace Antiques and Collectibles** (252-728-2325), 131 Turner Street. Dozens of dealers display estate

THE DOCK HOUSE FRONTING ON THE BOARDWALK HOSTS SUNSET MUSIC MOST NIGHTS

BEAUFORT'S FRONT STREET, FACING THE HARBOR, IS THE SCENE OF DINING, SHOPPING, AND FESTIVALS

pieces from local and New Orleans families, plus a fun selection of folk art, at this indoor flea mall.

Taylor's Creek Antiques & Collectibles (252-728-2275), 513 Front Street. Get a peek inside an old Beaufort mansion while shopping for vintage furniture, china, and bottles.

ART GALLERIES **Craving Art Studio** (252-728-024; www.cravingartstudio .com), 121 Craven Street. Artist Heather Sink invites you to visit her studio in this historic home.

Handscapes Gallery (252-728-6805; www.handscapesgallery.com), 410 Front Street. Exquisite selection of pottery, jewelry, art glass, and works in other media created by more than 200 artists across the nation. Special section of Banker pony–themed art.

Mattie King Davis Art Gallery (252-728-5225; www.beauforthistoricsite .org), 130 Turner Street. Occupying the 1732 **Rustell House** on the grounds of the Beaufort Historic Site, this gallery displays juried works by over 100 local and regional artists.

SPECIAL SHOPS **Jarrett Bay Boathouse** (252-728-6363; www.jarrettbay.com/

boathouse), 507 Front Street. Retail store of a local boatbuilder carries classic yachting garb, plus gifts and Jarrett Bay–commissioned art and prints.

Old Beaufort Shop (252-728-5225; www.beauforthistoricsite.org), 130 Turner Street. Shop at the Beaufort Historic Site stocks history-related gifts and toys, as well as books on local and regional history.

❄ 🐾 **Seagrass Whimsical Gift Shop** (252-728-2775), 519 Front Street. Fun shop that welcomes dogs offers a wide variety of fun clothing and accessories, plus local art, books, and handmade decor. Upstairs, a Christmas shop carries unique holiday decorations.

Tierra Fina (252-504-2789 or 1-877-504-2789; www.tierrafinanc.com), 415 Front Street. Bright and bold ceramics from around the world, including popular Spanish ceramic house-number tiles.

❄ Special Events

Check the **Crystal Coast visitors website** (www.crystalcoastnc.org) for an updated list of events during your stay.

April: **Beaufort Wine and Food Weekend** (www.beaufortwineandfood.org).

Five-day event includes wine and food tastings, seminars, dinners, art shows, and more.

🔖 **Easter Egg Hunt** (www .beauforthistoricsite.org), Beaufort Historic Site. Free event for children seven and under.

Publick Day (www.beauforthistoric site.org), Beaufort Historic Site. Colonial-style flea market and period children's games. Free.

Whales and Whaling Symposium (www.ncmaritimemuseum.org), North Carolina Maritime Museum.

May: **Beaufort Music Festival** (www .beaufortmusicfestival.com). A weekend of free music and family fun featuring national and local performers.

Wooden Boat Show (www.ncmaritime museum.org), North Carolina Maritime Museum. Free.

June: **Beaufort Old Homes & Gardens Tour** (www.beauforthistoricsite.org), Beaufort Historic Site.

Maritime Day (www.maritimefriends .org), Gallants Channel, 172 W. Beaufort Road. Music, old-fashioned picnic, and rides aboard wooden boats at this free festival.

July: **Barta Boys & Girls Club Billfish Tournament and Art Show** (252-808-2286; www.bartabillfish.com), Beaufort Docks.

Carteret County Arts and Crafts Coalition Art Show (www.ccartsandcrafts .com), outdoor art show held on the Beaufort Historic Site grounds.

Independence Day Parade on Front Street followed by **July 4th Fireworks** at Gallants Channel. (www.beinbeaufort .com).

Spanish Mackerel & Dolphin Fishing Tournament (www.carteretsmt.com), The Boathouse at **Front Street Village** (www .frontstreetvillage.com); 2400 Lennoxville Road. Family fishing tournament benefits Carteret Community College.

August: **Beaufort Pirate Invasion** (252-728-3917; www.beaufortpirateinvasion

.com). Captain Sinbad fires on the town docks, then invades with his buccaneer crew for a weekend of feasting, dancing, and other pirate merriment.

September: **Beaufort's Brewin'** (www .beaufortwineandfood.org). Annual beer festival features regional crafts.

October: **Beaufort Historical Association Fall Gala and Art Show** (www .beauforthistoricsite.org).

November: **Community Thanksgiving Feast** (www.beauforthistoricsite.org).

Beaufort Food & Wine Oyster Roast (www.beaufortwineandfood.org).

December: **Beaufort Holiday Art-Walk and Historic Beaufort Candlelight Homes Tour** (www.beauforthistoricsite .org).

Christmas Parade and Tree Lighting on Front Street (www.beinbeaufort.com).

Crystal Coast Christmas Flotilla (www.maritimefriends.org). Decorated boats parade along the Beaufort and Morehead City waterfronts.

PIRATES, READY TO INVADE

MOREHEAD CITY AND NEWPORT

J ust across the bridge from Beaufort lies the commercial center of Morehead City, one of North Carolina's two deepwater state ports. The adjacent waterfront area is home to an active charter fishing fleet, as well as seafood restaurants and markets featuring fish fresh from the sea. Several of these, including the **Sanitary Fish Market** and **Captain Bill's**, have been in operation since before World War II and are landmarks along the coast. The town is a center for marine research as well, with several government and university facilities.

The tracks of Governor Morehead's railroad run right down the center of the town's main drag, **Arendell Street**, US 70. Many of Morehead City's attractions, restaurants, and shops lie along either side.

GUIDANCE The ❀ ☙ **Visitor Center for Carteret County and the Crystal Coast** (252-726-8148; www.crystalcoastnc.org) at 3409 Arendell Street in Morehead City has helpful counselors and lots of local information, as well as restrooms, a boat ramp, and a pleasant picnic area overlooking Bogue Sound.

THE CRYSTAL COAST VISITOR CENTER PROVIDES A FREE BOAT RAMP FOR VISITORS

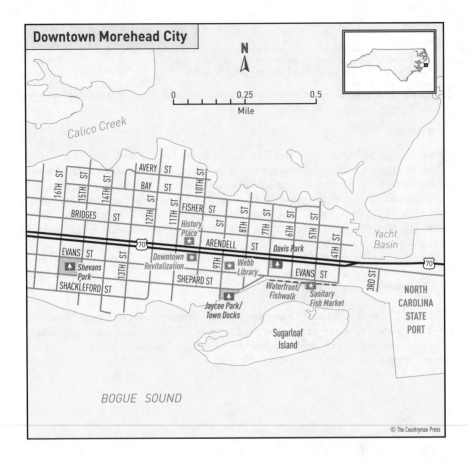

The Downtown Morehead City Revitalization Association (252-808-0440; www
.downtownmoreheadcity.com), 1001 Arendell Street, Morehead City. Visitor center
housed in a historic 1904 train depot has information on Morehead City's history, maps
of the historic downtown, and other info.

Morehead City Town Hall (252-726-6848; www.moreheadcitync.org), 706 Arendell
Street, Morehead City.

Carteret County Chamber of Commerce (252-726-6350 or 1-800-622-6278; www
.nccoastchamber.com), 801 Arendell Street, Morehead City.

POST OFFICE The **Morehead City U.S. Post Office** (252-726-0920) is at 3500 Bridges
Street. The zip code in Morehead City is 28557.

The **Newport U.S. Post Office** (252-223-4638) is at 460 Howard Boulevard. The zip
code in Newport is 28570.

PUBLIC RESTOOMS Public facilities in Morehead City are found at the Crystal Coast
visitor center, 3409 Arendell Street; the community center, 1600 Fisher Street; and the
Downtown Morehead City visitor center, 1001 Arendell.

PUBLIC LIBRARY ✄ ♂ ☂ ((•)) **The Webb Library** (252-726-3012; www.thewebblibrary
.com), 812 Evans Street. Morehead City's historic library makes a good rainy-day

destination. The **Kids' Room** has many books for young children, plus games and computers filtered for appropriate content. The **Sports, Exploration, and Adventure (S.E.A.) Room** displays artifacts from local shipwrecks and contains documents of interest to historians, boaters, and divers.

GETTING THERE US 70 enters Morehead City from the west, becoming Arendell Street and running straight down the center of town and over the causeway to Beaufort. NC 24 follows the shore of Bogue Sound east from Swansboro and Cape Carteret, joining US 70 at a major intersection.

The downtown section of Newport lies along US 70 north of Morehead City, while another, unconnected, section of Newport, often called Ocean, lies along NC 24 and the shores of Bogue Sound. The **Croatan National Forest** lies just beyond the development on the north side of NC 24 from Morehead City to Cape Carteret.

GETTING AROUND The waterfront area in Morehead City's downtown is fun to walk around in, strolling along the waterfront to see the fishing fleet, poking around in the area's shops, then checking out the bars and restaurants that line Arendell Street just a block or two away.

MEDICAL EMERGENCY **Carteret General Hospital** (252-499-6000; www.carteret health.org), 3500 Arendell Street, Morehead City. Full-service hospital offers inpatient, outpatient, and emergency services 24 hours a day all year.

✳ To See

ARCHITECTURE The **Morehead City Historic District**, running along Fisher and Bridges streets, is a mix of Victorian mansions and Craftsman bungalows. Between 10th and 12th streets, the area known as the **Promise Land** has cottages in the Banker style, some of them ferried across Bogue Sound after hurricanes in the 1890s. The **Downtown Morehead City Revitalization Association** (see *Guidance*) sponsors an annual Homes and Heritage Tour every May.

ART **The Fish Walk**, a series of bas-relief sculptures created by local artists Keith Lambert and Willie Baucom of **Shipyard Earthworks Studio** (252-241-2613; www.shipyardearthworks.com) celebrating the region's fishing heritage, runs along the city's boardwalk beginning at S. Fourth and Arendell, ending at S. Seventh and Shepard. There the new **Jib Plaza** features a triangular fountain topped by a 17-foot statue of a leaping marlin, celebrating the **Big Rock Blue Marlin Tournament's** new home.

A SERIES OF SCULPTURES ALONG THE MOREHEAD CITY WATERFRONT MAKE UP THE FISH WALK

EXCURSIONS
NEW BERN—NORTH CAROLINA'S COLONIAL CAPITAL

New Bern, located at the junction of US 17 and US 70 about 40 miles from Morehead City, is one of the oldest towns in North Carolina and a must for history buffs, the capital of the colony at the outbreak of the **Revolutionary War.** **Tryon Palace** (www.tryonpalace.org), the home of royal governor William Tryon, a magnificent Georgian structure designed by architect John Hawks, has been reconstructed based on the original 1767 plans and archaeological evidence, and its 16 acres of gardens replanted in the Colonial Revival style. A one-day pass includes admission to the palace, plus three nearby historic houses, the surrounding gardens, the **New Bern Academy Museum**, and the **North Carolina History Center**. The objects on display in the palace and other buildings are considered one of the top 10 collections of American and European decorative arts in the United States. Other sights to visit in the city include **the soda fountain where Pepsi-Cola was invented, now a museum** (www.pepsistore.com). Walking and trolley tours visit colonial and Civil War sites in the historic downtown. Watch for the numerous bear mascots that dot the town. The **city's website** (www.visitnewbern.com) has more options and info.

ONE OF THE MANY BEAR MASCOTS FOUND ALL OVER NEW BERN

TRYON PALACE, HOME OF NORTH CAROLINA'S LAST ROYAL GOVERNOR, WAS RECONSTRUCTED FROM THE ORIGINAL 1767 PLANS

The Arts Council of Carteret County (252-726-9156; www.artscouncilcarteret.org), 812 Evans Street, Morehead City, sponsors changing exhibits of artwork in local businesses. Consult the website or visit the Arts Council gallery for the latest art news.

More local art can be found at the **Morehead City Curb Market** (www.facebook .com/MoreheadCityCurbMarket), 13th & Evans Streets, open on Saturday mornings from May to October, with special markets throughout the year.

✒ ♿ ⬆ **History Museum of Carteret County** (252-247-7533; www.carterethistory .org), 1008 Arendell Street, Morehead City. Open Tuesday–Friday 10–4. Operated by the Carteret County Historical Society, this is a museum of both history and art. Exhibits explore the history and traditions of the region, including menhaden fishing, duck hunting, the first yacht club, the railroad, the porcelain dolls of Sally Beatty, and artifacts relating to local Confederate spy Miss Emeline Pigott.

North Carolina Coastal Federation (252-393-8185; www.nccoast.org), 3609 NC 24, Newport. Nonprofit sponsors many conservation and coastal restoration projects. The headquarters building is open to the public and houses exhibits explaining the organization's programs, plus an exhibit of some 15,000 shells, a library dedicated to works and videos on nature and conservation, and a shop with eco-friendly books and gifts for all ages. The **Patsy Pond Nature Trail** is located directly across the street.

North Carolina State Port (252-726-3158; www.ncports.com), 113 Arendell Street, Morehead City. Groups can schedule tours in advance by contacting communications@ncports.com. Free tours are also offered during the annual North Carolina Seafood Festival. Adults must show photo ID upon entry.

✒ **Outer Banks Wildlife Shelter** (252-240-1200; www.outerbankswildlifeshelter .com), 100 Wildlife Way, off NC 24, Newport. Tours of the OWLS hospital that cares for injured, sick, and orphaned wild animals are offered for a small fee. A nature trail leads to outdoor exhibits on the grounds.

Sugarloaf Island, off the downtown Morehead City waterfront. Easily visible across the water from the downtown boardwalk, this uninhabited island belongs to the Town of Morehead City. There are boat docks, a bathhouse with restrooms, and a nature trail on the island. You can reach Sugarloaf by ferry, private boat, or kayak.

University of North Carolina Institute of Marine Sciences (252-726-6841; ims.unc .edu), 3431 Arendell Street, Morehead City. Free seminars on marine topics offered weekly during the school year.

✳ To Do

BICYCLING The **Morehead Alternative Transportation System (MATS)**, a multiuse trail for bikes and pedestrians, runs along Bridges Road between Country Club Road and North 35th Street in Morehead City, connecting with the Calico Creek Boardwalk and the Rotary Park Fitness Trail.

Bike rentals are available from **EJW Outdoors** (252-247-4725; www.ejwoutdoors .com), 4667Arendell Street, Morehead City.

BOATING ♿ **North Carolina Wildlife Intracoastal Waterway Boat Ramp** (www.nc wildlife.org), 3407 Arendell Street, Morehead City. Facility behind the Crystal Coast visitor center has restrooms and a shady picnic area.

South 10th Street Water Access and Boat Ramp (252-726-5083; www.morehead citync.org), 1001 Shepard Street, Morehead City. City-operated facility has parking, a pier, and a boat ramp for boats up to 16 feet.

Morehead City Docks (252-726-7678; www.moreheadcitync.org), 807 Shepard Street. Transient slips at S. Ninth Street, adjacent to Jaycee Park, in the heart of the downtown action.

(ᵗᵖ) **Morehead City Yacht Basin** (252-726-6862 or 1-888-726-6292; www.morehead cityyachtbasin.com), 208 Arendell Street, Morehead City. Transient slips at the foot of the causeway to Beaufort.

Portside Marina (252-726-7678; www.portsidemarina.com), 209 Arendell Street, Morehead City. Harbor tours, Carolina skiff rentals, transient slips, and a ship's store, plus ferries to Sugarloaf Island.

BOAT TOURS AND RENTALS **Morehead City Ferry Service** (252-504-2488; www .moreheadcityferryservice.com), 709 Shepard Street, downtown Morehead City. Ferry service to Sand Dollar Island for a day of shelling sails with the tide. Marine encounter and sunset cruises also available.

✎ *Good Fortune* **Coastal Ecology Charters** (252-241-6866; www.goodfortunesails .com), Peltier Creek Marina, Morehead City. During the summer season, this 41-foot yacht sails on coastal ecology charters conducted by biologist Ron White. Cruises may include snorkeling, shelling, bird and dolphin watching, and kayaking.

FISHING PIERS Public fishing piers are located all along the downtown Morehead City waterfront, at the north ends of Seventh and 11th streets and the south ends of Ninth and 10th streets. You'll need a North Carolina Coastal Recreational Fishing License if you are 16 years old or over.

FITNESS CENTER **Morehead City Community Center** (252-726-5083; www .moreheadcitync.org), 1600 Fisher Street, Morehead City. Nonresident passes are available at this city facility, offering a wide range of exercise classes and a fully equipped fitness room.

FOR FAMILIES ✎ **The Morehead City Parks and Recreation Department** (252-726-5083; www.moreheadcity.nc.gov) sponsors a summer camp program for children ages 3–15.

✎ **Sea of Dreams public playground**, designed by kids for kids, is located at **Shev-ans Park** (252-726-5083; www.moreheadcitync.org) at 16th and Evans streets in More-head City.

GOLF **Brandywine Bay Golf Club** (252-247-2541; www.brandywinegolf.com), 224 Brandywine Boulevard, Morehead City. Award-winning semiprivate course.

The Golf Farm (252-223-3276; www.facebook.com/thegolffarm), 612 Tom Mann Road, Newport. Driving range set amid old-growth pines offers lessons and clinics with LPGA pro Nina Foust. Special days for ladies, seniors, and military.

HEADBOAT FISHING *Carolina Princess* (252-726-5479 or 1-800-682-3456; www .carolinaprincess.com), 604 Evans Street, Sixth Street Waterfront, Morehead City. Full- and half-day trips to the edge of the Gulf Stream. For hard-core fishers, the *Princess* also offers an 18-hour bottom-fishing marathon.

KAYAKING The most popular paddle in Morehead City is out to uninhabited **Sugar-loaf Island**, just off the downtown waterfront, where visitors can enjoy a nature trail, floating dock, and restrooms. A great spot for a picnic.

Numerous launch sites are located all along the southern waterfront of **Morehead City** (252-726-5083; www.moreheadcitync.org). Popular spots to put in include **Conchs Point** (608 Bay Street), **South Sixth Street Day Docks** (S. Sixth and Evans), the small sandy beach at the **South 11th Street canoe launch** (S. 11th and Shepard), and **South 13th Street Boardwalk and Dock** (S. 13th and Shackleford).

SNORKELING AND SCUBA DIVING **Olympus Dive Center** (252-726-9432; www .olympusdiving.com), 713 Shepard Street, Morehead City. Three dive boats docked at the Morehead City waterfront next to a full-service dive shop offer day and night dives to the area's many wrecks, lobster and spearfishing charters, and popular shark dives. A diver's lodge nearby provides inexpensive bunk rooms.

SURFING **Action Surf Shop** (252-240-1818; www.actionsurf.com), 4130 Arendell Street, Morehead City. Surfboards hand-shaped on-site by owner Bob Webb, plus skateboards, motocross, and accessories.

TENNIS Lighted tennis courts are found in Morehead City at **Swinson Park** (252-808-3301; www.ccparksrec.com), 4319 Country Club Road, and **Shevans Park** (252-726-5083; www.moreheadcitync.org), 16th and Evans streets. In Newport, **Fort Benjamin** (252-808-3301; www.ccparksrec.com), 100 McQueen Avenue, has lighted courts, plus a walking trail, shuffleboard, playground, band shell, and restroom.

✳ Green Space

Croatan National Forest (252-638-5628; www.fs.usda.gov/nfsnc), 141 E. Fisher Avenue, New Bern. The 160,000-acre forest is the natural habitat of carnivorous plants such as the Venus flytrap and pitcher plant. Numerous recreational opportunities include camping, hiking, mountain biking, fishing, paddling, and swimming. Two of the forest's campgrounds have hookups for RVs. Primitive camping is also available at numerous sites. The 21-mile **Neusiok Trail** for hikers runs across the forest; other trails include the **Pine Cliff Equestrian Trail** and the **Black Swamp OHV Trail. Flanners Beach on the Neuse River** is a popular spot for freshwater swimming. Other areas of interest within the forest include **Fisher's Landing**, off US 70, site of the 1862 Battle of New Bern and a historic CCC camp; and **Long Point Recreation Area** on the White Oak River, once the site of a large Native American village. The Croatan ranger station, with maps and further information, is on US 70, about 10 miles south of New Bern and 30 miles north of Morehead City.

TRAILS **Neusiok Trail** (252-638-5628; www.neusioktrail.org), Croatan National Forest. The 20.4-mile Neusiok Trail, running between the Neuse and Newport rivers, features carnivorous plants and cypress wetlands. Primitive camping is allowed at three camping shelters along the trail and at other undeveloped sites.

OWLS Nature Trail (252-240-1200; www.outerbankswildlifeshelter.com), 100 Wildlife Way, Newport. Half-mile loop passes 40 labeled plant species, a duck pond, raptor enclosures, and interactive exhibits. In-depth guided tours of the wildlife shelter are offered Tuesday, Thursday, and Saturday for a small fee.

KING NEPTUNE PRESIDES OVER THE MOREHEAD CITY WATERFRONT AND ITS MANY FESTIVALS

Patsy Pond Nature Trail (252-393-8185; www.nccoast.org), 3609 NC 24, Newport. The trailhead for this easy 3.7-mile hike through longleaf pines is on NC 24 between Morehead City and Cape Carteret, across from the North Carolina Coastal Federation. Maps and restrooms available at the federation office.

Sugarloaf Island Nature Trail (252-726-5083; www.moreheadcitync.org). Located across from the Morehead City waterfront and accessible only by boat.

WALKS **Calico Creek Boardwalk** (252-726-5083; www.moreheadcitync.org), N. 19th and Bay streets to N. 22th Street, Morehead City. Easy mile-long walk with good bird-watching opportunities. Restrooms at community center, 1600 Fisher Street.

Fish Walk (252-808-0440; www.downtownmoreheadcity.com). Stroll along the Morehead City Waterfront Boardwalk, beginning at Fourth Street and Evans, to see 12 glazed plaques depicting sea life species common to the area.

Promise Land Waterfront Walk (252-808-0440; www.downtownmoreheadcity .com). Easy 2.3-mile fitness heritage trail leads from Morehead City Park along Bogue Sound through a neighborhood where many of the houses were ferried over from Shackleford Banks. Maps and restrooms are available at the office of the **Morehead City Downtown Revitalization Association** at 811 Arendell Street.

Rotary Park Exercise Trail (252-726-5083; www.moreheadcitync.org), 2200 Mayberry Loop Road, Morehead City. This 0.89-mile loop with fitness stations circles Rotary Park and Big Rock Stadium.

✳ Lodging

Morehead City is the home of numerous national chain hostelries, including **Econo Lodge, Budget Inn, Hampton Inn, Comfort Inn, Quality Inn,** and **Holiday Inn Express and Suites.**

CAMPGROUNDS ♿ **Neuse River Campground in the Croatan National Forest** (252-638-5628; www.fs.usda.gov/ nfsnc), located off US 70, has 40 sites, 24 with electric hookups, flush toilets, warm showers, drinking water, and a dump station. Sites are first come, first served. A stairway leads down to sandy **Flanners Beach,** a popular spot for swimming and picnicking. A **handicapped-accessible paved path** circles the campground, and the longer **Beede Loop Trail,** for hiking or mountain biking, runs on a boardwalk through a tupelo swamp. $.

✻ ✦ **Oyster Point Campground in the Croatan National Forest** (252-638-5628; www.fs.usda.gov/nfsnc), FR 181 off SR 1154, Newport. Tent and dry RV campground along the Newport River has 16 campsites, handicapped-accessible restrooms, drinking water, and a shallow-water launch for kayaks and canoes. This is the southern trailhead for the 21-mile-long **Neusiok Trail** and also a popular spot to rake for oysters. $.

✻ **Water's Edge RV Park** (252-247-0494 or 252-247-0709; www.watersedgenorthcarolina.com), 1463 NC 24, Newport. Campers enjoy full hookups, a pier on Bogue Sound, paddleboats, kayaks, and planned activities.

✻ ✿ **Whispering Pines RV Park and Campground** (252-726-4902; www.wprvpark.com), 25 Whispering Pines Road, Newport. Situated amid tall pines, full-hookup RV and tent sites include access to a large pool and a freshwater fishing pond.

✻ Where to Eat

DINING OUT ✎ ♈ **Floyd's 1921 Restaurant** (252-727-1921; www.floyds1921.com), 400 Bridges Street, Morehead City. Chef/owner Floyd Olmstead serves dishes inspired by, but not limited to, traditional Southern cuisine in this historic house built in 1921. Favorites include the fried green tomato and mozzarella stack, Grandma's deviled eggs, and the Lowcountry meat loaf. The popular patio features live music, fire pits, and a menu of tapas. Lunch $; dinner $$–$$$$.

✎ ✦ ♈ **Sanitary Fish Market Restaurant** (252-247-3111; www.sanitaryfishmarket.com), 501 Evans Street, Morehead City. A landmark on the Morehead City waterfront since 1938, when the first 12-seat counter opened in the fish market here, Sanitary now seats 600, plus new expanded outdoor seating, but waits can be long when the tour buses roll in. Lunch features fish sandwiches, shrimp and oyster burgers,

plus salads made of shrimp and fresh tuna. This is a good place to sample some of the more unfamiliar fish favored by locals, such as bluefish, jumping mullet, spots, wahoo, king mackerel, or mahi-mahi, all available in-season. The hush puppies here are famous: you can buy a bag of mix to take home. The **Tall Tales Pub** hosts live music. Overnight moorage available at the dock. Lunch and dinner $–$$$.

✎ ✦ ♈ ✦ **Southern Salt Seafood Company** (252-499-9528; www.southernsaltseafood.com), 701 Evans Street, Morehead City. The venerable Capt. Bill's, oldest restaurant on the Morehead City waterfront, returns in a new incarnation, still serving the freshest local seafood, available steamed, broiled, blackened, or fried, and carrying on the tradition of making everything from scratch. New owner Sammy Boyd, who also operates **Sammy's Seafood House**

THE SANITARY FISH MARKET BEGAN SERVING THE FRESHEST SEAFOOD IN 1938

and Oyster Bar (252-648-8399; www
.sammysseafoodhouse.com) nearby
at 109 Sixth Street, has renovated the
dining area and expanded the bar area,
which now hosts live music, including
many big-name regional bands. The
oysters are shucked in cold water, and
you can taste the difference. Lunch and
dinner $$–$$$.

EATING OUT ✐ **Beach Bumz Pub & Pizzeria** (252-726-7800; www.beachbumzpub
.com), 515 Arendell Street, Morehead City.
Located at the corner of Arendell and
Sixth streets in the downtown district,
this casual spot is a great place for a quick
bite and a beer before or after a fishing
trip or a visit to Sugarloaf Island. $.

✐ **Grumpy's** (252-726-5100; www
.grumpysmorehead.com), 907-A Arendell Street. Longtime local favorite for
breakfast skillets, omelets, and hand-
patted burgers. $.

Promise Land Market (252-222-0422;
www.promiselandmarket.com), 909-B
Arendell Street. Specialty grocery offers
an all-day menu of house-made salads,
sandwiches, and snacks, plus charcuterie
platters and a tempting Sunday brunch.
Check out the expanded seating in the
back bar. $–$$.

❄ ↝ **Ruddy Duck Tavern** (252-726-
7500; www.ruddyducktavern.com), 509
Evans Street, Morehead City. Casual
waterfront spot in the original Sanitary
Fish Market building serves a wide variety of creative cuisine, much of it with a
spicy twist, from seafood-laden jambalaya to crispy duck to the ever-popular
fish taco. You can eat outside on a deck
overlooking Bogue Sound. Local produce
is featured, and much of the seafood
comes off the owner's boat. Full bar. $–$$.

Shuckin' Shack Oyster Bar (252-222-
3811; www.theshuckinshack.com), 707
Arendell Street. A native of the North
Carolina coast, this concept is spreading
fast, with franchises in several states.
And why not? Sports pub atmosphere?
Check. Great cocktails with funny
names? Check. Fresh local seafood?

Check. The menu is creative in a way
that seafood usually isn't, with sampler
platters, lobster rolls, crabcake sliders,
and its own version of surf and turf (oysters or shrimp with wings). Try the oyster
sampler with local crustaceans served
three different ways (raw, steamed, and
chargrilled).

BEACH FAST FOOD **El's Drive-In** (252-
726-3002; www.elsdrivein.com), 3706
Arendell Street, Morehead City. Family-
owned fast food joint, home of the original Superburger, has been serving since
1959. Waitresses deliver burgers, barbecue, shrimp burgers, rootbeer floats, and
more right to your car, or you can eat at a
shady picnic table. Open late. $.

COFFEE AND SWEETS **The Infusion
Cafe** (252-240-2800; www.facebook
.com/TheInfusionCafe), 1012 Arendell
Street, Morehead City. Elegant tearoom
next door to the history museum stocks
more than 120 whole-leaf and herbal
teas, single-origin coffees, and other
infusions from around the world, and
serves light lunches, desserts, and afternoon tea with scones and savories. Make
reservations in advance for a formal high
tea, served 2–4 PM. Live acoustic music is
scheduled most weekend evenings. $.

ELEGANT TEA ROOM NEXT TO THE HISTORY MUSEUM
OFFERS HIGH TEA BY RESERVATION

Slice Bakery (252-726-2253; www
.alexandbretts.com), 513 Arendell Street,
Morehead City. Sweet spot in downtown
Morehead City features delicious pastries, both savory and sweet, baked on
the premises. Try the tomato pie, a local
delicacy.

((ŋ)) ¥ **Sweet Beans Coffee & Café**
(252-247-6020; www.facebook.com/
sweetbeanscafe), 2302-G Arendell Street,
Morehead City. Internet hotspot has a
full menu of coffee and tea drinks, a nice
selection of sandwiches, and open mic
nights.

HEALTHY MEALS ↬ **Akai Hana** (252-
222-3272; www.akaihana.com), 909
Arendell Street. This full-service Japanese restaurant is a member of Carteret
Catch, using the freshest local seafood
for sushi rolls, nigiri, and sashimi.
Lunch features unique sushi burritos
wrapped in soy paper. The dinner menu
includes teriyaki, tempura, and noodle
dishes. Many vegetarian and vegan
options are available. Lunch $–$$; din-
ner $$–$$$.

MARKETS **Morehead City Curb Market**
(978-621-5436; www.facebook.com/
MoreheadCityCurbMarket), 1213 Evans
Street, Morehead City. Shop for local produce, fresh seafood, flowers, and baked
goods at the oldest continuously operating curb market in North Carolina from
7:30 to noon Saturday from May to Labor
Day. A demonstration garden is located
next door.

🐚 **Beaufort Olive Oil Company** (252-
222-3414; www.beaufortoliveoil.com),
413 Evans Street, Morehead City. Locally
owned store stocks carefully selected
olive oils, vinegars, and salts, plus local
culinary treats, all available for tasting.
Owner-chef Clarke Merrell looms large
on the local culinary scene, with three
other locations of his Olive Oil Company
in Beaufort, Swansboro, and Emerald
Isle, as well as his tapas bar, **Circa 81**
(www.circa-81.com) in downtown Morehead City, and his food truck, the **Dank**

Burrito (www.thedankburrito.com), so
popular that Merrell has expanded to
permanent locations in both Morehead
City and on the Beaufort waterfront.

SEAFOOD MARKET ↬ **Captain Jim's
Seafood** (252-726-3454; www.captjims
seafood.com), 4665 Arendell Street,
Morehead City. The motto here is, "If it
swims, we've got it." A certified Carteret
Catch (www.carteretcatch.org) retailer.

WINE AND BEER **Lake Road Winery**
(252-622-0930; www.lakeroadwinery
.com), 1120 Lake Road. Winery in Newport specializes in wines made from
North Carolina fruits and berries. Wine
tastings available.

Somerset Cellars Winery (252-
725-0029 or 252-727-4800; www
.somersetcellars.com), 3906 Arendell
Street, Morehead City. The Crystal
Coast's first federally bonded winery
offers tours and tastings. Nearly two
dozen private label wines are made
on-site from imported grapes and juice at
this well-hidden spot downtown.

¥ **Tight Lines Pub & Brewing Co.**
(252-773-0641; www.tightlinesbrewing
.com), 709 Arendell Street. Local brewery
offers 30 beers on tap, including several
of their own crafts. Try the Bogue Sound
Watermelon seasonal for a real taste of
the Crystal Coast. Fun beer pub menu
and live music make this a winner.

✱ Entertainment

Spots to look for live entertainment in
Morehead City and Newport include
Floyd's 1921 Restaurant, the Infusion
Cafe, Southern Salt Seafood Company,
the Tall Tales Pub at Sanitary Fish Mar-
ket, Tight Lines Pub & Brewing Co., and
Sweet Beans Coffee & Café.

CONCERT SERIES **American Music
Festival** (252-728-6152; www.american
musicfestival.org). Chamber music
series sponsors performances by top

regional and national artists in Morehead City from September to May.

Carteret Arts Forum (252-354-5537; www.carteretartsforum.com). Annual subscription series brings professional music and theatrical performances to the Crystal Coast. Individual tickets $35.

Down East Folk Arts Society Concert Series (252-412-1703; www.downeast folkarts.org). Folk and roots music concerts are held September to May at Joslyn Hall at Carteret Community College in Morehead City and at Trent River Coffee Company in New Bern.

FILMS **CCCF International Film Series** (www.carteret.edu/foundation), Joslyn Hall, on the Carteret Community College campus, 3505 Arendell Street, Morehead City. Series of four foreign films are preceded by live music and refreshments. The Dinner and a Movie option includes a dinner themed on the nationality of the film served in the historic Camp Glenn Building on campus. Reservations required (252-222-6056).

MUSIC AND THEATER **Carteret Community Theatre** (252-497-8919; www .carteretcommunitytheatre.com), 1311 Arendell Street. Amateur theatrical group with an impressive 50-year history mounts an average of three productions each year, including musicals and children's plays, and hosts music concerts and other events in its 500-seat theater.

Crystal Coast Choral Society (910-324-6864; www.crystalcoastchoral society.org). This chorus of 70 voices, recently guest artists at New York's Carnegie Hall, performs several concerts annually, including a Christmas performance of Handel's *Messiah*.

♂ **Crystal Coast Civic Center** (252-247-3883; www.crystalcoastcivicctr.com), 3505 Arendell Street, Morehead City. Hosts concerts by regional and national touring groups, plus many annual events, at its location on the waterfront.

NIGHTCLUBS ♈ **Arendell Room** (252-240-2753; www.arendellroom.com), 715 Arendell Street, Morehead City. Hole-in-the-wall downtown bar is surprisingly plush and has the most creative mixologists—and best selection of liquors—in town.

❄ ♈ ↩ **Bistro-By-The-Sea** (252-247-2777; www.bistro-by-the-sea.com), 4031 Arendell Street, Morehead City. This popular eatery hosts a piano bar on Friday and Saturday nights all year.

♈ **Jack's Waterfront Bar** (252-247-2043; www.jackswaterfrontbar.com), 513 Evans Street, Morehead City. Locally owned spot offers live bands every weekend, plus daily drink specials and a great waterfront deck to enjoy them on. In accordance with North Carolina law, this is a private club. Bring your ID.

🐟 ♈ **Off the Hook** (252-732-5986; www .offthehookmoreheadcity.com), 105 S. Seventh Street. Cool spot across from the Morehead City docks blends waterfront dining and live music on its big patio. Lunch $$; dinner $$–$$$.

OUTDOOR CONCERTS **Alive at 5** (252-808-0440; www.downtownmoreheadcity .com), Jaycee Park, 807 Shepard Street. Free twilight concerts take place on first and third Fridays, spring to fall.

Saturday in the Park Concert Series (252-726-5083; www.moreheadcitync .org), Jaycee Park, Ninth and Shepard streets, Morehead City. Free concerts every Saturday evening from Memorial Day to Labor Day at 7 PM.

❋ Selective Shopping

On **Evans Street** in Morehead City, a stroll takes you past a variety of fascinating shops located in historic surroundings. Along the docks you'll find a cluster of seafood restaurants and galleries.

ANTIQUES **Downtown Morehead City** has quite a nice selection of antiques shops, all within a few blocks of the waterfront along Evans and Arendell streets, most in the 500 to 700 blocks, including **Seaport Antique Market** (252-726-6606; www.facebook.com/SeaportAntiques) and **Blue Gardenia Antique Company** (1208 Arendell Street). Several art galleries are found in the same area. The **Downtown Morehead City website** (www.downtownmoreheadcity.com) has current listings.

ART GALLERIES **Arts & Things Gallery** (252-240-1979; www.arts-things.com), 704 Evans Street, downtown Morehead City. Gallery exhibits works by many local artists, as well as the Shona sculptors of Zimbabwe. Also offers the area's largest selection of art supplies, fine art printing, custom framing, and classes in many media.

  ✒ **BluSail Gallery** (252-723-9516; www.blu-sail.com), 903 Arendell Street, Morehead City. Light-filled gallery in downtown Morehead City offers lovely local art, a wide range of classes in various art forms, and a fully equipped pottery studio.

  Carolina Artists Studio Gallery (252-726-7550; www.carolinaartistgallery.com), 800 Evans Street, downtown Morehead City. The area's largest gallery displaying original local art welcomes visiting artists and art lovers to participate in open studios. This artists' cooperative offers classes and workshops and operates the **Special Hands Pottery** community outreach, with art created by special needs clay artists for sale in the gallery.

  Carteret Contemporary Art (252-726-4071; www.twogalleries.net), 1106 Arendell Street, and **Vision Gallery** (252-247-5550), 4426 Arendell Street. Sister galleries in Morehead City hang changing exhibits of original, cutting-edge artwork, with many pieces by local artists.

  Marc Montocchio Gallery (252-515-0886; www.marcmontocchio.com), 712 Arendell Street. Photographer and former Navy diver displays stunning underwater scenes in his museum-quality gallery.

BOOKS **The Book Shop** (252-240-1163; www.moreheadcitybookshop.com), Kmart Plaza, 4915 Arendell Street, Morehead City. Inventory includes more than 50,000 used books, plus new books, DVDs, and audiobooks; trade-ins accepted.

  Dee Gee's Gifts and Books (252-726-3314 or 1-800-DEE-GEES; www.deegees.com), 508 Evans Street, Morehead City. Established in 1934, this is one of the oldest continuously operating bookstores in the state. Selections and events showcase the many writers living in the region.

SHOPPING CENTERS AND MALLS In recent years, Morehead City has seen many big box stores, such as **Walmart** and **Lowe's**, move in, making it the shopping destination for the region. These are concentrated in **Cypress Bay Shopping Center** at the junction of US 70 and NC 24, with **Sears**, **Belk**, and a number of specialty stores. Another center, **Pelletier Harbor Shops**, 4426 Arendell Street/US 70, has a concentration of upscale shops.

  ❋ ♁ **Newport Flea Mall** (252-223-2085; www.newportfleamall.com), 196 Carl Garner Road, hosts dozens of vendors in covered stalls every weekend. A restaurant is on-site.

SPECIAL SHOPS **St. Andrew's Episcopal Thrift Shop** (252-726-4747), 1107 Arendell Street. Established in 1953, this thrift has great prices on secondhand stuff, and profits go to good causes in the community.

❋ Special Events

Check the **Crystal Coast visitors website** (www.crystalcoastnc.org) for an updated list of events during your stay.

  January: **Bridal Fair** (252-247-3883; www.crystalcoastcivicctr.com), Crystal Coast Civic Center, Morehead City.

  Escoffier Chefs Dinner Series (www.cccfoundation.org), Crystal Coast

Civic Center. Monthly gourmet dinners (January through April) featuring French cuisine created by faculty and students from the Carteret Community College Culinary Arts program. Proceeds send culinary students to study in France.

February: **Art from the Heart** (252-726-9156; www.artscouncilcarteret.org).

Carolina Chocolate Festival (252-354-9500; www.carolinachocolatefestival.com). Chocolate dinners, cooking demonstrations, and other events surround the main tasting festival at the Crystal Coast Civic Center.

March: **Coastal Home and Garden Show** (252-247-3883; www.crystalcoastcivicctr.com), Crystal Coast Civic Center.

April: **Newport Pig Cookin'** (252-223-3112; www.newportpigcooking.com), Newport Community Park. Newport goes whole hog with more than 80 pigs on the grill.

May: **Cherry Point Air Show** (www.cherrypointairshow.com), Marine Air Corps Station Cherry Point, Havelock. The state's largest air show features two days of military and civilian aerobatic demonstrations, aircraft on display, live music, and the famous "Night Show" featuring skydivers and aerial pyrotechnics topped off by the region's largest fireworks display.

Crystal Coast Boat Show (www.crystalcoastboatshow.com), Downtown Morehead City waterfront. Free.

June: **Big Rock Blue Marlin Fishing Tournament** (252-247-3575; www.thebigrock.com). Weeklong event includes men's and ladies' divisions, social mixers, and a fireworks display.

July: **Morehead City Fourth of July Fireworks on Sugarloaf Island** (www.downtownmoreheadcity.com). View from the downtown waterfront.

N.C. Ducks Unlimited Band the Billfish Tournament (252-237-3717; www.ncdubillfish.com), Crystal Coast Civic Center.

October: **North Carolina Seafood Festival** (252-726-6273; www.ncseafoodfestival.org), Morehead City waterfront. Weekend celebrating the commercial fishing industry includes seafood tastings, live music, fishing and sailing competitions, free boat show, Flounder Fling, and Blessing of the Fleet.

Promise Land Festival (252-241-4767), Morehead City Train Depot, 1001 Arendell Street. Free festival celebrates the history of the Promise Land neighborhood with guided tours, storytellers, and live music, plus food and crafts from local vendors.

November: **Veterans Day Parade** (www.downtownmoreheadcity.com), Arendell Street, Morehead City.

December: **Christmas Flotilla** (www.maritimefriends.org), downtown Morehead City waterfront, early December.

Morehead City Christmas Parade (www.downtownmoreheadcity.com), Arendell Street.

BOGUE BANKS

niquely situated along the Carolina coast, **Bogue Banks**, composed of the beach towns of Atlantic Beach, Pine Knoll Shores, Indian Beach, Salter Path, and Emerald Isle, runs 24 miles east to west, so both sunrise and sunset can be enjoyed from your oceanfront balcony. The long, white-sand beaches that gave the area its Crystal Coast nickname face south, bringing warmer water and different surf than ocean beaches farther north. On the north side of Bogue, quiet sound waters make this a great destination for paddling and boating, and provide a breeding ground for many birds, as well as the seafood that has made this coast famous.

While the original resort on Bogue Banks, located opposite Morehead City, had its first beach pavilion back in the 1880s, military forts have occupied the eastern tip of the island since before the Revolutionary War. Today's **Fort Macon**, an impressive pentagon-shaped masonry structure, is also North Carolina's most popular state park, thanks to its fine public beach.

ATLANTIC BEACH

The heart of Atlantic Beach lies at the end of the causeway from Morehead City. The oceanfront here was famous as **The Circle**, a collection of rides, dance halls, taverns, and hotels. Most of the establishments were demolished to make way for a mixed-use project dubbed **The Grove**, which will include several condominium towers and commercial buildings. Some of the local color, including an ice cream shop, a few taverns, and the area's best diner, remain, however, as does the public boardwalk and the wide, white-sand beach adjacent to public parking. Plans for The Grove proceed, but very slowly, thanks to a number of environmental concerns.

PINE KNOLL SHORES

Just west of Atlantic Beach, dense growths of twisted live oaks shield most of Pine Knoll Shores (often referred to as PKS) from passing eyes. This was once the private estate of heiress Alice Hoffman, who willed the land to her cousins, the children of President Theodore Roosevelt. The kids of the national parks founder followed in their father's footsteps, setting aside much of the maritime forest as the **Theodore Roosevelt Natural Area**, now the home of the **North Carolina Aquarium**, and developing the rest with an eye on ecology. The island's only golf course is located on stunning terrain here.

INDIAN BEACH AND SALTER PATH

In these two towns, located in the middle of the island, the past and future of Bogue Banks meet. Salter Path, one of the oldest villages on the island, is home to descendants of the original settlers, some of whom floated their houses over from **Diamond City**, the lost town of Shackleford Banks. Officially part of the Hoffman estate, the land was awarded to the established families through a series of court cases. Today, the residents continue their traditional lifestyle as commercial fishermen, selling their catch at local markets. To take advantage of the increasing tourist trade, they've also branched out into Jet Ski and kayak rentals, and offer a variety of water sports adventures.

The modern world crept up on the fishing port, however, with several large condominium projects built on either side. In 1973, these areas incorporated as the town of Indian Beach, wrapping unincorporated Salter Path in a doughnut of upscale development. Together, the two towns offer a range of accommodation and dining options, from down-home to world-class.

EMERALD ISLE

Developed as a resort in the 1950s, Emerald Isle was named for the dense maritime forest that dominated the area. Today this is a family-oriented destination, with many kid-friendly activities and a large selection of beach cottages in every size and price range. The town has several public parks along both the ocean and sound, all the way down to the western tip of the island, and a new system of multiuse paths. NC 58 crosses back to the mainland on the scenic **Cameron Langston Bridge**, intersecting with NC 24 at a busy shopping corner of big box stores.

GUIDANCE The **Visitor Center for Carteret County and the Crystal Coast** (252-726-8148; www.crystalcoastnc.org), 3409 Arendell Street, Morehead City. The **Emerald Isle branch of the visitor center** (252-393-2008) is located at 8401 Emerald Isle Drive.

Atlantic Beach Town Hall (252-726-2121; www.atlanticbeach-nc.com), 125 W. Fort Macon Road, Atlantic Beach.

Pine Knoll Shores Town Hall (252-247-4353; www.townofpks.com), 100 Municipal Circle, Pine Knoll Shores. Discover the fascinating history of Pine Knoll Shores and the Rockefeller family at www.pineknollhistory.blogspot.com.

Indian Beach Town Hall (252-247-3344; www.indianbeach.org), 1400 Salter Path Road, Indian Beach.

Emerald Isle Town Hall (252-354-3424; www.emeraldisle-nc.org), 7500 Emerald Drive/NC 58, Emerald Isle.

MEDICAL EMERGENCY **Med First Urgent Care** (252-354-6500; www.thinkmedfirst .com), 7901 Emerald Drive/NC 58.

POST OFFICES The **Atlantic Beach U.S. Post Office** (252-726-5630) is at 1516 W. Fort Macon Road. The zip code for both Atlantic Beach and Pine Knoll Shores is 28512. The zip code for both Salter Path and Indian Beach is 28575.

The **Emerald Isle U.S. Post Office** (252-354-6677) is located at 142 Eastview Drive. The zip code for Emerald Isle is 28594.

PUBLIC LIBRARY ✐ ☂ (ᵖ) **Bogue Banks Public Library** (252-247-4660; carteret.cpclib .org), 320 Salter Path Road, Pine Knoll Shores. Services include children's story time, faxing, public-use computers, free Wi-Fi, a changing exhibit of local art, and a free paperback exchange.

PUBLIC RESTROOMS In Emerald Isle, both the ♿ **Eastern and Western Regional Beach Accesses** have public restrooms, as does **Blue Heron Park** behind the Town Hall; ♿ **Emerald Isle Woods Park** (9404 Coast Guard Road); Merchant's Park (8401 NC 58); and the ♿ **Emerald Isle Boating Access** (6800 NC 58).

GETTING THERE Two high-rise bridges join Bogue Banks with the mainland. The **Atlantic Beach Causeway** begins in downtown Morehead City, linking to the eastern end of Bogue Banks. The **Cameron Langston Bridge**, at the western end of Bogue Banks, joins Emerald Isle with Cape Carteret. NC 58 runs about 25 miles down the Banks between the bridges. Numerous beach access points are located along the south side of NC 58. Look for the signs with a pelican flying in an orange circle. (In our beach sections, we list accesses with bathhouses and restrooms.)

GETTING AROUND A series of mile markers (MM) helps judge distances along NC 58. MM 0 is at Fort Macon at the eastern end of the island. The road has several different names along its length—it is called Fort Macon Road in Atlantic Beach, changing from East to West at the Atlantic Beach Causeway. It is Salter Path Road in PKS and Emerald Drive in Emerald Isle. We'll call it NC 58 to avoid confusion.

✷ To See

ATLANTIC BEACH

✷ ⚲ ✐ ♿ **Fort Macon State Park** (252-726-3775 or 252-726-2295; www.ncparks.gov), 2300 E. Fort Macon Road, Atlantic Beach. Open all year, daily 9–5; closed Christmas Day. Hours for the surrounding grounds, bathhouse, and swimming area vary by season. The eastern tip of Bogue Banks was fortified as early as 1715. The present pentagon-shaped fort was begun in 1826, fell to Union forces in the Civil War, and was garrisoned for the final time during World War II. Today it is the second-oldest state park in the North Carolina system and the most visited. The 27 vaulted casements in the restored fort house a comprehensive museum detailing the history of the facility and the men who saw service here. Guided tours, musket- and cannon-firing demonstrations, and nature walks are offered, and Civil War reenactments take place in July and September. The **Friends of Fort Macon** (www.friendsoffortmacon.org) hosts a very popular free Friday night summer concert series on the fort's parade ground. The **Coastal Education and Visitor Center** houses ecology exhibits. Free.

PINE KNOLL SHORES

⚲ ✐ ♿ ♟ **North Carolina Aquarium at Pine Knoll Shores** (252-247-4003 or 1-866-294-3477; www.ncaquariums.com), 1 Roosevelt Boulevard, Pine Knoll Shores. This branch of the state aquariums takes visitors on a journey from a waterfall in the North Carolina mountains, down through many streams and bays, to the deep offshore realm of the big saltwater game fish. Along the way, visitors meet live native brown trout, giant catfish, playful river otters, sea turtles, sharks, and red drum. Several huge tanks hold replicas of famous wrecks located on the floor of the ocean nearby, including a German U-boat; the *Caribsea*, torpedoed in 1942; and Blackbeard's flagship, *Queen Anne's Revenge*, discovered on the bottom just off Fort Macon, all now home to tiger sharks and other large fish. Outdoors, a boardwalk leads over the marsh to a snake exhibit and Bogue Sound overlook. Free programs are offered daily; kayak and SUP trips,

THE CANNONS AT FORT MACON CONTINUE TO GUARD THE COAST

marsh explorations, sea turtle treks, and fishing lessons require a small additional fee. Adults, $11; seniors 62 and over, $10; children 3–12, $9; children 2 and under free. Free admission on Martin Luther King Jr. Day and Veterans Day. Closed Thanksgiving and Christmas days.

THE PINE KNOLL SHORES BRANCH OF THE NC AQUARIUM INCLUDES AN EXHIBIT ON BLACKBEARD'S FLAGSHIP, DISCOVERED ON THE BOTTOM JUST OFF FORT MACON

IN EMERALD ISLE

Bogue Inlet Fishing Pier (252-354-2919; www.bogueinletpier.com), 100 Bogue Inlet Drive. Emerald Isle's last pier is the state's longest and one of the most beloved, a family tradition that stretches across generations, with the Stanley family rebuilding numerous times. King mackerel fishing is especially good here, with the state record sea mullet, weighing in at 3 pounds 8 ounces, landed in 1971. After a brush with the developer's wrecking ball, the pier's future seems secure, at least for the time being. It was completely rebuilt in 2011 after the visit of Hurricane Irene, and again for the 2017 season, with an improved king and Spanish mackerel area and an upper observation deck. The funky old Bushwackers Lounge has been replaced with the **Surf's Up! Grill &**

Bar, with a large deck overlooking the ocean. Spectators can stroll down the pier to watch the action for free.

✳ To Do

BICYCLE RENTALS **Beach Wheels Bike Rentals** (252-240-2453; www.beach wheelsbikerentals.com), 1420 Salter Path Road, Indian Beach. Free baskets, helmets, locks, and delivery.

BEACH READING

Duncan, Pamela. *The Big Beautiful*. New York: Dial Press, 2007. A romantic comedy set in Salter Path.

Morris, Bill. *Saltwater Cowboys*. Winston-Salem, NC: John F. Blair, 2004. A fun fish tale set on the Crystal Coast.

Beach Butler Rentals (252-241-0590; www.beachbutlerrentals.com), 7229 Archers Creek Drive. Rent beach bikes or a golf cart for your week at the beach. Free delivery within Emerald Isle.

Hwy 58 Bicycles (252-354-9006; www.hwy58bicycles.com), 8802 Reed Road, off US 58. Dedicated bike shop goes beyond basic beach cruisers, offering a variety of bikes to meet your needs, from geared and mountain bikes to tandems and adult trikes—all nicely maintained.

Island Essentials (252-354-8887 or 1-888-398-8887; www.islandessentials.com), 208 Bogue Inlet Drive. Rents bikes by the week for the whole family, plus beach equipment, linens, and baby gear. Kayaks and bodyboard rentals also available.

BIKE TRAILS In keeping with its family-friendly identity, the town of Emerald Isle has wide multiuse paths stretching alongside many of its roads, including **Emerald Drive** (NC 58) and **Coast Guard Road**. **Emerald Path**, a 10-foot-wide paved trail, runs for 11 miles from the Indian Beach town line to the Point at Bogue Inlet. Restrooms, bike racks, and parking can be found at ♿ **Emerald Isle Woods Park** (9404 Coast Guard Road) at the west end of the path; **Merchant's Park** (8401 NC 58); and the ♿ **East Ocean Regional Access** (2701 NC 58). The paths can be used by pedestrians, bikers, in-line skaters, and handicapped-accessible motorized vehicles. Maps of the paths can be found on the **Emerald Isle website** (www.emerald isle-nc.org).

Ocean Drive, one block back from the beach, is another good biking option in Emerald Isle, with paths connecting the occasional dead ends.

BOATING Atlantic Beach has several public boat ramps. **Pelican Drive Dock** is the town dock. Other ramps with limited parking are located at **Moonlight Drive** and at **W. Bogue Sound Drive**. Kayaks can launch into the sound from the **Hoop Pole Creek Nature Trail** next to the Atlantic Station Shopping Center.

Anchorage Marina (252-726-4423; www.anchoragemarina.net), 517 E. Fort Macon Road, Atlantic Beach. Boat ramp, transient slips, ship's store.

The ♿ **Emerald Isle Boating Access** (www.ncwildlife.org), located on Bogue Sound/ICW at 6800 NC 58, MM 18, about 3 miles east of the causeway, is the largest on the North Carolina coast, with four free ramps; 112 boat trailer spaces, plus additional spaces for passenger vehicles; a kayak/canoe launch; and a fishing pier, playground, and picnic area with restrooms.

Kayaks can also launch from the floating dock in **Emerald Isle Woods** (9404 Coast Guard Road).

FISHING **Captain Stacy Fishing Center and Headboat** (1-800-533-9417; www.capt stacy.com), Atlantic Beach Causeway, Atlantic Beach. Family-owned *Captain Stacy IV* headboat specializes in full-day and 24-hour excursions and night shark-hunting trips. Charter fishing also available.

Emerald Isle Adventures (910-538-2749; www.emeraldisleadventures.com), 6800 US 58, Emerald Isle. Family-owned business offers pontoon boat rentals and light-tackle fishing charters.

((•)) **Fisherman's Inn Charters** (252-726-2273; www.fishermansinn.net), 200 Atlantic Beach Causeway, Atlantic Beach. Inshore and offshore fishing charters, boat slips, inexpensive motel rooms, and a bunkhouse are available.

Saltwater Bait and Tackle (252-222-0670; www.saltwaterbaitandtackle.com), 601 Atlantic Beach Causeway, Atlantic Beach. Shop established by fishing writer Captain Joe Shute specializes in helping you fish the local waters.

FISHING PIERS Once the home of several popular oceanfront piers, Emerald Isle is down to just one, the **Bogue Inlet Fishing Pier**. However, there is a movement afoot to save the family tradition of pier fishing, and the state and town are working together to build a new 1,000-foot concrete fishing pier at the former site of the Emerald Isle Pier, currently the Eastern Regional Ocean Access. To be called the **Aquarium Pier**, the new facility will be operated as an outreach of the North Carolina Aquarium in Pine Knoll Shores, following the general blueprint of Jennette's Pier in Nags Head. The first part of the project, which will stretch across the island, has already been built—**a fishing pier in Cedar Street Soundside Park**, directly north of the beach access.

Bogue Inlet Fishing Pier (252-354-2919; www.bogueinletpier.com), 100 Bogue Inlet Drive. Emerald Isle's last remaining oceanfront pier (for now, see above) remains open 24/7 during the fishing season, which typically stretches from March to November. Daily passes are available for bottom fishing and king fishing. Spectators can watch the action for free. The all-new pier house offers an expanded selection of bait and tackle, beverages and snacks, as well as rental rods and reels. The new **Surf's Up! Grill & Bar**, open year-round, provides full meals and a full bar with ocean views.

✄ ((•))Y **Oceanana Fishing Pier** (252-726-0863; www.oceananapier.com), 700 E. Fort Macon Road, Atlantic Beach. The 1,000-foot Oceana pier, centerpiece of the family-friendly **Oceanana Resort**, is open to the public and offers rod and reel rentals. The **Pier House Restaurant** serves breakfast, lunch, and dinner. The **Barnacle Bar** at the end of the pier serves up the famous frozen Painkiller cocktail and live music.

Soundside Piers. Emerald Isle has a number of public piers on the Bogue Sound side where you can cast a line or dip for crabs, including those at **Bluewater Drive** and **Emerald Woods**. Fishing license required.

FOR FAMILIES ✄ ((•)) **Atlantic Beach Town Park** (www.atlanticbeach-nc.com), 915 W. Fort Macon Road. New park across from Atlantic Station has a large playground area, merry-go-round, splashpad, basketball hoop, and a free skateboard and BMX park, plus a shady and well-lighted picnic area. The new 18-hole mini-golf course ($3) has restrooms and a concession stand.

Emerald Isle Disc Golf Course (252-354-6350; www.emeraldisle-nc.org), 9404 Coast Guard Road. New nine-hole course at Emerald Isle Woods Park. Free.

✄ **Kites Unlimited & Bird Stuff** (252-247-7011; www.kitesandbirds.com), 1010 W. Fort Macon Road, Atlantic Station, Atlantic Beach. Full-service kite store sponsors kite-flying events every Sunday morning at Fort Macon State Park.

✄ The **North Carolina Aquarium at Pine Knoll Shores** (252-247-4003) sponsors annual Holiday Adventure Camps at Thanksgiving and Christmas.

✐ **Professor Hacker's Lost Treasure Golf & Raceway** (252-247-3024; www .losttreasuregolf.com), 976 NC 58, Salter Path. A full day of fun with 36 holes of mini-golf, a mining train ride, go-karts, bumper boats, arcade games, ice cream parlor, and picnic area.

❄ ✐ **Emerald Isle Parks and Recreation** (252-354-6350; www.emeraldisle-nc.org), 7500 NC 58, sponsors a year-round program of family-oriented Friday Free Flicks on the second Friday of the month at 7 PM. Admission is free; popcorn and a drink are just $1.

GOLF ⛳ The **Country Club of the Crystal Coast** (252-726-1034; www.crystalcoastcc .com), 152 Oakleaf Drive, Pine Knoll Shores. Semiprivate course set amid maritime forest with views of Bogue Sound. Rental clubs available. Restaurant with patio overlooking Bogue Sound serves lunch and dinner.

PARASAILING **Dragonfly Parasail** (252-422-5500; www.dragonflyparasail.com), 517 E. Fort Macon Road, Atlantic Beach. Located at the Anchorage Marina.

SCUBA DIVING **Atlantic Beach Diving Services** (443-255-3775; www.atlanticbeach diving.com). The comfortable dive boat *Mutiny II*, offering charters to the numerous wrecks in the region, docks next to the Fisherman's Inn on the Atlantic Beach Causeway, Atlantic Beach.

♿ **Atlantis Charters** (252-728-6244; www.atlantischarters.net), Atlantic Beach Causeway, Atlantic Beach. The spacious *Atlantis IV* dive boat carries up to six passengers out to dive World War II wrecks or to snorkel at the Cape Lookout jetties. The boat also goes out on fishing charters, including bluefin tuna trips every winter.

Diver Down Diving Charters (252-240-2043; www.diverdownscubadiving .com), 212 Atlantic Beach Causeway, Atlantic Beach. Trips include shark dives, live bottom hunting, World War II wrecks, and artificial reef dives. Walk-ons available.

SURFING **AB Surf Shop** (252-726-9382; www.absurfshop.com), 515 W. Fort Macon Road, Atlantic Beach. The Crystal Coast's oldest surf shop stocks over 300 boards, including the house brand, Outer Banks Custom Shapes.

Bert's Surf Shop (252-726-1730; www .bertsurfshop.com), 304 W. Fort Macon Road, Atlantic Beach; **two additional locations** in Emerald Isle at 8202 Emerald Drive (252-354-2441) and 300 Islander Drive (252-354-6282). Shops carry surf-board and skateboard equipment and accessories, as well as the popular Bert's logo wear.

Hot Wax Surf Shop and Surf Camp (252-354-6466; www.hotwaxsurf.com), 200 Mallard Drive, Emerald Isle. Shop

PARASAILING IS A POPULAR ACTIVITY FROM THE MARINAS ON BOGUE BANKS

with 30 years' experience on the water carries the region's largest selection of surf-boards, stand-up paddleboards, and kayaks for rent. They offer kayak fishing tours, SUP ecotours, and surfing and paddle surfing instruction, including the five-day Instant Karma camp, featured in the *Wall Street Journal*, taught by experienced locals who are on the water daily.

TENNIS **Country Club of the Crystal Coast** (252-499-9048; www.crystalcoastcc.com), 152 Oakleaf Drive, Pine Knoll Shores. Semiprivate club offers court time and lessons to nonmembers on a fee basis.

In Emerald Isle, free lighted tennis courts are found at **Blue Heron Park**, behind the **Emerald Isle Town Hall** (252-354-6350), 7500 NC 58. Other facilities here include a grill and picnic area, playground, basketball court, and fossil pit.

WATER SPORTS **Carolina Kitesurfing and Emerald Isles Paddle Tours** (252-876-2595; www.carolinakitesurfing.com; www.emeraldislepaddletours.com), 142 Fairview Drive, Emerald Isle. Take a kiteboarding lesson out on Emerald Isle Point, paddle out on a SUP ecotour, or try stand-up paddle surfing. SUP rentals available. Morning yoga classes on SUPs take stretching to a new level.

✐ **Island Water Sports Rentals** (252-247-7303; www.h2osportsrentals.com), 1960 NC 58, MM 12.5, Indian Beach, near the Emerald Isle border. Rent a Jet Ski, SUP, or kayak, or sign up for a Banana Boat ride at this full-service water sports mecca. Younger kids dig the bumper boats. You can launch into Bogue Sound from the 200-foot pier, then return for a sunset cocktail at the two-story **Dolphin Deck and Tiki Bar**, a cool way to end the day, and one of the best sunset views on Bogue Banks.

✳ Green Space

BEACHES ♿ **Fort Macon State Park Beach Access** (252-726-3775; www.ncparks.gov), 2300 E. Fort Macon Road, Atlantic Beach. One of the state's most popular beaches offers an accessible bathhouse and refreshment stand, with lifeguards on duty during the summer season. Free.

The Circle Regional Access at the Circle (201 W. Atlantic Boulevard) is the main beach access in Atlantic Beach, with a boardwalk, sand volleyball, on-the-sand swings, and three lifeguard stands. There is a fee to park in the lots here during the summer.

Additional Atlantic Beach bathhouses are located at ♿ **Fort Macon State Park**, the **Les and Sally Moore Public Beach Access** (177 New Bern Street), and the new ♿ **Tom Doe Memorial Beach Access** on Ocean Boulevard. Driving is allowed on Atlantic Beach sands from October 1 to March 15 with a permit, $75 for nonresidents.

Pine Knoll Shores has a bathhouse with 50 parking spaces at **Iron Steamer Regional Beach Access** (345 US 58, MM 7.5). Parking fees may apply. Smaller beach access points in PKS, with free parking, can be found at the Beacons Reach and Knollwood Public Beach Accesses.

In **Indian Beach/Salter Path**, outside showers, restrooms, and 75 parking places are located at **Salter Path Regional Public Beach Access** (1050 NC 58). The **Indian Beach Regional Public Access** (1425 NC 58) has a four-wheel-drive access ramp.

Emerald Isle has a public ocean access at the southern end of nearly every cross street, a total of about 90. Two larger areas have bathhouses, picnic pavilions, grills, large parking lots, and other amenities: the ♿ **Eastern Regional Access** (2701 NC 58) and the ♿ **Western Regional Access** (299 Islander Drive). Both have lifeguards on duty Memorial Day to Labor Day and charge $10 for parking on weekends and holidays, April through September. Beach wheelchairs can be checked out from **Emerald Isle Fire Station No. 1** (7508 NC 58). Dogs are permitted on the beach but must be leashed at all times. Fires and fireworks are not allowed. Driving on the beach is permitted from September 15 to April 30, with the exception of the 10-day period around the Easter holiday. Permits are required and cost $80 for nonresidents. Handicapped individuals are eligible to receive a free permit, with appropriate documentation. To get a permit, go in person to the **Town Administration Building** (252-354-3424) at 7509 NC 58. You can find detailed information on Emerald Isle's numerous public beach accesses at the **town's website**, www.emeraldisle-nc.org.

THE SAGA OF SALTER PATH

For a beach soundtrack, listen to Mark Fielding Darden's 2004 CD, *Will This Town Survive? Songs and Stories from Salter Path*, released by Salter Path Records (www.salterpathnc.com). The disc comes with a 60-page book recounting the fast-disappearing life of one of the Banks' original fishing villages.

TRAILS **Alice Hoffman Nature Trail** (252-247-4003; www.ncaquariums.com), 1 Roosevelt Boulevard, Pine Knoll Shores. Half-mile trail leads along marsh to a brackish pond frequented by white ibis and other wading birds. Access is through the North Carolina Aquarium with an entrance fee.

Emerald Isle Woods Park (252-354-6350; www.emeraldisle-nc.org), 9404 Coast Guard Road, Emerald Isle. Nature trail leads from Coast Guard Road to Bogue Sound. The area is a stop on the **North Carolina Birding Trail** (www.ncbirdingtrail.org).

Fort Macon State Park Trails (252-726-3775; www.ncparks.gov), 2300 E. Fort Macon Road, Atlantic Beach. Hiking opportunities include 1.5 miles of ocean beach, home to numerous bird species; the **Elliott Coues Nature Trail** linking the fort area with the swimming beach; and **Yarrow's Loop**, a short quarter-mile nature trail with informational signs.

Hoop Pole Creek Clean Water Preserve Nature Trail (252-393-8185; www.nccoast.org), NC 58, Atlantic Beach. Easy half-mile walk to the shore of Bogue Sound begins in the parking lot of Atlantic Station Shopping Center. Interpretive signs explain the maritime forest.

Theodore Roosevelt Nature Trail (252-726-3775), Theodore Roosevelt State Recreation Area, Pine Knoll Shores. The 1.5-mile trail leads through maritime forest and marsh frequented by painted buntings and songbirds. Trailhead is located in the North Carolina Aquarium's parking lot, and access is free.

BOARDWALK AT THE ATLANTIS LODGE LEADS OVER THICK MARITIME FOREST BEFORE REACHING THE BEACH

✳ Lodging

OCEANFRONT INN ✳ 🦞 🖋 🐾 ♿ (ɯ)
Atlantis Lodge (252-726-5168 or 1-800-682-7057; www.atlantislodge.com), 123 Salter Path Road/US 58, Pine Knoll Shores. The family of A. C. and Dot Hall, longtime innkeepers of the first hotel along this stretch of coast, continue to operate this retro retreat designed by A. C. and his friend, modernist North Carolina architect Donald Stewart. The lodge is set amid the live oaks along the oceanfront and exudes a warm and welcoming vibe. Pets of all kinds are welcome here as long as they are well behaved, and many guests return every year, so reservations should be made in advance. Standard rooms with two doubles or a king bed, and completely equipped efficiencies, open onto balconies or a peaceful, grassy courtyard where feeders attract many birds. A wooden boardwalk leads to a wide beach with complimentary lounges, chairs, and umbrellas during the summer months, in addition to complimentary beach toys, boogie boards, kayaks, and mountain bikes. A sand wheelchair is available for disabled guests. Lovely landscaping surrounds a heated saltwater pool, where a little waterfall leads to a baby pool. High atop the three-floor building, a sundeck and lounge with pool table, ping-pong, library, and big-screen TV provides a gathering spot where guests can socialize. Non-pet rooms are also available, and all rooms have coffeemakers and cable TV. Off-season $–$$; in-season $$$.

MOTOR INN 🖋 🐾 (ɯ) **Caribbe Inn** (252-726-0051; www.caribbe-inn.com), 309 E. Fort Macon Road, Atlantic Beach. Brightly painted and immaculately clean, the Caribbe Inn is a favorite among bargain hunters, with prices half of what you'd pay in a chain hotel. The inn is located across the street and a short walk from the beach, but it backs up to Bogue

Sound, with its own boat dock and slips. If you fish, you can use the fish-cleaning station, then store your catch in the deep freezer or cook it up on the grill in the waterfront barbecue area. Rooms here are cheerfully decorated with murals of sea life, a hit with kids. Two children under 12 stay free. $–$$.

🐾 (((•))) **William and Garland Motel** (252-247-3733; www.williamandgarlandmotel .com), 1185 NC 58, Salter Path. This small family-owned and family-operated hotel offers simple, clean lodgings, personal service, and great rates and location. Direct access to the beach is via a lovely nature trail. The property is pet friendly. $.

CAMPING 🐾 (((•))) **Holiday Trav-L-Park Resort** (252-354-2250; www.htpresort .com), 9102 Coast Guard Road, Emerald Isle. Oceanfront resort, awarded five-stars by Woodall's, offers 325 sites with full hookups, Wi-Fi, and cable TV. Planned activities, a pool, Frisbee golf course, raceway, beach concessions, and modern bathhouse are among the amenities. Rentals of on-site travel trailers available. $–$$.

CONDO RESORT ❄ 🐾 🐾 (((•))) ⊹ **The Ocean Club Resort**, 1700 NC 58, Indian Beach. Stretching across Bogue Banks with both oceanfront and soundfront units, the centrally located Ocean Club rents villas with one to three bedrooms in mostly three-story buildings with elevators and covered parking. This unique resort employs ecologically advanced technology to cause the least impact on the local environment. Outdoor amenities include pool complexes on both the beach and sound, with a heated pool and whirlpool, a children's pool, a golf putting course, lighted clay tennis courts, and a fishing pier great for sunset views. A state-of-the-art fitness center and a luxurious spa are on the property. Check with local realty companies for available units.

RETREAT **Pelican House at the Trinity Center** (1-888-874-6287; www.trinityctr

.com/pelican), 618 Salter Path Road, Pine Knoll Shores. Part of the lovely property stretching from the sound to the ocean given to the Episcopal Diocese of East Carolina by Alice Hoffman and the heirs of Theodore Roosevelt, Pelican House offers guided spiritual retreats, silent retreats, and individual "personal time" for people of all faiths. Guests have access to the paths that thread the property's maritime forest, a prayer garden, ocean beach, soundside docks, and other facilities. Rates include meals in the Trinity Center dining room. $$.

VACATION RENTALS **Atlantic Beach Realty** (252-240-7368 or 1-800-786-7368; www.atlanticbeachrealty.net), 513 Atlantic Beach Causeway, Atlantic Beach. Voted Best Beach Cottage & Condo Company on the Crystal Coast, Atlantic handles over 200 properties.

Atlantic Sun Properties (252-808-2786; www.atlanticsunproperties.com), 205 Atlantic Beach Causeway, Atlantic Beach.

🐾 ❄ **Emerald Isle Realty** (252-354-3315 or 1-800-849-3315; www .emeraldislerealty.com), 7501 NC 58. Representing 700 cottages, condos, and luxury "sand castles," this company has a "no worries" policy that minimizes extra fees and adds free perks such as continental breakfast, free ice cream, and concierge services.

Shorewood Real Estate (252-354-7873 or 1-888-557-0172; www.shorewood realestate.net), 7703 NC 58. Specializes in Emerald Isle properties.

❄ Where to Eat

ATLANTIC BEACH

DINING OUT 🐾 ♿ ♟ ⊹ **Amos Mosquito's Restaurant & Bar** (252-247-6222; www.amosmosquitos.com), 703 E. Fort Macon Road, Atlantic Beach. Cleverly decorated, fun restaurant has great views over the sound. The menu ranges from sushi to brown sugar–glazed meat loaf. Kids have a great time at "Skeeters," ordering Slimewiches (grilled cheese) and Snake Skins (buttered noodles) off the children's menu. For dessert, s'mores, cooked over a brazier at the table, are another kid favorite. Adults without children in tow may want to dine in the bar or on the patio, as the dining room is often packed with family groups. Gluten-free options available. Dinner only, $$–$$$.

❄ ♈ **Channel Marker Restaurant & Lounge** (252-247-2344; www.thechannel marker.com), 718 Atlantic Beach Causeway, Atlantic Beach. Waterfront spot with a big deck and great view at the foot of the causeway is a favorite gathering spot for locals. Try the she-crab soup or clam chowder, and the seafood lasagna if it's on special. Dinner $$–$$$$.

⌗ ↣ **Crab's Claw Restaurant** (252-726-8222; www.crabsclaw.com), 201

DECK DINING AT THE CRAB CLAW OVERLOOKS THE SURF AT ATLANTIC BEACH

W. Atlantic Boulevard, Atlantic Beach. Awesome beachfront location next to the Circle public access teams with fresh seafood and Caribbean spices at this longtime favorite, with decks overlooking the waves. Appetizers range from local littleneck clams from Harkers Island to a spicy crab dip praised by *Southern Living*. Steamer pots with seafood and vegetables are a specialty. Lunch and dinner $$–$$$.

❄ **The Island Grille** (252-240-0000; www.igrestaurant.net), 401 Money Island Drive, Atlantic Beach. Hugely popular BOGO entrées, including filet mignon stuffed with feta and bacon, and a special shrimp and scallop pasta dish offered every Monday and Tuesday night all year, pack this little seaside spot with avid fans. Certified local seafood and prime steaks top the menu every night, while a variety of Benedicts, smoked Gouda grits and duck hash line up at Sunday brunch. Reservations recommended. Sunday brunch $–$$; dinner $$–$$$$.

Pescara Wood Oven Kitchen (252-499-9300; www.pescararestaurant.com), 208 West Drive, Atlantic Beach. Located in a historic cottage near the ocean, this new entry to the dining scene offers Italian coastal cuisine, blending local seafood and produce into dishes that might be found in an Italian seaside café. The traditional wood-fired oven adds wonderful flavor to roasted eggplant Parmesan as well as a variety of pizzas, including one topped with clams, bacon, and garlic. Try the seafood-filled lasagna, if on special, accompanied by one of the wine cellar's unusual Italian varietals. Dinner only, $$–$$$.

EMERALD ISLE

♈ ↣ **Caribsea Restaurant** (252-424-8400; www.caribsearestaurant.com), 8921 Crew Drive, Emerald Isle. Located on the third floor of the new Transportation Impact headquarters in Emerald Isle, this new restaurant, named for a nearby

KATHRYN'S BISTRO IN EMERALD ISLE IS A LOCAL FAVORITE FOR SPECIAL OCCASIONS

shipwreck, was a success before it opened, thanks to its chef. Patrick Hogan is the talent behind the various Carlton's restaurants and markets, and creator of legendary crabcakes, wildly believed to be the best in the country, possibly the world. Hogan is a managing partner at the new venture, and the famous crab-cakes are front and center on the Carib-sea menu, along with shrimp and grits, prime steaks, and local fish and shellfish certified sustainable by Carteret Catch. The adjacent **Torpedo Lounge** is the area's only rooftop bar, offering ocean-to-sound views, live music, and spectacular sunsets. Lunch and dinner $$-$$$$.

    & **Kathryn's Bistro & Martini Bar** (252-354-6200; www.kathrynsbistro .com), 8002 NC 58. A favored destina-tion for date nights or special occasions, Kathryn's keeps its wood-fired grill busy searing fork-tender steaks, fresh local seafood, and free-range chicken. If you're just looking for something light, sit at the elegant mahogany and granite bar and enjoy your choice of 30 martinis, plus a lengthy list of excellent appetiz-ers ranging from baked stuffed oysters

to Firecracker Shrimp. Dinner only, $$$-$$$$.

EATING OUT

ATLANTIC BEACH/PINE KNOLL SHORES

    ⚓ & ⛾ **Clam Digger Restaurant** (252-247-4155 or 1-800-338-1533; www.the innatpks.com), The Inn at Pine Knoll Shores, 511 Salter Path Road/US 58, Atlantic Beach. Popular with locals for its daily specials and Calabash-style seafood, the restaurant serves breakfast favorites from 6:30 AM. Full bar with DJ dance parties in the **Cutty Sark Lounge** on weekends. Breakfast $; lunch $-$$; dinner $-$$$.

    ⚓ **4 Corners Diner** (252-240-8855; www.4cornersdiner.com), 100 E. Fort Macon Road, Atlantic Beach. Breakfast is served all day at this classic diner located at the Circle. Breakfast and lunch $; dinner $-$$.

    ⚓ ⛾ **The Shark Shack** (252-726-3313; www.facebook.com/SharkShack AtlanticBeach), 100 S. Durham Avenue, Atlantic Beach. Serving burgers and bas-kets, this is fast food with a difference: live music on the grassy lawn; a beachy menu of oyster, shrimp, and scallop burg-ers; plus beer and wine. $-$$.

EMERALD ISLE

    ⚓ & ⛾ **RuckerJohn's** (252-354-2413; www .ruckerjohns.com), 8700 NC 58, Emerald Plantation. Overlooking the lake behind Emerald Plantation Shopping Center, RuckerJohn's has a huge menu of popu-lar favorites, including many dishes pre-pared on a charcoal grill. Music plays on the lakeside patio on summer evenings. Lunch and dinner $-$$$.

    ⚓ ⛾ **The Trading Post** (252-424-8284; www.thetradingpostei.com), 8302 NC 58. Spot near the Bogue Inlet Pier offers Southern food and spirits, serving full breakfast and lunch menus with dishes like chicken and waffles, green tomato BLTs, and lunch plate specials. For

STOP AT BIG OAK DRIVE IN FOR THE BEST SHRIMP BURGER ON THE COAST

dinner, local seafood and a rib eye in whiskey butter join the menu. Live music and cocktails are featured some evenings. Breakfast and lunch $–$$; dinner $$–$$$.

BEACH TAKEOUT **Big Oak Drive-In & Bar-B-Q** (252-247-2588; www.bigoak drivein.com), 1167 NC 58, Salter Path. The specialty at this old-time take-out stand is the shrimp burger, reputed to be the best on the coast. *US Airways* magazine named this the best drive-in in the country. $

White Swan Bar-B-Q & Fried Chicken (252-726-9607; www .whiteswanatlanticbeach.com), 2500A W. Fort Macon Road, Atlantic Beach. Slow-cooked Eastern North Carolina–style barbecue, ribs, and barbecue chicken star on the menu, along with fried shrimp, flounder, and chicken, plus a wide range of Southern sides. Most folks get take-out since seating is limited. $

COFFEE AND INTERNET ✆ ☎ (((•))) **Stir It Up Coffee Shop** (252-354-2643; www .stiritupei.com), 8700 NC 58, Emerald Plantation, Emerald Isle. Cool spot with free Wi-Fi access serves fair trade organic coffees and teas hot and iced, frappes, and lattes, plus local muffins and breakfast specials. Comfy seating indoors and out make this a nice place to hang out and check your email. $

ICE CREAM AND CANDY **AB Ice Cream and Candy Shoppe** (252-648-8324; www.abicecream.com), 1010 W. Fort Macon Road, Atlantic Station, Atlantic Beach. Cool off with a banana split, sundae, smoothie, or 40 flavors of hand-dipped cone, or satisfy your sweet tooth with saltwater taffy or homemade fudge. *Conde Nast Traveler* readers named this one of the best ice cream shops in the world. $.

✆ ☎ **Sweet Spot Ice Cream Parlor and Candy Shoppe** (252-354-6201; www .sweetspotei.com), 8201 NC 58, MM 19.5, Emerald Isle. Ice cream parlor features 48 flavors of Hershey's premium ice cream, frozen yogurt, Italian ice, and 46 flavors of saltwater taffy, plus lots of specialty coffees, teas, and candies, as well as a wide range of gifts, artwork, and jewelry to browse. Kids have their own corner full of toys.

PIZZA ✐ **Michaelangelo's Pizza** (252-354-7424; www.michaelangelosinc.com), 8700 NC 58, Emerald Plantation, Emerald Isle. Local favorite serves New York–style pizza, whole or by the slice; pasta dishes; salads; gyros; and subs. Gluten-free pies and delivery available. Second location (252-240-3333) in Atlantic Beach at 1010 W. Fort Macon Road. $–$$.

Roma Pizza & Subs (252-247-2020), 100 Charlotte Avenue, Atlantic Beach. Locally owned spot serves great pizza, hot subs, and Italian specialties, all made from scratch. Try the house-made chips. Delivery available. $–$$.

SEAFOOD ❄ **Cap'n Willis Seafood Market** (252-354-2500), 7803 NC 58, Emerald Isle. Operated by the Willis family, providing seafood to Bogue Banks for four generations, this shop stocks local fish and shellfish depending on what's in season, plus tartar sauce, slaw, crabcakes, and fab Key lime pie made with secret family recipes.

WINES AND BEER **Emerald Isle Wine Market** (252-354-8466; www.eiwine market.com), 9102 Coast Guard Road. Located inside the Holiday Trav-L-Park RV resort, this wine store stocks micro-brews and wines from around the world, handcrafted mixers and bitters, as well as gourmet chocolates and ready-to-eat items from the famed Beaufort Grocery. Check the schedule for wine tastings.

❄ Entertainment

CONCERT SERIES **Emerald Fest** (www.seasideartscouncil.com), Western Ocean Regional Beach Access, Emerald Isle. Free music concerts, ranging from reggae to country, most Thursdays, June through August, 6:30 to 8 PM. Bring your lawn chairs and picnics, but no alcohol is allowed.

Fort Macon Summer Concert Series (252-726-3775; www.friendsoffortmacon .org), Atlantic Beach. Free concerts sponsored by the Friends of Fort Macon are held inside the fort Friday 7–8 PM, June to August.

FILM SERIES ✐ During the summer, the town of **Atlantic Beach** (252-726-2121; www.atlanticbeachnc.com) sponsors free family movies on an outdoor screen at the Circle Beach Access. Free.

NIGHTCLUBS ❄ ⍦ **Beach Tavern Bar and Grill** (252-247-4466; www .BTsBarAndGrill.com), 413 W. Fort Macon Road, Atlantic Beach. Known to locals at BT's, this dive bar, serving burgers and beers around its horseshoe bar since 1972, has moved on up to beach bar status in the still-in-the-works Grove project. Beachside patio is a definite plus, and you'll still find that sports bar vibe with poker, pinball, pool, darts, foosball, and sports on TV, along with entertainment and daily specials on food and drink. Lunch and dinner $–$$.

⍦ **Emerald Club Beach & Tiki Bar** (252-354-2929; www.emeraldclubei.com), 8102 NC 58, Emerald Isle. Indoor and outdoor stages and the largest patio on Bogue host live music and top DJs.

⍦ **Frank and Clara's Restaurant & Lounge** (252-773-0901), 1440 NC 58, Salter Path. Tucked behind an old live oak, this classic surf-and-turf place has an upstairs lounge with a balcony and a reputation as a fun spot to party. New owners are booking live bands every Saturday night with no cover.

❄ ⍦ **Memories Beach Club** (252-240-7424; www.memoriesbeachclub .net), 128 E. Fort Macon Road, Coastal Plaza, Atlantic Beach. DJs spin beach rhythm and blues, otherwise known as shag music, and top beach bands make frequent live appearances. The big hardwood dance floor hosts free dance lessons and meetings of the **Atlantic Beach Shag Club** (www.atlanticbeachshagclub .com). Check out the Shaggers Hall of Fame.

⍦ **Molly's Beachside Bar & Grill** (252-240-1155; www.facebook.com/

MollysAtlanticBeach), 2717 W. Fort Macon Road, Atlantic Beach. Seasonal spot located on the pier at the Doubletree Hilton.

Other spots with live music on Bogue Banks include **Amos Mosquito's**, the **Shark Shack**, **Clam Digger**, and **Channel Marker** in Atlantic Beach; and **Caribsea**, the **Trading Post**, and **RuckerJohn's** in Emerald Isle.

✳ Selective Shopping

SHOPPING CENTERS Shopping options abound in **Atlantic Station Shopping Center**, 1010 W. Fort Macon Road/NC 58 at MM 3, where you'll also find several restaurants. The **Atlantic Station Cinema** (252-247-7016; www.atlantic stationcinema.com) screens first-run films.

Both sides of the causeway to **Morehead City** are lined with docks, water sports, and fishing tackle stores, plus several restaurants with waterfront decks.

The **Emerald Plantation Shopping Center**, a huge collection of shops and services at 8700 Emerald Drive, MM 20 on NC 58, is an inevitable stop in Emerald Isle. There you'll find the **Emerald Plantation Cinema** (252-354-5012; www .emeraldplantationcinema.com), as well as a Food Lion supermarket, restaurants, and numerous gift, book, toy, and clothing stores that make for great browsing.

ART GALLERIES **Leni Newell Studios** (252-269-1804; www.leninewell.com). Internationally known mixed media and fiber artist offers workshops in batik and collage at her working studio in Salter Path. A small gallery exhibits her works.

🖋 ⛵ **Turtle's Nest Gallery** (252-269-1702; www.facebook.com/turtlesnest gallery), 8700 US 58, Emerald Plantation, Emerald Isle. Artists' collective features local art, music, jewelry, and more. Frequent workshops are offered in a variety of techniques.

BOOKS 🖋 **Beach Book Mart** (252-240-5655; www.beachbookmart.com), 1010 Atlantic Station, Atlantic Beach. Adults enjoy the best-sellers and local-interest books, while kids are crazy for the action figures and other toys at this independent bookstore. Comic books and graphic novels a specialty.

🖋 **Emerald Isle Books & Toys** (252-354-5323; www.emeraldislebooks.com), Emerald Plantation. Family-run independent bookshop sponsors book clubs for children and adults, besides stocking a wide variety of toys, pirate loot, and bath items.

SPECIAL SHOPS **Coastal Crafts Plus** (252-247-7210), 16 Atlantic Station, Atlantic Beach. A wide selection of gifts, including lots of nautical and collegiate items, shares space with the area's largest selection of knitting supplies in this family-owned shop.

THE ANNUAL CAROLINA KITE FEST BRINGS HUGE KITES TO ATLANTIC BEACH FROM AROUND THE WORLD

Flip Flops Gift Shop (252-354-3446; www.flipflopsgifts.com), 7702 NC 58, Emerald Isle. Cute shop carries all things flip-flop, from sandals you can wear to flip-flop wall hangings.

Island Furniture & Accessories (252-727-4778; www.shopislandfurniture.com), 407 Causeway Shopping Center, Atlantic Beach. Big selection of wicker and lawn furniture, plus nautically themed decor and locally made shell art.

✳ Special Events

Check the **Crystal Coast visitors website** (www.crystalcoastnc.org) for an updated list of events during your stay.

February: **Atlantic Beach Shaggers Hall of Fame Induction Weekend** (www.memoriesbeachclub.net).

March: **St. Patrick's Day Celebration** (www.emeraldisle-nc.org), Emerald Plantation Shopping Center.

July: **Atlantic Beach Fourth of July Fireworks** (www.atlanticbeach-nc.com), the Circle. Family event includes amusement rides and waterslides.

Emerald Isle Fourth of July Fireworks (www.emeraldisle-nc.org), Bogue Island Pier.

"The Buddy" Longboard Classic (www.buddypelletier.com). Surfing competition honors the memory of a local East Coast Surfing Hall of Fame member, Buddy Pelletier.

September: **Emerald Isle Beach Music Festival** (www.emeraldisle-nc.org).

October: 🐟 **Carolina Kite Fest** (www.kitesandbirds.com), 1400 E. Fort Macon Road. Held on the beach in front of the Sands Villa Resort, this fun event includes a Night Fly with illuminated kites, daytime events with huge character kites, and a Candy Drop.

Atlantic Beach King Mackerel Saltwater Slam (www.abkmsaltwaterslam.com). A long tradition on the coast, this family-friendly competition, with divisions for flounder, Spanish mackerel, trout, and puppy drum, benefits the local volunteer fire department.

Bogue Inlet Pier King Mackerel Tournament (www.bogueinletpier.com).

Gordie McAdams Speckled Trout Surf Fishing Tournament (www.emeraldisle-nc.org).

🐟 **Trick-or-Treat Under the Sea** (www.ncaquariums.com), North Carolina Aquarium at Pine Knoll Shores.

November: **Emerald Isle Christmas Parade and Christmas Tree Lighting** (www.emerald isle-nc.org), Merchant's Park. Weekend events include caroling, visits with Santa, merchant open houses, and a Holiday Arts and Crafts Fair in the parks and rec gymnasium.

December: **Atlantic Beach Christmas by the Sea** (www.atlantic beach-nc.com), Atlantic Beach Town Park. Visits from Santa and the illumination of the town tree.

SWANSBORO, CEDAR POINT, AND CAPE CARTERET

Back on the mainland, NC 58 continues north through the Croatan National Forest after crossing NC 24 coming from Morehead City. From the junction, home to a variety of national chain stores and an entertainment complex, NC 24 continues west over the White Oak River to **Swansboro**, another historic fishing village with an eclectic downtown. Just to the west of town, **Hammocks Beach State Park** offers daily boat trips to Bear Island, site of some of the most impressive and unspoiled natural dunes on the East Coast.

Swansboro sits at the eastern edge of Onslow County, home of the Marine training base **Camp Lejeune**. The camp itself has many historic sites; however, NC 172 across the base is generally closed due to security concerns. The impressive and moving Beirut, Vietnam, and World Trade Center monuments in Jacksonville, however, are open to all.

GUIDANCE For information on Swansboro, visit the **official visitor website** at www .visitswansboro.org, or contact the **Swansboro Area Chamber of Commerce** (910-326-1174; www.swansborochamber.org), 203 W. Church Street, Swansboro, or **Onslow County Tourism** (1-800-932-2144; www.onlyinonslow.com), 1099 Gum Branch Road, Jacksonville.

More sources of local information:

Cape Carteret Town Hall (252-393-8483; www.townofcapecarteret.com), 102 Dolphin Street, Cape Carteret.

Cedar Point Town Hall (252-393-7898; www.cedarpointnc.org), 427 Sherwood Avenue, Cedar Point.

Swansboro Town Hall (910-326-4428; www.swansboro-nc.org), 502 Church Street, Swansboro.

POST OFFICE The **Swansboro U.S. Post Office** (910-326-5959) is at 664 W. Corbett Avenue. The zip code in Swansboro, Cedar Point, and Cape Carteret is 28584. The telephone area code in Swansboro changes to 910.

PUBLIC LIBRARY ✍ ((ŋ)) **Western Carteret Public Library** (252-728-2050; carteret.cpclib .org), 230 Taylor Notion Road, Cape Carteret. Services include children's story time, faxing, public-use computers, free Wi-Fi, changing exhibits of local art, and a free paperback exchange.

((ŋ)) **Onslow County Library–Swansboro Branch** (910-326-4888; www.onslowcountync .gov), 1460 W. Corbett Avenue, Swansboro.

GETTING THERE NC 58, coming over the bridge from Emerald Isle, and NC 24 meet in the town of Cape Carteret. The communities known as Bogue and Ocean are to the east of this junction; the town of Cedar Point lies to the west on the banks of the White Oak River. Swansboro is just across the river.

MUST SEE

Hammocks Beach State Park (910-326-4881; www.ncparks .gov), 1572 Hammocks Beach Road, Swansboro. Located just outside Swansboro, this state park includes several uninhabited islands. **Bear Island**, the most popular, is a barrier island about 3 miles long and less than a mile wide with a pristine beach, extensive dune system, and pockets of maritime forest. Accessible only by boat, the island is a popular spot for ocean swimming, primitive camping, kayaking, and birding. On the mainland, the park visitor center, with ecological exhibits, is free and open daily all year (except on Christmas Day); however, the ferry to Bear Island runs only April through October on a variable schedule. Fares are $5 round-trip for adults; $3 for seniors ages 62 and up and children ages 6–12.

UNSPOILED AND UNDEVELOPED, BEAR ISLAND CAN BE REACHED ONLY BY BOAT

GETTING AROUND *By boat:* **Marsh Cruises and Water Taxi** (910-330-8750; www .marshcruises.com). Traveling by water is the best way to get around the Crystal Coast. This company will take you out to Bear Island, to dinner along the docks in Swansboro, or on a sunset cruise.

On foot: Swansboro's historic downtown, located along the west bank of the White Oak River, is ideal for a walking tour.

✳ To See

Carteret County Speedway and Entertainment Complex (252-436-7223; www .carteretspeedway.com), 501 Whitehouse Forks Road, Swansboro. Historic racetrack, recently renovated, hosts the NASCAR Racing Series, plus concerts, car shows, and other fun events.

Swansboro Historic District and Bicentennial Park (910-326-1174; www .swansborohistory.blogspot.com), bounded by NC 24 and the White Oak River. Listed on the National Register of Historic Places, Swansboro's waterfront is home to an eclectic selection of architectural styles. Bicentennial Park, located on the waterfront at the base of the NC 24 bridge, features a statue of native son Otway Burns, captain of the *Snap Dragon* privateer during the War of 1812 and the first person to build a steamboat in North Carolina. The 1901 **William Edward Mattocks House**, 107 Front Street, now houses the Tidewater Gallery.

Swansboro Historic Site and Heritage Center (www.swansborohistoricsite.org), 502 Church Street, Swansboro. New museum in the historic Emmerton School houses a growing collection of exhibits on the town's rich history.

✳ To Do

BICYCLING The 25-mile **Swansboro Bicentennial Bicycle Trail** makes a loop into the Croatan National Forest before returning to the historic fishing village. The 19-mile signed **City to the Sea Bike Trail** (www.onlyinonslow.com) runs from Jacksonville to Hammocks Beach State Park. Maps of these trails can also be ordered from the **North Carolina Department of Transportation website** (www.ncdot.org).

BOATING The **North Carolina Wildlife Service** (www.ncwildlife.org) maintains free boat ramps at ♿ **Cedar Point** (144 Cedar Point Boulevard/NC 24), a large facility that also has a canoe/kayak launch, a fishing pier, and restrooms. A smaller boat ramp is located at **Shell Rock Landing** (250 Shell Rock Landing Road, Hubert), south of Hammocks Beach State Park. Free boat ramps are located throughout the **Croatan National Forest** (252-638-5628; www.fs.usda.gov/nfsnc). Those at Catfish Lake, Great Lake, and Oyster Point are best suited to shallow-bottom boats.

Dudley's Marina (252-393-2204; www.dudleysmarinanc.com), 106 NC 24, Cedar Point. Family-owned marina offers dockage for transients, courtesy car, charter fishing fleet, and ship's store. Several charter fishing boats dock here. Check www .nccharterfishing.com for options.

ECOTOURS ⚓ **Sandbar Safari Eco-Tours** (252-725-4614; www.sandbarsafari.com), 328 Live Oak Drive, Cape Carteret. Custom-designed boat tours from Dudley's Marina can include shelling, shrimping, crabbing, digging for clams, dolphin- and bird-watching, or some light-tackle fishing.

Second Wind Eco-Tours (910-325-3600; www.secondwindecotours.com), 208 W. Main Street, Swansboro. Tours combine yoga and kayaking. SUP and kayak rentals, introduction to kayak fishing, plus SUP yoga and other yoga classes, also available.

FITNESS CENTER ⚕ **Cape Carteret Aquatic and Wellness Center** (252-393-1000; www.ccaw.net), 300 Taylor Notion Road, Cape Carteret. Temporary memberships and day passes are offered at this full-service fitness facility, with an indoor pool, hot tub, steam room, and fitness equipment.

FOR FAMILIES The many military families based at Camp Lejeune ensure that there's lots of fun for families in the area. A day at the farm, learning about what rural life was like, is a popular family activity. Visit ⚓ **Mike's Farm** (910-324-3422; www.mikesfarm .com), 1600 Haw Branch Road, Beulaville, to meet a variety of farm animals, see a bakery in action, then have a fried chicken family-style meal at the on-site restaurant.

EXCURSIONS

A short trip from Swansboro, **Jacksonville**, the support community for the Marine Corps Base Camp Lejeune and Marine Corps Air Station New River, is home to the moving **Beirut Memorial** (www.beirut-memorial.org), carved with the words, THEY CAME IN PEACE, and the nearby memorials to Vietnam and the World Trade Center. The Memorial Park is located at the Camp Johnson Gate entrance of the Marine Corps' Camp Lejeune. You can also visit the oldest USO in the nation still in operation and follow the African-American Heritage Trail. Visit the **Onslow Tourism website** (www.onlyinonslow.com) for guidance and more suggestions.

THE BEIRUT MEMORIAL IS A MOVING TRIBUTE TO THE SOLDIERS WHO SERVED THEIR COUNTY IN THE MIDDLE EAST. NEARBY, THE VIETNAM MEMORIAL HONORS VETERANS OF THAT WAR, WHILE A PIECE OF TWISTED METAL FROM THE WORLD TRADE CENTER COMMEMORATES THE LIVES LOST ON 9/11

Golfin' Dolphin Family Recreation Center (252-393-8131; www.thegolfindolphin.com), 134 Golfin' Dolphin Drive, at the corner of NC 58 and NC 24, Cape Carteret. Features mini-golf, driving range, go-karts, bumper boats, batting cages, and a summertime water wars area.

Mac Daddy's Bowling Center (252-393-6565; www.mymacdaddys.com), 130 Golfin' Dolphin Drive, Cape Carteret. Bowling center with a huge video game arcade, plus a sports bar and grill with beer for the grown-ups.

GOLF **Paradise Point Golf Course** (910-451-5445; www.mccslejeune-newriver.com), Brewster Boulevard, Camp Lejeune. The general public is invited to play the two 18-hole courses on the Marine Corps base just west of Swansboro, including the Gold

Course, designed by George Cobb, renowned architect of Augusta National and a former marine.

Silver Creek Golf Club (252-393-8058; www.golfemeraldisle.com), 601 Pelletier Loop Road, Swansboro. Club rentals and driving range available at this course designed by North Carolina Golf Hall of Famer Gene Hamm.

Star Hill Golf Club (252-393-8111; www.starhillgolf.com), 202 Clubhouse Drive, Cape Carteret. Semiprivate club offers 27 holes of golf with bentgrass greens.

HEADBOAT FISHING **Nancy Lee Fishing Center** (910-326-4304; www.nancylee fishingcharters.com), 128 W. Corbett Avenue, Swansboro. ♂ The *Nancy Lee V* and her captain Lee Manning offer five-hour morning or afternoon fishing trips from a dock between the bridges in Swansboro, as well as private fishing charters.

HORSEBACK RIDING ♂ **Equine Country USA** (910-347-4511; www.equinecountryusa .com), 1259 McAllister Road, Jacksonville. Horse resort offers trail and carriage rides, plus lessons with English or Western tack. Inexpensive cabin rentals available.

KAYAKING The area around Swansboro is one of the best for kayaking and canoeing on the East Coast, with opportunities for paddling both open saltwater inlets and slow-flowing blackwater rivers. On the saltwater side, two marked paddle trails in the protected waters of **Hammocks Beach State Park** (910-326-4881; www.ncparks.gov) thread their ways from the dock at the visitor center to Bear Island, with its unspoiled dunes, and to Huggins Island, with a large maritime forest of many live oaks. Both are great spots for birding and shelling.

The White Oak River Paddle Trail (1-800-932-2144; www.onlyinonslow.com) travels down the upper regions of this blackwater stream, through cypress swamps draped in Spanish moss, ending at Stella, about 10 miles north of Swansboro. The 20-mile trail begins at the **White Oak River Campground** (910-595-4163; www.white oakrivercampground.com), US 17, Maysville, where **White Oak River Outfitters** (910-743-2744) rents kayaks and canoes, and offers guided tours and a shuttle service. Below Stella the White Oak widens to over a mile, becoming first a freshwater, then a saltwater tidal estuary. Paddlers can continue to the Cedar Island campground or beyond, to the Swansboro waterfront.

The New River Paddle Trail (910-347-5332; www.onlyinonslow.com), with unusual limestone formations along its upper course, begins in Richlands and ends in downtown Jacksonville, about 20 miles from Swansboro.

Ambitious paddlers will enjoy the **Croatan Saltwater Adventure Trail**, a 100-mile route that can take up to seven days. Beginning at the Brice's Creek Paddle Trail near New Bern, it almost circumnavigates Croatan National Forest, traversing the Trent River, Neuse River, historic Harlowe Canal, Bogue Sound, and White Oak River in turn, visiting historic sites and camping along the way. A search of the **US Forest Service website** (www.fs.fed.us) will turn up a map.

Barrier Island Kayaks (252-393-6457; www.barrierislandkayaks.com), 160 NC 24, Swansboro. This Nigel Dennis Kayaks Expedition Center rents kayaks and stand-up paddleboards, and offers lessons and tours, including a marsh ecotour and a paddle to Bear Island. Excursions around the tip of Cape Lookout, into the Atlantic to listen to dolphins, and longer island-to-island trips are also available.

MUD BOGGING AND RACING Dirt trail bikes and mud racing are popular in the Camp Lejeune area north of Swansboro. Two facilities in the area are **Halfmoon**

Motorcross Track (910-382-4394; www
.facebook.com/HalfmoonMX), 1037
Ramsey Road, Jacksonville, and *Jumping Run Creek Mudbog* (910-389-4159;
www.promud.com), Riggs Road, Hubert.

In the **Croatan National Forest** (252-
638-5628; www.fs.usda.gov/nfsnc), the
8-mile **Black Swamp Trail** is designed for
off-road vehicles. A $5 permit, available
at the district office in New Bern (141 E.
Fisher Avenue), is required.

PRIMITIVE CAMPING Fourteen primitive campsites are located on Bear Island
in **Hammocks Beach State Park** (910-
326-4881; www.ncparks.gov). Water and
restroom facilities are available on the
island, except mid-November to mid-
March. Fires are not permitted. Reservations are highly recommended.

Numerous primitive campsites are
available in the **Croatan National Forest** (252-638-5628; www.fs.fed.us). Those
accessible by US 58 from Cape Carteret
include Long Point Landing along the
White Oak River, as well as Catfish Lake
and Great Lake, blackwater pocosin
ponds in the forest's interior.

THE MARITIME FOREST ON BEAR ISLAND IS SO DENSE THAT
TRAILS TUNNEL THROUGH IT

TENNIS Lighted tennis courts are found at **Western Park** (252-808-3301; www
.ccparksrec.com), on Old Highway 58 in Cedar Point, along with a picnic area, playground, and restrooms.

✳ Green Space

For additional information on the **Croatan National Forest**, home to numerous carnivorous plant species, see the listing in the "Morehead City" section.

BEACHES **The beach at Bear Island**, part of **Hammocks Beach State Park** (910-326-
4881; www.ncparks.gov), south of Swansboro, is one of the wildest and least touched
of any barrier island. It can only be reached by boat, and no vehicles are allowed. On
the ocean side of the island, a boardwalk connects shaded picnic pavilions and a bathhouse with restrooms, drinking water, and cold water showers. A concession stand is
open Memorial Day to Labor Day, when lifeguards are also on duty. Primitive camping
sites are available ($13) year-round. Reservations recommended.

TRAILS **Tideland Trail** (252-638-5628; www.trailsofnc.com/croatan), Croatan
National Forest. This designated National Recreation Trail winds through the marsh
on boardwalks from Cedar Point Campground.

SWANSBORO HARBOR AT SUNSET

✳ Lodging

BED & BREAKFASTS ♿ ⟨ɰ⟩ **Harborlight Guest House** (252-393-6868; www.harborlightnc.com), 332 Live Oak Drive, Cape Carteret. Selected as one of the best undiscovered bed & breakfasts in the country by BedandBreakfast.com, the Harborlight sits slightly off the beaten track on a peninsula jutting into Bogue Sound. The isolation and gracious amenities make this a favorite for romantic getaways. Seven elegantly appointed suites offer two-person whirlpool tubs, fireplaces, waterfront decks, and awesome views. Gourmet breakfasts, served in your suite or on the deck, include creative dishes such as baked grapefruit, peach-glazed French toast, and sausage-stuffed mushrooms. One ground-floor suite is handicapped accessible. Guests may use the inn's beach chairs, umbrellas, and fishing rods.

Romance packages with in-room massage available. $$–$$$$.

MOTEL ♿ ⟨ɰ⟩ **Waterway Inn** (252-393-8027 or 1-877-216-4206; www.waterwayinn.net), 160 Cedar Point Boulevard/NC 24, Cape Carteret. Motel with 16 recently remodeled rooms sits directly on the Intracoastal Waterway (Marker 46), making it a favorite with boaters and kayakers. A boat pier and 90-foot fishing pier are on the property. $.

MOTOR INN 🐾 ♿ ⟨ɰ⟩ **Best Western Plus Silver Creek Inn** (252-393-9015 or 1-877-459-1448; www.bestwestern.com), 801 NC 24, Swansboro. Conveniently located to both Swansboro and Emerald Isle, this hotel has all the amenities, plus a friendly staff of locals. The AAA three-diamond hotel has an elevator, an outdoor pool and whirlpool, and serves free continental breakfast daily. Children ages 17 and under stay free. $$.

BOGUE SOUND WATERMELONS

Grown only in the sandy soil along Bogue Sound, these unique watermelons are sweeter and juicier than the average melon, with an old-fashioned goodness not found in today's hybrids. Almost extinct, the melons were rescued by the formation of the **Bogue Sound Watermelon Growers Association**, which supports and encourages local farmers to grow them. Watch for these local delicacies at roadside stands. Each melon bears a distinctive label and is only available from local farmers. Visit the association's website (www.boguesoundwatermelons.com) to find out where they are available.

RV CAMPGROUNDS ✽ ♿ **Cedar Point Campground in Croatan National Forest** (252-638-5628; www.fs.usda.gov/nfsnc). Campground near Swansboro has 42 sites, all with electric hookups, a bathhouse with warm showers and flush toilets, drinking water, and a boat ramp for kayaks or other shallow-bottomed boats.

✽ ✍ **Goose Creek Resort** (252-393-2628 or 1-866-839-2628; www.goosecreekcamping.com), 350 Red Barn Road, Ocean. A favorite with families and anglers thanks to its large swimming pool, 135-foot waterslide, beach area, Jet Skis, boat ramp, and a 250-foot fishing pier. Open all year.

✽ Where to Eat

DINING OUT ✍ ♈ **Icehouse Waterfront Restaurant** (910-325-0501; www.swansboroicehouse.com), 103 Moore Street. Huge landmark on the harbor offers wonderful views and sunsets to go with meals. Fish and shellfish, certified local by Carteret Catch, dominate the menu, which stars an excellent seafood jambalaya and a whole flounder stuffed with shrimp, crab, and aromatic herbs. Plenty of steamed and fried seafood as well, plus chargrilled beef that is all-natural and antibiotic-free. Creative pastas and salads fill out the menu. Live music and a late-night menu liven up evenings on the deck or large covered porch several night a week. Vegetarian and vegan menus available. Lunch and Sunday brunch $–$$; dinner $$–$$$.

✍ ♿ ✍ **Riverside Steak & Seafood** (910-326-8847; www.the-riverside-swansboro.com), 506 W. Corbett Avenue, NC 24, Swansboro. Daily specials supplement a menu of fresh local seafood and hand-cut aged beef at this longtime favorite. Try the Carpetbagger, a rib eye stuffed with jumbo shrimp. All meals come with famous homemade sweet potato muffins. Reservations recommended. Dinner only, $$–$$$$.

EATING OUT ✍ **The Carteret Cafe** (252-764-0304; www.facebook.com/TheCarteretCafe), 1000 NC 24, Cape Carteret. Hard-to-miss bright yellow building on NC 24 serves satisfying breakfast and lunch at easy-on-the-wallet prices. Southern-style breakfasts and peach fritters like the ones at sister restaurant Yana's in Swansboro keep locals coming back. $.

🍴 ✍ **Church Street Irish Pub & Deli** (910-326-7572; www.churchstreet-deli-pub-inn.com), 105 Church Street, Swansboro. This local favorite with a nice patio is a deli and an Irish pub where you can lift a pint of Guinness. You can even spend the night. The adjacent **Church Street Inn** (910-326-7573) offers five uniquely decorated suites overlooking the historic downtown. Sandwiches $–$$. Rooms $$$.

BREAKFAST **Yana's Ye Olde Drugstore Restaurant & '50s Memorabilia Shoppe** (910-326-5501), 119 Front Street, Swansboro. Locals rave about the fruit fritters at this cool soda shop, complete with milkshakes and a jukebox loaded with rock 'n' roll hits. Fans of Elvis, Marilyn,

Betty Boop, the Lone Ranger, and many more '50s icons will find plenty to admire. Breakfast and lunch $.

PRODUCE STANDS **Guthrie Farm Stand** (252-393-2254 or 252-241-4918), 5417 NC 24, Bogue. Farmer Guthrie was the founder of the Bogue Sound Watermelon Growers Association, and his family continues to offer the fruits of their farm, in the family for more than 150 years, at this roadside stand.

Winberry Farm (252-393-2281; www.ncagr.gov/ncproducts), 1006 NC 24, Cedar Point. An old tobacco barn houses one of the area's largest stands, a great place to find local tomatoes and Bogue Sound watermelons.

✲ Entertainment

SwanFest (www.seasideartscouncil.com). Free concerts are held every Sunday evening in Swansboro's Olde Town Square, May to September.

Ψ **Saltwater Grill** (910-326-7300; www.saltwatergrillswansboro.com), 99 W. Church Street. Sweet spot on the Swansboro waterfront serves up certified local fresh seafood and a fun summer music series, plus daily drink and dinner specials.

✲ Selective Shopping

Historic **Front Street** in Swansboro is home to an eclectic group of gift shops specializing in one-of-a-kind items.

ANTIQUES **Swansboro Antiques & Uniques** (252-326-0043; www.swansboroantiques.com), 675 W. Corbett Avenue, NC 24, Swansboro. Art glass and pottery, sterling, jewelry, and much more, selected by top "pickers."

Sterling Auction House (910-545-9831; www.auctionhousesterling.com), 1786 Wilmington Highway, Jacksonville. Estate auctions offer unique opportunities to buy local antiques and collectibles.

SPECIAL SHOPS **Russell's Olde Tyme Shoppe** (910-326-3790), 116 Front Street, Swansboro. Artist Maxinne Russell creates marvelous hand-painted objects for every room in the house, besides stocking decorative items by other local artisans.

✲ Special Events

March: **Oyster Roast** (910-326-6175; www.swansbororotary.com), Swansboro Rotary Civic Center.

April: **Swansboro Rotary Beach Bash** (910-326-6175; www.swansbororotary.com), Swansboro Rotary Civic Center. **Historical Home Tour** (www.swansborohistoricsite.org).

May: **King Mackerel Bluewater Fishing Tournament** (www.fishswansboro.com). Memorial Day weekend competition is one of the country's largest.

June: **Arts by the Sea Festival** (910-326-7370; www.swansborofestivals.com). Arts, crafts, and storytelling in downtown Swansboro.

July: **Fourth of July Fireworks** (910-326-7370; www.swansborofestivals.com), downtown Swansboro.

October: **Swansboro Mullet Festival** (910-326-7370; www.swansborofestivals.com), downtown Swansboro. **Five-O King Mackerel Tournament** (www.swansboro50.com).

November: **Holiday Flotilla** (910-326-7370; www.swansborofestivals.com), downtown Swansboro. Decorated boat parade along the Swansboro waterfront on Thanksgiving weekend.

INDEX

dogs: and beaches, 33, 105, 135, 379; and Camp Hatteras RV Resort & Campground, 238; and Cyber Dog USA Holistic Pet Shop & School for Dogs, 169; and Dajio Restaurant and Patio Bar, 309; and dog parks, 92, 124, 138, 238; and Duck Town Park and Soundside Boardwalk, and fountains for, 92; and Emerald Isle beach, 379; and Island Ferry Adventures, 345; and Kitty Hawk beaches, 135; and Kitty Hawk Park, 124; and Lucky Duck's Guide Service, 327; and Morning View Coffee House, 157; and Nags Head Woods Ecological Preserve, 138; and Otway House Bed & Breakfast, 329; and Outer Barks, 103; and pet accommodations, 308; and Salty Paws Dog Biscuits, 160; and Seagrass Whimsical Gift Shop, 355; and South Beach Grille, 153; and Southern Shores beaches, 105; and Sting Wray's Bar & Grill, 240; and The Dancing Turtle Coffee Shop, 278

dolphins (mahi mahi), 27, 154, 204, 272, 356

dolphins, and North Carolina Marine Mammal Stranding Network, 32

dolphins, and watching: and Barrier Island Kayaks, 392; and Cape Carteret, 390; and *Capt. Johnny's* Outer Banks Dolphin Cruises, 195; and Carolina Ocean Studies, 345; and Carolina Ocean Studies, 345; and central beaches, 121, 135; and Crystal Coast Lady Cruises, 345; and Crystal Coast Lady Cruises, 345; and Crystal Coast, 346, 392; and Good Fortune Coastal Ecology Charters, 362; and Hatteras, 270, 273; and Island Express Ferry Service, 336; and Kitty Hawk Watersports, 121, 135; and Lookout Cruises, 345; and Lookout Cruises, 346; and Manteo and Pirate's Cove, 195; and *Miss Bodie Island* Dolphin Watch Cruises, 195; and *Miss Hatteras*, 273; and Morehead City, 362; and Nags Head Dolphin Watch, 121; and Ocracoke, 297; and Paradise Dolphin Cruises,

217; and Rudy Austin, *297*, 298; and Sandbar Safari Eco-Tours, 390; and Seabirding Pelagic Trips, 270; and Thicket Lump Marina, 219; and Wanchese, 217, 219

donuts, 97, 167

Down East, 21, 30, 323, 368

Downeast Rover, 194

dunes, 42–43, 59; and Currituck National Wildlife Refuge, 77; largest, 113, and Penny's Hill, 75; unspoiled system of, 322, 388, 389, 92. *See also* Jockey's Ridge

Duplin Winery, 192

E

E. S. Newman, 53, 186

ecotourism: and Albemarle Peninsula, 200–1; and Alice Hoffman Nature Trail, 379; and Alligator River, 200–1; and Buxton Woods Coastal Reserve, 255–56; and Cape Carteret, 390; and Carolina Ocean Studies, 345; and Cedar Island National Wildlife Refuge, 326, 328; and Coastal Studies Institute, 217; and Corolla, 76, 77, 79; and Currituck, 77; and Dismal Swamp Canal Welcome Center, 131; and eco-cruise, 91; and *Good Fortune* Coastal Ecology Charters, 362; and Hatteras Island Ocean Center Ecology Park, 270; and Jennette's Pier, 116, *116*; and Jockey's Ridge State Park, 117; and kayaks, 76, 134, 195; and Museum of the Albemarle, 131; and Museum of the Sea, 252; and Nags Head Woods Ecological Preserve, 138; and North Beaches, 76; and Oregon Inlet, 171; and Outer Banks Wildlife Shelter, 361; and Pea Island National Wildlife Refuge, 228; and Pine Knolls, 379; and Pirate's Cove, 193; and Rachel Carson National Estuarine Research Reserve, 344, 348; and Roanoke Island, 195; and Sea Gate Woods Preserve, 349; and SUPs, 133; and Swansboro, 390; and Theodore Roosevelt Nature Trail, 379

Edenton, 49